SVG Programming:
The Graphical Web

KURT CAGLE

Apress™

SVG Programming: The Graphical Web
Copyright © 2002 by Kurt Cagle

ISBN (pbk): 1-59059-019-8
Printed and bound in the United States of America 12345678910

Trademarked names may appear in this book. Rather than use a trademark symbol with every occurrence of a trademarked name, we use the names only in an editorial fashion and to the benefit of the trademark owner, with no intention of infringement of the trademark.

Technical Reviewer: Don Demcsak
Editorial Directors: Dan Appleman, Peter Blackburn, Gary Cornell, Jason Gilmore, Karen Watterson, John Zukowski
Project Manager: Tracy Brown Collins
Copy Editor: Kim Wimpsett
Production Editor: Grace Wong
Compositor: Impressions Book and Journal Services, Inc.
Indexer: Ron Strauss
Cover Designer: Kurt Krames
Manufacturing Manager: Tom Debolski
Marketing Manager: Stephanie Rodriguez

Distributed to the book trade in the United States by Springer-Verlag New York, Inc., 175 Fifth Avenue, New York, NY, 10010 and outside the United States by Springer-Verlag GmbH & Co. KG, Tiergartenstr. 17, 69112 Heidelberg, Germany.
In the United States, phone 1-800-SPRINGER, email orders@springer-ny.com, or visit http://www.springer-ny.com.
Outside the United States, fax +49 6221 345229, email orders@springer.de, or visit http://www.springer.de.

For information on translations, please contact Apress directly at 2560 Ninth Street, Suite 219, Berkeley, CA 94710. Phone 510-549-5930, fax: 510-549-5939, email info@apress.com, or visit http://www.apress.com.

The source code for this book is available to readers at http://www.apress.com in the Downloads section.

To Katherine and Jennifer—may this be a part of your world—and to Anne, after a decade of building dreams.

Contents at a Glance

Contents

Michael Bierman's Foreword

As I write this, SVG 1.0 is almost one year old. Of course, SVG really began well before that. If Sept. 4, 2001 is SVG's birthday, the date of conception would have to be April 1998, when the W3C formally accepted the first proposal for a vector-based language for Web graphics.[1]

My journey with SVG began three years ago when I joined Adobe to shape a product strategy for this nascent technology. The first SVG demo I ever saw was a Web site for a fictitious San Francisco–based coffee house. When a visitor searched for store locations, little coffee cups appeared on the map to indicate store locations. When the mouse was over a given coffee cup, steam wafted up and the address appeared in the steam. You could zoom and pan the map image or search for street names. (A personal favorite since I often have trouble finding the street I am looking for on a map—especially on low-resolution GIFs!) There were marvelous filter effects that one usually associates with Photoshop and raster formats. The user interface was unconfined by the limitations of HTML widgets such as checkboxes and radio buttons. The demo seems so primitive compared to what has been produced since, but it made me stop and think . . .

SVG is an XML-based declarative programming language for interactive, animated, two-dimensional graphics. That places it somewhere between Adobe PostScript or Portable Document Format (PDF), Macromedia Flash (SWF), and Sun's Java. It is no accident or coincidence that all three companies contributed to the development of SVG.

So, this little coffee house demo raised my curiosity. What could Web designers and programmers do with a human-readable language for graphics? How close could SVG come to HTML's impressive adoption curve? What would it be like to have information graphics and user interfaces that can be easily and cheaply dynamically generated, translated, and updated? How would designers and programmers use such a language to change the Web? How would they change the world?

Hyperbole? Try to imagine a world without HTML. Now think about the possibilities of an equivalent markup language for graphics and then add to that, a "platform- and language-neutral interface that will allow programs and scripts

---

1. Adobe, IBM, Netscape, and Sun submitted Precision Graphics Markup Language (PGML) on April 10, 1998. Autodesk, Hewlett-Packard, Macromedia, Microsoft, and Visio Corporation submitted Vector Markup Language (VML) on May 13, 1998.

to dynamically access and update the content, structure, and style of documents,"[2] or the DOM.

Back then, I could only hope for the success SVG has achieved. As one would expect, there was also not much awareness of SVG at that time. For those who heard about it, there was a mixture of excitement and skepticism. Now, do not get me wrong, I think some skepticism is healthy. It tempers excitement over bad ideas. But, like any discontinuous innovation, there are those who resist change even when change is an improvement. By definition, discontinuous innovations disrupt the status quo, and they succeed when the value they bring outweighs the disruption they cause. Disruptions include learning new skills, building new systems, and buying new equipment, software, or books. Even SVG supporters like myself were not sure the market would accept SVG—even if it was superior to the other solutions. Yes, Virginia, the "best" solution does not always win in the marketplace—for example, VHS vs. Beta.

With uncertainty came more questions: Where would a user agent (viewer) come from? Was it possible for anyone to achieve enough viewer distribution to allow content developers to trust that their content would be usable by everyone? **Okay, I thought, requirement one: viewer ubiquity.** Would SVG ever achieve the market momentum necessary for commercial success? Adobe could not successfully go down this path alone. Would anyone else produce authoring tools and servers? **Requirement two: a complete complement of authoring tools and server solutions. The more the better.** Like HTML, SVG was about making the best tools around, not creating a proprietary format that locked people to one company. What was the unique value of SVG? What industries would benefit most from it, and which would be among the first to wade into an unproven technology with a weighty specification that was still only in draft form. **Requirement three: an audience of content developers (a.k.a. early adopters) who would derive benefit from this unproven technology.** Aside from questions about the ubiquity of a viewing solution and the lack of tools, there were several other important pieces missing. Early adopters, like everyone, need education. With most successful technologies, early adopters learn from each other. Forums such as groups.yahoo.com/group/svg-developers/ soon emerged from the well of early beta testers of the Adobe SVG Viewer. Still, that was not enough. For SVG to be embraced by the masses, good references and tutorials needed to be written. **Requirement four: Books like this one**. The weight of these questions and requirements often seemed too much for this infant to endure, and it looked like SVG could be stillborn.

From that time until now, people have worked hard to answer to the questions and meet the requirements. SVG is now a W3C recommendation. The Adobe SVG Viewer, distributed with all Adobe products including Adobe Acrobat and Acrobat Reader, is now on hundreds of millions of desktops and climbing

---

2.   www.w3.org/DOM/

rapidly. There are already several companies so anxious to develop solutions for the wireless and mobile space that they are developing solutions for these platforms even though the process to develop a recommendation for SVG Mobile is not yet complete. **Requirement one: Complete.** Hundreds of authoring tools and servers offer support for SVG in some way or another (even if some of them hide that by saying they support XML, JavaScript, Perl, and so on.) Hint: Your favorite editor may already be a powerful SVG tool! **Requirement two: Complete (enough).**[3]

SVG adoption is going well. Google.com and HotBot.com return thousands of hits in response to *SVG* or *scalable vector graphics.* In addition to these public examples of SVG, I have had the privilege to talk with many developers regarding internal intranet projects that will dramatically reduce the cost of building and maintaining their Web applications while making data more accessible and more meaningful than ever before possible. SourceForge.net currently shows 11 active SVG projects with 22 new projects awaiting more help. Yahoo groups,[4] the most popular place for SVG developers to share their extensive knowledge, now boasts thousands of members from around the world. What is sparking their interest? Interest in XML, and SVG specifically, increases all of the time as people strive to produce, synthesize, and maintain fantastic amounts of information across a huge number of devices, with smaller budgets and resources. SVG will most certainly prosper because it solves problems that current formats do not. **Requirement three: Well underway!**

But perhaps the best indicator that SVG is taking off is that we are now meeting my fourth requirement. Talented authors are now choosing to take on the challenge of learning SVG and skillfully sharing their knowledge with the rest of us. In May of 2001, developers on the SVG group started talking about Kurt Cagle's XML books. Eventually, Kurt joined the conversation himself and became a valuable contributor to archive. I sometimes wondered when he would put pen to paper on an SVG book. When I heard he was doing just that, I was delighted. Kurt has written or contributed to more than a dozen books, including ones on XML and Flash. This gives Kurt a unique background for writing about SVG. SVG, by its nature, simultaneously attracts graphic designers, programmers, and often the rare breed that lies somewhere in between—sometimes known as *Flash developers.* These folks often have found themselves in the confines of the SWF world. So given Kurt's background, I was particularly interested in reading what he would say about SVG.

I am not disappointed. For many people, this will make an excellent SVG primer. As I said, SVG appeals to both developers and designers. Kurt's approach to the subject matter is accessible to everyone. He provides enough pointers for

---

3. This is not meant to imply that the perfect SVG editor exists yet. Many companies are working their concept of the "ultimate" SVG integrated development environment.
4. `groups.yahoo.com/group/svg-developers/`

programmers to know where to get started and how to exploit their previous experience with JavaScript, Perl, and XSLT. If you are a designer, some of this information is still useful as you will want to want to have enough background in how SVG programming works to design your work to fit into the bigger workflow. Because SVG covers so much ground, it is a complex and far-reaching topic. So, if you encounter something in the book that puzzles you, have no fear. Continue reading and experiment with the examples provided. Some of later chapters will likely answer your question!

It goes without saying that none of this would be possible without and the rest of the SVG working group; my thanks to them for their vision.

I have had the extraordinary pleasure to work with Chris Lilley, chairman of the SVG Working Group, and Jon Ferraiolo, editor of SVG 1.0. Without them and the rest of the working group, SVG would not exist. I have also had the opportunity to interact with designers and developers all over the world. They are a devoted and ingenious group. They too are crucial to SVG's success. SVG has gone from a theoretical standard to a living industry. There are few times that one has the chance to affect the way millions of people communicate. I am glad to have had such an opportunity and look forward to what comes next.

—*Michael Bierman*
SVG Technologist
LinguaGrafica.com

Don XML's Foreword

IF YOU HAVE OPENED (and hopefully bought) this book, you obviously have heard a little something about Scalable Vector Graphics. You may have heard that SVG is an exciting new technology developed by the W3C and a group of corporate partners that include Adobe, Corel, and Kodak. You may have heard that SVG is an XML-based language that you can use to create and animate graphics and that it offers high-resolution for printing or Web browsers, but the file sizes are amazingly small. And you have probably heard a word or two about the comparisons between Flash and SVG. Yes, the buzz is starting to build about SVG. But I am here to tell you that SVG is everything the hype has it made out to be, and more. It is not fad, or the language nouveau of the day, but part of a new way to build computer systems using open XML standards. And what is a computer system without a way to present information graphically? Thus, SVG was born. Well, it was not really born, but it is something that has slowly matured from various other formats and ideas at the W3C over the past couple years. Out of this slowly evolving process developed a grassroots movement to educate the masses about this really cool graphics format. Enter Kurt Cagle.

Kurt Cagle: He is the author or coauthor of 14 books and a couple hundred articles on XML, XSLT, and Web-related technologies and open-source issues. I have known Kurt for quite some time now, through various discussions on the Web and from his books and articles. This book is not a rehash of the W3C's SVG specification (you can go to the Web and read that for free), but it is a book of SVG programming how-to exercises and best practices. Kurt does a good job keeping the reader's attention through what can be a dry subject (if you do not believe me, try reading the SVG specification). This book is geared toward the developer, but it could also be used by a graphics artist who likes to dabble in programming. The first half of the book covers the SVG basics, without delving too deeply in the gory details of the SVG specification. The second half is all about different programming techniques. I use the word *programming* loosely because XML and SVG start to blur the traditional definition of programming. By the end of the book Kurt gives you a little taste of the future. You see, SVG by itself is pretty cool and worth learning, but combining SVG along with other formats (such as XHTML, XSLT, SMIL, and MathML) and scripting languages (such as JavaScript or ECMAScript) is where the future lies.

There is an old saying that a picture is worth a thousand words, but with SVG, the picture is constructed of a thousand words.

—*Don XML*
Active participant
SVG-Developers Yahoo Group
`groups.yahoo.com/group/svg-developers/`

About the Author

KURT CAGLE HAS WRITTEN 14 books and more than 200 articles on a wide variety of topics in the technical arena, most recently specializing in the various XML technologies. He is working with the OASIS HumanML Technical Committee to develop a standard for intelligent agenting systems built around XML, and he moderates a number of online newsgroups. He also runs his own consulting company, Cagle Communications, in Olympia, Washington. When not writing for profit, he writes science fiction novels, draws serial narratives, and helps take care of two rambunctious daughters.

About the Technical Reviewer

DON XML IS THE MUCH more memorable pen name of independent consultant Don Demcsak. He specializes in architecting and programming multitier applications using Microsoft's .NET Framework. You can find Don pontificating the benefits of XML, SVG, and the .NET Framework on various discussion groups across the Web. When not working, Don can usually be found playing with some new beta software or just hanging out and enjoying life with his wife, Melissa, and their two daughters, Amanda and Rebecca. Don would like to thank his friends and family for all their support. It is not easy living with a young, entrepreneurial technocrat. You can contact Don at don@donxml.com.

Acknowledgments

A BOOK IS A COLLABORATIVE EFFORT, one that involves the work of a great number of people to make happen. This book is no exception. Apress is not a large publisher (though it is one of the fastest growing in the computer book industry), but it is easily one of the best I have worked with in 10 years of writing. I want to thank Gary Cornell, one of the founders of Apress, for the opportunity to write for Apress and for being supportive in trying to get what has been a complex book out the door. Thanks also to Jason Gilmore, who was the acquisition editor for the book and has been remarkably patient, all things considered.

Tracy Brown Collins has had the unenviable position of being my project manager. The purpose of a project manager is to make sure that everything gets in on time, to specification, and in good shape, which means unavoidably that there will be some hair pulling. Still, she has shaped the manuscript in ways that will probably not be obvious but are crucial nonetheless.

Don Demcsak served as the technical editor for the book and wrote a most excellent foreword (thanks, Don!). The technical editor position is part tester, part guru, and part wordsmith, and he has done exceptionally in all three positions. He is also currently heading an open-source development project on Source Forge to port SVG to the .NET C# architecture and is an active leader in the various SVG development groups across the country.

Similarly, I want to thank Michael Bierman, who was the product manager for the Adobe SVG Viewer 3.0 and consented to write the foreword for this book. Michael is one of the leading authorities on SVG in the world, and his comments in the SVG mailing lists and to me personally have given me a much deeper understanding of SVG and the Adobe SVG Viewer than I would have been able to reach otherwise.

Pity the poor copy editor, who has to make sure that all of the i's are properly dotted and the t's properly crossed (a thankless job at best when looking at several hundred pages of manuscript). She is also often the one least thanked because she comes into the process so late. I want to give a special note of thanks to Kim Wimpsett, who worked well beyond the call of duty on this, as well as Grace Wong, who helped coordinate the book from the time it left my hands to the time it got into yours.

I want to also thank the Starbucks coffee shops in Olympia, Lacey, and Tacoma, Washington, and Red Robin in Olympia. I have consumed way too many Venti Hazelnut Nonfat Lattes over the course of this book, but the good barristas and servers there put up with me typing away at the manuscript for the better part of five months.

Finally, and most importantly, I want to thank my wife, Anne, and my daughters Katie and Jennifer. If you think being a writer is tough, try being married to one.

Introduction

THE PROCESS OF WRITING A book always looks radically different at the beginning than it does at the end. In the beginning, if you are smart, you have an outline, a general roadmap of the terrain you want to cover, a well thought-out document that usually survives for about the first third of the book. Writing a book also entails learning a subject; the best books are usually not written by people who intimately know the subject because they often find they have little common ground to describe their experiences. Rather, they are written by people who know enough about a topic to devote the time and energy into *becoming* experts and along the way recording their experiences for others who will be traversing the path with this book as their guide.

When I started writing *SVG Programming : The Graphical Web*, I envisioned a much larger book, of which SVG was just a small part. It was a book intended to cover the whole explosion of XML-based "publishing" languages. However, the more I delved into the nuances of SVG, the more I began to appreciate both how sophisticated and how complex the language really was. Originally I had seen it primarily as a target for XSL transformations to draw graphs and charts, but few graphics tools come with the ability to do alpha channel transparencies, interactive scripting, animation, live text manipulation, or kernel convolution filters, all in real time.

I soon began to see that SVG is a language that is, in its own way, as richly nuanced as Dynamic HTML, and the fact that it was written in XML makes it well suited to the evolving panorama of Web design. Moreover, there are a number of indications that SVG is approaching the cusp—that point in a technology's evolution where it goes from being a specialist's domain to where it becomes ubiquitous. A large and growing number of conversion tools are available for mapping a host of formats (from Flash and Illustrator to Windows Meta-Files, TIFF, PDF, and many more) to SVG—with relatively few going in the other direction. Software developers are beginning to recognize that SVG may end up being to vector graphics what formats such as JPEG are to bitmap graphics: the default graphic format of choice.

At any rate, this has had a profound influence upon the direction of the book. The introduction, written at the end even if it is placed at the beginning, allows me a chance to survey what I have produced (with a *lot* of help from editors, colleagues, and gurus in the field). With this in mind, I want to answer a few questions in the following sections.

Who Will Benefit from This Book?

Everyone! I should sell a million copies that way! Seriously, the book is written primarily for the person who is familiar with HTML and has at least a basic understanding of JavaScript (though this is not strictly necessary for the first seven chapters or so). It is an introductory to middling complexity programming book, with SVG as the programming language.

I should clarify something here, however. For the past 25 years, programming has been focused primarily on procedural languages, most derived from the "mother tongues" of C, BASIC, Fortran, and Pascal. Of the principal languages of the 1990s, two, Java and C++, derive directly from the C language, and Visual Basic and Delphi have their roots in the 40-year-old BASIC and Pascal languages, respectively.

However, a quiet revolution has been taking place in the so-called declarative languages, a revolution radically reshaping the way we program. XML makes it possible to describe not just data, but the entire evolution of an application over time. HTML has become the standard language for interface development, and XML-based Web services are challenging the notions about the boundaries of programming.

Much of this book looks at SVG from the standpoint of its value as a declarative language. This too was a conscious decision on my part as an author. There is a fair amount of scripting later in the book (for those itching to get into DOM manipulation), but my experience as I learned more about the language is that the most efficient use of SVG is to take advantage of its XML origins and nature first and then slip into DOM only when you absolutely must.

This is not a reference book—there are a number of them beginning to come out, and if you are looking for the specific attributes of the `<feTurbulence/>` filter, you can probably find a better source for that type of information than you can here. On the other hand, this book intends to teach the methodology of how to work with SVG, how to make it sing and dance for you, and to outline a few of the myriad possibilities that the language holds.

So, if you are a programmer looking at mastering this language in your own applications, this book is for you. If you are a Web designer who wants to add some panache to your creations, this book is for you. If you are an XML developer looking at getting a handle on one of the graphical sides of the XML revolution, this book is for you.

How Is This Book Organized?

As you can probably tell, this book has an overall tone that is considerably more informal than is typical for computer books (blame the author—he has a serious dislike for ties). I make no apologies for that. Programming has gained a reputation for being complicated, a charge that has no doubt come about in part because complicated programs require rich consulting fees and service contracts and specialized applications to simplify the complexity. There *are* some areas of programming that are hard, most ultimately having to do with the boundaries between programming, linguistics, mathematics, and philosophy, but in most cases programming is harder than it has to be.

Consequently, this book meanders a bit, but it covers most of the important pieces of SVG. I start out with a basic history of SVG and how it relates to the rest of the world (Chapter 1, "Why SVG?"). In Chapter 2, "Getting Started: An SVG Tutorial," I provide a couple of tutorials illustrating how you write SVG, with examples. Chapter 3, "You Are Here: Coordinate Systems and Transformations," looks at coordinate systems, an important facet in being able to work with SVG directly and to making it more programmatically useful. Chapter 4, "Shaping the Spiral Path: Shapes and Paths," and Chapter 5, "Painting and Drawing," look at the core building blocks of the language—creating shapes and paths (and filling (and stroking) them with color. Chapter 6, "The Basics of Text," deals with the various manifestations of text and how to best use it in SVG, and Chapter 7, "Incorporating Texture," looks at *texturing*, masks, and filters. You can think of Chapters 3 through 7 as looking at the part of SVG involved with static rendering.

Chapter 8 and later look at the dynamic aspects of SVG. Chapter 8, "Animating SVG," explores animation (though it is used throughout earlier sections) as well as interactivity. In Chapter 9, "Integrating SVG and HTML," I look at integrating SVG with HTML because, at least in this fairly early stage, SVG application will most likely end up playing more of a supporting role. In Chapter 10, "SVG Components," I deal with what I consider the most important aspect of SVG—the ability to use the language to create sophisticated components. Finally, Chapter 11, "The Future of SVG," explores the directions that SVG is going, and outlines in greater detail a number of "design pattern" concepts meant to expand the use of SVG in light of other XML standards.

Conventions in This Book

This book follows a number of basic conventions that should make it easier for you to get useful material out of it. Blocks of code are written with a standard monospaced, code font, as follows:

```
<svg xmlns="http://www.w3.org/2000/svg"
     xmlns:xlink="http://www.w3.org/1999/xlink">
    <rect fill="blue" x="100" y="100" width="200" height="100"
        opacity="1">
      <animate attributeName="opacity" attributeType="CSS" from="1"
           to="0" begin="3s" dur="4s" fill="freeze"/>
    </rect>
</svg>
```

As most of the code listed is XML based (and usually SVG), I have tried to use indenting patterns consistent with XML to make it easier to follow. With the exception of spaces within quotes, whitespace such as carriage returns or tabs are ignored by XML, so you can consequently break the lines any way you want. Note that this is not always the case with JavaScript, however, and in general I have tried to make it clear when a line is cut prematurely in a JavaScript routine. Most code blocks are given as listings. A listing is a complete SVG "program" (it can run within an SVG viewer) and is indicated with a listing header, as follows:

Listing 8-1. `Jabberwocky.svg`

```
<svg ="http://www.w3.org/2000/svg"
     xmlns:xlink="http://www.w3.org/1999/xlink">
<g transform="translate(100,100)" font-size="20">
<text x="0" y="0" visibility="hidden">
<set attributeName="visibility" attributeType="CSS"
to="visible" begin="1s" fill="freeze"/>
T'was brillig and the slithy toves
</text>
```

The filename given with the listing is a more descriptive name for the file. You can download the code from the Apress site, either by its listing number (`Listing8-1.svg`) or by its name (`Jabberwocky.svg`).

I have also tried to follow the convention of including element names within brackets (such as `<feGaussianBlur>`) as well as having all inline code use the same code style as blocks of text.

There are three kinds of "iconic" notes:

NOTE *Notes are points that may be of interest to the reader but that do not necessarily follow the flow of the narrative.*

TIP *These are ideas, tips, or techniques you may want to apply in your own code.*

CAUTION *There are few things in SVG that will bring your system crashing to a halt, but they do exist. These icons warn when you may want to tread carefully, as well as letting you know when limitations exist in a specific implementation.*

Sidebars

Additionally, topics I think are germane to the thread but not necessarily part of the existing narrative are called out as sidebars. Sidebars employ a different font and size than normal body text and are usually fairly short.

Following Up

A book is a snapshot in time (though admittedly one with a four-month exposure interval), and given the emergent nature of SVG, it is difficult to keep content current. All of the examples contained in this book are also available for free download from Apress at `www.apress.com`, with the code also mirrored at `www.kurtcagle.net` (also known as the Metaphorical Web). Additional samples, links to resources, and news about *SVG Programming : The Graphical Web* and any subsequent works can be found on the Apress site as well. If you have any questions, you can also contact me directly via e-mail at `kurt@kurtcagle.net` or through a Q&A interface on either the Apress and Metaphorical Web site.

Let me know what you think. SVG is special, a phenomenon primed to happen, and I hope with my book that you can be a part of it.

CHAPTER 1

Why SVG?

THE FIRST WORDS that you, as the reader, see are in many respects the most important words in the book. If written well, they invite you in, motivating you to undertake the sometimes arduous task of learning, which any such book in fact requires. On the other hand, when written poorly, these same words can dissuade you, perhaps to the extent of not even purchasing the book. Hence, I must write these words with care.

This book is about pictures . . . and words. This includes not only the words that appear in presentations, alongside graphs, or on buttons but also the words used to describe and build these other words and graphics—the "programming" words, if you will.

The axiom *A picture is worth a thousand words,* when coined, was meant to illustrate the principle that we humans are fundamentally visual rather than literary beings. Yet with Scalable Vector Graphics (SVG), this simple thought takes on a life of its own, as we use words to generate the very pictures we are using to illustrate. SVG is essentially a language: It's a way of using the particular grammar imposed by Extensible Markup Language (XML) to draw pictures (and words), animate them, make them responsive to external events, generate new SVG on the fly, and interact with other languages and environments.

This is a book about SVG, but it is also about a concept beginning to gain some currency even in the workaday realm of commercial software: the idea that perhaps the real nature of programming is not to find the most efficacious way of optimizing the limited set of programming languages to accomplish a task, but rather to see language itself as a medium to be manipulated. In other words, it is not so much about programming with a language as it is about programming our concept of language.

Most people, when first encountering SVG, will try to judge it against existing applications. SVG vs. Adobe PostScript, SVG vs. Macromedia Flash. SVG vs. Microsoft PowerPoint. All of these are valid comparisons, but to view SVG this way is to miss its true applicability. Ultimately, SVG is a standard way to describe graphics and graphical interactions; it's one particular dialect of the incredibly rich family of XML technologies. It's a way of encoding a visual image that can be transported as a single unit or in pieces and a way of describing interfaces that can be built at a moment's notice, existing only so long as it's needed and then melting away in transformation.

Conceptually, this may be a hard concept to wrap your brain around because for 50 years the concept of interfaces has been (and continues to be) oriented around the idea that an interface is built. SVG is one piece of a dramatic change in the way you develop applications, use computers, work with networks, and otherwise deal with these marvelously sophisticated communication devices. Yet increasingly, these open, distributed systems tend to evolve their own priorities and protocols in response to needs over time.

Software vendors have derided Hypertext Markup Language (HTML) as being extremely simplistic and insufficient to the task of building the complex tools needed for binding communities, ensuring electronic commerce, and policing the resultant infrastructure. The irony is that HTML is still (by a wide margin) the single most widely used computer language, with several billion pieces of HTML "software" being deployed every day. Meanwhile, most vendor-driven applications have been rendered irrelevant (along with, in many cases, the vendors themselves) just a meager 10 years from the time HTML first appeared on the scene.

You can make similar arguments for other open protocols, languages, and associated tools. For instance, the most widely used Web server on the planet (by about a five-to-two margin) is the Apache Web server. Additionally, the Post Office Protocol/Simple Mail Transfer Protocol (POP3/SMTP) e-mail has not completely eliminated alternative mail systems, but there are few proprietary mail formats on the planet that don't at least have a gateway for converting mail to the open standard; otherwise, these service providers would cease to be relevant.

For that matter, the prevalent infrastructure protocols such as the Transport Control and Internet Protocols (the ubiquitous TCP/IP) have so completely rendered other network protocols obsolete that meaningful development of proprietary network protocols has all but ground to a halt. The only protocol likely to challenge TCP/IP in the long term is Block Extensible Exchange Protocol (BEEP) format, perhaps with a Simple Object Access Protocol (SOAP) layer sitting on top of it.

As I write this, SVG is roughly one year old. It has already engendered fierce controversy as well as a host of naysayers who have a vested interest in seeing that it does not succeed. In this chapter, I look at the 10,000-foot view of SVG, especially how it relates to other known protocols (including the de facto protocol PostScript) and products such as Flash. Additionally, much of this book (as much of XML itself) revolves around the notion of context. To understand where SVG is going, it doesn't hurt to understand its history. With that in mind, let's get started.

A Short History of XML and SVG

XML has sprung into existence seemingly overnight, but this appearance is deceptive. XML has, much like the Internet, gestated under a number of different forms since the late 1960s. During that decade, Charles Goldfarb, Edward Mosher, and Raymond Lorie of IBM faced a conundrum: how to effectively store electronic documentation. The solution they came up with soon came to be known as General Markup Language (GML), which was a way of providing a logically cohesive structure to a document that could in turn provide metadata about that document.

GML proved to be something of a hit in the early 1970s, and others began to provide their own implementations of GML. Unfortunately, although there was a great deal of similarity between these various markup languages, there were also a sufficient number of differences to make building tools for GML next to impossible. As a consequence, the adopters of this technology agreed to create a standard, called Standardized Generalized Markup Language (SGML), which was adopted by the United Nations (through the International Standards Organization) as a key standard for markup languages worldwide in the early 1980s.

SGML was an extremely powerful way of expressing a wide range of documents, but the growth and fracturing of SGML meant that the standard was also so sufficiently complex that it was difficult to implement on any but the largest machines. SGML consequently went into a decline after becoming a standard; it was still widely used but with far less activity going toward improving it during the period of intense growth in the computer industry between 1980 and 1992.

Examining PostScript

Another standard emerged in that same interval, however: PostScript. This language is a page-description language, or a theoretically human-readable standard for describing graphical content, including both pictures and the letters of words. Adobe Systems created PostScript in the early 1980s as a way for printers to universally describe how a page looked, and it was such a success that PostScript-based printers currently dominate the printer market.

It's worth examining PostScript in some detail because PostScript provided an interesting paradigm that has made its way into SVG: the use of plain text to describe graphical information. For example, Listing 1-1 shows a PostScript document (generated for this particular chapter out of Open Office). The document is legible, but it looks far more like a programming language than a way of linguistically describing a page.

Listing 1-1. A PostScript Document

```
%!PS-Adobe-3.0
%%BoundingBox: 0 0 595 842
%%Creator: OpenOffice.org 641
%%For: seatails
%%CreationDate: Mon Apr 29 19:46:28 2002
%%Title: xmlSVGHistory.svg.sxw
%%LanguageLevel: 2
%%DocumentData: Clean7Bit
%%Pages: (atend)
%%PageOrder: Ascend
%%EndComments
%%BeginProlog
/ISO1252Encoding [
/psp_definefont { exch dup findfont dup length dict begin { 1 index
/FID ne
{ def } { pop pop } ifelse } forall /Encoding 3 -1 roll def
currentdict end exch pop definefont pop } def

/pathdict dup 8 dict def load begin
/rcmd { { currentfile 1 string readstring pop 0 get dup 32 gt { exit }
{ pop } ifelse } loop dup 126 eq { pop exit } if 65 sub dup 16#3 and 1
add exch dup 16#C and -2 bitshift 16#3 and 1 add exch 16#10 and 16#10
eq 3 1 roll exch } def
/rhex { dup 1 sub exch currentfile exch string readhexstring pop dup 0
get dup 16#80 and 16#80 eq dup 3 1 roll { 16#7f and } if 2 index 0 3
-1 roll put 3 1 roll 0 0 1 5 -1 roll { 2 index exch get add 256 mul }
for 256 div exch pop exch { neg } if } def
/xcmd { rcmd exch rhex exch rhex exch 5 -1 roll add exch 4 -1 roll add
1 index 1 index 5 -1 roll { moveto } { lineto } ifelse } def end
/readpath { 0 0 pathdict begin { xcmd } loop end pop pop } def

systemdict /languagelevel known not {
/xshow { exch dup length 0 1 3 -1 roll 1 sub { dup 3 index exch get
exch 2 index exch get 1 string dup 0 4 -1 roll put currentpoint 3 -1
roll show moveto 0 rmoveto } for pop pop } def
/rectangle { 4 -2 roll moveto 1 index 0 rlineto 0 exch rlineto neg 0
rlineto closepath } def
/rectfill { rectangle fill } def
/rectstroke { rectangle stroke } def } if
%%Trailer
%%Pages: 1
%%EOF
```

Of course, plain text does not always mean that the text is intelligible. To describe graphics, PostScript uses Reverse Polish Notation, a language especially well suited for programming structures called *stacks*. A stack is probably familiar to you in the context of a bunch of cafeteria trays sitting on springs—as a tray is added, the weight of the tray pushes the stack down, and pulling (or popping) the topmost tray off the stack pushes the remaining trays back up.

Stacks are remarkably efficient ways of handling any number of programming problems, but they have long been central to programming graphics. In a stack-based graphic system, when you want to draw something, you create a *graphical context* (think of it as one of those trays) and perform what drawing you need. At some point, you may need to change the context—perhaps the coordinate system (or the way the coordinate system is oriented) or some other property for that specific context. So, you create a *new* graphical context and push the old context onto the stack until you're done. When finished, you remove the active context and return to the previous coordinate system, variables, and so forth in the older context.

One advantage of such an approach is that you can essentially add as many contexts onto the stack as you need to perform short-term calculations, without having to spend a lot of time dealing with state maintenance. This was the approach that PostScript first used (and ultimately is the approach that SVG uses two decades later).

Another characteristic of such a stack-based graphical system is that you can describe how to draw an entire document by simply keeping track of what happens when a stack is added or removed. You can think of a PostScript document as (more or less) the history of creating the document in the first place, optimized somewhat to take into account changes that were made but then undone. In other words, PostScript is also a *declarative* language; you are describing the entire state transition set that the drawing has gone through, correlating time with a position in the document. Declarative programming differs from *procedural programming*, which makes up the bulk of what most people today consider "real" programming languages: C, C++, Java, Python, and so on.

> **NOTE** *I'd throw Perl into that mix, too, but Perl is so heavily built upon regular expressions—another form of declarative (also known as* functional*) programming—that you can think of Perl as having a foot in both worlds.*

By the way, in comparison to PostScript, Listing 1-2 shows a short SVG program (simplified a little).

Listing 1-2. A Simplified SVG Program

```
<svg width="1024" height="768">
    <defs>
        <linearGradient id="backgroundGradient" gradientTransform="rotate(90)">
            <stop offset="0%" stop-color="blue"/>
            <stop offset="100%" stop-color="navy"/>
        </linearGradient>
        <rect x="0" y="0' width="100%" height="100%" id="background"
                fill="url(#backgroundGradient)"/>
        <text dominant-baseline="mathematical" text-anchor="center" x="50%"
                y="50%" fill="yellow" id="helloWorld">
            Hello, SVG World!
        </text>
    </defs>
    <g>
        <use xlink:href="#background"/>
        <use xlink:href="#helloWorld"/>
    </g>
</svg>
```

The stack model still exists here, but it is hidden within the container/contained paradigm of XML. A <defs> section includes defined objects made available for later use by other entities. Graphical contexts are pushed on the stack to draw things and then released, hidden within the abstraction of the <use> element. An SVG document involves the creation of a tiny little world, for the most part a self-contained one, with the added benefit of persistence (that is to say, when you define an object, that object stays defined over the scope of the document). It's a powerful paradigm and is consistent with the surprisingly rich world of both HTML and XML.

The Rise of Web Markup Languages

The creation of HTML is so well documented that most grade-school children are aware of it, but I want to look at HTML as it relates to SVG and at the somewhat lesser-known underside of HTML. The original HTML that Tim Berners-Lee wrote was an extremely limited language, with perhaps a dozen tags or so. Most of the staples you think of as "crucial" to HTML, in fact, didn't even exist; form elements, tables, images, scripting blocks, and event handlers were not a part of the initial draft that Berners-Lee wrote back in the late 1980s.

Moreover, although people said HTML was written in SGML, that's actually a bit of revisionist history. Berners-Lee was attempting to solve a problem: how to make physics abstracts (summaries of articles) available to the researchers at the Center for European Nuclear Research (CERN) in Switzerland, which was where Berners-Lee worked when developing the HTTP and HTML specifications. He had encountered SGML and developed an SGML-like solution to what he perceived to be a small-scale problem. What he hadn't counted on was how quickly HTML would take off.

Meanwhile, in the United States, the U.S. Defense Advanced Research Projects Agency (DARPA) had been quietly seeding the nascent Arpanet (the precursor of the Internet) with projects to utilize SGML as a way of describing more generic entities than simple documents. In fact, DARPA was a major contributor to the National Centers for Supercomputing Applications research laboratories across the country, including the one at the University of Illinois that helped fund the creation of the Mosaic browser. It is entirely possible that had Berners-Lee not written HTML, an SGMLish language would have emerged soon thereafter because the research community had been working with SGML as data structures even around that time.

NOTE *This is not to discount the real contribution that Berners-Lee made to the effort, which was as much to give away Hypertext Transfer Protocol (HTTP) and its systems rather than charge for it as it was to develop the language in the first place.*

Unfortunately, the standards battles of the 1970s with respect to GML were repeated in the early 1990s with respect to HTML. As the number of applications for HTML increased exponentially, entrepreneurial-minded Internet browser vendors added new features to the HTML model, eventually getting to the point where there were nearly as many different versions of HTML as there were browsers.

In response to this, Berners-Lee founded a new organization, made up principally by those same vendors as well as a host of SGML experts who had wrestled with many of the same problems a generation earlier. The World Wide Web Consortium (W3C) took shape in 1994 and immediately set to work trying both to stabilize the still-morphing HTML and to try to solve some of the more egregious problems besetting the standard.

By 1996, the W3C had established a stylistic language called Cascading Style Sheets (CSS) that made it possible to separate the logical structure from its media representation. Additionally, the SGML community had attempted to create an alternative language that would use HTML/SGML-like syntax and sundry tools but would be more generalized. This language, called HyTime, started out with noble goals—to build a cohesive mechanism for linking both across a network and over time—but for the most part failed to produce more than a specification for describing music in SGML terms (an effort that has been recast in XML, by the way). However, in the process, it spawned a couple of interesting child technologies. Specifically, a superb programmer named James Clark (who also appears later in the section) created a scripting language called Document Style Semantics and Specification Language (DSSSL) that you can use to perform more complex transformations on SGML-like documents.

In that same year, the W3C recognized that if HTML were to truly evolve, it would need to become far more flexible; essentially, it would need to become a meta-language itself, like SGML. The unfortunate downside of SGML, though, came from the twenty-plus years of legacy adaptations that had made writing an SGML application still an exercise requiring complex parsers (the programs that interpret the SGML to create the document structures in memory). SGML was simply too big and flexible to fit nicely on the Web. So, the W3C stripped out all but the most basic parts of SGML to create a new language: XML.

XML was originally envisioned as being a way of creating various document structures, and consequently the first XML experts were the SGML gurus who had worked so heavily with the older language. By December 1997, the W3C had published a formal XML specification, and the language emerged to . . . well, yawns. Sold originally as a way of replacing HTML (a goal that it is in fact finally beginning to do), XML was simply too abstract and document-oriented for most people to really care.

However, one of the characteristics of XML (which had been foreseen by DARPA several years earlier) was that a consistent, simple-to-use markup language could actually encode a large number of things beyond documents. For example, it could describe data structures such as those used in object-oriented programming, and it could readily describe stack structures. Programmers (myself included, at the time) saw an XML parser as a superb way of being able to describe binary trees and hierarchical data. By late 1998, the revolution had been hijacked, and XML became synonymous with data.

By late 1998, the W3C started putting together the pieces of the Web "as they should have been built." If HTML was a page-description language with links, it would be much better to have a whole language that existed to style XML documents into a specific media representation. This effort led to the creation of the XML Stylesheet Language (XSL), which in turn consisted of one part that described the specific layout, PostScript-like, called XSL and one part for styling the XSL from the XML based on DSSSL but using XML as its description language. This language was in turn called the XML Stylesheet Language for Transformations (XSLT) and was shaped in great part by the aforementioned James Clark.

Remember those data guys? The programmers who saw XML as a way of representing data? They recognized a very subtle truth: XSLT is a compiler.

XSLT takes a string (an XML document), parses it into lexical units (XML nodes), arranges those nodes in a tree structure, and then maps that tree structure onto a new string—the output stream. Compilers are nice tools to have, especially when the output of those streams could in fact be another XML document (it doesn't have to be HTML). XSLT soon ballooned out of proportion to its XSL sibling to such an extent that XSL became interchangeable with the transformation language. Belatedly, XSL became XSL-Formatting Objects (XSL-FO), which is a way of describing page content that may end up becoming more important to the printing industry than it would be to browser manufacturers.

From Stormy Beginnings, a Common Standard

1998 was a good year for XML. Not only did it see the publication of the XML specification in December 1997, but people began looking for potential needs that weren't being met by HTML but that might be met by XML. A big one loomed in the need for a vector graphics standard.

PostScript has long been the de facto standard for describing *vector-based graphics*, or graphics that use equations rather than pixels to depict images. However, as is demonstrated previously, PostScript is a little too low level; it is a language that an expert could potentially write, but in general was far too optimized for machine use to be useful in the same way that HTML can be. HTML, however, includes nothing in the way of graphics primitives for drawing, so the field was largely ceded to proprietary standards written by third-party vendors.

A few years before, a small company named Future Splash worked out a way of encoding vector graphics in a small bundle to allow for dynamic animations without the tedious download times of digital video. Future Splash became popular—so popular that in 1996 Macromedia (one of the largest established players in the multimedia field) purchased it, renaming it Flash. Flash, rendered through Macromedia's Shockwave plug-in, has become the most common piece of proprietary software on the planet.

Adobe and Macromedia have traditionally had a rivalry, and arguably they have been battling back and forth in the multimedia production and playback arena for several years. In 1998, Adobe submitted a proposal called the Precision Graphics Markup Language (PGML) to the W3C that basically described an XML-based graphics language.

That same year, Microsoft had been looking at creating a vector markup language standard to complement its efforts with the XML, XSLT, and XML Schema (a way of defining data types associating with specific XML elements or attributes) specifications currently under submission. Macromedia at the time had released the specification for Flash but because it wasn't XML-based had chosen instead to support Microsoft's alternative: the Vector Markup Language (VML). As a proof of concept, Microsoft also created a viewer for VML that could be run as a COM component and then incorporated this viewer into Internet Explorer and Microsoft Office (where it is to this day).

The issue came to a head in the spring of 1999 within the newly formed W3C Graphics Working Group. The final consensus of the group (though one reached only after a great deal of argument) was that neither submission would be considered final. Instead, the two standards would merge into a new working draft document called the Scalable Vector Graphics language. Although both Macromedia and Microsoft were signatories to the original group and the resulting document, both companies essentially ceased to participate in the development of the standard after this point, and currently neither has provided any indication that they will support SVG in their line of products (the computer world can change overnight, however; this may not be true by the time you read this book). The SVG 1.0 Working Draft became a formal recommendation in September 2001.

Despite the apparent discord, the people and companies who participated in developing the standard is an exhaustive list of the key Internet players in the late 1990s. In addition to those mentioned earlier, other participants included Autodesk, IBM, Netscape, Apple, Sun Microsystems, Xerox, Corel, Visio, Hewlett-Packard, and Quark, as well as the XML standards organization OASIS, Oxford Brookes University, and a number of experts on graphical standards such as David Dodds, Chris Lilley, Philip Mansfield, and David Duce. This broad base of support has meant that SVG has had a chance to evolve across a number of different applications and uses even before it became widely known to the public.

The formal SVG standard is now about a year old, and its impact is already beginning to be felt. SVG is a critical part of the open-source Apache XML Project (supported heavily by IBM) and is in use with both Cocoon (the Apache Web publishing platform) and Batik (an open-source SVG component). The Adobe SVG component, which is the primary SVG platform used in this book, provides perhaps the most complete implementation of the SVG standard for multimedia playback, and graphic tool manufacturers such as Adobe, Corel, AutoDesk, and others are now incorporating it as either an import or an export format (and in most companies as both).

SVG is very much a version 1.0 technology. Like all 1.0 technologies, that means that far from being the ultimate graphics format, SVG is really just beginning to be truly field tested. Already this process has revealed a few deficiencies in the language; but as these are discovered, they are being incorporated into the SVG 1.1 specification currently underway. The working group has also proposed significant new functionality for SVG 2.0, a document that acts more as a way of defining the goals for the next generation of SVG applications. Additionally, the

W3C is likely to adopt the second versions of W3C recommendations, such as XSLT 2.0, XML Query, and XPath 2.0, within 2002 or early 2003. Further, a number of working drafts of new technologies such as XML Forms and XSL-FO either have just been recommended or are close to being so, and the W3C Graphics Working Group is coordinating closely with these other groups to ensure compatibility between the various standards.

SVG as a Piece of the Puzzle

I've been talking about SVG as a graphical format, but this is in fact somewhat misleading. You can certainly describe a graphic using SVG (indeed, almost every graphic in this book was originally generated using SVG), but it is important to realize that SVG is a language intended to work *in conjunction with* other languages, most notably the Synchronized Multimedia Integration Language (SMIL) but also scripting languages such as JavaScript, statically typed languages such as Java or C#, XSLT, XHTML (the XML version of HTML), and many others.

To that end, it's worthwhile to think of SVG as being a way of exposing graphical objects that other applications can use. For instance, SMIL is an XML-based language that in essence provides a way of correlating other languages and time- or event-based processes. The SVG animation elements work by providing an SVG structure on which to hang SMIL properties. Similarly, the SVG `<script>` element serves as a way to not only run programs within SVG documents but also to manipulate the SVG using a Document Object Model (DOM) that the SVG viewer exposes. Chapter 9, "Integrating SVG and HTML," and Chapter 10, "SVG Components," in this book also explore the fairly intimate way that SVG can work in conjunction with HTML or XHTML and how SVG can enhance HTML without replacing the benefits of using it.

Finally, XSLT is a powerful tool for both generating SVG from XML resources and for extracting key information from SVG documents. You should not overlook this particular point because it opens up a view of a world where many significant processes are actually handled through the transformation of XML data into a variety of forms, including SVG. XSLT is quietly performing a transformation on programming and application development as well, increasingly appearing as a core component in both Web and stand-alone applications, serving as a generic engine within embedded systems, and performing more of the necessary but seemingly unimportant programming that makes networked computer systems interoperate.

Consequently, when working with SVG, you should always remember that SVG by itself is far less powerful than SVG used in conjunction with something else. This is a point I hope to prove throughout this book.

Using SVG and Flash

Chances are pretty good that if you have heard anything about SVG, you will have heard about how SVG is sort of like Flash and may even be a "Flash killer."

I'll confess here, in the name of full disclosure. I worked as the Technical Editor for the *Macromedia User Journal* and am intimately familiar with both Macromedia Director and Flash applications. I personally think that Flash is a superb product and has a well-deserved reputation for producing some of the most cutting-edge multimedia on the Internet. Moreover, I think that in the area where Flash has initially been targeted, it is the dominant mechanism for both creating and displaying multimedia far and away.

So why am I not writing a book about the next version of Flash? There are actually any number of reasons, but most of them boil down to the fact that the principle thing that the Web really needs is not a superb way of building flashy presentations . . . instead, SVG will succeed because it satisfies the need for an easy-to-use, inexpensive, dynamic, nonproprietary way to build graphical inter-faces.

Let me address each of these four points individually.

Simplicity

HTML became popular not because it was the most powerful solution out there; as mentioned earlier, HTML was originally intended to describe physics abstracts, documents that no one but maybe a practicing scientist is ever likely to see. What was more important for HTML's success was that it originally had a small enough set of tags and a simple enough way of using them that you didn't *have to be* a programmer to build sophisticated applications.

This is the HyperCard principle. HTML owes a great deal to HyperCard, Apple's groundbreaking application tool that defined everything from hypertext linking to drag-and-drop language development. The people who took to HyperCard weren't programmers (at least such programmers wouldn't admit it); they were grade-school students and teachers, soldiers, and small-store owners. It was a language that let people who didn't know the arcane syntax and convo-luted logic of C++ still write applications that solved *their* needs.

The HyperCard principle is one I personally think has been forgotten (or deliberately displaced) by software vendors. In the rush to build into the business sector, to get those all important e-commerce systems contracts, the creators of too many software tools have sought to create "solutions" that are incredibly complex and only manageable by other tools (which of course those vendors provide). This holds as much for Web application development as it does for stand-alone, shrink-wrapped software. Declarative language solutions may help here, but these solutions will likely emerge from the open-source community before the commercial software industry rediscovers why it's no longer making any money.

Inexpensive

Expensive tools are another facet of this same problem. For example, my oldest daughter is nine years old. She's learning how to build Web pages on her computer (a hand-me down) on which I installed Linux. The tools she's using to build the pages are open-source—part of a distribution I paid about $50 for, primarily for the convenience of not having to burn CDs. She's now teaching her classmates how to do the same thing on the Apple computers at school, this time using inexpensive software that the school purchased.

The pages aren't fancy (unless you *really* like the Powerpuff Girls and Sailor Moon), but that's unimportant. HTML is both simple enough that she can learn it with relatively little instruction and inexpensive enough that she doesn't have to be wealthy to learn how to work with this technology.

SVG is a lot like that. Because it is an open standard, there are numerous tools emerging for the creation of SVG, some of them bare-bones, some of them quite sophisticated. If you want a full Integrated Development Environment (IDE) and development suite to create SVG applications, then you can (and should) pay a premium for them. But just as you can create HTML applications in a text editor, you can also do so with SVG (as I did in almost every instance in this book). This means the people learning SVG may not necessarily be the ones with the deepest pockets but rather the people who are most motivated to learn, and that is one of the keys that will likely make SVG the HTML of this decade.

Dynamic

Dynamic is one of those great marketing words that has been rendered largely meaningless in this day and age, but in this particular case *dynamic* has a strict technical meaning. SVG is a highly mutable language because of the combination of its XML foundation and its DOM interfaces. In many respects, SVG is one giant text string, with pieces that can be pulled out or added in as the need arises. This means it is in fact an ideal language for the broad category of graphics that are least well served on the Net: information graphics.

Information is not static; it has relevance only in a limited context and typically for only a limited duration. Some of that information can be readily expressed as text, yet the irony is that the Web is actually relatively information-poor. We are visual beings, yet most of the information on the Web is still presented to us in the form of text. Using an XSLT transformation, you can generate graphics based upon dynamic information, and you can even show how specific data points change over time, either dynamically (through DOM) or based upon previous history (by setting specific animation points within a SMIL statement). Such animations are easy to do in SVG, but they would be challenging at best within Flash or even a dedicated chart component.

Moreover, it is possible to build SVG using external libraries (though currently you need to use a lot of DOM to help the process along—see Chapter 10, "SVG Components"), and you can make the mechanisms for describing the links to these resources dynamic. This means you could configure the same core SVG document to display different kinds of output depending upon user preferences, the type of data involved, and the kind of browser being used.

Nonproprietary

Who owns the Web? This is not an academic question, and SVG was actually a central case around which this question hinged. The W3C, since its inception, has adopted a uniform and open license on all standards it has published—in essence stating that the W3C acts as the owner of all W3C material licenses and makes them freely available to anyone who wants to use them, with the proviso that no one can consequently license modified versions of these standards.

This principle is a variant upon the General Public License (GPL, or CopyLeft, as it is sometimes known) that recognizes that the standards being published are essentially being kept as part of a public trust.

An attempt was made to seriously undermine that principle in September 2001, though the issue had surfaced with SVG a few months earlier. In essence, the SVG case involved Adobe making a claim of prior patent on the SVG specification, saying it could prove it had a patent on key technologies used within SVG and consequently could enforce that patent if need be.

The implications of this are not clear, though they probably wouldn't have been good. W3C patents had, up until that point, been strictly royalty-free; that is to say, even if a member company had prior patent claims, they would need either to declare that such patents were royalty-free and not claim royalties for the use of the patent or to withdraw that particular technology from the specification.

During one meeting of the W3C Patent Working Group, a second category of license agreements was created called the Reasonable and Non-Discriminatory (RAND) license. RAND licenses would give the licensees the opportunity to charge a reasonable fee if someone used the standard in an application. The problem of course comes down to such terms as *reasonable* and *non-discriminatory*. A reasonable fee could easily bankrupt a smaller company that did lots of SVG, and a non-discriminatory license was essentially unenforceable.

SVG (and potentially other already-extant standards) were quietly shifted into the RAND category, and an accelerated response period was instituted to get it into the bylaws as quickly as possible. Fortunately, an alert reader notified the Web community through a number of developer Web sites (most notable Slashdot), and the response was enormous . . . and highly critical of the RAND license. More than 5,000 respondents wrote, including many of the major names in the Web and XML communities. As of January 2002, the W3C rescinded the RAND licenses and converted to royalty-free licenses on SVG, with Adobe giving up its claim to any prior technology that could have been used against other companies or individuals.

Why is an obscure legalistic question about patents so important to SVG developers? A RAND license, if it had been allowed to continue, would have essentially meant that any person who created anything using the standard (such as an SVG graphic or an application for editing the same) would have had to pay Adobe a usage fee—even if they weren't using any Adobe-developed software. It would have also meant that companies could not use SVG to create applications without the possibility that they would have to pay license fees to Adobe, even if they weren't planning on using the Adobe SVG Viewer.

The real effect of such an action wouldn't have been the enrichment of Adobe's coffers (save perhaps via legal fees). Instead, it would have meant that both people and companies would have simply stopped doing anything with SVG, and the language would have become just one more has-been technology.

As it stands now, however, with the RAND issue rendered moot, a number of companies (even small one- or two-person companies) are looking at SVG not just as a way to deploy multimedia presentations but also as the foundation for core technology or as an integral part of new applications. This doesn't mean that people can use the Adobe SVG Viewer as part of their own work; the Adobe SVG Viewer is very much Adobe's own implementation of the SVG standard and should by all rights be licensable. However, should you implement your own version of SVG (or license someone else's), you do not have to worry about the possibility, sometime in the future, that all of your work could be invalidated on the basis of a "prior claim." Nor do you have to worry that Adobe will change the specification beneath you in an unadvertised fashion so that your work will no longer work with the language itself.

In the debate between Flash and SVG, the status of Macromedia's Flash is considerably murkier in this regard. Macromedia has openly published the Flash format, which means you could in theory write applications that consume or produce Flash without potential litigation. However, Macromedia still holds all patents to Flash itself and has not submitted the format to any recognized standards group—and to be honest should not be expected to do so. This may prove to be more problematic as Macromedia attempts to position Flash as an alternative to complete Web page development, especially as a key provision within the Macromedia Flash license states: "You may not decompile, reverse engineer, disassemble, or otherwise reduce the Macromedia software to a human-perceivable form."

This particular story is far from over. The impetus that open-source software licenses have had on the development of new technology is forcing many people to reconsider the conditions under which they both create and license technology. It is entirely possible (though in the realm of speculation at this point) that Macromedia could choose to make SVG a format for at least reading and potentially writing Flash content. Here again, Macromedia would own the patents on its own engine, but the data format that it's using would be open-source and could only be altered through extensive public debate within the overall development community. In many ways it is this ability to have the debate in public, with the potential for input on the part of all interested parties, that illustrates why SVG should remain a royalty-free standard.

Programming and SVG

This book isn't filled with lots of fancy graphics—indeed, in comparison to what you can do with the language, the content here is distinctly pedestrian. One reason for that (my own inability as a graphic designer notwithstanding) is that I wanted to place more focus on the task of working with SVG from the standpoint of a programmer.

Programming with SVG might well be seen as something of an oxymoron, especially given that I don't really start into serious DOM programming until Chapter 8, "Animating SVG," or so in this book. However, this actually misses the point about SVG, in that the language itself includes any number of features that make it a valid programming environment even before you write the first line of JavaScript or Java.

Declarative programming differs considerably from procedural programming in that regard. In a procedural program, you focus upon specific actions: You assign this variable to this value, you turn this flag on or off, you perform this calculation, and then you move the frog over the result in pixels. In essence, procedural programming involves the creation of a running thread of actions, and you can typically, at any point in the program, say that this event will happen at this time.

Declarative programming, on the other hand, involves the creation of environments: You build primitive objects that in turn go toward the making of more complex objects, which in turn build even more complex objects. However, at any stage, the increasing complexity is also handled at an increasingly high level of abstraction so that by the time you reach the end of the document, you are in fact dealing with objects at an abstract level.

One side effect of such declarative programming arises over the issue of time. Traditional procedural programming by its nature correlates the position of the code in a routine with time; in other words, any coding written following a particular line of code will be executed after that code (within the same routine, of course).

The declarative nature of SVG is much less temporal in nature—to the extent that you could easily invert the structure of an SVG document so the definitions for objects occur after the objects themselves are invoked, with no real effect on the way the world is rendered. Because of this, in the SVG model, time becomes just one more parameter to work with (usually as part of the various SMIL animation elements). Consequently, creating multimedia applications using SVG is surprisingly easy, especially once you understand that in multimedia programming, the graphics, sound, and video are easy. Unfortunately, it's time management that generally proves to be the nightmare.

Coding against the DOM breaks this model somewhat because you reintroduce time into the equation. Currently, that is unavoidable; the language is still evolving dramatically, and most practitioners of SVG would rather have something that requires patches now than an idealized version of the language that would never actually appear. As more the growing number of SVG developers raise more issues, you'll likely begin seeing less of a need to jump into procedural code to extend the functionality of the language.

As you begin to play with SVG, you should keep this idea in your head: The best SVG code is the one that least breaks the declarative nature of the language. When I started working with SVG, I had a tendency to assume that the language was too simplistic for what I wanted to do, only to discover after having coded some hairy procedure in JavaScript that a little more digging would have revealed an already existing capability that did pretty much everything I had needed. I've rewritten a lot of the code in this book as I've become more adept with the language, and I'm astonished and amused to find that my final SVG code is much less procedural than when I started out. I hope as you get a chance to play with this technology that you will discover this same realization. It's a powerful one, Zen-like in its profundity, and it provides a good indication why I think declarative language programming will become the predominant way to "program."

Installing the Adobe SVG Viewer

Adobe has been one of the major backers of the SVG standard since its inception, and if it succeeds, it will almost certainly be directly because of the efforts of Adobe. One of the key pieces of Adobe's strategy with regard to SVG is the Adobe SVG Viewer.

The Adobe SVG Viewer 3.0 is actually two distinct products: an automation component COM object (EXE) used by Internet Explorer and a set of Java classes used by the Mozilla 0.94+ browser, as well as any Netscape browser that uses that engine (Netscape 6.0+). The components are available for free directly from Adobe at `www.adobe.com/svg`.

Installation is straightforward. Either load the application file to your system and double-click it to run the installation wizard or choose the Open option to run it once it downloads. This component is roughly 3.2MB.

Loading the Adobe SVG Viewer under Linux is a little less straightforward. From the SVG download page, you'll see a paragraph at the bottom indicating archives of older versions:

> *Older, unsupported versions of the Adobe SVG Viewer are available for developers and users who are not yet able to upgrade to the latest version of the Viewer. These versions are not supported by Adobe, and Adobe recommends that you install the latest version, above, unless you are sure that you need to install an older version. Click here to download an older version of the Adobe SVG Viewer.*

This text is a little misleading because the link also contains binaries for the Red Hat Linux distribution (Red Hat 7.3, though it works fine under Mandrake 8.1 and Suse 7.3) and a Solaris version. To install the Linux viewer, you should do the following:

1. In a terminal console, switch to super-user by typing **su**, followed by your root password.

2. Download the file `adobe-svg3.0-linux-i386.tar.gz` to a temporary directory.

3. Run **tar adobe-svg3.0-linux-i386.tar.gz** to extract it to a folder.

4. Enter **./install.sh** to run the installation routine. This will place the relevant files into the Netscape 6.0 and Mozilla 0.9.4 browser's plug-in folders.

5. Exit the console, create or download an SVG file, and then pass the URL to Mozilla. Depending upon the speed of your computer, a few seconds to a minute will pass before a license screen appears. Indicate your assent, and you should then be

able to see your SVG (the license screen is only shown the first time you view an SVG document).

NOTE   *If you include an* <embed> *tag pointing to an SVG document from HTML, you'll similarly be able to start the viewer. More details about embed tagging are covered in Chapter 2, "Getting Started: An SVG Tutorial," and Chapter 10, "SVG Components."*

Adobe SVG Viewer 3.0 enables you to view SVG 1.0 documents. Check back on the site for updates that will support SVG 1.1 and SVG 2.0.

Summary

Context is everything. This chapter looked at how and why SVG was created and some of the design principles underlying it. Understanding these principles is paramount to using SVG for anything more complex than the creation of static graphics. But even with static graphics it can turn an autogenerated monstrosity into a rich library of reusable objects. Additionally, the open-source nature of SVG means that there will be many different implementations of the specification for any number of different target applications—from printing to full multimedia extravaganzas and from interface design to page descriptions.

SVG can be a little daunting. The next chapter provides a step-by-step walk-through of several SVG documents and applications to show what goes into them. There's not a lot of how or why available yet (that's why I wrote the book in the first place), but in trying the exercises you'll get a little better feel for the language's flow. It's still early in the game, so sit back, pull up a chair, and immerse yourself in SVG.

CHAPTER 2

Getting Started: An SVG Tutorial

THE BEST WAY to learn is to do. Although it is not always possible within this book to create step-by-step walk-throughs, you can get up and running with SVG surprisingly quickly. This chapter in particular is not meant for deep insight into the creative process or programming models—instead, it is a set of simple recipes you can use to create more sophisticated applications.

Whenever possible, I also point you to the primary area that each example most heavily uses. Like any real meaningful languages, even the simplest of Scalable Vector Graphics (SVG) code requires the use of integrated concepts. Try playing with the examples, seeing if you can come up with the solutions to the problems posed at the end of each exercise (answers are available on my Web site at `www.kurtcagle.net`).

To work through the examples in this chapter, you will need to download and install the Adobe SVG Viewer 3.0 for both Windows- and Linux-based systems. Also, the examples covered in this chapter assume Internet Explorer 5.0 for the client and Internet Information Services (IIS) for the server (when a server is needed), but the same principles can easily be ported over to Apache on Linux.

Starting with a Stop

Creating a simple stop sign is remarkably useful for illustrating a number of different concepts. You can use stop signs to do everything from creating static images that enhance the *STOP* message to a creating a forum for political commentary by replacing the *STOP* word with some other text on a rollover. Moreover, you can go with the simple, flat stop sign or instead create a graphic with a fairly high degree of realism with SVG.

Creating a Simple, Flat Stop Sign

You have to start somewhere, and a basic sign is the simplest place to begin:

1. Install the Adobe SVG Viewer 3.0 from `www.adobe.com/svg`.

2. Open your favorite text editor to an empty document, and save it as **tutStopSign1.svg**.

3. Enter the script from Listing 2-1 into `tutStopSign1.svg`.

4. Save the file, and then open Internet Explorer or Mozilla 1.0. If this is the first SVG file you have ever viewed, a dialog box will first appear containing the licensing agreement for the viewer. Accept it (the viewer will not work if you do not—though by all means read the fine print), and you will see an SVG image that looks like Figure 2-1.

Listing 2-1. `tutStopSign1.svg`

```
<svg xmlns="http://www.w3.org/2000/svg"
     xmlns:xlink="http://www.w3.org/1999/xlink"
     width="300" height="400" viewBox="0 0 300 400"
     preserveAspectRatio="none">
<desc>Stop Sign 1</desc>
<rect x="0" y="0" width="300" height="400"
        fill="black" id="background"/>
<g transform="translate(150,150)">
    <rect x="-10" y="0" width="20" height="250"
        fill="gray" id="pole"/>
    <path id="signShape"
        d="m0,-100 l40,0 l60,60 l0,80 l-60,60 l-80,0 l-60,-60
                    l0,-80 l60,-60z"/>
    <use xlink:href="#signShape" x="0" y="0"
        fill="white" id="signWhite"/>
    <use xlink:href="#signShape" x="0" y="0" fill="red"
        transform="scale(0.95)" id="signRed"/>
    <text x="0" y="0"
        font-size="72"
        font-family="Arial Narrow"
        fill="white"
        text-anchor="middle"
        dominant-baseline="mathematical">
    STOP
```

Figure 2-1. A simple stop sign with flat shapes and vectors

```
</text>
    </g>
</svg>
```

So what is going on here? A quick step-by-step analysis demonstrates how easy SVG can be to create. The first part of the <svg> sets the stage, so to speak, identifying the namespaces and the coordinate system:

```
<svg xmlns="http://www.w3.org/2000/svg"
    xmlns:xlink="http://www.w3.org/1999/xlink"
    width="300" height="400" viewBox="0 0 300 400"
    preserveAspectRatio="none">
```

Perhaps the best way of thinking about a *namespace* is to envision that it serves the same role to Extensible Markup Language (XML) as a ProgID or class name serves to COM or Java, respectively—it both uniquely identifies the role that elements with that prefix have and tells the respective processors what engine to run to make the XML actually do something useful. In this case, there are two namespaces: the default namespace that identifies SVG (www.w3.org/2000/svg) and a linking namespace for creating internal references to existing blocks of SVG code (www.w3.org/1999/xlink).

NOTE *The formal definition of a namespace is remarkably complicated because a namespace essentially defines and identifies the vocabulary used to describe a specific object, procedure, or mechanism. Informally, the namespace Uniform Resource Identifier (or namespace URI) is frequently called the namespace as well, but this URI is , in fact, a way of uniquely labeling the more conceptual namespace itself. Finally, the namespace prefix is a convenient nonunique label to identify elements in the namespace and is mapped to a namespace through an expression such as* `xmlns:svg=http://www.w3.org/2000/svg` *for the SVG name-space.*

After this and a brief internal description, the various elements are defined. The black background is established as a rectangle element:

```
<rect x="0" y="0" width="300" height="400" fill="black" id="background"/>
```

The pole is similarly a rectangle, though a gray one:

```
<rect x="-10" y="0" width="20" height="250" fill="gray" id="pole"/>
```

The sign is a more complicated shape and uses the <path> element to define the specific points that the sign uses:

```
<path id="signShape"
d="m0,-100 l40,0 l60,60 l0,80 l-60,60 l-80,0 l-60,-60 l0,-80 l60,-60z"/>
```

Because the shape is used twice—once for the external white part of the sign and again for the internal red part—rather than duplicating it, the SVG document invokes the <use> element to employ the path as a shape, scaling the dimensions of the shape down by 5 percent to draw the smaller red portion:

```
<use xlink:href="#signShape" x="0" y="0" fill="white" id="signWhite"/>
 <use xlink:href="#signShape" x="0" y="0" fill="red"
transform="scale(0.95)" id="signRed"/>
```

Finally the text element is drawn, positioned so that it will always be centered with respect to the sign:

```
<text x="0" y="0"
      font-size="72"
      font-family="Arial Narrow"
      fill="white"
      text-anchor="middle"
      dominant-baseline="mathematical">STOP</text>
```

The next several chapters discuss the specific properties discussed in this section in considerably greater depth. For now, experiment with changing various properties to see what effects they have.

....

Debugging SVG

If everything goes properly, you should in fact see the image in Figure 2-1. However, in the real world, things seldom go completely as planned—especially with large blocks of SVG. Furthermore, the Adobe SVG Viewer does not help matters much because it is what is known as a "lazy" parser. In other words, it will basically draw the document up to the point where an error occurs, rather than just failing outright. Although this can mean you can get *most* of your graphic on the screen, it also means that tracking down problems often requires the recognition that there is a problem in the first place, something that is not always immediately obvious.

One of the best advantages of working with SVG is the fact that it is XML. If you utilize an XML processor, you can determine whether you have well-formed XML (which is where a significant portion of all problems with SVG usually stem from). Fortunately, both Internet Explorer and Mozilla 1.0 include such processors, but they are (at least on the Windows side) typically only triggered if the file itself has an .xml extension.

So, if you are having problems in the previous file, change the name from tutStopSign1.svg to tutStopSign1.xml and view it in either of the two browsers (Internet Explorer is probably more reliable on this front, but both will do). If the document is not well formed, you will probably get a message that looks something like Figure 2-2. In that case, make sure the end tags match the start tags and that nothing is improperly contained. Once you are done, check again, and if it works, rename the file to **tutStopSign1.svg** and trying viewing it again.

Figure 2-2. A common error message

Creating a More Realistic Stop Sign

The stop sign you just created is . . . well, less than living up to its full potential. Frankly, it is ugly. Specifically, it has no sense of depth, shading, texture, or any of the other cues that help in making graphics appear more realistic. Additionally, it does not begin to show off the real capabilities of SVG. Consider a real stop sign: It is usually on some kind of metallic pole, with screws holding it into place, the light is seldom uniform over its surface, and it is usually at least a little dirty.

Is that doable in SVG? Sure, though to do so well, you have to create a little more complex SVG document:

1. Open your favorite text editor to an empty document, and save it as **tutStopSign2.svg**.

2. Enter the SVG code in Listing 2-2 into tutStopSign2.svg.

3. Open Internet Explorer or Mozilla and view the file (see Figure 2-3).

Listing 2-2. tutStopSign2.svg

```
<svg xmlns="http://www.w3.org/2000/svg"
    xmlns:xlink="http://www.w3.org/1999/xlink"
    width="300" height="400" viewBox="0 0 300 400"
    preserveAspectRatio="none">
    <defs>
```

```
<linearGradient id="signGrad" gradientTransform="rotate(45)">
    <stop offset="0%" stop-color="white" stop-opacity="0"/>
    <stop offset="100%" stop-color="black" stop-opacity=".4"/>
</linearGradient>
<radialGradient id="boltGrad"
        gradientTransform="translate(-0.2,-0.2)">
    <stop offset="0%" stop-color="#E0E0E0"/>
    <stop offset="70%" stop-color="#808080"/>
    <stop offset="100%" stop-color="black"/>
</radialGradient>
<linearGradient id="steel">
    <stop offset="0%" stop-color="#C0C0C0"/>
    <stop offset="20%" stop-color="#404040"/>
    <stop offset="30%" stop-color="#FFFFFF"/>
    <stop offset="60%" stop-color="#808080"/>
    <stop offset="65%" stop-color="#202020"/>
    <stop offset="70%" stop-color="#C0C0C0"/>
    <stop offset="100%" stop-color="#8080"/>
</linearGradient>
<linearGradient id="steelShadow" gradientTransform="rotate(90)">
    <stop offset="0%" stop-color="black" stop-opacity="1"/>
    <stop offset="40%" stop-color="black" stop-opacity="1"/>
    <stop offset="42%" stop-color="black" stop-opacity="0"/>
    <stop offset="100%" stop-color="black" stop-opacity="0"/>
</linearGradient>
  <filter id="Turb5" filterUnits="objectBoundingBox"
          x="0%" y="0%" width="100%" height="100%">
    <feTurbulence type="fractalNoise" baseFrequency="0.3" numOctaves="4"/>
  </filter>
<image xlink:href="ForbiddingTrimmed.jpg" x="0" y="0"
                width="300" height="400" fill="black"
                id="background"/>
<path id="signShape" d="m0,-100 l40,0 l60,60
l0,80 l-60,60 l-80,0 l-60,-60 l0,-80 l60,-60z"/>
<mask maskUnits="objectBoundingBox" id="signMask">
            x="0%" y="0%" width="100%" height="100%">
    <use xlink:href="#signShape" x="0" y="0" width="100%"
            height="100%" fill="white"/>
</mask>
<circle cx="0" cy="0" r="4" fill="url(#boltGrad)" id="bolt"/>
<g transform="translate(150,150)" id="sign">
    <rect x="-10" y="0" width="20" height="250"
            fill="url(#steel)" id="pole"/>
```

```
            <rect x="-10" y="0" width="20" height="250"
                    fill="url(#steelShadow)" id="pole"/>
            <use xlink:href="#signShape" x="0" y="0" fill="white"
                    id="signWhite"/>
            <use xlink:href="#signShape" x="0" y="0" transform="scale(0.95)"
                    id="signInner"/>
            <text x="0" y="0" font-size="72" font-family="Arial Narrow"
                    fill="white" text-anchor="middle"
                    dominant-baseline="mathematical">
                STOP
                </text>
            <use xlink:href="#signShape" x="0%" y="0%" filter="url(#Turb5)"
                    id="signShade"  mask="url(#signMask)" opacity="0.4"/>
            <use xlink:href="#signShape" x="0%" y="0%" fill="url(#signGrad)"
                    id="signShade"  mask="url(#signMask)"/>
            <use xlink:href="#bolt" x="0" y="-80"/>
            <use xlink:href="#bolt" x="0" y="80"/>
        </g>
        </defs>
        <use xlink:href="#background" x="0" y="0"/>
        <use xlink:href="#sign" x="0" y="0" fill="red"/>
    </svg>
```

Figure 2-3. A richer stop sign, combined with a bitmap graphic

This is a little more like it. The image in the background (done in a 3D-rendering program) gives a sense of foreboding and makes the sign seem considerably more solid. The sign itself has a subtle overlay gradient that makes it appear to be slightly warped (perhaps someone did not stop quite soon enough). The pole now has depth and solidity, down to the shadow that the sign casts on it, and the steel bolts on the sign now seem to actually hold it to the pole. If you look closely enough, you will also see a faint patina of dirt on the sign.

This illustrates a little more of the true power of SVG. You can combine fairly complex gradients with Photoshop-like filters and bitmap graphics to create both realistic and abstract graphics. The fascinating thing about all of this is that the second stop sign is not all that much more complicated than the first sign in terms of the SVG document, as a little analysis will reveal. The `<svg>`-containing element is the same, defining the image as having a height of 400 pixels and a width of 300 pixels:

```
<svg xmlns="http://www.w3.org/2000/svg"
     xmlns:xlink="http://www.w3.org/1999/xlink"
     width="300" height="400" viewBox="0 0 300 400" preserveAspectRatio="none">
```

The `<defs>` element defines elements to be used later in the graphic without displaying the pieces ahead of time; think of it as a place where templates are stored for defining more complex elements.

In this example, the first things to define are *gradients*: shades of color that can be assigned to specific objects. You can create gradients that run in a line from starting to ending color (`<linearGradient>` elements) or that grow in a circle (technically an oval) from a central point outward (`<radialGradient>`). Gradients can also combine varying levels of opacity in the mix, as illustrated in the `#signGrad` gradient:

```
<linearGradient id="signGrad" gradientTransform="rotate(45)">
    <stop offset="0%" stop-color="white" stop-opacity="0"/>
    <stop offset="100%" stop-color="black" stop-opacity=".4"/>
</linearGradient>
<radialGradient id="boltGrad" gradientTransform="translate(-0.2,-0.2)">
    <stop offset="0%" stop-color="#E0E0E0"/>
    <stop offset="70%" stop-color="#808080"/>
    <stop offset="100%" stop-color="black"/>
</radialGradient>
<linearGradient id="steel">
    <stop offset="0%" stop-color="#C0C0C0"/>
    <stop offset="20%" stop-color="#404040"/>
    <stop offset="30%" stop-color="#FFFFFF"/>
    <stop offset="60%" stop-color="#808080"/>
```

```
                <stop offset="65%" stop-color="#202020"/>
                <stop offset="70%" stop-color="#C0C0C0"/>
                <stop offset="100%" stop-color="#8080"/>
        </linearGradient>
        <linearGradient id="steelShadow" gradientTransform="rotate(90)">
                <stop offset="0%" stop-color="black" stop-opacity="1"/>
                <stop offset="40%" stop-color="black" stop-opacity="1"/>
                <stop offset="42%" stop-color="black" stop-opacity="0"/>
                <stop offset="100%" stop-color="black" stop-opacity="0"/>
        </linearGradient>
```

The `<filter>` element makes it possible to apply a number of special effects
to one of the various SVG shape elements, making an object blur, creating highlights and lighting effects, generating drop shadows and glows, and composing
multiple elements (and potentially bitmaps) into single blocks. Filters tend to be
expensive (in terms of processing time), but for static graphics they can create
extremely powerful effects (see Chapter 10, "SVG Components"). The following
filter, #Turb5, was responsible for creating the "dirty" surface on the sign:

```
<filter id="Turb5" filterUnits="objectBoundingBox"
        x="0%" y="0%" width="100%" height="100%">
    <feTurbulence type="fractalNoise" baseFrequency="0.3" numOctaves="4"/>
</filter>
```

The image element makes it possible to combine vector graphics with
bitmaps. Using the XML Xlinking notation, images can reference JPEG, GIF, or
PNG images universally and can also load in SVG graphics as static images:

```
<image xlink:href="ForbiddingTrimmed.jpg" x="0" y="0"
        width="300" height="400" fill="black" id="background"/>
```

As with tutStopSign1.svg, the `<path>` element in tutStopSign2.svg defines
the octagonal shape of the stop sign. But in addition to its use by the white and
red portions of the sign, this image also uses `<path>` to create a mask so that when
the filter or gradients are applied to it they are only drawn within the dimensions
of the sign itself, and not in the rest of the signs bounding rectangle:

```
        <path id="signShape"
          d="m0,-100 140,0 160,60 l0,80 l-60,60
                l-80,0 l-60,-60 l0,-80 160,-60z"/>
        <mask maskUnits="objectBoundingBox" x="0%" y="0%"
                width="100%" height="100%" id="signMask">
            <use xlink:href="#signShape" x="0" y="0"
                width="100%" height="100%" fill="white"/>
        </mask>
```

The shape definition and layering is similar between the first and second version but makes more extensive use of the <use> element to build multiple sandwiched layers of predefined components: sign, post, text, shading and textures, and bolts, all tied together in a single package called #sign. For example:

```
<circle cx="0" cy="0" r="4" fill="url(#boltGrad)" id="bolt"/>
<g transform="translate(150,150)" id="sign">
    <rect x="-10" y="0" width="20" height="250"
            fill="url(#steel)" id="pole"/>
    <rect x="-10" y="0" width="20" height="250"
            fill="url(#steelShadow)" id="pole"/>
    <use xlink:href="#signShape" x="0" y="0"
            fill="white" id="signWhite"/>
    <use xlink:href="#signShape" x="0" y="0"
            transform="scale(0.95)" id="signInner"/>
    <text x="0" y="0" font-size="72" font-family="Arial Narrow"
            fill="white" text-anchor="middle"
           dominant-baseline="mathematical">
           STOP
    </text>
    <use xlink:href="#signShape" x="0%" y="0%"
            filter="url(#Turb5)" id="signShade"
            mask="url(#signMask)" opacity="0.4"/>
    <use xlink:href="#signShape" x="0%" y="0%"
            fill="url(#signGrad)" id="signShade"  mask="url(#signMask)"/>
    <use xlink:href="#bolt" x="0" y="-80"/>
    <use xlink:href="#bolt" x="0" y="80"/>
</g>
</defs>
```

Once outside the <defs> element, all elements that are listed actually render to the canvas of the SVG:

```
<use xlink:href="#background" x="0" y="0"/>
<use xlink:href="#sign" x="0" y="0" fill="red"/>
</svg>
```

Here the graphic is rendered through two simple calls: one to draw the background, and the other to draw the sign. In well-defined SVG, abstraction—hiding the irrelevant details of a drawing at successive points in the document—provides the key to both programmatic capabilities and ease of design. I will return to this point throughout the book.

Adding a Sunset or Sunrise

SVG is not just for static graphics, though as `tutStopSign2.svg` illustrates, you can create impressive two-dimensional graphics with SVG. However, one of the goals of the SVG language is to do more than simply provide an alternative to PostScript. Although never explicitly stated within the SVG charter, certainly one area where there is significant overlap in functionality comes from the vector animation program Flash, which utilizes a binary format for storing and manipulating shapes, images, and text. Flash started as Future Splash, which recognized that if you could just keep track of the changes in vector characteristics of an animated graphic, you could send an animation over the wire in a fraction of the space that you would need to send a digital video animation or even a GIF image.

This saving was not lost to the SVG development committee. The SVG recommendation incorporates portions of the Synchronized Multimedia Integration Language (SMIL) to perform a novel function: providing a method to indicate when specific animations should take place, how they take place, and against which properties.

You can modify the stop sign graphic through the use of these SMIL elements to perform any number of different tasks, such as changing the position of elements, changing their opacities, changing text contents, or even reacting to mouse clicks. For instance, try typing in `tutStopSign3.svg` (Listing 2-3) and see what happens (see Figure 2-4).

Listing 2-3. `tutStopSign3.svg`

```
<svg xmlns="http://www.w3.org/2000/svg"
    xmlns:xlink="http://www.w3.org/1999/xlink"
               width="300" height="400" viewBox="0 0 300 400"
               preserveAspectRatio="none">
    <defs>
      <filter id="Turb5" filterUnits="objectBoundingBox"
             x="0%" y="0%" width="100%" height="100%">
        <feTurbulence type="fractalNoise" baseFrequency="0.3"
               numOctaves="4"/>
      </filter>
      <linearGradient id="signGrad" gradientTransform="rotate(45)">
          <stop offset="0%" stop-color="white" stop-opacity="0"/>
          <stop offset="100%" stop-color="black" stop-opacity=".4"/>
      </linearGradient>
      <radialGradient id="boltGrad" gradientTransform="translate(-0.2,-0.2)">
          <stop offset="0%" stop-color="#E0E0E0"/>
          <stop offset="70%" stop-color="#808080"/>
          <stop offset="100%" stop-color="black"/>
      </radialGradient>
```

```
<linearGradient id="steel">
    <stop offset="0%" stop-color="#C0C0C0"/>
    <stop offset="20%" stop-color="#404040"/>
    <stop offset="30%" stop-color="#FFFFFF"/>
    <stop offset="60%" stop-color="#808080"/>
    <stop offset="65%" stop-color="#202020"/>
    <stop offset="70%" stop-color="#C0C0C0"/>
    <stop offset="100%" stop-color="#8080"/>
</linearGradient>
<linearGradient id="steelShadow" gradientTransform="rotate(90)">
    <stop offset="0%" stop-color="black" stop-opacity="1"/>
    <stop offset="40%" stop-color="black" stop-opacity="1"/>
    <stop offset="42%" stop-color="black" stop-opacity="0"/>
    <stop offset="100%" stop-color="black" stop-opacity="0"/>
</linearGradient>
<image xlink:href="ForbiddingTrimmed.jpg" x="0" y="0"
        width="300" height="400" fill="black" id="background"/>
<image xlink:href="SandDune.jpg" x="0" y="0"
        width="300" height="400" fill="black" id="background2"/>
<path id="signShape"
        d="m0,-100 l40,0 l60,60 l0,80 l-60,60
            l-80,0 l-60,-60 l0,-80 l60,-60z"/>
<mask maskUnits="objectBoundingBox" x="0%" y="0%"
        width="100%" height="100%" id="signMask">
    <use xlink:href="#signShape" x="0" y="0"
        width="100%" height="100%" fill="white"/>
</mask>
<circle cx="0" cy="0" r="4" fill="url(#boltGrad)" id="bolt"/>
<rect id="night" x="0" y="0" width="300" height="400" fill="black"/>
<g transform="translate(150,150)" id="sign">
    <rect x="-10" y="0" width="20" height="250"
            fill="url(#steel)" id="pole"/>
    <rect x="-10" y="0" width="20" height="250"
            fill="url(#steelShadow)" id="pole"/>
    <use xlink:href="#signShape" x="0" y="0"
            fill="white" id="signWhite"/>
    <use xlink:href="#signShape" x="0" y="0"
            transform="scale(0.95)" id="signInner"/>
    <text x="0" y="0" font-size="72" font-family="Arial Narrow"
            fill="white" text-anchor="middle"
            dominant-baseline="mathematical">
            STOP
    </text>
```

```
            <use xlink:href="#signShape" x="0%" y="0%"
                    filter="url(#Turb5)" id="signShade"
                    mask="url(#signMask)" opacity="0.4"/>
            <use xlink:href="#signShape" x="0%" y="0%"
                    fill="url(#signGrad)" id="signShade"  mask="url(#signMask)"/>
            <use xlink:href="#bolt" x="0" y="-80"/>
            <use xlink:href="#bolt" x="0" y="80"/>
    </g>
    <g transform="translate(150,150)" id="sign2">
        <rect x="-10" y="0" width="20" height="250"
                    fill="url(#steel)" id="pole"/>
        <rect x="-10" y="0" width="20" height="250"
                    fill="url(#steelShadow)" id="pole"/>
        <use xlink:href="#signShape" x="0" y="0" fill="white" id="signWhite"/>
        <use xlink:href="#signShape" x="0" y="0"
                    transform="scale(0.95)" id="signInner"/>
        <text x="0" y="0" font-size="72" font-family="Arial Narrow"
                    fill="white" text-anchor="middle"
                    dominant-baseline="mathematical">
                    GO
        </text>
        <use xlink:href="#signShape" x="0%" y="0%"
                    filter="url(#Turb5)" mask="url(#signMask)"
                    opacity="0.4" id="signShade"/>
        <use xlink:href="#signShape" x="0%" y="0%"
                    fill="url(#signGrad)" mask="url(#signMask)"
                    id="signShade"  />
        <use xlink:href="#bolt" x="0" y="-80"/>
        <use xlink:href="#bolt" x="0" y="80"/>
    </g>
    </defs>
    <use xlink:href="#background" x="0" y="0">
        <set attributeName="xlink:href" attributeType="XML"
                to="#background2" begin="15s" fill="freeze"/>
    </use>
    <use xlink:href="#night" x="0" y="0" opacity="0">
        <animate attributeName="opacity" attributeType="CSS"
                values="0;0.9;0.9;0" dur="30s" fill="freeze"/>
    </use>
    <use xlink:href="#sign" x="0" y="0" fill="red">
        <set attributeName="xlink:href" attributeType="XML"
                to="#sign2" begin="15s" fill="freeze"/>
```

Figure 2-4. Changing opacity, text, and even background bitmaps

```
        <set attributeName="fill" attributeType="CSS"
                to="green" begin="15s" fill="freeze"/>
    </use>
    <use xlink:href="#night" x="0" y="0" opacity="0">
        <animate attributeName="opacity" attributeType="CSS"
values="0;0.9;0.9;0" dur="30s" fill="freeze"/>
    </use>
</svg>
```

There are relatively few differences between this and the previous sign in the `<defs>` section: A second sign (#sign2) was added that was identical to the first except that instead of the word *STOP*, the sign has the word *GO* on it. Additionally, I have defined a black rectangle entitled #night to handle some special effects.

The primary changes, however, come in the *rendered* portion of the graphic. Each of the visible `<use>` elements now include a set of animations that tell that element to change the value of a particular property, either continuously (such as changing the opacity of the #night graphic) or via discreet jumps (changing the xlink property in the middle of the animation sequence to point to a different graphic):

```
<use xlink:href="#background" x="0" y="0">
    <set attributeName="xlink:href" attributeType="XML"
            to="#background2" begin="15s" fill="freeze"/>
</use>
```

```
<use xlink:href="#night" x="0" y="0" opacity="0">
    <animate attributeName="opacity" attributeType="CSS"
            values="0;0.9;0.9;0" dur="30s" fill="freeze"/>
</use>
<use xlink:href="#sign" x="0" y="0" fill="red">
    <set attributeName="xlink:href" attributeType="XML"
            to="#sign2" begin="15s" fill="freeze"/>
    <set attributeName="fill" attributeType="CSS"
            to="green" begin="15s" fill="freeze"/>
</use>
<use xlink:href="#night" x="0" y="0" opacity="0">
    <animate attributeName="opacity" attributeType="CSS"
            values="0;0.9;0.9;0" dur="30s" fill="freeze"/>
</use>
```

The animation in the <use> element that references #background changes the background 15 seconds after the document is loaded. The #night referencing element (essentially a black rectangle that sits behind the sign but in front of the background) fades up from being completely transparent to nearly completely opaque. At 15 seconds after the show begins, the sign changes color from red to green while simultaneously changing the referenced text from *STOP* to *GO*. Finally, another #night layer sits on top of the sign itself, providing a different level of "sunset" effects for the sign than for the background.

NOTE *Although the opacity patterns are the same in both cases, the opacities multiply for the background. In other words, at the darkest point, the sign is only 90-percent opaque, while the background becomes 99-percent opaque [100%-(100%–90%)*(100%–90%)=99%].*

Generating a Graph

You can often overlook the fact that SVG is an XML format when you are using it to create "artistic" pieces, but it is in fact a powerful reason for exploring SVG as a way of creating *information graphics.* Graphs, charts, and maps all lend themselves to *auto-generation,* or using an XML data source to drive the way that such a map gets displayed and then using XML Stylesheet Language for Transformations (XSLT) to actually performing the mapping of the data into the SVG structure. Certainly you can use XSLT to handle translation to other graphics formats (such as PostScript), but the difficulty is that XSLT is really optimized for working with XML (or XML-like languages such as HTML). The mix of XML, SVG, and XSLT thus makes for a potent combination in the development of information graphics that can change in a timely fashion.

For example, consider a graph that displays traffic volume for an Internet service. The purpose of the graph is to determine, at any given time of day, whether the volume is extraordinarily higher or lower than the average for that time. This graph displays the activity as two bars: a blue bar that shows the current activity and an overlaying red bar (slightly transparent) that shows the expected average for that time of day. Significant discrepancies between the two will show up clearly in such a graph (see Figure 2-5).

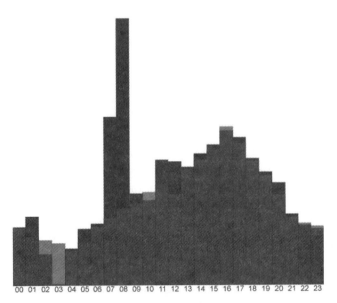

Figure 2-5. Creating an information graphic

To create an information graphic, follow these steps:

1. Create the following XML file (or load it from the Web site at www.kurtcagle.net or the Apress site at www.apress.com) and save it as **activity.xml**:

```
<activity>
    <report time="2002-04-05T00:00:00" current="1824" average="1792"/>
    <report time="2002-04-05T01:00:00" current="2159" average="1524"/>
    <report time="2002-04-05T02:00:00" current="981" average="1412"/>
    <report time="2002-04-05T03:00:00" current="52" average="1316"/>
```

```
        <report time="2002-04-05T04:00:00" current="1152" average="1102"/>
        <report time="2002-04-05T05:00:00" current="1762" average="1355"/>
        <report time="2002-04-05T06:00:00" current="1922" average="1825"/>
        <report time="2002-04-05T07:00:00" current="5255" average="2101"/>
        <report time="2002-04-05T08:00:00" current="7332" average="2411"/>
        <report time="2002-04-05T09:00:00" current="2864" average="2557"/>
        <report time="2002-04-05T10:00:00" current="2655" average="2903"/>
        <report time="2002-04-05T11:00:00" current="3912" average="3152"/>
        <report time="2002-04-05T12:00:00" current="3855" average="2825"/>
        <report time="2002-04-05T13:00:00" current="3688" average="3604"/>
        <report time="2002-04-05T14:00:00" current="4102" average="3902"/>
        <report time="2002-04-05T15:00:00" current="4387" average="4217"/>
        <report time="2002-04-05T16:00:00" current="4822" average="4943"/>
        <report time="2002-04-05T17:00:00" current="4611" average="4421"/>
        <report time="2002-04-05T18:00:00" current="3951" average="3871"/>
        <report time="2002-04-05T19:00:00" current="3527" average="3402"/>
        <report time="2002-04-05T20:00:00" current="3194" average="2814"/>
        <report time="2002-04-05T21:00:00" current="2219" average="2107"/>
        <report time="2002-04-05T22:00:00" current="1865" average="1924"/>
        <report time="2002-04-05T23:00:00" current="1755" average="1825"/>
    </activity>
```

2. For the next part, you will need a command-line XSLT processor. Although there are several you can use, I like the Saxon Java-based parser (specifically, Saxon7), which you can download from Michael Kay's Saxon project on Source Forge (saxon.sourceforge.org). To use Saxon, you also need to have a version of Java, generally 1.2 or above (I use 1.3.1 in these samples).

3. Enter the following stylesheet, or download it from www.kurtcagle.net:

```
<xsl:stylesheet xmlns:xsl="http://www.w3.org/1999/XSL/Transform"
    xmlns="http://www.w3.org/2000/svg"
    version="1.0">
    <xsl:output method="xml" media-type="image/svg-xml"
            omit-xml-declaration="yes" indent="yes"/>
    <xsl:variable name="maxValue">
        <xsl:call-template name="max">
            <xsl:with-param name="list"
                    select="//report/@current|//report/@average"/>
        </xsl:call-template>
    </xsl:variable>
    <xsl:template match="/">
```

```
        <xsl:apply-templates/>
</xsl:template>


<xsl:template match="activity">
    <svg>
        <g transform="translate(50,50)">
        <svg x="0" y="0" width="500" height="500"
                viewBox="0 0 1000 {$maxValue * 1.2}"
                preserveAspectRatio="none">
        <g transform="translate(0,{$maxValue * 1.2}),scale(1,-1)">
        <xsl:apply-templates select="report"/>
        </g>
        </svg>
        <g transform="translate(0,510)">
            <xsl:apply-templates select="report" mode="labels"/>
        </g>
        </g>
    </svg>
</xsl:template>


<xsl:template match="report">
    <rect
            x="{format-number((position() - 1)
             *1000 div count(//report),'0.0')}"
             y="0"
             width="{format-number(1000 div count(//report),'0.0')}"
             height="{@current}"
             fill="blue" stroke="black" stroke-width="2"/>
    <rect
            x="{format-number((position() - 1)
            *1000 div count(//report),'0.0')}"
             y="0"
             width="{format-number(1000 div count(//report),'0.0')}"
             height="{@average}"
             fill="red" stroke="black"
             stroke-width="2" opacity="0.7"/>
</xsl:template>


<xsl:template match="report" mode="labels">
    <text
            x="{format-number((position() - 0.5)
            * 500 div count(//report),'0')}"
            y="0"
```

```
                                   text-anchor="middle">
                                <xsl:value-of select="substring(@time,12,2)"/>
          </text>
      </xsl:template>

      <xsl:template name="min">
          <xsl:param name="list"/>
          <xsl:variable name="minValue">
          <xsl:for-each select="$list">
              <xsl:sort select="." order="ascending" data-type="number"/>
              <xsl:if test="position()=1">
              <item><xsl:value-of select="number(.)"/></item>
              </xsl:if>
          </xsl:for-each>
          </xsl:variable>
          <xsl:value-of select="$minValue"/>
      </xsl:template>

      <xsl:template name="max">
          <xsl:param name="list"/>
          <xsl:variable name="maxValue">
          <xsl:for-each select="$list">
              <xsl:sort select="." order="descending" data-type="number"/>
              <xsl:if test="position()=1">
              <item><xsl:value-of select="number(.)"/></item>
              </xsl:if>
          </xsl:for-each>
          </xsl:variable>
          <xsl:value-of select="$maxValue"/>
      </xsl:template>


  </xsl:stylesheet>
```

4. Apply the stylesheet to the data via a command-line call, saving the file
    as **activity.svg** (you will need to change the location given to reflect the
    path to your XSLT processor):

```
c:\> java -jar c:\winnt\saxon7.jar activity.xml
                        showActivity.xsl > activity.svg
```

5. View the results in Listing 2-4 in Internet Explorer or Mozilla (the result should look like Figure 2-4).

Listing 2-4. Resulting SVG Output (Reformatted for Legibility)

```
<svg xmlns="http://www.w3.org/2000/svg">
    <g transform="translate(50,50)">
        <svg x="0" y="0" width="500" height="500"
                    viewBox="0 0 1000 9998.4"
                    preserveAspectRatio="none">
            <g transform="translate(0,9998.4),scale(1,-1)">
                <rect x="0.0" y="0" width="41.7" height="1824"
                        fill="blue" stroke="black" stroke-width="2"/>
                <rect x="0.0" y="0" width="41.7" height="1792"
                        fill="red" stroke="black" stroke-width="2" opacity="0.7"/>
                <rect x="41.7" y="0" width="41.7" height="2159"
                        fill="blue" stroke="black" stroke-width="2"/>
                <rect x="41.7" y="0" width="41.7" height="1524"
                        fill="red" stroke="black" stroke-width="2" opacity="0.7"/>
                <rect x="83.3" y="0" width="41.7" height="981"
                        fill="blue" stroke="black" stroke-width="2"/>
                <rect x="83.3" y="0" width="41.7" height="1412"
                        fill="red" stroke="black" stroke-width="2" opacity="0.7"/>
                <rect x="125.0" y="0" width="41.7" height="52"
                        fill="blue" stroke="black" stroke-width="2"/>
                <rect x="125.0" y="0" width="41.7" height="1316"
                        fill="red" stroke="black" stroke-width="2" opacity="0.7"/>
                <rect x="166.7" y="0" width="41.7" height="1152"
                        fill="blue" stroke="black" stroke-width="2"/>
                <rect x="166.7" y="0" width="41.7" height="1102"
                        fill="red" stroke="black" stroke-width="2" opacity="0.7"/>
                <rect x="208.3" y="0" width="41.7" height="1762"
                        fill="blue" stroke="black" stroke-width="2"/>
                <rect x="208.3" y="0" width="41.7" height="1355"
                        fill="red" stroke="black" stroke-width="2" opacity="0.7"/>
                <rect x="250.0" y="0" width="41.7" height="1922"
                        fill="blue" stroke="black" stroke-width="2"/>
                <rect x="250.0" y="0" width="41.7" height="1825"
                        fill="red" stroke="black" stroke-width="2" opacity="0.7"/>
                <rect x="291.7" y="0" width="41.7" height="5255"
                        fill="blue" stroke="black" stroke-width="2"/>
                <rect x="291.7" y="0" width="41.7" height="2101"
                        fill="red" stroke="black" stroke-width="2" opacity="0.7"/>
```

```
<rect x="333.3" y="0" width="41.7" height="8332"
      fill="blue" stroke="black" stroke-width="2"/>
<rect x="333.3" y="0" width="41.7" height="2411"
      fill="red" stroke="black" stroke-width="2" opacity="0.7"/>
<rect x="375.0" y="0" width="41.7" height="2864"
      fill="blue" stroke="black" stroke-width="2"/>
<rect x="375.0" y="0" width="41.7" height="2557"
      fill="red" stroke="black" stroke-width="2" opacity="0.7"/>
<rect x="416.7" y="0" width="41.7" height="2655"
      fill="blue" stroke="black" stroke-width="2"/>
<rect x="416.7" y="0" width="41.7" height="2903"
      fill="red" stroke="black" stroke-width="2" opacity="0.7"/>
<rect x="458.3" y="0" width="41.7" height="3912"
      fill="blue" stroke="black" stroke-width="2"/>
<rect x="458.3" y="0" width="41.7" height="3152"
      fill="red" stroke="black" stroke-width="2" opacity="0.7"/>
<rect x="500.0" y="0" width="41.7" height="3855"
      fill="blue" stroke="black" stroke-width="2"/>
<rect x="500.0" y="0" width="41.7" height="2825"
      fill="red" stroke="black" stroke-width="2" opacity="0.7"/>
<rect x="541.7" y="0" width="41.7" height="3688"
      fill="blue" stroke="black" stroke-width="2"/>
<rect x="541.7" y="0" width="41.7" height="3604"
      fill="red" stroke="black" stroke-width="2" opacity="0.7"/>
<rect x="583.3" y="0" width="41.7" height="4102"
      fill="blue" stroke="black" stroke-width="2"/>
<rect x="583.3" y="0" width="41.7" height="3902"
      fill="red" stroke="black" stroke-width="2" opacity="0.7"/>
<rect x="625.0" y="0" width="41.7" height="4387"
      fill="blue" stroke="black" stroke-width="2"/>
<rect x="625.0" y="0" width="41.7" height="4217"
      fill="red" stroke="black" stroke-width="2" opacity="0.7"/>
<rect x="666.7" y="0" width="41.7" height="4822"
      fill="blue" stroke="black" stroke-width="2"/>
<rect x="666.7" y="0" width="41.7" height="4943"
      fill="red" stroke="black" stroke-width="2" opacity="0.7"/>
<rect x="708.3" y="0" width="41.7" height="4611"
      fill="blue" stroke="black" stroke-width="2"/>
<rect x="708.3" y="0" width="41.7" height="4421"
      fill="red" stroke="black" stroke-width="2" opacity="0.7"/>
<rect x="750.0" y="0" width="41.7" height="3951"
      fill="blue" stroke="black" stroke-width="2"/>
<rect x="750.0" y="0" width="41.7" height="3871"
      fill="red" stroke="black" stroke-width="2" opacity="0.7"/>
```

```
        <rect x="791.7" y="0" width="41.7" height="3527"
                fill="blue" stroke="black" stroke-width="2"/>
        <rect x="791.7" y="0" width="41.7" height="3402"
                fill="red" stroke="black" stroke-width="2" opacity="0.7"/>
        <rect x="833.3" y="0" width="41.7" height="3194"
                fill="blue" stroke="black" stroke-width="2"/>
        <rect x="833.3" y="0" width="41.7" height="2814"
                fill="red" stroke="black" stroke-width="2" opacity="0.7"/>
        <rect x="875.0" y="0" width="41.7" height="2219"
                fill="blue" stroke="black" stroke-width="2"/>
        <rect x="875.0" y="0" width="41.7" height="2107"
                fill="red" stroke="black" stroke-width="2" opacity="0.7"/>
        <rect x="916.7" y="0" width="41.7" height="1865"
                fill="blue" stroke="black" stroke-width="2"/>
        <rect x="916.7" y="0" width="41.7" height="1924"
                fill="red" stroke="black" stroke-width="2" opacity="0.7"/>
        <rect x="958.3" y="0" width="41.7" height="1755"
                fill="blue" stroke="black" stroke-width="2"/>
        <rect x="958.3" y="0" width="41.7" height="1825"
                fill="red" stroke="black" stroke-width="2" opacity="0.7"/>
    </g>
</svg>
<g transform="translate(0,510)">
    <text x="10" y="0" text-anchor="middle">00</text>
    <text x="31" y="0" text-anchor="middle">01</text>
    <text x="52" y="0" text-anchor="middle">02</text>
    <text x="73" y="0" text-anchor="middle">03</text>
    <text x="94" y="0" text-anchor="middle">04</text>
    <text x="115" y="0" text-anchor="middle">05</text>
    <text x="135" y="0" text-anchor="middle">06</text>
    <text x="156" y="0" text-anchor="middle">07</text>
    <text x="177" y="0" text-anchor="middle">08</text>
    <text x="198" y="0" text-anchor="middle">09</text>
    <text x="219" y="0" text-anchor="middle">10</text>
    <text x="240" y="0" text-anchor="middle">11</text>
    <text x="260" y="0" text-anchor="middle">12</text>
    <text x="281" y="0" text-anchor="middle">13</text>
    <text x="302" y="0" text-anchor="middle">14</text>
    <text x="323" y="0" text-anchor="middle">15</text>
    <text x="344" y="0" text-anchor="middle">16</text>
    <text x="365" y="0" text-anchor="middle">17</text>
    <text x="385" y="0" text-anchor="middle">18</text>
    <text x="406" y="0" text-anchor="middle">19</text>
```

```
            <text x="427" y="0" text-anchor="middle">20</text>
            <text x="448" y="0" text-anchor="middle">21</text>
            <text x="469" y="0" text-anchor="middle">22</text>
            <text x="490" y="0" text-anchor="middle">23</text>
        </g>
    </g>
</svg>
```

To understand what is going on in this example, it is probably best to start from the final SVG document and work backward. In `activity.svg`, the structure is divided into two distinct sections. The first contains the graph itself, with no text contents. For ease of display, this particular code shifts the graphic down and to the right by 50 pixels through the use of a translation transform on a containing <g> element:

```
<svg xmlns="http://www.w3.org/2000/svg">
    <g transform="translate(50,50)">
```

In the second section, the graph in turn takes advantage of "local" coordinate systems. It makes the assumption that the "interior" height of the graph (in other words, the height as seen by the graph elements themselves) is sized to be about 20-percent taller than the height of the highest element. This ensures that the graph will always show all of the data for each time period, though it does so at the cost of no longer being consistent in scale. The external dimensions, on the other hand, are set to be a consistent 500x500 pixels. This automatically forces the page to rescale itself to fit in that dimension, regardless of the dimensions used within the SVG:

```
<svg x="0" y="0" width="500" height="500"
    viewBox="0 0 1000 9998.4" preserveAspectRatio="none">
```

The real goal in working with SVG is to try to do as little work in computation as possible. One of the problems in creating graphs is the fact that the coordinate system that SVG uses (one in which vertical coordinates go *down* the page rather than up) are well suited to computer graphics but not at all suited to most charts (which work in the reverse direction). Consequently, rather than trying to calculate the difference in height between the top of the document and the baseline—a pretty complicated undertaking—I simply draw the boxes down from a given baseline and then flip the entire picture along the horizontal axis with the command scale (1,-1). Once this happens, the graphic is now *above* the top of the graphic, so I have to move it (translate) back down by the generated height of the graph:

```
<g transform="translate(0,9998.4),scale(1,-1)">
```

The graphic rectangles themselves are actually straightforward. The width is calculated so that however many you have in the sample (in this case, 24), the total will always add up to 500, give or take a few pixels from rounding. Each graph point consists of two rectangles, one blue and solid, the other red and 70-percent opaque. The opacity makes it easy to overlay one over the other to see where the greatest discrepancies are between the average and the actual value:

```
<rect x="0.0" y="0" width="41.7" height="1824"
                    fill="blue" stroke="black" stroke-width="2"/>
<rect x="0.0" y="0" width="41.7" height="1792"
                    fill="red" stroke="black" stroke-width="2" opacity="0.7"/>
<rect x="41.7" y="0" width="41.7" height="2159"
                    fill="blue" stroke="black" stroke-width="2"/>
<rect x="41.7" y="0" width="41.7" height="1524"
                    fill="red" stroke="black" stroke-width="2" opacity="0.7"/>
<!-- more along this line -->
```

I deliberately separated out the labels from the rest of the graph because of the reflection and translation issue; drawing the text into the graph would have made the letters appear upside down in the final output. Instead, a new <g> element was defined to move the starting positions of the letters to just under the graph, and each text item was positioned to be centered under their corresponding block. Note that the hours are given in military time, ranging from 00 for midnight to 23 for 11 p.m. Not only is this the easiest way to generate this information (in essence, reading it from the activity timestamps), but it also keeps the labels both big enough to see and small enough to avoid overlap. For example:

```
<g transform="translate(0,510)">
    <text x="10" y="0" text-anchor="middle">00</text>
    <text x="31" y="0" text-anchor="middle">01</text>
    <text x="52" y="0" text-anchor="middle">02</text>
    <text x="73" y="0" text-anchor="middle">03</text>
        <!-- more along this line -->
```

That is it. You could do more with this graph, of course—making the elements dynamic, including coordinate grids, and so forth, but the principle in working with those elements is essentially the same as shown in this section.

Examining the XSLT

The XSLT to generate such a graph is fairly simple, though it can be daunting if you have not worked a lot with XSLT in the past. Because XSLT is somewhat outside of the immediate scope of this chapter, I want to just briefly discuss what each template does.

The initial header creates the stylesheet namespaces and also identifies the namespace for SVG, something that is reinforced by the `<xsl:output>` object that defines the `method` attribute (which describes the overall structural language) as being `xml` and the media-type as being `images/svg-xml`:

```
<xsl:stylesheet xmlns:xsl="http://www.w3.org/1999/XSL/Transform"
    xmlns="http://www.w3.org/2000/svg"
    version="1.0">
    <xsl:output method="xml" media-type="image/svg-xml"
        omit-xml-declaration="yes" indent="yes"/>
```

Perhaps the only really flashy part of the XSLT transformation involves the generation of the maximum value from the data sets. Because the maximum could in fact come from either the current timestamps (an extraordinarily high-hit response) or from the average timestamp for that period (if, for instance, a denial of service attack hit the server for more than a day), the maximum value needs to be calculated from the union of the two sets and is then assigned into the variable $maxValue:

```
<xsl:variable name="maxValue">
    <xsl:call-template name="max">
        <xsl:with-param name="list"
                        select="//report/@current|//report/@average"/>
    </xsl:call-template>
</xsl:variable>
```

NOTE *XSLT variables start with the dollar ($) sign except at the time of their definition, and I use the same notation to refer to them within the text body.*

The routine that actually does the sorting, well, er . . . cheats. It takes the list of nodes in the XML source, then uses the `<xsl:sort>` attribute on an `<xsl:for-each>` to automatically order the nodes by the requisite attributes.

By indicating whether the sorted list is ascending or descending in order, you can then be sure that the first element will always be either the lowest or highest value in the list. For example:

```
<xsl:template name="min">
    <xsl:param name="list"/>
    <xsl:variable name="minValue">
    <xsl:for-each select="$list">
        <xsl:sort select="." order="ascending" data-type="number"/>
        <xsl:if test="position()=1">
        <item><xsl:value-of select="number(.)"/></item>
        </xsl:if>
    </xsl:for-each>
    </xsl:variable>
    <xsl:value-of select="$minValue"/>
</xsl:template>
```

The root template match passes the processing to the next node, `activity`, which lays out the initial SVG document structure, then processes the records twice—first to generate the graph, then to generate the labels. Note the use of bracketed XPath evaluations to calculate the height and offset of the graph region:

```
<xsl:template match="/">
    <xsl:apply-templates/>
</xsl:template>

<xsl:template match="activity">
    <svg>
        <g transform="translate(50,50)">
        <svg x="0" y="0" width="500" height="500"
                    viewBox="0 0 1000 {$maxValue * 1.2}"
                    preserveAspectRatio="none">
        <g transform="translate(0,{$maxValue * 1.2}),scale(1,-1)">
        <xsl:apply-templates select="report" mode="graph"/>
        </g>
        </svg>
        <g transform="translate(0,510)">
            <xsl:apply-templates select="report" mode="labels"/>
        </g>
        </g>
    </svg>
</xsl:template>
```

The `report` template, graph mode, is where the heavy lifting is done. Normally, calculations done on numbers return those numbers with a mantissa of eight significant figures. Unfortunately, although more accurate, this makes things much harder to read; thus, most of the calculations are cleaned up with the format-number XPath function:

```
<xsl:template match="report" mode="graph">
    <rect
            x="{format-number((position() - 1)*1000 div count(//report),'0.0')}"
            y="0"
            width="{format-number(1000 div count(//report),'0.0')}"
            height="{@current}"
            fill="blue" stroke="black" stroke-width="2"/>
    <rect
            x="{format-number((position() - 1)
            *1000 div count(//report),'0.0')}"
            y="0"
            width="{format-number(1000 div count(//report),'0.0')}"
            height="{@average}"
            fill="red" stroke="black" stroke-width="2"
            opacity="0.7"/>
</xsl:template>
```

The label generator is in fact a fairly simple variant of the rectangle drawing routine. The positioning mechanism is nearly identical, save for a half-bar offset to ensure that the text is centered on the bar's midpoint rather than on the bar's leftmost point. The routine that retrieves the hour extracts the hour field from the @time attribute for each report (as substring(@time,12,2)):

```
<xsl:template match="report" mode="labels">
    <text
            x="{format-number((position() - 0.5)
            * 500 div count(//report),'0')}"
            y="0"
            text-anchor="middle">
                    <xsl:value-of select="substring(@time,12,2)"/>
    </text>
</xsl:template>
```

That is pretty much it. As with XSLT in general, the trick to using SVG with XSLT is to pass to each language the task that they are best suited for—in other words, SVG for rendering, changing graphical context, and defining entities, and XSLT for positioning, identifying pieces, building core objects, and performing conditional logic.

Summary

The tutorials in this chapter were intended to give you a blitz of what real SVG documents look like, and a great deal of information was glossed over in the interest of trying to pull together a sampler of what you can do with the language.

The next several chapters look at the various pieces of the SVG puzzle: coordinate systems, shapes, fills, strokes, images, and text, as well as animation, interactivity, the DOM, and then ultimately back to XSLT again. If you have trouble understanding this chapter, I recommend you come back here after each chapter and see how later explanations relate to this content.

Learning is seldom a linear process, no matter how much you may try to make it so. Instead, knowledge and wisdom come only when a solid foundation exists upon which to build.

CHAPTER 3
You Are Here: Coordinate Systems and Transformations

IN 1649, THE FRENCH PHILOSOPHER and mathematician Rene Descartes took a position with the Swedish Queen Christina as Royal Mathematician (see Figure 3-1). A few months into his stay, however, the cold and gloom of that northern country soon forced him into an extended bed-rest while he struggled (ultimately unsuccessfully) against a cold that turned into pneumonia. One day, while in bed, he watched an ant as it made its way up a wall and onto the ceiling, and he began wondering what the shortest path that the ant could take across the walls was to get from one point to another. The ruminations proved to be the foundation for Cartesian coordinate systems, where every point in a plane is assigned a pair of numbers corresponding to specific locations. Other than providing the morale that laying in bed all day can actually accomplish something useful, this development also laid the ground for most of modern mathematics and computer graphics.

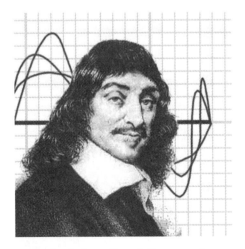

Figure 3-1. Rene Descartes, the father of analytic geometry

Much of Scalable Vector Graphics (SVG) involves either setting or modifying the coordinates of an object, of an object's container, or of the whole view space. Intimately tied into the notion of a coordinate system is the concept of a transformation, which determines how those coordinates are moved, resized (scaled), rotated, or squashed. In this chapter I introduce the concept of coordinate systems, transformations, and coordinate attributes and animations involving transformations. This is something of a core chapter, as almost everything that comes after it will involve working with coordinates in some form, so it is worth taking the time to understand the concepts involved.

Understanding Coordinate Systems and Transformations

A computer screen consists of an array of pixels, with each pixel having a width of anywhere from $1/72$ to $1/96$ of an inch, depending upon the monitor and the resolution of the graphics card. This in turn determines the screen "size," which can be 640×480, 800×600, 1024×768, and up, usually in a ratio of 4×3 (called the *aspect ratio*). Because this 4×3 aspect ratio has become the dominant one in monitors, there are few screens that do not fit into this ratio.

Computer monitors from the earliest days worked by drawing *rasters* (the Cathod Ray Tube excitation beam) from left to right and top to bottom, with each point on the screen specified as an absolute position in memory (with that memory usually mirroring the position on the screen). Thus, a 320×240-pixel screen would locate the position (24,135) as 24 * 320+135 or an offset of 7,815 from the starting point in memory. Because it is generally easy to give the position as a pair of x and y coordinates, the top-down arrangement of pixels meant that the resulting coordinate system works contrary to most mathematical coordinate systems by having the positive y axis going down rather than up. This is often referred to as the *pixel* (or *screen*) coordinate system.

The pixel coordinate system has become the default format that most, if not all, computers current use. In such a system, the origin is given as the point (0,0) and is set to the upper-left corner of the screen. The x axis runs from left to right in a one-to-one relationship with the pixels on the screen, and the y axis starts with 0 at the top and increases as you move down. Note that this is the opposite of the format that is used in most graphs, where the y axis moves up the page.

NOTE *Because most 3D graphics packages also assume that the third dimension, usually called the z axis, extends from the screen to the user, the pixel coordinate system is an example of a* left-hand system. *In other words, if the thumb moves along the positive x axis and the index finger points along the positive y axis, the middle finger (when curled perpendicular to the other two) will face toward the positive z axis.*

The default coordinate system is a map to the pixel positions, but there are some fundamental differences between the map and the display. A computer display can only show integral pixels. You can read or write the pixel located at (400,250) 400 pixels from the left and 250 pixels down, but you cannot have a pixel at (400.42,250,375).

However, the coordinate system is different in that it *does* permit such partial points. Moreover, the screen itself is limited to only those points in the range (0,0)–(799,599) on an 800x600 screen, but the coordinate system can in fact extend from negative infinity (–∞) to positive infinity (+∞) in either direction. The coordinate system describes an infinitely long, infinitely wide plane (Figure 3-2).

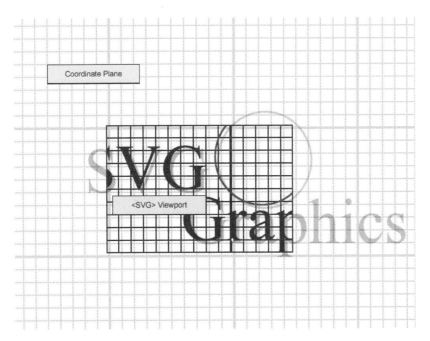

Figure 3-2. Placing a viewport on a near infinitely large, infinitely precise coordinate system

In practice, the SVG coordinate plane is neither completely continuous nor completely infinite, but it is instead limited to the data types used to describe coordinates on the particular computer system. For instance, on a typical Windows or Unix computer system, the coordinates are actually described as of type double and as such can go from roughly -2^{127} to 2^{127} and to a granularity of 2^{-128}. In other words, they can go from $-340,282,366,920,938,463,463,374,607,431,770,000,000$ to $340,282,366,920,938,463,463,374,607,431,770,000,000$ at a resolution of $0.0000000000000000000000000000000000003$ units. However, unless you are attempting to create a galactic-sized computer chip that utilizes quarks as building blocks, this should generally be more than satisfactory for your needs.

Of course, in practice, the discrete resolution of the physical devices means that the SVG engine needs to compensate for the fact that a 0.5-pixel line is smaller than the smallest element that can display that line. It does this by using anti-aliasing—approximating the appearance of a line or edge by combining pixels of differing shades, as shown in Figure 3-3. Of course, if a line or edge is too fine, then it may not show up at all in the output.

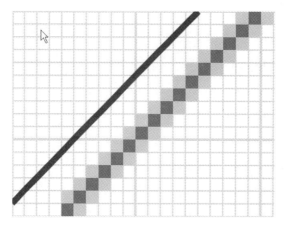

Figure 3-3. A finer resolution than the pixel dimensions would suggest

 NOTE *The internal model that SVG uses maintains the precision regardless of what is drawn on the screen. Consequently, if you zoom into a graphic, anti-aliased lines and edges will become more distinct, and lines too fine to render in the original will appear.*

When you create an SVG document, the implicit assumption that the SVG processor makes (unless you explicitly change it) is that the coordinate system maps one *user unit* to one pixel. This is the base coordinate system. You can think of a coordinate system as being a map: It describes the terrain, of course, but a map also provides three other useful services:

- A map gives you a set of measures, letting you know the distance from one point to another in an appropriate unit.

- It defines the location of at least one point relative to the rest of the world, an origin relative to a larger coordinate system.

- It provides an orientation—the direction of the "top" of the map relative to North.

Each map defines its own units (usually inches or centimeters but not always) along with a conversion system that maps these units to "real-world" distances: miles, kilometers, meters, feet, inches, and so forth. Maps can thus define structures or features relative to these local, or user units. The mapmaker employs these user units to scale other features; for instance, if the mapmaker takes his information from an aerial photograph, he only needs to be concerned about the scale of the map relative to the photograph. If the map shows a lake 3 inches to the right of a town in the reference photograph, the cartographer can create a map that scales the distance between lake and town to 6 user units (that may or may not be inches) on his map, without needing to worry about the actual distance between the real-world lake and town.

Moreover, suppose you had three maps: one of the United States, one of Washington state, and one of Olympia, Washington. The dimensions of the maps themselves may well be the exact same size (assume for the moment that they are all in an atlas). However, the user units for each map differs considerable—and not coincidentally, so does the level of detail that can be shown. A street map of Olympia for instance, could easily show my street, whereas you would need a microscope to see the same street from the U.S. map. It is much easier for the mapmaker to create streets when using the map of Olympia than when using the map of the United States.

This principle carries over to SVG. In general, it is preferable to define elements relative to a local origin, orientation, and scale than it is to use the same units universally and orientation. For instance, suppose you have a graphic intended to be $3\frac{1}{2}$-inches wide by 2-inches high. You can, with SVG, create a coordinate system that has a width of 3.5 and a height of 2.5 that maps internally to the pixel coordinate system; you do not need to know that on this system, 1 inch equates to 80 pixels or 96 pixels—when you specify a square that is a half-inch on a side and located 1.5 pixels to the right and down from the origin, you do not need to perform the calculations to determine how many pixels that is. In essence, you have created a temporary second coordinate system that overlays the first.

Taking this one step further, suppose you had a map of Washington state within the graphic. With an atlas, you could determine the position (in miles) relative to the upper-left corner of the state of the border, and you could compile this information in turn into an SVG path object. However, if the picture of just the state was meant to be an inch wide, then each coordinate in the path would have to be rescaled in a normal graphic. In SVG, on the other hand, you can in fact change the coordinate system *again*, this time going from a system-based on inches to one based on miles. By just creating a new map, relative to the old, you can retain the path information in miles (basically, by telling the SVG parser that 1 inch equals roughly 400 miles). Figure 3-4 shows that each map has its own coordinate system to best express features. A map can thus be considered a viewport into that local coordinate system.

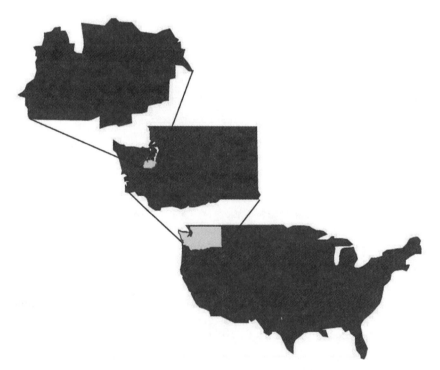

Figure 3-4. Using the most appropriate coordinate system for a given map

TIP *This brings up another interesting potential use for SVG. You can nest such maps arbitrarily deep, raising the possibility of building "maps" with multiple layers of information, each coupled to its containing map by transformation information. Such maps do not necessarily have to be geographical in nature—you could in fact hide hierarchical topic trees within SVG graphics in this same way, using as coordinates less tangible metrics such as how closely related the topics are. Chapter 11, "The Future of SVG," will discuss this in some detail.*

Working with Viewports

The concept of a *viewport* is simple. You can think of a viewport as a virtual screen—everything within the bounds of that screen is visible, and everything outside of it is not. From the standpoint of the SVG engine, though, a viewport involves the concept of a clipping region—every time the screen refreshes, the processor checks to see if the point about to be drawn is within the clipping region. If it is, then the pixel is painted; otherwise it is not.

 NOTE *The clipping region does not have to be rectangular, by the way. Chapter 7, "Incorporating Texture," will explore how you can make an irregular clipping region.*

The <svg> element performs three services. It determines the dimensions of the viewport that all child elements of that SVG element share. Any element within <svg> abides by that viewport; if part of the graphic lies outside of the viewport, then that part will not be displayed. The <svg> element also defines the coordinate system to be used in the viewport, relative to the external viewport. Finally, it defines the global coordinates to be used by the viewport associated with the browser window or embedded control, and in that capacity acts as the root node for the rest of the document.

The SVG element has a number of standard attributes though it is important to note that *no* attributes are explicitly required on the <svg> element (see Table 3-1). The bare <svg> tag by itself will define a default coordinate system that matches the pixel-based coordinate system that the screen uses. Moreover, by not specifying dimensions, the <svg> element will automatically expand to the extent of the graphics within that element.

Table 3-1. Attributes of the <svg> *Element*

ATTRIBUTE NAME	TYPE/DEFAULTS	WHAT DOES IT DO?
width	length | percentage (100%)	Sets the width of the viewport, either in absolute units or current container units. Percentage should be given as "35%", for instance.
height	length | percentage (100%)	Sets the height of the viewport, either in absolute units or current container units.
x	length | percentage (0)	Sets the horizontal position of the viewport, either in absolute units or current container units.
y	length | percentage (0)	Sets the vertical position of the viewport, either in absolute units or current container units.
viewBox	(x y width height)	Gives the unit dimensions of the bounding box in new coordinates.
preserveAspectRatio	none | xMinYMin | xMinYMid | xMinYMax | ... xMaxYMax (xMidYMid) meet | slice(meet)	Forces uniform scaling. Set this to none to allow anisotropic scaling. The meet or slice subattribute controls truncation behavior.
zoomAndPan	disable | (magnify)	This determines whether the graphic permits zooming on the element in question.
contentScriptType	qname (text/ecmascript)	This gives the type of scripting language used by default within the document.
contentStyleType	(text/css)	Gives the default style language in use. Currently this can only be text/css.
xmlns	www.w3.org/2000/svg	Defines the default namespace of the Extensible Markup Language (XML) document (in this case SVG 1.0). This is not required, but it is a good habit.
xmlns:link	www.w3.org/1999/xlink	Defines the xLink namespace and sets it to the link prefix. This is only needed if you are going to use the xLink namespace within this document, but it does not hurt if you leave it in and do not use it (another good habit).

The `width` and `height` attributes provide the dimensions to the SVG viewport, relative to the external coordinate system. This means that, unless you specify dimensions with units, the values you give for the width and height are those of the containing coordinate system. Thus, the following code:

```
<svg xmlns="http://www.w3.org/2000/svg" width="4in" height="2in">
```

will create a viewport that is 4-inches wide and 2-inches high, regardless of the coordinate system. But it does not change the internal coordinates to a scale of inches. An SVG document like this one:

```
<svg xmlns="http://www.w3.org/2000/svg"  width="4in" height="2in">
    <rect width="1" height="1"/>
</svg>
```

will display a rectangle at the upper-left corner that is 1-pixel wide by 1-pixel high. You can use these same internal coordinates with each attribute internally. For example, this SVG document:

```
<svg xmlns="http://www.w3.org/2000/svg"  width="4in" height="2in">
    <rect width="1in" height="1in"/>
</svg>
```

will properly display a 1-inch-by-1-inch box within a viewport that is 4 inches by 2 inches.

SVG recognizes the same absolute units that Cascading Style Sheets (CSS) does, as shown in Table 3-2.

Table 3-2. SVG Coordinate Systems

UNIT NAME	UNIT DESCRIPTION	ABSOLUTE OR RELATIVE?
Inch (in)	English inch	Absolute
Centimeter (cm)	Metric centimeter (1in=2.54cm)	Absolute
Millimeter (mm)	Metric millimeter (1in = 25.4mm)	Absolute
Pixel (px)	The length of one pixel, which changes depending upon the resolution of the screen (the default coordinate system for SVG)	Relative
Point (pt)	Printer's point (1in = 72.72pts)	Absolute
Em (em)	The width of the capital M in the current font	Relative
En (en)	The width of the capital N in the current font = half of 1 em	Relative

However, the following code:

```
<svg xmlns="http://www.w3.org/2000/svg"  width="400" height="200">
```

will use the default coordinate system (in this case, pixel coordinates) to set the units.

The viewBox in turn defines the internal coordinate system used by anything within the width and height of the <svg> element. These values are given as a list of four space-separated values, containing the coordinate of the left-top corner in the new units, then the width and height of the bounding box in the new units. For instance, this code:

```
<svg xmlns="http://www.w3.org/2000/svg"
        width="400" height="200"
        viewBox="0 0 10 5">
```

will create a view box where the upper-left corner has a coordinate position of (0,0), the width of the box is 10 user units, and the height of the box is 5 user units. The conversion is straightforward: At a width of 400 pixels, each user unit will be 40-pixels wide (ditto for the height). Thus, if you draw a rectangle that starts at x="2" y="1" and has a width of "5" and height of "3" pixels:

```
<svg xmlns="http://www.w3.org/2000/svg"
    width="400" height="200" viewBox="0 0 10 5">
    <rect x="2" y="1" width="5" height='3' fill="blue" stroke="black"/>
</svg>
```

the box would have a corresponding dimension in the "original" coordinates of x="80", y="40", width="200", and height="120".

Things get a little more complicated when the starting position for the new coordinates is non-zero. The first two coordinates describe the location of the viewport *in the new coordinate system*. This means if you set the two initial coordinates to (2,3), you are indicating that the only those elements that have an x value greater than 2 and a y value greater than 3 will appear within the bounding rectangle. Thus, the following code:

```
<svg xmlns="http://www.w3.org/2000/svg"  width="400" height="200"
    viewBox="2 3 10 5">
        <rect x="2" y="1" width="5" height='3' fill="blue" stroke="black"/>
</svg>
```

displays only a portion of the rectangle. Note that the display area is still 10 user units wide and 5 high, however, which means that the lower-right corner of the display area is now (12,8), which is (10+2,5+3). Thus, the second sets of coordinates is the position of the lower-right part of the view box *relative* to the upper-left.

CAUTION *This distinction needs to be maintained. The temptation is to think of the lower-right corner as being given in absolute coordinates, which can often cause great angst and suffering as your images seem to be preternaturally extended.*

Leaving the viewBox attribute off gives you the same effect as if you had declared a view box with a width and height of the same value as the values in the width and height attributes, positioned so that the upper-left corner is at (0,0). If no such attributes are declared, then the coordinates of the view box are given in pixels.

Aspect Ratios

The proportion of width to height is called the *aspect ratio*. Normally, if the inner coordinate system's aspect ratio is the same as the outer system's aspect ratio, the contents displayed within the inner coordinate system will be scaled proportionately. Things get a little more complicated, however, when the two aspect ratios are different. At that point, the SVG rendering engine has to figure out how to make the two ratios compatible. It does this through the preserveAspectRatio attribute.

This property lets you specify the part of a graphic that is most important to appear in the image. For instance, the hint of "xMinYMax" will mean you want to make sure the minimum x value (the leftmost part of the image) is visible, while the maximum y value (the bottommost part of the image) is also visible. On the other hand, xMidYMid would indicate that the middle of the image must be displayed, regardless of what else is shown.

The impact of this property depends upon which of two modes are specified: meet and slice. In the meet mode, the processor will try to ensure that the whole image appears by scaling the largest dimension to fit into the external display region. Listing 3-1 demonstrates how the meet mode displays two <svg> contexts, one where the internal ratio of width to height is greater than 1 (the solid rectangles), the other where the ratio is less than 1 (the dashed rectangles). The meet attribute ensures that the largest dimension of the graphic will always be displayed (see Figure 3-5).

Listing 3-1. `preserveAspectRatioMeet.svg`

```
<svg xmlns="http://www.w3.org/2000/svg"  x="0" y="0"
        width="100" height="100" viewBox="0 0 10 5"
              preserveAspectRatio="xMidYMin meet">
    <rect fill="none" stroke="red" x="0" y="0" width="10"
              height="5" stroke-width="0.5"/>
</svg>

<svg xmlns="http://www.w3.org/2000/svg"  x="0" y="0"
        width="100" height="100" viewBox="0 0 5 10"
              preserveAspectRatio="xMidYMin meet">
    <rect fill="none" stroke="blue" x="0" y="0" width="5" height="10"
              stroke-width="0.5" stroke-dasharray="0.2 0.2"/>
</svg>
```

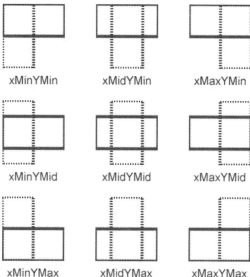

Figure 3-5. Preserving aspect ratios with meet

In general, with the meet attributes, when the aspect ratio (`width`/`height`) of the inner coordinate system is greater than that of the outer coordinate system, the y part of the descriptor will determine where in the bounding box the rectangle will appear. For instance, the expression `"xMaxYMin meet"` will make the graphic appear at the top of the bounding box. On the other hand, if the aspect ratio of the inner coordinate system is less than that of the outer system, then the x part predominates (xMaxYMin here would cause the contents to shift all the way to the right).

The slice mode will scale the image so that the smaller of the two dimensions gets displayed in full, but the larger one gets "sliced off." In this case, the descriptors determine which portion of the image remains visible, which is again tied into whether the aspect ratio of the outer coordinate system or the inner one is larger (see Figure 3-6).

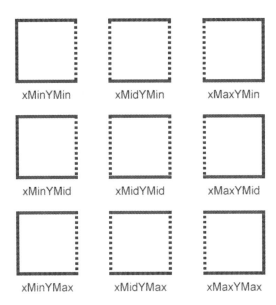

Figure 3-6. Preserving aspect ratios with slice

You can give the format for preserveAspectRatio either as "xMinYMax slice" or "slice xMinYMax". Although order is unimportant here, case is very much significant.

Of course, in many cases, it is actually better if the internal image expanded or contracted to completely fit the container, but to do that, the aspect ratios must be made to match. This, consequently, means that either the width or the height must end up being rescaled to compensate, contracting or extending the internal graphic in one or the other dimension. You can accomplish this by setting preserveAspectRatio to the value "none".

NOTE *Transformations that preserve the aspect ratio are called* isomorphic, *meaning equal change. Those that do not preserve the aspect ratio are called* anisomorphic. *Isomorphic transformations also have the useful property that they preserve angles, as well (in other words, they are isogonal).*

Zooming and Panning

Like everybody, I am getting older. My eyes are just not as clear as they used to be, and type that once upon a time seemed perfectly right seems to have shrunk to being absurdly small. The zoom-and-pan feature (A rather awkwardly named feature that simultaneously handles both characteristics) built into SVG is actually just right for my eyes. Zoom-and-pan actually provides two operations: zooming, which involves increasing or decreasing the scale of the viewport, and panning, which lets you move an image around by dragging on it.

You can usually accomplish panning by holding down the Alt key (the Option key on a Macintosh) and dragging on the image. You can use this to good effect when you have an embedded SVG object within a Hypertext Markup Language (HTML) document without having to write a lot of complex scripting code.

You can invoke the zoom feature, on the other hand, by holding down the Control key (the Command key on a Macintosh) to zoom in, by holding down the Shift and Control keys simultaneously to zoom out, or by right-clicking on the graphic and selecting Zoom Out or Zoom In from the context menu that appears.

The zoomAndPan attribute lets you control these features. By setting this attribute to "magnify" (or not giving any zoomAndPan attribute at all), you enable the default behavior. To turn it off, you would simply set zoomAndPan to disable. This disables the zoom features in the context menu and turns off the graphic's ability to accept the Control or Alt keys for zooming or panning, respectively.

Abstracting with ‹g› and ‹use›

In most programming languages, one of the most critical elements you can work with are the block or grouping elements. For instance, in JavaScript the grouping elements are the braces ({ and }). In SVG, there is plenty of need for grouping, but the grouping itself should be done within the context of XML. Thus, the language introduces the ‹g› element, known as either the *grouping* (the SVG formal name for it) or *graphics context* (my name for it) element. Table 3-3 shows the attributes of the ‹g› element.

Table 3-3. Attributes of the `<g>` *Element*

ATTRIBUTE NAME	TYPE/DEFAULTS	WHAT DOES IT DO?
transform	translate() | scale() | rotate() | skewX() | skewY() | matrix()	Sets the width of the viewport, either in absolute units or current container units.
id	qname	This provides an identifier that other elements can reference (and that can be used in SVG DOM code).
CSS properties	Varied	CSS properties can be applied to all elements within a `<g>` element.

The `<g>` elements are somewhat more sophisticated than ordinary brackets, for three reasons:

- **Identity**: You can name a `<g>` grouping element via the `id` attribute and then refer to the entire block by that name in subsequent `<use>` elements.

- **CSS Property Pass-Through**: Any CSS property applied to a `<g>` element also applies to any child elements within the `<g>` element, which is as concise a definition of what CSS really is as any that I can construct.

- **Transformations**: You can also apply transformations to a graphics context, and the transformation will affect everything within that context. This makes it possible to shift the coordinate systems locally for easier rendering of content.

Identity Programming, Defs, and Uses

Identity is an integral part of SVG, especially once you start using it for programming purposes. It makes code reuse possible, which in turn leads to smaller (and more legible) files and, not coincidentally, a more functional model of programming that has some long-term implications for program development with SVG.

The reuse of code comes about by dividing your SVG into two sections: a definitions section that lets you create primitive objects (as well as aggregate objects based upon those primitives) and an instance section where the definitions are rendered into the viewport. Elements declared within the `<defs>` section (for *definitions*) are not explicitly rendered to the viewport; instead, they exist as templates, akin to *classes* in object-oriented languages.

NOTE *The class analogy here can be a little misleading. In at least the declarative portion of SVG, one of the limitations of an item defined within a* <defs> *block is that any properties explicitly assigned to that item (such as a* fill="red"*) become fixed—you cannot override that property in some subordinate item that is instantiated from the initial item. Several examples of this limitation will be brought up through the book.*

Each element (or grouping of objects) in the <defs> tag can then be referenced through a <use> tag elsewhere in the document, including in another definition. For instance, Listing 3-2 shows how a composite object (a button with an associated fill) can be defined, then an instance made of that definition (see Figure 3-7).

Listing 3-2. useButtons1.svg

```
<svg xmlns="http://www.w3.org/2000/svg"
        xmlns:link="http://www.w3.org/1999/xlink" >
  <defs>
    <linearGradient id="testGrad">
        <stop stop-color="blue" offset="0%"/>
        <stop stop-color="navy" offset="100%"/>
    </linearGradient>

    <rect id="buttonBase" fill="url(#testGrad)" x="0" y="0"
                    width="150" height="30"
                    rx="5" ry="5" stroke="black"/>

    <text id="buttonText" text-anchor="middle"
            fill="yellow" font-size="20">Button</text>

    <g id="button">
        <use xlink:href="#buttonBase" x="0" y="0"/>
        <use xlink:href="#buttonText" x="75" y="20"/>
    </g>

  </defs>
  <g>
    <use xlink:href="#button" x="100" y="100"/>
  </g>
</svg>
```

Button

Figure 3-7. Defining an element and reusing it later with the <use> *statement*

The first definition is for a linear gradient called #testGrad, which provides a two-tone gradient that sweeps from blue on the left to navy (dark blue) on the right. The second definition (#buttonBase) defines a rounded rectangle that uses the gradient as a fill. In this particular instance, the reference is made as if the test gradient was references as part of a URL: The notation myFile.svg#testGrad is a shorthand way for specifying an XML file that has an element with id of testGrad. The unqualified url(#testGrad) indicates that an element in the same document as the <use> element with the id="testGrad" should be used.

 NOTE *In general, when referring to an element with an* id *value of* "foobar", *I will usually use the notation* #foobar *to indicate that item.*

Similarly, a <text> element is defined with its own id. It is useful to think of text elements as being similar to labels in languages such as Visual Basic or Java. In other words, the contents of the label may only be peripherally related to the name of that label (as given here by its id attribute).

The next element declaration, the formal button, illustrates the usage of the <g> element as both a container and a bracketing agent, and it also shows how the <use> element is, well, <use>d (sorry):

```
<g id="button">
    <use xlink:href="#buttonBase" x="0" y="0"/>
    <use xlink:href="#buttonText" x="75" y="20"/>
</g>
```

The <g> element acts as a wrapper, indicating that whenever #button is invoked, then all of the elements within the wrapper should be rendered instead. In that respect, the <g> element has a certain similarity to a function. The same expression could be represented in pseudo-code as something like this:

```
define button{
    draw(#buttonBase,x=0,y=0);
    draw(#buttonText,x=75,y=75);
    }
```

where draw() would in turn be a function that renders the item at the indicated position (and is the functional analog to the <use> element).

The <use> element that follows employs a slightly different syntax for referencing which object it is rendering:

```
<use xlink:href="#buttonBase" x="0" y="0"/>
```

The xlink:href attribute is the first (and most common) manifestation of XLink in the SVG specification. XLink, a language for defining the links between documents or elements within documents, is implicitly defined within SVG's DTD. In other words, when you create the initial <svg> element that contains the rest of the document, what you are in fact creating is a document with two implied namespaces:

```
<svg xmlns="http://www.w3.org/2000/svg"
xmlns:xlink="http://www.w3.org/1999/xlink"/>
```

Most validating SVG parsers automatically assume the existence of these namespace declarations, as they are defined in the namespace, but unfortunately, if an XML parser does not have access to the DTD (which will likely happen for efficiency purposes), then the use of the xlink: prefix will have to be explicitly declared if you want to manipulate your internally linked SVG with an XML parser.

The fill attribute can have one of a number of different types of resources: either colors declared using CSS valid names (such as red or blue), hex triplets (#FF00FF for purple) or RGB functional declarations (255,0,255 for purple), or linked references to color, gradient, or pattern definitions. Because of this, the url() notation is needed to distinguish between these possibilities. The attribute xlink:href on the other hand will always point to an element referenced by an id attribute, so the url() notation is not needed in that case.

The position expressed by the x and y attributes of the <use> element tell the renderer where to draw the origin of the <g> element. This in turn hints at another purpose of the <g> element: It implicitly defines an origin. Any element within the <g> element thus inherits this origin so that the element coordinates are given relative to the location of the <g> element, not the global coordinate system. This property is critical in the discussion of transformations (as covered in the "Understanding Transformations" section later in this chapter).

None of the elements or groupings of elements thus defined are yet rendered to the screen. To do that, you need to move out of the definitions block and actually create rendered instances of the object in question:

```
    </defs>
    <g id="context">
        <use xlink:href="#button" x="100" y="100" id="myButton"/>
    </g>
</svg>
```

Again, it is noteworthy here to see the use of the <g> elements, this time as generic brackets. As a personal style, I prefer to make sure any elements actually rendered are contained in a <g> element, simply because it continues to reinforce the concept of modularity. And it is handy in case you want to change the position of all of the elements rendered to the screen.

The <use> element #myButton references the composite button declared earlier, which in turn is made up of other <use> elements from even farther down the tree. As a matter of principle, I actually place id elements on the new instances as well (because ids have to be unique, the name of the instance cannot be the name of the declared class here—I could not name this <use> element #button). This not only makes it easier to refer to the appropriate <g> or <use> element, but it becomes highly useful in situations where you are manipulating these elements using JavaScript or other scripting language.

SVG and Functional Programming

Functional programming goes back almost to the beginning of computing with the cybernetics movement of the 1950s and early 1960s and the use of languages such as Lisp (for List Processing). Such functional languages usually have a number of common characteristics:

- Every *object* is a functional entity, with inheritance typically being either aggregational (big objects made up of little objects) or restrictive (child functions constrain what makes up valid data).

- The languages are usually dynamically typed—the type of any given object is basically determined at runtime rather than design time (in other words, statically typed languages such as C++ or Java), making for more flexibility in programming at the cost of more intensive processing requirements.

- Manipulation is usually performed across sets of objects, rather than on one object at a time. Thus, lists, hashes, and trees are far more common in a functional programming paradigm than in the single object focus of procedural programming. Consequently, many of the operations that work in such languages employ pattern matching and recursion to do their processing (hence languages such as Perl are not functional per se, but Perl's powerful regular expression engine most certainly is).

- Functional languages have no "side effects"; an object declaration cannot transparently change global quantities. Put another way, there are no globals in functional languages.

XML by itself is not a programming language, but many of the XML instance languages, such as XHTML, XML Stylesheet Language for Transformations (XSLT), and SVG, are. Moreover, they are predominantly functional in nature. XSLT is perhaps the most obvious example of this, but even languages such as SVG evince many of the characteristics of functional programming. Although some limitations in the language mean that occasional forays into procedural programming are necessary with SVG, the best way of making programming-friendly SVG involves understanding the same principles as used in other programming language: modular design, object-oriented design with strong relational associations, and a minimum of side effects.

Cascading Properties

One principle of SVG that shares similarities with HTML is the use of cascading styles. In essence, when you change such characteristics as the fill (the color, gradient, or pattern used on a shape), the stroke (the color of the edge), the opacity (the degree of transparency), or some other similar quality on a grouping element, this change of property cascades down to all elements within the group that *do not have that property set*. If a child element is also a group element, this cascading occurs on all of its associated children, as well.

For instance, in Listing 3-3, the fill attribute "cascades" into the child <use> boxes so that any child of #g1 that does not explicitly define a fill attribute will have a red fill (see Figure 3-8).

Listing 3-3. cascades.svg

```
<svg xmlns="http://www.w3.org/2000/svg"
    xmlns:link="http://www.w3.org/1999/xlink"  >
    <defs>
        <rect id="box" width="100" height="100" stroke-width="2"/>
    </defs>
    <g fill="red" id="g1">
        <use xlink:href="#box" x="100" y="100" id="box1"/>
        <use xlink:href="#box"  x="200" y="100" fill="blue" id="box2"/>
```

Figure 3-8. Propagating styles down to any elements in that container

```
<g stroke="blue" stroke-width="6" id="g2">
    <use xlink:href="#box" x="250" y="250" id="box3"/>
    <use xlink:href="#box" x="350" y="250" stroke="green" id="box4"/>
    <use xlink:href="#box" x="450" y="250"
        stroke="green" fill="yellow" id="box5"/>
    <rect id="rect1" x="550" y="250" width="100" height="100"/>
    </g>
</g>
</svg>
```

The first grouping object, #g1, sets the fill attribute to the value red. Where the fill is not otherwise specified (in other words, except for #box2 and #box5), all of the squares are red, even those in the child grouping #g2. In #g2, on the other hand, the stroke color is set to "blue" and the stroke's width is set to 6. However, although the stroke color gets set correctly (except when explicitly overruled), the only place where the stroke's width is actually displayed to its correct value of 6 is in #rect1 . . . all other elements have a stroke width of "2".

The reason for this can be seen in the definition of #box. There, the stroke width is explicitly defined as having the value "2". This hints at an important principle: Any CSS property that is defined within a <defs> section will overrule any properties that are applied to instances of that object.

Here, stroke width is defined; it consequently becomes fixed as that value, even though I attempt to redefine it as having a value of "6" in the containing <g> element. This can be a pain. In general, as a rule of thumb, you should never define properties that you want to change via animation within <defs> blocks (though you can override this limitation if you use an external scripting language, as will be discussed in Chapter 10, "SVG Components").

Abstracting with Stylesheets

CSS has another utility in SVG, one having to do with abstraction. When you use a graphics application such as Adobe Illustrator to generate SVG, the SVG that's created tends to be flat, verbose, and generally uninformative. This is not a limitation of the product; this is in fact the most efficient way of generating SVG automatically. However, when you are creating SVG content for use in programming, in general it is preferable to *abstract* the process as much as possible.

That is to say, the best SVG for programming should actually know little about the stylistic considerations applied to an object. For instance, if you had a button that had three states—a resting state, a highlighted state (when the mouse hovers over the button), and a depressed state (when the mouse button is clicked) —it is generally preferable to designate the colors used for those states by names such as "normal", "highlight", and "depressed" rather than "maroon", "red", and "black".

Why is it preferable? The first names are functional abstractions; they provide a context or meaning to each of the possible states, regardless of what those colors actually are. The second set, on the other hand, only tells you about the colors that were selected—you have to do potentially a lot of searching to determine the significant of those colors.

When you go with states such as "resting", "highlight", and so on, it also means that if you can assign specific values to these states independent of the SVG document itself, then changing the visual appearance of an interface (its skin, if you will) can be accomplished as simply as changing the pointer to a different document.

If this principle sounds familiar, it is because it lies at the heart of what CSS is all about. CSS includes support for an attribute called class, which makes it possible to associate a label with a set of CSS properties. For instance, suppose you wanted to define the three possible states of a button as given previously. You could do so with a normal SVG document as in Listing 3-4.

Listing 3-4. CSSButton1.svg

```
<svg xmlns="http://www.w3.org/2000/svg"
        xmlns:link="http://www.w3.org/1999/xlink" >
    <defs>
        <rect id="buttonNormal" width="120" height="30" rx="5" ry="5"
              stroke-width="2" stroke="black" fill="maroon"/>
        <rect id="buttonHighlight" width="120" height="30" rx="5" ry="5"
              stroke-width="2" stroke="yellow" fill="red"/>
        <rect id="buttonDepressed" width="120" height="30" rx="5" ry="5"
              stroke-width="2" stroke="yellow" fill="black"/>
    </defs>
    <g>
```

```
            <use xlink:href="#buttonNormal" x="100" y="100" id="ButtonNormal"/>
            <use xlink:href="#buttonHighlight" x="100" y="150" id="ButtonHighlight"/>
            <use xlink:href="#buttonDepressed" x="100" y="200" id="ButtonDepressed"/>
        </g>
</svg>
```

However, if you use CSS and the class attribute, this can be simplified considerably (see Listing 3-5). Figure 3-9 shows what this code looks like.

Listing 3-5. `CSSButton2.svg`

```
<?xml-stylesheet type="text/css" href="CSSButton2.CSS"?>
<svg xmlns="http://www.w3.org/2000/svg"
     xmlns:link="http://www.w3.org/1999/xlink" >
    <defs>
        <rect id="buttonNormal" width="120" height="30" rx="5" ry="5"
            class="CSSButtonNormal"/>
        <rect id="buttonHighlight" width="120" height="30" rx="5" ry="5"
            class="CSSButtonHighlight"/>
        <rect id="buttonDepressed" width="120" height="30" rx="5" ry="5"
            class="CSSButtonDepressed"/>
    </defs>
    <g>
        <use xlink:href="#buttonNormal" x="100" y="100" id="ButtonNormal"/>
        <use xlink:href="#buttonHighlight" x="100" y="150" id="ButtonHighlight"/>
        <use xlink:href="#buttonDepressed" x="100" y="200" id="ButtonDepressed"/>
    </g>
</svg>
```

Figure 3-9. Setting the three states of the button using an external CSS stylesheet

The fill, stroke, and stroke-width properties are eliminated, replaced by a single class attribute. Not only is this a little easier to read, but you have also abstracted the media presentation. You now know that the style is appropriate to the CSSButtonNormal class, *regardless of what the components of that style really are*. However, these classes by themselves contain no implicit information; they must in some way reference a list of definitions that define these classes. You can incorporate stylistic information either through the use of <style> elements in the SVG (see Chapter 6, "Text") or through an external CSS stylesheet invoked with an xml-stylesheet processing instruction, of this form:

```
<?xml-stylesheet type="text/css" href="CSSButton2.css"?>
```

where the type gives the MIME-type of the stylesheet (typically either text/css for CSS or text/xsl for the XSL), and href is a pointer to the requisite CSS definition. For instance, CSSButton2.css may look as follows:

```
.CSSButtonNormal {fill:maroon;stroke:black;stroke-width:2;}
.CSSButtonHighlight {fill:red;stroke:yellow;stroke-width:2;}
.CSSButtonDepressed {fill:black;stroke:yellow;stroke-width:2;}
```

The expression CSSButtonNormal is the selector for the CSSButtonNormal class, with the period at the beginning of the term indicating the name refers to a class attribute rather than an element. If you just wanted to restrict the particular stylesheet rule (the selector along with its definition) to only be applicable for <use> elements, for instance, you would use the selector use.CSSButtonNormal. If you wanted the style to apply to all <use> elements, you would just use the selector use with no class extensions.

The properties that can be changed are generally the ones that do not change the shape or position of an element. For instance, using CSS to set the width or height has no effect on an element, nor does setting the x and y positions, nor can you set a <path> element's i*d* attribute. However, you can set most text properties. (You can argue that the stroke-width attribute changes the shape of an object, but it is actually supported as a valid CSS property).

By decoupling these visual properties from the underlying structural composition, one other advantage that external CSS stylesheets offer is that you can associate different stylesheets for different environments. For instance, the same script could have a completely different set of attributes if viewed on a grayscale display screen:

```
.CSSButtonNormal {fill:gray;stroke:black;stroke-width:2;}
.CSSButtonHighlight {fill:white;stroke:black;stroke-width:2;}
.CSSButtonDepressed {fill:black;stroke:black;stroke-width:2;stroke-dasharray:5 5;}
```

In this case the default button state is gray. When the mouse moves over the button, the interior turns white, and when the button is pressed, the button turns black with a dashed border. You can see these particular actions in Listing 3-6, which also utilizes a second minor bit of abstraction to make reduce the number of core button templates to one. Figure 3-10 shows what this code looks like.

Listing 3-6. CSSButton3.svg

```
<?xml-stylesheet type="text/css" href="CSSButton3.CSS"?>
<svg xmlns="http://www.w3.org/2000/svg"
           xmlns:link="http://www.w3.org/1999/xlink" >
    <defs>
        <rect id="buttonBase" width="120" height="30" rx="5" ry="5"/>
        <use id="buttonNormal" xlink:href="#buttonBase" class="CSSButtonNormal"/>
        <use id="buttonHighlight" xlink:href="#buttonBase"
              class="CSSButtonHighlight"/>
        <use id="buttonDepressed" xlink:href="#buttonBase"
              class="CSSButtonDepressed">
<!-- Uncomment this next line to see an interesting special effect -->
<!--             <animate attributeName="stroke-dashoffset" attributeType="CSS"
                     from="100%" to="0%" dur="5s" repeatCount="indefinite"/> -->
        </use>
    </defs>
    <g>
        <use xlink:href="#buttonNormal" x="100" y="100" id="ButtonNormal">
            <set attributeName="xlink:href"
                  attributeType="XML" to="#buttonHighlight"
                  begin="mouseover;mouseup" end="mouseout"/>
            <set attributeName="xlink:href"
                  attributeType="XML" to="#buttonDepressed"
                  begin="mousedown" end="mouseup;mouseout"/>
        </use>
    </g>
</svg>
```

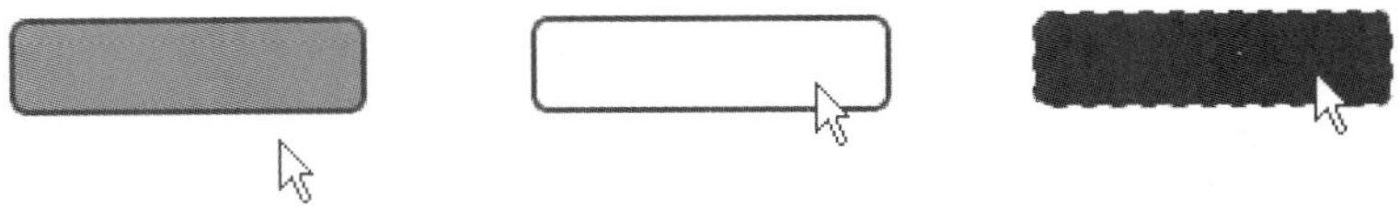

Figure 3-10. Creating different appearances with the same functionality

The CSS file `CSSButton3.css` is spartan and is designed for use in high-contrast settings:

```
.CSSButtonNormal {fill:gray;stroke:black;stroke-width:2;}
.CSSButtonHighlight {fill:white;stroke:black;stroke-width:2;}
.CSSButtonDepressed {fill:black;stroke:black;stroke-width:2;stroke-dasharray:5 5;}
```

TIP   *For a little more visual excitement, uncomment the* `<animate>` *element and see what happens.*

TIP   *When you are designing your own applications, keep these multiple layers of abstraction in mind, as they can often radically simplify the code (and hence make it far easier to maintain).*

Understanding Transformations

The `transform` attribute, which can be applied to shape elements but is most typically applied to `<g>` elements, makes it possible to create a local coordinate system for ease of construction, to move, scale, skew, or rotate that system relative to the outer coordinate system.

For instance, suppose you wanted to draw the tick marks of a clock, lines that start from the outer edge of the circle and head radially inward for a distance of about 10 percent or so. The hard way to do this is to calculate the x and y positions of the outer and inner points of each tick mark using a complex set of trigonometric relationships. The simpler way to do it, on the other hand, is to draw a line vertically from about 90 percent of the circle's radius to 100 percent, then rotate that to the required angular position through a transformation, as shown in Listing 3-7.

Listing 3-7. `ticks.svg`
```
<svg xmlns="http://www.w3.org/2000/svg"
      xmlns:link="http://www.w3.org/1999/xlink">
    <defs>
        <!-- define a vertical tick mark, offset from the origin by 80 units -->
```

```
    <g id="tick">
        <line x1="0" y1="-80" x2="0" y2="-100"/>
    </g>
    <!-- create a circular face -->
    <circle cx="0" cy="0" r="100" fill="none" stroke-width="4"
            stroke="black" id="face"/>
    <!-- for each tick mark, draw it,
            then rotate it by 30 degree increments -->
    <g id="ticks" stroke="black" stroke-width="2">
        <use xlink:href="#tick" x="0" y="0" transform="rotate(0)"
            stroke="blue" stroke-width="4"/>
        <use xlink:href="#tick" x="0" y="0" transform="rotate(30)"/>
        <use xlink:href="#tick" x="0" y="0" transform="rotate(60)"/>
        <use xlink:href="#tick" x="0" y="0" transform="rotate(90)"/>
        <use xlink:href="#tick" x="0" y="0" transform="rotate(120)"/>
        <use xlink:href="#tick" x="0" y="0" transform="rotate(150)"/>
        <use xlink:href="#tick" x="0" y="0" transform="rotate(180)"/>
        <use xlink:href="#tick" x="0" y="0" transform="rotate(210)"/>
        <use xlink:href="#tick" x="0" y="0" transform="rotate(240)"/>
        <use xlink:href="#tick" x="0" y="0" transform="rotate(270)"/>
        <use xlink:href="#tick" x="0" y="0" transform="rotate(300)"/>
        <use xlink:href="#tick" x="0" y="0" transform="rotate(330)"/>
    </g>
    </defs>
    <!-- draw the boundary of the "clock" -->
    <use xlink:href="#face" x="200" y="200"/>
    <!-- draw the collection of tick marks -->
    <use xlink:href="#ticks" x="200" y="200"/>
</svg>
```

By controlling the transformations of the coordinate system, you can dramatically simplify what would otherwise be ugly problems, such as drawing radial elements such as a clock's tick marks (see Figure 3-11).

Figure 3-11. Coordinate systems transformations

The initial tick element drew a line straight up, starting at 80 pixels above the origin (–80, because the orientation of the default coordinate y axis is down) to 100 pixels above the origin (–100). The important thing to keep in mind is that the origin is not located where the visible part of the graphic starts, but is in fact 80 units below that. When you rotate that, the rotation is made relative to the origin of that local coordinate system.

In essence, when you say `transform="rotate(150)"`, what you are in fact doing is rotating the local coordinate system (in this case the one referenced by the <use> element) relative to the external coordinate system. This is the case with all transformations; in effect, what you are doing is defining a local coordinate system (usually centered around a <g> element), taking a snapshot of that system rendered, and the moving (translating), scaling, rotating, or skewing that snapshot.

Table 3-4 summarizes the transformations, transformation functions, but all generally have the following format:

```
<element transform="transformFn(arg1,arg2, ... )"/>
```

For instance, a transform to scale an object defined earlier as #grid to 50 percent of its size might look like:

```
<use xlink:href="#grid" transform="scale(0.5)"/>
```

Table 3-4. Transformation Functions

TRANSFORMATION FUNCTION	ARGUMENTS	DESCRIPTION
translate	translate(tx,ty)	Moves the location of the element or group by the amount (tx,ty) in the current coordinate system.
scale	scale(s) or scale(sx,sy)	Scales all points in the element or group by a factor of *s*, relative to the origin. If two values are given, these scale the x and y axis values, respectively, relative to the origin.
rotate	rotate(∞)	Rotates the element or graph clockwise by the angle ∞, about its origin.
skewX	skewX(∞)	Skews the bottom-left of an element or group left or right by the angle ∞, relative to the origin of the graphic.
skewY	skewY(∞)	Skews the top-left of an element or group up or down by the angle ∞, relative to the origin of the graphic.
matrix	matrix(a,b,c,d,e,f)	Performs a matrix transformation on an element or group. See "The Matrix" section for details.

Although the use of most of these are straightforward, to the following sections explore each of the transformation methods in a little more detail to point out their utility in various situations.

Translation

The translate() function is perhaps one of the most common (and certainly most useful) transformations because it lets you build objects relative to a local coordinate system, then move these objects en mass to some other point in the containing coordinate system. This technique is especially useful when working with elements programmatically: Programs such as Adobe Illustrator position all elements relative to the top-left portion of the page (the viewport) because these values can be easily calculated from mouse actions, but calculating absolute positions of every element manually can get to be . . . ugly.

For instance, consider a situation where you have five rectangular buttons positioned so that the first button's upper-left corner is at (87,72). Each button is 120-pixels wide and 30-pixels high, and there is an 8-pixel horizontal gap between buttons. This could be given as shown in Listing 3-8.

Listing 3-8. `translateCoords1.svg`

```
<svg xmlns="http://www.w3.org/2000/svg"
    xmlns:link="http://www.w3.org/1999/xlink"  >
   <defs>
       <rect id="button"  x="0" y="0" width="120" height="30"
             fill="blue" stroke="black" stroke-width="2" />
       <text id="button1Text" font-size="18" fill="yellow"
             dominant-baseline="mathematical" text-anchor="middle">
             Button 1
       </text>
       <text id="button2Text" font-size="18" fill="yellow"
             dominant-baseline="mathematical" text-anchor="middle">
             Button 2
       </text>
       <text id="button3Text" font-size="18" fill="yellow"
             dominant-baseline="mathematical" text-anchor="middle">
             Button 3
       </text>
       <text id="button4Text" font-size="18" fill="yellow"
             dominant-baseline="mathematical" text-anchor="middle">
             Button 4
       </text>
   </defs>
```

```
    <use xlink:href="#button" x="82" y="72"/>
    <use xlink:href="#button1Text" x="142" y="87"/>
    <use xlink:href="#button" x="210" y="72"/>
    <use xlink:href="#button2Text" x="270" y="87"/>
    <use xlink:href="#button" x="338" y="72"/>
    <use xlink:href="#button3Text" x="398" y="87"/>
    <use xlink:href="#button" x="466" y="72"/>
    <use xlink:href="#button4Text" x="526" y="87"/>
</svg>
```

Absolute positioning often makes it difficult to tell at a glance what your code is doing, makes it difficult to reuse code, and is error prone (see Figure 3-12).

Figure 3-12. Absolutely positioned buttons

 NOTE *The attributes* dominant-baseline="mathematical" *and* text-anchor="middle" *position the text so that the origin of the text is in the middle of the expression, both horizontally and vertically. Chapter 6, "Text," will explain this in detail.*

The problem with this comes in the coordinates within the <use> block. Even if you know what the element is, the position of each element seems arbitrary, and adding another button to this mix would require knowing a lot about the position of the last button in the list. However, you can rewrite this to make the structure much more obvious with the use of a few well-placed translations, as in Listing 3-9.

Listing 3-9. translateCoords2.svg

```
<svg xmlns="http://www.w3.org/2000/svg"
    xmlns:link="http://www.w3.org/1999/xlink" >
    <defs>
        <rect id="button" x="0" y="0" width="120" height="30"
            fill="blue" stroke="black" stroke-width="2" />
        <g transform="translate(60,15)" id="button1Text">
```

```
            <text font-size="18" fill="yellow"
                    dominant-baseline="mathematical" text-anchor="middle">
                    Button 1
            </text>
        </g>
        <g transform="translate(60,15)" id="button2Text">
            <text font-size="18" fill="yellow"
                    dominant-baseline="mathematical" text-anchor="middle">
                    Button 2
            </text>
        </g>
        <g transform="translate(60,15)" id="button3Text">
            <text font-size="18" fill="yellow"
                    dominant-baseline="mathematical" text-anchor="middle">
                    Button 3
            </text>
        </g>
        <g transform="translate(60,15)" id="button4Text">
            <text font-size="18" fill="yellow"
                    dominant-baseline="mathematical" text-anchor="middle">
                    Button 4
            </text>
        </g>
    </defs>
    <g transform="translate(82,72)" id="Buttons">
        <g transform="translate(0,0)" id="Button1">
            <use xlink:href="#button"/>
            <use xlink:href="#button1Text"/>
        </g>
        <g transform="translate(128,0)" id="Button2">
            <use xlink:href="#button"/>
            <use xlink:href="#button2Text"/>
        </g>
        <g transform="translate(256,0)" id="Button3">
            <use xlink:href="#button"/>
            <use xlink:href="#button3Text"/>
        </g>
        <g transform="translate(384,0)" id="Button4">
            <use xlink:href="#button"/>
            <use xlink:href="#button4Text"/>
        </g>
    </g>
</svg>
```

Employing relative positioning can make both automation and code maintenance much easier (see Figure 3-13).

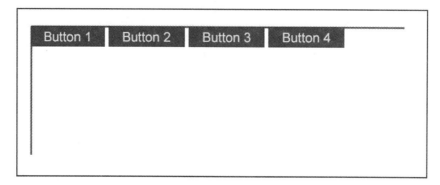

Figure 3-13. Employing grouped relative coordinates

Not only is the structure much more explicit in the previous example, but adding a new button would be as simple as creating another <g> structure with a transformation of "translate(512,0)" and referencing the text. In the initial <text> elements, they have a format of the following:

```
<g transform="translate(60,15)" id="button4Text">
    <text font-size="18" fill="yellow"
            dominant-baseline="mathematical" text-anchor="middle">
            Button 4
    </text>
</g>
```

In this case, the translate will move the text so that the origin is 15 pixels up and 60 pixels to the left of where it was initially. In general, when you set the translation values, you end moving the origin in the opposite direction, both horizontally and vertically, from the translation.

The first grouping element <g> outside of the <defs> section performs an initial translation, moving the new origin 82 pixels to the right of the old one and 72 pixels down:

```
<g transform="translate(82,72)" id="Buttons">
```

Consequently, the start of any new drawing commands (in other words, the new origin) is now at (82,72), even though internal to that grouping element the starting point is still (0,0).

Within that grouping element (#Buttons), the first button is translated to (0,0), relative to the new origin set by #Buttons . . . in other words, it does not move at all. This is included only to make it explicit that this is what is happening—the transform="translate(0,0)" statement could be left off entirely with the same effect. On the other hand, #Button2 provides a nontrivial example of the use of translate:

```
<g id="Button2" transform="translate(128,0)">
        <use xlink:href="#button"/>
        <use xlink:href="#button2Text"/>
</g>
```

The button #Button2 is positioned 128 pixels to the right of the origin defined in #Buttons, or 210 pixels = 128 + 82 pixels from the origin of the initial graphic. However, the internal elements are where the benefits from the transformed groupings play off. The default x and y values of the <use> element (and any shape element, for that matter) are (0,0). This means that, by intelligent definition of the objects in the <defs> block, you can get by without having to explicitly set the coordinates in the instance section. One side effect of this is that, once again, your code becomes easier to read and maintain—and also, not coincidentally, becomes easier to program against, as will be discussed in Chapter 9, "Integrating SVG and HTML," and Chapter 10, "SVG Components").

Rotation

The rotate() function has already been demonstrated and does what you would expect rotation to do. The important point to keep in mind is that a rotation is performed around the internal origin of the coordinate system. This means that performing a rotation of 90° on a rectangle positioned at (0,0) will rotate the rectangle about its upper-left corner, as shown in the (a) and (b) diagram of Listing 3-10.

Listing 3-10. rotations1.svg

```
<svg xmlns="http://www.w3.org/2000/svg"
    xmlns:link="http://www.w3.org/1999/xlink" >
   <g transform="translate(150,150)">
       <line x1="0" y1="-100" x2="0" y2="100" stroke="blue"/>
       <line x1="-100" y1="0" x2="100" y2="0" stroke="blue"/>
       <text x="-120" y="-60" font-size="20">a) rotate(0)</text>
       <g transform="rotate(0)">
           <rect x="0" y="0" width="100" height="50"/>
       </g>
   </g>
```

```
        <g transform="translate(400,150)">
            <line x1="0" y1="-100" x2="0" y2="100" stroke="blue"/>
            <line x1="-100" y1="0" x2="100" y2="0" stroke="blue"/>
            <text x="-120" y="-60" font-size="20">b) rotate(90)</text>
            <g transform="rotate(90)">
                <rect x="0" y="0" width="100" height="50"/>
            </g>
        </g>
        <g transform="translate(150,400)">
            <line x1="0" y1="-100" x2="0" y2="100" stroke="blue"/>
            <line x1="-100" y1="0" x2="100" y2="0" stroke="blue"/>
            <text x="-120" y="-60" font-size="20">c) rotate(0)</text>
            <g transform="rotate(0)">
                <rect x="-50" y="-25" width="100" height="50"/>
            </g>
        </g>
        <g transform="translate(400,400)">
            <line x1="0" y1="-100" x2="0" y2="100" stroke="blue"/>
            <line x1="-100" y1="0" x2="100" y2="0" stroke="blue"/>
            <text x="-120" y="-60" font-size="20">d) rotate(90)</text>
            <g transform="rotate(90)">
                <rect x="-50" y="-25" width="100" height="50"/>
            </g>
        </g>
    </g>
</svg>
```

Rotations occur around the origin of the contained object, not necessarily the center—to set them explicitly, you need to relocate the elements relative to the origin (or move the origin with a translate statement), as shown in Figure 3-14.

In the (c) and (d) diagrams of Figure 3-14, on the other hand, the rectangle's position was set to (–50, –25), which means that the center of the rectangle rather

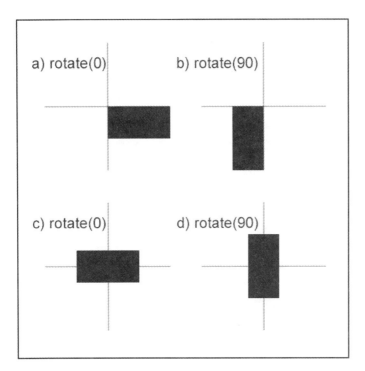

Figure 3-14. Different rotations

than the upper-left corner is now located at (0,0). Rotating the image by 90° in this case causes the rotation to take place around the rectangle's midpoint.

The rotations apply equally to everything contained within the rotated <g> elements: text, collections of shapes, even bitmapped images. For instance, in Listing 3-11, a fairly detailed bitmap image is shown in its initial position as well as rotated by 30° (see Figure 3-15).

Listing 3-11. `rotatedImage1.svg`

```
<svg xmlns="http://www.w3.org/2000/svg"
     xmlns:link="http://www.w3.org/1999/xlink"  >
    <defs>
        <image id="merPicture" xlink:href="SweaterMer3.png"
             width="237" height="484" x="-124" y="-242"/>
    </defs>
    <g transform="translate(200,250)">
        <use xlink:href="#merPicture"/>
    </g>
```

```
<g transform="translate(500,250)">
    <g transform="rotate(30)">
        <use xlink:href="#merPicture"/>
    </g>
</g>
</svg>
```

Rotations are powerful, but not perfect, especially when used in conjunction with images (see Figure 3-15).

Figure 3-15. Rotating a graphical figure

 NOTE *Chapter 7, "Incorporating Texture," will cover images in far greater detail.*

Rotations are powerful, but not perfect, especially when used in conjunction with images. The drawback of rotating bitmaps should be obvious upon inspection: The SVG renderer has to map one set of pixels to an entirely different set, so rotations of images are both slow and likely to be of poor quality compared to simpler bitmap renders. However, the beauty of SVG is that the complex set of calculations is handled by the render engine; you as a designer need only concern yourself with specifying the rotation angle.

The angles that the rotation(), skewX, and skewY functions use are given in degrees. There is no practical limit to the values, positive or negative, which the angle itself can take, and of course 360° is the same as 0° from the standpoint of the rotate function.

Scaling

The scale() function provides a multiplier or set of multipliers to change the size of the graphics in the outer coordinate system. Unlike translate() and rotate(), scale can be of two forms: scale(s), where s is a multiplier that changes both x and y coordinates equally, or scale(s_x, s_y), where s_x is a multiplier that changes only the x axis and s_y is a multiplier that changes only the y axis.

In Listing 3-12, the use of the scale() transform property is shown. The image itself is depicted at a scale of s=1 (that is to say, at its initial size), then is displayed at (s_x = 1, s_y=0.5), (s_x=0.5, s_y=1), and s=0.5 (see Figure 3-16).

Listing 3-12. scaleImage1.svg

```
<svg xmlns="http://www.w3.org/2000/svg"
     xmlns:link="http://www.w3.org/1999/xlink" >
    <defs>
        <text id="scale1" font-size="18" x="-124" y="-220">scale(1)</text>
        <text id="scale05_1" font-size="18" x="-124" y="-220">scale(0.5,1)</text>
        <text id="scale1_05" font-size="18" x="-150" y="-90">scale(1,0.5)</text>
        <text id="scale05" font-size="18" x="-140" y="-50">scale(0.5)</text>
        <image id="merPicture" xlink:href="SweaterMer3.png"
               width="237" height="484" x="-124" y="-242"/>
    </defs>
    <g transform="translate(180,250)">
        <use xlink:href="#scale1"/>
        <use xlink:href="#merPicture"/>
    </g>
    <g transform="translate(380,250)">
        <use xlink:href="#scale05_1"/>
```

```
            <g transform="scale(0.5,1)">
                <use xlink:href="#merPicture"/>
            </g>
        </g>
    <g transform="translate(580,130)">
        <use xlink:href="#scale1_05"/>
        <g transform="scale(1,0.5)">
            <use xlink:href="#merPicture"/>
        </g>
    </g>
    <g transform="translate(580,400)">
        <use xlink:href="#scale05"/>
        <g transform="scale(0.5)">
            <use xlink:href="#merPicture"/>
        </g>
    </g>
    </g>
</svg>
```

Figure 3-16. Scaling along one or both axes using the scale() *translation*

In each case, the transformation uses the local origin as the point of expansion or contraction; the hot-point (the origin of the graphic relative to scaling or other transformation) remains the same as every other part becomes half as large.

The use of the scale attribute can also do more than just shrink or grow elements. A negative-valued scaling factor causes values to flip to the other side of the imaginary axis centered at the local origin. Thus, a scale factor of $(s_x=-1, s_y=1)$ will flip the contained image along the vertical axis, $(s_x=1, s_y=-1)$ will flip the contents along a horizontal axis, and $s = -1$ (which is the same as $(s_x=-1, s_y= -1)$) will flip both horizontally and vertically, as demonstrated in Listing 3-13. Figure 3-17 shows what this code looks like.

Listing 3-13. `ScaleImage2.svg`

```
<svg xmlns="http://www.w3.org/2000/svg"
        xmlns:link="http://www.w3.org/1999/xlink"   >
    <defs>
        <text id="scale1" font-size="18" x="-124" y="-100">scale(1)</text>
        <text id="scaleN1_1" font-size="18" x="-124" y="-100">scale(-1,1)</text>
        <text id="scale1_N1" font-size="18" x="-150" y="-90">scale(1,-1)</text>
        <text id="scaleN1" font-size="18" x="-140" y="-50">scale(-1)</text>
        <image id="merPicture" xlink:href="SweaterMer3.png"
                    width="124" height="242" x="-62" y="-121"/>
    </defs>
    <g transform="translate(180,150)">
        <use xlink:href="#scale1"/>
        <use xlink:href="#merPicture"/>
    </g>
    <g transform="translate(380,150)">
        <use xlink:href="#scaleN1_1"/>
        <g transform="scale(-1,1)">
            <use xlink:href="#merPicture"/>
        </g>
    </g>
    <g transform="translate(180,400)">
        <use xlink:href="#scale1_N1"/>
        <g transform="scale(1,-1)">
            <use xlink:href="#merPicture"/>
        </g>
    </g>
    <g transform="translate(380,400)">
        <use xlink:href="#scaleN1"/>
        <g transform="scale(-1)">
            <use xlink:href="#merPicture"/>
        </g>
    </g>
</svg>
```

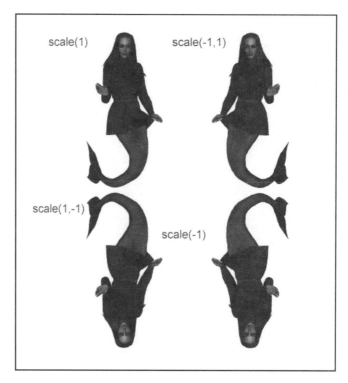

Figure 3-17. Flipping an image around the appropriate axis

Skewing

You can think of a *skew* as a mixture of a rotation and scaling. In normal rectangular coordinates, the x and y axes meet one another at right angles. However, in a skewed transformation, one axis is rotated by a certain amount while the other remains fixed, causing the entire coordinate system to collapse like an old-style egg-carton (the ones that used slotted cardboard grids rather than molded Styrofoam).

There is no generalized skew function. Instead, there are two axis skews: skewX() and skewY(). This has to do with the fact that in a two-dimensional system, one axis can always be considered as the *fixed* axis while the other's angle changes from 90° to something other less than or greater than 90°. Thus, if you hold the x axis fixed, then the y axis will rotate to the specified angle, moving the skew horizontally . . . the result of skewX(∞). Similarly, the skewY(∞) function actually holds the y axis constant and instead skews the x axis by that amount. This can be seen in Listing 3-14, which shows how an image can be skewed along one or the other axis. Figure 3-18 illustrates this code.

Listing 3-14. `ImageSkew1.svg`

```
<svg xmlns="http://www.w3.org/2000/svg"
        xmlns:link="http://www.w3.org/1999/xlink"   >
    <defs>
        <line x1="0" y1="0" x2="200" y2="0"
                id="horizontal_line" stroke-linecap="square"/>
        <use xlink:href="#horizontal_line" transform="rotate(90)"
                id="vertical_line"/>
        <g id="grid" stroke-width="2">
            <use xlink:href="#horizontal_line" x="0" y="0" stroke-width="4"/>
            <use xlink:href="#horizontal_line" x="0" y="20"/>
            <use xlink:href="#horizontal_line" x="0" y="40"/>
            <use xlink:href="#horizontal_line" x="0" y="60"/>
            <use xlink:href="#horizontal_line" x="0" y="80"/>
            <use xlink:href="#horizontal_line" x="0" y="100"/>
            <use xlink:href="#horizontal_line" x="0" y="120"/>
            <use xlink:href="#horizontal_line" x="0" y="140"/>
            <use xlink:href="#horizontal_line" x="0" y="160"/>
            <use xlink:href="#horizontal_line" x="0" y="180"/>
            <use xlink:href="#horizontal_line" x="0" y="200" stroke-width="4"/>
            <use xlink:href="#vertical_line" y="0" x="0" stroke-width="4"/>
            <use xlink:href="#vertical_line" y="0" x="20"/>
            <use xlink:href="#vertical_line" y="0" x="40"/>
            <use xlink:href="#vertical_line" y="0" x="60"/>
            <use xlink:href="#vertical_line" y="0" x="80"/>
            <use xlink:href="#vertical_line" y="0" x="100"/>
            <use xlink:href="#vertical_line" y="0" x="120"/>
            <use xlink:href="#vertical_line" y="0" x="140"/>
            <use xlink:href="#vertical_line" y="0" x="160"/>
            <use xlink:href="#vertical_line" y="0" x="180"/>
            <use xlink:href="#vertical_line" y="0" x="200" stroke-width="4"/>
        </g>
        <text id="skewX0" font-size="18"
                dominant-baseline="mathematical" text-anchor="middle">
            skewX(0)
        </text>
        <text id="skewX45" font-size="18">skewX(45)</text>
        <text id="skewY0" font-size="18">skewY(0)</text>
        <text id="skewY45" font-size="18">skewY(450)</text>
        <g id="merPicture">
        <use xlink:href="#grid" x="-100" y="-100" stroke="blue"/>
```

```
                        <image xlink:href="SweaterMer3.png" width="124" height="242"
                        x="-62" y="-121"/>
                         </g>
            </defs>
            <g transform="translate(180,150)">
                <use xlink:href="#skewX0" x="-80" y="-120"/>
                <use xlink:href="#merPicture"/>
            </g>
            <g transform="translate(500,150)">
                <use xlink:href="#skewX45" x="20" y="-120"/>
                <g transform="skewX(45)">
                    <use xlink:href="#merPicture"/>
                </g>
            </g>
            <g transform="translate(180,400)">
                <use xlink:href="#skewY0" x="-100" y="-110"/>
                <g transform="skewY(0)">
                    <use xlink:href="#merPicture"/>
                </g>
            </g>
            <g transform="translate(500,400)">
                <use xlink:href="#skewY45" x="20" y="-100"/>
                <g transform="skewY(45)">
                    <use xlink:href="#merPicture"/>
                </g>
            </g>
        </svg>
```

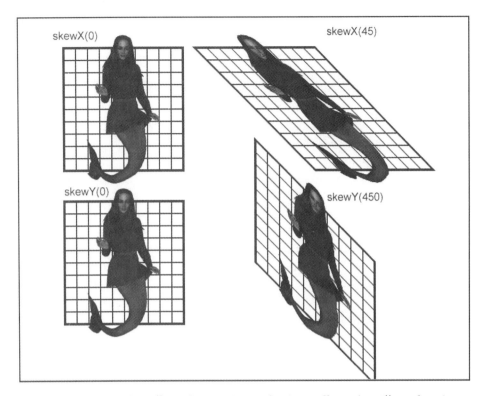

Figure 3-18. Using skewX() *to skew an image horizontally or* skewY() *to skew it vertically*

A grid is included with this to illustrate the warping of the underlying coordinate system whenever a skew is used.

The Matrix

When I was first writing the first draft of this chapter, I included extensive discussions about the underlying mathematics of transformations, complete with dot-and-cross product notations, complex matrices, and enough Greek letters to choke a graduate student. Other than discovering that most What-You-See-Is-What-You-Get (WYSWIG) editors still do not hold a candle to LaTeX when it comes to formatting mathematical text and that there is absolutely no standardization anywhere when it comes to mathematical formula expression between different versions of Word, I found that it was pretty much an exercise in futility. You can understand transformations without needing to know anything about complex mathematics, with one minor exception.

All of the transformations that SVG supports fall into the category of being *affine* transformations. An affine transformation is essentially one that can be produced by some combination of scaling, rotation, skewing, or translation. Specifically, an affine transformation is any transformation that can be written in this form:

```
x' = ax + cy + e
y' = bx + dy + f
```

where the coefficients *a* through *f* are considered to be part of a *matrix* of numbers, (x, y) are the original coordinate values and (x', y') the transformed values. For instance, scaling the x axis by 2 and the y axis by $\frac{1}{2}$ could be done if a = 2, d = 0.5, and all the other coefficients are 0. Rotations and skews are a little more complex, as they require the results of trigonometric sine and cosine functions in all four initial values a through d, and translations are perhaps easiest, with a translation by (dx, dy) being represented as:

```
x' = 1 · x + 0 · y + dx
y' = 0 · x + 1 · y + dy
```

or a matrix of this, respectively:

a	c	e	=	1	0	dx
b	d	f	=	0	1	dy

The `matrix()` function is especially useful in autogenerated SVG because you can create transformations by multiplying them together using matrix multiplication (look at any good book on linear algebra for more information), then just pass the resulting matrix of numbers into a `matrix()` function. The `matrix()` function, as you might guess, takes six arguments, one for *a* through *f* in the previous list.

For instance, suppose you wanted to create a function that rotated an image 30° clockwise, then flipped it about its y axis. You could use functional composition (discussed in the next section) or you could just get out your handy-dandy Hewlett-Packard calculator, do a few quick calculations, and determine the coefficients as the following:

```
a = - cos (30) = - 0.866
b = - sin (30) = - 0.5
c = - sin (30) = 0.5
d =   cos (30) = 0.866
e =   0
f =   0
```

The matrix transform could then be invoked by passing these numbers in:

```
<g transform="matrix(-0.866, -0.5, 0.5, 0.866, 0 0)">
```

In practice, especially when working programmatically, it is usually preferable to apply multiple transformations using the other methods, unless you need to retain state information about a current complex set of transformations applied by a user.

Note that all affine transformations are isometric in nature. That is to say, if you apply an affine transformation to a grid, you can select a rectangular region of the new grid and move it so that it matches up with both the angle and dimensions of any other part of the grid. Although affine transformations make up a significant portion of the total number of operations you can do on a grid, they are not all inclusive. For instance, you cannot, using an affine transformation, turn a rectangle into a *frustrum*, where the length of the base is larger than that of the top. Unfortunately, as exactly this kind of operation is necessary to create perspective effects, one upshot is that, at least with version 1.0, you have to create any perspective shapes directly with a path or polygon tool, rather than relying upon a transformation.

 NOTE *There is some discussion for SVG 2.0 to include a larger class of transformations that would let you do such things as perspective effects.*

Chaining Transformations

As has been illustrated earlier, you can apply multiple transformations to the same set of objects by applying the transformations to <g> elements from the inside out. Thus, if you wanted to flip an image about the y axis and then rotate it by 30 degrees, you would work from the outside in:

```
<g transform="rotate(30)">
    <g transform="scale(-1,1)">
        <!-- graphics content -->
    </g>
</g>
```

In many cases, this is actually the best strategy because each transformation operation usually serves some distinct semantic purpose, and breaking the transformations into their associated steps make it possible to retain the semantics. Similarly, it is usually easier to both animate such transformations—as discussed in Chapter 8, "Animating SVG" —and to program against them—as discussed in Chapter 9, "Integrating SVG and HTML," and Chapter 10, "SVG Components". However, if you do want to combine the transformations, you can using the , operator:

```
<g transform="rotate(30), scale(-1,1) ">
    <!-- graphics content -->
</g>
```

The order goes from right to left: The scale (actually a flip) operation is performed first, then the rotation is performed. You can chain as many such transformations as you want in this way, going from right to left. An example of this in practice is as given in Listing 3-15. Figure 3-19 shows what this code looks like.

Listing 3-15. `chainedTransforms.svg`

```
<svg xmlns="http://www.w3.org/2000/svg"
        xmlns:link="http://www.w3.org/1999/xlink" >
    <defs>
        <line x1="0" y1="0" x2="200" y2="0"
                id="horizontal_line" stroke-linecap="square"/>
        <use xlink:href="#horizontal_line"
                transform="rotate(90)" id="vertical_line"/>
        <g id="grid" stroke-width="2">
            <use xlink:href="#horizontal_line" x="0" y="0" stroke-width="4"/>
            <use xlink:href="#horizontal_line" x="0" y="20"/>
            <use xlink:href="#horizontal_line" x="0" y="40"/>
            <use xlink:href="#horizontal_line" x="0" y="60"/>
            <use xlink:href="#horizontal_line" x="0" y="80"/>
            <use xlink:href="#horizontal_line" x="0" y="100"/>
            <use xlink:href="#horizontal_line" x="0" y="120"/>
            <use xlink:href="#horizontal_line" x="0" y="140"/>
            <use xlink:href="#horizontal_line" x="0" y="160"/>
            <use xlink:href="#horizontal_line" x="0" y="180"/>
            <use xlink:href="#horizontal_line" x="0" y="200" stroke-width="4"/>
            <use xlink:href="#vertical_line" y="0" x="0" stroke-width="4"/>
            <use xlink:href="#vertical_line" y="0" x="20"/>
            <use xlink:href="#vertical_line" y="0" x="40"/>
            <use xlink:href="#vertical_line" y="0" x="60"/>
            <use xlink:href="#vertical_line" y="0" x="80"/>
```

```
            <use xlink:href="#vertical_line" y="0" x="100"/>
            <use xlink:href="#vertical_line" y="0" x="120"/>
            <use xlink:href="#vertical_line" y="0" x="140"/>
            <use xlink:href="#vertical_line" y="0" x="160"/>
            <use xlink:href="#vertical_line" y="0" x="180"/>
            <use xlink:href="#vertical_line" y="0" x="200" stroke-width="4"/>
        </g>
        <svg id="image" preserveAspectRatio="xMinYMax meet"
                width="200" height="200" viewBox="0 0 242 242"
                x="-100" y="-100">
            <use xlink:href="#grid" stroke="blue"/>
            <image xlink:href="SweaterMer3.png" width="124" height="242"
              x="0" y="0"/>
        </svg>
    </defs>
    <g id="unchainedTransforms">
        <g transform="translate(150,200)">
            <use xlink:href="#image" x="0" y="0"/>
        </g>
        <g transform="translate(300,200)">
            <g transform="scale(-1,1)">
                <use xlink:href="#image" x="0" y="0"/>
            </g>
        </g>
        <g transform="translate(500,200)">
            <g transform="rotate(45)">
                <g transform="scale(-1,1)">
                    <use xlink:href="#image" x="0" y="0"/>
                </g>
            </g>
        </g>
    </g>
    <g id="chainedTransforms">
        <g transform="translate(150,400)">
            <use xlink:href="#image" x="0" y="0"/>
        </g>
        <g transform="translate(300,400),scale(-1,1)">
            <use xlink:href="#image" x="0" y="0"/>
        </g>
        <g transform="translate(500,400),rotate(45),scale(-1,1)">
            <use xlink:href="#image" x="0" y="0"/>
        </g>
    </g>
</svg>
```

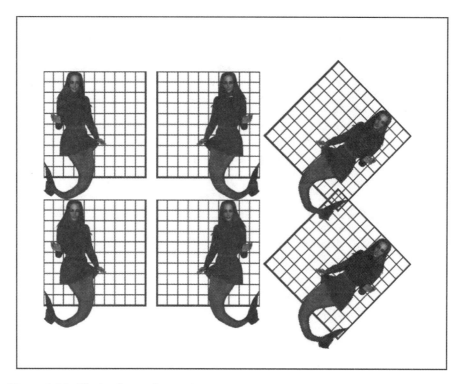

Figure 3-19. Chained transformations

In the <g> element #unchainedTransforms, the grouping operators each carry one primitive transformation per group, while in #chainedTransforms, the operations are grouped into chains. Note again that although there is less code involved, it is a little harder operationally to figure out what's going on with the following:

```
<g transform="translate(500,400),rotate(45),scale(-1,1)">
        <use xlink:href="#image" x="0" y="0"/>
</g>
```

than it is with this:

```
<g transform="translate(500,200)">
        <g transform="rotate(45)">
            <g transform="scale(-1,1)">
                <use xlink:href="#image" x="0" y="0"/>
            </g>
        </g>
</g>
```

because you're generally used to reading left to right rather right to left.

CAUTION   *One other aspect that makes chained transformations less than desirable is that they are incredibly difficult to debug because an errant transformation may make an element move off screen or evince other behavior that is not immediately obvious from the transformation itself. This is especially true of rotations.*

NOTE   *A proposal currently in front of the SVG committee for SVG 2.0 is the possibility of creating aggregate-named transformation functions, just as you would create named CSS functions. I should also note that transformations are not CSS attributes, so you cannot create stylesheets that perform transformations on element based upon its class.*

Summary

Coordinate systems act as the canvases upon which you create your work. Just as a painter primes her canvas with the appropriate gessos (the medium to which the paint is actually applied) or sands it to get the appropriate ground, the ability to create and transform coordinate systems can be useful for controlling the surface upon which you both create your graphics and develop your programming.

However, beyond just establishing coordinate systems, the structure of SVG gives you the ability both to create classes of objects using referenced elements and to abstract the actual presentation of information by associating an SVG document with a CSS stylesheet. These features are of secondary importance to generating graphics through tools, but they are the necessary precursors to programming, and gaining mastery of the use of viewports and graphic contexts will give you much more control over building your applications.

Of course, SVG is a graphics language, and most of its operations involve understanding the principles of SVG *as* a graphics language. As a consequence, in Chapters 4 through 6, I will explore how you draw SVG shapes, how you work with fills, masks, colors, and strokes, and how you manipulate text. Consequently, these chapters may belie the "programming" part of the title, but they are worth studying in their own right because having a good handle on how SVG uses these objects can give you some truly powerful tools for application development.

CHAPTER 4

Shaping the Spiral Path: Shapes and Paths

ONE OF THE CENTRAL PROBLEMS with HTML is that it is rectilinear. Everything is in a box. Although Cascading Style Sheets (CSS) begins to push the boundaries of those boxes out a bit—you can, for instance, rotate text elements in the W3C CSS 2 recommendation, but few browsers support this feature—the language has no real concept of handling nonrectangular shapes.

Applications such as Adobe Illustrator or Macromedia FreeHand both work by letting users define their own shapes. A few basic primitives are included—rectangles (straight and rounded), ovals, occasionally stars, polygons, or similar elements—but in most cases the expectation is that you will be creating your own shapes from scratch. The primitives are there primarily as the foundation tools on which to build your own more elaborate shapes.

This chapter looks at the core shapes, as well as how to "roll your own" shapes using the <path> element. It also explores the <defs> and <use> elements in more depth, along with <symbol> and <marker>, to better create libraries of shapes. Finally, I show how you can use shape elements to create more complex objects.

A brief caveat here is in order. Certain attributes such as fill and stroke are quite rich and complex, falling as they do into the realm of painting. Throughout this chapter I use fills and strokes because they are necessary for visualization purposes, but if some aspect of either confuses you, please see Chapter 5, "Painting and Drawing."

Using Shape Primitives

SVG defines a set of six primitive shapes:

- <rect>: A rectangle element, potentially with rounded corners.

- <circle>: A circle element, defined by giving the center coordinate and the radius of the circle.

- `<ellipse>`: An ellipse element, which is like a circle except that you can specify both the horizontal and vertical radius independently.

- `<line>`: A line element, which lets you join two points together. You can also use lines in conjunction with markers to create arrows.

- `<polyline>`: An open shape made of a series of connected line segments.

- `<polygon>`: A closed shape made of a series of connected line segments.

Additionally, any shape (whether made of line segments or arcs) can consist of the `<path>` element, although the specific path parameters are a language unto themselves and are discussed in Chapter 5, "Painting and Drawing."

Because each of the elements has a number of attributes that differ significantly from the baseline, it is worth exploring each in turn.

The `<rect>` *Element*

Rectangles are perhaps the easiest SVG elements to work with, in great part because they reflect most of the standard CSS conventions with which Web developers are familiar. Table 4-1 lists the attributes for `<rect>`.

NOTE   *The primary* fill *and* stroke *properties indicate whether a given shape supports fills, strokes, or both. If they support the primary* fill *property, they also support the subordinate fill such as* fill-opacity; *similarly, shapes supporting* stroke *also support all stroke properties such as* stroke-width. *Chapter 5, "Painting and Drawing," will cover fills and strokes more extensively.*

Table 4-1. The `<rect>` *Element Attributes*

ATTRIBUTE NAME	ATTRIBUTE TYPE	DESCRIPTION
x	SVGLength	The horizontal coordinate of the upper-left point of the rectangle in the appropriate coordinate system. This can be negative.
y	SVGLength	The vertical coordinate of the upper-left point of the rectangle. This can be negative.
width	SVGLength	The width of the rectangle. This must be non-negative.
height	SVGLength	The height of the rectangle. This must be non-negative.
id	ID	An identifier for the element. Note that you can have more than one element with the same ID, but in that case they are referenced as an array .
rx	SVGLength	The x radius of a circle that rounds the edges of the rectangle. This must be non-negative.
ry	SVGLength	The y radius of a circle that rounds the edges of the rectangle. This must be non-negative.
class	NMToken	The name of a particular CSS class that specifies relevant attributes for the rectangle.
style	String	A set of CSS style attributes that describe relevant attributes for the rectangle.
fill	SVGColor I URL	The fill attribute describes the color, pattern, or gradient that fills the shape. Chapter 5, "Painting and Drawing," discusses it in greater detail.
stroke	SVGColor	This sets the color of the line bordering the shape.

A simple rectangle, 100-pixels wide by 36-pixels high, with a red background and a 3-pixel wide black border, would be described as the following:

```
<svg xmlns="http://www.w3.org/2000/svg"
            xmlns:xlink="http://www.w3.org/1999/xlink"
            width="100" height="36"
            viewBox="0 0 100 36"
            preserveAspectRatio="none">
```

```
    <g>
        <rect width="100" height="36" fill="red"
                stroke="black" stroke-width="3"/>
    </g>
</svg>
```

The <svg> element, included here with the namespaces defining SVG itself and the W3C XLink standard for linking, serves as a wrapper that defines the graphic context (its dimensions and coordinate system). The color of the rectangle is given by its fill attribute, an attribute that is actually far more versatile than it appears on the surface. Similarly, the stroke attribute handles the creation of the border around the rectangle. On the other hand, if you wanted to create a button with rounded corners (with each corner having a radius of 12 pixels), you would describe it like this:

```
<svg xmlns="http://www.w3.org/2000/svg"
            xmlns:xlink="http://www.w3.org/1999/xlink"
            width="100" height="36"
            viewBox="0 0 100 36"
            preserveAspectRatio="none"
    <g>
        <rect width="100" height="36" fill="red"
                stroke="black" stroke-width="3"
                rx="12" ry="12"/>
    </g>
</svg>
```

Figure 4-1 shows the effects of the rx and ry parameters. In general, the larger you make rx and ry, the more rounded and lozenge-like the rectangle becomes. You can set the two parameters independently; you are essentially setting the x and y radii of an ellipse for each corner, as shown in Figure 4-2.

Figure 4-1. Effects of changing rounded rectangle parameters

Figure 4-2. Defining the rounded rectangle

The `<circle>` Element

Circles have a slightly different syntax than rectangles. With a circle, you basically specify the location of the circle's origin, relative to the current coordinate system, then give a radius value, as covered in Table 4-2.

Table 4-2. The `<circle>` Element Attributes

ATTRIBUTE NAME	ATTRIBUTE TYPE	DESCRIPTION
cx	SVGLength	The horizontal coordinate of the center of the circle.
cy	SVGLength	The vertical coordinate of the center of the circle.
r	SVGLength	The radius of the circle. This must be non-negative.
id	ID	An identifier for the element. Note that you can have more than one element with the same ID, but in that case they are referenced as an array.
class	NMToken	The name of a particular CSS class that specifies relevant attributes for the circle.
style	String	A set of CSS style attributes that describe relevant attributes for the circle.
fill	SVGColor	URL	The `fill` attribute describes the color, pattern, or gradient that fills the shape. Chapter 5, "Painting and Drawing," discusses it in greater detail.
stroke	SVGColor	This sets the color of the line bordering the circle.
transform	rotate	translate	scale	skewX	skewY	matrix	Transforms the circle according to the transformation operator.

Thus, if you wanted to create a red, black-stroked circle located at (150,150) and a radius of 100, you would use the following expression:

```
<svg xmlns="http://www.w3.org/2000/svg"
    xmlns:xlink="http://www.w3.org/1999/xlink" >
    <g>
        <circle cx="150" cy="150" r="100" fill="red"
                stroke="black" stroke-width="3"/>
    </g>
</svg>
```

Note that you can also use the <rect> element to draw a circle within a specific bounding square. To do this, set the rx and ry values of the rounded rectangle element to be half of the height and width, respectively:

```
<svg xmlns="http://www.w3.org/2000/svg"
      xmlns:xlink="http://www.w3.org/1999/xlink">
    <g>
        <rect width="150" height="150" rx="75" ry="75" fill="red"
              stroke="black" stroke-width="3"/>
    </g>
</svg>
```

This technique works best in situations where you do not want to have to calculate the center point of a circle but know the bounding rectangle and radius of the circle.

The <ellipse> Element

The <ellipse> element, much like the <circle> element, creates a shorthand notation for creating an ellipse positioned around the center of the ellipse rather than the upper-left corner of the ellipses-bounding rectangle. It is in fact nearly identical, except that rather than the ellipse having one radius, it has two (rx and ry) specifying the x and y axis radius respectively. Table 4-3 shows the <ellipse> element attributes.

Table 4-3. The `<ellipse>` *Element Attributes*

ATTRIBUTE NAME	ATTRIBUTE TYPE	DESCRIPTION
cx	SVGLength	The horizontal coordinate of the center of the ellipse.
cy	SVGLength	The vertical coordinate of the center of the ellipse.
rx	SVGLength	The radius of the ellipse along the x axis. This must be non-negative.
ry	SVGLength	The radius of the ellipse along the y axis. This must be non-negative.
id	ID	An identifier for the element. Note that you can have more than one element with the same ID, but in that case they are referenced as an array.
class	NMToken	The name of a particular CSS class that specifies relevant attributes for the ellipse.
style	String	A set of CSS style attributes that describe relevant attributes for the ellipse.
fill	SVGColor | URL	The fill attribute describes the color, pattern, or gradient that fills the ellipse. Chapter 5, "Painting and Drawing," discusses this in more detail.
stroke	SVGColor	This sets the color of the line bordering the ellipse.
transform	rotate | translate | scale | skewX | skewY | matrix	Transforms the ellipse according to the transformation operator.

Creating a red ellipse with a black stroke is nearly as straightforward as building a circle (see Figure 4-3):

```
<svg xmlns="http://www.w3.org/2000/svg"
     xmlns:xlink="http://www.w3.org/1999/xlink">
  <g>
      <ellipse rx="100" ry="50" cx="150" cy="150"
          fill="red" stroke="black"/>
  </g>
</svg>
```

Figure 4-3. Specifying the rx *and* ry *axes of the ellipse separately*

You can also transform the ellipse using the transform attribute. Note that the cx and cy attributes do not change the center of rotations or scaling, which means that if you want to rotate an ellipse, you need to position it within a graphical context <g> and set the cx and cy attributes both to 0, as follows (see Figure 4-4):

```
<svg xmlns="http://www.w3.org/2000/svg"
     xmlns:xlink="http://www.w3.org/1999/xlink">
   <g transform="translate(150,150)">
       <ellipse rx="100" ry="50" cx="0" cy="0"
           fill="red" stroke="black" transform="rotate(30)"/>
   </g>
</svg>
```

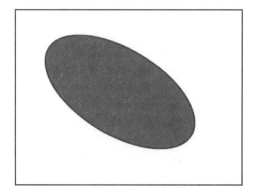

Figure 4-4. Setting cx *and* cy *to 0*

Note again that the ellipse tag is a "convenience" tag. You can also create an ellipse from a rectangle with rounded edges by setting with rx and ry radii to half the width and height, respectively, of the rectangle. Thus, the ellipse in Figure 4-3 could just as easily have been rendered as this:

```
<svg xmlns="http://www.w3.org/2000/svg"
        xmlns:xlink="http://www.w3.org/1999/xlink">
    <g>
        <!-- The ellipse  -->
        <ellipse rx="100" ry="50" cx="150" cy="150"
            fill="red" stroke="black"/>
        <!-- is the same as the rounded rectangle -->
        <rect width="200" height="100" x="100" y="100"
            rx="100" ry="50" fill="red" stroke="black"/>
    </g>
</svg>
```

The advantage to one over the other is chiefly whether you want to position an element relative to the center (`<ellipse>`) or upper-left corner (`<rect>`).

The `<line>` Element

Lines are straightforward elements to work with (sorry). A line, in SVG, basically consists of two points (x1,y1) and (x2,y2). A line does not have an associated fill, although you can set the stroke property. Table 4-4 shows the <line> element attributes.

Table 4-4. The `<line>` Element Attributes

ATTRIBUTE NAME	ATTRIBUTE TYPE	DESCRIPTION
x1	SVGLength	The horizontal (x) coordinate of the starting point of the line.
y1	SVGLength	The vertical (y) coordinate of the starting point of the line.
x2	SVGLength	The horizontal (x) coordinate of the ending point of the line.
y2	SVGLength	The vertical (y) coordinate of the ending point of the line.
id	ID	An identifier for the element. Note that you can have more than one element with the same ID, but in that case they are referenced as an array.
class	NMToken	The name of a particular CSS class that specifies relevant attributes for the line.
style	String	A set of CSS style attributes that describe relevant attributes for the line.
stroke	SVGColor | URL	This sets the color of the line.
transform	rotate | translate | scale | skewX | skewY | matrix	Transforms the line according to the relevant transformation operator.

For instance, the following will let you draw a red line from (100,50) to (320,240):

```
<svg xmlns="http://www.w3.org/2000/svg"
        xmlns:xlink="http://www.w3.org/1999/xlink">
    <g>
        <line x1="100" y1="50" x2="320" y2="240" stroke="red"/>
    </g>
</svg>
```

The line element is a primitive, useful for quick line and rule generation, but should not be used for creating shapes or paths (to do that, use a polyline, polygon, or path element instead).

The <polyline> and <polygon> Elements

The <polyline> element is useful when you want to create an open path using straight-line segments, although the path element covered in the next section may be more versatile. A polygon is a polyline that is closed—has a fill as well as a stroke—whereas polylines are just collections of connected lines. Because the two use the same syntax, they can be treated together. Table 4-5 shows the <polyline> and <polygon> element attributes.

Both polygons and polylines provide a simple syntax for creating shapes quickly. You create a shape with either form by specifying the coordinates of each point in the shape. For instance, the following polygon will create a stellated (star-shaped) pentagon shape within a pentagon (as shown in Figure 4-5):

```
<svg xmlns="http://www.w3.org/2000/svg"
        xmlns:xlink="http://www.w3.org/1999/xlink">
    <g>
        <polygon points="50,0 97,35 79,91 20,91 2,35"
                stroke="black" fill="blue"/>
        <polygon points="50,0 79,91 2,35 97,35 20,91"
                stroke="black" fill="yellow"/>
    </g>
</svg>
```

Table 4-5. The `<polyline>` *and* `<polygon>` *Element Attributes*

ATTRIBUTE NAME	ATTRIBUTE TYPE	DESCRIPTION
x	SVGLength	The horizontal (x) coordinate of the upper-left corner of the shape's bounding box.
y	SVGLength	The vertical (y) coordinate of the upper-left corner of the shape's bounding box.
points	SVGLength array	A set of whitespace-separated coordinate pairs of the form `"x1,y1 x2,y2 x3,y3 . . . "`.
id	ID	An identifier for the element. Note that you can have more than one element with the same ID, but in that case they are referenced as an array.
class	NMToken	The name of a particular CSS class that specifies relevant attributes for the shape.
style	String	A set of CSS style attributes that describe relevant attributes for the shape.
stroke	SVGColor | URL	This sets the color of the line bordering the shape.
fill	SVGColor | URL	The `fill` attribute describes the color, pattern, or gradient that fills the shape (polygon only).
transform	rotate | translate | scale | skewX | skewY | matrix	Transforms the shape according to the relevant transformation operator.

Figure 4-5. A pentagon within a pentagon

If the last point in a polygon is not the starting point, then the SVG renderer will automatically draw a line between that point and the starting point. This makes it easy to write routines that will generate regular polygon shapes. The JavaScript function `getRegularPolygon()` in the HTML document `shapeRoutine.htm` lets you generate a regular polygon of n-sides (see Figure 4-6). Listing 4-1 shows the Polygon Generator (`polygonGenerator.htm`) that will create the necessary path information for generating simple regular polygons.

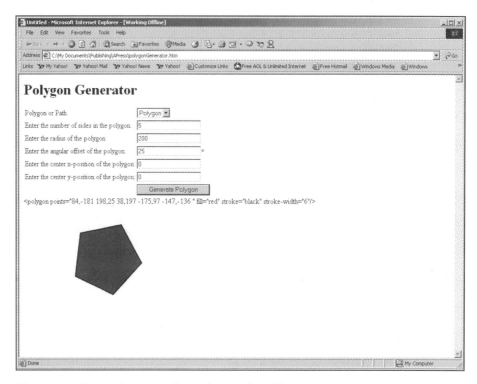

Figure 4-6. Generating a regular polygon of n-sides

*Listing 4-1. Polygon Generator (*polygonGenerator.htm*)*

```
<html>
<head>
    <title>Untitled</title>
    <script language="JavaScript">//<![CDATA[
function passBackSVG(){
    var embedNodes=document.embeds;
    for (var i=0;i<embedNodes.length;i++){
        embedNode=embedNodes[i];
        if(embedNode.window.passState){
            embedNode.window.passState(embedNode);
            }
        }
    }
//]]>    </script>
</head>

<body onload="passBackSVG()">
<h1>Polygon Generator</h1>
<table>
<tr>
    <td>Polygon or Path</td>
    <td><select id="polytype">
            <option id="polygon" selected">Polygon</option>
            <option id="path" selected">Path</option>
        </select>
    </td>
</tr>
<tr>
    <td>Enter the number of sides in the polygon:</td>
    <td><input type="text" id="sides" value="5"/></td>
</tr>
```

```
<tr>
    <td>Enter the radius of the polygon:</td>
    <td><input type="text" id="radius" value="200"/></td>
</tr>
<tr>
    <td>Enter the angular offset of the polygon:</td>
    <td><input type="text" id="angleOffset" value="0"/>&deg;</td>
</tr>
<tr>
    <td>Enter the center x-position of the polygon:</td>
    <td><input type="text" id="cx" value="0"/></td>
</tr>
<tr>
    <td>Enter the center y-position of the polygon:</td>
    <td><input type="text" id="cy" value="0"/></td>
</tr>
<tr>
    <td> </td>
    <td><input type="submit" value="Generate Polygon"
        onclick="buffer.innerHTML=getRegularPolygon
        (sides.value,radius.value,angleOffset.value,cx.value,cy.value)"/>
    </td>
</tr>

</table>
<div id="buffer"></div>
<script language="Javascript">
function getRegularPolygon(n, r, angleOffset,cx,cy){
    var polyBuf="";
    polyTypeNode=document.all("polytype");
    elementType=polyTypeNode.options.item(
            polyTypeNode.options.selectedIndex).id;
    for (var i=0;i<n;i++){
        var angle=(2*3.1415927*i/n) + (angleOffset/180)*3.1415927;
        var x= parseFloat(cx) + Math.floor(parseFloat(r) * Math.sin(angle));
        var y= parseFloat(cy) - Math.floor(parseFloat(r) * Math.cos(angle));
        if (elementType=="path"){
```

```
            if (i==0){
                polyBuf="m";
                }
            else {
                polyBuf += "L";
                }
            }
        polyBuf += x+"," + y + " ";
        }
    if (elementType=="polygon"){
        buf = '&lt;polygon points="' +polyBuf + '" fill="red"
                            stroke="black" stroke-width="6"/&gt;';
        }
    else {
        buf = '&lt;path d="' +polyBuf + '" fill="red"
                            stroke="black" stroke-width="6"/&gt;';
        }
    buffer.innerHTML=buf;
    var shape=window.display_polygon;
    shape.setPoints(polyBuf);
    return buf;
    }
</script>
<embed src="polygon.svg" width="400" height="400"
            wmode="transparent" points="50,0 97,35 79,91 20,91 2,35"
            id="display_polygon"
            style="position:absolute;top:200;left:0"/>
</body>

</html>
```

Listing 4-1 will create a polygon element with the appropriate point set, though you will still need to set any stroke or fill coordinates. It was used in fact to generate the polygon coordinates given previously. The routine can also generate regular polygons using <path> coordinates, covered later in this chapter.

The generator makes use of an embedded SVG to display the resulting polygon (Internet Explorer 5+ only). The SVG document in Listing 4-2 employs a number of techniques developed later in this book (Chapter 9, "Integrating SVG and HTML," and on) to respond to parametric changes.

Listing 4-2. `Polygon.svg`

```
<svg xmlns="http://www.w3.org/2000/svg"
    xmlns:xlink="http://www.w3.org/1999/xlink"
    width="500"
    height="500"
    viewBox="0 0 1000 1000"
    preserveAspectRatio="none"
    onload="initSVG(evt)">
    <script language="JavaScript" scriptImplementation="Microsoft"
                type="text/javascript">//<![CDATA[

var svg=null;
function initSVG(evt){
    svg=evt.target.ownerDocument;
    }

function passState(extObject){
    extObject.setPoints=setPoints;
    }

function setPoints(pointList){
    var shape=svg.getElementById("base_polygon");
    var path=svg.getElementById("base_path");
    if (pointList.charAt(0)=="m"){
        shape.setAttribute("visibility","hidden");
        path.setAttribute("d",pointList+"z");
        path.setAttribute("visibility","visible");
        }
    else {
        path.setAttribute("visibility","hidden");
        shape.setAttribute("points",pointList);
        shape.setAttribute("visibility","visible");
        }
    }
//    ]]></script>
    <g transform="translate(500,500)">
        <polygon points="0,-200 190,-61 117,162 -118,162 -191,-61"
                    fill="red" stroke="black" stroke-width="6"
                    id="base_polygon"/>
        <path d="m0,0" fill="red" stroke="black"
                    stroke-width="6" id="base_path"/>
    </g>
</svg>
```

You can leverage <polygon> and <polyline> elements to quickly create basic shapes. However, both elements are extremely limited: You cannot create curved elements with polygons, nor can you create disconnected shapes. These are elements that are defined as being a part of a single element, but visually they are broken into two or more regions. In fact, both polygons and polylines are special instances of another SVG element: <path>.

Creating Paths, Splines, and Curves

Most of the SVG shape elements tend to be fairly bland. Although there are always uses for rectangles, ellipses, circles, and even simple lines and polygons, the primary elements are hardly adequate for the task of describing the richness of form that can be found in even the simplest of graphics. Fortunately, underlying all other shapes in the SVG repertoire is the <path> element, which can best be described as the "every other shape" shape. Table 4-6 shows the <path> element attributes.

Table 4-6. The <path> *Element Attributes*

ATTRIBUTE NAME	ATTRIBUTE TYPE	DESCRIPTION
d	SVGPathExpression	The set of flags and coordinates that describe the path being drawn.
pathLength	SVGLength	This value describes the total length of a given path in user-defined units. This value is used in animation and DOM calculations.
id	ID	An identifier for the element. Note that you can have more than one element with the same ID, but in that case they are referenced as an array.
class	NMToken	The name of a particular CSS class that specifies relevant attributes for the rectangle.
style	String	A set of CSS style attributes that describe relevant attributes for the shape.
stroke	SVGColor | URL	This sets the color of the line bordering the shape.
fill	SVGColor | URL	The fill attribute describes the color, pattern, or gradient that fills the shape (polygon only).
transform	rotate | translate | scale | skewX | skewY | matrix	Transforms the shape according to the relevant transformation operator.

The <path> element actually uses a language-within-a-language approach to generating output. Instead of simply specifying the coordinates, you work with the <path> element by following the tracings of an imaginary "pen." You specify the movement from one position to another, along with a flag indicating whether the movement is drawing a line using L (**Line to**) as the flag or simply moving without drawing a line, using M (**Move to**) as the flag, within the d attribute, as illustrated in the "Creating Simple Path Shapes" section. (Note: the letter's case does matter, but you will get to that in the next section.) Table 4-7 shows the commands used to draw lines within the path element.

Table 4-7. The <path> *Element's Move and Line Commands*

PATH PROPERTY	SYNTAX	DESCRIPTION
Move to	Mx,y	Moves to the absolute position x,y in the local coordinate system without drawing a line
Line to	Lx,y	Moves to the absolute position x,y in the local coordinate system while drawing a line from the last point
Close Path	z	Closes the current working path, drawing a line from the current point to the starting point of the current path

Creating Simple Path Shapes

Follow these steps to create simple path shapes:

1. In your text editor, create the following SVG file and name it **path1.svg**:

```
<svg xmlns="http://www.w3.org/2000/svg"
    xmlns:xlink="http://www.w3.org/1999/xlink" >
    <defs>
        <line x1="0" y1="0" x2="100%" y2="0"
                    stroke="cyan" stroke-width="1" id="hline"/>
        <line x1="0" y1="0" x2="0" y2="100%"
                    stroke="cyan" stroke-width="1" id="vline"/>
        <g id="grid">
            <use xlink:href="#hline" y="0"/>
            <use xlink:href="#hline" y="50"/>
            <use xlink:href="#hline" y="100"/>
            <use xlink:href="#hline" y="150"/>
```

```
            <use xlink:href="#hline" y="200"/>
            <use xlink:href="#hline" y="250"/>
            <use xlink:href="#hline" y="300"/>
            <use xlink:href="#hline" y="350"/>
            <use xlink:href="#hline" y="400"/>
            <use xlink:href="#hline" y="450"/>
            <use xlink:href="#hline" y="500"/>
            <use xlink:href="#vline" x="0"/>
            <use xlink:href="#vline" x="50"/>
            <use xlink:href="#vline" x="100"/>
            <use xlink:href="#vline" x="150"/>
            <use xlink:href="#vline" x="200"/>
            <use xlink:href="#vline" x="250"/>
            <use xlink:href="#vline" x="300"/>
            <use xlink:href="#vline" x="350"/>
            <use xlink:href="#vline" x="400"/>
            <use xlink:href="#vline" x="450"/>
            <use xlink:href="#vline" x="500"/>
            <use xlink:href="#vline" x="550"/>
            <use xlink:href="#vline" x="600"/>
            <use xlink:href="#vline" x="650"/>
            <use xlink:href="#vline" x="700"/>
            <use xlink:href="#vline" x="750"/>
        </g>
    </defs>
    <g transform="translate(0,0)">
        <use xlink:href="#grid"/>
    </g>
    <g>
        <path id="testpath" d="M50,100 L250,100 L250,200 L50,200"
                fill="red" stroke="black" stroke-width="2"/>
    </g>
</svg>
```

The bold <path> element (with id="testpath") should draw a rectangle 200-units wide and 100-units high, starting at (50,100), as shown in Figure 4-7. It also includes a grid in the background drawn in 50-pixel-wide units for reference. When viewed in an SVG browser, you should note that one side of the rectangle is missing: the line from the end of the data to the beginning.

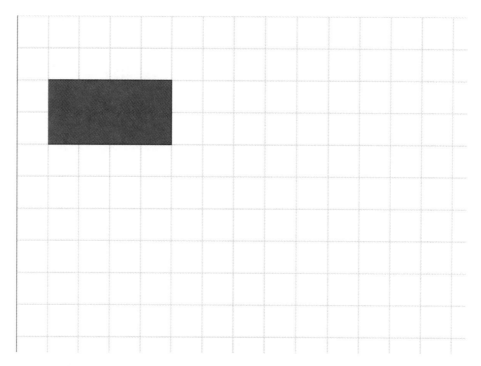

Figure 4-7. Drawing a rectangle 200-units wide and 100-units high

2. The reason for the gap has to do with the fact that a normal path is by default "open"—although it has an associated fill, the path extends only from the first coordinate to the last one. By closing a shape, you implicitly finish the path to the beginning coordinate. The z command indicates that the shape should be closed as that point. Add a z to the end of the path #testpath:

```
<g>
    <path id="testpath"
        d="M50,100 L250,100 L250,200 L50,200z"
        fill="red" stroke="black" stroke-width="2"/>
</g>
```

3. Save the file as **path2.svg**, and try viewing it again. Figure 4-8 shows the results. A completed path (terminated with the z element) will draw a final line from the last point to the first, and additionally will treat this path as closed.

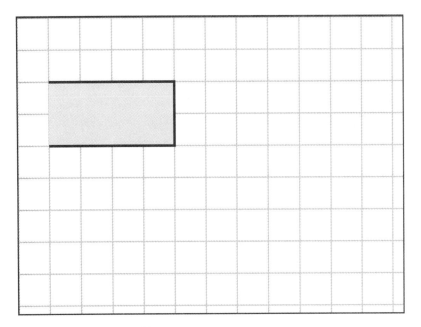

Figure 4-8. The Path2.svg *file*

The ability to close a shape is important in SVG, because it means that you can define more than one region with a single command.

4. Add a new path string after the one just terminated, using the **M** to reposition the pen, **L** to draw the lines, and **z** to close the second region, making a shape that is split into two distinct pieces. Save the file as **path3.svg**:

```
<g>
    <path d="M50,100 L250,100 L250,200 L50,200z M300,100 L450,100 L300,250z"
        fill="red" stroke="black" stroke-width="4"/>
</g>
```

Figure 4-9 shows a single path element can encompass disconnected areas by using multiple z flags.

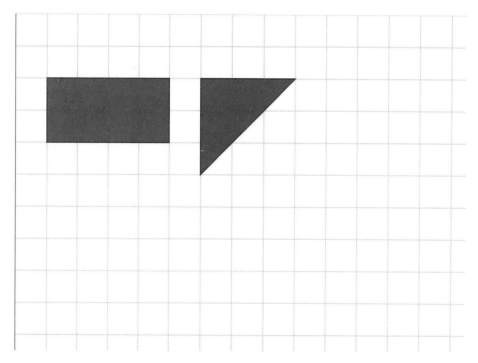

Figure 4-9. A disconnected path

Working with Relative Coordinates

The pen described in the previous section relied upon absolute coordinates. As with so much of SVG, the <path> element will be in a <g> element that may set up local coordinates, but from that origin the path assumes that all coordinates are absolute. However, notice that this makes it a little more difficult to frame the problem: From a starting point, you have to manually calculate the coordinates of each point from the condition "Draw a rectangle with a width of 200 and a height of 100."

Relative coordinates, on the other hand, let you describe the coordinates relative to the previous coordinate (or the current origin for the first coordinate) in the path. For instance, consider the rectangle described in the previous section. The absolute coordinates are given as these:

- M50,100: Move to the point 50,100.

- L250,100: Line to the point 250,100.

- L250,200: Line to the point 250,200.

- L50,200: Line to the point 50,200.

- z: Return to the starting point.

Relative coordinates, on the other hand, would be given as these:

- m50,100: Move 50 units to the right and 100 units down.

- l200,0: Line 200 units to the right and 0 units down.

- l0,100: Line 0 units to the right and 100 units down.

- l-200,0: Line 200 units to the left and 0 units down.

- z: Return to the starting point.

You use the lowercase *m* and *l* to indicate that relative coordinates are used instead of absolute ones. Note the *l* is a lowercase *L*, not a one (1); this unfortunate similarity in many different fonts has led the SVG Working Group to consider providing a synonym that is not so easily confused in casual reading for the SVG 2.0 specification. Table 4-8 shows the `<path>` element's relative move and line commands.

Table 4-8. The `<path>` *Element's Relative Move and Line Commands*

PATH PROPERTY	SYNTAX	DESCRIPTION
Move to (relative)	m*dx*,*dy*	Moves dx units to the right and dy units down in the local coordinate system without drawing a line
Line to (relative)	l*dx*,*dy*	Moves dx units to the right and dy units down in the local coordinate system while drawing a line from the last point

You can cast any absolute path as a relative one (and vice versa). For instance, you can rewrite the combination rectangle and triangle in the previous example as this (with the altered path in bold):

```
<path d="m50,100 l200,0 l0,100 l-200,0z m250,0 l150,0 l0,l-150,150z"
    fill="red" stroke="black" stroke-width="2"/>
```

CAUTION *You can also combine relative and absolute coordinates, but this is generally a recipe for disaster, as it becomes much more difficult to visualize the movements involved. In general, stick with either all absolute or all relative coordinates.*

Seeking Closure: More on z

Closing a path is not quite the same as simply making sure that the ending point and the starting point are the same. Although fills are generally not a problem, certain stroke properties are handled differently depending upon whether the last point is coincident with the first as opposed to the path being closed with z. In particular, the stroke-linejoin and stroke-cap properties at the end of a path change depending upon whether the path is opened or closed.

This can be seen in the file strokeZ.svg (shown in Figure 4-10):

```
<svg xmlns="http://www.w3.org/2000/svg"
     xmlns:xlink="http://www.w3.org/1999/xlink" >
   <g>
      <path d="m100,100 l100,0 l0,100 l-100,0z" stroke-linejoin="round"
            fill="red" stroke="black" stroke-width="30"/>
      <path d="m300,100 l100,0 l0,100 l-100,0 l0,-100"
            stroke-linejoin="round"
            fill="red" stroke="black" stroke-width="30"/>
   </g>
</svg>
```

Figure 4-10. The termination of a stroke using the z command

The first path illustrates a closed path. All four corners are identically rounded because the "round" line-join is applied to each segment of the path, including the implicit segment from the final to the starting point.

In the second path, showing an open shape, the last point is coincident with the first but is not actually joined to it. In this case, the butt uses the default `stroke-linecap` for the end points of the path but the "round" `stroke-linejoin`, making the starting point look broken.

An additional advantage of using z has been noted before: You can actually create a path that contains more than one shape in it, simply by making sure that each noncontiguous shape has its own z terminator. These shapes will work together as a unit and can also be used for masking purposes (which comes in handy for all kinds of interesting special effects). Chapter 5, "Painting and Drawing," will show more examples of this.

Coming Round the Bend: Cubic Beziers

So far, there is not a lot of difference here between the <path> element and the <polygon> or <polyline> elements. Indeed, for many shapes, resorting to <polygon> or <polyline> elements may actually seem to be better then getting wrapped up in the sometimes-cryptic path notation used by <path>. However, this all changes if you want to create any kind of curved line.

SVG defines three types of curves: cubic Bezier curves, quadratic Bezier curves, and elliptical arcs. Bezier curves are mathematical curves that have found a great deal of application in most forms of computer graphics because they are remarkably simple to generate but can describe a fairly wide set of curved lines. The fact that SVG offers three types of Bezier curves may seem to be a little overkill, but in fact, each type of curve has its own application where it works well.

The simpler of the Bezier curves, cubic Beziers, depend upon an implicit starting point, an explicit ending point, and two *control* points, which control both the direction and the "strength" of the curve as it leaves the initial point or enters into the final point. Table 4-9 shows the cubic Bezier commands for the <path> element.

Table 4-9. Cubic Bezier Commands for the `<path>` *Element*

PATH PROPERTY	SYNTAX	DESCRIPTION
Cubic Bezier to (absolute)	$Cx_1,y_1\ x_2,y_2\ x',y'$	Creates a Bezier curve starting from the current position, using the points x_1,y_1 and x_2,y_2 as the control points (in absolute coordinates) and the point x',y' as the final point of the curve. The point x',y' becomes the new current position for any subsequent paths.
Cubic Bezier to (relative)	$cdx_1,dy_1\ dx_2,dx_2\ dx',dy'$	Creates a Bezier curve starting from the current position, using the offsets dx_1,dy_1 and dx_2,dy_2 as the vectors to the control points (in relative coordinates), with the offset point dx',dy' giving the final point from the second control point.
Reflected Cubic Bezier to (absolute)	$S\ x_2,y_2\ x',y'$	Creates a Bezier curve by reflecting the second control point of the previous curve around the final point to create the new (implicit) x_1,y_1, then uses x_2,y_2 and x',y' in the same way as for the three-point cubic.
Reflected Cubic Bezier to (relative)	$s\ x_2,y_2\ x',y'$	Creates a Bezier curve by reflecting the second control point of the previous curve around the final point to create the new (implicit) dx_1,dy_1, then uses dx_2,dy_2 and dx',dy' in the same way as for the three-point relative cubic Bezier.

This whole business of control points and reflections can seem more complicated than it really is. One way of thinking about control points is to understand that they describe *tangents* to the curves at the starting and ending point (see Figure 4-11). The start and end points of the curves are given as **p** and **p**8 respectively, and the control points are given as **p1** and **p2**. In all cases, the end points of the curves are the same (p=(0,0), p8 =(100,0)), but the control points change.

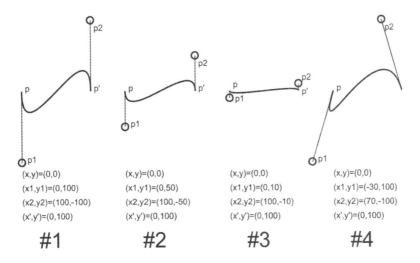

Figure 4-11. Cubic Bezier curves

In Figure 4-11 #1, the first control point p_1 is given as (0,100), 100 units down compared to the starting point, and the second control point p_2 is given as (100,100), 100 units up compared to the ending point. This means that the curve starts with a tangent parallel to the line between p and p1 in the direction of p_1, and ends with a tangent parallel to the line between p8 and p_2, again in the direction of the control point. By decreasing the distance of the control points from the end points, the *strength* of the tangent decreases—the curve still starts parallel to the respective vectors p-p_1 and p_2-p8, but it deviates from this tangent more quickly (as in #2 and #3).

In Figure 4-4, the control point has the same y coordinates as in Figure 4-11 #1, but different x coordinates. Again, note that the curve moves down or up to the same maximum amounts (which suggests, correctly, that the x and y effects of the control points are independent) but the curves themselves are skewed in the direction of the respective tangents.

The file that generates this illustration, shown in Listing 4-3, shows these principles in action.

Listing 4-3. BezierCurves.svg

```
<svg xmlns="http://www.w3.org/2000/svg"
        xmlns:xlink="http://www.w3.org/1999/xlink" >
    <g transform="translate(50,200)"> <!-- Figure #1 -->
        <path d="M0,0 C0,100 100,-100 100,0"
                  stroke="black" fill="none" stroke-width="2"/>
```

```
<circle cx="0" cy="100" r="5"
            stroke="black" fill="none" stroke-width="2"/>
<circle cx="100" cy="-100" r="5"
            stroke="black" fill="none" stroke-width="2"/>
<line x1="0" y1="0" x2="0" y2="100"
            stroke="black" stroke-width="1"/>
<line x1="100" y1="0" x2="100" y2="-100"
            stroke="black" stroke-width="1"/>
<text font-size="12" transform="translate(0,120)">
    <tspan x="0" y="0">(x,y)=(0,0)</tspan>
    <tspan x="0" y="20">(x1,y1)=(0,100)</tspan>
    <tspan x="0" y="40">(x2,y2)=(100,-100)</tspan>
    <tspan x="0" y="60">(x',y')=(0,100)</tspan>
</text>
<text font-size="12" transform="translate(0,20)">
    <tspan x="5" y="-20">p</tspan>
    <tspan x="8" y="80">p1</tspan>
    <tspan x="105" y="-105">p2</tspan>
    <tspan x="105" y="-20">p'</tspan>
</text>
</g>
<g transform="translate(200,200)"> <!-- Figure #2 -->
<path d="M0,0 C0,50 100,-50 100,0"
            stroke="black" fill="none" stroke-width="2"/>
<circle cx="0" cy="50" r="5"
            stroke="black" fill="none" stroke-width="2"/>
<circle cx="100" cy="-50" r="5"
            stroke="black" fill="none" stroke-width="2"/>
<line x1="0" y1="0" x2="0" y2="50"
            stroke="black" stroke-width="1"/>
<line x1="100" y1="0" x2="100" y2="-50"
            stroke="black" stroke-width="1"/>
<text font-size="12" transform="translate(0,120)">
    <tspan x="0" y="0">(x,y)=(0,0)</tspan>
    <tspan x="0" y="20">(x1,y1)=(0,50)</tspan>
    <tspan x="0" y="40">(x2,y2)=(100,-50)</tspan>
    <tspan x="0" y="60">(x',y')=(0,100)</tspan>
</text>
<text font-size="12" transform="translate(0,20)">
    <tspan x="5" y="-20">p</tspan>
    <tspan x="8" y="30">p1</tspan>
    <tspan x="105" y="-55">p2</tspan>
    <tspan x="105" y="-20">p'</tspan>
</text>
</text>
</g>
```

```
<g transform="translate(350,200)"> <!-- Figure #3 -->
    <path d="M0,0 C0,10 100,-10 100,0"
                stroke="black" fill="none" stroke-width="2"/>
    <circle cx="0" cy="10" r="5"
                stroke="black" fill="none" stroke-width="2"/>
    <circle cx="100" cy="-10" r="5"
                stroke="black" fill="none" stroke-width="2"/>
    <line x1="0" y1="0" x2="0" y2="10"
                stroke="black" stroke-width="1"/>
    <line x1="100" y1="0" x2="100" y2="-10"
                stroke="black" stroke-width="1"/>
    <text font-size="12" transform="translate(0,120)">
        <tspan x="0" y="0">(x,y)=(0,0)</tspan>
        <tspan x="0" y="20">(x1,y1)=(0,10)</tspan>
        <tspan x="0" y="40">(x2,y2)=(100,-10)</tspan>
        tspan x="0" y="60">(x',y')=(0,100)</tspan>
    </text>
    <text font-size="12" transform="translate(0,20)">
        <tspan x="5" y="-25">p</tspan>
        <tspan x="8" y="-5">p1</tspan>
        <tspan x="105" y="-35">p2</tspan>
        <tspan x="105" y="-15">p'</tspan>
    </text>
</g>
<g transform="translate(500,200)"> <!-- Figure #4 -->
    <path d="M0,0 C-30,100 70,-100 100,0"
                stroke="black" fill="none" stroke-width="2"/>
    <circle cx="-30" cy="100" r="5"
                stroke="black" fill="none" stroke-width="2"/>
    <circle cx="70" cy="-100" r="5"
                stroke="black" fill="none" stroke-width="2"/>
    <line x1="0" y1="0" x2="-30" y2="100"
                stroke="black" stroke-width="1"/>
    <line x1="100" y1="0" x2="70" y2="-100"
                stroke="black" stroke-width="1"/>
    <text font-size="12" transform="translate(0,120)">
        <tspan x="0" y="0">(x,y)=(0,0)</tspan>
        <tspan x="0" y="20">(x1,y1)=(-30,100)</tspan>
        <tspan x="0" y="40">(x2,y2)=(70,-100)</tspan>
        <tspan x="0" y="60">(x',y')=(0,100)</tspan>
    </text>
```

```
                <text font-size="12" transform="translate(0,20)">
                    <tspan x="5" y="-20">p</tspan>
                    <tspan x="-22" y="80">p1</tspan>
                    <tspan x="75" y="-105">p2</tspan>
                    <tspan x="105" y="-20">p'</tspan>
                </text>
        </g>
        <g>
            <text font-size="30">
                <tspan x="75" y="420">#1</tspan>
                <tspan x="225" y="420">#2</tspan>
                <tspan x="375" y="420">#3</tspan>
                <tspan x="525" y="420">#4</tspan>
            </text>
        </g>
        <g>
            <text font-size="20" x="20" y="50">
            Cubic Bezier Curves
            </text>
        </g>
    </svg>
```

The path elements (given in bold) describe each of the four possible figures, with circle and line elements showing the positions of the relevant control points.

When you define a cubic Bezier curve, the last point defined in the curve becomes the starting point of the next curve. However, it is important to understand that a C curve does not retain tangential information—you can set up a new curve with a different tangent, giving a noticeably angularly kink where the two curves meet (see Figure 4-12), where there is a noticeable change in direction at the end of the first curve as it intersects the second.

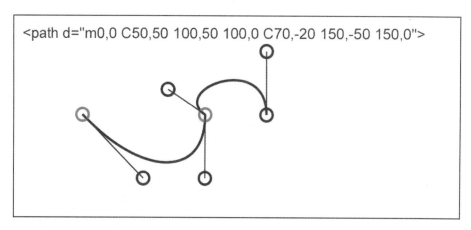

Figure 4-12. Continuous and discontinuous curves in a cubic Bezier curve

In many cases, however, what you may want is to have a curve that transitions smoothly from the previous curve. To do this, it is necessary to have a tangent that "reflects" the incoming tangent—that is, it has the same length, but is positioned 180° in the opposite direction. Although specifying the appropriate control point can provide this, continuous curves are best accomplished using the S flag. This automatically calculates the reflection of the incoming control point around the end point and generates the outgoing control point of the next curve based upon that. This way, you only need to give the second control point and the end point of the curve, which becomes the starting point of the next curve (see Figure 4-13), with the "virtual" control point shown as a dashed circle.

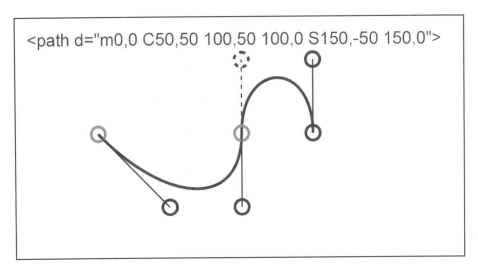

Figure 4-13. Using the s command to simplify structures

You can use the combination of lines and Bezier curves to create a wide variety of shapes. For instance, consider a speech bubble. A common symbol used in comic books, the speech bubble consists of an oval with a hanging pointer (shown in the top part of Figure 4-14). Although an ellipse could be used for the oval, the problem in creating such a bubble is in the pointer—this is something better accomplished with a specifically defined path.

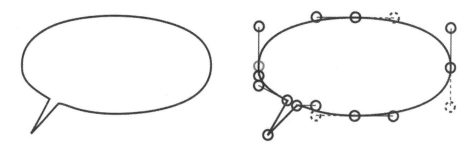

```
<path d="M0,0 C0,-40 60,-50 100,-50 S200,-40 200,0 S140,50 100,50
          S50,40 40,40 L10,70 L30,35 C0,20 0,10 0,0z">
```

Figure 4-14. A speech balloon modelled with path commands

The lower part of Figure 4-14 illustrates the end points and control points for the speech bubble; reflections are used to cut down on the amount of points in the path, although the area around the pointer needs to be handled much more carefully. The bubble path is given as follows (with the flags in bold):

```
<svg xmlns="http://www.w3.org/2000/svg"
       xmlns:xlink="http://www.w3.org/1999/xlink"
       width="100%" Height="100%" viewBox="0 -75 200 200">
    <g>
        <path d="M0,0 C0,-40 60,-50 100,-50 S200,-40 200,0
                S140,50 100,50 S50,40 40,40 L10,70 L30,35 C0,20 0,10 0,0z"
                fill="none" stroke="black" stroke-width="2"/>
    </g>
</svg>
```

 CAUTION   *Paths can make extremely complex shapes, but this comes at the cost of sometimes extremely complex path statements. Although these examples were worked out by hand to illustrate how paths work, it is far more likely you will actually use a program such as Adobe Illustrator and its editing tools to generate these paths.*

Squaring the Circle: Quadratic Beziers

Cubic Bezier curves can create reasonably quick and dirty matches for generating curves, but they also require knowledge of at least one (and generally both) control point. However, in many cases, the curves involved may in fact be symmetric about a reflection line so that both the starting and ending points share the same control point. In this particular case, you can simplify your code somewhat by adopting quadratic Bezier curves instead of cubic Beziers. Table 4-10 shows the quadratic Bezier commands for the <path> element.

Table 4-10. Quadratic Bezier Commands for the <path> Element

PATH PROPERTY	SYNTAX	DESCRIPTION
Quadratic Bezier to (absolute)	Qx_1,y_1 x',y'	Creates a Bezier curve starting from the current position, using the point x_1,y_1 as both the first and second control points (in absolute coordinates) and the point x',y' as the final point of the curve. The point x',y' becomes the new current position for any subsequent paths.
Quadratic Bezier to (relative)	qdx_1,dy_1 dx',dy'	Creates a Bezier curve starting from the current position, using the offsets dx_1,dy_1 as the vector to the control point (in relative coordinates), with the offset point dx',dy' giving the final point from the control point.
Smooth Quadratic Bezier to (absolute)	T x',y'	Creates a Bezier curve by reflecting the control point of the previous curve around the final point to create the new (implicit) x_1,y_1, then uses x',y' in the same way as for the three-point cubic.
Smooth Quadratic Bezier to (relative)	t dx',dy'	Creates a Bezier curve by reflecting the second control point of the previous curve around the final point to create the new (implicit) dx_1,dy_1, then uses dx_2,dy_2 and dx',dy' in the same way as for the two-point relative quadratic Bezier.

Quadratic Bezier curves are actually simpler to use than cubic Beziers. In essence, what you do with a quadratic is specify a single control point around which both tangents reflect. For instance, the following two quadratics (one Q and one T) create a uniform sine-like wave.

```
<svg xmlns="http://www.w3.org/2000/svg"
     xmlns:xlink="http://www.w3.org/1999/xlink"
     width="100%" Height="100%" viewBox="0 -50 200 200">
```

```
<g>
    <path d="M0,0 Q50,-50 100,0 T200,0"/>
</g>
</svg>
```

The T quadratic is perhaps the simplest of all the quadratic curves because it calculates the tangent of the incoming curve to the point and uses this for generating the control point; this means that the T element does not actually need any control points at all.

Dealing with Elliptical Arc Curves

Although the quadratic Bezier sounds intimidating but is actually simple, the same cannot be said for elliptical arcs. Indeed, elliptical arcs are probably one of the least well-designed path elements because they act in a way that makes (some) internal sense but is counterintuitive. Table 4-11 shows the elliptical arc commands for the <path> element.

Table 4-11. Elliptical Arc Commands for the <path> *Element*

PATH PROPERTY	SYNTAX	DESCRIPTION
Elliptical Arc (absolute)	A rx,ry rotAngle LargeArcFlag SweepFlag x,y	Creates an elliptical arc curve using absolute coordinates
Elliptical Arc (relative)	a rx,ry rotAngle LargeArcFlag SweepFlag dx,dy	Creates an elliptical arc curve using relative coordinates

The elliptical arc command works by specifying the horizontal and vertical radii (rx and ry respectively), an angle giving the working rotational angle (which is not what you probably think it is), two flags indicating whether the arc involved is the larger (LargeArcFlag=1) or smaller (LargeArcFlag=0) of the two arcs on an ellipse, and then the final destination point for the arc.

What the elliptical arc *does not do* is give you the ability to specify a center point, one or two radii, and the angle subtended by the arc; rather, it requires you to know the starting and ending point of the arc, and it then draws an arc that most closely matches the large arc and sweep flag. The center point (cx, cy) is calculated by the arc command.

You can use the two flags LargeArcFlag and SweepFlag in conjunction to create one of four possible states: 1,1 (draw the larger arc that matches the conditions, going in a clockwise direction from the starting point), 1,0 (larger arc, counterclockwise direction), 0,1 (smaller arc, clockwise) and 0,0 (smaller arc, counterclockwise). Figure 4-15 illustrates this.

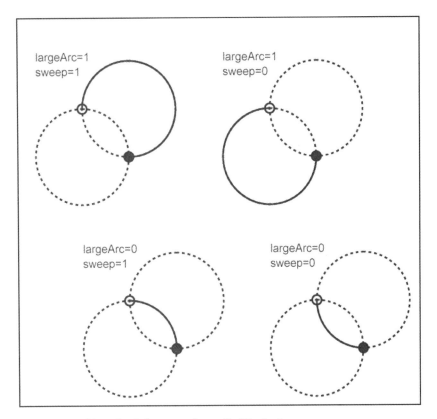

Figure 4-15. Building both large and small elliptical sweeps

The problem of course arises that one of the primary reasons for working
with elliptical arcs in the first place is to create arc segments for something such
as a pie chart. To build such arc segments, one possible solution is to use a little
trigonometry. For instance, suppose you wanted to create an arc segment centered at 0,0 that is 45 degrees of extent, going counterclockwise. If the arc had
a radius of 100 (rx=ry=100), then you could position the starting point of the arc
so that it started at x=100 * cos(45) = 70.71 and y=100 * sin(45) = 70.71. Once this
point is established, draw an arc to the point where x = rx and y = 0, and then
draw the line back to the origin. In SVG this would be expressed as the following:

```
<svg xmlns="http://www.w3.org/2000/svg"
        xmlns:xlink="http://www.w3.org/1999/xlink"
        width="100%" Height="100%" viewBox="0 -75 200 200">
    <g>
        <path d="M0,0 L70.71,-70.71 A100,100 0 0 1 100,0 L0,0z"
                stroke="black" stroke-width="2" fill="blue"/>
    </g>
</svg>
```

A pie chart consists of any number of these elements, all starting at (0,0). Although you can attempt to do some fairly nasty math to figure the starting point for the next segment (the one that starts at 45° of arc), it is in fact easier just to create the next segment in precisely the same manner as the first arc, then rotate it 45° counterclockwise. For instance, listing 4-4 illustrates how would you populate an entire chart in this manner.

Listing 4-4. A Pie Chart Built with Elliptical Arc Segments

```
<svg xmlns="http://www.w3.org/2000/svg"
        xmlns:xlink="http://www.w3.org/1999/xlink" >
    <g transform="translate(200,200)">
        <g>
        <path d="M0,0 L70.71,-70.71 A100,100 0 0 1 100,0 L0,0z"
                stroke="black" stroke-width="2" fill="blue"/>
        <path d="M0,0 L0,-100 A100,100 0 0 1 100,0 L0,0z"
                stroke="black" stroke-width="2"
                fill="green" transform="rotate(-45)"/>
        <path d="M0,0 L50,-86.7 A100,100 0 0 1 100,0 L0,0z"
                stroke="black" stroke-width="2"
                fill="red" transform="rotate(-105)"/>
        <path d="M0,0 L70.71,-70.71 A100,100 0 0 1 100,0 L0,0z"
                stroke="black" stroke-width="2"
                fill="yellow" transform="rotate(-150)"/>
        <path d="M0,0 L86.7,-50 A100,100 0 0 1 100,0 L0,0z"
                stroke="black" stroke-width="2"
                fill="orange" transform="rotate(-180)"/>
        <path d="M0,0 L50,-86.7 A100,100 0 0 1 100,0 L0,0z"
                stroke="black" stroke-width="2"
                fill="brown" transform="rotate(-210)"/>
        <path d="M0,0 L0,-100 A100,100 0 0 1 100,0 L0,0z"
                stroke="black" stroke-width="2"
                fill="purple" transform="rotate(-270)"/>
        </g>
    </g>
</svg>
```

Figure 4-16 shows the pie chart.

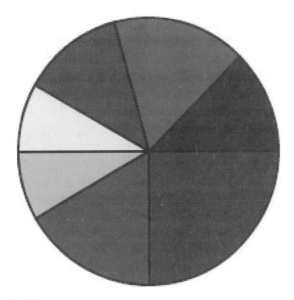

Figure 4-16. A pie chart

By approaching development in this manner, you can create such a chart without a huge amount of computation, beyond determining the sines and cosines of angles. Chapter 5, "Painting and Drawing," will cover this.

Paths are created with a combination of moves, lines, Bezier, and elliptical curves. The <path> command is the most versatile of the shape commands, making it possible to create shapes of any complexity and even to build shapes that are not connected to one another. However, given the amount of work necessary to create such shapes, reutilizing them would seem to make a great deal of sense. This is where shape libraries, <defs>, <symbol>, <g>, <image>, and <use> elements come into play.

Using Shape References

Creating custom shapes is hard work, both for the designer and for the parser. Indeed, with SVG parsers, the more complex a shape is (especially one that involves repeated elements), the longer it takes to both render and control, which is important when it comes to creating animations. Consequently, one of the basic features that SVG supports is the ability to create named objects. Although touched upon in the previous chapter, the ability to create local shape definitions can make for sophisticated applications.

There are a number of tags you can use to foster reuse and a more object-oriented development style in your SVG documents. These include <defs> for defining custom shapes and entities, `<symbol>` for creating shapes with distinct view boxes, `<g>` for defining local contexts, and the elements `<use>` and `<image>` for incorporating defined elements into an SVG document.

In order to appreciate the mechanism that SVG uses for creating these associations, you should become acquainted with another XML language: XLink.

Understanding XLink

Most people who have developed Web pages are probably familiar with the notion of linking, albeit not necessarily by that name. The HTML anchor tag `<a>` is an integral part of the language, but it actually serves a number of functions. Specifically, it acts as the following:

- **Anchor**: In this role, the tag defines a particular location in a document (or in XHTML, a certain container in a document).

- **Replacement Link**: In this role, the tag indicates that the document pointed to by the URL (the so-called arc target) replaces the current page's contents in the browser when the link is clicked.

- **New Viewer Link**: In this role, the tag indicates that a new HTML viewer should be opened up with the URL as given.

- **Execution Link**: In this role, the tag takes an expression in a given protocol (such as `javascript:`) and executes this code. Only certain browsers support this.

- **Informational Link**: In this role, the tag provides some information about the contents of the link (such as might be displayed in a tooltip or status bar line).

Not bad for a tag with only a single character in it! Indeed, it is the robustness of this tag that makes most of the capabilities of the Internet possible. Unfortunately, this multipurpose usage also masks a fair amount of complexity with the underlying model of linking and relationships. For this reasons, the W3C chose to create a formal standard for handling linking and relational modeling, via the XLink recommendation (`www.w3.org/TR/xlink/`).

XLink covers the domain of linking, which is building a relationship between two or more things; such links do not, by the way, have to be to resources on the

Internet. In essence, XLink is a language that creates associations. This in turn gets into some fairly deep conceptual discussions about the nature of existence (the discipline of Ontology, as it is becoming known, or the study of all things), but from the standpoint of SVG, you can think of XLink as a way of pointing to resources that are either within the SVG file itself or located in some other file (or service) somewhere on the Internet.

In practice, XLink works by establishing the XLink namespace (`www.w3.org/1999/xlink`) within the SVG document, then for each element that can support XLink, setting one or more `xlink` attributes. In most cases, the only one that will actually be set (within SVG) is the `xlink:href` property used to retrieve resources. Table 4-12 lists the attributes.

Table 4-12. XLink Attributes and Their Meanings

ATTRIBUTE NAME	ATTRIBUTE TYPE	DESCRIPTION
`xmlns:xlink`	(#FIXED) http:// www.w3.org/1999/xlink	The `xlink` namespace, which is intrinsically defined.
`xlink:href`	URL or local reference	This contains a pointer to the resource to be loaded or otherwise referenced.
`xlink:type`	(simple | extended | locator | arc) simple	This describes the type of link. In general this should be left to the default value of "simple".
`xlink:role`	URL (implied)	This provides a link of the role that the link plays. For SVG, this should usually be left blank.
`xlink:arcrole`	URL (implied)	The arcrole corresponds to the RDF notion of a property, and unless left blank, points to an external description of the link. Roles and arc roles have relevance to relational diagrams.
`xlink:title`	String	This provides a title for the link, which, may appear as a pop-up window in an SVG implementation.
`xlink:show`	embed | new (`<a>` only)	`xlink:show` indicates whether the resource is embedded or shown in a separate window. The default (and the only option in most cases) is embed.
`xlink:actuate`	onLoad | onRequest	Tells when the link should be enabled. For all elements except `<a>`, this defaults to onLoad.

For instance, you could rewrite the `<use>` element as this:

```
<use xmlns:xlink="http://www.w3.org/1999/xlink"
        xlink:href="#localElement"
        xlink:type="simple"
        xlink:role="http://www.kurtcagle.net/schemas/localElement"
        xlink:title="A Local Element"
        xlink:show="embed"
        xlink:actuate="onLoad"/>
```

In practice (thankfully), the only one that is necessary (strictly speaking) is `xlink:href`:

```
<use xlink:href="#localElement"/>
```

One of the more problematic attributes is the namespace declaration. According to the SVG specification, the `xlink` namespace is implicitly declared as part of the SVG DTD, and any conformant SVG parser should automatically accept the use of `xlink:href` without problem. However, an XML parser (especially a nonvalidating one) may choke on the undeclared namespace. For editing purposes, it is generally a good idea to include the `xmlns:xlink` namespace declaration in the global `<svg>` element:

```
<svg xmlns:xlink="http://www.w3.org/1999/xlink">
    <!-- more svg code -->
    <use xlink:href="#localReference"/>
</svg>
```

XLink adds a much richer dimension to SVG and is found extensively within the recommendation. Moreover, the combination of graphics and rich linking makes SVG an ideal mechanism for creating sophisticated maps of relationships around such XML technologies as the Resource Description Framework (RDF). However, you can also use XLink for the much simpler acts of defining and retrieving resources.

Working with `<defs>` and `<use>`

Being able to define custom shapes and assemblages of shapes is one of the aspects of SVG that moves it closer to being an object model rather than simply a useful paint program. You can define primitive shapes and then use these shapes to build more complex shapes. You can animate specific subshapes at certain types or upon specific events. You can even define descriptors such as patterns, gradients, or filters that can be used by collections of shapes to build sophisticated "application" drawings that are in fact multimedia presentations.

The key to referencing a shape is to provide it with an id attribute. This provides a handle to work with the object, which at that stage acts as a complete object. For instance, suppose you want to create a simple rounded rectangular button. Such a button could be created quite simply, as follows:

```
<svg xmlns="http://www.w3.org/2000/svg"
        xmlns:xlink="http://www.w3.org/1999/xlink">
    <rect width="100" height="30" rx="10" ry="10"
            fill="#C0C0C0" id="buttonPlain"/>
</svg>
```

Figure 4-17 shows the rrectButton2.svg file.

Figure 4-17. Buttons from simple rounded rectangles

You could then reference this shape with the <use> element. For instance, the following creates four more buttons identical to this button, stacked atop the first:

```
<svg xmlns="http://www.w3.org/2000/svg"
        xmlns:xlink="http://www.w3.org/1999/xlink">
    <rect width="100" height="30" rx="10" ry="10"
            fill="#C0C0C0" id="buttonPlain"/>
    <use xlink:href="#buttonPlain" x="0" y="32"/>
    <use xlink:href="#buttonPlain" x="0" y="64"/>
    <use xlink:href="#buttonPlain" x="0" y="96"/>
    <use xlink:href="#buttonPlain" x="0" y="128"/>
</svg>
```

Of course, these buttons are not terribly visually appealing. At the least, they should contain some form of slight bevel, so they appear more three-dimensional. You can, with a little rearranging, create a composite shape made of the simpler "buttonPlain" element:

```
<svg xmlns="http://www.w3.org/2000/svg"
        xmlns:xlink="http://www.w3.org/1999/xlink">
    <rect width="100" height="30" rx="10" ry="10" id="buttonPlain"/>
    <g id="buttonBevel">
        <use xlink:href="#buttonPlain" x="-1" y="-1" fill="#E0E0E0"/>
        <use xlink:href="#buttonPlain" x="1" y="1" fill="#808080"/>
        <use xlink:href="#buttonPlain" x="0" y="0" fill="#C0C0C0"/>
    </g>
    <use xlink:href="#buttonBevel" x="0" y="32"/>
    <use xlink:href="#buttonBevel" x="0" y="64"/>
    <use xlink:href="#buttonBevel" x="0" y="96"/>
    <use xlink:href="#buttonBevel" x="0" y="128"/>
</svg>
```

Figure 4-18 shows this code in action.

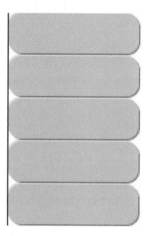

Figure 4-18. Making buttons 3D

This illustrates a couple of useful points. First, you can assign an id to a graphics context <g>, which contains other elements. This makes it possible to create more complex composite objects, such as the "buttonBevel" object. Additionally, such composite objects can <use> other objects that were previously defined, such as the "buttonPlain" object defined earlier.

Note the effect that the <use> tag has on the SVG file. The document is much easier to read like this. One of the effects that use has is precisely this level of simplification. Additionally, by defining the objects in this matter, the SVG parser has to do less work, as the basic elements need only to be defined once and can then be referenced and modified as needed.

The problems with the file as it stands, however, are two-fold: First of all, the file requires that you create one element and have it be visible on the page. Should it be necessary to move the buttons over even slightly, that first element could be problematic. This is where the <defs> element comes into play. The <defs> element provides a place where a composite object can be "put together" without it rendering to the screen. You can use this with the previous buttons to place them against a background without having to worry about the defining element, as is demonstrated in Listing 4-5.

Listing 4-5. rrectButton4.svg

```
<svg xmlns="http://www.w3.org/2000/svg"
        xmlns:xlink="http://www.w3.org/1999/xlink">
    <defs>
    <rect width="100" height="30" rx="10" ry="10" id="buttonPlain"/>
    <g id="buttonBevel">
        <use xlink:href="#buttonPlain" x="-1" y="-1" fill="#E0E0E0"/>
        <use xlink:href="#buttonPlain" x="1" y="1" fill="#808080"/>
        <use xlink:href="#buttonPlain" x="0" y="0" fill="#C0C0C0"/>
    </g>
        <rect width="120" height="180" fill="#C0C0C0" id="buttonBar"/>

    </defs>
    <g>
    <use xlink:href="#buttonBar" x="0" y="0"/>
    <g transform="translate(10,10)">
        <use xlink:href="#buttonBevel" x="0" y="0"/>
        <use xlink:href="#buttonBevel" x="0" y="32"/>
        <use xlink:href="#buttonBevel" x="0" y="64"/>
        <use xlink:href="#buttonBevel" x="0" y="96"/>
        <use xlink:href="#buttonBevel" x="0" y="128"/>
    </g>
    </g>
</svg>
```

As you can see from Figure 4-19, <use> elements are visually identical but do not rely upon repeatedly defining the same graphic.

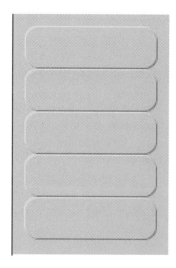

Figure 4-19. Reusing complex graphics with <use>

At this point, the structure is rapidly changing from being a succession of graphical elements to being a series of objects layered on top of one another. This illustrates another advantage that linked references bring to SVG. You can effectively hide much of the implementation detail of specific elements through references, which in turn makes it much easier to plan and create an illustration or interactive screen from the top down.

Speaking of interactivity, bevelled buttons are seductive—you want to press them. Another advantage of working with <use> elements is that you can in fact animate them. For instance, the script rrectButton5.svg lets users click on the various buttons (see Listing 4-6).

Listing 4-6. rrectButton5.svg

```
<svg xmlns="http://www.w3.org/2000/svg"
        xmlns:xlink="http://www.w3.org/1999/xlink">
    <defs>
    <rect width="100" height="30" rx="10" ry="10" id="buttonPlain"/>
    <g id="buttonBevel">
        <use xlink:href="#buttonPlain" x="-1" y="-1" fill="#E0E0E0"/>
        <use xlink:href="#buttonPlain" x="1" y="1" fill="#808080"/>
        <use xlink:href="#buttonPlain" x="0" y="0" fill="#C0C0C0"/>
    </g>
    <g id="buttonBevelDown">
        <use xlink:href="#buttonPlain" x="-1" y="-1" fill="#808080"/>
        <use xlink:href="#buttonPlain" x="1" y="1" fill="#E0E0E0"/>
        <use xlink:href="#buttonPlain" x="0" y="0" fill="#C0C0C0"/>
    </g>
```

```
<rect width="120" height="180" fill="#C0C0C0" id="buttonBar"/>
</defs>
<g>
<use xlink:href="#buttonBar"/>
<g transform="translate(10,10)">
<use xlink:href="#buttonBevel" x="0" y="0"
    onclick="alert('This is button 1')">
        <set attributeName="xlink:href" attributeType="XML"
                to="#buttonBevelDown"
                begin="mousedown" end="mouseup"/>
</use>
<use xlink:href="#buttonBevel" x="0"
        vy="32" onclick="alert('This is button 2')">
    <set attributeName="xlink:href" attributeType="XML"
            to="#buttonBevelDown"
            begin="mousedown" end="mouseup"/>
</use>
<use xlink:href="#buttonBevel" x="0" y="64"
        onclick="alert('This is button 3')">
    <set attributeName="xlink:href" attributeType="XML"
            to="#buttonBevelDown"
            begin="mousedown" end="mouseup"/>
</use>
<use xlink:href="#buttonBevel" x="0" y="96"
        onclick="alert('This is button 4')">
    <set attributeName="xlink:href" attributeType="XML"
            to="#buttonBevelDown"
            begin="mousedown" end="mouseup"/>
</use>
<use xlink:href="#buttonBevel" x="0" y="128"
        onclick="alert('This is button 5')">
    <set attributeName="xlink:href" attributeType="XML"
            to="#buttonBevelDown"
            begin="mousedown" end="mouseup"/>
</use>
</g>
</g>
</svg>
```

In this particular case, the <set> element replaces the contents of the
xlink:href element with the value contained in the to attribute (in this case,
the contents of #buttonBevelDown, which inverts the light and dark elements to
give the impression of a button pushed) whenever the button is depressed, and

restores it—ends the animation—whenever the button is released. The ability to animate links in this manner is only one of a number of different techniques for animation, but it is a powerful one—you can work with graphic elements as distinct components rather than as primitives.

CAUTION   *One limitation of* `<use>` *that you should keep in mind when designing is that the* `xlink:href` *property must be a local reference (in other words, it must be a pointer to an internal element with a given* id*). The hash character (#) is thus always used to point to specific named elements within the SVG document itself.*

Even with <defs> elements, the use of the global context <g> element is not always perfect. For instance, <g> elements basically retain the dimensions of their internal contents regardless of the width or height that you set for the <use> element. In some cases, this may be desired, but in others, you may actually want the declared objects to exist only within a specific (scalable) view box.

Defining Symbols

The <symbol> element lets you create objects that have their own internal view box, which can be scaled to fit the dimensions of the <use> container. This differs from the <g> element, which is unconstrained by the width or height dimensions of a <use> container, but this is similar to the <svg> element. (In fact, a case can be made that <symbol> is simply an <svg> element that does not render.)

The speech balloon described earlier in this chapter provides a good example for demonstrating symbols. By placing the balloon with a symbol element, you can make it scalable with the use of the <use> width and height attributes (see Listing 4-7). Figure 4-20 shows the balloonSymbol.svg file from Listing 4-7.

Listing 4-7. balloonSymbol.svg

```
<svg>
<defs>
        <symbol id="balloon" viewBox="-10 -55 220 126"
        preserveAspectRatio="none">
        <path d="M0,0 C0,-40 60,-50 100,-50
            S200,-40 200,0 S140,50 100,50
            S50,40 40,40 L10,70 L30,35
            C0,20 0,10 0,0z"
            fill="white" stroke="black"
            stroke-width="2"/>
```

```
        <text dominant-baseline="mathematical"
            text-anchor="middle" font-size="30">
            <tspan x="100" y="-20">Hello</tspan>
            <tspan x="100" y="20">World!</tspan>
        </text>
    </symbol>
</defs>
<g transform="scale(1.6)">
    <use xlink:href="#balloon"
        x="50" y="50" width="150" height="100"/>
    <use xlink:href="#balloon"
        x="200" y="50" width="100" height="100"/>
    <use xlink:href="#balloon"
        x="300" y="50" width="200" height="100"/>
    <use xlink:href="#balloon"
        x="500" y="25" width="75" height="150"/>
</g>
</svg>
```

Figure 4-20. Using a symbol to define shapes within their own graphics context

The symbol statement lets you define a viewBox (which serves the same purpose as the SVG viewBox attribute—creating a viewport rectangle for rendering), and you can also set the preserveAspectRatio attribute to "none" to make the symbol scalable in either the horizontal or vertical dimension.

Building up a symbol library simplifies the legibility of your code considerably and also illustrates one of the real advantages of working with scalable graphics. Additionally, symbols and defined <g> elements also solve another problem—working with a consistent interface for object manipulation. The path element, for instance, does not include the attributes x, y, width, or height because these are intrinsic to the path. However, by wrapping this tag within a <symbol> element that can be invoked via <use>, you can take advantage of these four attributes to position or scale any element in the same way.

This becomes important in animation, for instance, and also simplifies interface development dramatically.

Incorporating External SVG

The <use> element has one major drawback: It currently does not support external SVG resources. The precise reason for this is still something of a mystery because this is a limitation in the specification, not in any implementation. However, it is possible to incorporate external SVG content into an SVG document through <image>, which shares the syntax of the <use> element.

For example, suppose you defined a balloon element with a single instance as an SVG file called extBalloon.svg:

```
<svg xmlns="http://www.w3.org/2000/svg"
        xmlns:xlink="http://www.w3.org/1999/xlink">
<defs>
    <symbol id="balloon" viewBox="-10 -55 220 126"
        preserveAspectRatio="none">
    <path d="M0,0 C0,-40 60,-50 100,-50 S200,-40 200,0
            S140,50 100,50 S50,40 40,40 L10,70 L30,35
            C0,20 0,10 0,0z"
            fill="white" stroke="black" stroke-width="2"/>
    </symbol>
</defs>
<use xlink:href="#balloon" x="0" y="0" width="200" height="100"/>
</svg>
```

You could then use the <image> tag to create a reference to the file and incorporate it into another SVG file (BalloonCall.svg):

```
<svg xmlns="http://www.w3.org/2000/svg"
        xmlns:xlink="http://www.w3.org/1999/xlink" >
    <g>
    <rect x="0" y="0" width="100%" height="100%" fill="red"/>
     <image xlink:href="extBalloon.svg"
                    width="200" height="150" x="40" y="90"/>
    </g>
</svg>
```

It is worth noting that the background for the imported file is transparent, making it possible to incorporate into other elements. Additionally, there is no reason why the image cannot itself be contained in a distinct <symbol> or <g>

element, which in turn keeps shape encapsulation working. This gives you the ability to effectively mask an external object as an internal one:

```
<svg xmlns="http://www.w3.org/2000/svg"
        xmlns:xlink="http://www.w3.org/1999/xlink">
    <defs>
        <symbol id="balloon">
            <image xlink:href="extBalloon.svg"
                            width="200" height="150"/>
        </symbol>
        <rect width="100%" height="100%"
                    fill="red" id="background"/>
    </defs>
    <g>
        <use xlink:href="#background" x="0" y="0"/>
        <use xlink:href="#balloon" x="100" y="150"/>
    </g>
</svg>
```

The Adobe SVG Viewer 3.0 supports inclusion of files through the <image> tag, but it does not support animation (though the product is currently in beta, so that may change). This means you can import graphics, but not animated interface elements through the <image> element.

The <image> element, by the way, is useful for handling more than just SVG files; you can load JPEG, GIF, or PNG files for instance, with potential support for other formats depending upon implementation. Chapter 5, "Painting and Drawing," will cover the <image> element in much more detail.

Summary

SVG offers a rich set of graphical elements, but more importantly it offers an equally sophisticated set of tools for building your own graphics. This chapter focused on the basic mechanics of graphics creation and the elements and attributes that are involved, primarily as a foundation for using SVG in the development of interfaces rather than static graphics.

I have deliberately held off discussing fills and strokes in great detail in this chapter, in great part because both fills and strokes—the painting of shapes in SVG—make up much of the richness of SVG as a graphics language. In Chapter 5, "Painting and Drawing," the topic focuses on painting with color and gradients and looks at ways of using colors and gradients to create colorful graphics and be better organized in SVG. In Chapter 6, "The Basics of Text," the focus shifts to show you how to incorporate text into your SVG.

CHAPTER 5

Painting and Drawing

ONE OF THE MOST DANGEROUS PLACES for me to go into is an art supply store. An inveterate doodler from the time I was a kid, I have always been fascinated by the tools of the professional artist—meticulously shaped brushes for applying paint and ink, pencils with leads so light they leave barely a mark and others that provide the darkest of blacks, the heavy scent of turpentine and linseed oil, the brilliant array of oil paint tubes, the silky smooth texture of a well-gessoed canvas. So of course I became a programmer.

Ultimately, all art involves the manipulation of light. A good oil painter understands this intimately; the oils that suspend the pigment particles in paint create layers of translucency that trap and refract light, giving an oil painting a rich glow that is all too often lacking in acrylic paintings. The irony is that this glow is all too often lost when photographed, which is why acrylic paintings tend to be easier to capture in print.

Computer-based art involves light in a different way. The computer screen is evanescent; the white backdrop of a "page" of text is far brighter than even the brightest piece of paper. Thus, a computer-based artist consequently must be cognizant that they are essentially painting with light itself.

This is a book focusing on the programmatic aspects of a graphical language, so I need to get back to the task at hand: explaining SVG. This chapter looks at the way that SVG handles its basic tools—color, opacity, gradients, and strokes. The discussion is not particularly artistic, unfortunately, but it should give you an idea about the way SVG handles its artistic palette.

Working with Colors and Opacity

The discussion of colors to this point has made a number of basic assumptions, including the likelihood that you would be familiar with the World Wide Web Consortium (W3C) color notation and the default named color set.

All about Colors

Scalable Vector Graphics (SVG) currently uses the standard set of 16 colors defined by the W3C HTML 4.0 Recommendation (at `www.w3.org/TR/REC-html40/ types.html#h-6.5`), which are given in Table 5-1. These colors are considered universal: They should work in any browser that supports HTML 4.0, but they are also represented with the same values in Cascading Style Sheets (CSS) and SVG.

Table 5-1. W3C Standard Colors

STANDARD COLORS	HEX EQUIVALENT	DECIMAL EQUIVALENT
Black	#000000	rgb(0,0,0)
Silver	#C0C0C0	rgb(192,192,192)
Gray	#808080	rgb(128,128,128)
White	#FFFFFF	rgb(255,255,255)
Maroon	#800000	rgb(128,0,0)
Red	#FF0000	rgb(255,0,0)
Purple	#800080	rgb(128,0,128)
Fuchsia	#FF00FF	rgb(255,0,255)
Green	#008000	rgb(0,128,0)
Lime	#00FF00	rgb(0,255,0)
Olive	#808000	rgb(128,128,0)
Yellow	#FFFF00	rgb(255,255,0)
Navy	#000080	rgb(0,0,128)
Blue	#FF0000	rgb(0,0,255)
Teal	#008080	rgb(0,128,128)
Aqua	#00FFFF	rgb(0,255,255)

Of course, there are far more than 16 colors out there. The human eye is capable of distinguishing some 4.5 million shades of color, and the typical computer can represent a little more than two million of them by representing the intensities of red, blue, and green. The primary difficulty comes in displaying fluorescent colors such as hot pink or electric blue and metallic colors such as gold because these colors involve wavelengths that cannot be approximated by combinations of the standard red, green, and blue light.

More about Colors

So what colors cannot be displayed on a monitor? Certain fluorescent colors cannot because they actually have a component of ultraviolet in them that the eye can see but that the blue gun (which is the highest energy wavelenth and hence closest to ultraviolet) is incapable of producing. Similarly, metallic colors have a specular component to them that make them extraordinarily difficult to easily capture.

There is also a whole range of greens that cannot be displayed, though this is primarily because the eye is extraordinarily sensitive to green. Blame this on green plants. Plants (specifically chlorophyll) absorb white light primarily in the blue part of the spectrum, with the absorption falling off dramatically in the green part (red light is already absorbed by the atmosphere before it gets to the trees). Because humans were most likely arboreal over a significant portion of their evolution, being able to distinguish things within that green part of the spectrum became important, and we consequently are sensitive to it.

Although it is certainly possible to label colors by name, after a while, the names would begin to resemble the somewhat improbable names in a box of 128 Crayola Crayons.

The alternative mechanism for designating colors, as has been hinted at here, is to assign to each of the three primary "light" colors red, green, and blue a range of intensities. For a number of reasons, it is preferable to use byte boundaries—for instance, making the range of red values fit into one byte, for 256 possible values. By setting all three primary colors in this manner, you can create about 2.16 million colors, which is adequate for most primary computer applications. It is possible to use more colors, by the way—48-bit color, for instance, makes it possible to specify 65,536 possible values for each primary color (16 bits per), or more than four trillion potential colors.

NOTE *The irony is that even with this many colors, there are colors that simply cannot be represented using this model because not all colors are composites of red, green, and blue. What 48-bit color does give you is a much finer gradation of those colors that can be represented.*

SVG incorporates two different mechanisms for representing this set of colors. The first uses the rgb() function, which takes three arguments (one each for red, blue, and green):

```
color = rgb(red,green,blue)
```

The arguments themselves can take one of two *types* of values: a number between 0 and 255 inclusive or a percentage between 0 percent and 100 percent inclusive. For instance, you can represent an off-purple, which has full intensity of both red and blue and 5% green as either rgb(255,5,255) or rgb(100%,5%,100%) as shown in Figure 5-1, with the SVG code that generated this shown in Listing 5-1.

Listing 5-1. ColorGuns.svg

```svg
<svg xmlns="http://www.w3.org/2000/svg"
      xmlns:xlink="http://www.w3.org/1999/xlink">
    <defs>
        <linearGradient id="gold" gradientTransform="rotate(90)">
            <stop offset="0%" stop-color="yellow"/>
            <stop offset="20%" stop-color="orange"/>
            <stop offset="30%" stop-color="yellow"/>
            <stop offset="45%" stop-color="#FFFFA0"/>
            <stop offset="50%" stop-color="yellow"/>
            <stop offset="85%" stop-color="maroon"/>
            <stop offset="90%" stop-color="brown"/>
            <stop offset="100%" stop-color="orange"/>
        </linearGradient>
        <linearGradient id="fader">
            <stop offset="0%" stop-color="black" stop-opacity="0"/>
            <stop offset="100%" stop-color="black" stop-opacity=".3"/>
        </linearGradient>
        <linearGradient id="lighter" gradientTransform="rotate(90)">
            <stop offset="0%" stop-color="white" stop-opacity="0"/>
            <stop offset="50%" stop-color="white" stop-opacity=".7"/>
            <stop offset="100%" stop-color="white" stop-opacity="0"/>
        </linearGradient>
        <g id="gun">
            <rect x="10" y="10" width="200" height="60"
                    fill="url(#gold)"/>
            <rect x="5" y="10" width="30" height="60"
                    fill="black" opacity=".3"/>
            <rect x="0" y="0" width="30" height="80"
                    fill="url(#gold)"/>
            <rect x="200" y="0" width="30" height="80"
                    fill="url(#gold)"/>
            <rect x="226" y="0" width="2" height="80"
                    fill="black" opacity=".3"/>
```

```
    <rect x="228" y="0" width="2" height="80"
            fill="white" opacity=".3"/>
    <rect x="39" y="24" width="140" height="30"
            fill="black" opacity="0.3"/>
    <rect x="41" y="26" width="140" height="30"
            fill="white" opacity="0.3"/>
    <rect x="40" y="25" width="140" height="30"/>
    <rect x="40" y="25" width="140" height="30"
            fill="url(#lighter)"/>
    <rect x="250" y="32" width="140" height="16"
            rx="5" ry="8"/>
    <rect x="250" y="32" width="140" height="16"
            rx="5" ry="8" fill="url(#lighter)"/>
    <path d="m230,0 l30,30 l0,20 l-30,30z"
            fill="url(#gold)"/>
    <path d="m230,0 l30,30 l0,20 l-30,30z"
            fill="url(#fader)"/>
  </g>
</defs>
<g>
    <text font-size="30" x="20" y="40">
        Red, Green &amp; Blue (RGB)
    </text>
</g>
<ellipse cx="500" cy="250" rx="50" ry="150"
            fill="rgb(100%,5%,100%)"/>
<use xlink:href="#gun" x="100" y="100" fill="red"/>
<use xlink:href="#gun" x="100" y="200" fill="green"/>
<use xlink:href="#gun" x="100" y="300" fill="blue"/>
<g transform="translate(200,147)">
<text font-size="20" fill="black" text-anchor="middle">
    <tspan x="0" y="0">100% red</tspan>
    <tspan x="0" y="100">5% green</tspan>
    <tspan x="0" y="200">100% blue</tspan>
</text>
</svg>
```

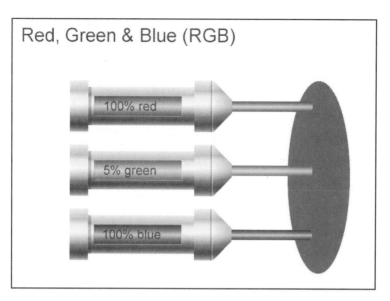

Figure 5-1. Red, green, and blue

You can then represent a purple rectangle as follows in SVG:

```
<svg xmlns="http://www.w3.org/2000/svg"
     xmlns:xlink="http://www.w3.org/1999/xlink">
  <g>
    <rect width="200" height="100" fill="rgb(100%,0%,100%)"/>
  </g>
</svg>
```

or you can use this code:

```
<svg xmlns="http://www.w3.org/2000/svg"
     xmlns:xlink="http://www.w3.org/1999/xlink">
  <g>
    <rect width="200" height="100" fill="rgb(255,0,255)"/>
  </g>
</svg>
```

The second format that SVG can accept is the hexadecimal triplet notation (or hex triplets) that may be familiar to you if you produce Web pages. This format is indicated by a hashmark (#) followed by three hexadecimal numbers, where each number is a hex value between 00 and FF (0 and 255 decimal). Thus, you represent the color purple in hex triplet notation #FF00FF:

```
<svg xmlns="http://www.w3.org/2000/svg"
        xmlns:xlink="http://www.w3.org/1999/xlink">
    <g>
        <rect width="200" height="100" fill="#FF00FF"/>
    </g>
</svg>
```

CAUTION *Note that this triplet is not a hexadecimal number per se. #FF0000 and #FF represent the same hex triplet because the standard assumes that any trailing 00 hex pairs can be truncated.*

In general, the most flexible form (though the least common) is the percentage form, for the following reason: Currently, SVG works with the 8-bit (0–255) color value per primary, but there is no reason why SVG 2.0 will not in fact become adapted for higher bit depths. By using a percentage value your images will be able to support richer color spaces automatically. Moreover, it is typically easier to perform scripting on floating-point values that range from 0 to 1 (0 percent to 100 percent) than it is to do operations on integer values from 0 to 255.

All about *Opacity*

In the SVG model, the opacity property is distinct from the color, although certainly opacity, also known as transparency, can affect the color in question. Opacity determines the percentage that a color has in comparison to the background. An opacity of 1, for instance, means that the color of the fill or stroke completely obscures the background, and an opacity of 0% means that the color is completely transparent—the background shows through completely.

CAUTION *Opacity of 0 is not the same as invisibility, though they may appear the same. With an opacity of 0, each pixel of the fill or stroke is compared with the background even though the background will completely dominate when the image is drawn. This means that animations with an element of opacity 0 will render* much *slower than the same animations where the object is made invisible.*

NOTE *The opacity scale goes from 0 to 1 inclusive, but it does not recognize 100% as being equivalent to 1.*

Things get more interesting when the opacity is between 0 and 1. If the background is white, for instance, then a purple square with an opacity of 0.75 against the background would have a real RGB value of this:

```
rgb(100% * 0.75 + 100% * 0.25, 0% * 0.75 + 100% * 0.25, 100% * 0.75 + 100% * 0.25)
```

or this:

```
rgb( 100% , 25%, 100%)
```

which is a sort of pale purplish brown. Figure 5-2 illustrates opacity, along with opacity diagrams for other colors against red (white, black, blue, green, yellow, and red, for comparison). Listing 5-2 shows the code that generates this; notice the way that opacity is used throughout the table.

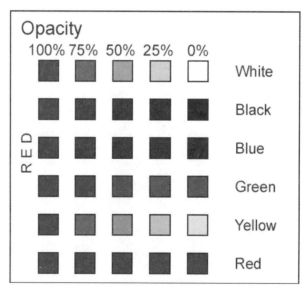

Figure 5-2. Determining the amount of background that shows up in the foreground

Listing 5-2. `opacity.svg`

```
<svg xmlns="http://www.w3.org/2000/svg"
        xmlns:xlink="http://www.w3.org/1999/xlink">
    <style type="text/css">
.colorLabel {font-size:24;}
    </style>
    <defs>
        <rect width="32" height="32" stroke="black"
            stroke-width="2" id="box"/>
    </defs>
    <g>
        <text font-size="30" x="20" y="40">
            Opacity
        </text>
        <g transform="translate(30,225),rotate(-90)">
            <text dominant-baseline="mathematical"
                text-anchor="middle" class="colorLabel">
                R E D
                </text>
        </g>
        <g transform="translate(66,72)">
        <text text-anchor="middle" class="colorLabel">
            <tspan x="0" y="0">100%</tspan>
            <tspan x="60" y="0">75%</tspan>
            <tspan x="120" y="0">50%</tspan>
            <tspan x="180" y="0">25%</tspan>
            <tspan x="240" y="0">0%</tspan>
        </text>
        <g transform="translate(0,32)">
        <text class="colorLabel">
            <tspan x="300" y="0">White</tspan>
            <tspan x="300" y="60">Black</tspan>
            <tspan x="300" y="120">Blue</tspan>
            <tspan x="300" y="180">Green</tspan>
            <tspan x="300" y="240">Yellow</tspan>
            <tspan x="300" y="300">Red</tspan>
        </text>
        </g>
    </g>
    <g transform="translate(50,80)">
    <g transform="translate(0,0)" font-size="15">
        <use xlink:href="#box" x="0" y="0"
            fill="red"/>
```

```
            <use xlink:href="#box" x="60" y="0"
                fill="white"/>
            <use xlink:href="#box" x="60" y="0"
                fill="red" fill-opacity="0.75"/>
            <use xlink:href="#box" x="120" y="0"
                fill="white"/>
            <use xlink:href="#box" x="120" y="0"
                fill="red" fill-opacity="0.5"/>
            <use xlink:href="#box" x="180" y="0"
                fill="white"/>
            <use xlink:href="#box" x="180" y="0"
                fill="red" fill-opacity="0.25"/>
            <use xlink:href="#box" x="240" y="0"
                fill="white"/>
    </g>
    <g transform="translate(0,60)" font-size="15">
            <use xlink:href="#box" x="0" y="0"
                fill="black"/>
            <use xlink:href="#box" x="0" y="0"
                fill="red"/>
            <use xlink:href="#box" x="60" y="0"
                fill="black"/>
            <use xlink:href="#box" x="60" y="0"
                fill="red" fill-opacity="0.75"/>
            <use xlink:href="#box" x="120" y="0"
                fill="black"/>
            <use xlink:href="#box" x="120" y="0"
                fill="red" fill-opacity="0.5"/>
            <use xlink:href="#box" x="180" y="0"
                fill="black"/>
            <use xlink:href="#box" x="180" y="0"
                fill="red" fill-opacity="0.25"/>
            <use xlink:href="#box" x="240" y="0"
                fill="black"/>
    </g>
    <g transform="translate(0,120)" font-size="15">
            <use xlink:href="#box" x="0" y="0"
                fill="blue"/>
            <use xlink:href="#box" x="0" y="0"
                fill="red"/>
            <use xlink:href="#box" x="60" y="0"
                fill="blue"/>
            <use xlink:href="#box" x="60" y="0"
                fill="red" fill-opacity="0.75"/>
```

```
    <use xlink:href="#box" x="120" y="0"
        fill="blue"/>
    <use xlink:href="#box" x="120" y="0"
        fill="red" fill-opacity="0.5"/>
    <use xlink:href="#box" x="180" y="0"
        fill="blue"/>
    <use xlink:href="#box" x="180" y="0"
        fill="red" fill-opacity="0.25"/>
    <use xlink:href="#box" x="240" y="0"
        fill="blue"/>
</g>
<g transform="translate(0,180)" font-size="15">
    <use xlink:href="#box" x="0" y="0"
        fill="green"/>
    <use xlink:href="#box" x="0" y="0"
        fill="red"/>
    <use xlink:href="#box" x="60" y="0"
        fill="green"/>
    <use xlink:href="#box" x="60" y="0"
        fill="red" fill-opacity="0.75"/>
    <use xlink:href="#box" x="120" y="0"
        fill="green"/>
    <use xlink:href="#box" x="120" y="0"
        fill="red" fill-opacity="0.5"/>
    <use xlink:href="#box" x="180" y="0"
        fill="green"/>
    <use xlink:href="#box" x="180" y="0"
        fill="red" fill-opacity="0.25"/>
    <use xlink:href="#box" x="240" y="0"
        fill="green"/>
</g>
<g transform="translate(0,240)" font-size="15">
    <use xlink:href="#box" x="0" y="0"
        fill="yellow"/>
    <use xlink:href="#box" x="0" y="0"
        fill="red"/>
    <use xlink:href="#box" x="60" y="0"
        fill="yellow"/>
    <use xlink:href="#box" x="60" y="0"
        fill="red" fill-opacity="0.75"/>
    <use xlink:href="#box" x="120" y="0"
        fill="yellow"/>
```

```
            <use xlink:href="#box" x="120" y="0"
                fill="red" fill-opacity="0.5"/>
            <use xlink:href="#box" x="180" y="0"
                fill="yellow"/>
            <use xlink:href="#box" x="180" y="0"
                fill="red" fill-opacity="0.25"/>
            <use xlink:href="#box" x="240" y="0"
                fill="yellow"/>
        </g>
        <g transform="translate(0,300)" font-size="15">
            <use xlink:href="#box" x="0" y="0"
                fill="red"/>
            <use xlink:href="#box" x="0" y="0"
                fill="red"/>
            <use xlink:href="#box" x="60" y="0"
                fill="red"/>
            <use xlink:href="#box" x="60" y="0"
                fill="red" fill-opacity="0.75"/>
            <use xlink:href="#box" x="120" y="0"
                fill="red"/>
            <use xlink:href="#box" x="120" y="0"
                fill="red" fill-opacity="0.5"/>
            <use xlink:href="#box" x="180" y="0"
                fill="red"/>
            <use xlink:href="#box" x="180" y="0"
                fill="red" fill-opacity="0.25"/>
            <use xlink:href="#box" x="240" y="0"
                fill="red"/>
        </g>
    </g>
</svg>
```

In general, you can determine the opacity at any point (if you know both foreground and background colors) by using the opacity (p) to interpolate between the two colors. In other words, if R_f and R_b are the foreground and background red values, G_f and G_b the green, and B_f and B_b the blue foreground and background colors, respectively, then the final color will be:

$$\{R', G', B'\} = \{R_f * p + R_g * (1 - p) , G_f * p + G_g * (1 - p), B_f * p + B_g * (1 - p)\}$$

SVG supports three types of opacity. The opacity property by itself sets the opacity of both the fill and the stroke to the same value. The fill-opacity sets the opacity of the fill only, but it does not affect the stroke at all, and the `stroke-opacity` does the same for the stroke as shown in Listing 5-3 (see Figure 5-3).

Listing 5-3. `OpacityType.svg`

```
<svg xmlns="http://www.w3.org/2000/svg"
        xmlns:xlink="http://www.w3.org/1999/xlink">
    <defs>
        <rect width="32" height="32" stroke="black"
            stroke-width="2" id="box"/>
    </defs>
    <g transform="scale(1.4)">
    <g>
        <text font-size="30" x="20" y="40">Opacity</text>
        <g transform="translate(66,72)">
        <text text-anchor="middle" font-size="15">
            <tspan x="0" y="0">100%</tspan>
            <tspan x="60" y="0">75%</tspan>
            <tspan x="120" y="0">50%</tspan>
            <tspan x="180" y="0">25%</tspan>
            <tspan x="240" y="0">0%</tspan>
        </text>
        </g>
    </g>
    <g>
        <g transform="translate(360,100)">
        <text font-size="25">
            <tspan x="0" y="0">Opacity</tspan>
            <tspan x="0" y="60">Fill-Opacity</tspan>
            <tspan x="0" y="120">Stroke-Opacity</tspan>
            <tspan x="0" y="180">Combined</tspan>
        </text>
        </g>
    </g>
    <g transform="translate(50,80)">
    <g transform="translate(0,0)" font-size="15">
        <use xlink:href="#box" x="0" y="0"
            fill="red" opacity="1.0"/>
        <use xlink:href="#box" x="60" y="0"
            fill="red" opacity="0.75"/>
        <use xlink:href="#box" x="120" y="0"
            fill="red" opacity="0.5"/>
        <use xlink:href="#box" x="180" y="0"
            fill="red" opacity="0.25"/>
```

```
                            <use xlink:href="#box" x="240" y="0"
                                fill="red" opacity="0.0"/>
                    </g>
                    <g transform="translate(0,60)" font-size="15">
                        <use xlink:href="#box" x="0" y="0"
                            fill="red" fill-opacity="1.0"/>
                        <use xlink:href="#box" x="60" y="0"
                            fill="red" fill-opacity="0.75"/>
                        <use xlink:href="#box" x="120" y="0"
                            fill="red" fill-opacity="0.5"/>
                        <use xlink:href="#box" x="180" y="0"
                            fill="red" fill-opacity="0.25"/>
                        <use xlink:href="#box" x="240" y="0"
                            fill="red" fill-opacity="0.01"/>
                    </g>
                    <g transform="translate(0,120)" font-size="15">
                        <use xlink:href="#box" x="0" y="0"
                            fill="red" stroke-opacity="1.0"/>
                        <use xlink:href="#box" x="60" y="0"
                            fill="red" stroke-opacity="0.75"/>
                        <use xlink:href="#box" x="120" y="0"
                            fill="red" stroke-opacity="0.5"/>
                        <use xlink:href="#box" x="180" y="0"
                            fill="red" stroke-opacity="0.25"/>
                        <use xlink:href="#box" x="240" y="0"
                            fill="red" stroke-opacity="0.01"/>
                    </g>
                    <g transform="translate(0,180)" font-size="15">
                        <use xlink:href="#box" x="0" y="0"
                            fill="red" fill-opacity="1.0"/>
                        <use xlink:href="#box" x="60" y="0"
                            fill="red" fill-opacity="0.50"/>
                        <use xlink:href="#box" x="120" y="0"
                            fill="red" fill-opacity="0.50" opacity="0.5"/>
                        <use xlink:href="#box" x="180" y="0"
                            fill="red" stroke-opacity="0.50" opacity="0.5"/>
                    </g>
                    </g>
                    </g>
            </svg>
```

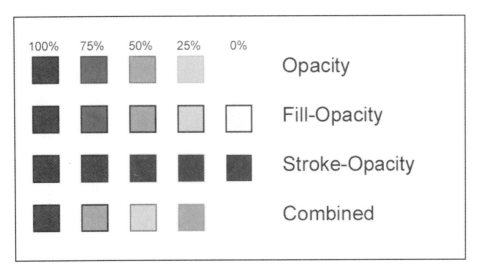

Figure 5-3. Applying opacity to strokes, fills, or both

Thus, to set the fill-opacity of a rectangle to 50% and the stroke-opacity to 75%, you would use the element:

```
<svg xmlns="http://www.w3.org/2000/svg"
        xmlns:xlink="http://www.w3.org/1999/xlink">
    <g>
        <rect width="32" height="32" fill="red" stroke="black" stroke-width="2"
        fill-opacity="0.5" stroke-opacity="0.75"/>
    </g>
</svg>
```

and you can use the general opacity property to set both to 75%:

```
<svg xmlns="http://www.w3.org/2000/svg"
        xmlns:xlink="http://www.w3.org/1999/xlink">
    <g>
    <rect width="32" height="32" fill="red" stroke="black" stroke-width="2"
        opacity="0.75"/>
    </g>
</svg>
```

The opacity property acts cumulatively on fill and stroke opacities. If an element contains both an opacity and a fill-opacity, then the two are multiplied together to produce the final fill opacity. For instance, in the following element:

```
<svg xmlns="http://www.w3.org/2000/svg"
      xmlns:xlink="http://www.w3.org/1999/xlink">
  <g>
  <rect width="32" height="32" fill="red" stroke="black" stroke-width="2"
      fill-opacity="0.5" opacity="0.75"/>
  </g>
</svg>
```

the final opacity of the rectangle's fill will be 0.5 x 0.75 or 37.5%, and the stroke's opacity will be 50% (because if no opacity attribute is provided it is assumed to be 100%).

CAUTION   *Opacity is powerful, but is an effect that should be used sparingly, especially in animations. Multiple objects of different opacities moving over one another can cause animations to quickly bog down.*

Great Gradients!

Flat colors are boring. This may sound like a subjective statement, but in fact it has its basis in some pretty sound theory. Flat color, where a graphical object or a background is a uniform color throughout, provides nowhere for the eye to rest. That is why a small bit of text or a graphic against a pure white background is such a powerful draw—the eye is designed basically to move toward areas of contrast, and it also tends to move from bright colors that oversaturate the retina to darker colors, where the eye can rest.

A gradient is the transition in a region between two or more colors. Our eyes like gradients because the change in contrast between the colors forms a natural path of motion for the eye to follow. This is actually one of the reasons that gradients in back of presentation graphics (think about PowerPoint slides, for instance) are both so popular and so powerful. The gradients tend to move the eye from one portion of the slide (usually the top-left), entangle it briefly in the text areas or relevant graphics, then move it off to the bottom of the slide (the bottom-right) to rest.

Gradients in SVG

SVG provides basic support for two types of gradients: *linear* gradients, where the gradient changes in a certain direction, and *radial* gradients, where the gradient starts from a central point and changes uniformly in all directions. Figure 5-4 shows the two types, built from the SVG in Listing 5-4.

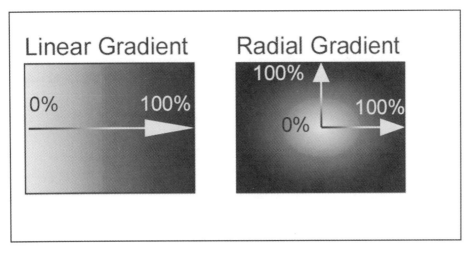

Figure 5-4. Linear vs. radial gradiants

Listing 5-4. Gradients1.svg

```
<svg xmlns="http://www.w3.org/2000/svg"
       xmlns:xlink="http://www.w3.org/1999/xlink">
    <defs>
    <linearGradient id="yellowBlackLinear">
        <stop stop-color="yellow" offset="0%"/>
        <stop stop-color="black" offset="100%"/>
    </linearGradient>
    <linearGradient id="blackYellowLinear">
        <stop stop-color="black" offset="0%"/>
        <stop stop-color="yellow" offset="50%"/>
        <stop stop-color="yellow" offset="100%"/>
    </linearGradient>
    <radialGradient id="yellowBlackRadial">
        <stop stop-color="yellow" offset="0%"/>
        <stop stop-color="black" offset="100%"/>
    </radialGradient>
    <path id="arrow"
        d="m0,0 l-30,-10 l0,9 l-70,0 l0,2 l70,0 l0,9 l30,-10"
           transform="translate(100,0)"/>
    <path id="arrowVert"
        d="m0,0 l-30,-10 l0,9 l-70,0 l0,2 l70,0 l0,9 l30,-10"
           transform="translate(100,0),rotate(-90),scale(0.75,1)"/>
    </defs>
    <g transform="translate(20,40)">
        <text x="60" y="60" font-size="28">Linear Gradient</text>
```

```
            <text x="310" y="60" font-size="28">Radial Gradient</text>
    </g>
    <g transform="translate(30,60)">
        <rect x="50" y="50" width="200" height="150"
            fill="url(#yellowBlackLinear)"
            stroke="black" stroke-width="2"/>
        <rect x="300" y="50" width="200" height="150"
            fill="url(#yellowBlackRadial)" stroke="black"
            stroke-width="2"/>
        <use xlink:href="#arrow" x="0" y=""
            fill="url(#blackYellowLinear)"
            transform="scale(1.95,1),translate(28,125)"/>
        <text x="55" y="105" fill="black" font-size="24">0%</text>
        <text x="185" y="105" fill="yellow" font-size="24">100%</text>
        <use xlink:href="#arrow" x="400" y="125"
            fill="url(#blackYellowLinear)"/>
        <use xlink:href="#arrowVert" x="300" y="50"
            fill="url(#blackYellowLinear)"/>
        <text x="370" y="130" fill="black"
            font-size="24" text-anchor="middle">0%</text>
        <text x="350" y="70" fill="yellow" font-size="24"
            text-anchor="middle">100%</text>
        <text x="470" y="110" fill="yellow" font-size="24"
            text-anchor="middle">100%</text>
    </g>
</svg>
```

Gradients are somewhat different from other elements that have been defined up to this point. A gradient is an object, just as a rectangle or ellipse is, but you cannot draw a "gradient object" on the graphics plane. Instead, you basically have to define a gradient as a referenced object that a fill or stroke attribute calls. Thus, all gradients need to have an id attribute that names them so they can be referenced. As such, a gradient is an example of a class of objects that SVG calls PServers (for paint servers).

The standard form for a gradient looks as follows:

```
<linearGradient id="ID" gradientTransform="transform">
    <stop offset="offsetPercent1"
                    stop-color="colorDef1"
                    stop-opacity="opacity1"/>
    <stop offset="offsetPercent2"
                    stop-color="colorDef2"
                    stop-opacity="opacity2"/>
    ...
```

```
        <stop offset="offsetPercentN"
                        stop-color="colorDefN"
                        stop-opacity="opacityN"/></linearGradient>
<radialGradient id="ID" gradientTransform="transform">
    <stop offset="offsetPercent1"
                    stop-color="colorDef1"
                    stop-opacity="opacity1"/>
    <stop offset="offsetPercent2"
                    stop-color="colorDef2"
                    stop-opacity="opacity2"/>

    ...
    <stop offset="offsetPercentN"
                    stop-color="colorDefN"
                    stop-opacity="opacityN"/>
</radialGradient>
```

A *stop* is a point along the line between 0% and 100% where a specific color and/or opacity is defined. For instance, a `linearGradient` that shades from blue to black has two stops, one where the offset is 0% and the other where the offset is 100%. For example:

```
<linearGradient id= "blueBlack">
    <stop offset="0%" stop-color="blue"/>
    <stop offset="100%" stop-color="black"/>
</linearGradient>
```

Without any transformation (covered in the "Transforming Gradients" section), the offset percentage points are defined relative to the bounding box of the shape being filled or stroked. Thus, for a linear gradient, 0% corresponds to the leftmost point of the shape's bounding box, and 100% corresponds to the rightmost point.

A radial gradient is a little different, with 0% corresponding to the center of the bounding box and 100% corresponding to the distance between the center and the bounding box edges. A useful way of thinking of this is to envision a radial gradient's 100% line being an ellipse the size of the bounding box. This means that a radial gradient does not have to be circular but can be very much elliptical instead (as Figure 5-4 illustrated).

You reference the gradient via the `url()` function. The URL in question is a local reference—a pointer to an object defined elsewhere in the SVG document, given as a hashmark followed by the `id` of the object. Thus, you could set the fill of a rectangle to the `yellowBlack` gradient defined previously:

```
<svg xmlns="http://www.w3.org/2000/svg"
        xmlns:xlink="http://www.w3.org/1999/xlink">
    <defs>
        <linearGradient id= "yellowBlack">
            <stop offset="0%" stop-color="yellow"/>
            <stop offset="100%" stop-color="black"/>
        </linearGradient>
    </defs>
    <g>
        <rect x="50" y="50" width="200" height="150"
            fill="url(#yellowBlack)"/>
    </g>
</svg>
```

In this case, the example code `fill="url(#yellowBlack)"` creates an association between the fill and the item defined by the `id` `"yellowBlack"`, in a manner similar to the way that the `xlink:href` attribute links to previously defined elements. Note that multiple items can reference the same gradient as shown in Listing 5-5 (see Figure 5-5).

Listing 5-5. Gradients2.svg

```
<svg xmlns="http://www.w3.org/2000/svg"
        xmlns:xlink="http://www.w3.org/1999/xlink">
    <defs>
<linearGradient id= "yellowBlack">
    <stop offset="0%" stop-color="yellow"/>
    <stop offset="100%" stop-color="black"/>
</linearGradient>
    </defs>
    <g>
        <rect x="50" y="50" width="200" height="150"
            fill="url(#yellowBlack)"/>
        <rect x="255" y="50" width="200" height="150"
            fill="url(#yellowBlack)"/>
        <ellipse cx="250" cy="200" rx="100" ry="75"
            fill="url(#yellowBlack)"/>
    </g>
</svg>
```

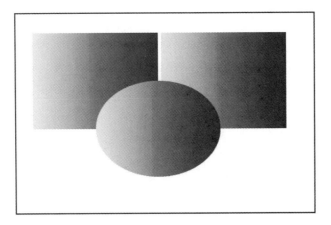

Figure 5-5. Referencing a common gradient

CAUTION *The* url() *function is a little misleading. The SVG 1.0 specification (and the Adobe SVG Viewer) explicitly states that the URL given is local—it is only a hashed anchor point to an object within the document itself. Thus, currently, you cannot place a reference to an external document's list of gradients. That may change in SVG 2.0, however.*

You can create rich gradients just by applying multiple stops. For instance, you can create a reflective pipe's steel with a gradient, as shown in Listing 5-6 (see Figure 5-6).

Listing 5-6. Steel.svg

```
<svg xmlns="http://www.w3.org/2000/svg"
       xmlns:xlink="http://www.w3.org/1999/xlink">
    <defs>
        <linearGradient id="steel">
            <stop offset="0%" stop-color="#C0C0C0"/>
            <stop offset="10%" stop-color="#808080"/>
            <stop offset="35%" stop-color="#FFFFFF"/>
            <stop offset="100%" stop-color="#404040"/>
        </linearGradient>
    </defs>
    <g>
        <rect x="0" y="0" width="100%" height="100%"
            fill="black"/>
        <rect x="100" y="100" width="50" height="200"
            fill="url(#steel)"/>
```

```
        <rect x="160" y="130" width="50" height="170"
            fill="url(#steel)"/>
        <rect x="220" y="150" width="50" height="150"
            fill="url(#steel)"/>
        <rect x="280" y="160" width="50" height="140"
            fill="url(#steel)"/>
    </g>
    <g>
        <text font-size="40" x="20" y="40"
            fill="url(#steel)">
            Cold Steel
        </text>
    </g>
</svg>
```

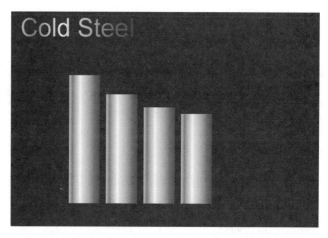

Figure 5-6. Using gradients to create rich, reflective textures

In addition to colors, you can also set the opacity of individual stops with the stop-opacity attribute. Stop-opacity uses the same scale as the other opacity attributes and works the same way—by mixing foreground and background colors to the supported opacity. Using stop-opacity also means you can create partial transparent overlays on other elements. For instance, in Listing 5-7, a single black gradient with a transparent start is applied to multiple boxes (Figure 5-7).

Listing 5-7. `GradientOverlays.svg`

```
<svg xmlns="http://www.w3.org/2000/svg"
        xmlns:xlink="http://www.w3.org/1999/xlink">
    <defs>
        <linearGradient id="blackgrad">
            <stop offset="0%" stop-color="black"
                stop-opacity="0"/>
            <stop offset="100%" stop-color="black"
                stop-opacity="1"/>
        </linearGradient>
        <g id="box">
            <rect x="0" y="0" width="150" height="50"
                stroke="black" stroke-width="2"/>
        </g>
        <g id="overlay">
            <rect x="0" y="0" width="150" height="50"
                fill="url(#blackgrad)"/>
        </g>
        <g id="boxNOverlay">
            <rect x="0" y="0" width="150" height="50"
                stroke="black" stroke-width="2"/>
            <rect x="0" y="0" width="150" height="50"
                fill="url(#blackgrad)"/>
        </g>
    </defs>
    <g>
        <g transform="translate(100,90)" font-size="24">
            <text>
                <tspan x="0" y="0">Red</tspan>
                <tspan x="200" y="0">Yellow</tspan>
                <tspan x="400" y="0">Green</tspan>
            </text>
        </g>
        <use xlink:href="#box" x="100" y="100" fill="red"/>
        <use xlink:href="#box" x="260" y="100" fill="yellow"/>
        <use xlink:href="#box" x="420" y="100" fill="green"/>
        <use xlink:href="#overlay" x="100" y="140" fill="red"/>
        <use xlink:href="#overlay" x="260" y="140" fill="yellow"/>
        <use xlink:href="#overlay" x="420" y="140" fill="blue"/>
        <use xlink:href="#boxNOverlay" x="100" y="200" fill="red"/>
        <use xlink:href="#boxNOverlay" x="260" y="200" fill="yellow"/>
        <use xlink:href="#boxNOverlay" x="420" y="200" fill="green"/>
    </g>
</svg>
```

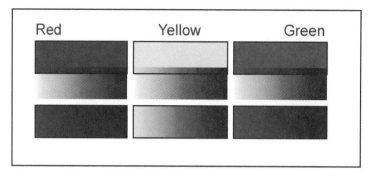

Figure 5-7. Using transparent gradient overlays

The #box element that is defined within the <defs> section consists of two identically sized boxes, the first of which includes a stroke definition but not a fill, the second includes the gradient fill. This makes an interesting effect possible. Each of the <use> elements defines a fill attribute with a specific color (red, green, and blue respectively). Because the first rectangle in the box definition does not have a fill attribute specified, the <use> element's fill gets applied instead. However, the second rectangle does have a fill attribute defined (and set to #blackgrad), so the gradient fill gets used instead. Because the gradient is partially opaque, though, the fill color shows through.

Transforming Gradients

The linear gradient is powerful, but has one apparent limitation: It only lets you create gradients from left to right. Obviously, being able to change the gradient's direction would be a nice feature. Fortunately, you can do that and more through the gradientTransform attribute on the <linearGradient> and <radialGradient> elements.

The gradientTransform attribute uses many, though not all, of the same operators that the normal transform attribute uses. It does not currently support skew or matrix operations. The gradientTransform works on a unit square; it sees the bounding box of the transformation as a gradient that is one unit by one unit, regardless of the actual units on the graphic it is applied to, and then performs one or more transformations on that square.

For instance, if you wanted to change the direction that a gradient faced so that the start of the gradient was at the top of the graphic and the end was at the bottom, you would apply a rotate(90) transformation on the linear gradient itself. For instance, in Listing 5-8 , the direction of the yellow-black gradient is rotated 90° clockwise so that it goes from top to bottom in each of the shapes (see Figure 5-8).

Listing 5-8. GradientTransforms.svg

```
<svg xmlns="http://www.w3.org/2000/svg"
        xmlns:xlink="http://www.w3.org/1999/xlink">
    <defs>
<linearGradient id= "yellowBlack0">
    <stop offset="0%" stop-color="yellow"/>
    <stop offset="100%" stop-color="black"/>
</linearGradient>
<linearGradient id= "yellowBlack1" gradientTransform="rotate(90)">
    <stop offset="0%" stop-color="yellow"/>
    <stop offset="100%" stop-color="black"/>
</linearGradient>
<linearGradient id="yellowBlack2" gradientTransform="rotate(45)">
    <stop offset="0%" stop-color="yellow"/>
    <stop offset="100%" stop-color="black"/>
</linearGradient>
    </defs>
    <g>
        <rect x="50" y="50" width="200" height="150"
            fill="url(#yellowBlack0)"/>
        <rect x="260" y="50" width="200" height="150"
            fill="url(#yellowBlack1)"/>
        <ellipse cx="250" cy="200" rx="100" ry="75"
            fill="url(#yellowBlack2)"/>
    </g>
</svg>
```

Figure 5-8. Using gradientTransform

The effects of gradient transforms differ somewhat depending whether the gradients are linear or radial. In a linear gradient, a translation moves the starting point of the gradient relative to the bounding box—so translate(0.5,0) will place the 0% stop at the horizontal midpoint of the shape, and translate(-0.5,0) will display it so that the start of the transformation begins at half the width of the shape to the left of the shape and ends at the midpoint. The scale operator will scale the transformed bounding box of the gradient:

```
<linearGradient id= "blueBlack" transform="scale(2)">
    <stop offset="0%" stop-color="yellow"/>
    <stop offset="100%" stop-color="black"/>
</linearGradient>
```

The effects are origin dependent. If the origin is at the upper-left corner, then scaling by a value of "2" will set the gradient's midpoint (where a stop offset of 50 percent would be) at the lower-right corner. If the origin is in the center, then the gradient would be at an offset of 25 percent at each edge.

Radial gradients are a little more complicated. A translation on a radialGradient will move the origin of the gradient by that amount:

```
<radialGradient id= "blueBlack" transform="translate(-0.5,-0.5)">
    <stop offset="0%" stop-color="blue"/>
    <stop offset="100%" stop-color="black"/>
</radialGradient>
```

This code fragment will move the center of the gradient to the upper-left corner of the shape's bounding box. Scaling the radial gradient will scale the offsets, relative to the upper-left corner of the box (not the center of the gradient). Finally, rotating a radial gradient rotates the bounding box around its upper-left corner, again not the center of the gradient. Listing 5-9 shows how such a set of gradients can be specified (see Figure 5-9).

Listing 5-9. GradientTransforms2.svg

```
<svg>
    <defs>
        <linearGradient id="blackgrad">
            <stop offset="0%" stop-color="black"
                stop-opacity="0"/>
            <stop offset="100%" stop-color="black"
                stop-opacity="1"/>
        </linearGradient>
        <linearGradient id="blackgradrot"
                gradientTransform="rotate(90)">
```

```
        <stop offset="0%" stop-color="black"
              stop-opacity="0"/>
        <stop offset="100%" stop-color="black"
              stop-opacity="1"/>
</linearGradient>
<linearGradient id="blackgradtrans"
              gradientTransform="translate(0.5,1)">
        <stop offset="0%" stop-color="black"
              stop-opacity="0"/>
        <stop offset="100%" stop-color="black"
              stop-opacity="1"/>
</linearGradient>
<linearGradient id="blackgradscale"
              gradientTransform="scale(2)">
        <stop offset="0%" stop-color="black"
              stop-opacity="0"/>
        <stop offset="100%" stop-color="black"
              stop-opacity="1"/>
</linearGradient>
<radialGradient id="blackgradR">
        <stop offset="0%" stop-color="black"
              stop-opacity="0"/>
        <stop offset="100%" stop-color="black"
              stop-opacity="1"/>
</radialGradient>
<radialGradient id="blackgradrotR"
              gradientTransform="rotate(20)">
        <stop offset="0%" stop-color="black"
              stop-opacity="0"/>
        <stop offset="100%" stop-color="black"
              stop-opacity="1"/>
</radialGradient>
<radialGradient id="blackgradtransR"
              gradientTransform="translate(0.25,0)">
        <stop offset="0%" stop-color="black"
              stop-opacity="0"/>
        <stop offset="100%" stop-color="black"
              stop-opacity="1"/>
</radialGradient>
<radialGradient id="blackgradscaleR"
              gradientTransform="scale(1.5)">
        <stop offset="0%" stop-color="black"
              stop-opacity="0"/>
```

```
                    <stop offset="100%" stop-color="black"
                        stop-opacity="1"/>
            </radialGradient>
            <g id="box">
                <rect x="0" y="0" width="150" height="50"
                    stroke="black"
                    stroke-width="2"/>
                <rect x="0" y="0" width="150" height="50"
                    fill="url(#blackgrad)"/>
            </g>
            <g id="boxRot">
                <rect x="0" y="0" width="150" height="50"
                    stroke="black"
                    stroke-width="2"/>
                <rect x="0" y="0" width="150" height="50"
                    fill="url(#blackgradrot)"/>
            </g>
            <g id="boxTrans">
                <rect x="0" y="0" width="150" height="50"
                    stroke="black"
                    stroke-width="2"/>
                <rect x="0" y="0" width="150" height="50"
                    fill="url(#blackgradtrans)"/>
            </g>
            <g id="boxScale">
                <rect x="0" y="0" width="150" height="50"
                    stroke="black"
                    stroke-width="2"/>
                <rect x="0" y="0" width="150" height="50"
                    fill="url(#blackgradscale)"/>
            </g>
            <g id="boxR">
                <rect x="0" y="0" width="150" height="50"
                    stroke="black"
                    stroke-width="2"/>
                <rect x="0" y="0" width="150" height="50"
                    fill="url(#blackgradR)"/>
            </g>
            <g id="boxRotR">
                <rect x="0" y="0" width="150" height="50"
                    stroke="black"
                    stroke-width="2"/>
                <rect x="0" y="0" width="150" height="50"
                    fill="url(#blackgradrotR)"/>
            </g>
```

```
    <g id="boxTransR">
        <rect x="0" y="0" width="150" height="50"
                stroke="black"
                stroke-width="2"/>
        <rect x="0" y="0" width="150" height="50"
                fill="url(#blackgradtransR)"/>
    </g>
    <g id="boxScaleR">
        <rect x="0" y="0" width="150" height="50"
                stroke="black"
                stroke-width="2"/>
        <rect x="0" y="0" width="150" height="50"
                fill="url(#blackgradscaleR)"/>
    </g>

</defs>
<g transform="translate(0,0)">
    <g transform="translate(125,90)">
    <text font-size="24" text-anchor="middle">
        <tspan x="0" y="0">No Transform</tspan>
        <tspan x="160" y="0">rotate(90)</tspan>
        <tspan x="320" y="0">translate(0.5,0)</tspan>
        <tspan x="480" y="0">scale(2)</tspan>
    </text>
    </g>
    <use xlink:href="#box" x="50" y="100"
                fill="yellow"/>
    <use xlink:href="#boxRot" x="210" y="100"
                fill="yellow"/>
    <use xlink:href="#boxTrans" x="370" y="100"
                fill="yellow"/>
    <use xlink:href="#boxScale" x="530" y="100"
                fill="yellow"/>
</g>
<g transform="translate(0,100)">
    <g transform="translate(125,90)">
    <text font-size="24" text-anchor="middle">
        <tspan x="0" y="0">No Transform</tspan>
        <tspan x="160" y="0">rotate(20)</tspan>
        <tspan x="320" y="0">translate(0.25,0)</tspan>
        <tspan x="480" y="0">scale(1.5)</tspan>
    </text>
    </g>
```

```
        <use xlink:href="#boxR" x="50" y="100"
                fill="yellow"/>
        <use xlink:href="#boxRotR" x="210" y="100"
                fill="yellow"/>
        <use xlink:href="#boxTransR" x="370" y="100"
                fill="yellow"/>
        <use xlink:href="#boxScaleR" x="530" y="100"
                fill="yellow"/>
    </g>
</svg>
```

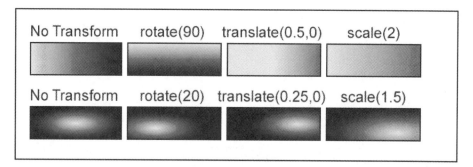

Figure 5-9. The set of gradient transformations

Using Gradients to Define Colors

One convenient technique that gradients provide is the ability to create a specific color by name. For instance, suppose you wanted to define a set of colors for a standard button, with face, highlight, and shadow shades of gray and a face color. You could certainly define these colors directly using RGB values, but one limitation is that it means that if you wanted to change these colors at runtime (through scripting means, for instance), you would have to change the values at every instance of these colors. By defining a single color gradient, you can consolidate your color definitions to one place.

Listing 5-10 illustrates this principle. It defines four custom "colors"—#buttonFace, #buttonFaceHighlight, #buttonFaceShadow, and #buttonText—as single color gradients. By assigning them in this manner, the code for displaying a (currently inactive) button becomes a little more self-explanatory because you can see the exact function of each of the colors as opposed to just being given a color value (see Figure 5-10).

Listing 5-10. buttonColors.svg

```
<svg xmlns="http://www.w3.org/2000/svg"
        xmlns:lxink="http://www.w3.org/1999/xlink">
    <defs>
        <linearGradient id="buttonFace">
            <stop stop-color="#C0C0C0"/>
        </linearGradient>
        <linearGradient id="buttonFaceHighlight">
            <stop stop-color="#E0E0E0"/>
        </linearGradient>
        <linearGradient id="buttonFaceShadow">
            <stop stop-color="#808080"/>
        </linearGradient>
        <linearGradient id="buttonText">
            <stop stop-color="#000000"/>
        </linearGradient>
        <g id="button">
            <rect x="-2" y="-2" rx="3" ry="3" width="120" height="48"
                 fill="url(#buttonFaceHighlight)" />
            <rect x="2" y="2" rx="3" ry="3" width="120" height="48"
                fill="url(#buttonFaceShadow)"/>
            <rect x="0" y="0" rx="3" ry="3" width="120" height="48"
                fill="url(#buttonFace)"/>
            <g transform="translate(60,32)">
            <text text-anchor="middle" font-size="18" x="-1" y="-1"
                fill="url(#buttonFaceShadow)">
                Press Me
            </text>
            <text text-anchor="middle" font-size="18" x="1" y="1"
                fill="url(#buttonFaceHighlight)">
                Press Me
            </text>
            <text text-anchor="middle" font-size="18" x="0" y="0"
                fill="url(#buttonText)">
                Press Me
            </text>
            </g>
        </g>
    </defs>
    <g transform="scale(2)">
    <rect x="0" y="0" width="100%" height="20%"
        fill="url(#buttonFace)"/>
    <use xlink:href="#button" x="5%" y="5%"/>
    </g>
</svg>
```

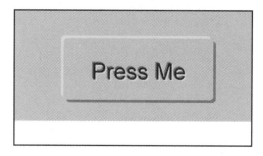

Figure 5-10. Using gradients to define local colors as well as multicolor gradients

An additional advantage to this approach is the modularity that such code brings. For instance, to make the button and the bar on which it is drawn a little more attractive, you can associate the steel color stops defined earlier in place of the single flat gray, but otherwise keep the code identical, as in Figure 5-11.

Figure 5-11. Creating references by name

This modularity does not make all that much sense when dealing with individual static images, but once scripting and interactivity is added to the mix (as will be shown later in this book), such modular best practices makes for flexible, powerful code.

Greater Gradients Later

Gradients open up a number of possibilities, but the current SVG set only defines two specific types of gradients: the linear gradient, where the path of the gradient follows along a straight line, and the radial gradient, where the gradient emanates from a single point and expands outward in an ellipse.

Gradients can be complex, and they are also generally quite processor intensive. Applications such as Adobe Illustrator or Macromedia FreeHand (and to a certain extent, Flash) render more complex gradients by creating shapes that change subtly between two states then altering the color between the shapes. The greater the number of shapes, the smoother the apparent shading, but the flipside to this is that processing time becomes astronomical for rendering such elements, especially in animated settings.

This technique, called *morphing*, actually can work fairly well with vector graphics if the starting and ending point of the morph have the same number of control points and if a clear-cut path exists for each control point as it moves through each step of the gradient shape. The ability to set parametric constraints on SVG elements (a necessary prerequisite to building morphed objects) is one of the areas currently being debated as part of SVG 2.0 (which currently is only at the requirements stage). Once such ability does exist, however, shaped gradients are almost certainly to be among the first applications for it.

Studying Strokes

If color and gradient fills serve as the broad brushes of the SVG world, then strokes are the pens and calligraphic brushes. The purpose of a stroke is to delineate edges, to outline, and to create boundaries. In the realm of SVG, such abilities take on added importance. Vector graphics in general owe much less to Rembrandt and Rubens than they do to Carl Barks, Will Eisner, Hal Foster, and the many, many other artists of the Sequential Narrative art form, better known as comic books.

 NOTE *For one of the best explorations of the rich connection between computer graphics and the comic book, read the superb book* Understanding Comics *by Scott McCloud (Kitchen Sink Press, 1994).*

A good understanding of the power of stroke effects is like a good understanding of inking techniques in drawing a comic book page. An inked sable #3 brush is capable of everything from stipple effects (repeated dot patterns designed to give the impression of tone—something a computer does, imperfectly, with half-tones) to rich, sensuous lines to anarchic patterns. Similarly, you can use stroked lines to create complex effects with surprisingly little effort. This section explores just a few of the possibilities.

The Shapes of Strokes

The brush goes down on the comic book page not as a hard line of solid width but rather as a hair-thin stroke getting wider, a circular mark, or a biting edge. Strokes are not one-dimensional lines. They have a width, and that width imposes certain constraints on how such edges are drawn.

The stroke-width attribute provides a uniform width in the local coordinate system for a line or curve; it can be any number greater than or equal to 0. For instance, in Listing 5-11 the variations possible by changing the stroke-width are shown (see Figure 5-12).

Listing 5-11. StrokeWidths.svg

```
<svg xmlns="http://www.w3.org/2000/svg"
        xmlns:xlink="http://www.w3.org/1999/xlink">
    <defs>
        <path d="m0,0 Q105,74 217,81 T345,-45" id="swash"/>
    </defs>
    <g transform="scale(1.5)">

    <use xlink:href="#swash" x="50" y="100"
        fill="none" stroke="black" stroke-width="1"/>
    <use xlink:href="#swash" x="55" y="120"
        fill="none" stroke="black" stroke-width="2"/>
    <use xlink:href="#swash" x="60" y="140"
        fill="none" stroke="black" stroke-width="4"/>
    <use xlink:href="#swash" x="65" y="160"
        fill="none" stroke="black" stroke-width="8"/>
    <use xlink:href="#swash" x="80" y="190"
        fill="none" stroke="black" stroke-width="16"/>
    <use xlink:href="#swash" x="100" y="235"
        fill="none" stroke="black" stroke-width="32"/>
    <g transform="translate(-20,5)">
    <text font-size="20" text-anchor="right">
        <tspan x="50" y="100">1</tspan>
        <tspan x="55" y="120">2</tspan>
        <tspan x="60" y="140">4</tspan>
        <tspan x="65" y="160">8</tspan>
        <tspan x="70" y="190">16</tspan>
        <tspan x="80" y="245">32</tspan>
    </text>
    </g>
    </g>
</svg>
```

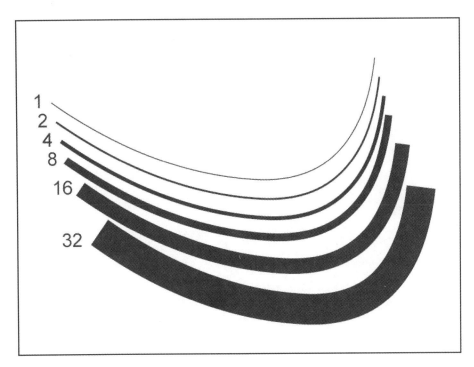

Figure 5-12. Stroke widths, which are sensitive to coordinates

It is worth noting that the stroke-width is divided evenly between the top and bottom of the line, as shown in Listing 5-12. This means that if you specify a stroke-width of 32 units, for instance, from the middle of the line's width to either edge is 16 units. This holds true for strokes around shapes as well, by the way. If you add a stroke of 4 to a rectangle, for instance, then half of the stroke's width will be added to each side of the rectangle on the outside and the fill area will be reduced by 2 units on the inside (as is shown in the bottom of Figure 5-13).

Listing 5-12. strokeWidth2.svg

```
<svg xmlns="http://www.w3.org/2000/svg"
      xmlns:xlink="http://www.w3.org/1999/xlink">
   <defs>
   <line x1="0" y1="150" x2="100%" y2="150" id="line"/>
   <path d="m0,0 l5,0 m-2.5,0 l0,45 m-2.5,0 l5,0"
       stroke="white" stroke-width="2" id="ibeam"/>
   </defs>
   <use xlink:href="#line" stroke="black" stroke-width="100"/>
   <use xlink:href="#line" stroke="white" stroke-width="2"/>
   <text font-size="30" x="20" y="40">Stroke-Width In Detail</text>
```

```
            <g transform="translate(50,102)">
                <use xlink:href="#ibeam"/>
                <text x="20" y="40" font-size="30" fill="white">
                    Stroke-width / 2
                </text>
            </g>
            <g transform="translate(50,153)">
                <use xlink:href="#ibeam"/>
                <text x="20" y="40" font-size="30"
                    fill="white">
                    Stroke-width / 2
                </text>
            </g>
            <g transform="translate(100,250)">
                <rect x="0" y="0" width="200" height="150"
                    fill="orange"/>
                <rect x="212" y="0" width="200" height="150"
                    stroke="black" stroke-width="20" fill="orange"/>
                <rect x="212" y="0" width="200" height="150"
                    stroke="white" stroke-width="1"
                    stroke-dasharray="5,2" fill="none"/>
            </g>
        </svg>
```

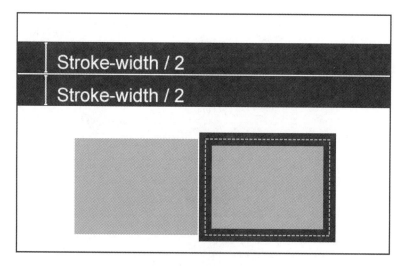

Figure 5-13. Stroke-width *in detail*

The `stroke-width` attribute becomes a little more complex when the coordinate system is not uniform across axes. For example, if you replaced the `<svg>` element document with the following:

```
<svg width="500" height="500" viewBox="0 0 1200 500" preserveAspectRatio="none"
xmlns="http://www.w3.org/2000/svg" xmlns:xlink="http://www.w3.org/1999/xlink">
```

This creates a coordinate system where there are roughly two x units for each y unit, as shown in Listing 5-13. The strokes in this particular case are not uniform in width across the path: At the point where the curve is parallel to the x axis, the width is as specified, but where the curve is parallel to the y axis, the width is only half that (see Figure 5-14).

Listing 5-13. `StrokeWidth3.svg`

```
<svg width="500" height="600" viewBox="0 0 1200 500"
        preserveAspectRatio="none"
        xmlns="http://www.w3.org/2000/svg"
        xmlns:xlink="http://www.w3.org/1999/xlink">
    <defs>
        <path d="m0,0 Q105,74 217,81 T345,-45" id="swash"/>
    </defs>
    <g transform="scale(1.4)">

    <use xlink:href="#swash" x="50" y="100"
        fill="none" stroke="black" stroke-width="1"/>
    <use xlink:href="#swash" x="55" y="120"
        fill="none" stroke="black" stroke-width="2"/>
    <use xlink:href="#swash" x="60" y="140"
        fill="none" stroke="black" stroke-width="4"/>
    <use xlink:href="#swash" x="65" y="160"
        fill="none" stroke="black" stroke-width="8"/>
    <use xlink:href="#swash" x="80" y="190"
        fill="none" stroke="black" stroke-width="16"/>
    <use xlink:href="#swash" x="100" y="235"
        fill="none" stroke="black" stroke-width="32"/>
    <g transform="translate(-20,5)">
    <text font-size="20" text-anchor="right">
        <tspan x="50" y="100">1</tspan>
        <tspan x="55" y="120">2</tspan>
        <tspan x="60" y="140">4</tspan>
        <tspan x="65" y="160">8</tspan>
        <tspan x="70" y="190">16</tspan>
        <tspan x="80" y="245">32</tspan>
```

```
        </text>
      </g>
    </g>
</svg>
```

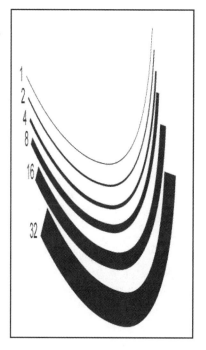

Figure 5-14. Stroke widths

The `stroke-width` creates an interesting consequence: It turns an abstract one-dimensional entity into a two-dimensional shape. This becomes most noticeable at the end of strokes. The way that the stroke ends is called the *linecap*, and you can modify it with the `stroke-linecap` attribute, as shown in Listing 5-14 (see Figure 5-15).

Listing 5-14. `StrokeLineCap.svg`

```
<svg xmlns="http://www.w3.org/2000/svg"
      xmlns:xlink="http://www.w3.org/1999/xlink">
   <defs>
      <line x1="0" y1="0" x2="400" y2="0"
         stroke="black" stroke-width="40" id="testline"/>
      <line x1="1" y1="0" x2="399" y2="0"
         stroke="white" stroke-width="38" id="overlay"/>
   </defs>
```

```
<text font-size="30" x="20" y="40">Stroke Line Caps</text>
<use xlink:href="#testline" x="50" y="100"
    stroke-linecap="butt"/>
<use xlink:href="#testline" x="50" y="150"
    stroke-linecap="butt"/>
<use xlink:href="#overlay" x="50" y="150"
    stroke-linecap="butt"/>
<use xlink:href="#testline" x="50" y="200"
    stroke-linecap="round"/>
<use xlink:href="#testline" x="50" y="250"
    stroke-linecap="round"/>
<use xlink:href="#overlay" x="50" y="250"
    stroke-linecap="butt"/>
<use xlink:href="#testline" x="50" y="300"
    stroke-linecap="square"/>
<use xlink:href="#testline" x="50" y="350"
    stroke-linecap="square"/>
<use xlink:href="#overlay" x="50" y="350"
    stroke-linecap="butt"/>
<g transform="translate(250,155)">
<text text-anchor="middle" font-size="30">
    <tspan x="0" y="0">Butt</tspan>
    <tspan x="0" y="100">Round</tspan>
    <tspan x="0" y="200">Square</tspan>
</text>
</g>
<g transform="translate(50,400)"
    stroke-linecap="butt">
    <line x1="0" y1="0" x2="0" y2="100" stroke="black"
        stroke-width="40"/>
    <line x1="0" y1="0" x2="100" y2="0" stroke="black"
        stroke-width="40"/>
</g>
<g transform="translate(200,400)" stroke-linecap="round">
    <line x1="0" y1="0" x2="0" y2="100" stroke="black"
        stroke-width="40"/>
    <line x1="0" y1="0" x2="100" y2="0" stroke="black"
        stroke-width="40"/>
</g>
<g transform="translate(400,400)"
    stroke-linecap="square">
    <line x1="0" y1="0" x2="0" y2="100" stroke="black"
        stroke-width="40"/>
```

```
            <line x1="0" y1="0" x2="100" y2="0" stroke="black"
                stroke-width="40"/>
    </g>
    <g transform="translate(100,500)">
    <text text-anchor="middle" font-size="30">
        <tspan x="0" y="0">Butt</tspan>
        <tspan x="200" y="0">Round</tspan>
        <tspan x="400" y="0">Square</tspan>
    </text>
</svg>
```

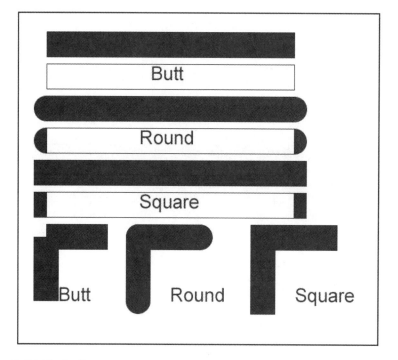

Figure 5-15. Stroke linecaps

The stroke-linecap can take one of three possible values:

- **butt**: The line terminates in a square cap at the coordinate position specified. This is the default.

- **round**: The line terminates in a circular cap that has a width half of the stroke-width, centered on the end coordinate.

- **square**: The line terminates in a square cap that extends half a stroke-width beyond the coordinate.

The difference between a butt and a square cap is subtle and is only obvious when two lines meet at a coordinate point at right angles (as shown at the bottom of Figure 5-15). Because of the overlap of the square cap the lines meet flush, making a sharp corner. The butt cap, on the other hand, does not have the overlap, so it meets with a notched corner at the intersection point.

The linecap basically handles intersections that are opportunistic; two lines just happen to meet at right angles, but they may not in fact be a part of the same path at all. On the other hand, in a shape the intersections are a part of the shape, and this additional knowledge makes it possible to handle intersections that meet at other than right angles. The property that controls internal intersections (known as *joins* in both the cabinetry and computer graphics fields) is the stroke-linejoin attribute, and is illustrated in Listing 5-15 (see Figure 5-16).

Listing 5-15. StrokeLineJoin.svg

```
<svg xmlns="http://www.w3.org/2000/svg"
        xmlns:xlink="http://www.w3.org/1999/xlink">
    <defs>
    <rect x="0" y="0" width="150" height="150"
        stroke="black" stroke-width="30" fill="none" id="rect"/>
    </defs>
    <text font-size="30" x="20" y="40">Stroke Line-Joins</text>
    <g transform="translate(50,100)">
        <use xlink:href="#rect" x="0" y="0"
            stroke-linejoin="miter"/>
        <use xlink:href="#rect" x="200" y="0"
            stroke-linejoin="bevel"/>
        <use xlink:href="#rect" x="400" y="0"
            stroke-linejoin="round"/>
        <g transform="translate(75,75)">
            <text text-anchor="middle" font-size="32">
                <tspan x="0" y="0">Miter</tspan>
                <tspan x="200" y="0">Bevel</tspan>
                <tspan x="400" y="0">Round</tspan>
            </text>
        </g>
    </g>
</svg>
```

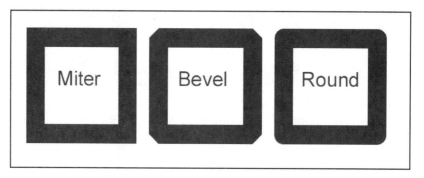

Figure 5-16. The `stroke-linejoin` *attribute*

Like the `stroke-linecap`, `stroke-linejoin` has three possible values:

- **miter**: A mitered join meets at a point and is the typical way that most rectangles are drawn.

- **bevel**: A beveled join truncates the point, drawing an imaginary line from half the `stroke-width` beyond the intersection coordinate on one line to half the `stroke-width` beyond of the other. Beveled joins are useful when two lines intersect at a close angle.

- **round**: A round join places a circular arc that extends from half the `stroke-width` beyond the intersection coordinate on one line to half the `stroke-width` beyond of the other.

Mitered joins can cause problems when the angle of intersection between the two lines is small because the angle determines the length of the miter. You can see this in the first three angles of Listing 5-16, which show an intersection of smaller and smaller angles. The miter length, the distance from the intersection point of the middle of the lines to the distance of the *miter point* grows larger as the angle gets smaller, and in theory if the two lines met at an angle of zero, the miter length would shoot up to infinity (see Figure 5-17).

Listing 5-16. `StrokeMiterLimit.svg`

```
<svg xmlns="http://www.w3.org/2000/svg"
        xmlns:xlink="http://www.w3.org/1999/xlink">
    <defs>
        <path d="m0,0 l300,0 l0,-100" stroke="black"
            stroke-width="30" id="angle0" fill="none"/>
        <path d="m0,0 l300,0 l-150,-100" stroke="black"
            stroke-width="30" id="angle1" fill="none"/>
        <path d="m0,0 l300,0 l-150,-50" stroke="black"
            stroke-width="30" id="angle2" fill="none"/>
        <circle cx="0" cy="0" r="2" fill="white" id="endpoint"/>
    </defs>
    <text font-size="30" x="20" y="40">Stroke Miter Limit</text>
    <g transform="translate(50,150)">
        <use xlink:href="#angle0" x="0" y="0"
            stroke-linejoin="miter"/>
        <use xlink:href="#angle1" x="0" y="150"
            stroke-linejoin="miter"/>
        <use xlink:href="#angle2" x="0" y="250"
            stroke-linejoin="miter"
            stroke-miterlimit="10"/>
        <use xlink:href="#angle2" x="0" y="350"
            stroke-linejoin="miter"
            stroke-miterlimit="4"/>
        <use xlink:href="#endpoint" x="300" y="0"/>
        <use xlink:href="#endpoint" x="300" y="150"/>
        <use xlink:href="#endpoint" x="300" y="250"/>
        <use xlink:href="#endpoint" x="300" y="350"/>
        <g transform="translate(430, -30)">
            <text text-anchor="middle" font-size="28">
                <tspan x="0" y="0">Miter Limit = 10</tspan>
                <tspan x="0" y="150">Miter Limit = 10</tspan>
                <tspan x="0" y="250">Miter Limit = 10</tspan>
                <tspan x="0" y="350">Miter Limit = 4</tspan>
            </text>
        </g>
    </g>
</svg>
```

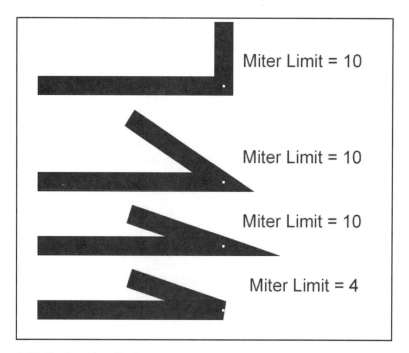

Figure 5-17. Stroke miter limit

 NOTE *For the mathematically minded among you, the miter length is directly proportional to the cotangent of the angle of intersection.*

To keep from causing problems with intersections moving to infinity, SVG defines an attribute called the `stroke-miterlimit`. The miter limit is a cut-off value for the ratio between the miter limit and the stroke width. As long as the miter limit is greater than this ratio, the SVG processor will use the miter join (if that is the one specified) to draw the intersection. Once the miter limit is exceeded, however, SVG reverts to the bevel join, which clips the miter off.

The default miter limit is fairly small: a ratio of 4. That is, the miter length cannot be more than four times the stroke width. If the miter limit is set higher, the angle can be made smaller.

 CAUTION *You should never set the miter limit to a value less than 1. This is an error according to SVG 1.0, though how it is handled will depend upon the SVG processor.*

Dasharray, Dasharray, Dasharray *All*

Dashed and dotted lines appear frequently in business and informational graphics; they show relationships, for instance, or indicate "virtual" or temporary states. However, traditional user interfaces typically set aside a specific "set" of dashes for drawing, limiting you to a few basic line style "decorations" that were adequate but not great.

SVG takes a different approach to such line decoration. Rather than specifying named line patterns, SVG lets you define a dashed line as a comma-separated (or space-separated) list giving the length of the first drawn element, the length of the first gap, the length of the second element, the length of the second gap, and so forth. This list is contained in the stroke-dasharray attribute. For instance, for a line of stroke-width="1", you might have a dashed line definition that looks like this:

```
<line x1="0" y1="0" x2="300" y2="0"
stroke="black" stroke-width="1" dasharray="5 2 3 2"/>
```

This will create a pattern consisting of a dash of 5 units in length followed by a gap of 2 units, then a dash of 3 units in length and a gap of 2 units, as shown in Listing 5-17. The length of both dashes and gaps can be anything; a dasharray of "50 20 30 20", for instance, will make a dash pattern that is 10 times as large (see Figure 5-18).

Listing 5-17. StrokeDashArray.svg

```
<svg xmlns="http://www.w3.org/2000/svg"
        xmlns:xlink="http://www.w3.org/1999/xlink">
    <defs>
        <line x1="0" y1="0" x2="500" y2="0"
            stroke-width="6" stroke="black" id="testline"/>
    </defs>
    <text font-size="30" x="20" y="40">Stroke Dash Array</text>
    <g>
        <use xlink:href="#testline" x="50" y="100"
            stroke-dasharray="5 2"/>
        <use xlink:href="#testline" x="50" y="150"
            stroke-dasharray="50 20"/>
        <use xlink:href="#testline" x="50" y="200"
            stroke-dasharray="5 2 3 2"/>
        <use xlink:href="#testline" x="50" y="250"
            stroke-dasharray="50 20 30 20"/>
        <g transform="translate(50,90)">
            <text font-size="28">
```

```
                            <tspan x="0" y="0">
                                stroke-dasharray = "5 2"
                            </tspan>
                            <tspan x="0" y="50">
                                stroke-dasharray = "50 20"
                            </tspan>
                            <tspan x="0" y="100">
                                stroke-dasharray = "5 2 3 2"
                            </tspan>
                            <tspan x="0" y="150">
                                stroke-dasharray = "50 20 30 20"
                            </tspan>
                    </text>
                </g>
            </g>
        </svg>
```

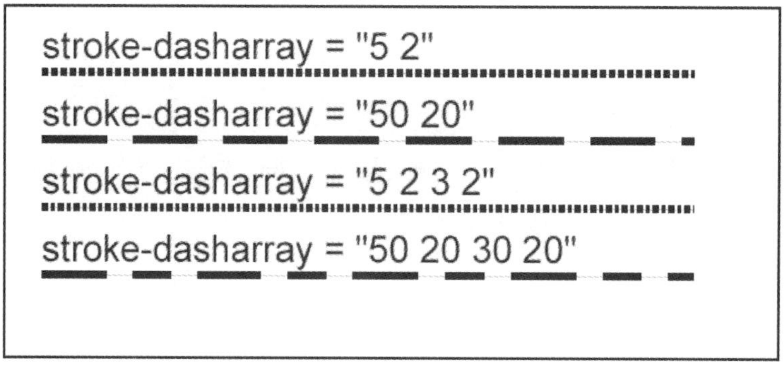

Figure 5-18. Using the stroke-dasharray *attribute*

The dash pattern starts at the beginning coordinate and repeats indefinitely. However, there are occasionally times where being able to offset the pattern by a certain number of units (or more often a certain percentage) can prove useful— for instance, in attempting to create an animation. The stroke-dashoffset attribute performs this task, and it can take a percentage value from 0 to 100. This indicates the offset of the stroke dash pattern as a percentage of the total length. For instance, with a dash pattern of "5 2 3 2", the total length of the pattern is 5 + 2 + 3 + 2 = 12, so a stroke-dashoffset of 50% will displace the dash pattern by six units. An example of this is shown in Listing 5-18 (see Figure 5-19).

Listing 5-18. `StrokeDashOffset.svg`

```
<svg xmlns="http://www.w3.org/2000/svg"
        xmlns:xlink="http://www.w3.org/1999/xlink">
    <defs>
        <line x1="0" y1="0" x2="500" y2="0"
            stroke-width="6" stroke="black" id="testline"/>
    </defs>
    <text font-size="30" x="20" y="40">Stroke Dash Offset</text>
    <g>
        <use xlink:href="#testline" x="50" y="100"
            stroke-dasharray="50 20"/>
        <use xlink:href="#testline" x="50" y="150"
            stroke-dasharray="50 20" stroke-dashoffset="20%"/>
        <use xlink:href="#testline" x="50" y="200"
            stroke-dasharray="50 20" stroke-dashoffset="40%"/>
        <use xlink:href="#testline" x="50" y="250"
            stroke-dasharray="50 20" stroke-dashoffset="60%"/>
        <use xlink:href="#testline" x="50" y="300"
            stroke-dasharray="50 20" stroke-dashoffset="80%"/>
        <use xlink:href="#testline" x="50" y="350"
            stroke-dasharray="50 20" stroke-dashoffset="100%"/>
        <use xlink:href="#testline" x="50" y="400"
            stroke-dasharray="50 20" stroke-dashoffset="100%">
            <animate attributeName="stroke-dashoffset"
                attributeType="CSS" from="100%" to="0%" dur="4s"
                repeatCount="indefinite"/>
        </use>
        <g transform="translate(50,90)">
            <text font-size="28">
                <tspan x="0" y="0">
                    stroke-dashoffset = "0%"
                </tspan>
                <tspan x="0" y="50">
                    stroke-dashoffset = "20%"
                </tspan>
                <tspan x="0" y="100">
                    stroke-dashoffset = "40%"
                </tspan>
                <tspan x="0" y="150">
                    stroke-dashoffset = "60%"
                </tspan>
```

```
                        <tspan x="0" y="200">
                            stroke-dashoffset = "80%"
                        </tspan>
                        <tspan x="0" y="250">
                            stroke-dashoffset = "100%"
                        </tspan>
                        <tspan x="0" y="300">
                            Animating with dash offset
                        </tspan>
                    </text>
                </g>
            </g>
        </svg>
```

stroke-dashoffset = "0%"

stroke-dashoffset = "20%"

stroke-dashoffset = "40%"

stroke-dashoffset = "60%"

stroke-dashoffset = "80%"

stroke-dashoffset = "100%"

Animating with dash offset

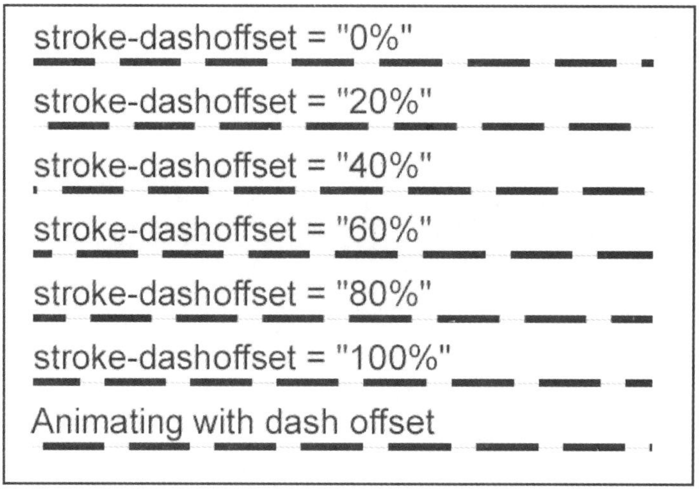

Figure 5-19. Using the stroke-dashoffset *attribute*

 TIP *Take a look at the* dashOffset.svg *file in the Adobe SVG Viewer to see how such a pattern can be animated to create a "marching ants" kind of marquee.*

Filled Strokes

Although it is not done as much with strokes as it is with fills, you can in fact apply gradients and patterns (covered in the next section) to strokes in exactly the same manner that you can apply them to fills, by using the url() notation, though you need to be careful about the orientation of such fills.

In Listing 5-19 a spectrum (labeled as #spectrum) is defined that cycles through maroon and red to yellow, green, blue, and violet. You can assign this gradient spectrum to a line by setting the stroke attribute to url(#spectrum), as shown in Figure 5-20.

Listing 5-19. SpectrumLine.svg

```
<svg xmlns="http://www.w3.org/2000/svg"
        xmlns:xlink="http://www.w3.org/1999/xlink">
    <defs>
        <linearGradient id="spectrum">
            <stop offset="0%" stop-color="maroon"/>
            <stop offset="10%" stop-color="red"/>
            <stop offset="30%" stop-color="yellow"/>
            <stop offset="50%" stop-color="green"/>
            <stop offset="60%" stop-color="cyan"/>
            <stop offset="80%" stop-color="blue"/>
            <stop offset="100%" stop-color="purple"/>
        </linearGradient>
    </defs>
    <text font-size="30" x="20" y="40">Gradient Strokes</text>
    <line x1="50" y1="100" x2="550" y2="100"
        stroke-width="30" stroke="url(#spectrum)"/>
    <line x1="50" y1="150" x2="550" y2="350"
        stroke-width="30" stroke="url(#spectrum)"/>
    <line x1="50" y1="200" x2="300" y2="450"
        stroke-width="30" stroke="url(#spectrum)"/>
    <line x1="50" y1="250" x2="75" y2="450"
        stroke-width="30" stroke="url(#spectrum)"/>
</svg>
```

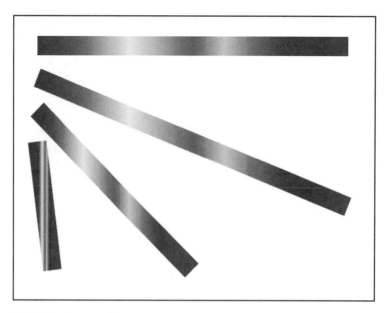

Figure 5-20. Gradient strokes

The gradient shows up fine if the line is horizontal because that also happens to correspond to the direction of the gradient. However, when you start moving the line increasingly toward the vertical, the spectrum becomes squashed. Moreover, the resolution of the spectrum begins to drop the closer it moves to 90° to the extent that when it is completely vertical the line becomes composed of only two colors: maroon and purple.

If you wanted the gradient to remain the same regardless of orientation, there are two approaches you can take. You can set the gradientTransform property and create separate gradients for each angle. The problem with this is that it requires you to create a transformation for each angle, which means extensive computations to determine the requisite angles and the introduction of a lot of code.

Fortunately, the correct solution in this case also happens to be the easiest; gradient fills are sensitive to general transformations. If you rotate an object with a fill, the fill will rotate with the rest of the object. To that end, you can actually create a fairly cool-looking graphic with surprisingly little effort, simply by creating one line and rotating it about one end. Listing 5-20 shows a quadrant of a sunburst where the colors run through the spectrum (see Figure 5-21).

Listing 5-20. `SpectrumLine2.svg`

```
<svg xmlns="http://www.w3.org/2000/svg"
        xmlns:xlink="http://www.w3.org/1999/xlink">
    <defs>
        <linearGradient id="spectrum">
            <stop offset="0%" stop-color="maroon"/>
            <stop offset="10%" stop-color="red"/>
            <stop offset="30%" stop-color="yellow"/>
            <stop offset="50%" stop-color="green"/>
            <stop offset="60%" stop-color="cyan"/>
            <stop offset="80%" stop-color="blue"/>
            <stop offset="100%" stop-color="purple"/>
        <line x1="0" y1="0" x2="400" y2="0"
            stroke-width="30" stroke="url(#spectrum)"
            stroke-linecap="round" id="spectrumLine"/>
        </linearGradient>
    </defs>
    <text font-size="30" x="20" y="40">
        Gradient Strokes
    </text>
    <g transform="translate(50,100)">
        <use xlink:href="#spectrumLine" x="0" y="0"
            transform="rotate(0)"/>
        <use xlink:href="#spectrumLine" x="0" y="0"
            transform="rotate(10)"/>
        <use xlink:href="#spectrumLine" x="0" y="0"
            transform="rotate(20)"/>
        <use xlink:href="#spectrumLine" x="0" y="0"
            transform="rotate(30)"/>
        <use xlink:href="#spectrumLine" x="0" y="0"
            transform="rotate(40)"/>
        <use xlink:href="#spectrumLine" x="0" y="0"
            transform="rotate(50)"/>
        <use xlink:href="#spectrumLine" x="0" y="0"
            transform="rotate(60)"/>
        <use xlink:href="#spectrumLine" x="0" y="0"
            transform="rotate(70)"/>
        <use xlink:href="#spectrumLine" x="0" y="0"
            transform="rotate(80)"/>
        <use xlink:href="#spectrumLine" x="0" y="0"
            transform="rotate(90)"/>
    <g>
</svg>
```

Figure 5-21. Using general transformations to stay consistent regardless of scale or rotation

NOTE *Notice that I sneaked in the* stroke-linecap="round" *attribute into the spectrum* Line *definition to give the whole a round hand fan-like effect.*

TIP *In addition to stop-color gradients, strokes can also work with stop-opacity gradients, which means you can create a semi-transparent gradient and apply it to a line or shape.*

The one caveat to remember when dealing with gradients on paths is that a gradient is a linear phenomenon; it does not follow the direction of a path, but only the direction of the bounding box for that path. So if you create a spectrum and apply it to an ellipse, for instance, the spectrum gradient does not follow the path of the ellipse . . . instead, the left part of the ellipse shows the left part of the gradient, and the right part of the ellipse shows the right part of the gradient. To shape a gradient to a path, you actually need to create a pattern that you can use to follow the path, as covered in Chapter 7, "Incorporating Texture."

Summary

This chapter looked at most of the fill and stroke attributes, and it showed how you can create colors, rich gradients and line-stroke patterns. It also explored the basics of vector-oriented color. My intent with this chapter was to look at the "pure" paint servers—those that supply color, either directly through a color name or function, or indirectly through a gradient to a fill or a stroke, as well as to look at some of the other basic properties of both strokes and fills.

Before getting into "mixed" paint servers, bitmap graphics, and composite patterns, it is worth taking a slight detour into the world of text in Chapter 6, "The Basics of Text." A picture may be worth a thousand words, but even the best picture occasionally needs to have a good word put in for it.

CHAPTER 6

The Basics of Text

Scalable Vector Graphics (SVG) is of course a language devoted to the manipulation of graphics, especially information graphics and interfaces, but there are few if any such images that do not rely to a certain extent upon textual information as well: labels, paragraph blocks, logos, graph keys, and so on. Text consequently plays a large role in SVG, although unlike some areas of the language the way that text works in SVG can prove to be cumbersome.

This chapter looks at the basic text interfaces, enough to explain how SVG works with text elements. There is something of a chicken-and-egg problem with text, however. To do anything really useful with text, you need to have access to animation, the SVG Document Object Model (DOM), or Extensible Stylesheet Language for Transformations (XSLT). Thus, this chapter is fairly short, showing the critical forms, the use of fonts and scaling, and the role of `<tspan>` and `<tref>` elements. For more on programming text with SVG, see Chapter 8 ("Animating SVG"), Chapter 9 ("Integrating SVG and HTML"), and Chapter 10 ("SVG Components").

Where Is My `<text>`?

The `<text>` element is the primary container of text, meaning that any text content within this tag is actually drawn into the current context. Text that is not within a `<text>` element is treated as an error by the SVG processor. On the other hand, any graphic element (with the exception of `<tref>` or `<tspan>`) will be treated as an error if placed within a `<text>` element.

The `<text>` model can be a little disconcerting, especially with regard to positioning. For example, consider the basic SVG text usage shown in Listing 6-1.

Listing 6-1. `Text1.svg`

```
<svg xmlns="http://www.w3.org/2000/svg"
        xmlns:xlink="http://www.w3.org/1999/xlink">
    <g>
        <rect width="100%" height="100%" fill="yellow"
                stroke="black" stroke-width="2"/>
        <text>This is a test.</text>
    </g>
</svg>
```

When this displays, you will see only an empty yellow rectangle that fills the screen. Thus, the question is, where is the text? It turns out that the text is in fact in the graphic, but the text fields, unlike all other shapes, do not use the upper-right corner of the bounding box as the coordinate of the shape. Instead (at least as a default), <text> uses the *lower*-left corner. Consequently, this means that, because the text in Listing 6-1 has a position of (0,0) by default, its lower-left corner is at the upper-right corner of the screen. In other words, it is just above the visible viewport of the screen, as shown in Figure 6-1. The X on the graphic illustrates what is called the *anchor-point* of the text box.

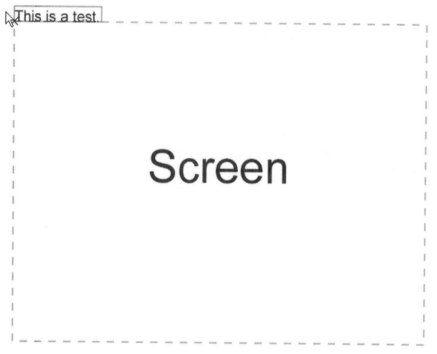

Figure 6-1. The default origin for text

As with any other shape (and text *is* a shape), the <text> element has both an x and y attribute that you can use to position it on the screen. Thus, to make the element visible, you just need to set its x and y positions so that they are fully within the screen—say at the position (100,100), as shown in Listing 6-2 and Figure 6-2.

Listing 6-2. `Text3.svg`

```
<svg xmlns="http://www.w3.org/2000/svg"
        xmlns:xlink="http://www.w3.org/1999/xlink">
    <g>
        <rect width="100%" height="100%" fill="yellow"
                stroke="black" stroke-width="2"/>
        <text x="100" y="100">This is a test.</text>
    </g>
</svg>
```

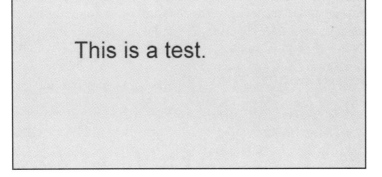

Figure 6-2. Positioning text

This is test text, but it is both fairly small and not terribly imposing. In all likelihood, you will want to change the size of the text element. Surprisingly, however, this code:

```
<text x="100" y="100" width="200" height="200">This is a test.</text>
```

has absolutely no effect. This stems from the fact that a text element has its own internal measure of the size of the elements, called the `font-size` attribute.

NOTE *Actually,* width *and* height *attributes do have an effect, but not the one you may expect. For more information, see the "Anchoring Text" section later in this chapter.*

If you are familiar with Cascading Style Sheets (CSS), then `font-size` may be quite familiar (it is in fact a standard CSS property). The `font-size` attribute in CSS is defined as being 120 percent of the height of a capital X in the font in question. This is somewhat different from the SVG usage of `font-size`, which defaults to the *point height* of the font—the number of points ($^1/_{72}$ of an inch) of height that a lowercase x has in a given font.

Unless specifically overridden, the `font-size` in SVG is based upon the coordinate system currently in use. For instance, in the default case, `font-size` uses pixels as the unit measure. So, a font-size of 50 indicates that the font height plus 20 percent will be 50-pixel units high.

On the other hand, if you change the coordinate system, you should change `font-size` accordingly. For instance, if the default height and width of the SVG context is 8 inches by 6 inches, then the coordinate system should be given in inches, including `font-size`. In Listing 6-3 and Figure 6-3, the `font-size` for the text is half an inch: `font-size="0.5`.

Listing 6-3. `Text4.svg`

```
<svg width="8in" height="6in" viewBox="0 0 8 6"
        preserveAspectRatio="none"
        xmlns="http://www.w3.org/2000/svg"
        xmlns:xlink="http://www.w3.org/1999/xlink">
    <g>
        <text x="1" y="1" font-size="0.5">This is a test.</text>
    </g>
</svg>
```

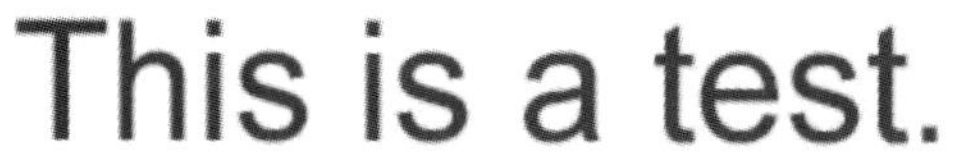

This is a test.

Figure 6-3. Specifying `font-size="0.5"`

The `font-size` attribute does run into much the same problem that the `stroke` attribute does under unequal coordinate axes. As illustrated in Chapter 5, "Painting and Drawing," if the size of your x unit is different from the y unit, then the real `font-size` along one axis is different from that in the other axis. You can use the scale transformation to correct for this, as shown in Listing 6-4 and Figure 6-4.

Listing 6-4. `Text5.svg`

```
<svg width="800" height="600" viewBox="0 0 1600 600"
        preserveAspectRatio="none"
      xmlns="http://www.w3.org/2000/svg"
      xmlns:xlink="http://www.w3.org/1999/xlink">
    <g>
        <text x="100" y="100" font-size="50">
                This is compressed 50% along the xaxis.
        </text>
        <text x="50" y="150" font-size="50" transform="scale(2,1)">
                This is the normal size.
        </text>
    </g>
</svg>
```

This is compressed 50% along the x axis.
This is the normal size.

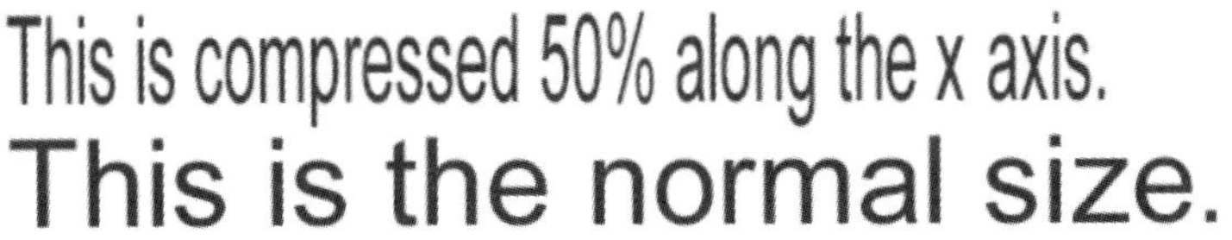

Figure 6-4. Using scale tranformation

While on the subject of transformations, it is worth noting that text, being a shape, can in fact be rotated in exactly the same manner as a rectangle, ellipse, path, or other shape element. This means you cannot only scale a <text> element, but you can also rotate, transform, skew, or perform any other matrix transformation on text. For instance, you can skew a selection of text by 30° in the x direction or rotate it by 30°, as shown in Listing 6-5 and Figure 6-5.

Listing 6-5. `Text5.svg`

```
<svg xmlns="http://www.w3.org/2000/svg"

        xmlns:xlink="http://www.w3.org/1999/xlink">
    <g>
        <text x="0" y="0" font-size="50"
                transform="translate(100,100),skewX(-30)">
                This is skewed text.
          </text>
        <text x="0" y="0" font-size="50"
                transform="translate(100,150),rotate(30)">
```

```
                              This is rotated text.
                </text>
           </g>
      </svg>
```

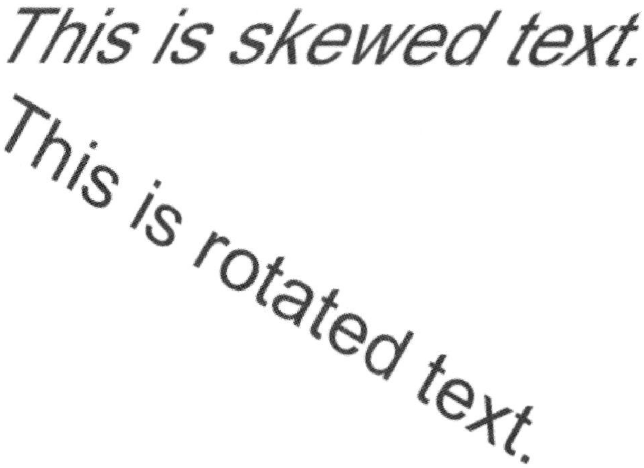

This is skewed text.

This is rotated text.

Figure 6-5. Skewing and rotating text

Spanning Text

You can think of the <text> element as the primary container for text elements, but there are often times when the text within such a block may need to have more than one format applied. For instance, suppose you wanted to have an expression that included 9-point Helvetica text, with a couple of words bolded or colored for emphasis. You could carefully calculate the position of the various words, as shown in Listing 6-6.

Listing 6-6. Badtext1.svg

```
<svg viewBox="0 -25 100 100"
        xmlns="http://www.w3.org/2000/svg"
        xmlns:xlink="http://www.w3.org/1999/xlink">
    <g>
        <text x="0" y="0" font-size="9">When in the course of</text>
        <text x="36" y="0" font-size="9" font-weight="bold">human events</text>
        <text x="45" y="0" font-size="9">it becomes necessary to  ... </text>
    </g>
</svg>
```

However, this can prove problematic; changing the text anywhere in the first two elements requires recalculating the position, as does changing the size. Additionally, to change any other formatting (font-size, for instance) requires changing it in three distinct places.

Fortunately, there exists a variant of the <text> element: the <tspan> (for text span) element. <tspan> functions in much the same way that the Hypertext Markup Language (HTML) <span> element does in comparison to a <div> element. It provides a generic class for text that is contained inline within an expression. Thus, the same expression can be rendered as shown in Listing 6-7 and Figure 6-6.

Listing 6-7. Tspan1.svg

```
<svg xmlns="http://www.w3.org/2000/svg"
      xmlns:xlink="http://www.w3.org/1999/xlink">
   <g transform="translate(100,100)">
   <text x="0" y="0" font-size="16">
   When in the course of <tspan font-weight="bold">human events</tspan>,
   it becomes necessary to . . .
   </text>
   </g>
</svg>
```

When in the course of **human events**, it becomes necessary to

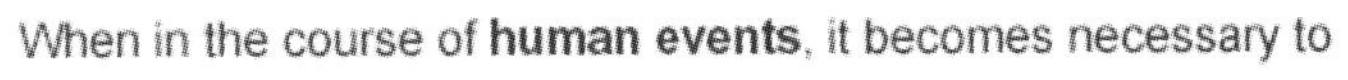

Figure 6-6. The <tspan> *element*

In Listing 6-7, the bulk of the text is contained in the <text> element, and the <tspan> element is only used to display those portions of the text that are in bold. Because it is a spanning element, <tspan> automatically handles the positioning of both its contained text and any following text, <tspan>, or <tref> element.

NOTE *You can use a* <tspan> *element only within a* <text> *element; you cannot use it independently.*

In addition to enhancing specific properties, the <tspan> element can also override an existing property. For instance, in Listing 6-8 and Figure 6-7, the purpose of the <tspan> element is to disable the italicized text for the word in question.

Listing 6-8. `Tspan2.svg`

```
<svg xmlns="http://www.w3.org/2000/svg"
        xmlns:xlink="http://www.w3.org/1999/xlink">
    <g transform="translate(100,100)">
    <text x="0" y="0" font-size="16" font-style="italic">
    When in the course of <tspan font-style="normal" >
        human events</tspan>,
    it becomes necessary to . . .
    </text>
    </g>
</svg>
```

When in the course of **human events**, *it becomes necessary to ...*

Figure 6-7. Overriding existing formatting with `<tspan>`

This will make the phrase *human events* appear as normal in comparison to the italicized text before and after the expression.

You can also use the `<tspan>` elements for positioning elements within a block of text . Because the span retains the previous relative position, you can use this for some interesting effects, as shown in Listing 6-9 and Figure 6-8.

Listing 6-9. `Tspan3.svg`

```
<svg xmlns="http://www.w3.org/2000/svg"
        xmlns:xlink="http://www.w3.org/1999/xlink">
    <g transform="translate(100,100)">
    <text font-size="11" font-style="italic">
            <tspan x="0" y="0">Once</tspan>
            <tspan y="10">there</tspan>
            <tspan y="20">was</tspan>
            <tspan y="30">a</tspan>
            <tspan y="40">little</tspan
            <tspan y="50">cat,</tspan>
            <tspan y="60">or</tspan>
            <tspan y="70">maybe</tspan>
            <tspan y="80">there</tspan>
            <tspan y="90">wasn't.</tspan>
```

```
        <tspan x="0" y="110">Ask Heisenberg.</tspan>
        <tspan y="110">He may know.</tspan>
    </text>
  </g>
```

Once
there
was
a
little
cat,
or
maybe
there
wasn't.

Ask Heisenberg. He may know.

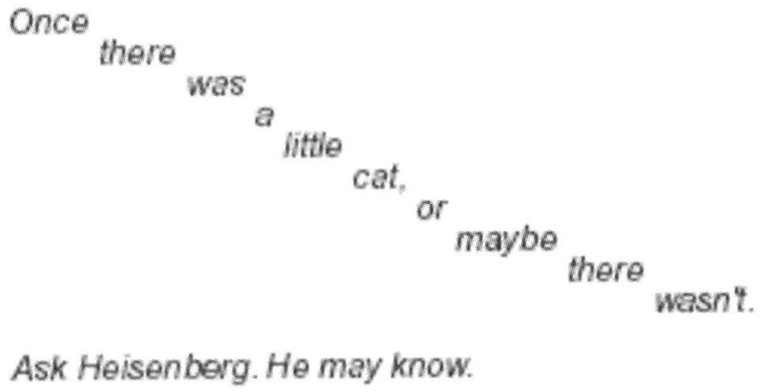

Figure 6-8. Retaining the position of the end of the previous element

```
</svg>
```

The horizontal position is calculated implicitly based upon the position of
the previous `<tspan>` element, and the vertical position is shifted down approximately one text "line" worth. In the last line, the x position is explicitly set,
resetting the relative offset for the next line. This relative context remains in force
until the end of the text block.

Referencing Text

As you may have noticed, one of the best ways of building SVG documents from
a programmatic standpoint is to define as many of the graphical elements ahead
of time, then build references to them in the "live" part of the document, the part
in the active graphic context. Text can initially prove to be somewhat problematic in this model because you can often have large blocks of text interspersed
with an extensive number of `<use>` declarations, rather defeating the whole purpose of object-oriented design.

However, text is an object in exactly the same way that rectangles, circles, or
other elements are objects. One implication of this is that a block of text can in
fact have its own ID and can in turn be referenced via a `<use>` element. For
instance, Listing 6-10 and Figure 6-9 illustrate a set of simple labeled button
faces, where all elements are referenced.

Listing 6-10. `RefText1.svg`

```
<svg xmlns="http://www.w3.org/2000/svg"
        xmlns:xlink="http://www.w3.org/1999/xlink">
    <defs>
        <rect x="0" y="0" width="120" height="40" rx="10" ry="10"
                fill="red" id="buttonFace" stroke="black"
                stroke-width="2"/>
        <text font-size="20" font-family="Helvetica"
                font-weight="bold" id="btnLbl1">Button 1</text>
        <text font-size="20" font-family="Helvetica"
                font-weight="bold" id="btnLbl2">Button 2</text>
        <text font-size="20" font-family="Helvetica"
                font-weight="bold" id="btnLbl3">Button 3</text>
        <g id="button1">
                <use xlink:href="#buttonFace" x="0" y="0"/>
                <use xlink:href="#btnLbl1" x="20" y="25"/>
        </g>
        <g id="button2">
                <use xlink:href="#buttonFace" x="0" y="0"/>
                <use xlink:href="#btnLbl2" x="20" y="25"/>
        </g>
        <g id="button3">
                <use xlink:href="#buttonFace" x="0" y="0"/>
                <use xlink:href="#btnLbl3" x="20" y="25"/>
        </g>
    </defs>
    <g transform="translate(100,100)">
        <use xlink:href="#button1" x="0" y="0"/>
        <use xlink:href="#button2" x="0" y="40"/>
        <use xlink:href="#button3" x="0" y="80"/>
    </g>
</svg>
```

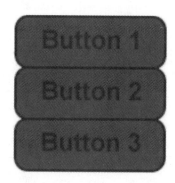

Figure 6-9. Using `<tref>` *elements*

The elements #btnLbl1, #btnLbl2, and #btnLbl3 define three distinct text labels. These elements are then referenced via the xlink:href attribute of the <use> tags, referenced in the <g> elements #button1, #button2, and #button3. The advantage of this approach is that you end up manipulating identifiable objects—#btnLbl—rather than concentrating on the specific text. This makes it far easier to animate the text (as discussed in Chapter 8, "Animating SVG"), and it also makes it easier to modularize text definition so that code localization—changing your interfaces for different languages and regions—becomes much simpler (as will be discussed in Chapter 10, "SVG Components").

You can also make use of references within <text> blocks, though with one caveat. Because the contents of a <text> element must only be text, the <use> element is too broad in its scope. Consequently, SVG also defines a <tref> element. The <tref> element must be a child of either a <text> or <tspan> element. It functions essentially as a <tspan> element that can point to a different selection of text.

The distinction is actually a more subtle than it may appear on the surface. The <tref> element references only text content, not text formatting, and <use> references the text object, formatting and all. Listing 6-11 and Figure 6-10 show this distinction.

Listing 6-11. RefText2.svg

```
<svg xmlns="http://www.w3.org/2000/svg"
        xmlns:xlink="http://www.w3.org/1999/xlink">
    <defs>
        <text id="item1" fill="blue" font-size="24">
                This is
                <tspan font-family="fantasy">referenced</tspan> text.
        </text>
    </defs>
    <desc>This illustrates referencing text via tref. Notice
                that the formatting gets lost -
                only the actual text content is retained.</desc>
    <g transform="translate(100,100)">
    <text>
        <tref xlink:href="#item1"/>
        <tspan>Referenced via &lt;tref&gt;</tspan>
    </text>
    </g>
    <g transform="translate(100,150)">
    <desc>Here the formatting is kept within the &lt;use&gt; statement.</desc>
    <use x="0" y="0" xlink:href="#item1"/>
    <text x="250" y="0">Referenced via <&lt;use&gt;></text>
    </g>
</svg>
```

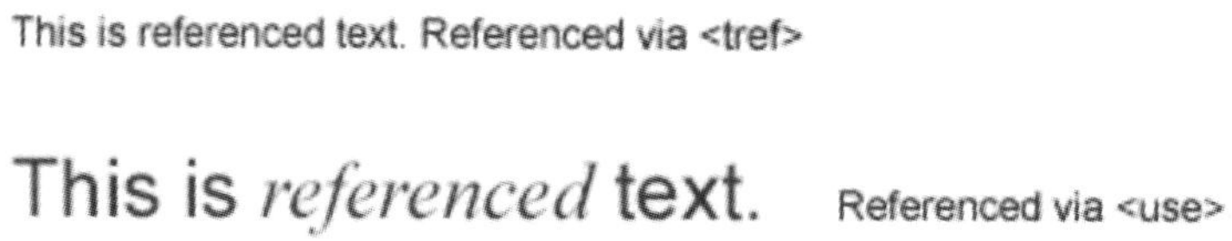

This is referenced text. Referenced via <tref>

This is *referenced* text.   Referenced via <use>

Figure 6-10. Retaining only content, not formatting

In this case, the first graphics context displays the use of the <tref> element to retrieve specific text content. The <tref> element extracts the text nodes from #item1 and concatenates them, independent of any <text> or <tspan> formatting information. On the other hand, in the second graphics context, the <use> element retains all formatting from the original #item1 object.

If the references were to be resolved (in other words, the appropriate contents replacing the referring elements), then Listing 6-11 would look like Listing 6-12.

Listing 6-12. RefText2Alt.svg

```
<svg xmlns="http://www.w3.org/2000/svg"
       xmlns:xlink="http://www.w3.org/1999/xlink">
    <!-- <tref> references resolved.-->
    <g transform="translate(100,100)">
    <text>
        <tspan>This is referenced text.</tspan>
        <tspan>Referenced via &lt;tref&gt;</tspan>
    </text>
    </g>
    <g transform="translate(100,150)">
<!-- <use> references resolved. -->
    <text fill="blue" font-size="24">
        This is <tspan font-family="fantasy">referenced</tspan>
        text.</text>
    <text x="250" y="0">Referenced via &lt;use&gt;</text>
    </g>
</svg>
```

You can apply CSS properties to <tref> elements just as you can <tspan> elements, as shown in Listing 6-13 and Figure 6-11.

Listing 6-13. `RefText3.svg`

```
<svg xmlns="http://www.w3.org/2000/svg"
        xmlns:xlink="http://www.w3.org/1999/xlink">
    <defs>
        <linearGradient gradientTransform="rotate(90)" id="chrome" >
            <stop stop-color="black" offset="0%"/>
            <stop stop-color="navy" offset="51%"/>
            <stop stop-color="lightBlue" offset="100%"/>
        </linearGradient>
        <text id="item1">This illustrates &lt;tspan&gt; formatting</text>
    </defs>
    <g transform="translate(100,100)">
        <text>
            <tref xlink:href="#item1" x="0" y="0"/>
            <tref xlink:href="#item1" x="0" y="20" font-size="18"/>
            <tref xlink:href="#item1" x="0" y="40" font-size="18"
                    fill="red"/>
            <tref xlink:href="#item1" x="0" y="60" font-size="18"
                    font-family="Impact"/>
            <tref xlink:href="#item1" x="0" y="120" font-size="40"
                    font-family="Impact" fill="url(#chrome)"
                    height="40"/>
        </text>
    </g>
</svg>
```

This illustrates <tspan> formatting
This illustrates <tspan> formatting
This illustrates <tspan> formatting
This illustrates <tspan> formatting

This illustrates <tspan> formatting

Figure 6-11. Formatting the `<tref>` *element as per* `<tspan>`

Two elements, a linear gradient (discussed in greater detail in Chapter 7, "Incorporating Texture") and a text element, are defined in the `<defs>` section. In the graphics context, the `<tref>` element illustrates how the same text can be presented in any number of different ways, including being drawn with a gradient fill. The `<tref>` element acts here as a `<tspan>` element for its referenced text.

TIP *The* <tref> *element can also be animated, as discussed in more detail in Chapter 8, "Animating SVG."*

Anchoring Text

SVG is an international standard, not just one applicable to English-speaking countries. Consequently, this graphics language has to deal with a number of different kinds of writing styles. For instance, throughout the Americas, Australia, most of Europe, and parts of Africa and Asia, the dominant writing style involves script that moves from right to left primarily, then from top to bottom secondarily. On the other hand, languages in Southeast Europe, the Arabian Peninsula, Northern Africa, and Southwest Asia use a script that moves from right to left. Finally, East Asian languages for the most part follow a top-down, right-to-left style.

These varying styles make the positioning and rendering of text considerably more complicated than it may appear at first glance. To accommodate this, SVG includes a number of attributes on the <text> element to provide for controls over everything from the horizontal and vertical starting positions to the direction that the text is drawn. Table 6-1 lists the relevant properties.

The text-anchor property controls the location within the text box that defines the horizontal origin for graphics. The default location of text-anchor is at the left side of the text box, which is consistent with English writing conventions. When a text region is rendered, it usually starts from the left and works right so that the rightmost part of the text box can be calculated as the leftmost part of any new box (such as might be calculated for a <tspan> element).

However, although such a convention makes it easier to create flowing blocks of text, there are often situations where being able to position an element relative to its middle or rightmost points is more useful. For instance, with buttons, it is usually much more useful to have the button text centered on the button, rather than having to position the elements relative to the left. Likewise, in presentations where text is right justified, positioning elements from the right makes far more sense.

The text-anchor attribute provides this support, as shown in Listing 6-14 and Figure 6-12.

Table 6-1. Text Positioning Properties

ATTRIBUTE NAME	ATTRIBUTE TYPE	DESCRIPTION
text-anchor	start | middle | end	The text-anchor property controls the horizontal location of the anchor point.
dominant-baseline	ideographic | alphabetic | hanging | mathematical | auto | autosense-script | no-change | reset-size	The dominant-baseline property controls the primary vertical location of the text.
alignment-baseline	ideographic | alphabetic | hanging | mathematical | auto | autosense-script | no-change | reset-size	This provides secondary baselines off of the dominate-baseline.
writing-mode	lr-tb | rl-tb | tb-rl | lr | rl | tb | inherit	This determines the direction that the characters in the text are laid down, with lr-tb being left to right, within lines going top to bottom.
direction	ltr | rtl	This determines whether text is drawn from left to right or right to left.
unicode-bidi	normal | embed | bidi-override | inherit	This determines whether bidirectional text is enabled in the processor (for efficiency).
baseline-shift	baseline | sub | super | <percentage> | <length> | inherit	This sets the position of the baseline of the current text element relative to its containing element.

Listing 6-14. TextAnchor.svg

```
<svg xmlns="http://www.w3.org/2000/svg"
      xmlns:xlink="http://www.w3.org/1999/xlink">
   <g>
   <text font-size="30" x="20" y="40">Text Anchor</text>
      <text x="350" y="100" font-size="30" text-anchor="start">
             text-anchor="start"</text>
      <text x="350" y="150" font-size="30" text-anchor="middle">
             text-anchor="middle"</text>
      <text x="350" y="200" font-size="30" text-anchor="end">
             text-anchor="end"</text>
      <line x1="350" x2="350" y1="50" y2="450" stroke="black"
             stroke-width="1"/>
      <line x1="100" x2="600" y1="100" y2="100" stroke="black"
             stroke-width="1"/>
```

```
        <line x1="100" x2="600" y1="150" y2="150" stroke="black"
                stroke-width="1"/>
        <line x1="100" x2="600" y1="200" y2="200" stroke="black"
                stroke-width="1"/>
    </g>
</svg>
```

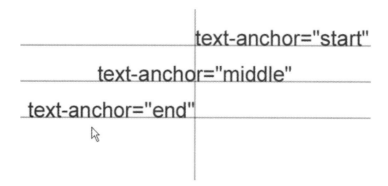

Figure 6-12. Using the text-anchor *attribute*

Notice that the values that text-anchor can hold are start |middle |end, not left |middle |right. This comes from the need to represent all languages, rather than just the left-to-right notation used in most European-based scripts. In a right-to-left language such as Hebrew, text-anchor="start" corresponds to the rightmost point in the text box, rather than the leftmost.

Again, one of the primary differences between text and other graphics comes in the fact that the text letters need to have some internal reference point that indicates where measurement begins. In printing, it is usually standard to use the bottom of the lowercase x character as this location. The line that extends from the base of this character underneath all other characters' bases is called, not surprisingly, the *baseline*.

However, things get complicated with baselines. A superscript or subscript sets the baseline up or down respectively from the dominant baseline, as do certain accent marks, especially in languages such as Arabic. Mathematical equations in particular can prove to be exceedingly rough on simple baselines. As such, SVG defines a *dominant baseline* that indicates the primary vertical position where the text is rendered, and *alternate baselines* that can be set for handling more complex typographical requirements.

The dominant-baseline attribute of the <text>, <tspan>, and <tref> elements sets this primary baseline, as illustrated in Listing 6-15 and Figure 6-13.

Listing 6-15. DominantBaseline.svg

```
<svg xmlns="http://www.w3.org/2000/svg"
        xmlns:xlink="http://www.w3.org/1999/xlink">
    <defs>
        <line x1="100" x2="600" y1="0" y2="0"
                stroke="black" stroke-width="1" id="vertline"/>
    </defs>
    <g>
        <text font-size="30" x="20" y="40">Dominant Baseline</text>
        <text x="350" y="100" font-size="20"
            dominant-baseline="ideographic">
            dominant-baseline="ideographic"</text>
        <text x="350" y="150" font-size="20"
            dominant-baseline="alphabetic">
            dominant-baseline="alphabetic"</text>
        <text x="350" y="200" font-size="20"
            dominant-baseline="hanging">
            dominant-baseline="hanging"</text>
        <text x="350" y="250" font-size="20"
            dominant-baseline="mathematical">
            dominant-baseline="mathematical"</text>
        <text x="350" y="300" font-size="20"
            dominant-baseline="auto">dominant-baseline="auto"</text>
        <line x1="350" y1="50" x2="350" y2="500" stroke="black"/>
        <use xlink:href="#vertline" x="0" y="100"/>
        <use xlink:href="#vertline" x="0" y="150"/>
        <use xlink:href="#vertline" x="0" y="200"/>
        <use xlink:href="#vertline" x="0" y="250"/>
        <use xlink:href="#vertline" x="0" y="300"/>
    </g>
</svg>
```

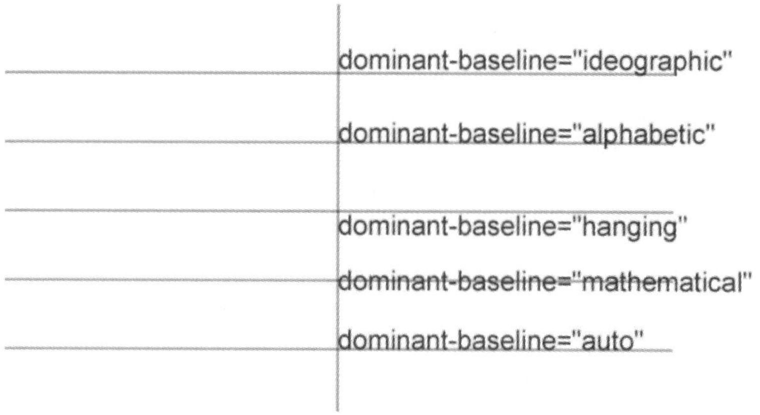

Figure 6-13. The `dominant-baseline` *attribute*

The four primary baselines include *alphabetic, ideographic, mathematical,* and *hanging.* The alphabetic baseline (the default with English, though not necessarily with all languages) uses the x character basis in positioning the baseline. The ideographic baseline is similar, save that it uses the bottom of the longest extender in the language (such as the tail of a g or y). This can have the side effect of making text appear to float slightly if drawn in the same position as a line.

The mathematical baseline assumes the baseline is located halfway between the highest part of the highest character (such as the handle of the h) and the lowest point of the lowest character (the end of the tail in the g or y character). The mathematical baseline is thus centered vertically. Finally, the hanging baseline assumes the top of the tallest character as the baseline, and all characters are drawn relative to this, appearing below a line at the same position.

The combination of baselines and text-anchors can thus be used to position text relative to its containing box. Listing 6-16 and Figure 6-14 illustrate the use of both of these properties together (as well as demonstrating how a simple multimedia application can be created in SVG).

Listing 6-16. `Anchoring.svg`

```
<svg xmlns="http://www.w3.org/2000/svg"
        xmlns:xlink="http://www.w3.org/1999/xlink">
    <defs>
        <radialGradient id="buttonUpFill">
            <stop offset="0%" stop-color="red"/>
        </radialGradient>
        <radialGradient id="buttonDownFill">
            <stop offset="0%" stop-color="yellow"/>
            <stop offset="65%" stop-color="orange"/>
```

```
        <stop offset="100%" stop-color="red"/>
</radialGradient>
<rect x="0" y="0" width="200" height="30" rx="10" ry="10"
        stroke="black" stroke-width="3" id="stdBtn"/>
<text id="taText1" text-anchor="middle"
    dominant-baseline="mathematical">start</text>
<text id="taText2" text-anchor="middle"
    dominant-baseline="mathematical">middle</text>
<text id="taText3" text-anchor="middle"
    dominant-baseline="mathematical">end</text>
<text id="dbText1" text-anchor="middle"
    dominant-baseline="mathematical">alphabetic</text>
<text id="dbText2" text-anchor="middle"
    dominant-baseline="mathematical">ideographic</text>
<text id="dbText3" text-anchor="middle"
    dominant-baseline="mathematical">mathematical</text>
<text id="dbText4" text-anchor="middle"
    dominant-baseline="mathematical">hanging</text>
    <use xlink:href="#stdBtn" id="stdBtnUp" fill="url(#buttonUpFill)"/>
    <use xlink:href="#stdBtn" id="stdBtnDown" fill="url(#buttonDownFill)"/>
<g id="taBtn1Up">
    <use xlink:href="#stdBtnUp"/>
    <use xlink:href="#taText1" x="100" y="15"/>
</g>
<g id="taBtn1Down">
    <use xlink:href="#stdBtnDown"/>
    <use xlink:href="#taText1" x="100" y="15"/>
</g>
<g id="taBtn2Up">
    <use xlink:href="#stdBtnUp"/>
    <use xlink:href="#taText2" x="100" y="15"/>
</g>
<g id="taBtn2Down">
    <use xlink:href="#stdBtnDown"/>
    <use xlink:href="#taText2" x="100" y="15"/>
</g>
<g id="taBtn3Up">
    <use xlink:href="#stdBtnUp"/>
    <use xlink:href="#taText3" x="100" y="15"/>
</g>
<g id="taBtn3Down">
    <use xlink:href="#stdBtnDown"/>
    <use xlink:href="#taText3" x="100" y="15"/>
</g>
```

```
                <g id="dbBtn1Up">
                    <use xlink:href="#stdBtnUp"/>
                    <use xlink:href="#dbText1" x="100" y="15"/>
                </g>
                <g id="dbBtn1Down">
                    <use xlink:href="#stdBtnDown"/>
                    <use xlink:href="#dbText1" x="100" y="15"/>
                </g>
                <g id="dbBtn2Up">
                    <use xlink:href="#stdBtnUp"/>
                    <use xlink:href="#dbText2" x="100" y="15"/>
                </g>
                <g id="dbBtn2Down">
                    <use xlink:href="#stdBtnDown"/>
                    <use xlink:href="#dbText2" x="100" y="15"/>
                </g>
                <g id="dbBtn3Up">
                    <use xlink:href="#stdBtnUp"/>
                    <use xlink:href="#dbText3" x="100" y="15"/>
                </g>
                <g id="dbBtn3Down">
                    <use xlink:href="#stdBtnDown"/>
                    <use xlink:href="#dbText3" x="100" y="15"/>
                </g>
                <g id="dbBtn4Up">
                    <use xlink:href="#stdBtnUp"/>
                    <use xlink:href="#dbText4" x="100" y="15"/>
                </g>
                <g id="dbBtn4Down">
                    <use xlink:href="#stdBtnDown"/>
                    <use xlink:href="#dbText4" x="100" y="15"/>
                </g>
                <text font-size="30" id="title">
                  Combining Text Anchor and Dominant-Baseline</text>
                <text font-size="20" id="taTextTitle">Text Anchor</text>
                <text font-size="20" id="dbTextTitle">Dominant Baseline</text>
            </defs>
                <use xlink:href="#title" x="20" y="40"/>
                <use xlink:href="#taTextTitle" x="20" y="80"/>
                <use xlink:href="#dbTextTitle" x="20" y="280"/>
                <g transform="translate(50,100)">
                <g id="taGroup">
```

```
                <use xlink:href="#taBtn1Up" x="0" y="0" id="taButton1">
                    <set attributeName="xlink:href" attributeType="XML"
                    begin="click" to="#taBtn1Down" end="taGroup.click"/>
            </use>
                <use xlink:href="#taBtn2Up" x="0" y="40" id="taButton2">
                    <set attributeName="xlink:href" attributeType="XML"
                    begin="click" to="#taBtn2Down" end="taGroup.click"/>
            </use>
                <use xlink:href="#taBtn3Up" x="0" y="80" id="taButton3">
                    <set attributeName="xlink:href" attributeType="XML"
                    begin="click" to="#taBtn3Down" end="taGroup.click"/>
            </use>
        </g>
        </g>
            <g transform="translate(50,300)">
        <g id="dbGroup">
            <use xlink:href="#dbBtn1Up" x="0" y="0" id="dbButton1">
                <set attributeName="xlink:href" attributeType="XML"
                 begin="click" to="#dbBtn1Down" end="dbGroup.click"/>
            </use>
                <use xlink:href="#dbBtn2Up" x="0" y="40" id="dbButton2">
                <set attributeName="xlink:href" attributeType="XML"
                 begin="click" to="#dbBtn2Down" end="dbGroup.click"/>
            </use>
                <use xlink:href="#dbBtn3Up" x="0" y="80" id="dbButton3">
                <set attributeName="xlink:href" attributeType="XML"
                 begin="click" to="#dbBtn3Down" end="dbGroup.click"/>
            </use>
                <use xlink:href="#dbBtn4Up" x="0" y="120" id="dbButton4">
                <set attributeName="xlink:href" attributeType="XML"
                 begin="click" to="#dbBtn4Down" end="dbGroup.click"/>
            </use>
        </g>
    </g>
</g>
<g transform="translate(400,200)">
    <line x1="-100" y1="0" x2="100" y2="0" stroke="black" stroke-width="2"/>
    <line y1="-100" x1="0" y2="100" x2="0" stroke="black" stroke-width="2"/>
    <text x="0" y="0" font-size="30">
        <set attributeName="text-anchor" attributeType="CSS"
        to="start"  begin="taButton1.click"/>
        <set attributeName="text-anchor" attributeType="CSS"
        to="middle"  begin="taButton2.click"/>
```

```
                        <set attributeName="text-anchor" attributeType="CSS"
                        to="end"  begin="taButton3.click"/>
                        <set attributeName="dominant-baseline" attributeType="CSS"
                        to="alphabetic"  begin="dbButton1.click"/>
                        <set attributeName="dominant-baseline" attributeType="CSS"
                        to="ideographic"  begin="dbButton2.click"/>
                        <set attributeName="dominant-baseline" attributeType="CSS"
                        to="mathematical"  begin="dbButton3.click"/>
                        <set attributeName="dominant-baseline" attributeType="CSS"
                        to="hanging"  begin="dbButton4.click"/>

                Example
                </text>
        </g>

</svg>
```

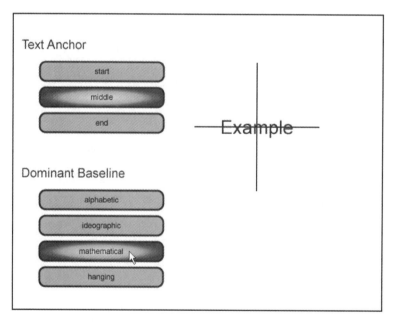

Figure 6-14. The combination of anchoring and using dominant-baseline

Clicking the relevant button in each of the two groups will show the location of the anchor point relative to the text.

TIP *For more information on the* <set> *element, see Chapter 8, "Animating SVG."*

You can also shift the baseline within a block of text. For instance, you can express Einstein's famous equation $E=mc^2$ and other elements with subscripts and superscripts in SVG as shown in Listing 6-17 and Figure 6-15.

Listing 6-17. `BaselineShift.svg`

```
<svg xmlns="http://www.w3.org/2000/svg"
        xmlns:xlink="http://www.w3.org/1999/xlink">
    <g transform="translate(100,100)">
        <text dominant-baseline="alphabetic" font-size="40">
        E=mc<tspan baseline-shift="50%" font-size="20">2</tspan>
        </text>
    </g>
    <g transform="translate(100,200)">
        <text dominant-baseline="alphabetic" font-size="40">
                H<tspan baseline-shift="sub" font-size="20">
                2</tspan>SO<tspan baseline-shift="sub" font-size="20">
                4</tspan>
        </text>
    </g>
    <g transform="translate(100,300)">
        <text dominant-baseline="mathematical" font-size="40">
        <tspan font-size="60" dominant-baseline="mathematical">
                &#8747;
        </tspan>
        e
        <tspan baseline-shift="60%" dominant-baseline="mathematical"
                font-size="20">-x<tspan baseline-shift="super"
                font-size="10">2</tspan>/2</tspan>dx
        </text>
    </g>
</svg>
```

$$E=mc^2$$

$$H_2SO_4$$

$$\int e^{-x^2/2} dx$$

Figure 6-15. Making superscripts, subscripts, and complex equations possible

The `baseline-shift` attribute can take on the values "sub" or "super," for subscript and superscript (respectively), and it can also take either an absolute value or a percentage of the current `font-size` to indicate the distance above the baseline that the shifted item will be drawn. Thus a `baseline-shift` of 60% for a `font-size` of 60 will move the new text up 60 x 60 percent, or 36 user units. Negative baseline shifts move the element down relative to the baseline.

Setting Writing Modes

Despite appearance to the contrary, neither the Internet nor computing in general is a solely American venture (thankfully). The need to write other languages, coupled with the need to simply orient text along more than the normal left to right angles, makes the ability to control the writing mode an imperative in SVG. There are a number of characteristics that can consequently control this writing mode, as shown in Table 6-2.

Table 6-2. Writing Mode Properties

ATTRIBUTE NAME	ATTRIBUTE TYPE	DESCRIPTION
writing-mode	lr-tb | rl-tb | tb-rl | lr | rl | tb | inherit	This determines the direction that the characters in the text are laid down, with lr-tb being left to right, within lines going top to bottom.
direction	ltr | rtl	This determines whether text is drawn from left to right or right to left.
glyph-orientation-vertical	auto | angle	This controls the orientation of each character in a line of text.

The writing-mode attribute applies only to the <text> element and controls the general positioning of the text and its orientation, though not the actual direction that it is rendered in. Listing 6-18 and Figure 6-16 illustrate the various combinations of left (l), right (r), top (t), and bottom (b) that are supported by SVG.

Listing 6-18. WritingMode.svg

```
<svg xmlns="http://www.w3.org/2000/svg"
      xmlns:xlink="http://www.w3.org/1999/xlink">
   <g transform="translate(200,100)">
      <text x="0" y="0" font-size="30" writing-mode="lr-tb">
           This is <tspan font-weight="bold">lr-tb</tspan> </text>
      <text x="0" y="30" font-size="30" writing-mode="rl-tb">
           This is <tspan font-weight="bold">rl-tb</tspan> </text>
      <text x="0" y="60" font-size="30" writing-mode="tb-rl">
           This is <tspan font-weight="bold">tb-rl</tspan></text>
      <text x="150" y="60" font-size="30" writing-mode="lr">
           This is <tspan font-weight="bold">lr</tspan></text>
      <text x="150" y="90" font-size="30" writing-mode="rl">
           This is <tspan font-weight="bold">rl</tspan></text>
      <text x="150" y="120" font-size="30" writing-mode="tb">
           This is <tspan font-weight="bold">tb</tspan></text>
   </g>
</svg>
```

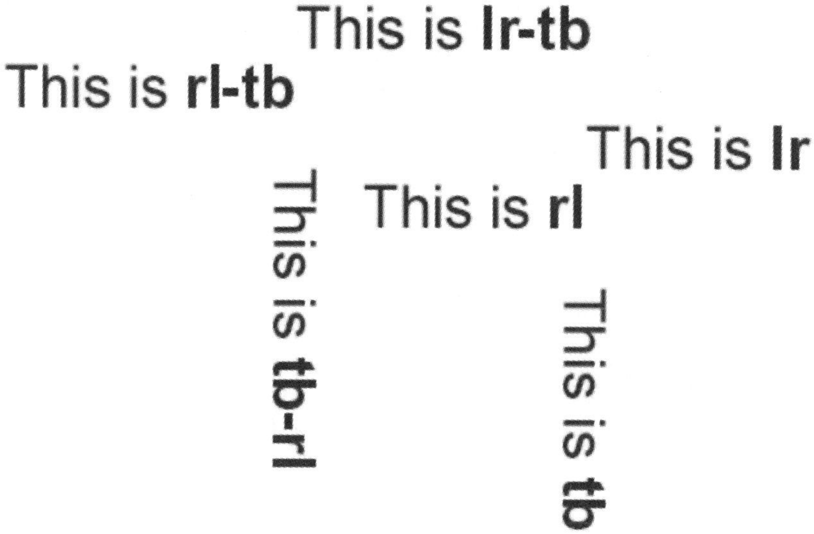

This is **lr-tb**

This is **rl-tb**

This is **lr**

This is **rl**

This is **tb-rl**

This is **tb**

Figure 6-16. Using writing-mode

You can set the direction of the text in one of two ways. The direction attribute actually affects the rendering of the glyphs—the characters in the text string. The direction can be set to ltr or rtl, independent of the writing mode, and direction can affect both <tspan> and <tref> elements as well as <use> elements. Listing 6-19 and Figure 6-17 illustrate this.

Listing 6-19. Direction.svg

```
<svg xmlns="http://www.w3.org/2000/svg"
     xmlns:xlink="http://www.w3.org/1999/xlink">
  <g transform="translate(300,100)">
    <text x="0" y="0" font-size="30" writing-mode="lr-tb"
        unicode-bidi="bidi-override" direction="ltr">
        This is ltr(lr-tb)</text>
    <text x="0" y="30" font-size="30" writing-mode="lr-tb"
        unicode-bidi="bidi-override" direction="rtl">
        This is rtlltr(lr-tb)</text>
    <text x="0" y="60" font-size="30" writing-mode="rl-tb"
        unicode-bidi="bidi-override" direction="ltr">
        This is ltrltr(rl-tb)</text>
    <text x="0" y="90" font-size="30" writing-mode="rl-tb"
        unicode-bidi="bidi-override" direction="rtl">
        This is rtlltr(rl-tb)</text>
```

```
<text x="0" y="120" font-size="30" writing-mode="tb"
      unicode-bidi="bidi-override" direction="ltr">
      This is ltrltr(tb)</text>
<text x="30" y="120" font-size="30" writing-mode="tb"
      unicode-bidi="bidi-override" direction="rtl">
      This is rtlltr(lr)</text>
    </g>
</svg>
```

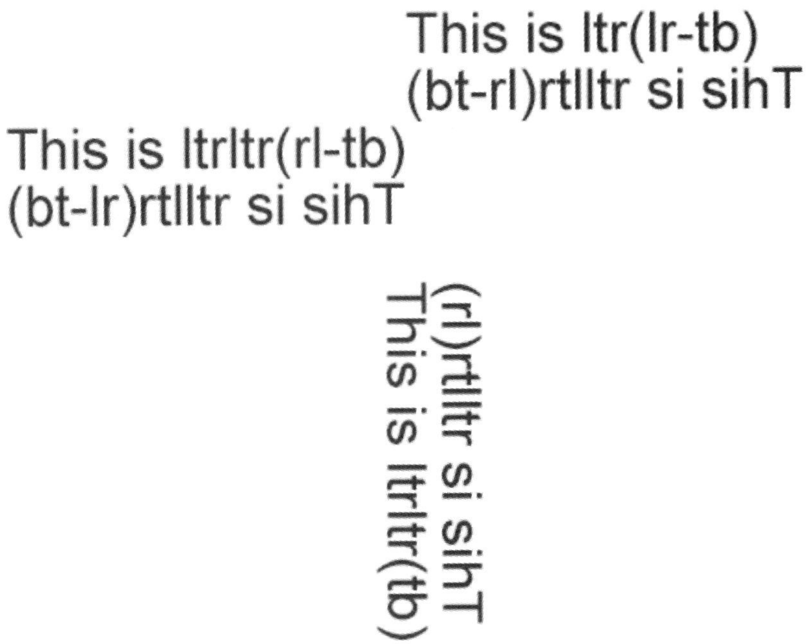

This is ltr(lr-tb)
(bt-rl)rtlltr si sihT

This is ltrltr(rl-tb)
(bt-lr)rtlltr si sihT

(rl)rtlltr si sihT
This is ltrltr(tb)

Figure 6-17. Using the direction and unicode-bidi attributes

 CAUTION *Because most systems are optimized for left-to-right rendering, another property,* unicode-bidi *must be set for right-to-left rendering to take place. You should set this to the value* "bidi-override," *where* bidi *stands for bi-directional.*

In addition to changing the orientation of the overall line of text, there are times where being able to change the orientation of the individual glyphs can come in handy. The glyph-orientation-vertical property can take as an argument any 90° angle increment ("0," "90," "180," "270," and so on) and orients the text accordingly. You can use this to good effect for creating labels that are oriented vertically (though you can also do this with a transformation).

Setting Font Properties

Most of the font properties that SVG supports should be apparent to anyone who has worked with CSS. In general, SVG uses the CSS properties almost completely unchanged, though it adds a few new characteristics as well. Table 6-3 lists the SVG font attributes.

Table 6-3. Font Properties

ATTRIBUTE NAME	ATTRIBUTE TYPE	DESCRIPTION
font-family	family-name | "serif" | "sans-serif" | "cursive" | "fantasy" | "monospace"	Either the name of the font to use or a generic family name such as "serif."
font-style	normal | italic | oblique | inherit	Whether the normal or italicized font face is used. The oblique style performs a skew on a normal font rather than using a dedicated italic font.
font-variant	normal | small-caps	Determines whether normal or small capitals are used within the text region.
font-weight	normal | bold | bolder | light | lighter | 100 | 200 | 300 | 400 | 500 | 600 | 700 | 800 | 900 | inherit	Determines the "boldness" of the text. A font-weight of 400 is considered to be normal, a font-weight of 700 is considered to be bold, and other weights range from "light" to "black" (100–900).
font-stretch	normal | wider | narrower | ultra-condensed | extra-condensed | condensed | semi-condensed | semi-expanded | expanded | extra-expanded | ultra-expanded | inherit	Determines the degree to which text is condensed or expanded to fill the available space.
font-size	absolute-size | relative-size | length | percentage | inherit	The distance from baseline to baseline of a given font when packed "tightly."
text-decoration	none | underline | underline | line-through | blink | inherit	Special effects for your text.

The font properties are straightforward and should be familiar to you if you have done much Web work. There are a couple of minor points that are worth noting, however.

The font-weight attribute is most often used to set the heaviness of a font to bold, but in fact it is intended to be a way of subtly shifting the heaviness from an extremely fine level (100) to an extremely heavy one (900). Unfortunately, it is not always implemented this way; the Adobe SVG Viewer for instance generally only recognizes normal (up to 500) and bold (600) and higher. Because the SVG processor has to change the geometry of a font extensively to support this fully (and because such changes are at best guesses), in general you are better off just using a font family with a wide range of different font faces. For instance, Franklin Gothic has a book, demi, medium, and heavy option that correspond roughly to 200, 400, 600, and 900 (respectively).

The font-stretch attribute can offset that somewhat. The font-stretch attribute performs a scaling upon the letters along the x axis, making them appear wider and heavier or narrower and lighter than the corresponding normal font. Listing 6-20 and Figure 6-18 show an example of this.

Listing 6-20. FontStretch.svg

```
<svg xmlns="http://www.w3.org/2000/svg"
        xmlns:xlink="http://www.w3.org/1999/xlink">
    <g transform="translate(50,100)">
        <text font-size="36" font-family="sans-serif">
            <tspan x="0" y="0" font-stretch="ultra-expanded">
            stretch is ultra-expanded</tspan>
            <tspan x="0" y="40" font-stretch="extra-expanded">
            stretch is extra-expanded</tspan>
            <tspan x="0" y="80" font-stretch="expanded">
            stretch is expanded</tspan>
            <tspan x="0" y="120" font-stretch="semi-expanded">
            stretch is semi-expanded</tspan>
            <tspan x="0" y="160" font-stretch="semi-condensed">
            stretch is semi-condensed</tspan>
            <tspan x="0" y="200" font-stretch="semi-condensed">
            stretch is condensed</tspan>
            <tspan x="0" y="240" font-stretch="condensed">
            stretch is extra-condensed</tspan>
            <tspan x="0" y="280" font-stretch="extra-condensed">
            stretch is ultra-condensed</tspan>
        </text>
    </g>
</svg>
```

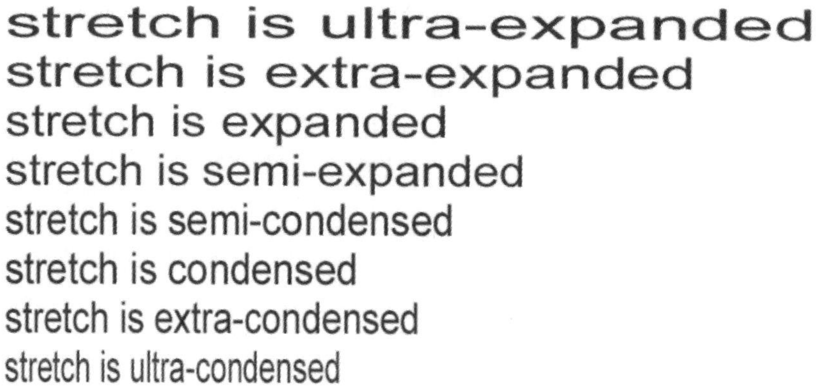

stretch is ultra-expanded
stretch is extra-expanded
stretch is expanded
stretch is semi-expanded
stretch is semi-condensed
stretch is condensed
stretch is extra-condensed
stretch is ultra-condensed

Figure 6-18. The font-stretch *attribute*

> **NOTE** *Although the vector orientation of SVG makes stretch-ing a font easier, expanded or condensed fonts produced in this way may not be as aesthetically appealing as using fonts that are specifically designed as condensed or expanded ver-sions. The same point holds true for oblique vs. italic fonts, where the first are generated programmatically and the latter are designed.*

Finally, the text-decoration attribute deserves some mention. This attribute is kind of a catchall for several different effects: underlining, overlining, line-throughs (as might be seen, for instance, in edited manuscripts), and blinking. Although it is certainly possible to use <line> elements to accomplish at least the first three of these features, the advantage to using text-decoration is that you do not have to calculate the positions of those lines.

The principal drawback to the use of such lining is that these lines are actu-ally shapes (very long rectangular shapes, essentially) and as such are treated like shapes with respect to the stroke properties such as stroke-dasharray, stroke, or stroke-width. Listing 6-21 and Figure 6-19 illustrate the usage of text decoration.

Listing 6-21. TextDecoration.svg

```
<svg xmlns="http://www.w3.org/2000/svg"
        xmlns:xlink="http://www.w3.org/1999/xlink">
    <g transform="translate(50,50)">
        <text font-size="36" font-family="sans-serif">
            <tspan x="0" y="0" text-decoration="underline">
            This text is <tspan font-weight="bold" fill="blue">
            underline</tspan>d.</tspan>
```

```
<tspan x="0" y="60" text-decoration="overline">
This text is <tspan font-weight="bold" fill="blue">
overline</tspan>d.</tspan>
<tspan x="0" y="120" text-decoration="overline underline">
This text is <tspan font-weight="bold" fill="blue">
underline</tspan>d &amp; <tspan font-weight="bold" fill="blue">
overline</tspan>d.</tspan>
<tspan x="0" y="180" text-decoration="line-through">
This text is <tspan font-weight="bold" fill="blue">
line-through</tspan>ed.</tspan>
<tspan x="0" y="240" text-decoration="blink">
This text might <tspan font-weight="bold" fill="blue">
blink</tspan>.</tspan>
<tspan x="0" y="300">
  <animate attributeName="visibility"
        attributeType="CSS" values="hidden;visible"
        begin="0s" dur="1s" repeatCount="indefinite"/>
This text will definitely <tspan font-weight="bold" fill="blue">
blink</tspan>.</tspan>
</text>
</g>
</svg>
```

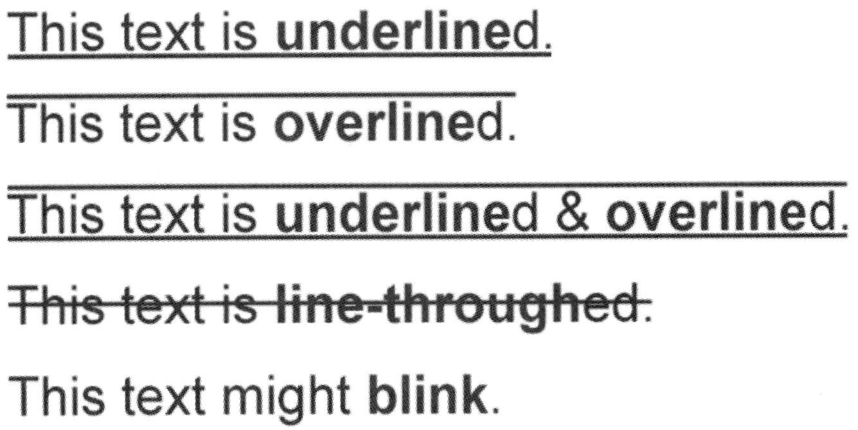

This text is **underlined**.

This text is **overlined**.

This text is **underlined** & **overlined**.

~~This text is **line-through**ed~~.

This text might **blink**.

Figure 6-19. The text-decoration *attribute*

You can apply more than one text-decoration effect at the same time by separating each value in the text-decoration attribute with a space. For instance, text-decoration="overline underline" will feature both overlining and underlining of the relevant text.

And then there is blink. CSS supports blink as an optional property, and in general few vendors of even dynamic SVG support the blink tag directly. This is probably a good thing, actually, but if you absolutely have to have blinking text, you can do so (with far better control) using an animate element. This is shown in the last line of text from Listing 6-21:

```
<tspan x="0" y="300">
        <animate attributeName="visibility" attributeType="CSS"
                values="hidden;visible" begin="0s" dur="1s"
                repeatCount="indefinite"/>
        This text will definitely <tspan font-weight="bold" fill="blue">
        blink</tspan>.</tspan>
</text>
```

You can control the duration of the blinking by setting the dur attribute to the time interval you want the blink to take. For more information about animations, read Chapter 8, "Animating SVG."

Setting Spacing and Kerning Properties

All characters are not created equal. If you place characters such as A and V together, for instance, a visual gutter forms that makes the characters appear farther apart than they actually are. Most fonts run into this problem to a greater or lesser degree, and to solve it, typographers employ *kerning*.

 NOTE *Originally, a* kern *was a thin sliver of lead that fit between lead type in the days when type was set by hand. Similarly, a strip of lead that fit underneath rows of set type was known as a* lead, *or* leader, *which is the reason why the space between lines is known as* leading.

In computer typesetting, the term *kerning* came to apply to the process of adding or subtracting space between characters. Most type definition files (and most especially Type 1 and True-Type fonts) include kerning tables that give, for specific combinations of problem characters, an offset that can be added or subtracted to the characters when they occur in that combination.

SVG implicitly accesses this kerning information; the default for kerning in SVG is "auto," However, applying kerning information is a relatively expensive task, especially given the amount of text information that may be present in an SVG file. You can use the kerning attribute to turn kerning off by setting it to the value "0." Once off, the bounding boxes of each individual character decide character spacing.

You can also use kerning to set an absolute width between each character by setting it to a value besides 0. Listing 6-22 and Figure 6-20 illustrate this, where the distance between the letters A and V is affected by the kerning value.

Listing 6-22. `Kerning.svg`

```
<svg xmlns="http://www.w3.org/2000/svg"
        xmlns:xlink="http://www.w3.org/1999/xlink">
    <g transform="translate(100,100)">
    <text font-size="100">
        <tspan kerning="auto" x="0" y="0" >AV</tspan>
        <tspan kerning="0" x="0" y="100">AV</tspan>
        <tspan kerning="10" x="0" y="200">AV</tspan>
        <tspan kerning="-20" x="0" y="300">AV</tspan>
        <tspan kerning="-38" x="0" y="400">AV</tspan>
    </text>
    <line x1="60" y1="0" x2="60" y2="-100"
            stroke="black" stroke-width="2"/>
    <line x1="66" y1="-100" x2="66" y2="300"
            stroke="black" stroke-width="1"/>
    <line x1="66" y1="0" x2="66" y2="100"
            stroke="black" stroke-width="2"/>
    <line x1="78" y1="100" x2="78" y2="200"
            stroke="black" stroke-width="2"/>
    <line x1="48" y1="200" x2="48" y2="300"
            stroke="black" stroke-width="2"/>
    </g>
    <g transform="translate(250,70)">
        <text font-size="20">
            <tspan x="0" y="0">kerning="auto"</tspan>
            <tspan x="0" y="100">kerning="0"</tspan>
            <tspan x="0" y="200">kerning="10"</tspan>
            <tspan x="0" y="300">kerning="-20"</tspan>
            <tspan x="0" y="400">kerning="-38"</tspan>
        </text>
    </g>
</svg>
```

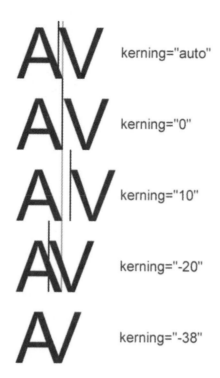

Figure 6-20. Kerning

The letter-spacing attribute provides an automatic space increment or decrement between letters that is independent of the kerning (either as a percentage of the font size or as an absolute length). You can use this to keep the kerning relationships intact while still providing a certain amount of spacing between letters.

Finally, the word-spacing attribute controls the extent of whitespace in the text string by increasing or decreasing the size just of the space character and similar whitespace characters. Note that in general whitespace is not preserved when SVG is rendered, which is a characteristic of Extensible Markup Language (XML), so sometimes increasing the amount of word-spacing in a <text>, <tspan>, or <tref> element is the only way to actually change the intervals between words.

Table 6-4 summarizes the various space attributes.

Table 6-4. Text Spacing Properties

ATTRIBUTE NAME	ATTRIBUTE TYPE	DESCRIPTION
kerning	auto | <length> | inherit	Either invokes the kerning table of the font to position characters of text (the default) or turns kerning off and uses an absolute value. Setting kerning="0" disables it.
letter-spacing	normal | <length> | inherit	Adds or subtracts a specific length from the distance between letters. Cumulative with kerning.
word-spacing	normal | <length> | inherit	Adds or subtracts a specific length from the width of whitespace in a text block.

Putting Text on a Path

Being vector graphics, text glyphs can be oriented in any direction without compromising their integrity. As such, placing text on a path is (relatively) easy with vector graphics. SVG actually simplifies the task even more because the fairly complex process of determining path normals is handled transparently.

The <textPath> element is a child of the <text> element. Its primary purpose is to associate with a selection of text (as either nodes of text, <tspan> elements, or <tref> elements) with a specific previously defined <path> element. Once associated, the text contained within the <textPath> element will be drawn over the path. For instance, Figure 6-21 draws the text expression *Understanding only comes with practice* onto a circle. The path #circlePath approximates the arcs of a circle using Bezier quadratic curves. The <textPath> attribute itself contains an xlink:href element pointing to the path by its id. See Listing 6-23 for the code.

Figure 6-21. Rendering text along a path

Listing 6-23. `PathText.svg`

```
<svg xmlns="http://www.w3.org/2000/svg"
        xmlns:xlink="http://www.w3.org/1999/xlink">
    <defs>
        <path d="M-100,0 C-100,-50 -50,-100 0,-100
                        C50,-100 100,-50 100,0 C100,50 50,100 0,100
                        C-50,100 -100,50 -100,0z"
            stroke="black" id="circlePath"/>
    </defs>
    <g transform="translate(300,200)">
        <circle cx="0" cy="0" r="100" stroke="red"
                    fill="none" stroke-width="5"/>
        <g>
        <text>
            <textPath xlink:href="#circlePath" font-size="34" >
            Understanding only comes with practice.</textPath>
        </text>
        </g>
    </g>
</svg>
```

Table 6-5 gives the `<textPath>` element's attributes.

Table 6-5. `<textPath>` *Attributes*

ATTRIBUTE NAME	ATTRIBUTE TYPE	DESCRIPTION
startOffset	<length> | <percentage>	This gives the starting point of the text on the path as either a specific length along the path or a percentage of the total length along the path.
method	align | stretch	If method is align, then the character glyphs align themselves with the path's tangents, and if it is to stretch, this lets the characters distort to retain ligatures.
spacing	auto | exact	Determines the set of rules to use when calculating the spacing of each character along the path.
xlink:href	uri	References a path element.

The `startOffset` attribute tells where on the path the text begins to render. It relies upon the idea of "unwrapping" the path: determining the length of the path by finding a straight line that most closely approximates a stretched-out version of the path. Thus, for instance, a circular path with a radius of 100 units would have a length of 628 (2π * 100). Specifying an absolute length of 157 ($^{628}/_4$) will begin the text one quarter of the way around the circle (in the example given in Listing 6-23). Similarly, a `startOffset` value of "25%" will position the text at one-fourth of the way around the circle, measured clockwise.

The `method` attribute controls the degree to which glyphs are distorted by the path. When `method` is set to "`align,`" the letters are rendered perpendicular to the path at the anchor point of the glyph but are kept otherwise intact. This can keep the shapes intact, but it has the disadvantage of breaking *ligatures* (the connections that combine letters such as *f* and *i* in certain fonts). On the other hand, setting `method` to "`stretch`" will keep characters connected by distorting the letter proportionally to the angle of difference between normals of the curve.

 NOTE *The* `method` *attribute is an optional property in SVG, and as such is not supported in the Adobe SVG Viewer 3.0 plug-in, as is the case with* `spacing,` *which controls whether spacing is determined along a path by kerning (exact) or by the curvature of the path (auto).*

Finally, as with most `xlink:href` attributes in SVG, the path in question must be local; in other words, you cannot reference a path contained in another file. (This may change in SVG 2.0, however.)

Text in SVG is something of a disappointment. Although you have unparalleled control over kerning, font attributes, and even the ability to move shape along a complex path, SVG by itself does not support word wrapping. You have to explicitly break lines of text. However, in some cases (and with a fair amount of work), you can cause text to break by using a disconnected path. For instance, in Figure 6-22, the path consists of three line segments, one under the other. When you apply a line of text to this path, the text will wrap across lines (see Listing 6-24).

Listing 6-24. `pathText2.svg`

```
<svg xmlns="http://www.w3.org/2000/svg"
       xmlns:xlink="http://www.w3.org/1999/xlink">
    <defs>
        <path d="M0,0 L300,0 M300,0 M0,40 L300,40
                M300,40 M0,80 L300,80 M300,80
                M0,120 L300,120 M300,120" id="rows"/>
    </defs>
```

```
<g transform="translate(300,200)">
    <circle cx="0" cy="0" r="100" stroke="red" fill="none" stroke-width="5"/>
        <g>
        <text>
            <textPath xlink:href="#rows" font-size="33" startOffset="0%">
            Understanding only comes with practice.
            We're trying to learn,of course.</textPath>
        </text>
        </g>
    </g>
</svg>
```

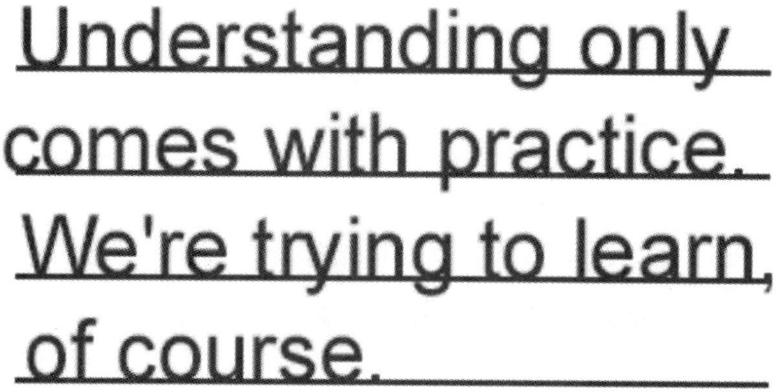

Understanding only comes with practice. We're trying to learn, of course.

Figure 6-22. Disconnecting text paths

Note that this is not true word wrapping. By luck and design, the font size is just such that the words wrap at the word boundaries. In general, it is better to wrap text using `<tspan>` blocks.

NOTE   *One of the features currently on the table for the SVG 2.0 specification is the expansion of the `<text>` element to include a text block. This would support such features as text wrapping and perhaps scrolling.*

Using Text and CSS

As you may have observed, specifying all of the attributes for a given <text> element can prove to be tedious at the best of times. Moreover, generic <text> elements give little indication about what specifically you want to do with the elements, making issues such as modularity that much more difficult to maintain. In an ideal world, it would be preferable to indicate that a given block of text is a headline, graph label, or button without having to define these characteristics explicitly every time.

This sounds like a ready-made solution for CSS, which of course defines many of the properties found in SVG, especially those related to text content. However, you can also use CSS explicitly to create *classes* that can then be assigned on the fly to relevant content. As with HTML, there are three distinct methods that can be used to apply stylistic information on a given node:

- **The style Attribute**: This attribute on most elements can set multiple CSS properties on that element and all its children.

- **The <style> Element**: This element lets you declare styled classes that can then be applied to an element via the class attribute.

- **The xml-stylesheet Processing Instruction**: This processing instruction, listed at the beginning of the SVG document prior to the <svg> element declaration, contains style class information that can be used across multiple documents.

Immediate Styling

In HTML, the style attribute passes various CSS properties to a particular element, though in most cases the same property also applies to any child elements that the original element contains. CSS in SVG works exactly the same way. For instance, consider the text elements shown in Listing 6-25 and Figure 6-23.

Listing 6-25. CSSText1.svg

```
<svg xmlns="http://www.w3.org/2000/svg"
     xmlns:xlink="http://www.w3.org/1999/xlink">
    <g transform="translate(100,100)">
        <text style="font-family:Garamond; font-size:24pt;fill:blue;">
            <tspan x="0" y="0">This is a sample of styled content.</tspan>
            <tspan x="0" y="24" style="fill:red;font-style:italic">
```

```
            <tspan x="0" y="48">This sample has inherited the
                font-family and size,</tspan>
            <tspan x="0" y="72">but overridden the fill attribute
                and added the </tspan>
            <tspan x="0" y="96">font-style attribute.</tspan>
        </tspan>
    </text>
  </g>
</svg>
```

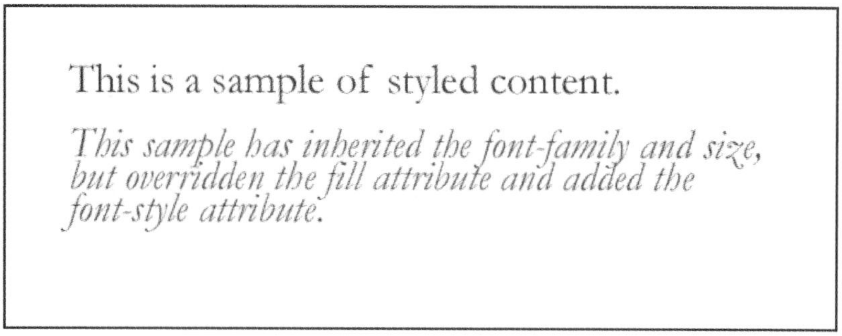

Figure 6-23. Expressing CSS properties inline within the style *attribute*

In this particular case, the CSS properties are assigned not through distinct attributes such as this:

```
<text font-family="Garamond" font-size="24"...
```

but rather through the style attribute, using the "propertyName:propertyValue;" notation:

```
<text style="font-family:Garamond;font-size:24"...
```

These two forms are functionally equivalent, by the way; internally, the SVG parser converts such style attribute properties into their equivalent singleton forms (in other words, style="font-family:Garamond" and font-family="Garamond" are both represented in the SVG DOM as the font-family property acting on a node of type SVGText). Thus, the use of the style attribute may only be of real value in compacting (slightly) the amount of space necessary to encode an expression. In some cases it may be useful from a DOM standpoint to have style information contained in a single container. Similarly, it may also be more useful to have distinct attributes that you can enumerate over, so the use of the style attribute versus explicit enumeration is largely driven by your requirements.

Internal Stylesheets and Classes

The style attribute by itself has fairly limited utility. Although it can make it a little easier to incorporate complex attributes, the benefits accruing from it are outweighed by denser code, limited animation support, and perhaps more importantly from a programming standpoint, no real understanding of why these properties are being set.

The style attribute in CSS is something of a compromise, bowing to the immediate needs of beginning (and unfortunately not so beginning) Web authors who want to make a particular font larger or smaller or ensure that the text is colored green, for example. CSS comes into its own, however, when styles are aggregated into classes.

As demonstrated initially in Chapter 2, "Getting Started: An SVG Tutorial," a CSS class consists of two distinct parts: a set of styles and a label for those styles. In SVG, these styles are collected into a distinct element called the <style> element. Each *rule*, which defines either a class or an element type, in turn consists of a rule name followed by the CSS attributes that define that rule. For instance, Listing 6-26 illustrates how the same content as shown in Listing 6-25 can be shown using CSS class rules.

Listing 6-26. CSSText2.svg

```
<svg xmlns="http://www.w3.org/2000/svg"
     xmlns:xlink="http://www.w3.org/1999/xlink">
    <style type="text/css"><![CDATA[
.mainText {font-family:Garamond; font-size:24pt;fill:blue;}
.subText {fill:red;font-style:italic}
]]>    </style>
    <g transform="translate(100,100)">
        <text class="mainText">
            <tspan x="0" y="0">This is a sample of styled content.</tspan>
            <tspan x="0" y="24" class="subText">
                <tspan x="0" y="48">This sample has inherited the
                        font-family and size,</tspan>
                <tspan x="0" y="72">but overridden the fill attribute
                        and added the </tspan>
                <tspan x="0" y="96">font-style attribute.</tspan>
            </tspan>
        </text>
    </g>
</svg>
```

In this case, the `<style>` element defines three class rules, one that applies to all text elements and two that `mainText` and `subText`:

```
<style type="text/css"><![CDATA[
text {font-family:Garamond; font-size:24;}
.mainText { fill:blue;}
.subText {fill:red;font-style:italic}
]]>    </style>
```

The selector for the rule (which maps a class or element name to a set of CSS properties) is given first, followed by the rule contents within braces ({}). To specify a type of element (such as `<text>` here) across the entire document, you would just make the name of that element the selector:

```
text {font-family:Garamond; font-size:24;}
```

On the other hand, if you wanted to apply a class definition to an element, you would create a class selector starting with a period (.). This is the case with both `mainText` and `subText`:

```
.mainText { fill:blue;}
.subText {fill:red;font-style:italic}
```

Note that more than one class can apply to a given element. For instance, the text class declaration applies to all `<text>` elements, as well as any child elements within that text element. All text unless otherwise explicitly overriding this will be 24-point Garamond. Meanwhile, you can use the `class` attribute to apply a specific named rule to any item with the name of that class as an attribute (or any children of that item):

```
<text class="mainText">
```

Thus, any content within this element will be 24-point Garamond but will also be blue (which is what `.mainText` does).

NOTE *The period (.) prefix of the class rule's name is not included when specifying the class in the* `class` *attribute.*

The subText rule illustrates a few other properties of class-based CSS. The rule sets the fill of any object within the element to which it is applied to red (unless that object has an explicit fill object declared) and sets the font style to italic. Because the <tspan> element that has the subText rule is contained within the text element that has the mainText rule, anything within the <tspan> will inherit the mainText properties save for fill or font-style, which are set by the subText rule. The full subText style basically then would look as follows:

```
font-size:24;font-family:Garamond;fill:red;font-style:italic;
```

 NOTE *Although the examples given in this section revolve primarily around text, it is worth noting that CSS classes (and element name classes) can apply to any object in the SVG tree.*

The <style> attribute type="text/css" is a strict requirement because it is possible, though not generally supported yet, for there to be other transformation engines that work on the document such as XSLT.

There are a number of significant benefits that classes bring to SVG developments. Perhaps one of the most important is the ability to modularize stylistic information, as well as structural content. For instance, Listing 6-27 and Figure 6-24 illustrate how a passage of text could be styled using simple CSS classes.

Listing 6-27. CSSText4.svg

```
<svg xmlns="http://www.w3.org/2000/svg"
        xmlns:xlink="http://www.w3.org/1999/xlink">
    <style type="text/css"><![CDATA[
.chapterNumber {font-family:Arial; font-size:18pt;font-weight:bold}
.chapterTitle {font-family:Arial; font-size:24pt;font-weight:bold}
.bodyText {font-family:Times;font-size:12pt;}
.emph {font-style:italic;}
]]>    </style>
    <defs>
        <text id="chNum" class="chapterNumber" x="0" y="0">
                Chapter 1
        </text>
        <text id="chHead" class="chapterTitle" x="0" y="0">
            Endings and Beginnings
        </text>
        <text id="Body" class="bodyText">
            <tspan x="0" y="0">Wiper blades arced back and forth in a
                fairly indifferent effort</tspan>
```

```
                    <tspan x="0" y="20">at keeping the rain off the windshield
                            of the VW Bug. The headlights </tspan>
                    <tspan x="0" y="40">made almost no difference, save
                            perhaps as feeble warning to other </tspan>
                    <tspan x="0" y="60">drivers that something resembling a
                            car was moving toward them</tspan>
                    <tspan x="0" y="80"> in the cold, inky darkness. Once, the
                            need for the car would have</tspan>
                    <tspan x="0" y="100"> been superfluous, but those days
                            were long gone, Liz thought ruefully</tspan>
                    <tspan x="0" y="120">as she looked in the rear-view
                            mirror.</tspan>
                    <tspan x="20" y="140">Sleep ... a few more nights of
                            that she'd hoped to have, before the end,</tspan>
                    <tspan x="0" y="160">but her time was near. A few
                            of them knew, of course. Dark, somber</tspan>
                    <tspan x="0" y="180">Morgan had come to her, a week
                            before, and they had spent the evening</tspan>
                    <tspan x="0" y="200">getting rip-roaring drunk together.
                            Morgan, her dearest friend,</tspan>
                    <tspan x="0" y="220">her oldest enemy, sitting by her
                            in front of the campfire,</tspan>
                    <tspan x="0" y="240">listening to the musicians singing
                            the real music of Woodstock,</tspan>
                    <tspan x="0" y="260">the music that, in various forms
                            had been sung around campfires</tspan>
                    <tspan x="0" y="280"> since the time Old Nick was a babe.
                            Liz thought that he guessed,</tspan>
                    <tspan x="0" y="300">he'd been there at the concert, a lame
                            old man who left merriment</tspan>
                    <tspan x="0" y="320">and laughter in his wake,
                            but his eyes were shaded even so.</tspan>
                    <tspan x="20" y="340">
                            <tspan class="emph">Yeah. He knew.</tspan>
                    </tspan

            </text>
        </defs>
        <g transform="translate(100,100)">
        <use xlink:href="#chNum" x="0" y="0"/>
        <use xlink:href="#chHead" x="0" y="30"/>
        <use xlink:href="#Body" x="0" y="60"/>

        </g>
    </svg>
```

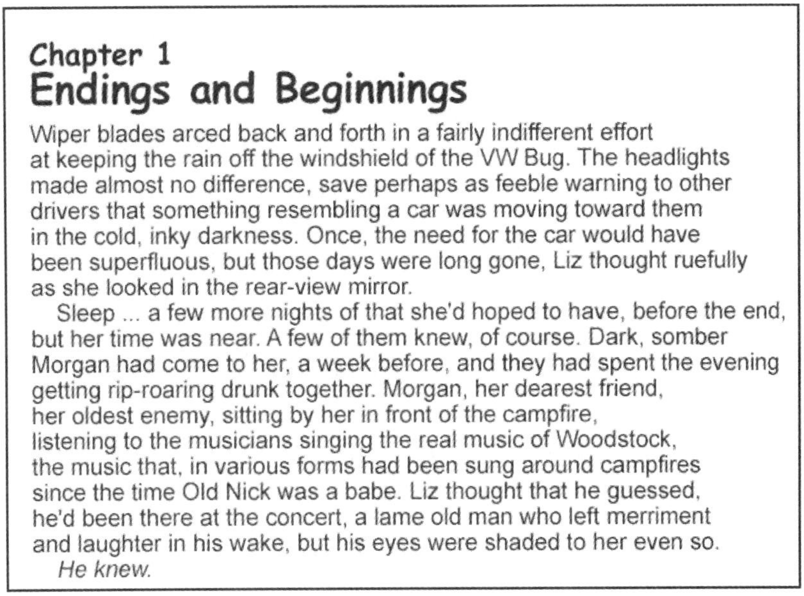

```
Chapter 1
Endings and Beginnings
Wiper blades arced back and forth in a fairly indifferent effort
at keeping the rain off the windshield of the VW Bug. The headlights
made almost no difference, save perhaps as feeble warning to other
drivers that something resembling a car was moving toward them
in the cold, inky darkness. Once, the need for the car would have
been superfluous, but those days were long gone, Liz thought ruefully
as she looked in the rear-view mirror.
      Sleep ... a few more nights of that she'd hoped to have, before the end,
but her time was near. A few of them knew, of course. Dark, somber
Morgan had come to her, a week before, and they had spent the evening
getting rip-roaring drunk together. Morgan, her dearest friend,
her oldest enemy, sitting by her in front of the campfire,
listening to the musicians singing the real music of Woodstock,
the music that, in various forms had been sung around campfires
since the time Old Nick was a babe. Liz thought that he guessed,
he'd been there at the concert, a lame old man who left merriment
and laughter in his wake, but his eyes were shaded to her even so.
      He knew.
```

Figure 6-24. The class *attribute, making the assignment of CSS classes both possible and simple*

In this case, four distinct classes are defined: chapterNumber, chapterTitle, bodyText, and emp. Because these are labeled conceptually rather than stylistically (in other words, "chapterNumber" vs. "mediumBigFont"), you have a little better idea about what the intent of the particular text element is, in addition to having a better ability to abstract out the style characteristics so that they can be changed without altering the content. Listing 6-28 is identical to Listing 6-27 except for the style block. Figure 6-25 shows this difference.

Listing 6-28. CSSText3.svg

```
<svg xmlns="http://www.w3.org/2000/svg
        xmlns:xlink="http://www.w3.org/1999/xlink">
<style type="text/css"><![CDATA[
.chapterNumber {font-family:Arial; font-size:18pt;font-weight:bold}
.chapterTitle {font-family:Arial; font-size:24pt;font-weight:bold}
.bodyText {font-family:Times;font-size:12pt;}
.emph {font-style:italic;}
]]>    </style>
    <style type="text/css"><![CDATA[
.chapterNumber {font-family:ComicSans; font-size:18pt;font-weight:bold}
.chapterTitle {font-family:ComicSans; font-size:24pt;font-weight:bold}
.bodyText {font-family:Arial;font-size:12pt;}
```

```
        .emph {font-style:italic;}
    ]]>    </style>
      <defs>
          <text id="chNum" class="chapterNumber" x="0" y="0">
              Chapter 1
          </text>
          <text id="chHead" class="chapterTitle" x="0" y="0">
              Endings and Beginnings
          </text>
          <text id="Body" class="bodyText">
              <tspan x="0" y="0">Wiper blades arced back and forth in a
                      fairly indifferent effort</tspan>
              <tspan x="0" y="20">at keeping the rain off the windshield
                      of the VW Bug. The headlights </tspan>
              <tspan x="0" y="40">made almost no difference, save
                      perhaps as feeble warning to other </tspan>
              <tspan x="0" y="60">drivers that something resembling a
                      car was moving toward them</tspan>
              <tspan x="0" y="80"> in the cold, inky darkness. Once, the
                      need for the car would have</tspan>
              <tspan x="0" y="100"> been superfluous, but those days
                      were long gone, Liz thought ruefully</tspan>
              <tspan x="0" y="120">as she looked in the rear-view
                      mirror.</tspan>
              <tspan x="20" y="140">Sleep . . . a few more nights of
                      that she'd hoped to have, before the end,</tspan>
              <tspan x="0" y="160">but her time was near. A few
                      of them knew, of course. Dark, somber</tspan>
              <tspan x="0" y="180">Morgan had come to her, a week
                      before, and they had spent the evening</tspan>
              <tspan x="0" y="200">getting rip-roaring drunk together.
                      Morgan, her dearest friend,</tspan>
              <tspan x="0" y="220">her oldest enemy, sitting by her
                      in front of the campfire,</tspan>
              <tspan x="0" y="240">listening to the musicians singing
                      the real music of Woodstock,</tspan>
              <tspan x="0" y="260">the music that, in various forms
                      had been sung around campfires</tspan>
              <tspan x="0" y="280"> since the time Old Nick was a babe.
                      Liz thought that he guessed,</tspan>
              <tspan x="0" y="300">he'd been there at the concert, a lame
                      old man who left merriment</tspan>
              <tspan x="0" y="320">and laughter in his wake,
                      but his eyes were shaded even so.</tspan>
```

```
            <tspan x="20" y="340">
                    <tspan class="emph">Yeah. He knew.</tspan>
            </tspan>
        </text>
    </defs>
    <g transform="translate(100,100)">
    <use xlink:href="#chNum" x="0" y="0"/>
    <use xlink:href="#chHead" x="0" y="30"/>
    <use xlink:href="#Body" x="0" y="60"/>

    </g>
</svg>
```

Chapter 1
Endings and Beginnings

Wiper blades arced back and forth in a fairly indifferent effort
at keeping the rain off the windshield of the VW Bug. The headlights
made almost no difference, save perhaps as feeble warning to other
drivers that something resembling a car was moving toward them
in the cold, inky darkness. Once, the need for the car would have
been superfluous, but those days were long gone, Liz thought ruefully
as she looked in the rear-view mirror.
   Sleep ... a few more nights of that she'd hoped to have, before the end,
but her time was near. A few of them knew, of course. Dark, somber
Morgan had come to her, a week before, and they had spent the evening
getting rip-roaring drunk together. Morgan, her dearest friend,
her oldest enemy, sitting by her in front of the campfire,
listening to the musicians singing the real music of Woodstock,
the music that, in various forms had been sung around campfires
since the time Old Nick was a babe. Liz thought that he guessed,
he'd been there at the concert, a lame old man who left merriment
and laughter in his wake, but his eyes were shaded to her even so.
   He knew.

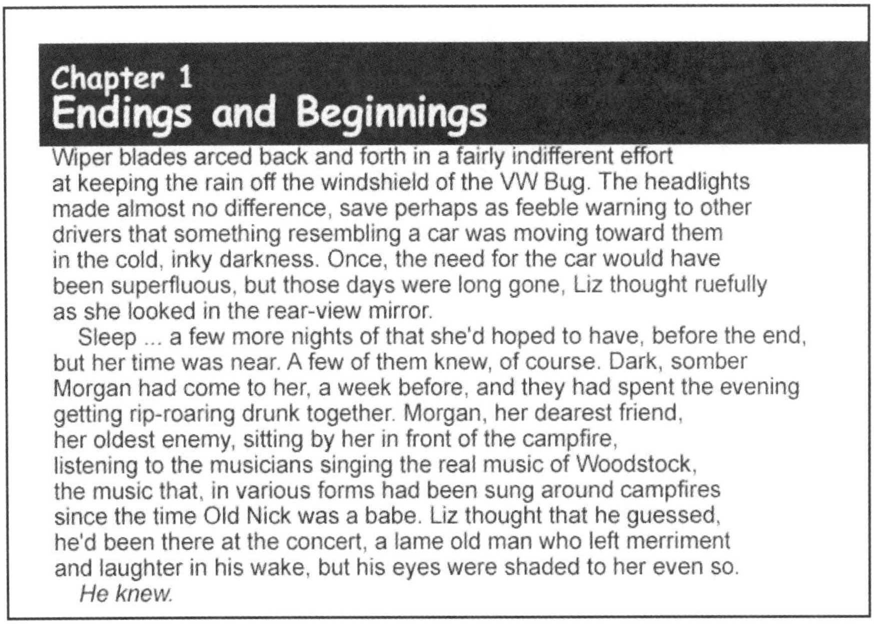

Figure 6-25. Changing large portions of an SVG document's presentation

NOTE   *With CSS, if you have rules with the same name
defined within an SVG or other source document, the last rule
with that name so defined becomes the active one. You can
see this in the previous example, where all four CSS rules are
actually listed twice, with the second rules overwriting the
effects of the first.*

What Cannot Be Changed via CSS

In some respects, CSS is less powerful in SVG than it is in HTML, especially in the area of setting coordinates and lengths. Put simply, SVG CSS does not support setting the x, y, rx, ry, cx, cy, r, width, or height attributes. There are some sound reasons for the World Wide Web Consortium (W3C) doing this with the specification (though there are also a few questionable reasons for doing it as well), most important being that the characteristics of width, height, and so on are crucial to the structural nature of the SVG document, and being able to control this from CSS weakens the SVG model considerably.

Unfortunately, one area where this does have an impact is modularity. It would be nice to define a shape's characteristics within a CSS <style> element or external CSS library (such as the dimensions of a leader line), but at least with SVG 1.0 that is simply not possible. As a consequence, when you are defining your CSS, you should always work from the assumption that you can only change the paint or font characteristics—fill, stroke, opacity, the various text attributes, and so on.

External Stylesheets

Internal stylesheets provide modularity at the document level, making it possible to define stylistic information that applies to all elements or to specific classes within those elements. However, an SVG document is much like a single HTML Web page: It does not usually exist in isolation. Instead, SVG documents usually tend to share common thematic and stylistic elements; a series of charts and graphs, for instance, may all share the same font family, type sizes, and font decorations (bold, italic, underline, and so on), as well as color conventions on bar or line charts.

Rather than redefining a <style> block for each graphic in such a case, it is usually preferable to create a single external stylesheet to which each graphic can then refer. You can use this technique to good effect with Web sites that use the HTML <link> attribute to associated CSS stylesheets with HTML documents. SVG does not have a similar <link> attribute (the underlying linking model is different), but it can employ a processing instruction to bind a CSS document with a page.

HTML, XML, and SVG use the <?xml-stylesheet?> processing instruction to *bind* (or associate) a particular stylesheet to a document. When the document is loaded into memory, the stylesheet is then loaded and acts as a filter for painting the final output. It should generally appear before the first element in the SVG document, though it may appear after the <?xml?> declaration that defines the XML model and encoding used.

For instance, in Listing 6-29, the graphic is associated with a stylesheet called
CSSText5.css through this processing instruction:

```
<?xml-stylesheet type="text/css" href="CSSText5.css"?>
```

Listing 6-29. CSSText5.svg

```
<?xml-stylesheet type="text/css" href="CSSText5.css"?>
<!-- Text from Midnight Rain, by Kurt Cagle -->
<svg xmlns="http://www.w3.org/2000/svg"
    xmlns:xlink="http://www.w3.org/1999/xlink">
    <defs>
        <linearGradient id="blueGrad" gradientTransform="rotate(90)">
            <stop offset="0%" stop-color="blue"/>
            <stop offset="100%" stop-color="navy"/>
        </linearGradient>
        <text id="chNum" class="chapterNumber"
              x="0" y="0">Chapter 1</text>
        <text id="chHead" class="chapterTitle"
              x="0" y="0">Endings and Beginnings</text>
        <text id="Body" class="bodyText">
            <tspan x="0" y="0">Wiper blades arced back and forth in a
                    fairly indifferent effort</tspan>
            <tspan x="0" y="20">at keeping the rain off the windshield
                    of the VW Bug. The headlights </tspan>
            <tspan x="0" y="40">made almost no difference, save
                    perhaps as feeble warning to other </tspan>
            <tspan x="0" y="60">drivers that something resembling a
                    car was moving toward them</tspan>
            <tspan x="0" y="80"> in the cold, inky darkness. Once, the
                    need for the car would have</tspan>
            <tspan x="0" y="100"> been superfluous, but those days
                    were long gone, Liz thought ruefully</tspan>
            <tspan x="0" y="120">as she looked in the rear-view
                    mirror.</tspan>
            <tspan x="20" y="140">Sleep . . . a few more nights of
                    that she'd hoped to have, before the end,</tspan>
            <tspan x="0" y="160">but her time was near. A few
                    of them knew, of course. Dark, somber</tspan>
            <tspan x="0" y="180">Morgan had come to her, a week
                    before, and they had spent the evening</tspan>
            <tspan x="0" y="200">getting rip-roaring drunk together.
                    Morgan, her dearest friend,</tspan>
```

```
                <tspan x="0" y="220">her oldest enemy, sitting by her
                        in front of the campfire,</tspan>
                <tspan x="0" y="240">listening to the musicians singing
                        the real music of Woodstock,</tspan>
                <tspan x="0" y="260">the music that, in various forms
                        had been sung around campfires</tspan>
                <tspan x="0" y="280"> since the time Old Nick was a babe.
                        Liz thought that he guessed,</tspan>
                <tspan x="0" y="300">he'd been there at the concert, a lame
                        old man who left merriment</tspan>
                <tspan x="0" y="320">and laughter in his wake,
                        but his eyes were shaded even so.</tspan>
                <tspan x="20" y="340">
                            <tspan class="emph">Yeah. He knew.</tspan>
                </tspan>
            </text>
            <rect id="backgroundBlock" width="100%" height="80"
                        x="-10" y="-35" class="chapterHeadBack"/>
        </defs>
        <g transform="translate(100,100)">
        <use xlink:href="#backgroundBlock" x="0" y="0"/>
        <use xlink:href="#chNum" x="0" y="0"/>
        <use xlink:href="#chHead" x="0" y="30"/>
        <use xlink:href="#Body" x="0" y="60"/>
        </g>
</svg>
```

When combined, the two create the output shown in Figure 6-26.

The stylesheet that this document is associated with, `CSSText5.css`, is essentially the same as the content of the `<style>` block, without the `<style>` tags around it. It is worth emphasizing here that the CSS document is not based in XML:

Listing 6-30. `CSSText5.css`

```
.chapterHeadBack {fill:url(#blueGrad)}
.chapterNumber {font-family:ComicSans;
        font-size:18pt;font-weight:bold;fill:white;}
.chapterTitle {font-family:ComicSans;
        font-size:24pt;font-weight:bold;fill:white;}
.bodyText {font-family:Arial;font-size:12pt;}
.emph {font-style:italic;}
```

Chapter 1
Endings and Beginnings

Wiper blades arced back and forth in a fairly indifferent effort at keeping the rain off the windshield of the VW Bug. The headlights made almost no difference, save perhaps as feeble warning to other drivers that something resembling a car was moving toward them in the cold, inky darkness. Once, the need for the car would have been superfluous, but those days were long gone, Liz thought ruefully as she looked in the rear-view mirror.

Sleep ... a few more nights of that she'd hoped to have, before the end, but her time was near. A few of them knew, of course. Dark, somber Morgan had come to her, a week before, and they had spent the evening getting rip-roaring drunk together. Morgan, her dearest friend, her oldest enemy, sitting by her in front of the campfire, listening to the musicians singing the real music of Woodstock, the music that, in various forms had been sung around campfires since the time Old Nick was a babe. Liz thought that he guessed, he'd been there at the concert, a lame old man who left merriment and laughter in his wake, but his eyes were shaded to her even so.

He knew.

Figure 6-26. External stylesheets

There is a bit of legerdemain in the first line of the CSS script. You can use CSS to apply such things as gradient and pattern fills to objects, provided that these fills or patterns are defined within the original SVG document. For instance, in the Listing 6-29 document, the gradient `#blueGrad` was defined. The line `.chapterHeadBack` in the CSS document then references this fill via a URL:

```
.chapterHeadBack {fill:url(#blueGrad)}
```

TIP *Currently, you cannot reference external SVG documents in this manner, so this ability has only limited utility. However, you can use the* `LoadExternalLibrary` *function defined in Chapter 10, "SVG Components," to load in external SVG content into the SVG document, which will then inherit the CSS and let you apply standard defined gradients, patterns, masks, and other fills in that manner.*

Classes and Interactivity (Advanced Topic)

Classes offer a number of advantages in creating static SVG documents, but they can also be used with a little bit of DOM to make dynamic interactions easier to create. For instance, consider the task of creating a button with three states: a normal (default) state, a highlighted state during a hover, and a pressed state when the mouse is clicked over the button. By using CSS, you can change multiple properties simultaneously in a coordinated fashion.

SVG by itself does not support the animation of CSS through the declarative language, but that does not mean it cannot be done. What you have to do is rely upon the fact that within SVG, the class attribute is just that, an *attribute*. By changing the underlying XML model upon which the SVG is built, you can switch the attribute itself on the fly, as shown in Listing 6-31 and Figure 6-27.

Listing 6-31. CSSClassButton1.svg

```
<svg xmlns="http://www.w3.org/2000/svg"
        xmlns:xlink="http://www.w3.org/1999/xlink">
    <style type="text/css">
.CSSButtonNormal {fill:red;stroke:black;stroke-width:2;}
.CSSButtonHighlight {fill:yellow;stroke:black;stroke-width:2;}
.CSSButtonDepressed {fill:maroon;stroke:black;stroke-width:2;
        stroke-dasharray:5 5;}
</style>
    <script language="JavaScript">
function setClass(evt,className){
    var item=evt.target;
    item.setAttribute("class",className);
    }
    </script>
    <defs>
        <rect id="buttonBase" width="120" height="30" rx="5" ry="5"/>
    </defs>
    <g>
        <use xlink:href="#buttonBase" x="100" y="100"
        id="Button1" class="CSSButtonNormal"
        onmouseover="setClass(evt,'CSSButtonHighlight')"
        onmousedown="setClass(evt,'CSSButtonDepressed')"
        onmouseup="setClass(evt,'CSSButtonHighlight')"
        onmouseout="setClass(evt,'CSSButtonNormal')"/>
    </g>
</svg>
```

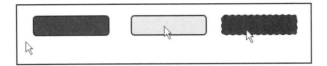

Figure 6-27. Controlling the `class` *attribute through the DOM*

When certain events occur (such as `onmouseover`, `onmouseout`, and so on), the routine invokes `setClass()`, passing into it an event identifier (the evt parameter) that contains information about what object called the event, what event was called, and other relevant information, and the `className` parameter to set the class to a new value.

The function itself is extremely straightforward:

```
<script language="JavaScript">
function setClass(evt,className){
    var item=evt.target;
    item.setAttribute("class",className);
    }
    </script>
```

The item being clicked on or rolled over can be retrieved from the event through the `target` property. Once this is retrieved, you can set the `class` attribute to the class name that you want to describe that element. This technique also works with external documents. CSS is pervasive in SVG and can play a significant role in both simplifying and modularizing text and graphical code. Unfortunately, space prohibits demonstrating some of the more sophisticated applications of CSS, such as the use of aural CSS to create SVG documents that have a literary component to them, but it is definitely a venue for exploration.

TIP *By the way, SVG mirrors HTML in the ability to pass more than one class name to the class attribute. For instance, if you had one class that set colors (for example, *`.warning`* sets the color to red) and another class that set font information (for example, *`.header`* sets the format of the block to 36-point Helvetica Bold), then you could pass both classes into *`setClass()`* by including a space between them:* `setClass("warning header")`.

Summary

A picture may be worth a thousand words, but what happens when the words become a part of the picture? You can anchor text in SVG to different points to support buttons or oddly aligned text, you can reference text to simplify code and ensure modularity, and you can style text with everything from bold and italic styles to strike-throughs, gradient fills, and (unfortunately) blinking. Finally, you can even coax that text so it flows along a complex path. Yet SVG is not terribly friendly for blocks of text, which often make up the bulk of all text used in SVG.

In addition to talking about text, I cheated here. I gave a couple examples of gradients, color flows that can be assigned to text, and other graphics. In Chapter 7, "Incorporating Texture," I review the whole issue of gradients, patterns, masks, and other related concepts, and after that, turn the static world dynamic with the power of SVG animation in Chapter 8, "Animating SVG."

CHAPTER 7

Incorporating Texture

VECTOR GRAPHICS HAVE A NUMBER of advantages over bitmapped graphics: You can encode complex information in a compact notation, you can specify subelements of graphics as their own distinct entities, and you can even change the characteristics of these elements on the fly. However, creating vector graphics (whether by using drawing programs, by writing the files by hand, or by generating them on the fly) takes considerably longer to do effectively than taking a photograph, dropping it onto a scanner, and pulling it up in your favorite graphics program.

What's more, what Scalable Vector Graphics (SVG)—or any other graphics protocol—does not give you is *texture*. Texture can be difficult to define in absolute terms, but from a graphics standpoint it is that quality that gives the illusion of a surface. Texture is difficult to create in a compelling fashion with SVG because texture has a random quality to it that is tricky to emulate with flat or graded colors by themselves. Even vector patterns (discussed in this chapter) are a little too regular to build a convincing model of reality.

Thus, for all of the advantages that vector graphics offer, there are times where you need to incorporate bitmaps. Fortunately, SVG incorporates the ability to work with bitmap images in a number of different capacities, both as discrete elements and as patterns for more complex elements. Moreover, SVG has the ability to create clipping zones that can shape a texture into a certain shape, and it also supports transparency levels with both Graphics Interchange Format (GIF) and Portable Network Graphics format (PNG) formats. This combination gives you the ability to create rich graphics that combine the best of both worlds.

The term *texture* here is fairly broad and open-ended. You can think of texture generally as those characteristics that cannot be established using basic colors or vector graphics alone. As such, this chapter looks at a number of texture generators: bitmap images, alpha channels, clip paths, and filters.

Getting Image Conscious

To add an image to an SVG document, you need to define an <image> element, a tag that incorporates a bitmap onto a specific graphic viewport for display. The syntax for using an image is easy and mirrors that of the <use> element:

```
<image xlink:href="targetImageFile" x="x-pos"  y="y-pos" width="width"/>
```

For instance, the following SVG loads in a file called mermaid1.jpg, drawing it to a dimension of 450 × 250 at a position of (100,50) and draws a background black fill that is slightly larger than the graphic itself to illustrate its position, as shown in Figure 7-1:

```
<svg xmlns="http://www.w3.org/2000/svg"
        xmlns:xlink="http://www.w3.org/1999/xlink">
    <g>
        <rect x="99" y="49" width="252" height="452" fill="black"/>
        <image xlink:href="SweaterMer3.png"
            width="250" height="450" x="100" y="50"/>
    </g>
</svg>
```

Figure 7-1. Incorporating an image into SVG

You can think of the surface on which the image is painted as being a piece of stretch rubber—the width and height of the image rendered may be different from the actual dimensions of the graphic. For instance, in Figure 7-1, the initial image is actually slightly more than twice the specified size (589x989) and is in fact scaled down to fit in the specified rectangle. You can see this more explicitly in the following code, where the scale is shifted so that the width and height are shown as 250×125 and 75×300 to illustrate the more extreme differences in the images (see Figure 7-2):

```
<svg xmlns="http://www.w3.org/2000/svg"
          xmlns:xlink="http://www.w3.org/1999/xlink">
    <g>
        <rect x="99" y="49"
                width="252" height="452" fill="black"/>
        <image xlink:href="mermaid1.jpg"
                width="250" height="450" x="100" y="50"/>
        <image xlink:href="mermaid1.jpg"
                width="250" height="125" x="400" y="50"/>
        <image xlink:href="mermaid1.jpg"
                width="75" height="300" x="400" y="200"/>
    </g>
</svg>
```

Figure 7-2. Changing the height and width coordinates and therefore the aspect ratio

Unlike HTML, the image does not automatically default to its stored size in SVG. If you fail to include both a height and a width, these values default to 0, making such images effectively invisible. This means that if you want the images to display proportionately, you must know the image's initial dimensions.

On a different note, scaling an image to a different dimension than its default can be an expensive option if the image is meant to animate (moving around, for instance). Part of the reason for this is that once the image is downloaded, it needs to be scaled to the appropriate size (a fairly complex operation). Additionally, large files take a while to download in the first place, although once loaded, the operation to draw images is not dependent upon the initial loading.

Moreover, the algorithms that SVG engine uses to scale the image are proprietary to the SVG processor, not specified within the SVG recommendation. Because of this, one processor may anti-alias the images, and another may not. Aliasing is an artifact of scaling bitmaps—especially when scaling larger. When doing this, the scaling algorithms by themselves usually create noticeable stair effects where contrasting border elements are located in the original. Anti-aliasing smooths these out by interpolating colors from around the transition into the final, but anti-aliasing is a expensive operation, especially in animations, as shown in the eye in Figure 7-3.

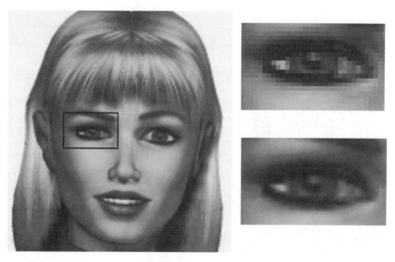

Figure 7-3. The distinctive stair pattern of aliasing

TIP *With the Adobe SVG Viewer, when you right-click a SVG file, the pop-up menu will include a Higher Quality option. When clicked, anti-aliasing is automatically applied to all images, but it is turned off when the image is unchecked.*

For all of these reasons, it is generally good practice in preparing source images for use with SVG to make them the same dimensions as the final displayed images (this is easiest when using pixels as coordinates, but of course becomes almost impossible when other units are used instead, unless you define the images ahead of time).

Working with Translucent Images

Translucent images are images that have *alpha channels*. An alpha channel is a measure of opacity and in fact can be treated as if it was a separate distinct color channel along with red, green, and blue. An alpha channel thus internally provides one or more bits that indicate whether a given pixel is completely opaque, completely transparent, or some value in between.

Certain graphics formats support alpha channels in one form or another. For instance, the venerable GIF, from at least 1987, has had the ability to incorporate a 1-bit alpha channel mask. Such a mask is fairly crude—if the bit is on for a given pixel, that pixel is rendered to the viewing surface. If the bit is off, it is not. The application that renders the GIF (such as a browser) will look at this bit to determine whether to paint each pixel against the background, as shown in Figure 7-4.

Figure 7-4. 1-bit alpha mask

On the other hand, certain formats such as the Tagged Image File Format (TIFF) or the PNG provide an 8-bit alpha channel. This means that each pixel within the image can have associated with it 256 possible shades of transparency, from fully opaque through translucent to completely transparent, as shown in Figure 7-5. The *masks* that these create make for considerably finer effects, not least of which being that a PNG document contains its own anti-aliasing information, which significantly minimizes the problems that GIF images have when displayed on a background with a different color from which it was generated.

Figure 7-5. An 8-bit alpha mask

SVG supports both 1-bit and 8-bit alpha channels with PNG and GIF images (though not with TIFF images). This means that the rendering engine that SVG uses will automatically take into account the alpha channel information when rendering an image, making it possible to combine transparent GIF or PNG images with vector graphics (or with other PNG or GIF images). This holds true regardless of whether these images are static or animated, by the way, which means you can use SVG to create a shell for moving even animated bitmaps around. Chapter 8, "Animating SVG," and Chapter 9, "Integrating SVG and HTML," discuss this in much greater detail.

You do not need to do anything special with a graphic that has an alpha channel to display it in SVG. For instance, the code to display a mermaid at various points in the sea (a blue gradient background) looks identical regardless of whether the image has an alpha channel or not, as is shown in Listing 7-1 and Figure 7-6.

Listing 7-1. Incorporating Both Bitmap and Vector Graphics

```
<svg xmlns="http://www.w3.org/2000/svg"
          xmlns:xlink="http://www.w3.org/1999/xlink">
    <defs>
        <linearGradient gradientTransform="rotate(90)" id="sea">
            <stop offset="0%" stop-color="lightBlue"/>
            <stop offset="100%" stop-color="navy"/>
        </linearGradient>
        <linearGradient gradientTransform="rotate(90)" id="ground">
            <stop offset="0%" stop-color="black" stop-opacity=".10"/>
            <stop offset="25%" stop-color="orangew" stop-opacity=".35"/>
        </linearGradient>
        <radialGradient gradientTransform="translate(0.04,-0.05)"
                id="bubbleGrad">
            <stop offset="0%" stop-color="white"
                      stop-opacity="0.10"/>
            <stop offset="100%" stop-color="white"
                      stop-opacity="0.35"/>
        </radialGradient>
        <g id="deepBlueSea">
            <rect fill="url(#sea)" x="0" y="0"
                      width="100%" height="100%"/>
            <rect fill="url(#ground)" x="0" y="75%"
                      width="100%" height="100%"/>
        </g>
        <svg id="bubble" width="20" y="20" viewBox="0 0 20 20">
            <circle fill="url(#bubbleGrad)" cx="0" cy="0" r="10"
                      transform="translate(10,10)" />
        </svg>
        <text x="82" y="222" font-size="72"
                font-family="Centaur" id="seaText">
                The Deep Blue Sea
        </text>

    </defs>
```

```
<g>
    <use xlink:href="#deepBlueSea" x="0" y="0"/>
    <use xlink:href="#bubble" x="360" y="50"
            width="16" height="16"/>
    <use xlink:href="#bubble" x="500" y="80"
            width="20" height="20"/>
    <image xlink:href="tshirtMer.png"
            width="400" height="400" x="190" y="65"
            opacity="1" fill="url(#sea)"/>
    <rect fill="url(#sea)" x="0" y="0"
            width="100%" height="100%" opacity="0.3"/>
    <use xlink:href="#bubble" x="380" y="140"
            width="24" height="24"/>
    <use xlink:href="#bubble" x="40" y="160"
            width="30" height="30"/>
    <image xlink:href="mermaid1.png"
            width="250" height="500" x="100" y="0"/>
    <use xlink:href="#seaText" fill="url(#sea)"
            x="0" y="0" stroke="black" stroke-width="1"/>
</g>
</svg>
```

Figure 7-6. Combining 8-bit images with both SVG overlays and underlays

The code in Listing 7-1 incorporates both alpha channel transparency and SVG opacity. Indeed, the right mermaid in the image is in a partially translucent blue rectangle to give the illusion of being farther away from the viewer than the left mermaid. Similarly, one of the fairly translucent bubbles sits in front of the farther mermaid's hair, again given a sense of depth.

NOTE   *The* <image> *element does support the SVG opacity attribute, but it only affects the global opacity of the image, not the opacity of any alpha channel masks that are implicit to the image file. There is no way for SVG to control the alpha channel directly.*

CAUTION   *As with opacity with vector graphics, opacity in bitmaps requires additional preprocessing. Consequently, bitmaps with alpha channels will render more slowly in both static and animated SVG.*

Referencing Images

One of the more potent abilities that images offer is the ability to create linked definitions of images, then utilize these referenced images in more than one place in a document. This principle is already well established for defining SVG graphics, but the same mechanism—the <use> element—can also reference bitmap images as well. For instance, you can rewrite Listing 7-1 to work via reference by defining the respective <image> elements in a <defs> block, then invoking the image via a <use> statement, as shown in Listing 7-2.

Listing 7-2. Referencing Images

```
<svg xmlns="http://www.w3.org/2000/svg"
          xmlns:xlink="http://www.w3.org/1999/xlink">
    <defs>
        <linearGradient gradientTransform="rotate(90)" id="sea">
            <stop offset="0%" stop-color="lightBlue"/>
            <stop offset="100%" stop-color="navy"/>
        </linearGradient>
        <linearGradient gradientTransform="rotate(90)" id="ground">
            <stop offset="0%" stop-color="black" stop-opacity=".10"/>
            <stop offset="25%" stop-color="orangew"
```

```
                  stop-opacity=".35"/>
    </linearGradient>
    <radialGradient gradientTransform="translate(0.04,-0.05)"
                  id="bubbleGrad">
        <stop offset="0%" stop-color="white"
                  stop-opacity="0.10"/>
        <stop offset="100%" stop-color="white"
                  stop-opacity="0.35"/>
    </radialGradient>
    <g id="deepBlueSea">
        <rect fill="url(#sea)" x="0" y="0"
                  width="100%" height="100%"/>
        <rect fill="url(#ground)" x="0" y="75%"
                  width="100%" height="100%"/>
    </g>
    <svg id="bubble" width="20" y="20" viewBox="0 0 20 20">
        <circle fill="url(#bubbleGrad)" cx="0" cy="0" r="10"
                  transform="translate(10,10)" />
    </svg>
    <text x="82" y="222" font-size="72" font-family="Centaur"
            id="seaText">The Deep Blue Sea</text>
    <image xlink:href="tshirtMer.png"
            width="400" height="400" x="0" y="0"
            opacity="1" fill="url(#sea)" id="tshirtmer"/>
    <image xlink:href="mermaid1.png"
            width="250" height="500" x="0" y="0"
            id="sweaterMer"/>
    <rect fill="url(#sea)" x="0" y="0"
            width="100%" height="100%" opacity="0.3"
            id="translucentSea"/>
</defs>
<g>
    <use xlink:href="#deepBlueSea" x="0" y="0"/>
    <use xlink:href="#bubble" x="360" y="50"
            width="16" height="16"/>
    <use xlink:href="#bubble" x="500" y="80"
            width="20" height="20"/>
    <use xlink:href="#tshirtmer" x="190" y="65"/>
    <use xlink:href="#translucentSea" x="0" y="0"/>
    <use xlink:href="#bubble" x="380" y="140"
            width="24" height="24"/>
    <use xlink:href="#bubble" x="40" y="160"
            width="30" height="30"/>
```

```
        <use xlink:href="#sweaterMer" x="100" y="0"/>
        <use xlink:href="#seaText" fill="url(#sea)"
                x="0" y="0" stroke="black" stroke-width="1"/>
    </g>
</svg>
```

In this case, the images are given the id attributes of #tshirtmer and #sweaterMer, respectively. Notice again one immediate consequence of working with references: seemingly without much effort, the whole viewable structure has been transformed into a collection of labeled <use> elements, and it also has the additional effect of simplifying the interfaces. By working via reference, you can use the same set of attributes (the same properties) for positioning, opacity, fill, and more, without having to worry about whether the element is an ellipse, an image, a shape, and so on.

NOTE *Although the context is perhaps a little different than in a language such as Java or C++, this example illustrates the principle of polymorphism in a declarative language. In essence, using references, you can get the advantages of detailed characteristics such as the radius or circle center position while at the same time being able to use more generalized code (such as the* x *or* width *properties). This has some implications for creating static graphics, but it really becomes important when dealing with SVG programmatically, as discussed in Chapter 9, "Integrating SVG and HTML," and Chapter 10, "SVG Components."*

Grouping Referenced Bitmaps

In addition to referencing single bitmaps, you can also group bitmaps together to create distinct functional units. For instance, suppose you have an application with a face where the eyes blink. Although the intricacies of setting up the animation to blink will be covered in the next section, the basic structure is essentially just a collection of bitmaps, as shown in Figure 7-7.

Figure 7-7. Grouping multiple <image> elements into a distinct unit

The code for doing this is straightforward, as illustrated in Listing 7-3.

Listing 7-3. Compositing Bitmaps

```
<svg xmlns="http://www.w3.org/2000/svg" xmlns:xlink="http://www.w3.org/1999/xlink">
    <defs>
        <svg id="faceEyesOpen" width="500" height="500" viewBox="0 0 500 500">
            <image xlink:href="MermaidFaceEyesOpen.png" x="0" y="0"
                width="500" height="500" id="faceEyesOpen"/>
        </svg>
        <svg id="faceEyesClosed" width="500" height="500" viewBox="0 0 500 500">
            <use xlink:href="#faceEyesOpen" x="0" y="0"
                width="500" height="500"/>
            <image xlink:href="EyeBlinkRight.jpg" x="180" y="180"
                width="80" height="50" id="rightEyeClosed"/>
            <image xlink:href="EyeBlinkLeft.jpg" x="280" y="180"
                width="80" height="50" id="leftEyeClosed"/>
        </svg>
```

```
                    <svg id="faceEyesWink" width="500" height="500" viewBox="0 0 500 500">
                        <use xlink:href="#faceEyesOpen" x="0" y="0"/>
                        <use xlink:href="#leftEyeClosed" x="0" y="0"/>
                    </svg>
            </defs>
            <g>
                    <text x="50" y="50" font-size="30">Using Grouped Images</text>
                    <use xlink:href="#faceEyesOpen" x="0" y="100"
                            width="250" height="250"/>
                    <use xlink:href="#faceEyesClosed" x="250" y="100"
                            width="250" height="250"/>
                    <use xlink:href="#faceEyesWink" x="500" y="100"
                            width="250" height="250"/>
            </g>
    </svg>
```

There are three states of the face here: one where the eyes are open (the default state), one where they are closed, and a wink where the left eye is closed (left relative to the actor, not the viewer). The #faceEyesOpen graphic constitutes the whole face, and if you had to download all three as separate graphics, it would require downloading three 500×500 pixel PNG files, an activity sure to slow down the deployment of your presentation.

In this particular case, the closed states of the left and right eye are loaded separately (these are each only 80×50 pixel JPG files, making them *much* smaller). Note how positional information is retained by the <use> element. For instance, the first time that the closed left eye is loaded (via the <image> tag with id of "rightEyeClosed"), its position is set to x="280", y="180", relative to the encompassing <svg> element:

```
<image xlink:href="EyeBlinkLeft.jpg" x="280" y="180" width="80" height="50"
    id="leftEyeClosed"/>
```

When this graphic is invoked via the <use> tag, however, the x and y positions are both set to a value of "0"—yet the graphic still positions itself correctly:

```
<use xlink:href="#leftEyeClosed" x="0" y="0"/>
```

The reason for this is that the graphic is initially positioned relative to the viewport it is in. When it is later referenced, the <use> element utilizes the offset position implicitly so that the x and y values give the position where the context starts, not just where the graphic begins. For instance, if the <use> statement had been the following:

```
<use xlink:href="#leftEyeClosed" x="100" y="50"/>
```

then the graphic would start at a position of (100+280,50+180) or (380,130)—relative to the local context—probably not the place that you would have expected.

TIP   *For this reason, if you have composite images, it is best to set the positions of all graphics relative to some (0,0) point, then use the <use> command to set the actual position of the composite on the page.*

Referencing SVG as Images

In addition to referencing bitmaps, the <image> tag can also be used to reference other SVG images. This is not as impressive as it sounds—basically what ends up happening with such referenced SVG (at least with the current Adobe SVG renderer) is that the SVG images are first converted into bitmaps that are then applied in exactly the same manner as a PNG image. For instance, if you had an SVG file called titlebar.svg, you could include it into another SVG document using the xlink:href attribute, just as you would with any other graphic format:

```
<image xlink:href="titlebar.svg" width="100%" height="100%"/>
```

This is useful if you want to build static SVG graphics, but currently the image that is loaded has no real intelligence; you cannot deal with elements that have id attributes defined in the included SVG. Moreover, if your SVG graphics are animated, this will only catch a snapshot of the graphic prior to any animations taking place.

It is possible that, when SVG 2.0 actually becomes a reality, this will change. One capability that SVG currently lacks is the ability to create libraries of interactive elements from external resources, but the inclusion of this ability is really critical for the true scalability of SVG on the Internet.

Using Masking

Okay, I have to make a confession. There are some aspects of SVG that are so cool that it is difficult not to want to jump to them immediately. Bitmap masks have this coolness factor (filters, which duplicate some of the same effects, are even more spectacular, but you will have to wait until Chapter 11, "The Future of SVG," to get to them).

The <mask> element is a container like elements <g> or <svg> that automatically converts its contents into a grayscale image of a specific height and width. This mask defines an alpha channel that can be applied to other objects, and has the attributes defined in Table 7-1.

Table 7-1. <mask> *Attributes*

ATTRIBUTE NAME	ATTRIBUTE TYPE	DESCRIPTION
x	SVGLength	The horizontal coordinate of the upper-left point of the rectangle in the appropriate coordinate system. This can be negative.
y	SVGLength	The vertical coordinate of the upper-left point of the rectangle. This can be negative.
width	SVGLength	The width of the rectangle. This must be non-negative.
height	SVGLength	The height of the rectangle. This must be non-negative.
id	ID	An identifier for the element. Note that you can have more than one element with the same ID, but that they are referenced as an array in that case.
maskUnits	userSpaceOnUse | objectBoundingBox	Indicates whether the coordinates given for the mask are those of the calling element or the pattern itself.
maskContentUnits	userSpaceOnUse | objectBoundingBox	Indicates whether the coordinates that the internal elements used in the pattern are those of the calling element or the mask itself.

A mask lets you create alpha channels on the fly. This is not an intuitive concept, especially if you have not done a lot of video postproduction work, but it is very powerful nonetheless. In essence, a mask lets you define a grayscale image using either bitmaps or SVG constructs, then use that as a mask to determine the percentage opacity that a fill applies over the size of the mask.

Confused? Perhaps the best example is to consider a drop shadow. Many of the mermaid (and related) figures you will see in this and other chapters of this book were generated in Curious Lab's superb figure modeler, Poser 4. One useful feature that it has is the ability to generate TIFF images with alpha channels for the portion of the graphic that is not specifically rendered (the background, typically). Most 3D graphic applications have similar capabilities, making them very useful for generating graphics for use with SVG.

Using an application such as Adobe Photoshop, you can actually extract the alpha channel mask very easily from a graphic that has one generated for it (usually TIFF formats). To create a drop shadow mask in Photoshop, follow these steps:

1. Open Adobe Photoshop and then open the graphic to which you want to apply a drop shadow (see Figure 7-8). It helps to have a graphic with a flat background that can be uniquely separated (such as white for a darker image).

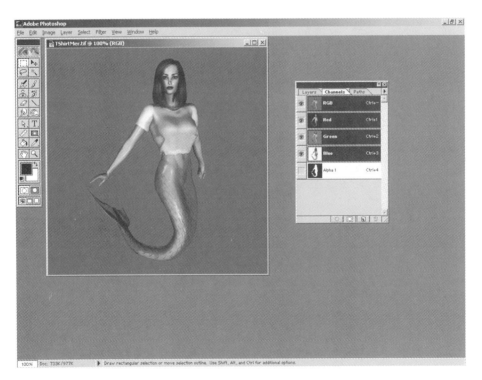

Figure 7-8. Loading the matted image into Photoshop

2. Select the background with the wand tool. Choose Select ➢ Invert, then choose Select ➢ Save Selection to save a new channel. Call this channel **Alpha**. Switch to the Channels palette to see the new channel (usually in position 4), as shown in Figure 7-9.

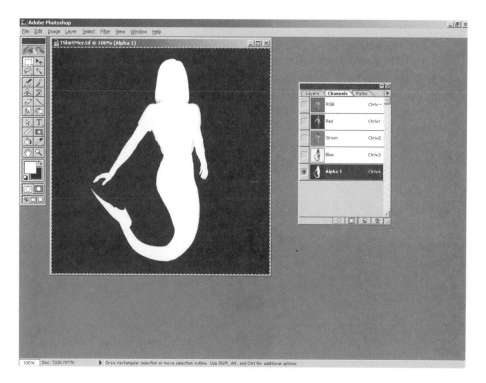

Figure 7-9. The alpha channel

3. From the Select menu, choose All (or press Ctrl+A) to select the graphic, then choose Edit ➢ Copy (or press Ctrl+C) to copy it to the clipboard.

4. Select File ➤ New to open a new window, which should automatically be set to the size of the graphic, and Paste (Edit ➤ Paste or Ctrl+V) the alpha channel into the new window (see Figure 7-10). Switch from the Channel to the Layer palette, and flatten the image using the palette's drop-down menu.

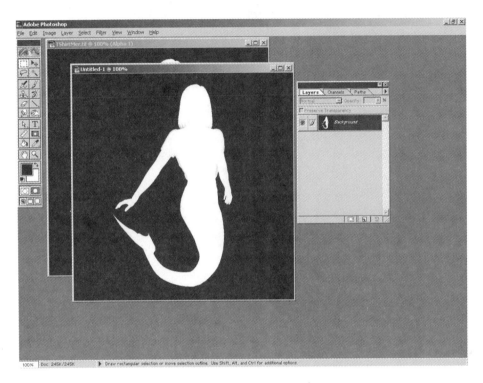

Figure 7-10. Isolate the alpha channel as a separate document

5. Choose Filter ➤ Gaussian Blur and set it so that the image blurs to the degree you want (usually between 5 and 10 is good), as shown in Figure 7-11.

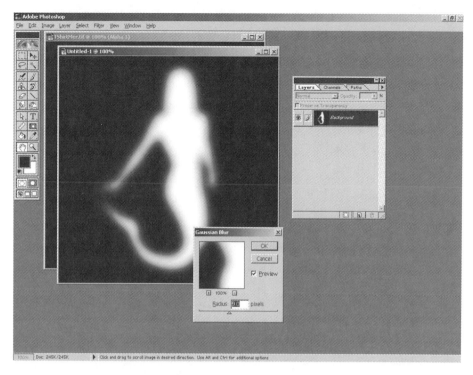

Figure 7-11. The alpha channel blurred

6. Save the new image as a JPEG file under a different name (such as `tshirtmermaid_blur.jpg`). Close the new graphic.

7. With the original graphic, set the channel back to RGB and save the original image as a PNG as well (`tshirtmermaid.png`). Close Photoshop.

You have just created both the original image and an associated drop-shadow alpha mask. Note that the PNG image still retains its initial alpha channel, which will mask the graphic proper.

For the image defined in the example, a mask can be built that creates a blurred drop shadow, as shown in Figure 7-12.

Figure 7-12. The final result of the process

Listing 7-4, which actually generates the file shown in Figure 7-12, shows the role of <mask>:

Listing 7-4. A Drop Shadow

```
<svg xmlns="http://www.w3.org/2000/svg"
xmlns:xlink="http://www.w3.org/1999/xlink">
    <defs>
        <linearGradient gradientTransform="rotate(90)" id="sea">
            <stop offset="0%" stop-color="lightBlue"/>
            <stop offset="100%" stop-color="navy"/>
        </linearGradient>
        <image x="0" y="0" width="500" height="500"
            xlink:href="tshirtMer.png" id="tshirtMer"/>
        <mask id="mermaidShadow" maskUnits="userSpaceOnUse"
            x="0" y="0" width="500" height="500">
            <image x="6" y="6" width="500" height="500"
                xlink:href="tshirtMermaid_Mask.jpg"/>
        </mask>
```

```
                <rect x="0" y="0" width="500" height="500" fill="black"
                        mask="url(#mermaidShadow)" id="shadow"/>
        </defs>
        <g>
                <text x="50" y="50" font-size="30">Drop Shadows</text>
                <use xlink:href="#shadow" x="0" y="50"/>
                <use xlink:href="#shadow" x="300" y="50"/>
                <use xlink:href="#tshirtMer" x="300" y="50"/>
        </g>
</svg>
```

The <mask> element #mermaidShadow loads in the tshirtMermaid_mask.jpg image (Listing 7-4), offsetting it six pixels to the right and down relative to the original image. This will make the drop shadow appear as if the light source is above and to the left of the graphic.

The alpha channel is applied to a rectangular element with an id of #shadow that both has a fill attribute of black and a mask attribute of "url(#mermaidShadow)", referring back to the mask just defined. The fill gives the actual color to be used as the base color for each pixel, with the mask's intensity at that pixel used to determine how much of that color is used compared to the background. Because the fill is black, it gives the illusion of a black drop shadow.

The maskUnits and maskContentUnits attributes set the scale that the mask and the elements within it use. The maskUnits attribute sets the way that the width, height, x, and y attributes of the <mask> element are interpreted and can take on either the values "userSpaceOnUse" or "objectBoundingBox". The first value, "userSpaceOnUse", indicates that the coordinates these qualities use should use the same system as the object that uses the mask.

For instance, in the previous sample, the mask element was given as this:

```
<mask id="mermaidShadow" maskUnits="userSpaceOnUse"
                x="0" y="0" width="500" height="500">
```

When the #mermaidShadow is invoked by the <rect> element, like so:

```
<rect x="0" y="0" width="500" height="500" fill="black"
                mask="url(#mermaidShadow)" id="shadow"/>
```

the maskUnits="userSpaceOnUse" indicates that the width, height, x, and y of the mask are given to the same scale as the rect—(in this case the default scale of pixels). Thus, a width of 500 units in the mask is treated as the same as a width of 500 units in the calling rectangle.

In many cases, however, you will not know (or want to know) the actual dimensions of the object being masked. In this particular case, you can set the maskUnits attribute to "objectBoundingBox". When this value is set, the width, height, x, and y coordinates are defined as being on the unit square (in other words, values going from 0.0 to 1.0), which is then scaled internally. This way, you can essentially set the mask to fit whatever element you want without worrying about dimensions:

```
<mask id="mermaidShadow" maskUnits="objectBoundingBox"
                x="0" y="0" width="1.0" height="1.0">
```

The maskContentUnits attribute works in a similar manner, but instead of affecting the coordinates of the <mask> elements, it affects the coordinates of the internal elements. Thus, with a value of userSpaceOnUse, the maskContentUnits attribute uses the internal coordinate system of the calling element:

```
<mask id="mermaidShadow" maskUnits="userSpaceOnUse" x="0" y="0"
                width="500" height="500"
                maskContentUnits="userSpaceOnUse">
    <image x="6" y="6" width="500" height="500"
                xlink:href="tshirtMermaid_Mask.jpg"/>
</mask>
```

But if you use objectBoundingBox, you would need to map to the unit square:

```
<mask id="mermaidShadow" maskUnits="userSpaceOnUse"
                x="0" y="0" width="500" height="500"
                maskContentUnits="objectBoundingBox">
    <image x="0.012" y="0.012" width="1" height="1"
                xlink:href="tshirtMermaid_Mask.jpg"/>
</mask>
```

where 0.012 in this case comes from 6/500.

It is worth noting that the drop shadow will be transparent if the alpha channel at a specific point on the graphic is a shade of gray. This means that the drop shadow will darken a background, but not set its color to black absolutely. You can see this a little more clearly in Listing 7-5, which shows the effects of both a drop shadow and a glow against an imported background image (see Figure 7-13).

Listing 7-5. Blurred Masks

```
<svg xmlns="http://www.w3.org/2000/svg"
       xmlns:xlink="http://www.w3.org/1999/xlink">
   <defs>
       <linearGradient gradientTransform="rotate(90)" id="sea">
          <stop offset="0%" stop-color="lightBlue"/>
          <stop offset="100%" stop-color="navy"/>
       </linearGradient>
       <image x="0" y="0" width="500" height="500"
              xlink:href="tshirtMer.png" id="tshirtMer"/>
       <mask id="mermaidShadow" maskUnits="userSpaceOnUse"
              x="0" y="0" width="500" height="500">
          <image x="6" y="6" width="500" height="500"
              xlink:href="tshirtMermaid_Mask.jpg" id="tshirtMerMask"/>
       </mask>
       <mask id="mermaidGlow" maskUnits="userSpaceOnUse"
              x="0" y="0" width="500" height="500">
          <image x="0" y="0" width="500" height="500"
              xlink:href="tshirtMermaid_Mask.jpg"
              id="tshirtMerMask"/>
       </mask>
       <rect x="0" y="0" width="500" height="500" fill="black"
              mask="url(#mermaidShadow)" id="shadow"/>
       <rect x="0" y="0" width="500" height="500" fill="yellow"
              mask="url(#mermaidGlow)" id="glow"/>
       <image xlink:href="pattern.jpg" x="0" y="0"
              width="100%" height="100%" id="background"/>
   </defs>
   <g>
       <use xlink:href="#background" x="0" y="0"/>
       <text x="50" y="50" font-size="30">Shadows and Glows</text>
       <use xlink:href="#shadow" x="0" y="50"/>
       <use xlink:href="#tshirtMer" x="0" y="50"/>
       <use xlink:href="#glow" x="300" y="50"/>
       <use xlink:href="#tshirtMer" x="300" y="50"/>
   </g>
</svg>
```

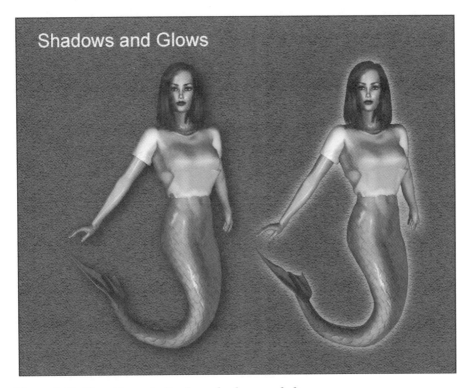

Figure 7-13. Blurred masks for drop shadows and glows

This also hints at other potential uses for masks. For instance, you could apply a masked texture to an image directly to make it look like the image is on canvas or brick, as shown in Listing 7-6 (see Figure 7-14).

Listing 7-6. Masking the Image

```
<svg xmlns="http://www.w3.org/2000/svg"
            xmlns:xlink="http://www.w3.org/1999/xlink">
    <defs>
        <mask id="texture" maskUnits="userSpaceOnUse"
            x="0" y="0" width="1024" height="768">
            <image xlink:href="patternBright.jpg"
                x="0" y="0" width="1024" height="768" id="background"/>
        </mask>
        <image x="0" y="0" width="500" height="500"
            xlink:href="tshirtMer.png" id="tshirtMer"/>
    </defs>
    <g>
        <text x="50" y="50" font-size="30">Applying Texture To An Image</text>
        <use xlink:href="#tshirtMer" x="0" y="50"/>
```

```
            <use xlink:href="#tshirtMer" x="300" y="50"
                    mask="url(#texture)"/>
            <rect width="600" height="50" x="100" y="530"
                    fill="black"/>
            <rect width="600" height="50" x="100" y="530"
                    fill="white" mask="url(#texture)"/>
      </g>
</svg>
```

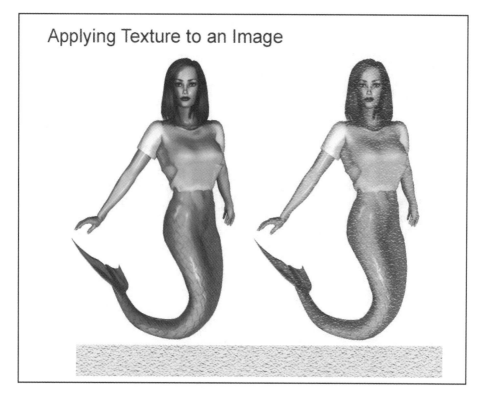

Figure 7-14. Compositing masked images

In this particular case, the texture shown at the bottom of Figure 7-14 is nearly white, with the exception of some gray elements that cut the opacity down somewhat at those points. The effect this has is to make the image partially transparent at those points, giving a canvas or concrete like effect to the whole.

Using Text Masks

From textures to text, one obvious application of masks comes from their use to create text masks, which permit images to appear within the confines of the text. The trick to doing this effectively is to understand that the text in fact acts as a mask. Because the mask intensity is proportional to the lightness of the image, it means the text should be white against a black background (the text would then be 100-percent opaque, the background 100-percent transparent). The code is shown in Listing 7-7, and Figure 7-15 illustrates this.

Listing 7-7. TextMask.svg

```
<svg xmlns="http://www.w3.org/2000/svg"
        xmlns:xlink="http://www.w3.org/1999/xlink">
    <defs>
        <mask id="texture" maskUnits="userSpaceOnUse"
                x="0" y="0" width="1024" height="768">
            <rect x="0" y="0" width="1024" height="768" fill="black"/>
            <text x="50" y="300" font-size="300" fill="white"
                font-family="Impact">SVG!</text>
        </mask>
    </defs>
    <g>
        <text x="50" y="50" font-size="30">
                Applying Images to Text
        </text>
        <image xlink:href="desktop.jpg" x="0" y="0"
                width="100%" height="100%" mask="url(#texture)"/>
    </g>
    <g>
        <rect x="25" y="320" width="400" height="200" fill="black"/>
        <text x="50" y="470" font-size="150" fill="white"
                font-family="Impact">SVG!</text>
    </g>
</svg>
```

Figure 7-15. Creating a text mask

The mask is then applied to the image in question. This technique works best when the image being displayed completely covers the extent of the text because otherwise the boundaries of the image will also show up in the text, something that is generally not desirable.

You will be revisiting masks frequently throughout the rest of this book because masks make it possible to build a number of special effect interfaces: drop shadows, glows, irregular *skins*, text filters and so forth. Using masks is actually one of three distinct techniques where you can combine text (or other graphics) and bitmaps. In the next section, I focus on the other two: patterned fills and clip paths.

Creating Patterns

If images represent one aspect of creating textures, then patterns represent another. A *pattern* in SVG parlance is a repeated graphic, whether drawn using SVG primitives or made up of image elements. Perhaps the easiest way to think of a pattern is to harken back to the background attribute in HTML. The background element tiles the background of a Web page, repeating the same rectangular element both left to right and top to bottom. An SVG pattern, similarly, will provide a tile pattern that can be used to fill any SVG shape element—a rectangle, circle, ellipse, path, or polygon. The `<pattern>` element syntax is similar to that of the mask, with attributes given in Table 7-2.

Table 7-2. `<pattern>` Attributes

ATTRIBUTE NAME	ATTRIBUTE TYPE	DESCRIPTION
x	SVGLength	The horizontal coordinate of the upper-left point of the rectangle in the appropriate coordinate system. This can be negative.
y	SVGLength	The vertical coordinate of the upper-left point of the rectangle. This can be negative.
width	SVGLength	The width of the rectangle. This must be non-negative.
height	SVGLength	The height of the rectangle. This must be non-negative.
id	ID	An identifier for the element. Note that you can have more than one element with the same ID, but that they are referenced as an array in that case.
patternUnits	userSpaceOnUse | objectBoundingBox	Indicates whether the coordinates given for the pattern are those of the calling element or the pattern itself.
patternContentUnits	userSpaceOnUse | objectBoundingBox	Indicates whether the coordinates that the internal elements used in the pattern are those of the calling element or the pattern itself.
xlink:href	Local URL	This is the address of a different pattern defined within the SVG document. This is used to make inheritance of patterns possible.

A very basic pattern works in a manner similar to a mask: An image is built up of SVG commands, bitmap <image> elements, text, and so forth that constitutes the pattern to be used. The <pattern> element defines the dimensions of the pattern, which will in turn be the width and height of each of the tiles when the pattern is used. Unlike a mask, however, a pattern is treated as a fill by SVG and consequently is called from the fill attribute just as a gradient would be (see Listing 7-8 and Figure 7-16).

Listing 7-8. Pattern1.svg

```
<svg xmlns="http://www.w3.org/2000/svg"
      xmlns:xlink="http://www.w3.org/1999/xlink">
    <defs>
        <pattern id="imagePattern" width="150" height="150"
                    patternUnits="userSpaceOnUse">
            <rect fill="blue" x="0" y="0" width="150" height="150"/>
            <image xlink:href="tshirtmer.png" x="0" y="0"
                    width="125" height="125"/>
        </pattern>
        <text fill="url(#imagePattern)" x="0" y="150"
                font-size="150" font-family="Impact" id="SVGText">
                SVG!
        </text>
    </defs>
    <rect fill="url(#imagePattern)" width="600" height="400" x="0" y="0"/>
    <use xlink:href="#SVGText" x="100" y="400"/>
</svg>
```

Figure 7-16. Creating a basic pattern from an image

The following <pattern> element given defines a pattern consisting of a blue filled rectangle (150×150 pixels in dimension) on which is placed the shape tshirtmer.png from the previous section, scaled down to fit within the dimensions:

```
<pattern id="imagePattern" width="150" height="150"
            patternUnits="userSpaceOnUse">
    <rect fill="blue" x="0" y="0" width="150" height="150"/>
    <image xlink:href="tshirtmer.png" x="0" y="0"
            width="125" height="125"/>
</pattern>
```

This element is assigned an id of #imagePattern, which is invoked both by another rectangle and by a text element. The effect of this is to fill both the shape and the text with the pattern, which is a mermaid swimming on a blue field. The pattern repeats itself every 150 pixels, which is, not coincidentally, both the width and height of the <pattern> element.

The `patternUnits` and `patternContentUnits` attributes serve the same function for patterns that the `maskUnits` and `maskContentUnits` serve for masks. If `patternUnits` has a value of `"userSpaceOnUse"`, then the coordinates of the `<pattern>` elements are those of the patterned object, and if it is set to `"objectBoundingBox"`, then the value is mapped to the unit square. (See the "Building Bitmap Masks" section later in this chapter for more information.)

One interesting consequence of this is that you can use the `patternUnits` attribute to fill a shape with a bitmap, as is shown in Listing 7-9 and Figure 7-17. Both `patternUnits` and `patternContentUnits` are set to `"objectBoundingBox"`, with width and height having a value of 1.0. This means that the pattern will scale itself to automatically fit to the dimensions of the bounding rectangle of the shape or text.

Listing 7-9. `Pattern2.svg`

```
<svg xmlns="http://www.w3.org/2000/svg"
        xmlns:xlink="http://www.w3.org/1999/xlink">
    <defs>
        <pattern id="imagePattern" width="1" height="1"
                patternUnits="objectBoundingBox"
                patternContentUnits="objectBoundingBox">
            <image xlink:href="tshirtmer.png" x="0" y="0" width="1" height="1"/>
        </pattern>
    </defs>
    <g>
    <text x="50" y="50" font-size="30">Using Bounding Box Patterns</text>
    <rect fill="url(#imagePattern)" width="300" height="300"
                x="10" y="100"
                stroke="black"/>
    <text fill="url(#imagePattern)" font-size="250"
                font-family="Impact" id="SVGText"
                stroke="black" x="310" y="310">SVG!</text>
    </g>
</svg>
```

Figure 7-17. Working with `patternUnits` *and* `patternContentUnits`

You can see the differences between `patternContentUnits` and `patternUnits` by varying the width and height of the `<pattern>` and its contained `<image>`, respectively. For instance, by setting the width and height of the pattern element to 0.5, you make the pattern repeat twice in each direction, as shown in Figure 7-18, but with the image itself still set to 1, only a quarter (half in each dimension) of the mermaid is visible. On the other hand, if you set the width and height of the enclosed image element, as shown in Figure 7-19, then you reduce the size of the image, but the bounding box of the `<pattern>` is still scaled to the size of the container. It is only when you set both to 0.5, shown in Figure 7-20, that you can increase the frequency *and* decrease the size of the pattern. Listing 7-10 shows the code.

Figure 7-18. `patternContentUnits` *with half-width and half-height*

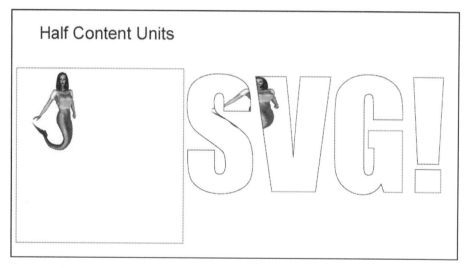

Figure 7-19. `patternUnits` *with half-width and half-height*

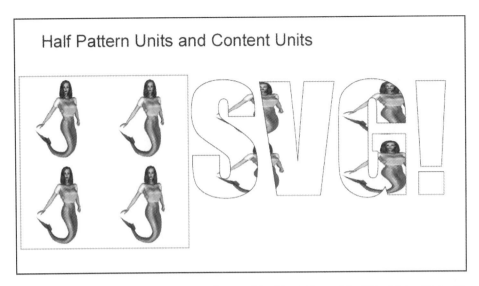

Figure 7-20. Both `patternContentUnits` *and half-width and half-height with half-width and half-height*

Listing 7-10. Doubling the Frequency and Halving the Pattern Size

```
<svg xmlns="http://www.w3.org/2000/svg"
       xmlns:xlink="http://www.w3.org/1999/xlink">
    <defs>
        <pattern id="imagePattern" width="0.5" height="0.5"
                patternUnits="objectBoundingBox"
                patternContentUnits="objectBoundingBox">
            <image xlink:href="tshirtmer.png" x="0" y="0"
                width="0.5" height="0.5"/>
        </pattern>
    </defs>
    <g>
    <text x="50" y="50" font-size="30">Half Pattern Units and Content Units</text>
    <rect fill="url(#imagePattern)" width="300" height="300"
                x="10" y="100" stroke="black"/>
    <text fill="url(#imagePattern)" font-size="250"
                font-family="Impact" id="SVGText"
                stroke="black" x="310" y="310">SVG!</text>
    </g>
</svg>
```

The xlink:href element makes it possible for one pattern to inherit a second pattern as a background. Figure 7-21 illustrates this, where the pattern.jpg texture (called #texture) creates a background for the mermaid figure in the #imagePattern pattern (see Listing 7-11).

Figure 7-21. The pattern xlink:href *attribute*

Listing 7-11. The xlink:href *Attribute*

```
<svg xmlns="http://www.w3.org/2000/svg"
        xmlns:xlink="http://www.w3.org/1999/xlink">
    <defs>
        <pattern id="texturePattern" width="1" height="1"
                patternUnits="objectBoundingBox"
                patternContentUnits="objectBoundingBox">
            <image xlink:href="pattern.jpg" x="0" y="0"
                width="1" height="1" id="texture"/>
        </pattern>
        <pattern id="imagePattern" width="0.5" height="0.5"
                patternUnits="objectBoundingBox"
                patternContentUnits="objectBoundingBox"
                xlink:href="#texture">
            <image xlink:href="tshirtmer.png" x="0" y="0"
                width="0.5" height="0.5"/>
        </pattern>
    </defs>
```

```
    <g>
    <text x="50" y="50" font-size="30">Half Pattern Units and Content Units</text>
    <rect fill="url(#imagePattern)" width="300" height="300"
                    x="10" y="100" stroke="black"/>
    <text fill="url(#imagePattern)" font-size="250"
                    font-family="Impact" id="SVGText"
                    stroke="black" x="310" y="310">SVG!</text>
    </g>
</svg>
```

CAUTION   *The Adobe SVG Viewer 3.0 does not currently properly support the inheritance of patterns. This is not a major limitation, however, as you can create an element in the* <defs> *section that duplicates the inherited pattern and reference it via a* <use> *element in the pattern that would otherwise inherit. Inheritance of patterns is thus fairly superfluous.*

Creating a Clipping Region

The distinction between creating a clipping region and creating a mask is pretty subtle, especially when you are dealing with static SVG. A mask creates an alpha channel, using the opacities of the elements within the <mask> element to determine the overall opacity of the alpha channel. A clip path, on the other hand, uses the boundaries of the objects within the <clipPath> element to determine what is painted to the screen. In other words, you can think of a clip path as a mask that can only have an opacity of 0 or 1 (not counting any edge anti-aliasing that may take place).

This may seem like a fairly useless element—after all, if you were going to define a clip path, why not just create a mask where all elements had opacities of 1? The answer to this question is that the primary purpose of a clip path is not to make an element transparent or opaque, but rather to determine whether a given element is within or outside a specific boundary. Scripts and Synchronized Multimedia Integration Language (SMIL) animation use this information to determine whether a mouse click, for instance, was within or outside of the relevant graphic.

TIP *Perhaps one of the best ways of visualizing a clip path is to think about the* <shape> *element in HTML, which creates an irregularly shaped boundary for a client-side image map. If you click within the boundary, then the browser will jump to the indicated URL. On the other hand, clicking outside of the boundary will do nothing.*

The <clipPath> element serves as a container for a clip path and has a structure similar to both a mask and pattern (see Table 7-3).

Table 7-3. Clip Path Attributes

ATTRIBUTE NAME	ATTRIBUTE TYPE	DESCRIPTION
x	SVGLength	The horizontal coordinate of the upper-left point of the rectangle in the appropriate coordinate system. This can be negative.
y	SVGLength	The vertical coordinate of the upper-left point of the rectangle. This can be negative.
width	SVGLength	The width of the rectangle. This must be non-negative.
height	SVGLength	The height of the rectangle. This must be non-negative.
id	ID	An identifier for the element. Note that you can have more than one element with the same ID, but that they are referenced as an array in that case.
clipPathUnits	userSpaceOnUse | objectBoundingBox	Indicates whether the coordinates given for the clip path are those of the calling element or the clip path itself.

For instance, consider a simple clip path that encloses an image (the mermaid) against a blue circle in a diamond, as is shown in Listing 7-12 and Figure 7-22.

Listing 7-12. `ClipPath1.svg`

```
<svg xmlns="http://www.w3.org/2000/svg"
        xmlns:xlink="http://www.w3.org/1999/xlink">
    <g>
        <clipPath id="MyClip" clipPathUnits="userSpaceOnUse">
        <path d="m0,150 l150,-150 l150,150 l-150,150 l-150,-150z"
                id="diamond"/>
        </clipPath>
    <g transform="translate(50,50)">
        <g transform="translate(0,0)">
            <circle cx="150" cy="150" r="120" fill="blue"/>
            <image xlink:href="tshirtmer.png" x="0" y="0"
                width="300" height="300"/>
            <use xlink:href="#diamond" stroke="black" fill="none"/>
        </g>
        <g clip-path="url(#MyClip)" onclick="alert('This is a test.')"
                transform="translate(300,0)">
            <circle cx="150" cy="150" r="120" fill="blue"/>
            <image xlink:href="tshirtmer.png" x="0" y="0"
                width="300" height="300"/>
        </g>
    </g>
    </g>
</svg>
```

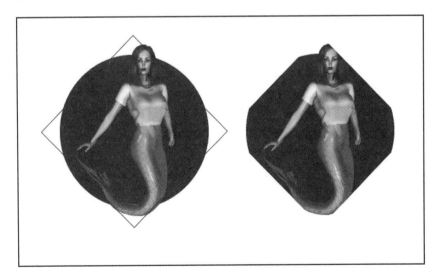

Figure 7-22. A basic clip path

The clip path definition includes a path object, but it should be noted that a path and a clip path have absolutely nothing to do with one another. The first describes the boundary of a shape, and the second describes the boundary of a clipping region. This sample would have worked just as well with a rectangle rotated 45 degrees to create a diamond.

The clip-path attribute is applied to any shape or context (<g>) element. When the element is rendered, only those portions of the elements that are within the boundaries of the clip path are displayed. In the example of Listing 7-11, the path clips everything within the <g> element, including both the circle and the mermaid image.

You can see the real power of the clip path with the use of the onclick attribute. Chapter 9, "Integrating SVG and HTML," will cover interactivity in greater detail, but this particular case illustrates the principle of what a clip path really does. When you click within the diamond in the right image of Figure 7-22, a message saying *This is a test* will be displayed. Anything outside of the diamond, even if it is in the associated bounding rectangle around the shape, will be ignored. In essence, the clip path indicates to the SVG environment that the only thing of interest lies within the boundary of the clip path.

Clip paths do not necessarily have to be just outer boundaries. You can actually create a clip path consisting of a shape with multiple "holes." For instance, in Listing 7-13 and Figure 7-23, the path object defines a diamond with a smaller diamond-shaped hole inside.

Listing 7-13. ClipPath2.svg

```
<svg xmlns="http://www.w3.org/2000/svg"
        xmlns:xlink="http://www.w3.org/1999/xlink">
    <g clip-rule="evenodd">
        <clipPath id="MyClip" clipPathUnits="objectBoundingBox">
        <path d="m0,.50 l.50,-.50 l.50,.50 l-.50,.50 l-.50,-.50z
                m0.4,0 l0.1,-0.1 l0.1,0.1 l-0.1,0.1 l-0.1,-0.1z"/>
        </clipPath>
    <g clip-path="url(#MyClip)" onclick="alert('This is a test.')">
        <circle cx="150" cy="150" r="120" fill="blue"/>
        <image xlink:href="tshirtmer.png" x="0" y="0"
                width="300" height="300"/>
    </g>
</svg>
```

Figure 7-23. An internal clip path

The trick in creating this path is to understand the principle of *winding*. One of the trickier aspects of working with irregular computer graphics is defining what exactly is meant by the word *within*. This in fact is one of the underlying questions that defines a key branch of mathematics called *topology*, so the intuitive concept is, like so many intuitive concepts, remarkably complex when viewed in depth.

The concept of winding involves understanding that vector graphics are, by definition, directed. You start at a certain point, move along a curve until you reach the end, which for closed paths could also be seen as the starting point. You can define the direction as having one of two states: It is either clockwise (+1) or counterclockwise (–1). Unfortunately, even *clockwise* and *counterclockwise* are a little hard to define, and mathematically they have to do with the direction of the cross-product vector of the direction of the tangent to the curve at the starting point and the direction of the radius of curvature at that same point. That is probably a little gorier than most people want out of a graphics book, however, so suffice it to say that in most cases, clockwise and counterclockwise actually act the way you would expect them to act.

The rules for determining whether a point within two contiguous curves can then come down to adding up the windings for each curve of which the point is a part. For instance, in the example in Listing 7-12, any point inside the outer diamond but outside the inner diamond has a winding of (+1) because the curve at that point is clockwise. On the other hand, the inner diamond also runs clockwise, so it too has an internal winding of +1. This means that for a point inside the inner diamond, the winding number is actually the winding of the outer diamond plus the winding of the inner diamond, or +2.

NOTE *This all makes the assumption that, relative to where the* clip-rule *attribute is defined, the space outside of the initial curve has a winding number of zero.*

SVG supports two distinct winding rules. The first rule, the *evenodd* rule, states that if the total winding number for a point is odd, then the point is considered to be a part of the area of the curve, and if the winding number is even, then the point is outside that curve and is consequently not rendered. This is the condition as shown in Listing 7-13, where the clip-rule attribute for the context that contains the clip path has been set to the value "evenodd".

However, another winding rule is a little more liberal. This rule—named, not surprisingly, the *nonzero* rule—says that if the total winding number is nonzero, then the point is considered a part of the curve, regardless of whether the winding number is positive or negative. Listing 7-14 and Figure 7-24 show where the clip-rule has been set to "nonzero".

Listing 7-14. ClipPath.svg

```
<svg xmlns="http://www.w3.org/2000/svg"
       xmlns:xlink="http://www.w3.org/1999/xlink">
    <g clip-rule="nonzero">
        <clipPath id="MyClip" clipPathUnits="objectBoundingBox">
        <path d="m0,.50 l.50,-.50 l.50,.50 l-.50,.50 l-.50,-.50z
                        m0.4,0 l0.1,-0.1 l0.1,0.1 l-0.1,0.1 l-0.1,-0.1z"/>
        </clipPath>
    </g>
    <g clip-path="url(#MyClip)" onclick="alert('This is a test.')">
        <circle cx="150" cy="150" r="120" fill="blue"/>
        <image xlink:href="tshirtmer.png" x="0" y="0" width="300" height="300" />
    </g>
</svg>
```

Figure 7-24. A nonzero clip rule fills interior curves

The nonzero and even-odd rules also work when you have paths that run both clockwise and counterclockwise. For instance, in Figure 7-25, the inner diamond has been drawn in reverse order to the outer diamond, so that it runs counterclockwise (–1) to the clockwise direction (+1) of the outer diamond. In Listing 7-15, the `clip-rule` attribute is set to nonzero, and the first path (terminated by the first z path command) runs in the opposite direction as the remaining path.

Figure 7-25. Negative clip path numbers

Listing 7-15. `ClipPath4.svg`

```
<svg xmlns="http://www.w3.org/2000/svg"
        xmlns:xlink="http://www.w3.org/1999/xlink">
    <g clip-rule="nonzero">
      <clipPath id="MyClip" clipPathUnits="objectBoundingBox">
        <path d="m0,.50 l.50,-.50 l.50,.50 l-.50,.50 l-.50,-.50z
                         m0.4,0 l0.1,0.1 l0.1,-0.1 l-0.1,-0.1 l-0.1,0.1z"/>
      </clipPath>
    </g>
    <g clip-path="url(#MyClip)" onclick="alert('This is a test.')">
        <circle cx="150" cy="150" r="120" fill="blue"/>
        <image xlink:href="tshirtmer.png" x="0" y="0" width="300" height="300" />
    </g>
</svg>
```

The interesting thing is that the winding number of a point inside the inner diamond is (+1 + -1) or 0. This means that regardless of the clip-rule, the area inside the inner diamond is considered not to be in the clip path region itself because it satisfies neither the evenodd rule (0 is even) nor the nonzero rule (0 is not nonzero). Thus, the inner diamond will never render.

 NOTE *Although this has been brought up in the context of clip paths, it is in fact true of fills in general, especially with paths. For that reason you can use a similar attribute,* `fill-rule`, *to set the winding behavior of fills.*

As with masks, clip paths have only limited utility in static graphics but have far more in interactive settings because clip paths also determine the mouse click region for a given graphic or graphic context. For that reason, it will appear fairly frequently in Chapter 8, "Animating SVG," and Chapter 9, "Integrating SVG and HTML."

Questioning the Use of Bitmaps

One of the big "pluses" that SVG is touted for is the efficiency that vector graphics bring to the table in comparison to bitmaps. Yet this chapter has gone to great lengths extolling the abilities of SVG to work with bitmaps, pointing out how you can make bitmap masks, work with bitmaps that have pre-existing alpha channels, incorporate bitmap textures into shapes and text, and so forth. This would seem to be a step backward, but in fact this actually points out that the vector-only advantage is not as significant a factor as some people would make it.

Most sophisticated vector graphics programs actually make provision for the use of bitmap imagery. SVG is a Web standard, true, but in many respects it is much more—it is an open standard for describing graphical information of any sort, whether bitmapped or vector based. Moreover, SVG is also an interactive language, especially when combined, as will be illustrated in the next few chapters, with SMIL animations and the SVG document object model.

You can create games, software interfaces, and more with SVG and other languages such as JavaScript. In many cases it is simply more efficient from a production standpoint to utilize bitmaps than to try to create complex SVG elements that will slow down both production and runtime performance compared to a simple bitmap (yes, you can make SVG that is too big!).

At the same time, bitmaps do introduce an overhead cost that should be evaluated carefully before using them in your productions. An SVG graphic that incorporates lots of bitmaps will tend to slow a download considerably, especially when you start moving to larger and richer PNG images. Similarly, graphics with complex alpha channels or that use alpha channel effects can adversely affect animation, sometimes dramatically.

There are a few things you can do to minimize either of these problems:

- If you have the same image used at fairly similar scales (within an order of two, generally), load the larger image in once and scale it down accordingly if you are looking for image quality, and go with the smaller image if you are looking at performance.

- If you do not need to use alpha channel graphics (in other words, rectangular or simply shape graphics are fine), then it may be preferable to loading in a compressed JPEG image rather than a comparatively expensive PNG. If the alpha channel needed is simple, it may even be worth your while to use a clip path or mask to handle the actual alpha channel work.

- SVG animations, covered in Chapter 8, "Animating SVG," can perform certain actions once a graphic is loaded. To that end, it may be worth creating SVG placeholders that get replaced with bitmap images once the load is completed.

- Look for places where you can reuse bitmaps. If you want to have a bitmap button, for instance, it is usually far better to load in a single button (or perhaps three button states: up, down, and highlighted) and then place SVG text on different instances of those bitmaps than it is to download different buttons for each need.

- Look for places where fills and patterns can be used to replace bitmaps. A silver gradient, for instance, is far more economical than trying to paint a silver bitmap.

- Similarly, look where you can replace differently shaded bitmaps with a single bitmap and varying opacities or masks.

- Finally, look at the use of filters (next section) for ways that you can combine various bitmaps and SVG blocks with special-purpose filters to create alternative bevels, lighting, blurs, glows, and other unusual effects.

With SVG, the tradeoffs typically come down to performance vs. graphical quality.

You can maximize performance by working with simplified graphics, keeping the size and depth of bitmaps at their default scale, using clip paths instead of masks (especially bitmap masks), reusing bitmaps through reference and in patterns, and using effective interactivity. Using larger bitmaps that can scale as needed, employing bitmap masks, and employing opacity to good effect can maximize graphical quality.

Adding Special Effects with Filters

Vector graphics in general have a reputation for being flat and cartoonish. You can use gradients to overcome this to a certain extent, but one of the principal differences between vector graphics and photographic bitmaps is the degree of noisiness, randomness, and "grit" in the images. Sometimes this can be added into the image through the use of bitmaps, but in many ways, adding bitmaps into the mix for such specialized effects is self-defeating.

That reason spurred the addition of filters into the SVG specification. A *filter* is a transformation that causes a change in the intermediate buffered image before it is rendered to the screen. To better understand this, it is worth re-examining the way that SVG renders an image:

1. An SVG document is initially loaded in as an XML resource.

2. Once loaded (typically using a DOM architecture), the SVG processor converts the XML into internal vectors, along with maps indicating how

each vector "shape" is to be rendered. Animated SVG does the same thing, but it creates a different map for each "tick" of the animation.

3. Each shape is rendered to a distinct temporary "off-screen" buffer, which also includes the requisite alpha channel and mask information.

4. Each shape is then composited (joined together) with previous shapes for that one particular "frame" in a secondary buffer.

5. Finally, this secondary buffer is written to the display screen, replacing what had been there before.

6. In an animation, this process is repeated.

The SVG filter works between step 3 and step 4. If a filter is applied to an individual element, then after an element is first rendered to its own off-screen buffer, the filter acts on this buffer to do things as diverse as add noise, lights, perform "wave" transformations, blur or otherwise transform the buffer, which is in turn composited into the displayed view.

Filters may be familiar to you if you have used filters for Adobe Photoshop or Macromedia FreeHand or in a 3D application such as 3D Studio Max or Maya. These applications tend to have explicit filter Application Programming Interfaces (APIs) that filter creators can use to work with the pixels in an image (or the alpha channels, in some cases) to perform almost any effect.

SVG is a specification, not an application, and as a specification it does not really have a formal API for building new filters. Instead, SVG defines a fairly comprehensive set of filter *primitives* that can be used individually to accomplish basic effects or can be chained together to handle more sophisticated effects. This solution is not perfect, and it is at least possible that SVG 2.0 will in fact establish a more formal mechanism for creating such filters.

A filter element acts as a container that both holds the collection of filter primitives and provides a label for referencing the filter in an external object. For instance, you can define a simple filter that blurs the object that it is attached to, as shown in Listing 7-16. The document shows two red squares, the first unfiltered, the second with a `<feGaussianBlur>` filter that makes it appear blurry and indistinct (see Figure 7-26). Such blurs are commonly used to create such special effects as drop shadows, glows, and back lighting.

Listing 7-16. `blurFilter1.svg`

```
<svg xmlns="http://www.w3.org/2000/svg"
    xmlns:xlink="http://www.w3.org/1999/xlink"
    width="100%" height="100%"
    viewBox="0 0 1024 768"
```

```
        preserveAspectRatio="none">
        <defs>
            <filter id="blurFilter1" filterUnits="userSpaceOnUse"
                    x="0" y="0" width="100%" height="100%">
                    <feGaussianBlur stdDeviation="6"/>
            </filter>
        </defs>
    <g transform="translate(100,100)">
    <rect id="box1" width="80" height="80" x="0"   y="20"
        fill="red" stroke="black" stroke-width="3"/>
    <rect id="box2" width="80" height="80" x="100"  y="20"
        fill="red" stroke="black" stroke-width="3"
        filter="url(#blurFilter1)"/>
    </g>
</svg>
```

Figure 7-26. Displaying a basic blur

The <filter> element uses a structure that is probably beginning to become familiar:

```
<filter id="blurFilter1" filterUnits="userSpaceOnUse"
        x="0" y="0" width="100%" height="100%">
```

A filter essentially describes a viewport over which the filter applies, depending upon whether the filterUnits are "userSpaceOnUse" or "objectBoundingBox". The x and y position similarly indicate where the filter effects begin relative to the object to which the filter is attached. This has special significance with filters because a filter may increase the extent of an object beyond the original dimensions of the object itself (as is the case with gaussian blurs).

The #blurFilter1 filter itself wraps a single filter primitive: <feGaussianBlur>. The fe prefix is short for *filter effect*, and its presence indicates that the tag is a filter primitive:

```
<feGaussianBlur stdDeviation="6"/>
```

Each primitive has its own set of attributes that perform a variety of actions. The <feGaussianBlur> element has the stdDeviation attribute (short for standard deviation), which describes the amount of blur that is applied. A stdDeviation of 0 indicates no blurring, with the amount of blurring increasing dramatically as the standard deviation also increases, as shown in Figure 7-27, with each number given being the value of the standard deviation for that rectangle.

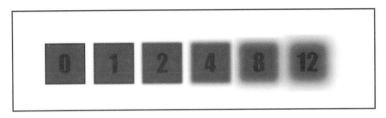

Figure 7-27. Changing the standard deviation in the gaussian blur filter

Once a filter is defined, an element can use the blur effect simply by referencing the filter in a filter attribute:

```
<rect id="box2" width="80" height="80" x="100"  y="20"
       fill="red" stroke="black" stroke-width="3"
       filter="url(#blurFilter1)"/>
```

The filter attribute is considered to be a Cascading Style Sheet (CSS) attribute. This has a number of interesting implications, not least of which being that you can create a CSS rule that includes a filter reference so that every element or group that calls that CSS class will also have the filter effect applied. The filter CSS rule syntax is essentially the same as that of the attribute:

```
<style type="text/css">
.myFilteredObject {filter:url(#myFilter); moreCSSPropertiesHere}
</style>
<rect class="myFilteredObject" . . . />
```

NOTE   *The drop shadow effect in the next section provides a working example of this.*

Chaining Filters

Anyone who has worked with Adobe Photoshop is probably familiar with the large number of potential filters that the application can use. I currently have around a hundred filters from a wide variety of manufacturers for doing everything from sharpening and blurring to creating bubbles to generating complex fractals for clouds, noise, or other effects. However, because SVG is a specification rather than an application, establishing all of the potential filters could easily end up overwhelming anything else in the SVG recommendation.

Consequently, SVG has a few basic filter primitives, with the idea that you can create a fairly varied set of potential filters by applying these primitives in various combinations. For instance, consider what steps would be required to creating a drop shadow using filters. The technique itself looks something like this:

1. Start with a black region with the same *outline* as the graphic that needs the drop shadow. This region could be called the SourceAlpha (for alpha channel).

2. Apply a gaussian blur to the SourceAlpha and store it in a temporary buffer called shadow.

3. Displace the shadow by a certain amount to the right and down, and save this in a new buffer called "offsetShadow".

4. Just as the black mask could be considered the SourceAlpha, the graphic itself could be considered the SourceGraphic.

5. Merge the SourceGraphic and the offsetShadow into a single object. At this point, you have a drop shadow.

As it turns out, this set of techniques describes exactly the way you would build an SVG drop shadow filter, as shown in Listing 7-17 and illustrated in Figure 7-28.

Listing 7-17. dropShadowFilter.svg

```
<svg xmlns="http://www.w3.org/2000/svg"
     xmlns:xlink="http://www.w3.org/1999/xlink">
     <style type="text/css">
.textDisplay {dominant-baseline:hanging;
             fill:red;
             stroke:black;
             stroke-width:2;
```

```
                font-size:100;
                font-family:Impact;
                filter:url(#dropShadow);
                }
    </style>
    <defs>
    <filter id="dropShadow" filterUnits="userSpaceOnUse"
            x="-15" y="-15" width="1000" height="1000">
      <feGaussianBlur stdDeviation="6"
            in="SourceAlpha" result="shadow"/>
      <feOffset dx="5" dy="5"
            in="shadow" result="offsetShadow"/>
      <feMerge>
        <feMergeNode in="offsetShadow"/>
        <feMergeNode in="SourceGraphic"/>
      </feMerge>
    </filter>
    </defs>
    <g transform="translate(100,100)">
        <rect id="box7" width="80" height="80" x="0" y="0"
            fill="red" stroke="black" stroke-width="3"
            filter="url(#dropShadow)"/>
        <g transform="translate(100,-10)">
            <text class="textDisplay" >
            Filters
            </text>
        </g>
    </g>
</svg>
```

Figure 7-28. A drop shadow filter

The key to this document, which can be applied to any shape from a rectangle to text, is in the drop shadow filter itself:

```
<filter id="dropShadow" filterUnits="userSpaceOnUse"
        x="-15" y="-15" width="1000" height="1000">
  <feGaussianBlur stdDeviation="6"
        in="SourceAlpha" result="shadow"/>
  <feOffset dx="5" dy="5"
        in="shadow" result="offsetShadow"/>
  <feMerge>
    <feMergeNode in="offsetShadow"/>
    <feMergeNode in="SourceGraphic"/>
  </feMerge>
</filter>
```

The <feGaussianBlur> element includes the stdDeviation attribute included earlier, but it also includes two other attributes: in and result.

The in attribute can be a little confusing. This attribute contains the name of a render surface, either one of the six predefined surfaces given in Table 7-4 or a surface that was defined in the result attribute of a previous filter primitive. It should be emphasized that in is not an XLink reference. With the exception of the standard surfaces, the in attribute can only refer to a surface explicitly defined within the current filter.

Table 7-4. Standard Filter Render Surfaces

SURFACE NAME	DESCRIPTION
SourceGraphic	The rendered version of the shapes or collections of shapes the filter acts on
SourceAlpha	The alpha channel of the source graphic
BackgroundImage	The image underneath the filter region
BackgroundAlpha	The alpha channel of the image underneath the filter region
FillPaint	The value of the fill attribute of the filtered element
StrokePaint	The value of the stroke attribute of the filtered element

The standard surfaces are actually quite complex, and each introduces its own wrinkles into the process of filtering:

SourceGraphic: This is the rendering of the initial shape or region before any filters are applied. If the region is irregular (such as text), the source graphic will likewise be irregular. If the source is a composite of multiple shapes, the region is defined by the intrinsic clip paths of all of the associated shapes. SourceGraphic is the default if no in parameter is given.

SourceAlpha: This is actually an inverted map of the alpha channel of the source graphic. The default alpha channel for a completely opaque object is black, with transparencies being shades of gray up to white for completely transparent. Otherwise this is similar to SourceGraphic.

BackgroundImage: This retrieves a snapshot of the background under the filter region. This differs from the SourceGraphic in that the background image may not actually be rendered within SVG itself. For instance, an SVG document may be contained in an HTML Web page as a transparent overlay. Using BackgroundImage in this case will actually pick up the HTML page *beneath* the SVG graphic, as well as any SVG that is rendered up to that point.

BackgroundAlpha: As with SourceAlpha, the BackgroundAlpha will pick up the extent of the background defined in BackgroundImage.

FillPaint: This mode uses the `fill` property that is either explicitly defined or inherited on the element in question. Note that fill here does not apply just to color. If the fill is a gradient or pattern, then that same gradient or pattern can be used as the source for the filter, making for some sophisticated possibilities. Note that if the gradient or pattern has an alpha channel (such as a gradient that uses a `stop-opacity` attribute with a value other than "1" in a `<stop>` element), then the `FillPaint` will likewise inherit that alpha channel in terms of its effects.

StrokePaint: This mode uses the `stroke` property that is either explicitly defined or inherited on the element in question. The same characteristics that apply to FillPaint also apply to StrokePaint.

The `result` attribute consequently lets you create new "named surfaces" that can consequently be used later in the filter. The `result` name cannot be the same as any previously defined surfaces—this will generate an error. If the `result` attribute is not included in a filter primitive, then the results of the filter are drawn to the painted canvas, which should be the case only if this primitive is the last one in the chain.

The `<feOffset>` element from Listing 7-17 illustrates an intermediate link in the filter chain:

```
<feOffset dx="5" dy="5"
          in="shadow" result="offsetShadow"/>
```

The effect of the filter is to offset the `in` rendered surface (in this case, "`shadow`") by the amount (dx,dy) = (5,5), moving it five units down and to the right of its previous position. The result is then rendered to the new named surface offsetShadow. It is worth noting here that these surfaces are temporary in nature; they will be *garbage collected* once the filter finishes processing.

The final filter primitive, <feMerge>, can be used to merge multiple rendered surfaces together into a single image, with the order of the child <feMergeNode> elements indicating the order that the graphic itself will be drawn. In this case the displaced "offsetShadow" surface is drawn first, then the resulting SourceGraphic is drawn on top of that:

```
<feMerge>
    <feMergeNode in="offsetShadow"/>
    <feMergeNode in="SourceGraphic"/>
</feMerge>
```

The <feMerge> node can have any number of surfaces merged together in this manner. Note that because this <feMerge> element also does not have a result attribute, it will be treated as the final filter to act on the element; however, the <feMerge> element could well have had a result attribute, which could in turn be referenced by other filter primitives.

Understanding the Filter Primitives

Okay, I have to admit something: The filter primitives are ugly, complex things that in many cases only make sense if you happen to have a good idea about the characteristics of high-end graphics programming. That is a terrible admission for a writer of a book on SVG to make, but it is worth emphasizing that the best real way to understand how the filters work—both alone and together—is to experiment with them. (The plus side of this is the fact that you can make some extremely impressive effects once you do invest in playing with the filters).

Table 7-5 briefly lists the filter primitives, with descriptions indicating roughly what each filter does, just to give you a general idea about the set of primitives. However, each one of the filters is worth exploring individually and will be done so thereafter. The filters are in thematic order.

Table 7-5. Filter Primitives

FILTER PRIMITIVE NAME	DESCRIPTION
feFlood	Fills the render surface with a single flat color and opacity. This is most often used as an intermediate filter.
feMerge	Merges two or more render surfaces together in a simple copy operation. More efficient than feBlend or feComposite.
feImage	Draws an external image from a file or other resource to a render surface, usually for secondary processing.
feBlend	Blends two render surfaces together using one of an established set of operations.
feTile	Fills a render surface with repeating tiles of the input surface.
feComposite	Combines two render surfaces in a number of different modes, incorporating constants that handle truncation of color when it exceeds a set boundary. feComposite is powerful but also quite complex in its use.
feColorMatrix	For each pixel in the input source, a transformation is made based upon the color matrix to set a new color for that pixel. It is useful for changing an image's saturation, hue, or luminance.
feComponentTransfer	For each color component (red, green, blue, alpha) of each pixel in the source, use a function to assign a new value to that component. feComponentTransfer is useful for handling brightness adjustment, changing contrast, color balance, and setting color thresholds.
feOffset	Displaces the input render surface by a fixed amount (dx,dy).
feDisplacementMap	A displacement map takes one channel of an image (such as the red or alpha channel in a color image) and displaces a given point by a factor proportional to the degree that the displacement map deviates from a 50-percent value. Displacement maps are useful for refraction effects in glass or waves of water, specialized blur effects (such as a zoom lens), and so forth.

(continued)

Table 7-5. Filter Primitives (continued)

FILTER PRIMITIVE NAME	DESCRIPTION
feConvolveMatrix	A convolution is a map that associates for each pixel in an image a value made up by weighted averages of surrounding values. This makes possible sharpening and blurring masks, fractal effects, edge detection, embossing, and much more.
feGaussianBlur	Performs a gaussian blur on an image, where the color and intensity of a color at a given pixel is a well-defined function acting on the neighbors of that pixel.
feMorphology	Although somewhat complex in effect, the morphology filter primitive can fatten or thin a given graphic. It is especially useful with alpha channels.
feDiffuseLighting	Places a "light" at a certain position relative to the input render surface. This light is diffuse; it affects the underlying color of the surface, and it can support distant lights, point lights, and spot lights.
feSpecularLighting	As with diffuse lighting, it places a light at a certain location, but this light affects the "reflective" characteristics of the object in question and is consequently used to make highlights, metallic reflections, and so forth.
feTurbulence	This filter adds "noise" to a given render surface. This can be used both to add a gritty or wavy characteristic surface or can be used in conjunction with other filters to create clouds, caustics (the patterns of light through surface waves), and similar effects.

The formal specification for the filters document runs to more than 60 pages, so I will not be able to cover more than a small part of the functionality inherent in filters. Instead I give you enough of an idea how to use these filters so that you can see how they can be useful to your own applications.

feFlood: *Quick Color Fills*

The <feFlood> filter primitive lets you easily create a render surface consisting of only one color and opacity value. The <feFlood> element takes only two attributes: flood-color, which specifies the color to apply to the filter, and flood-opacity, which specifies the opacity of the filter against any background elements.

Listing 7-18 shows how you can use `<feFlood>`. In this case, there are two elements: a square and an associated text field with the word *Filters* in it (get used to this—you will see a lot of variations of this by the time this chapter is over). The feFlood filter simply replaces that element with a filled region that goes to the extent of the source object. The resulting image is shown in Figure 7-29.

Listing 7-18. `feFlood.svg`

```
<svg xmlns="http://www.w3.org/2000/svg"
     xmlns:xlink="http://www.w3.org/1999/xlink">
    <style type="text/css">
.textDisplay {dominant-baseline:hanging;
              fill:yellow;
              stroke:black;
              stroke-width:2;
              font-size:100;
              font-family:Impact;
              }
.lightLabel {
              fill:black;
              font-size:30;
              font-family:Arial;
              font-weight:bold;
              }
    </style>
    <filter id="grayFlood" filterUnits="objectBoundingBox"
            x="0" y="-0" width="1" height="1">
            <feFlood flood-color="#C0C0C0" flood-opacity="0.7"
                in="SourceGraphic"/>
    </filter>
    <filter id="blueFlood" filterUnits="objectBoundingBox"
            x="0" y="-0" width="1" height="1">
            <feFlood flood-color="blue" flood-opacity="0.4"
                in="SourceGraphic"/>
    </filter>
    <g transform="translate(0,25)">
    <text class="lightLabel" x="75" y="25">Unfiltered</text>
    <g transform="translate(100,50)">
    <rect id="box7" width="80" height="80" x="0" y="0"
        fill="red" stroke="black" stroke-width="3"/>
    <text class="textDisplay" x="100">
        Filters
    </text>
    </g>
    </g>
```

```
        <g transform="translate(0,225)">
        <text class="lightLabel" x="75" y="25">With feFlood Applied</text>
        <g transform="translate(100,50)">
        <rect id="box7" width="80" height="80" x="0" y="0"
            fill="red" stroke="black" stroke-width="3"
            filter="url(#grayFlood)"/>
        <text class="textDisplay" x="100"
            filter="url(#blueFlood)">
            Filters
        </text>
        </g>
        </g>
</svg>
```

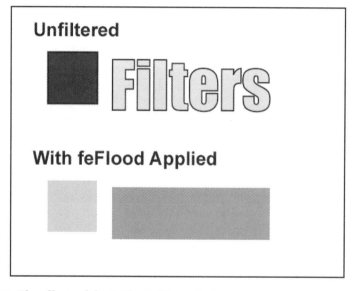

Figure 7-29. The effects of the feFlood *filter primitive*

feMerge: *Merging Multiple Surfaces*

The <feMerge> filter primitives combine multiple surfaces together and is perhaps the most efficient way of doing so, if all you are doing is layering one on top of the next. In essence, what feMerge does is to combine the result of multiple filter chains. <feMerge> works by setting up two or more <feMergeNode> child elements, each of which have an in parameter that can reference a named rendering surface. The <feMerge> element then respects position, alpha channels, and clipping paths to create the final rendered output.

For instance, in Listing 7-19, a blue rectangle is created from the bounding box of a text area using the `<feFlood>` filter. Applying a gaussian blur to this filter creates the named render surface "BlurredBack". You can then use the `<feMerge>` element to combine the initial SourceGraphic surface with the blurred background. The resulting image is shown in Figure 7-30.

Listing 7-19. `feMerge.svg`

```
<svg xmlns="http://www.w3.org/2000/svg"
     xmlns:xlink="http://www.w3.org/1999/xlink">
    <style type="text/css">
.textDisplay {dominant-baseline:hanging;
              fill:yellow;
              stroke:black;
              stroke-width:2;
              font-size:100;
              font-family:Impact;
              }
.lightLabel {`
              fill:black;
              font-size:30;
              font-family:Arial;
              font-weight:bold;
              }
    </style>
    <filter id="blueFlood" filterUnits="userSpaceOnUse"
            x="-60" y="-60" width="390" height="220">
            <feFlood flood-color="blue" in="SourceGraphic"
                result="blueBack" x="0" y="0"
                width="270" height="100"/>
            <feGaussianBlur stdDeviation="15" in="blueBack"
                result="blurredBack" x="-60" y="-60"
                width="390" height="220"/>
            <feMerge>
                <feMergeNode in="blurredBack"/>
                <feMergeNode in="SourceGraphic"/>
            </feMerge>
    </filter>

    <g transform="translate(0,25)">
    <text class="lightLabel" x="75" y="25">Unfiltered</text>
    <g transform="translate(100,50)">
    <text class="textDisplay" x="100">
        Filters
    </text>
```

```
        </g>
        </g>
        <g transform="translate(0,225)">
        <text class="lightLabel" x="75" y="25">With feMerge Applied</text>
        <g transform="translate(200,50)">
        <text class="textDisplay"
            filter="url(#blueFlood)">
                Filters
        </text>
        </g>
        </g>
    </svg>
```

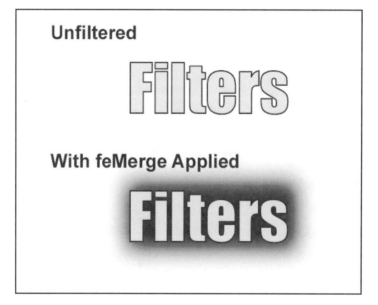

Figure 7-30. Multiple filter chains with feMerge

feImage: *Importing Images as Filters*

The <feImage> filter primitive provides a way of loading in an external file (or other external resource, such as the result of an HTTP call) as a rendering surface. This has a number of applications, beyond simply compositing an image into other rendering surfaces. For instance, the pixels of an external image may be used as a filter for some other filter process (such as a convolution, discussed shortly, or a displacement map).

The <feImage> syntax is almost identical to that of the <image> element; you must specify width and height, and you can specify x and y positions (to give the starting point within the bitmap of the render area). The primary difference is the fact that the <feImage> filter can specify a result attribute, naming the image for use by other filters.

In Listing 7-20, the code from the feMerge section is modified slightly so that an image (the top half of the mermaid used earlier in this chapter) is composited into the background of the text (see Figure 7-31). Note that the image (which includes alpha channel support along the outline of the PNG-based figure) merges seamlessly into the blue blur from the previous gaussian blur filter.

Listing 7-20. feImage.svg

```
<svg xmlns="http://www.w3.org/2000/svg"
     xmlns:xlink="http://www.w3.org/1999/xlink">
     <style type="text/css">
.textDisplay {dominant-baseline:hanging;
               fill:yellow;
               stroke:black;
               stroke-width:2;
               font-size:100;
               font-family:Impact;
               }
.lightLabel {
               fill:black;
               font-size:30;
               font-family:Arial;
               font-weight:bold;
               }
     </style>
     <filter id="blueFlood" filterUnits="userSpaceOnUse"
             x="-60" y="-60" width="390" height="220">
             <feFlood flood-color="blue" in="SourceGraphic"
                 result="blueBack" x="0" y="0"
                 width="270" height="100"/>
             <feGaussianBlur stdDeviation="15" in="blueBack"
                 result="blurredBack" x="-60" y="-60"
                 width="390" height="220"/>
             <feImage xlink:href="SweaterMer3.png" y="-60"
                 width="237" height="484" result="image"/>
             <feMerge>
                 <feMergeNode in="blurredBack"/>
                 <feMergeNode in="image"/>
                 <feMergeNode in="SourceGraphic"/>
             </feMerge>
     </filter>
```

```
            <g transform="translate(0,25)">
            <text class="lightLabel" x="75" y="25">Unfiltered</text>
            <g transform="translate(100,50)">
            <text class="textDisplay" x="100">
                    Filters
            </text>
            </g>
            </g>
            <g transform="translate(0,225)">
            <text class="lightLabel" x="75" y="25">
                <tspan x="75" y="0">With</tspan>
                <tspan x="75" y="40">feImage</tspan>
                <tspan x="75" y="80">Applied</tspan>
            </text>
            <g transform="translate(200,50)">
            <text class="textDisplay"
                filter="url(#blueFlood)">
                    Filters
            </text>
            </g>
            </g>
        </svg>
```

Figure 7-31. Using external bitmaps as filters with feImage

feBlend: *Blending Images Using Standard Tools*

The <feBlend> filter primitive makes it possible to combine two render surfaces through one of five possible operations: normal, multiply, screen, darken, or lighten. These modes correspond to their Photoshop equivalents, as given in Table 7-6. feBlend has two inputs, the source in and the secondary in2.

Table 7-6. Blend Modes

FILTER PRIMITIVE NAME	DESCRIPTION
normal	The render surface in2 replaces the render surface in where there is overlap, with the alpha channels multiplying together to determine the final opacity. This is the default.
multiply	On a pixel-by-pixel basis, each channel in the source is multiplied by the channel in the in2 surface, then divided by the source word length (in other words, 256 for a 24-bit color image).
screen	The channels are inverted before performing the multiply, then inverted again. This tends to produce a brighter image.
darken	Like multiply, but uses the minimum of the four channel values to perform the multiplication.
lighten	Like multiply, but uses the maximum of the four channel values to perform the multiplication.

The <feBlend> element is a specialized version of the <feComposite> element that lets you use predefined named operations to combine surfaces together. Listing 7-21 illustrates this principle in action, by combining the mermaid image and the text through a multiply blend (see Figure 7-32).

Listing 7-21. feBlend.svg

```
<svg xmlns="http://www.w3.org/2000/svg"
     xmlns:xlink="http://www.w3.org/1999/xlink">
     <style type="text/css">
.textDisplay {dominant-baseline:hanging;
              fill:yellow;
              stroke:black;
              stroke-width:2;
              font-size:100;
              font-family:Impact;
              }
```

```
.lightLabel {
            fill:black;
            font-size:30;
            font-family:Arial;
            font-weight:bold;
            }
  </style>
  <filter id="blueFlood" filterUnits="userSpaceOnUse"
          x="-60" y="-60" width="390" height="220">
          <feFlood flood-color="blue" in="SourceGraphic"
              result="blueBack" x="0" y="0"
              width="270" height="100"/>
          <feGaussianBlur stdDeviation="15" in="blueBack"
              result="blurredBack" x="-60" y="-60"
              width="390" height="220"/>
          <feImage xlink:href="SweaterMer3.png" y="-60"
              width="237" height="484" result="image"/>
          <feBlend in="image" in2="SourceGraphic"
              mode="darken" result="blended"/>
          <feMerge>
              <feMergeNode in="blurredBack"/>
              <feMergeNode in="blended"/>
          </feMerge>
  </filter>

  <g transform="translate(0,25)">
  <text class="lightLabel" x="75" y="25">Unfiltered</text>
  <g transform="translate(100,50)">
  <text class="textDisplay" x="100">
        Filters
  </text>
  </g>
  </g>
  <g transform="translate(0,225)">
  <text class="lightLabel" x="75" y="25">
      <tspan x="75" y="0">With</tspan>
      <tspan x="75" y="40">feImage</tspan>
      <tspan x="75" y="80">Applied</tspan>
  </text>
  <g transform="translate(200,50)">
  <text class="textDisplay"
```

```
        filter="url(#blueFlood)">
            Filters
        </text>
        </g>
        </g>
</svg>
```

Figure 7-32. `<feBlend>`

feComposite: *Compositing Master Control*

The `<feComposite>` filter primitive is a more generalized version of the `feBlend` and `feMerge` filters. `<feBlend>` gives you control of the merging process using well-established graphical terms, and `<feComposite>` performs bitwise operations on two render surfaces. As with `feBlend`, `feComposite` has two inputs, the source in and the secondary in2. However, unlike `feBlend`, `feComposite` uses the operator attribute rather than the mode attribute, with this attribute indicating one of six potential operations: over, in, out, atop, xor, and arithmetic. The "over" operator performs standard compositing and is the default value for the operator attribute.

The arithmetic operator is perhaps most pertinent of the operators from a control standpoint. When operator is "arithmetic", the `<feComposite>` element can also make use of four constants, k1 through k4, that control the result intensity as follows:

```
result = k1*i1*i2 + k2*i1 + k3*i2 + k4
```

where i1 and i2 are vectors consisting of the four channels (R_1,G_1,B_1,A_1) and (R_2,G_2,B_2,A_2) respectively. These values all default to 0.

> **NOTE** *For more information on the* feComposite *filter, see section 15.12 in the SVG 1.0 specification at* www.w3.org/TR/SVG/filters.html.

feColorMatrix: *Transforming Color*

The <feColorMatrix> filter primitive defines a matrix for transforming each pixel in the source graphic in a uniform manner. It treats each pixel's color value (r, g, b, a) as a vector to which the color matrix is applied as a transformation to create a new color vector for that pixel. To handle complex transformations, the vector also includes a fifth value (initially set to 1) to make the math work (i.e., the new vector is (r,g,b,a,1)):

```
| R' |     | a00 a01 a02 a03 a04 |    | R |

| G' |     | a10 a11 a12 a13 a14 |    | G |

| B' |  =  | a20 a21 a22 a23 a24 | *  | B |

| A' |     | a30 a31 a32 a33 a34 |    | A |

| 1 |      |  0   0   0   0   1  |    | 1 |
```

The transformation matrix itself does not have to be specified. The <feColorMatrix> filter primitive includes three default matrices: saturate, hueRotate, and luminanceToAlpha, specified in the type attribute, as well as the generic "matrix" type.

The saturate type controls the degree of color saturation in the image and can be set via the values attribute to have a value between 0 and 1. For example, this code:

```
<feColorMatrix  type="saturate" value="0"/>
```

sets the saturation to 0, in effect converting a color image into a (visual) black-and-white image, "bleaching" the color out of the image. Setting values to 1 will "oversaturate" the image, boosting the color while simultaneously reducing the amount of gray in the image.

The hueRotate type, on the other hand, cycles the image through the spectrum as if that spectrum was a full circle. Consequently, the values argument here is an angle between 0 and 360. You can use this to change the color of each pixel of a bitmap by the same amount, for example.

The luminanceToAlpha type is useful for turning an image into an alpha channel for another image. Those places where the intensity of the image is highest (color is closest to white) map to a fully transparent alpha channel equivalent, and those where the intensity is lowest (color is closest to black) map to a fully opaque alpha equivalent.

Finally, when type is matrix, then values needs to be a 5×4 collection of numbers. That is to say, you need 20 numbers separated by whitespace. Note that because SVG sees carriage returns as whitespace, you can create tables in your SVG code proper:

```
<feColorMatrix type="matrix" in="SourceGraphic"
values=".33 .33 .33 0 0
                .33 .33 .33 0 0
                .33 .33 .33 0 0
                .33 .33 .33 0 0"/>
```

Listing 7-22 (initially from Listing 7-21) shows how the filter can turn the flesh-colored parts of the mermaid image green, and this is illustrated in Figure 7-33.

Listing 7-22. feColorMatrix.svg

```
<svg xmlns="http://www.w3.org/2000/svg"
     xmlns:xlink="http://www.w3.org/1999/xlink">
     <style type="text/css">
.textDisplay {dominant-baseline:hanging;
                fill:yellow;
                stroke:black;
                stroke-width:2;
                font-size:100;
                font-family:Impact;
                }
.lightLabel {
                fill:black;
                font-size:30;
                font-family:Arial;
                font-weight:bold;
                }
     </style>
```

```
<filter id="fleshToGreenFilter" filterUnits="userSpaceOnUse"
        x="-60" y="-60" width="390" height="220">
    <feFlood flood-color="blue" in="SourceGraphic"
        result="blueBack" x="0" y="0"
        width="270" height="100"/>
    <feGaussianBlur stdDeviation="15" in="blueBack"
        result="blurredBack" x="-60" y="-60"
        width="390" height="220"/>
    <feImage xlink:href="SweaterMer3.png" y="-60"
        width="237" height="484" result="image"/>
    <feColorMatrix type="hueRotate" values="90" in="image"
        result="colorRotatedImage"/>
    <feBlend in="SourceGraphic" in2="colorRotatedImage"
        mode="normal"
        result="blended"/>
    <feMerge>
        <feMergeNode in="blurredBack"/>
        <feMergeNode in="blended"/>
    </feMerge>
</filter>

<g transform="translate(0,25)">
<text class="lightLabel" x="75" y="25">Unfiltered</text>
<g transform="translate(100,50)">
<text class="textDisplay" x="100">
    Filters
</text>
</g>
</g>
<g transform="translate(0,225)">
<text class="lightLabel" x="75" y="25">
    <tspan x="30" y="0">With</tspan>
    <tspan x="30" y="40">feColorMatrix</tspan>
    <tspan x="30" y="80">Applied</tspan>
</text>
<g transform="translate(200,50)">
<text class="textDisplay"
    filter="url(#fleshToGreenFilter)">
    Filters
</text>
</g>
</g>
</svg>
```

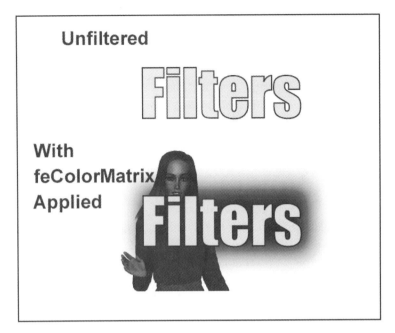

Figure 7-33. The feColorMatrix hueRotate *type*

feComponentTransfer: *Functional Assignment of Colors*

The <feComponentTransfer> filter primitive performs some of the same functions as the feColorMatrix filter, but rather than using a matrix (predefined or otherwise), it uses a set of predefined functions to perform the assignments. This makes it possible to handle areas that matrix transformations generally do not do well, such as defining cutoff values.

The mappings are basically done directly from channel to channel; there is no cross bleed between channels that you see with feColorMatrix. Put another way, with feComponentTransfer, you have functions of the following form:

```
R' = rf(R)
G' = gf(G)
B' = bf(B)
A' = af(A)
```

where rf(), gf(), and so on are functions that affect the red, green, blue, and alpha channels, respectively. feComponentTransfer defines five types of functions: identity, discrete, table, linear and gamma. These act as follows:

Identity: The result value is the same as the starting value. This is the default. This would be invoked through the component declarations:

```
<feComponentTransfer>
    <feFuncR type="identity"/>
    <feFuncG type="identity"/>
    <feFuncB type="identity"/>
    <feFuncA type="identity"/>
</feComponentTransfer>
```

Discrete: This is a lookup table that extracts a value from a set of values (defined in the attribute tableValues), with n *intervals* given by n+1 values. For instance, you could create a mapping that looked like tableValues="0 0.1 0.2 0.4 0.8 0.4 0.2 0.1 0", for eight intervals (nine values). The component values are given as values between 0 and 1, rather than between 0 and 255, thus vastly simplifying the map. For a source component value of 0.6, the nearest interval before that starts at 0.5 (the fifth interval) and has a value of 0.8. The following will set the R and G to discrete values, and keep the blue and alpha channels identical to the source:

```
<feComponentTransfer>
    <feFuncR type="discrete" tableValues="0 0.1 0.2 0.4 0.8 0.4 0.2 0.1 0"/>
    <feFuncG type="discrete" tableValues="0 0.1 0.2 0.4 0.8 0.4 0.2 0.1 0"/>
    <feFuncB type="identity"/>
    <feFuncA type="identity"/>
</feComponentTransfer>
```

Table: The Table type is similar to Discrete, but rather than retrieving a specific value from the table, the table entries provide the end points of a linear interpolation. For instance, for tableValues="0 0.1 0.2 0.4 0.8 0.4 0.2 0.1 0", a source R value of 0.6 is in the fifth source interval (0.5, 0.625), which is mapped to the new lookup values of (0.8,0.4). The new value then is the linearly interpolated value defined by the following, where v_k is the value of the kth interval in the list, N is the total number of intervals (one more than the total number of points), and C is the component value:

```
C' = vₖ + (C - k/N)*N * (vₖ₊₁ - vₖ)
   = 0.8 + (0.6 - (4/8))*8*(0.4 - 0.8)
   = 0.4
```

The Table mode is useful for creating approximations to exact functions without having to tie up resources in the SVG engine to build in a function evaluator. You can also set up cutoff values. For instance, if you wanted to reduce the range of a color so that it started from a value of 0 at 0.2 and ended at a value of 1 at 0.8, you would set up a table value over the range "0 0 0.33333 0.6666 1 1". The following will set the R and G to interpolated values, and keep the blue and alpha channels identical to the source:

```
<feComponentTransfer>
    <feFuncR type="discrete" tableValues="0 0.1 0.2 0.4 0.8 0.4 0.2 0.1 0"/>
    <feFuncG type="discrete" tableValues="0 0.1 0.2 0.4 0.8 0.4 0.2 0.1 0"/>
    <feFuncB type="identity"/>
    <feFuncA type="identity"/>
</feComponentTransfer>
```

Linear: The Linear type defines an equation of the form:

```
C' = slope * C + intercept
```

where slope and intercept are attributes defined on the <feFuncX> tag. If C' is less than 0, it is truncated to 0; if greater than 1, it is truncated to 1. Thus, the following on the R channel will set the value C' to 0 for C values between 0 and 0.2, set to 1 for values between 0.8 and 1.0, and set to increase linearly between 0 and 1 from 0.2 to 0.8.

```
<feComponentTransfer>
    <feFuncR type="linear" slope="1.3333" intercept="-0.3333"/>
            <!-- etc. -->
</feComponentTransfer>
```

You can determine the slope and intercept with a little algebra. If **a** is the slope and **b** the intercept, like so:

```
0 = 0.2*a + b
1 = 0.8*a + b
```

Subtracting the second equation from the first gives you this:

```
1=0.6 * a
```

or this:

```
a = slope = 5/3
```

Substituting **a** back in, you get this:

```
0 = (1/5)(5/3)+b
```

or this:

```
b = intercept = -1/3.
```

Gamma: Gamma corrections usually need to occur because of the different intensities of monitors with respect to color matching. The gamma function itself is an exponential one and is given as follows:

```
C' = amplitude * pow(C, exponent) + offset
```

where `amplitude`, `exponent`, and `offset` are attributes, reflected in the `<feFuncX>` form:

```
<feFuncR type="gamma" amplitude="1" exponent="1" offset="0"/>
```

If no attributes are supplied, this produces the same curve as the `identity` function.

feOffset: *Simple Displacement*

The `feOffset` filter primitive is the first in this list that alters the position of a given pixel, rather than its color value. The structure for `feOffset` is simple; if you want to change the location of a given surface five units to the right and five units up, you pass it in through the `in` parameter, with a attribute of `dx="5"` and `dy="5"`:

```
<feOffset in="mySurface" dx="5" dy="-5" result="offsetSurface"/>
```

Note that the filter moves the surface on a plane of infinite extent, so if the offset pushes an image so that it exceeds the boundaries of its viewport, the graphic that "moves in" is a blank area with an opacity of 0.

feTile: *Tiling Graphics*

The feTile filter primitive lets you define a rectangular region that can then be filled with the input surface, tiled repeatedly in both x and y dimensions:

```
<feTile in="mySurface" x="0" y="0" width="128" height="128"
            result="tiledSurface"/>
```

Tiling performs the same role for filters that <pattern> elements do for SVG fills.

feDisplacementMap: *Sophisticated Warping*

If feOffset is the equivalent of a Ford Escort, feDisplacementMap is a Ferrari. A displacement map is an image or render surface that the feDisplacementMap filter uses to determine the displacement of each pixel in the source surface. The filter reads two channels (which can be set by the xChannelSelector and yChannelSelector) from a pixel on an image map specified by the in2 attribute. For each coordinate, the filter then sets the new position of the graphic through a simple formula:

$$P_x'(x,y) = P_x(x,y) + S * (C_{Mx} - 0.5)$$
$$P_y'(x,y) = P_y(x,y) + S * (C_{My} - 0.5)$$

where P_x and P_y are the initial x and y coordinates, P_x' and P_y' are the new coordinates, S is a scale factor, and C_{Mx} and C_{My} are the channel values (normalized between 0 and 1) for the map's pixel.

If the color of the map is 50-percent gray, then no displacement takes place. If a pixel is black (or 0-percent gray), the displacement at that pixel is 0.5 to the left or the top (=C_{Mx} - 0.5 = 0 - 0.5 = -0.5). If a pixel is white, the displacement is 0.5 in the other direction.

Because a displacement of half a pixel is probably not even significantly noticeable, a scale factor can be applied to multiply the effects of the displacement. Thus, if a given pixel is 0.2 gray and you apply a scale of "100", the displacement will be 30 pixels (= S * (C_{Mx} - 0.5) = 100 * (0.2 - 0.5) = - 30). This can make for a significant displacement, especially if the next pixel over is a completely different color.

Any graphic in SVG has four channels, so even if an image file is grayscale, SVG will internally convert it into an RGBA image. The xChannelSelector and yChannelSelector can each be set to one of the four channels by giving the letter of that channel. Thus, to set the xChannelSelector to the red channel of an image, you would use xChannelSelector = "R". You can also specify the alpha channel with yChannelSelector="A". xChannelSelector defines the map to be used for displacement in the x direction, and yChannelSelector does the same for the y direction.

An example can illustrate how powerful this filter really is. Created in Photoshop, Figure 7-34 uses noise to generate a random deviation from a gray starting value, then gaussian blurs and other effects within Photoshop completed the image.

Figure 7-34. A "noisy" bitmap

NOTE   *With the* feTurbulance *filter, you can create similar effects, as will be demonstrated shortly.*

You can use this image with the feDisplacementMap filter to create a sophisticated dissolve effect of the word *Filters*, as shown in Listing 7-23. It relies on the <animate> elements to animate the scale attribute of the <feDisplacementMap> object, one frame of which is shown in Figure 7-35 (see Chapter 8, "Animating SVG," for more on animation).

Listing 7-23. feDisplacementMap.svg

```
<svg xmlns="http://www.w3.org/2000/svg"
     xmlns:xlink="http://www.w3.org/1999/xlink">
    <style type="text/css">
.textDisplay {dominant-baseline:hanging;
              fill:yellow;
              stroke:black;
              stroke-width:2;
              font-size:100;
              font-family:Impact;
              }
.lightLabel {
              fill:black;
              font-size:30;
              font-family:Arial;
              font-weight:bold;
              }
    </style>
    <filter id="displaceFilter" filterUnits="userSpaceOnUse"
            x="-60" y="-60" width="390" height="220">
            <feFlood flood-color="blue" in="SourceGraphic"
                    result="blueBack" x="0" y="0"
                    width="270" height="100"/>
            <feGaussianBlur stdDeviation="15" in="blueBack"
                    result="blurredBack" x="-60" y="-60"
                    width="390" height="220"/>
            <feImage xlink:href="SweaterMer3.png" y="-60"
                    width="237" height="484" result="image"/>
            <feImage xlink:href="DisplacementMapX.jpg"
                    width="400" height="400"
                    result="displacementImage"/>
            <feDisplacementMap in="SourceGraphic"
                    in2="displacementImage"
                    xChannelSelector="G" yChannelSelector="G"
                    result="displacedText" scale="50" >
```

```
                              <animate attributeName="scale" a
                               ttributeType="XML" dur="10s"
                               values="0;100;0;0" repeatCount="indefinite"/>
                      </feDisplacementMap>
                      <feMerge>
                          <feMergeNode in="blurredBack"/>
                          <feMergeNode in="image"/>
                          <feMergeNode in="displacedText"/>
                      </feMerge>
              </filter>

              <g transform="translate(0,25)">
              <text class="lightLabel" x="75" y="25">Unfiltered</text>
              <g transform="translate(100,50)">
              <text class="textDisplay" x="100">
                    Filters
              </text>
              </g>
              </g>
              <g transform="translate(0,225)">
              <text class="lightLabel">
                  <tspan x="15" y="0">With</tspan>
                  <tspan x="15" y="40">Displacement</tspan>
                  <tspan x="15" y="80">Map</tspan>
                  <tspan x="15" y="120">Applied</tspan>
              </text>
              <g transform="translate(200,50)">
              <text class="textDisplay"
                  filter="url(#displaceFilter)">
                    Filters
              </text>
              </g>
              </g>
      </svg>
```

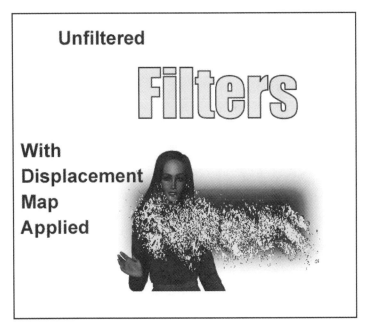

Figure 7-35. Repositioning pixels based on channel values

The displacement map is defined in the listing as follow:

```
<feDisplacementMap
        in="SourceGraphic"
        in2="displacementImage"
        xChannelSelector="G"
        yChannelSelector="G"
     scale="50"
     result="displacedText">
```

where "displacementImage" is the named surface that refers to the random graphic, and "displacedText" is the resulting image read by the <feMerge> primitive. Because the image is a grayscale, any channel will display the same values, so both xChannelSelector and yChannelSelector are set to the Green channel.

You can use displacement maps effectively in animations. The scale property shown here can be animated, as can the channel of the map and the source surface, making it possible to do such effects as waving flags, water vibrations, noise, and interactive perturbations.

One point that should be raised, however, is that such displacement map effects are extremely expensive in terms of memory and performance. In general, if you use such effects, it may be worth it to set the performance of the SVG document to optimize for speed and performance over quality of rendering.

feConvolveMatrix: *Know Your Neighbors*

The displacement map performs a mapping from one pixel in a source image to a different pixel in the result image. The feConvolveMap takes the opposite approach: It reads in a point and its *neighborhood* (the values of the points around it), and based upon a matrix (called a *kernel matrix*, or just *kernel*), sets the color of the point to a new value.

Convolutions may sound esoteric, but in fact they are found at the heart of almost all graphic processing algorithms used in modern graphics software: blurring, sharpening, embossing, edge detection, fractals, and much more. Thus, you can think of the feConvolveMatrix filter as the workhorse of SVG image processing.

To get an idea about how a convolution works, consider a small piece of an image channel as an array of values between 0 and 255:

255	248[b]	248	252	64
32	168	72[a]	255	225
32	212	254	211	215
64	128	4	38	219

A kernel matrix can be defined that will place a bias that will cause colors to the left of a point to leech into the value of a point, while the colors to the right are removed:

```
    1    0   -1
V =      1    4   -1
    1    0   -1
```

For the point marked *a* in the previous graph, the center of the convolution matrix is placed on that point, with the outlying matrix members occupying the same positions with the point's neighbors. Each point's values are multiplied by the convolution matrix for that point and the products are then added together. Finally, the whole is divided by the sum of the elements in the convolution array. In other words, for *a*, the new value is as follows:

```
      1 * 248 + 0 * 248 + -1 * 252 +
a' =      1 *   32 + 4 *   72 + -1 * 255 +
      1 * 313 + 0 * 254 + -1 * 215

    = (248 -252 +32 +288 - 255 +313  - 215) /4
    = 40.25 rounded to 40.
```

Thus, by examining the weighted average of neighbor values, a new color value a little less than the initial value is given. This particular convolution array is weighted heavily toward the central value, so the effects of neighbors will generally be fairly minor.

The order attribute indicates the dimensions of the matrix itself. If only one number is provided for order, then that number describes both the number of columns and the number of rows. Two order attributes separated by a space will set the number of columns and rows respectively. If no order attribute is given, the matrix is assumed to be 3×3.

The kernelMatrix attribute defines the matrix itself, and the number of items in the kernel *must* match the product of the row and column numbers (i.e., n × m) or an error will be generated. The kernel values can be separated either by white space or commas. Thus the kernel matrix for the previous sample would be given as

```
<feConvolveMatrix order="3" kernelMatrix="1 0 -1 1 4 -1 1 0 -1" ... />
```

Kernel matrices can be any dimensions, though obviously the larger the matrix (and the more complex, consequently, the rules associated with that matrix), the slower the processing will be. The number that divides the matrix—contained, not unexpectedly, in the divisor attribute—can also be changed from its default value of the sum of all weights, though it cannot be set either explicitly or implicitly to 0. Note that the values given previously are relative to 256-bit words. Internally, the feConvolveMatrix always normalizes the values of each channel, dividing them by the pixel word length (usually 8 bits or 256 bits) so that they have an internal value between 0 and 1.

The bias attribute provides a specific value to be added to the result after the weighted sum is divided by the divisor. For instance, it may be desirable to add 0.5 to the result so that the value is relative to 50-percent gray (this is useful when working with displacement maps . . . hint, hint!). The default value for bias is 0; that is, it does not add anything to the results.

The targetX and targetY attributes indicate the position of the pixel to be processed relative to the upper-left corner of the convolution matrix, starting from 0. In the previous example, the pixel to be processed was always the pixel at position (1,1) relative to the matrix (position (0,0) is the upper-left corner, indicate by the superscript *b*). By default, the pixel is assumed to be at the position floor((N-1)/2), where N is the number of rows or columns and floor() is the largest integer less than or equal to the expression.

The edgeMode indicates how pixels along the edges of the graphic are treated, with potential values of "duplicate", "wrap", and "none".

When edgeMode="duplicate", the convolve matrix assumes that the first row or column is repeated beyond the edge of the graphic for as many rows or columns as needed to complete the transformation.

When edgeMode="wrap", the graphic is assumed to be a torus—the row immediately after the bottom row is the top row, the column immediately after the right column is the left column. This mode is especially useful for creating tiled patterns.

Setting edgeMode="none" assumes that the value of each pixel outside the graphic is 0. This has the effect of darkening the edges in many convolution matrices.

Normally, the convolution matrix acts on all four RGBA channels of a pixel. However, there may be times where it is preferable to keep the alpha channel untouched. To do this, the preserveAlpha attribute can be set to a value of "true". This essentially removes the channel from processing. The default is "false".

The previous convolution is not visually interesting, but by replacing the central value (currently 4) with 0.01, you can create an "edgy" piece of art on the current sample, given in Listing 7-24 and shown in Figure 7-36.

Listing 7-24. feConvolveMatrix.svg

```
<svg xmlns="http://www.w3.org/2000/svg"
     xmlns:xlink="http://www.w3.org/1999/xlink">
     <style type="text/css">
.textDisplay {dominant-baseline:hanging;
              fill:yellow;
              stroke:black;
              stroke-width:2;
              font-size:100;
              font-family:Impact;
              }
.lightLabel {
              fill:black;
              font-size:30;
              font-family:Arial;
              font-weight:bold;
              }
     </style>
     <filter id="convolvedFilter" filterUnits="userSpaceOnUse"
             x="-60" y="-60" width="390" height="220">
             <feFlood flood-color="blue" in="SourceGraphic"
                  result="blueBack" x="0" y="0"
                  width="270" height="100"/>
             <feGaussianBlur stdDeviation="15" in="blueBack"
                  result="blurredBack" x="-60" y="-60"
                  width="390" height="220"/>
```

```
            <feImage xlink:href="SweaterMer3.png" y="-60"
                width="237" height="484" result="image"/>
            <feConvolveMatrix in="image" order="3"
                kernelMatrix="1 0 -1 1 0.01 -1 1 0 -1"
                edgeMode="none" result="convolvedImage"/>
            <feMerge>
                <feMergeNode in="blurredBack"/>
                <feMergeNode in="convolvedImage"/>
                <feMergeNode in="SourceGraphic"/>
            </feMerge>
        </filter>

        <g transform="translate(0,25)">
        <text class="lightLabel" x="75" y="25">Unfiltered</text>
        <g transform="translate(100,50)">
        <text class="textDisplay" x="100">
                Filters
        </text>
        </g>
        </g>
        <g transform="translate(0,225)">
        <text class="lightLabel">
            <tspan x="15" y="0">With</tspan>
            <tspan x="15" y="40">Convolve</tspan>
            <tspan x="15" y="80">Matrix</tspan>
            <tspan x="15" y="120">Applied</tspan>
        </text>
        <g transform="translate(200,50)">
        <text class="textDisplay"
            filter="url(#convolvedFilter)">
            Filters
        </text>
        </g>
        </g>
    </svg>
```

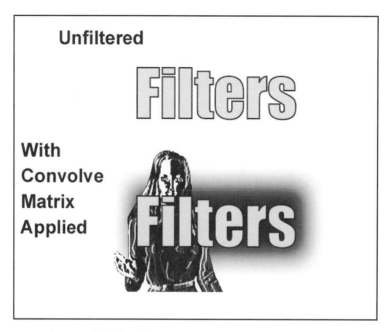

Figure 7-36. Edgy, psychedelic effects with convolve matrices

feMorphology: *Thin and Fat*

The <feMorphology> filter primitive is actually pretty cool. It causes a graphic to either expand (dilate) or contract (erode) by a certain amount, which in turn causes the graphic's alpha channel to similarly expand or contract. In the case of complex shapes such as text, one consequence of this is that the shape of the letters can be changed.

The <feMorphology> element has two distinct attributes beyond the standard filter attributes of in and result. The operator attribute can have the values of "dilate" or "erode", which causes the graphic to grow or shrink in extent. Meanwhile, the radius operator provides the amount (when divided by two) that the graphic shrinks or grows. Think of this radius as specifying a ball that moves along the perimeter of the graphic; the shape traced by the outside edge of the ball gives the dilated shape, and the inner edge traced by the ball gives the eroded shape.

You can see this effect in Listing 7-25, which actually includes the dilated text (saying *Filters*), the original text, and the eroded text overlaid on one another, as shown in Figure 7-37. Notice that this is not a simple scaling effect; the eroded shape is dramatically different from the original shape. Also notice that the width of the stroke is unaffected; the stroke property is a decorative element and has no correlation to the shape itself.

Listing 7-25. `feMorphology.svg`

```
<svg xmlns="http://www.w3.org/2000/svg"
     xmlns:xlink="http://www.w3.org/1999/xlink">
     <style type="text/css">
.textDisplay {dominant-baseline:hanging;
              fill:yellow;
              stroke:black;
              stroke-width:2;
              font-size:100;
              font-family:Impact;
              }
.lightLabel {
              fill:black;
              font-size:30;
              font-family:Arial;
              font-weight:bold;
              }
     </style>
     <filter id="morphFilter" filterUnits="userSpaceOnUse"
             x="-60" y="-60" width="390" height="220">
             <feFlood flood-color="blue" in="SourceGraphic"
                 result="blueBack" x="0" y="0"
                 width="270" height="100"/>
             <feGaussianBlur stdDeviation="15" in="blueBack"
                 result="blurredBack" x="-60" y="-60"
                 width="390" height="220"/>
             <feImage xlink:href="SweaterMer3.png" y="-60"
                 width="237" height="484" result="image"/>
             <feMorphology in="SourceGraphic" radius="4"
                 operator="dilate" result="fatImage"/>
             <feMorphology in="SourceGraphic" radius="4"
                 operator="erode" result="thinImage"/>
             <feMerge>
                 <feMergeNode in="blurredBack"/>
                 <feMergeNode in="image"/>
                 <feMergeNode in="fatImage"/>
                 <feMergeNode in="SourceGraphic"/>
                 <feMergeNode in="thinImage"/>
             </feMerge>
     </filter>

     <g transform="translate(0,25)">
     <text class="lightLabel" x="75" y="25">Unfiltered</text>
```

```
        <g transform="translate(100,50)">
        <text class="textDisplay" x="100">
             Filters
        </text>
        </g>
        </g>
        <g transform="translate(0,225)">
        <text class="lightLabel">
            <tspan x="15" y="0">With</tspan>
            <tspan x="15" y="40">Convolve</tspan>
            <tspan x="15" y="80">Matrix</tspan>
            <tspan x="15" y="120">Applied</tspan>
        </text>
        <g transform="translate(200,50)">
        <text class="textDisplay"
            filter="url(#morphFilter)">
             Filters
        </text>
        </g>
        </g>
    </svg>
```

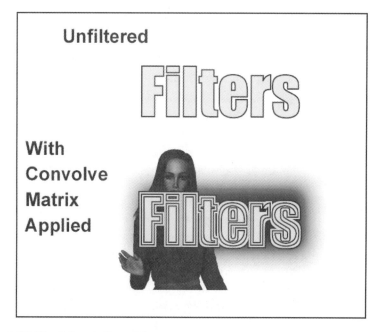

Figure 7-37. The feMorphology *filter*

Lighting: feDiffuseLighting *and* feSpecularLighting

feDiffuseLighting places a "light" at a certain position relative to the input render surface. This light is diffuse; it affects the underlying color of the surface and can support distant lights, point lights, and spot lights.

The notions of light is an odd one in two-dimensional graphics because the concept of a light is only meaningful if it is above the page, and hence in a third dimension. However, by adding light, you can actually create a pseudo-three dimensionality that both makes for more sophisticated graphics and that lays the possibility that SVG may one day leap from the page and merge with 3D graphical standards.

SVG currently defines two distinct kinds of light related filters: feDiffuseLighting and feSpecularLighting. With respect to SVG, the two operate in similar ways, but have slightly different results. In both cases, the lights take advantage of the alpha channels of the elements being illuminated to generate *bump maps*. With a bump map, the regions of transition between light and dark areas on the map are treated as being the equivalent of topographical maps, which means that lighting acting on such a bitmap will create a highlight when the apparent angle caused by the gradient between regions is positive and will create a shadow when the apparent angle is negative.

The principal difference between the two comes in the result. A diffuse light converts the surface to an opaque one with no alpha channel, and a specular light performs the illumination but keeps the alpha channel information intact so that the resulting surface is partially transparent where the shadows are located. One advantage of this is that you can composite the specular image over the diffuse image to get both shadows and highlights in the same image.

The <feDiffuseLight> element defines two attributes that determine the characteristic of the light: surfaceScale and diffuseConstant. The surfaceScale determines the degree to which the alpha channel gradient affects the apparent bumpiness of the bump map. When surfaceScale = 0, the alpha channel has no effect. A surfaceScale = 10 would basically treat an opacity jump from 1 to 0 as a 10-unit high hill. The diffuseConstant attribute, on the other hand, determines the smoothness of the Phong rendering, which is used for shading the gradients.

The <feSpecularLight> element has three attributes that determine the characteristic of the light: surfaceScale, specularConstant, and specularExponent. The surfaceScale acts like the surfaceScale attribute of the diffuse light, determining the degree to which the alpha channel gradient affects the apparent bumpiness of the bump map. The specularConstant on the other hand determines the smoothness of the Phong rendering, which is used for shading the gradients. Finally, the specularExponent determines how "shiny" the surface is. A specularExponent of 1 is a flat mat color, and an exponent of 128 is maximally shiny, with tight highlights appropriate for reflective surfaces.

Listing 7-26 shows the way these lights work. Both a specular and a diffuse light are created, then the surfaces are combined in a way that emphasizes the diffuse layer, the specular layer, and the composite layer (see Figure 7-38).

Listing 7-26. feMixedLighting.svg

```
<svg xmlns="http://www.w3.org/2000/svg"
    xmlns:xlink="http://www.w3.org/1999/xlink">
    <style type="text/css">
.textDisplay {dominant-baseline:hanging;
              fill:yellow;
              stroke:black;
              stroke-width:2;
              font-size:100;
              font-family:Impact;
              }
.lightLabel {
              fill:black;
              font-size:30;
              font-family:Arial;
              font-weight:bold;
              }
    </style>
    <filter id="distantLight" filterUnits="userSpaceOnUse"
            x="-15" y="-15" width="400" height="120">
        <feSpecularLighting in="SourceGraphic" lighting-color="white"
                surfaceScale="1" specularConstant="1"
                specularExponent="32" result="distantSpecLight1">
            <feDistantLight azimuth="25" elevation="25">
                <animate attributeName="azimuth" attributeType="XML"
                    values="0;180;0" dur="9s"
                    repeatCount="indefinite"/>
                <animate attributeName="elevation" attributeType="XML"
                    values="0;180;0" dur="13s"
                    repeatCount="indefinite"/>
            </feDistantLight>
        </feSpecularLighting>
        <feDiffuseLighting in="SourceGraphic" lighting-color="blue"
                result="distantDifLight1">
            <feDistantLight azimuth="25" elevation="25">
                <animate attributeName="azimuth" attributeType="XML"
                    values="0;180;0" dur="9s"
                    repeatCount="indefinite"/>
```

```
                <animate attributeName="elevation" attributeType="XML"
                        values="0;180;0" dur="13s"
                        repeatCount="indefinite"/>
        </feDistantLight>
    </feDiffuseLighting>
    <feComposite in="distantDifLight1" in2="distantSpecLight1"
                operator="arithmetic" k1="0" k2="1" k3="0" k4="0"
                 result="light"/>
    <feImage xlink:href="SweaterMer3.png" x="-60"
            width="237" height="484"
            result="image"/>

    <feMerge>
        <feMergeNode in="light"/>
        <feMergeNode in="image"/>
    </feMerge>
</filter>
<filter id="distantLight2" filterUnits="userSpaceOnUse"
        x="-15" y="-15" width="400" height="120">
    <feSpecularLighting in="SourceGraphic"
            lighting-color="white"
          surfaceScale="1" specularConstant="1"
           specularExponent="32"
          result="distantSpecLight1">
        <feDistantLight azimuth="25" elevation="25">
            <animate attributeName="azimuth" attributeType="XML"
                    values="0;180;0" dur="9s"
                    repeatCount="indefinite"/>
            <animate attributeName="elevation" attributeType="XML"
                    values="0;180;0" dur="13s"
                    repeatCount="indefinite"/>
        </feDistantLight>
    </feSpecularLighting>
    <feDiffuseLighting in="SourceGraphic" lighting-color="blue"
          result="distantDifLight1">
        <feDistantLight azimuth="25" elevation="25">
            <animate attributeName="azimuth" attributeType="XML"
                    values="0;180;0" dur="9s"
                    repeatCount="indefinite"/>
            <animate attributeName="elevation" attributeType="XML"
                    values="0;180;0" dur="13s"
                    repeatCount="indefinite"/>
        </feDistantLight>
    </feDiffuseLighting>
```

```
                        <feComposite in="distantDifLight1" in2="distantSpecLight1"
                                operator="arithmetic" k1="0" k2="0.2" k3="0.8" k4="0"
                                        result="light"/>
                        <feImage xlink:href="SweaterMer3.png" x="-60"
                                width="237" height="484" result="image"/>
                        <feMerge>
                            <feMergeNode in="light"/>
                            <feMergeNode in="image"/>
                        </feMerge>
                    </filter>
                    <filter id="distantLight3" filterUnits="userSpaceOnUse"
                            x="-15" y="-15" width="400" height="120">
                        <feSpecularLighting in="SourceGraphic"
                                lighting-color="white" surfaceScale="1"
                                specularConstant="1" specularExponent="32"
                                result="distantSpecLight1">
                            <feDistantLight azimuth="25" elevation="25">
                                <animate attributeName="azimuth" attributeType="XML"
                                        values="0;180;0" dur="9s" repeatCount="indefinite"/>
                                <animate attributeName="elevation" attributeType="XML"
                                        values="0;180;0" dur="13s" repeatCount="indefinite"/>
                            </feDistantLight>
                        </feSpecularLighting>
                        <feDiffuseLighting in="SourceGraphic" lighting-color="blue"
                                result="distantDifLight1">
                            <feDistantLight azimuth="25" elevation="25">
                                <animate attributeName="azimuth" attributeType="XML"
                                        values="0;180;0" dur="9s" repeatCount="indefinite"/>
                                <animate attributeName="elevation" attributeType="XML"
                                        values="0;180;0" dur="13s" repeatCount="indefinite"/>
                            </feDistantLight>
                        </feDiffuseLighting>
                        <feComposite in="distantDifLight1" in2="distantSpecLight1"
                                operator="arithmetic" k1="0.5" k2="0.8" k3="0.8" k4="0"
                                result="light"/>
```

```
            <feImage xlink:href="SweaterMer3.png" x="-60"
                     width="237" height="484" result="image"/>

        <feMerge>
            <feMergeNode in="light"/>
            <feMergeNode in="image"/>
        </feMerge>
    </filter>
    <g transform="translate(0,25)">
    <text class="lightLabel" x="75" y="25">Mixed Light</text>
    <g transform="translate(100,50)" filter="url(#distantLight)">
    <rect id="box7" width="80" height="80" x="0" y="0"
        fill="red" stroke="black" stroke-width="3"/>
    <text class="textDisplay" x="100">
            Filters
    </text>
    </g>
    <g transform="translate(100,250)" filter="url(#distantLight2)">
    <rect id="box7" width="80" height="80" x="0" y="0"
        fill="red" stroke="black" stroke-width="3"/>
    <text class="textDisplay" x="100">
            Filters
    </text>
    </g>
    <g transform="translate(100,450)" filter="url(#distantLight3)">
    <rect id="box7" width="80" height="80" x="0" y="0"
        fill="red" stroke="black" stroke-width="3"/>
    <text class="textDisplay" x="100">
            Filters
    </text>
    </g>
</svg>
```

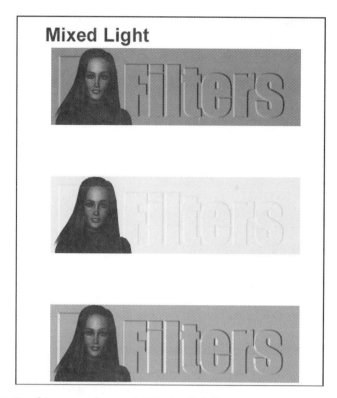

Figure 7-38. Combine specular and diffusive lighting

The light filters let you define three distinct types of lights: distant lights, point lights, and spot lights. These types of light are fairly standard in three-dimensional packages and function as follows:

Distant Lights: A distant light comes from an extremely bright light source located a large distance away so that the light rays coming in are mostly parallel to one another when they illuminate an image. Distant lighting is basically flat and diffuse. You can think of sunlight as being a type of distant light.

`<feDistantLight>` defines two attributes for specifying the direction of light. An azimuth defines the position of the light in the plane where the graphic is located, starting from a position of 3 o'clock and moving clockwise. This value can go from 0° to 360°. Meanwhile, elevation describes the angle between the ground and the light, assuming that the light is at right angles to the ground. The elevation can range from 0 (on the ground) to 90, directly overhead, to 180, back on the ground in the opposite direction.

Point Lights: A point light provides a spherical layer of illumination emanating from a single point in the three-dimensional space around the graphic, with the origin at the origin of the graphics surface. Point lights give off gradiated illumination and can be used in conjunction with other point lights to provide a richer light environment.

`<fePointLight>` defines three attributes: x, y, and z, which give the coordinates of the light on the plane, with a z offset up above the plane. The farther away the light, the less effect it has on the graphic.

Spot Lights: A spot light is a light with a radial extent that can be used to point to a particular position (not necessarily a position on the plane, by the way).

`<feSpotLight>` both defines the location of the light (through the same x, y and z coordinates that `<fePointLight>` uses) and the target of the spot (via attributes pointsAtX, pointsAtY, pointsAtZ). Additionally, `<feSpotLight>` includes the specularExponent (the same as that used by the `<feSpecularLighting>` element and the limitingConeAngle, which gives a cone of diffusion that defines how spread out the light is when it hits the target.

In Listing 7-27, the three types of lights are shown in action, along with animations that show how they vary over time. Figure 7-39 shows the effects of the three lights at a certain time in the animation.

Listing 7-27. feComplexLighting.svg

```
<svg xmlns="http://www.w3.org/2000/svg"
     xmlns:xlink="http://www.w3.org/1999/xlink">
    <style type="text/css">
.textDisplay {dominant-baseline:hanging;
              fill:yellow;
              stroke:black;
              stroke-width:2;
              font-size:100;
              font-family:Impact;
              }
.lightLabel {
              fill:black;
              font-size:30;
              font-family:Arial;
              font-weight:bold;
              }
    </style>
```

```
<filter id="distantLight" filterUnits="userSpaceOnUse"
        x="-15" y="-15" width="400" height="120">
    <feDiffuseLighting in="SourceGraphic" lighting-color="blue"
            result="distantDiffLight">
        <feDistantLight azimuth="45" elevation="45">
            <animate attributeName="azimuth" attributeType="XML"
                    values="0;180;0" dur="9s"
                    repeatCount="indefinite"/>
            <animate attributeName="elevation" attributeType="XML"
                    values="0;180;0" dur="13s"
                    repeatCount="indefinite"/>
        </feDistantLight>
    </feDiffuseLighting>
    <feImage xlink:href="SweaterMer3.png"
            width="237" height="484"
            result="image"/>
    <feComposite in="image" in2="distantDiffLight" operator="arithmetic"
            k1="1" k2="1" k3="1" k4="0"/>
</filter>
<filter id="pointLight" filterUnits="userSpaceOnUse"
        x="-15" y="-15" width="400" height="120">
    <feDiffuseLighting in="SourceGraphic" lighting-color="white"
            result="pointDiffLight">
        <fePointLight x="100" y="50" z="30">
            <animate attributeName="x" attributeType="XML"
                    values="0;400;0" dur="10s" repeatCount="indefinite"/>
        </fePointLight>
    </feDiffuseLighting>
    <feImage xlink:href="SweaterMer3.png" width="237" height="484"
            result="image"/>
    <feComposite in="image" in2="pointDiffLight" operator="arithmetic"
            k1="0.3" k2="0.2" k3="1" k4="0">
        <animate attributeName="k2"
                attributeType="XML" dur="10s"
                values="1;0.2;1;1;1;1;0.2;1"
                repeatCount="indefinite"/>
    </feComposite>
</filter>
<filter id="spotLight" filterUnits="userSpaceOnUse"
        x="-15" y="-15" width="400" height="120">
    <feDiffuseLighting in="SourceGraphic"
            lighting-color="red" result="spotDiffLight">
```

```
        <feSpotLight x="-10" y="50" z="40"
             pointsAtX="300" pointsAtY="50" pointsAtZ="10"
                  specularExponent="10" limitingConeAngle="30">
           <animate attributeName="specularExponent"
                  attributeType="XML"
                  values="0;10;0" dur="10s" repeatCount="indefinite"/>
           <animate attributeName="limitingConeAngle"
                  attributeType="XML"
                  values="10;90;10" dur="11s" repeatCount="indefinite"/>
           <animate attributeName="pointsAtX"
                  attributeType="XML"
                  values="-10;300;-10" dur="10s" repeatCount="indefinite"/>
        </feSpotLight>
     </feDiffuseLighting>
     <feImage xlink:href="SweaterMer3.png"
             width="237" height="484"
             result="image"/>
     <feComposite in="image" in2="spotDiffLight"
             operator="arithmetic" k1="1" k2="1" k3="1" k4="0"/>
  </filter>
  <g transform="translate(0,25)">
  <text class="lightLabel" x="75" y="25">Distant Light</text>
  <g transform="translate(100,50)" filter="url(#distantLight)">
  <rect id="box7" width="80" height="80" x="0" y="0"
     fill="red" stroke="black" stroke-width="3"/>
  <text class="textDisplay" x="100">
        Filters
  </text>
  </g>
  <text class="lightLabel" x="75" y="225">Point Light</text>
  <g transform="translate(100,250)" filter="url(#pointLight)">
  <rect id="box7" width="80" height="80" x="0" y="0"
     fill="red" stroke="black" stroke-width="3"/>
  <text class="textDisplay" x="100">
        Filters
  </text>
  </g>
  <text class="lightLabel" x="75" y="425">Spot Light</text>
  <g transform="translate(100,450)" filter="url(#spotLight)">
  <rect id="box7" width="80" height="80" x="0" y="0"
     fill="red" stroke="black" stroke-width="3"/>
  <text class="textDisplay" x="100">
```

```
          Filters
      </text>
      </g>
      </g>
  </svg>
```

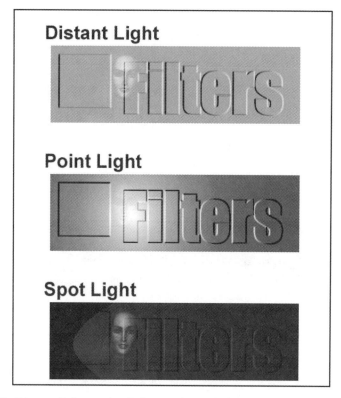

Figure 7-39. Distant lights, point lights, and spot lights

feTurbulence: *Tapping into Chaos*

We live in turbulent times. It is only appropriate we have a filter to match <grin/>. The <feTurbulence> filter adds a bit of chaos into the otherwise stately world of SVG graphics . . . quite literally. Benoit Mandelbrot first laid down the principles of fractals to the general public in the 1980s with the publication of his epochal book, *Fractal Geometry of Nature* (WH Freeman & Co., 1988). Self-repeating structures and nonlinear algorithms were tailor-made for use by computers, and in the two decades since chaos first began to be studied, the most significant strides have been in the graphics arena. Fractals, and the related arena of noise, can add texture to otherwise featureless graphics and can mimic anything from clouds to waves to trees.

The <feTurbulence> filter is not that comprehensive, of course, but it is quite fully capable of creating a variety of different effects (especially when used in conjunction with other filters). Beyond the standard filter primitive types, <feTurbulence> defines several attributes:

type: You can specify that the filter applies either "fractalNoise" or "turbulence" to the source image. Turbulence is generally smooth, with eddies appearing in the structure. Turbulence here is also frequently referred to as *caustics*, for the pattern that light makes when reflected through turbulent water. Fractal noise, on the other hand, is grainy and discrete and can be used to emulate stone, rock, sand, brick, or other granular textures.

baseFrequency: Although appearing random, noise (of either type) does have a certain structure, and one parameter determining that structure is a base frequency. This is roughly the number of times that a noise *cell* is "repeated" in either direction over its extent. The higher the frequency, the more random the noise is. But it is also more expensive to create the turbulence. The default is 0.

numOctaves: Fractal turbulence and noise tend to share a lot of musical terms that describe similar concepts. For instance, an *octave* in noise occurs when the fractal structure of the noise is self-similar when scaled up or down. The higher the number of octaves, the "busier" the resulting noise, and the longer it takes to compute the fractal in question. The default is 1.

seed: Fractals are functions iterated repeatedly against themselves. What this means is that if you start with the same input, or *seed*, you will always get the same output. Choice of seed is important (even critical) because the seed's value (especially at certain points) can often produce extremely divergent behavior. The default value is 0.

stitchTiles: The algorithms that handle feTurbulence do so by creating smaller tiles of results. The stitchTiles attribute can either be set to "stitch", in which case the Perlin algorithm attempts to smooth the boundaries between each time, and "noStitch" turns this behavior off.

Listing 7-28 shows the combination of these attributes and especially demonstrates the difference between turbulence and fractal noise (see Figure 7-40).

Listing 7-28. Turbulence.svg

```
<svg width="450px" height="325px" viewBox="0 0 450 325"
     xmlns="http://www.w3.org/2000/svg">
  <title>Example feTurbulence - Examples of feTurbulence operations</title>
  <desc>Six rectangular areas showing the effects of
        various parameter settings for feTurbulence.</desc>
  <g  font-family="Verdana" text-anchor="middle" font-size="10" >
    <defs>
        <filter id="Turb1" filterUnits="objectBoundingBox"
                x="0%" y="0%" width="100%" height="100%">
          <feTurbulence type="turbulence" baseFrequency="0.05"
                numOctaves="2"/>
        </filter>
        <filter id="Turb2" filterUnits="objectBoundingBox"
                x="0%" y="0%" width="100%" height="100%">
          <feTurbulence type="turbulence" baseFrequency="0.1"
                numOctaves="2"/>
        </filter>
        <filter id="Turb3" filterUnits="objectBoundingBox"
                x="0%" y="0%" width="100%" height="100%">
          <feTurbulence type="turbulence" baseFrequency="0.05"
                numOctaves="8"/>
        </filter>
        <filter id="Turb4" filterUnits="objectBoundingBox"
                x="0%" y="0%" width="100%" height="100%">
          <feTurbulence type="fractalNoise" baseFrequency="0.1"
                numOctaves="4"/>
        </filter>
        <filter id="Turb5" filterUnits="objectBoundingBox"
                x="0%" y="0%" width="100%" height="100%">
          <feTurbulence type="fractalNoise" baseFrequency="0.4"
                numOctaves="4"/>
        </filter>
        <filter id="Turb6" filterUnits="objectBoundingBox"
                x="0%" y="0%" width="100%" height="100%">
          <feTurbulence type="fractalNoise" baseFrequency="0.1"
                numOctaves="1"/>
        </filter>
    </defs>
```

```
<rect x="1" y="1" width="448" height="323"
        fill="none" stroke="blue" stroke-width="1"/>

<rect x="25" y="25" width="100" height="75"
                filter="url(#Turb1)"/>
<text x="75" y="117">type=turbulence</text>
<text x="75" y="129">baseFrequency=0.05</text>
<text x="75" y="141">numOctaves=2</text>

<rect x="175" y="25" width="100" height="75"
                filter="url(#Turb2)"/>
<text x="225" y="117">type=turbulence</text>
<text x="225" y="129">baseFrequency=0.1</text>
<text x="225" y="141">numOctaves=2</text>

<rect x="325" y="25" width="100" height="75"
                filter="url(#Turb3)"/>
<text x="375" y="117">type=turbulence</text>
<text x="375" y="129">baseFrequency=0.05</text>
<text x="375" y="141">numOctaves=8</text>

<rect x="25" y="180" width="100" height="75"
                filter="url(#Turb4)"/>
<text x="75" y="272">type=fractalNoise</text>
<text x="75" y="284">baseFrequency=0.1</text>
<text x="75" y="296">numOctaves=4</text>

<rect x="175" y="180" width="100" height="75"
                filter="url(#Turb5)"/>
<text x="225" y="272">type=fractalNoise</text>
<text x="225" y="284">baseFrequency=0.4</text>
<text x="225" y="296">numOctaves=4</text>

<rect x="325" y="180" width="100" height="75"
                filter="url(#Turb6)"/>
<text x="375" y="272">type=fractalNoise</text>
<text x="375" y="284">baseFrequency=0.1</text>
<text x="375" y="296">numOctaves=1</text>
    </g>
</svg>
```

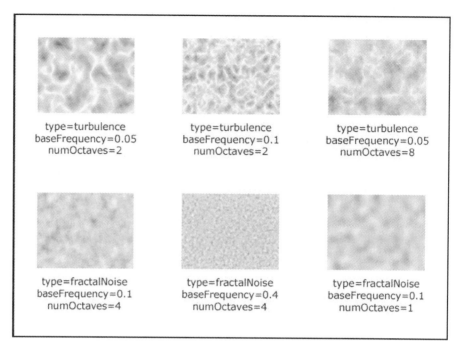

Figure 7-40. Adding texture into both images and alpha channels with noise

There is not enough space here to experiment with the possibilities that both turbulence and noise open up, but they include such projects as creating underwater lights, adding textures to rough up surfaces without the use of bitmaps, dissolves, hair (by performing a motion blur on noise), ragged edges (in conjunction with the morphology erode property), and many more.

Incorporating Filters

Filters are much like syrup in a latte—a little bit is great for cutting the bitterness of SVG itself, but when used too much, filters can overwhelm the taste of the coffee (or the presentation). Filters replace loading of images with computations, and just as with working with images, there are a few tips you can use to optimize your SVG:

- Animating alpha channels can be an incredibly expensive operation. Balance your need for "cool" drop shadows and glows against this reality.

- feTurbulence, feDiffuseLighting, feSpecularLighting, feGaussianBlur, feColorMatrix, and feDisplacementMap all involve lengthy computations that can significantly slow down your work. Sometimes it is better to create partially translucent graphics in paint packages and then incorporate them into your SVG, rather than attempting to build the graphics on the fly.

- Many SVG implementations do not fully support filters (especially animated filters), so test out your filtered applications on your target platforms before committing to a filtered approach.

- Filters can cause trouble with memory, so again, use them judiciously.

- Finally, use filters wisely. If, by animating, you can get a much smaller part of a screen through filters rather than the whole screen, the filter will work pretty well.

Having said all that, filters can give you exquisite control over your graphics, and especially in conjunction with other filters can provide the groundwork for some truly exceptional special effects.

Summary

One of the distinguishing marks between an amateur artist and a professional is the level of detail (and the contrast of detail and simplicity) that a professional artist will place in their work. This texture can be overdone—realism for the sake of realism is not always a laudable goal—but knowing how to apply just enough texture to a piece of artwork can turn an average work into an exceptional one.

This chapter looked at the ways that textures could be applied: through the use of images, patterns, alpha channel masks, clip paths, and filters. It says something that a topic seemingly so mundane could end up taking up a major portion of the book.

This is the last chapter in the first part of this book, concentrating on the process of creating (primarily) static graphics. From here on, things whiz around, bang together, emerge and disappear like ethereal ghosts, and otherwise become far more intriguing and lifelike. Chapter 8 makes all this happen: "Animating SVG."

CHAPTER 8

Animating SVG

IN THE FIRST YEARS OF THE 20th century, long before Mickey Mouse, Popeye the Sailor, Betty Boop, Bugs Bunny, and Krazy Kat flitted around on the silver screen, a quiet, unassuming comic strip artist named Windsor McKay had an intriguing idea. A few years earlier, McKay had gained a reputation as one of the first strip artists of the age, combining surrealism and Art Nouveau sensibilities with a deft sense of humor in such strips as *Little Nemo* and *Dreams of a Rarebit Fiend* for William Randolph Hearst's newspapers.

Becoming quite popular, McKay went onto the lecture circuit, where he did an interesting skit with rapid drawings on a newsprint pad. After seeing one of the new movies that were becoming all of the rage in theaters, he began playing with the idea of transcribing his rapid sketch artwork onto frames of film, and in the process he created the first animated cartoon. Called *Gertie the Dinosaur*, it featured a young Brontosaurus as she ambled across the prehistoric landscape, eating trees, drinking up lakes, and giving an animated McKay a lift as the film ended (see Figure 8-1).

Figure 8-1. Gertie the Dinosaur

Animation has of course come a long, long way since Gertie first trudged (and danced) her way to fame. Yet ironically, the most effective animations use many of the same principles first pioneered by McKay. The process of animation is, at its heart, the ability to control time.

SMIL: You're on SVG Camera

In Scalable Vector Graphics (SVG), animation basically involves changing one or more properties of a graphic over time, usually relative to either a specific starting time or a given event such as a mouse click or the completion of another animation. This animation could be the change of position (motion animation), but could just as readily be a transformation rotation such as rotating or scaling an object, cycling through various colors, replacing a reference from one graphic (or text block) to another, making an object more or less opaque, changing the fill or stroke that a given graphic uses, or even changing the path that a given animation follows.

SVG accomplishes animations by adopting an Extensible Markup Language (XML) language specifically intended to handle animations: the Synchronous Multimedia Integration Language (SMIL). SMIL was originally designed to solve one of the more vexing problems facing most presentation languages, including Hypertext Markup Language (HTML): how to schedule specific events or actions in various media.

Ideally, such a language should be able to describe when a given object should begin animating, when it should stop, and whether it should repeat (and how many times). It should also describe what happens when the animation completes. SMIL does this via the `<animation>` element, along with the specialized elements `<set>`, `<animateMotion>`, `<animateColor>`, and `<animateTransform>`. For instance, the following SMIL/SVG code causes the opacity of an element to fade to nothing, starting three seconds after the presentation and ending four seconds later:

```
<svg xmlns="http://www.w3.org/2000/svg"
     xmlns:xlink="http://www.w3.org/1999/xlink">
<rect fill="blue" x="100" y="100" width="200" height="100"
    opacity="1">
<animate attributeName="opacity" attributeType="CSS" from="1"
    to="0" begin="3s" dur="4s" fill="freeze"/>
</rect>
</svg>
```

The `<animate>` tag in this code specifies that the property in the `attributeName` attribute will change uniformly from one value (the value `"1"` specified in the from attribute) to another value (the value "0" specified in the to attribute). The attributeType "CSS" indicates that the attribute is part of the CSS set (the alternative is "XML", for values not specifically defined as part of CSS).

 NOTE *The specific reason for the* attributeType *property is somewhat mysterious because the divisions between Cascading Style Sheets (CSS) and XML are not terribly clear-cut. For instance, the* x *attribute used for specifying location is considered an XML property, not a CSS property. In general, when building your animations, if you cannot get a specific property to work as CSS, try changing this to XML or vice versa.*

There are two time attributes in this sample animation: begin and dur. The begin attributes gives the event that starts the animation (in this case, when the time from the loading of the SVG to the current time equals three seconds), and the dur attribute provides the interval for the animation to remain in effect.

Once the indicated interval is reached, then the animation needs to know whether to return back to its original position (fill="restore") or to stay in the last state of the animation (fill="freeze"). For example, in the current ani mation, with fill="freeze", once the four second duration for transitioning from an opacity of "1" to an opacity of "0" is up, the opacity will remain set to "0". On the other hand, with fill="restore", the opacity will immediately return to "1" when time is up.

 CAUTION *The animation* fill *attribute is not the same as a shape's fill. This unfortunate confluence of terms arose because the animation language uses the SMIL namespace (without declaring it as such), and in SMIL, fill is used in the context of "filling" an animation score.*

Not all animations are transitional in nature. For instance, suppose you wanted a line of text to pop up in the graphic after five seconds. A common programming trick to make this happen is to set the visibility attribute to "hidden" and then use another animation element, the <set> element, to make the element visible.

For instance, in Listing 8-1 (a snippet from Lewis Carroll's "Jabberwocky" from *Through the Looking-Glass and What Alice Found There*), each line of the poem appears a second after the previous one, using the set command to determine the animation timing (see Figure 8-2).

Listing 8-1. Jabberwocky.svg

```
<svg ="http://www.w3.org/2000/svg"
     xmlns:xlink="http://www.w3.org/1999/xlink">
    <g transform="translate(100,100)" font-size="20">
        <text x="0" y="0" visibility="hidden">
            <set attributeName="visibility" attributeType="CSS"
                 to="visible" begin="1s" fill="freeze"/>
                 T'was brillig and the slithy toves
        </text>
        <text x="0" y="20" visibility="hidden">
            <set attributeName="visibility" attributeType="CSS"
                 to="visible" begin="2s" fill="freeze"/>
                 Did gyre and gymbol in the wabe.
        </text>
        <text x="0" y="40" visibility="hidden">
            <set attributeName="visibility" attributeType="CSS"
                 to="visible" begin="3s" fill="freeze"/>
                 All mimsy were the borogroves,
        </text>
        <text x="0" y="60" visibility="hidden">
            <set attributeName="visibility" attributeType="CSS"
                 to="visible" begin="4s" fill="freeze"/>
                 And the mome raths outgrabe.
        </text>
        <text x="0" y="100" visibility="hidden">
            <set attributeName="visibility" attributeType="CSS"
                 to="visible" begin="5s" fill="freeze"/>
                 Beware the Jabberwock, my son!
        </text>
        <text x="0" y="120" visibility="hidden">
            <set attributeName="visibility" attributeType="CSS"
                 to="visible" begin="6s" fill="freeze"/>
                 The jaws that bite, the claws that catch!
        </text>
        <text x="0" y="140" visibility="hidden">
            <set attributeName="visibility" attributeType="CSS"
                 to="visible" begin="7s" fill="freeze"/>
```

```
                        Beware the Jub-jub bird and shun
            </text>
            <text x="0" y="160" visibility="hidden">
                <set attributeName="visibility" attributeType="CSS"
                        to="visible" begin="8s" fill="freeze"/>
                    The frumious Bandersnatch!
            </text>
        </g>
</svg>
```

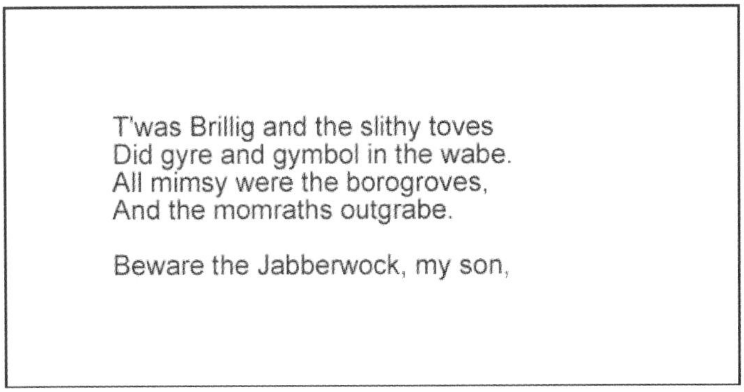

T'was Brillig and the slithy toves
Did gyre and gymbol in the wabe.
All mimsy were the borogroves,
And the momraths outgrabe.

Beware the Jabberwock, my son,

Figure 8-2. Animating opacity for any number of effects

The syntax for <set> is pretty much identical to that of <animate>, save that it acts all at once, rather than providing a continuous transition.

It is possible to have more than one animation associated with a given item. For example, in the previous animation, suppose you wanted each line to fade away after it had been displayed for two seconds. You can do this by combining <set> and <animate> statements, as in Listing 8-2 (see Figure 8-3).

Listing 8-2. Jabberwocky2.svg

```
<svg ="http://www.w3.org/2000/svg"
     xmlns:xlink="http://www.w3.org/1999/xlink">
    <g transform="translate(100,100)" font-size="20">
        <text x="0" y="0" visibility="hidden">
            <set attributeName="visibility" attributeType="CSS"
                    to="visible" begin="1s" fill="freeze"/>
                <animate attributeName="opacity"
                        attributeType="CSS"
                        from="1" to="0" begin="3s"
```

```
                              dur="3s" fill="freeze"/>
                   T'was Brillig and the slithy toves
            </text>
            <text x="0" y="20" visibility="hidden">
                <set attributeName="visibility" attributeType="CSS"
                        to="visible" begin="2s" fill="freeze"/>
                    <animate attributeName="opacity"
                            attributeType="CSS"
                            from="1" to="0" begin="4s"
                            dur="3s" fill="freeze"/>
                    Did gyre and gymbol in the wabe.
            </text>
            <text x="0" y="40" visibility="hidden">
                <set attributeName="visibility" attributeType="CSS"
                        to="visible" begin="3s" fill="freeze"/>
                    <animate attributeName="opacity"
                            attributeType="CSS"
                            from="1" to="0" begin="5s"
                            dur="3s" fill="freeze"/>
                    All mimsy were the borogroves,
            </text>
            <text x="0" y="60" visibility="hidden">
                <set attributeName="visibility"
                        attributeType="CSS"
                        to="visible" begin="4s"
                        fill="freeze"/>
                <animate attributeName="opacity"
                        attributeType="CSS"
                        from="1" to="0" begin="6s"
                        dur="3s" fill="freeze"/>
                And the momraths outgrabe.
            </text>
        <!-- And so on -->
    </g>
</svg>
```

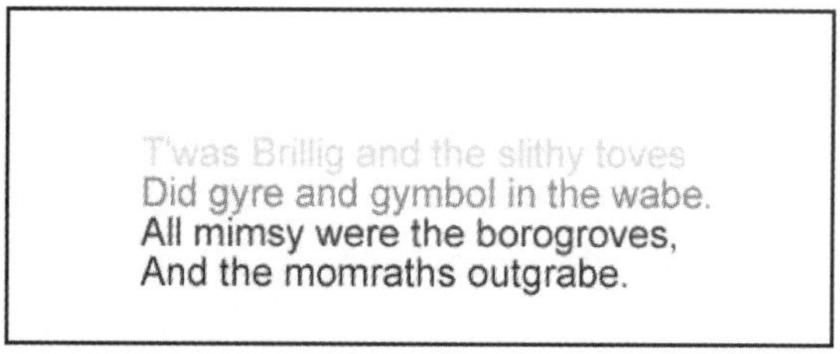

Figure 8-3. Poetically animating opacity

Creating Simple Event-Driven Animations

Timed animations by themselves can make for interesting visual eye candy, but from the standpoint of programming SVG, they are not all that useful. Chances are, you would prefer to be able to make animations work in response to a mouse click or a key press—or, put another way, you want to make your code event driven.

SVG was designed with event-driven interactions in mind, either through assigning event handlers to element tags (as you would find in HTML) or by starting or stopping animations using specific events. The former case, where you might have something like an onclick attribute, as in this:

```
<rect onclick="foobar()"/>
```

will be covered extensively in Chapter 9 ("Integrating SVG and HTML"). This section, on the other hand, looks at the use of events to start or stop animations.

The begin attribute normally takes a time in seconds. However, this duration is actually in response to a specific event: the time at which the SVG is first instantiated. You could thus think of this time as in fact being a shorthand for the longer expression "load + 0s". It is this form that forms the basis for all event-driven programming. For instance, in the following SVG document, the rectangle will fade away to nothing when it is clicked.

```
<svg xmlns="http://www.w3.org/2000/svg"
     xmlns:xlink="http://www.w3.org/1999/xlink">
<rect x="100" y="100" width="200" height="100" fill="blue">
<animate attributeName="opacity" attributeType="CSS" from="1"
    to="0" begin="click + 0s" dur="1s" fill="restore"/>
</rect>
</svg>
```

When there is no delay like this, the expression "+ 0s" can be dropped:

```
<svg xmlns="http://www.w3.org/2000/svg"
     xmlns:xlink="http://www.w3.org/1999/xlink">
<rect x="100" y="100" width="200" height="100" fill="blue">
```

```
<animate attributeName="opacity" attributeType="CSS" from="1"
    to="0" begin="click" dur="1s" fill="restore"/>
</rect>
</svg>
```

With respect to mouse events, the SVG recommendation defines several event handlers:

- **click:** Called when the user clicks on an element with the mouse and releases the mouse while still over the element.

- **mousedown:** Called when the user presses down on the mouse button while over the element.

- **mouseup:** Called when the user releases the mouse button while over the element.

- **mouseover:** Called when the user moves into an element with the mouse.

- **mouseout:** Called when the user moves out of an element with the mouse.

- **mousemove:** Called whenever the mouse moves while within the element. Note that if the mouse does not move, no event is registered.

- **activate:** Called whenever the element is clicked or (if text) selected.

- **focusin:** Called whenever the element receives the focus (typically acts like a mouseover, except for text).

- **focusout:** Called whenever the element loses the focus (typically acts like a mouseover, except for text).

With these primary events, you can actually create highly interactive applications. For example, consider the simple case of a prototypical button—in this case, a blue rectangle (see Listing 8-3).

When the mouse enters the button, the border changes to red. When the mouse is depressed, the rectangle fill color changes to navy until the button is released, at which point it is restored to the brighter blue. Finally, when the mouse moves out, the border returns to its original black (see Figure 8-4).

Listing 8-3. `colorButton1.svg`

```
<svg xmlns="http://www.w3.org/2000/svg"
     xmlns:xlink="http://www.w3.org/1999/xlink">
<rect x="100" y="100" width="100" height="100" fill="blue"
    stroke="black" stroke-width="2">
<set attributeName="stroke" attributeType="CSS" to="red"
    begin="mouseover" end="mouseout"/>
<set attributeName="fill" attributeType="CSS" to="navy"
    begin="mousedown" end="mouseup"/>
</rect>
</svg>
```

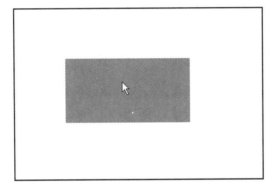

Figure 8-4. The mouseover *and* mouseout *commands*

The begin and end attributes provide the cues that start and end the animation. In the first case, the stroke attribute is set to red when the mouseover event gets sent to the rectangle element (in other words, when the mouse moves over it). This condition stays in effect until the end condition is reached—the mouse moves out of the rectangle (mouseout). Notice that these two events do not care what the state of the mouse button itself is—they will work regardless of whether the mouse button is down or up.

The second case is similar, though it points to a distinction that needs to be made. The mousedown event is called only when the mouse button is pressed while the mouse is within the rectangle—if the mouse button is pressed outside then dragged in, the event is not called.

This typically is not a problem, but the mouseup event can be. The difficulty comes when you click on a button, then drag off of the button before releasing. The problem is that the element only retains knowledge about the button while it is within its focus area (typically its bounding rectangle, though this can be changed through clip paths). Once the mouse moves out of that focus area, the button never receives the mouseup event, which means it stays in the depressed position.

Fortunately, SVG (actually SMIL, but SVG uses the same conventions) recognizes that sometimes there is a need for more than one event to either start or end an animation. You can solve the problem of the sticky button by adding a mouseout event to the fill-changing animation. You do this by expanding the end attribute's value with a semicolon list:

```
<svg>
    <rect x="100" y="100" width="100" height="100" fill="blue"
        stroke="black" stroke-width="2">
    <set attributeName="stroke" attributeType="CSS" to="red"
        begin="mouseover" end="mouseout"/>
    <set attributeName="fill" attributeType="CSS" to="navy"
        begin="mousedown" end="mouseup;mouseout"/>
    </rect>
</svg>
```

Notice that both the stroke and fill animations now include a mouseout end event. In general, this is not a problem—the same event can be used for more than one animation within the same element, provided that the event is not involved in setting the same attribute more than once for a given element. Moreover, the same event cannot be used for both the begin and the end attributes unless the end has a time offset greater than the begin.

For instance, in Listing 8-4, the click event starts the animation, setting the color of the blue button to yellow. The end attribute then specifies that three seconds after the click event, the animation will stop (see Figure 8-5).

Listing 8-4. ColorButton2.svg

```
<svg xmlns="http://www.w3.org/2000/svg"
    xmlns:xlink="http://www.w3.org/1999/xlink">
    <rect x="100" y="100" width="100" height="100" fill="blue"
        stroke="black" stroke-width="2">
        <set attributeName="fill" attributeType="CSS" to="red"
            begin="click" end="click + 3s" fill="restore"/>
    </rect>
</svg>
```

Figure 8-5. Combining mouse and timing actions

This in turn gives a hint as to how to make one event start an animation and the same kind of an event end it. You can set the difference between the begin and the end events to be small—say 0.1 seconds. For instance, Listing 8-5 illustrates how you can set or reset a selection of buttons by clicking them on and off (see Figure 8-6).

Listing 8-5. ColorButton3.svg

```
<svg xmlns="http://www.w3.org/2000/svg"
     xmlns:xlink="http://www.w3.org/1999/xlink">
    <g transform="translate(100,100)">
        <rect x="0" y="0" width="30" height="30" fill="blue"
            stroke="black" stroke-width="2" id="bt1">
            <set attributeName="fill" attributeType="CSS" to="red"
                    begin="click" end="click + 0.1s"
                    fill="restore"/>
        </rect>
        <rect x="0" y="30" width="30" height="30" fill="blue"
            stroke="black" stroke-width="2">
            <set attributeName="fill"
                    attributeType="CSS" to="red"
                    begin="click" end="click + 0.1s"
                    fill="restore"/>
        </rect>
        <rect x="0" y="60" width="30" height="30" fill="blue"
            stroke="black" stroke-width="2">
            <set attributeName="fill" attributeType="CSS" to="red"
                    begin="click" end="click + 0.1s"
                    fill="restore"/>
        </rect>
```

```
                <rect x="0" y="90" width="30" height="30" fill="blue"
                    stroke="black" stroke-width="2">
                        <set attributeName="fill"
                            attributeType="CSS" to="red"
                            begin="click" end="click + 0.1s"
                            fill="restore"/>
                </rect>
                <rect x="0" y="120" width="30" height="30" fill="blue"
                    stroke="black" stroke-width="2">
                        <set attributeName="fill"
                            attributeType="CSS" to="red"
                            begin="click" end="click + 0.1s"
                            fill="restore"/>
                </rect>
        </g>
</svg>
```

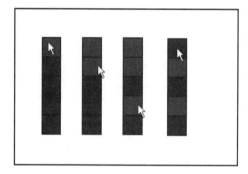

Figure 8-6. Catching click events

Introducing Event Bubbling and Cascading

When you click upon a particular point in the screen that has one or more elements underneath, that click can go in one of two directions—down the tree or up the tree. Think of an event in this case as a cookie: chocolate chip, peanut butter, or oatmeal raisin. Each element along the way has a preference for zero or more of these kinds of cookies (an element may not like any cookies at all, of course).

The cookie is passed up or down the tree, and at each point the element needs to decide whether it wants to eat the cookie (has an event handler for that event). If he does eat the cookie, it cannot be passed on—it gets consumed.

In the event bubbling model, the cookie eater either eats the cookie or passes it to its parent (a rectangle element passes the event to its containing <g>

element, which in turn passes it to its containing <svg> element). The event is said to *bubble up* until it gets consumed. If no one likes the cookie, it simple goes uneaten and passes to the garbage collector (which of course eats everything, but does nothing with what it eats).

The event bubbling model is the default mode for interaction—an event moves up the tree until it passes to the root node, and from there it moves out to the garbage collector.

You can use this default event bubbling behavior to simplify your animations somewhat. For instance, consider Listing 8-6. which displays the bubbling principle at work (see Figure 8-7).

Listing 8-6. ColorButton4.svg

```
<svg xmlns="http://www.w3.org/2000/svg"
    xmlns:xlink="http://www.w3.org/1999/xlink">
    <g transform="translate(100,100)">
        <g transform="translate(0,0)">
            <rect x="0" y="0" width="30" height="30" fill="blue"
                    stroke="black" stroke-width="2" id="bt1">
                <set attributeName="fill"
                        attributeType="CSS" to="red"
                        begin="click" end="click + 0.1s"
                        fill="restore"/>
            </rect>
            <text x="15" y="15" font-size="25" text-anchor="middle"
                    dominant-baseline="mathematical">
                    1
            </text>
        </g>
        <g transform="translate(0,30)">
            <rect x="0" y="0" width="30" height="30" fill="blue"
                    stroke="black" stroke-width="2" id="bt1">
                <set attributeName="fill"
                        attributeType="CSS" to="red"
                        begin="click" end="click + 0.1s"
                        fill="restore"/>
            </rect>
            <text x="15" y="15" font-size="25"
                    text-anchor="middle"
                    dominant-baseline="mathematical">
                    2
            </text>
        </g>
```

```
<g transform="translate(0,60)">
    <rect x="0" y="0" width="30" height="30" fill="blue"
            stroke="black" stroke-width="2" id="bt1">
            <set attributeName="fill"
                    attributeType="CSS" to="red"
                    begin="click" end="click + 0.1s"
                    fill="restore"/>
    </rect>
    <text x="15" y="15" font-size="25"
            text-anchor="middle"
            dominant-baseline="mathematical">
            3
    </text>
</g>
<g transform="translate(0,90)">
    <rect x="0" y="0" width="30" height="30" fill="blue"
            stroke="black" stroke-width="2" id="bt1">
            <set attributeName="fill"
                    attributeType="CSS" to="red"
                    begin="click" end="click + 0.1s"
                    fill="restore"/>
    </rect>
    <text x="15" y="15" font-size="25"
            text-anchor="middle"
            dominant-baseline="mathematical">
            4
    </text>
</g>
<g transform="translate(0,120)">
    <rect x="0" y="0" width="30" height="30" fill="blue"
            stroke="black" stroke-width="2" id="bt1">
            <set attributeName="fill"
                    attributeType="CSS" to="red"
                    begin="click" end="click + 0.1s"
                    fill="restore"/>
    </rect>
    <text x="15" y="15" font-size="25"
            text-anchor="middle"
            dominant-baseline="mathematical">
            5
    </text>
</g>
</svg>
```

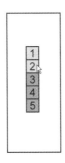

Figure 8-7. Bubbling events

If you build and run this SVG graphic, you will have the buttons from the previous example, but with numbers from 1 to 5. Clicking in the rectangle will cause the color of the rectangle to toggle from blue to red and vice versa, but if you click on the number, nothing happens. Why? The problem is that the text element's events bubble upward from text to g to svg, but the event handler is in the rectangle object, which is not in this chain. Because the event cookie never bubbles into the rectangle, there is nothing to eat it.

However, you can modify this by placing the fill color on the ⟨g⟩ element and letting all descending elements either inherit or override that property explicitly. The ⟨animate⟩ tag, in turn, can be placed as a child of the ⟨g⟩ element as in Listing 8-7 and Figure 8-8.

Listing 8-7. `ColorButton5.svg`

```
<svg xmlns="http://www.w3.org/2000/svg"
        xmlns:xlink="http://www.w3.org/1999/xlink">
    <defs>
        <style type="text/css">
.buttonText {font-size:18;
                    text-anchor:middle;
                    dominant-baseline:mathematical;
                    fill:yellow;}
        </style>
        <rect id="rectBase" x="0" y="0"
                    width="100" height="30" stroke="black"
                    stroke-width="2"/>
        <text id="button1Text" class="buttonText"
                    x="50" y="15">Button 1</text>
        <text id="button2Text" class="buttonText"
                    x="50" y="15">Button 2</text>
        <text id="button3Text" class="buttonText"
                    x="50" y="15">Button 3</text>
```

```
                <text id="button4Text" class="buttonText"
                        x="50" y="15">Button 4</text>
                <text id="button5Text" class="buttonText"
                        x="50" y="15">Button 5</text>
        </defs>
        <g transform="translate(100,100)">
            <g id="button1">
                <set attributeName="fill"
                        attributeType="CSS" to="blue"
                        begin="load" fill="freeze"/>
                <set attributeName="fill" attributeType="CSS" to="red"
                        begin="click" end="click + 0.1s" fill="restore"/>
                <use xlink:href="#rectBase" x="0" y="0"/>
                <use xlink:href="#button1Text" x="0" y="0"/>
            </g>
            <g id="button2" transform="translate(100,0)">
                <set attributeName="fill" attributeType="CSS" to="blue"
                        begin="load" fill="freeze"/>
                <set attributeName="fill" attributeType="CSS" to="red"
                        begin="click" end="click + 0.1s" fill="restore"/>
                <use xlink:href="#rectBase" x="0" y="0"/>
                <use xlink:href="#button2Text" x="0" y="0"/>
            </g>
            <g id="button3" transform="translate(200,0)">
                <set attributeName="fill" attributeType="CSS" to="blue"
                        begin="load" fill="freeze"/>
                <set attributeName="fill" attributeType="CSS" to="red"
                        begin="click" end="click + 0.1s" fill="restore"/>
                <use xlink:href="#rectBase" x="0" y="0"/>
                <use xlink:href="#button3Text" x="0" y="0"/>
            </g>
            <g id="button4" transform="translate(300,0)">
                <set attributeName="fill" attributeType="CSS" to="blue"
                        begin="load" fill="freeze"/>
                <set attributeName="fill" attributeType="CSS" to="red"
                        begin="click" end="click + 0.1s" fill="restore"/>
                <use xlink:href="#rectBase" x="0" y="0"/>
                <use xlink:href="#button4Text" x="0" y="0"/>
            </g>
            <g id="button5" transform="translate(400,0)">
                <set attributeName="fill" attributeType="CSS" to="blue"
                        begin="load" fill="freeze"/>
```

```
        <set attributeName="fill" attributeType="CSS" to="red"
                begin="click" end="click + 0.1s" fill="restore"/>
        <use xlink:href="#rectBase" x="0" y="0"/>
        <use xlink:href="#button5Text" x="0" y="0"/>
    </g>
  </g>
</svg>
```

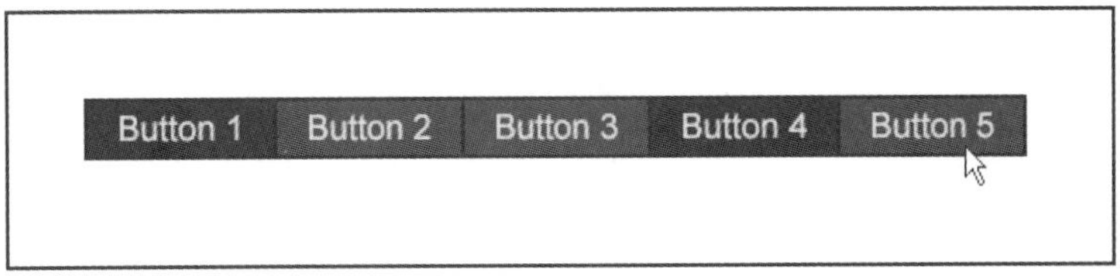

Button 1	Button 2	Button 3	Button 4	Button 5

Figure 8-8. Intelligent use of element cascading

Once you make these changes, the animation event handler for the click event is now contained in the <g> element rather than in the rectangle itself. Thus, anything that is contained within that same <g> element will pass the cookie up to the graphics context element, unless it specifically overrides it with its own click handler.

Event cascading, on the other hand, passes any event that occurs down from the background to any child elements that have the focus (in other words, usually the element that is clicked on or moved over). This model can be likened to a chain letter—the one where you are asked to send the letter on to all of your friends (or here, your children), with encouragement for them to do the same. If a given element consumes the event token, it does not pass it on, otherwise, it makes as many copies as it has children and passes the event on to each of them.

The event cascading model differs from the event bubbling model in one important respect: More than one element can receive and act on the same event. This will usually be somewhat counterintuitive. A click event, for instance, would always start with the <svg> node and then apply to all elements that have click event handlers—regardless of whether that element is beneath the mouse at the time. There are a few specialized cases where passing events in cascades makes sense (such as unload or abort calls), but they usually occur only in context of DOM programming. For that reason, there is no way to change the event handling model from an event bubbling one to an event cascading (also known as *event capturing*) one within declarative SVG; however, you can do it using DOM.

Animating Key Presses

The mouse is perhaps the most obvious Graphical User Interface (GUI) device, but the keyboard is certainly far from unimportant in these transactions. Indeed, even in the point-and-click world of today's modern GUIs, keyboard control is still typically much faster than a mouse could ever be.

The accessKey() event handler makes it possible to trap specific key events. For instance, the following expression:

```
accessKey(a)
```

will be called whenever the lower case *a* character is pressed on the keyboard, and accessKey(A) traps the uppercase *A* character.

Going back to the button example, Listing 8-8 and Figure 8-9 present five buttons labeled 1 through 5. Pressing these number keys will activate the buttons (turn the blue background to red), and pressing the Shift key and these numbers will deactivate the respective button.

Listing 8-8. ColorButton6.svg

```
<svg>
    <g transform="translate(100,100)">
        <g transform="translate(0,0)" fill="blue">
            <set attributeName="fill" attributeType="CSS" to="red"
                    begin="accessKey(1)"/>
            <set attributeName="fill" attributeType="CSS" to="blue"
                    begin="accessKey(!)" fill="freeze"/>
            <rect x="0" y="0" width="30" height="30" stroke="black"
                    stroke-width="2" id="bt1">
            </rect>
            <text x="15" y="15" fill="black" font-size="25"
                    text-anchor="middle"
                    dominant-baseline="mathematical">
                    1
            </text>
        </g>
        <g transform="translate(0,30)" fill="blue">
                <set attributeName="fill"
                        attributeType="CSS" to="red"
                        begin="click" end="click+0.1s"/>
                <set attributeName="fill"
                        attributeType="CSS" to="red"
                        begin="accessKey(2)"/>
```

```
            <set attributeName="fill"
                    attributeType="CSS" to="blue"
                    begin="accessKey(@)" fill="freeze"/>
            <rect x="0" y="0" width="30" height="30"
                    stroke="black" stroke-width="2" id="bt2">
            </rect>
            <text x="15" y="15" fill="black" font-size="25"
                    text-anchor="middle"
                    dominant-baseline="mathematical">
                    2
            </text>
    </g>
    <g transform="translate(0,60)" fill="blue">
            <set attributeName="fill"
                    attributeType="CSS" to="red"
                    begin="click" end="click+0.1s"/>
            <set attributeName="fill"
                    attributeType="CSS" to="red"
                    begin="accessKey(3)"/>
            <set attributeName="fill"
                    attributeType="CSS" to="blue"
                    begin="accessKey(#)" fill="freeze"/>
            <rect x="0" y="0" width="30" height="30"
                    stroke="black" stroke-width="2" id="bt3">
            </rect>
            <text x="15" y="15" fill="black" font-size="25"
                    text-anchor="middle"
                    dominant-baseline="mathematical">
                    3
            </text>
    </g>
    <g transform="translate(0,90)" fill="blue">
            <set attributeName="fill"
                    attributeType="CSS" to="red"
                    begin="click" end="click+0.1s"/>
            <set attributeName="fill"
                    attributeType="CSS" to="red"
                    begin="accessKey(4)"/>
             <set attributeName="fill"
                    attributeType="CSS" to="blue"
                    begin="accessKey($)" fill="freeze"/>
            <rect x="0" y="0" width="30" height="30"
                    stroke="black" stroke-width="2" id="bt4">
            </rect>
```

```
                              <text x="15" y="15" fill="black" font-size="25"
                                    text-anchor="middle"
                                    dominant-baseline="mathematical">
                                    4
                              </text>
                  </g>
                  <g transform="translate(0,120)" fill="blue">
                              <set attributeName="fill"
                                    attributeType="CSS" to="red"
                                    begin="click" end="click+0.1s"/>
                              <set attributeName="fill"
                                    attributeType="CSS" to="red"
                                    begin="accessKey(5)"/>
                              <set attributeName="fill"
                                    attributeType="CSS" to="blue"
                                    begin="accessKey(%)" fill="freeze"/>
                              <rect x="0" y="0" width="30" height="30"
                                    stroke="black" stroke-width="2"
                                    id="bt5">
                               </rect>
                               <text x="15" y="15" fill="black" font-size="25"
                                    text-anchor="middle"
                                    dominant-baseline="mathematical">
                                    5
                              </text>
                  </g>
         </g>
</svg>
```

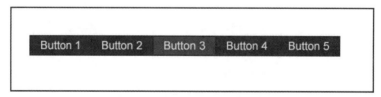

Figure 8-9. Using the accessKey() *function to capture key events*

In the fifth button, for instance, there are three specific animations:

```
<set attributeName="fill"
     attributeType="CSS" to="red"
     begin="click" end="click+0.1s"/>
<set attributeName="fill"
     attributeType="CSS" to="red"
     begin="accessKey(5)"/>
<set attributeName="fill"
     attributeType="CSS" to="blue"
     begin="accessKey(%)" fill="freeze"/>
```

The first animation handles the setting and resetting of the button through the mouse. The second animation uses accessKey(5)—called when the key 5 is pressed—to set the fill to red. The third animation uses the accessKey(%)—which is invoked when the Shift and the 5 key are pressed—at least on U.S. keyboards.

CAUTION   *This was something of a compromise. By all rights, the end attribute should be able to accept an access key to stop an animation, but at least with the current version of Adobe SVG Viewer, this does not seem to happen.*

Some whitespace and special characters can also be caught using the accessKey() function; to do this, you need to use the HTML encoding form &#NN; where NN is the ASCII character code for the characters in question. For instance, this code:

```
accessKey(&#13;)
```

will capture the carriage return character that is sent when someone presses the Enter key, and this code:

```
accessKey(&#32;)
```

will capture the space character. Additionally, you can use the standard encodings for the ampersand (&) and bracket (< and >) characters—&, <, and >, respectively.

NOTE *The set of whitespace characters is somewhat overly restrictive. Essentially, you can catch the space character ( ), tab (	), and carriage return (&13;), but that seems to be it, at least in Internet Explorer. This may be partially because IE captures most of the other characters for its own purposes, but this gets to be problematic for doing things such as capturing arrow keys (you cannot) or function keys.*

Animating Simple Motion

One of the reasons that I like SVG is its ability to create presentations. The traditional presentation is usually fairly text heavy (perhaps too much so), and all too often this text is also static. Sometimes, spicing up a presentation can be as simple as animating some of the more salient bullet points or headlines.

There are in fact several different ways you can create motion-based animations. Perhaps the simplest involves changing the position/dimension-related properties of a given element—the attributes x, y, width, and height. For instance, you could set up an animation in which a text headline started off-screen and flew horizontally into a final position on a page, as shown in Listing 8-9 (see Figure 8-10).

Listing 8-9. MotionAnim1.svg

```
<svg xmlns="http://www.w3.org/2000/svg"
     xmlns:xlink="http://www.w3.org/1999/xlink">
    <text x="100" y="50" font-size="48" font-family="serif">
        <animate attributeName="x" attributeType="XML" from="1024"
            to="50" dur="3s" fill="freeze" begin="load"/>
        Welcome to My World!
    </text>
</svg>
```

Welcome to My World!

Figure 8-10. Motion animation

In this code, the x attribute (of `attributeType="XML"`) starts from the horizontal position 1024 and over three seconds moves to the position 50, at which point it freezes its motion. The animation only begins once all of the elements of the SVG document have loaded (the `begin="load"` statement), thus guaranteeing that the animation precedes smoothly if there is a delay in downloading.

You can have more than one coordinate being animated simultaneously. For instance, in Listing 8-10, the headline comes from the upper-left corner, with both the x and y coordinates changing simultaneously (see Figure 8-11).

Listing 8-10. `MotionAnim2.svg`

```
<svg xmlns="http://www.w3.org/2000/svg"
    xmlns:xlink="http://www.w3.org/1999/xlink">
    <text x="100" y="50" font-size="48" font-family="serif">
        <animate attributeName="x" attributeType="XML" from="-100"
            to="50" dur="3s" fill="freeze" begin="load"/>
        <animate attributeName="y" attributeType="XML" from="-100"
            to="50" dur="3s" fill="freeze" begin="load"/>
        Welcome to My World!
    </text>
</svg>
```

Figure 8-11. Applying motion animation to both coordinates simultaneously

More complex motion animations are possible through the use of the `values` attribute. This attribute lets you define a series of semicolon-delimited values that make it possible to animation continuously between values. For instance, the animation in Listing 8-11 will move the text in a diamond pattern (see Figure 8-12).

Listing 8-11. `MotionAnim2.svg`

```
<svg xmlns="http://www.w3.org/2000/svg"
    xmlns:xlink="http://www.w3.org/1999/xlink">
    <text x="100" y="50" font-size="48" font-family="serif"
        text-anchor="middle">
```

```
                        <animate attributeName="x"
                            attributeType="XML"
                            values="400;500;400;300;400" dur="3s"
                            fill="freeze" begin="load"
                            repeatCount="indefinite"/>
                        <animate attributeName="y"
                            attributeType="XML"
                            values="100;200;300;200;100" dur="3s"
                            fill="freeze" begin="load"
                            repeatCount="indefinite"/>
                        Welcome to My World!
                </text>
        </svg>
```

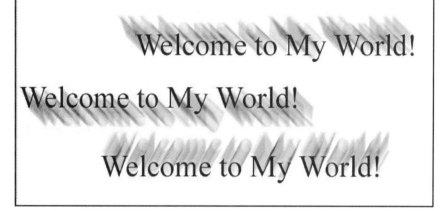

Figure 8-12. The values *attribute*

The x value varies between five values: 400, 500, 400, 300, and 400, as defined in the values attribute. The values attribute basically provides a continuous iteration between each of the values, considered key-frame values so that they are spread out across the duration involved. The animation reaches a value of 500 at 0.75 seconds, 400 at 1.5 seconds, 300 at 2.25 seconds, and back to 400 at 3 seconds, and then it repeats this pattern indefinitely.

The y animation similarly has five values in it, but that is not in fact strictly necessary; the importance here is that the values are interpolated so that the sequence takes place within the allotted time.

A key-frame can then be considered a specific well-defined point in an animation. Most contemporary animation software actually works upon the principle of defining specific keyframes at critical points in the animation, then letting the computer perform interpolations "tweening" to determining the position or some other quality of an animation at the intermediate points between the keyframes.

In addition to being able to define the value of a specific animation at fixed points along an animation, SVG makes it possible to set the key timing of an animation as well, with the keyTimes attribute. This particular attribute contains a semicolon-delimited list of numbers between 0 and 1, giving the relative time (the absolute time given by the dur attribute times the respective keyTimes value. There must be one such number for each value in the values list.

For instance, in Listing 8-12, the three figures move over the same interval in the same period of time: five seconds. However, each has a different keyTimes value. In the first, the sequence is bunched up around the midpoint of the animation (in other words, around the value 0.5) and sparse around the beginning or end of the sequence. This has the effect of making the animation faster as it moves to the right and slower as it moves back to the left (see Figure 8-13).

Listing 8-12. MotionAnim3.svg

```
<svg xmlns="http://www.w3.org/2000/svg"
      xmlns:xlink="http://www.w3.org/1999/xlink">
    <image xlink:href="SweaterMer_0001.png" width="160" height="160">
        <animate attributeName="x" attributeType="XML"
              values="0;100;200;300;400;500;400;300;200;100;0"
              dur="5s" keyTimes="0;.2;.35;.45;.48;.5;.52;.55;.65;.8;1"
              begin="load" repeatCount="indefinite"/>
    </image>
    <image xlink:href="SweaterMer_0001.png"
          width="160" height="160" y="160">
        <animate attributeName="x" attributeType="XML"
              values="0;100;200;300;400;500;400;300;200;100;0"
              keyTimes="0;.025;.05;.1;.2;.5;.8;.9;.95;.975;1"
              begin="load" dur="5s"  repeatCount="indefinite"/>
    </image>
    <image xlink:href="SweaterMer_0001.png"
          width="160" height="160" y="320">
        <animate attributeName="x" attributeType="XML"
              values="0;100;200;300;400;500;400;300;200;100;0"
              dur="5s" begin="load" repeatCount="indefinite"/>
    </image>
  </svg>
```

Figure 8-13. The keyTimes *element*

On the other hand, the second figure has the values bunched around the end points, making the animation appear to slow down as it moves toward the right (the middle of the animation sequence) and speed back up again as it moves toward the left. The final image moves regularly to provide a benchmark for movement of the other two.

Creating Motions on a Path

You can create fairly complex simple-motion animations just by changing the x and y properties, but unless the object is traveling along a straight line (or along a simple polygon) the action can appear jerky. Curved animation paths (or animating along a shape) in particular are almost impossible to do with single property animations.

The <animateMotion> element is specifically intended to handle more complex animations. Although it can be used in much the same way as the <animate>

element to set individual (x,y) points, its real power comes in the ability to assign an animation path using the SVG path language. This path could move an object across a complex trajectory that might loop around itself or potentially even jump from one continuous path segment to another, disconnected one.

Listing 8-13 illustrates this. A graphic (in this case, a red circle with internal white, blue, green, and yellow lines, moves along a complex split path that is defined by the path attribute (see Figure 8-14).

Listing 8-13. AnimPath1.svg

```
<svg xmlns="http://www.w3.org/2000/svg"
     xmlns:xlink="http://www.w3.org/1999/xlink">
    <g transform="translate(200,200)">
        <g>
            <animateMotion
                    path="m-100,0 C0,-100 0,-100 100,-100 L100,0z
                             m300,0 l100,0 l0,-100 l-100,0z"
                    dur="8s" fill="freeze"/>
            <circle cx="0" cy="0" r="50" fill="red"
                    stroke="black" stroke-width="4"/>
            <line x1="0" y1="0" x2="50" y2="0"
                    stroke="blue" stroke-width="4"/>
            <line x1="0" y1="0" x2="-50" y2="0"
                    stroke="green" stroke-width="4"/>
            <line x1="0" y1="0" x2="0" y2="50"
                    stroke="yellow" stroke-width="4"/>
            <line x1="0" y1="0" x2="0" y2="-50"
                    stroke="white" stroke-width="4"/>
        </g>
        <path d="m-100,0 C0,-100 0,-100 100,-100 L100,0z
                    m300,0 l100,0l0,-100 l-100,0z"
                 stroke="black" stroke-width="3" fill="none"/>
    </g>
</svg>
```

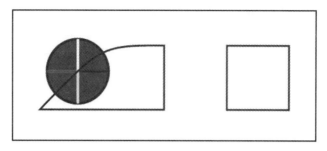

Figure 8-14. The `<animateMotion>` *element*

> **NOTE** *The path itself illustrates the expected motion, but the actual path that the object takes is invisible.*

It is noteworthy that the path itself is split into two disconnected portions. This makes it possible for an object to move along a number of different locations even if they are not contiguous. Also, both the animation path and the demonstration path terminate the respective subpaths with the z command. The object moving along that animation path will also follow the termination subpath as a consequence.

The strange radial lines on the circle are designed to indicate the orientation of the circle. In the example of Listing 8-13, the circle (any graphic, for that matter) always points in one direction—the white line (always points North). However, you can affect the orientation of a graphic along a path. For instance, you may want the orientation to always point to 45 degrees clockwise from North. To do this, you would use the rotate attribute to set the angle explicitly:

```
<animateMotion path="m-100,0 C0,-100 0,-100 100,-100 L100,0z
m300,0 l100,0 l0,-100 l-100,0z" rotate="45" dur="8s" fill="freeze"/>
```

On the other hand, what may prove more useful would be for the graphic to align itself along the direction of motion. For instance, a small car graphic could be made to drive along a complex course, changing direction according to the path. The value to set the rotate property to do this is "auto" (no pun intended—well, not much, anyway). Listing 8-14 illustrates this principle in action (see Figure 8-15).

Listing 8-14. `AnimPath2.svg`

```
<svg xmlns="http://www.w3.org/2000/svg"
    xmlns:xlink="http://www.w3.org/1999/xlink">
    <g transform="translate(200,200)">
        <g>
            <animateMotion
                    path="m-100,0 C0,-100 0,-100 100,-100 L100,0z
                            m300,0 l100,0 l0,-100 l-100,0z"
                    rotate="auto" dur="8s" fill="freeze"/>
            <circle cx="0" cy="0" r="50" fill="red"
                    stroke="black" stroke-width="4"/>
            <line x1="0" y1="0" x2="50" y2="0"
                    stroke="blue" stroke-width="4"/>
            <line x1="0" y1="0" x2="-50" y2="0"
                    stroke="green" stroke-width="4"/>
            <line x1="0" y1="0" x2="0" y2="50"
                    stroke="yellow" stroke-width="4"/>
            <line x1="0" y1="0" x2="0" y2="-50"
                    stroke="white" stroke-width="4"/>
        </g>
         <path
            d="m-100,0 C0,-100 0,-100 100,-100 L100,0z
                m300,0 l100,0 l0,-100 l-100,0z"
            stroke="black" stroke-width="3" fill="none"/>
    </g>
</svg>
```

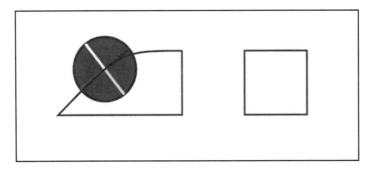

Figure 8-15. Using `rotate="auto"`

The "`auto`" value forces the graphic to stay aligned with the path's current travel vector at the appropriate point of the animation. Consequently, the changes are abrupt at angular connections in the path and smooth at curved connections.

The `rotate` attribute can hold either a specific angle value or the expression "`auto`" but not both. If you want to add a specific rotation angle to auto-rotate an animation with a specific angular offset, you need to place the whole graphic into a `<g>` element with the relevant transformation applied to the shell, then rotate the context containing that context, as shown in Listing 8-15 (see Figure 8-16).

Listing 8-15. `AnimPath3.svg`

```
<svg xmlns="http://www.w3.org/2000/svg"
     xmlns:xlink="http://www.w3.org/1999/xlink">
    <g transform="translate(200,200)">
        <g>
            <animateMotion
                    path="m-100,0 C0,-100 0,-100 100,-100 L100,0z
                            m300,0 l100,0 l0,-100 l-100,0z"
                    dur="8s" fill="freeze" rotate="auto"/>
            <g transform="rotate(45)">
                <circle cx="0" cy="0" r="50" fill="red"
                        stroke="black" stroke-width="4"/>
                <line x1="0" y1="0" x2="50" y2="0"
                        stroke="blue" stroke-width="4"/>
                <line x1="0" y1="0" x2="-50" y2="0"
                        stroke="green" stroke-width="4"/>
                <line x1="0" y1="0" x2="0" y2="50"
                        stroke="yellow" stroke-width="4"/>
                <line x1="0" y1="0" x2="0" y2="-50"
                        stroke="white" stroke-width="4"/>
            </g>
        </g>
        <path d="m-100,0 C0,-100 0,-100 100,-100 L100,0z
                    m300,0 l100,l0,-100 l-100,0z"
                    stroke="black" stroke-width="3" fill="none"/>
    </g>
</svg>
```

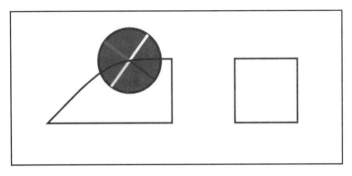

Figure 8-16. Rotating the graphic, not the animation

The keyTimes can be applied to complex paths in the same way that it can with linear paths, but because the path trajectory is mapped out using a path rather than a discrete set of values, a second attribute, keyPoints, is needed. The keyPoints attribute consists of values between 0 and 1. These values provide positions along the path relative to the whole. In other words, the beginning of the path is 0, the end of the path is 1, and the point x, where 0 is less than or equal to x (which is less than or equal to 1), specifies the length from the beginning point to the current point. This is a *normalized* value: If you multiply this value by the total length of the path, it will give you the length of the path traversed so far.

Listing 8-16 and Figure 8-17 demonstrate this.

Listing 8-16. AnimPath4.svg

```
<svg xmlns="http://www.w3.org/2000/svg"
    xmlns:xlink="http://www.w3.org/1999/xlink">
    <g transform="translate(200,200)">
        <g>
            <animateMotion
                    path="m-100,0 C0,-100 0,-100 100,-100 L100,0z
                            m300,0 l100,0 l0,-100 l-100,0z"
                    keyTimes="0;.05;.1;.3;.6;1.0"
                    keyPoints="0;.2;.4;.6;.8;1"
                    dur="8s" fill="freeze" rotate="auto"/>
            <g transform="rotate(45)">
                    <circle cx="0" cy="0" r="50" fill="red"
                            stroke="black" stroke-width="4"/>
```

```
            <line x1="0" y1="0" x2="50" y2="0"
                    stroke="blue" stroke-width="4"/>
            <line x1="0" y1="0" x2="-50" y2="0"
                    stroke="green" stroke-width="4"/>
            <line x1="0" y1="0" x2="0" y2="50"
                    stroke="yellow" stroke-width="4"/>
            <line x1="0" y1="0" x2="0" y2="-50"
                    stroke="white" stroke-width="4"/>
        </g>
    </g>
    <path d="m-100,0 C0,-100 0,-100 100,-100 L100,0z
                m300,0 l100,0 l0,-100 l-100,0z"
            stroke="black" stroke-width="3" fill="none"/>
    </g>
</svg>
```

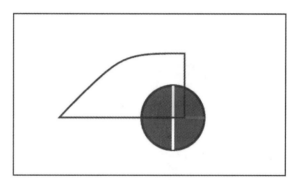

Figure 8-17. Combining keyTimes *and* keyPoints

 CAUTION   *The Adobe SVG Viewer does not currently support the* keyPoints *and* keyTimes *attributes on*
`<transformAnimation>`.

To enhance modularity, you can also use a secondary form of the
`<animateMotion>`, one in which the path of motion is referenced through an external link. This is actually accomplished via the child tag `<mpath>`, which contains as its primary attribute an `xlink:href`. Figure 8-18 and Listing 8-17 demonstrate the syntax for `<mpath>`.

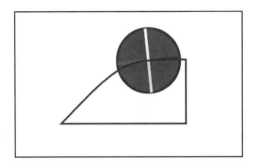

Figure 8-18. The <mpath> *element*

Listing 8-17. AnimPath5.vg

```
<svg xmlns="http://www.w3.org/2000/svg"
     xmlns:xlink="http://www.w3.org/1999/xlink">
     <defs>
          <path d="m-100,0 C0,-100 0,-100 100,-100 L100,0z"
               id="path1" />
     </defs>
     <g transform="translate(200,200)">
          <g id="orientedCircle">
               <animateMotion dur="4s" fill="freeze" rotate="auto">
                    <mpath xlink:href="#path1"/>
               </animateMotion>
               <g>
                         <circle cx="0" cy="0" r="50" fill="red"
                              stroke="black" stroke-width="4"/>
                         <line x1="0" y1="0" x2="50" y2="0"
                              stroke="blue" stroke-width="4"/>
                         <line x1="0" y1="0" x2="-50" y2="0"
                              stroke="green" stroke-width="4"/>
                         <line x1="0" y1="0" x2="0" y2="50"
                              stroke="yellow" stroke-width="4"/>
                         <line x1="0" y1="0" x2="0" y2="-50"
                              stroke="white" stroke-width="4"/>
               </g>
          </g>
          <path d="m-100,0 C0,-100 0,-100 100,-100 L100,0z"
                         stroke="black" stroke-width="3" fill="none"/>
     </g>
</svg>
```

TIP   *The <mpath> element cannot have an animation subelement, so currently it is not possible to swap one externally referenced path for another, unless you resort to Document Object Model (DOM) manipulation. However, that may change in a future version of SVG. (Chapter 9, "Integrating SVG and HTML," contains some hints as to how to create such a path swap using programmatic methods).*

Swapping Graphics

The true art of animation is of course a little more complex than setting a trajectory and moving a graphic across it. From the animation of Windsor McKay through the adventures of Mickey Mouse and Bugs Bunny and into the sophisticated two-dimensional animations of today involve changing the actual graphics themselves over time.

Traditional film animation generally requires that you create a background (in one or more layers), and then over that lay your animated figures. Each figure in turn consists of a series of drawings in which each drawing changes subtly from one frame to the next, being drawn relative to a given point on the screen (typically called the *registration point*). There is usually one unique drawing for each character per cel, with the total of background and foreground characters at any given time being called a *frame*.

Game animation and children's multimedia takes advantage of this same frame-based animation with the use of *sprites*. A sprite is essentially a single contained set of animation for a character or object. For instance, if you have a character walking, the character itself is considered the sprite, with each drawing of the character—known as a *cel*—being a snapshot of the movement of the character at a specific point in time.

NOTE   Cel *derives from* celluloid, *the name of the plastic on which animators drew, inked, and painted their characters. Movie animation cels are commanding top dollar nowadays, especially as computer animation (either rendered or via scanned images) has almost completely replaced traditional cel-based animation.*

Creating cel-based animation in SVG is surprisingly simple, even though it is not immediately obvious when looking at the SVG recommendation how to do it. Among other properties that can be animated, one of the more powerful is the xlink:href attribute of the <image> and <use> elements. By changing the value of this particular attribute, you can exchange one previously defined item for another, in essence, swapping the one element for another.

It turns out, however, that you can actually do much more sophisticated work than just swapping out simple button graphics using the xlink:href attribute. For instance, consider the case of a person walking. This action actually describes the prototypical sprite. Each frame of the sprite is a snapshot of the walking motion—the more snapshots between the start and end of the walking sequence (which may actually loop), the more fluid the animation but also the longer the initial download time.

Listing 8-18 and Figure 8-19 show an example of this.

Listing 8-18. DustyWalking1.svg

```
<svg xmlns="http://www.w3.org/2000/svg"
     xmlns:xlink="http://www.w3.org/1999/xlink">
    <defs>
        <image xlink:href="Dusty_0001.png" id="d01"
            width="320" height="320" x="0" y="0"/>
        <image xlink:href="Dusty_0002.png" id="d02"
            width="320" height="320" x="0" y="0"/>
        <image xlink:href="Dusty_0003.png" id="d03"
            width="320" height="320" x="0" y="0"/>
        <!-- and so forth -->
            <image xlink:href="Dusty_0029.png" id="d29"
            width="320" height="320" x="0" y="0"/>
            <image xlink:href="Dusty_0030.png" id="d30"
            width="320" height="320" x="0" y="0"/>
        <linearGradient id="grayGrad">
            <stop offset="0%" stop-color="white"/>
                    <stop offset="100%" stop-color="black"/>
        </linearGradient>
    </defs>
    <rect fill="url(#grayGrad)" x="0" y="0"
            width="100%" height="100%"/>
    <use xlink:href="#d30" x="0" y="0" id="animLeft">
        <animate attributeName="xlink:href"
            attributeType="XML" fill="freeze"
```

```
                    values="#d01;#d02;#d03;#d04;#d05;#d06;#d07;#d08;
                        #d09;#d10;#d11;#d12;#d13;#d14;#d15;#d16;
                        #d17;#d18;#d19;#d20;#d21;#d22;#d23;#d24;
                        #d25;#d26;#d27;#d28;#d29;#d30"
                begin="onload" dur="1.5s" repeatCount="indefinite"/>
        </use>
    </svg>
```

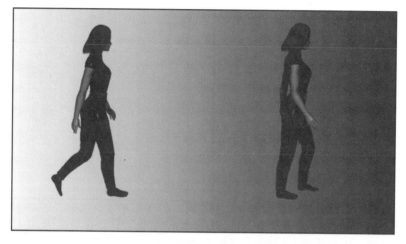

Figure 8-19. Switching graphics to create complex graphic actions

In Listing 8-18, 30 frames of an animation are first downloaded into the `<defs>` section and assigned id values from "d01" to "d30". Each frame is one step in an animation and is sized to be 320 pixels on a size and located at the origin (relative to its calling function).

The hard work, relatively speaking, in creating such an animation comes in preloading the graphics. Once the graphics are loaded, then the actual animation is done by a single `<animate>` element.

The `values` attribute contains a semicolon-separated list of the 30 frames in order, from #d01 to #d30. These are displayed one after the other over the duration specified in the `dur` attribute—in this case, 1.5s. This means that each frame is displayed for a period of 0.05 seconds per frame (in other words, 20 frames per second). This is about at the limit of human visual perception; the eye refreshes its view about 24 times a second, so the animation in Listing 8-18 will appear to be relatively seamless.

CAUTION *There is another factor that plays into this. The video chip speed comes into the equation; if there is not enough onboard RAM on the video chip, only part of the image may end up displaying before the screen refreshes, making the animation seem to flicker somewhat. This generally is not a problem when the animation involves fairly small movements, but it can be significant when the graphics change dramatically in presentation or location.*

There are two other aspects of the `<animate>` element that need to be explored. The "onload" value of the `begin` attribute in this case indicates that the animation will only begin once the last graphic has been loaded. If you arbitrarily set the time of the begin to "0s", the result may end up being that the animation starts out slowly as frames load, then suddenly jumps to the final speed when all of the graphics have loaded.

The last frame of the animation, #d30, is actually loaded as a placeholder while the animation itself is loaded. The reason for this is that when the animation begins, it will automatically transition into the first frame of the animation without an admittedly small delay. However, once the animation begins, the placeholder graphic does not explicitly have to appear again (it does in this case, but that is actually coincidental). In some applications, it may be worth making the placeholder a graphic with some kind of "loading" indicator on it, which will not be shown once the actual animation takes place.

The walking character shown here would appear to be walking on treadmill that keeps her stationary. However, you can apply more than one animation on the sprite at the same time. For instance, in Listing 8-19, there are two animations that act on the character Dusty, the first being a 30-frame stationary animation, the second being the movement of the whole sprite from right to left (see Figure 8-20).

Listing 8-19. `DustyWalking2.svg`

```
<svg xmlns="http://www.w3.org/2000/svg"
    xmlns:xlink="http://www.w3.org/1999/xlink">
    <defs>
        <pattern id="bricks" patternUnits="userSpaceOnUse"
            width="128" height="48" x="0" y="0"
            viewBox="0 0 128 48">
            <image xlink:href="bricks.png" width="128" height="48" x="0" y="0"/>
        </pattern>
```

```
                        <svg id="sidewalk" x="0" y="0" width="512" height="100"
                        viewBox="0 0 512 100" preserveAspectRatio="none">
                            <image xlink:href="sidewalk.png"
                                    width="512" height="100" x="0" y="0"/>
                        </svg>
                        <image xlink:href="Dusty_0001.png" id="d01"
                            width="320" height="320" x="0" y="0"/>
                        <image xlink:href="Dusty_0002.png" id="d02"
                            width="320" height="320" x="0" y="0"/>
                        <image xlink:href="Dusty_0003.png" id="d03"
                            width="320" height="320" x="0" y="0"/>
                            <!-- and so forth -->
                        <image xlink:href="Dusty_0029.png" id="d29"
                            width="320" height="320" x="0" y="0"/>
                        <image xlink:href="Dusty_0030.png" id="d30"
                            width="320" height="320" x="0" y="0"/>
                        <linearGradient id="grayGrad">
                            <stop offset="0%" stop-color="white"/>
                            <stop offset="100%" stop-color="black"/>
                        </linearGradient>
                </defs>
                <line x1="0" x2="100%" y1="280" y2="280" stroke="black"/>
                <line x1="0" x2="100%" y1="330" y2="330"
                    stroke="black" stroke-width="3"/>
                <rect x="0" y="0" width="1024" height="280"
                    fill="url(#bricks)"/>
                <use xlink:href="#sidewalk" x="0" y="280"
                        width="100%" height="50"/>
                <use xlink:href="#d30" x="0" y="0" id="walker">
                        <animate attributeName="x" attributeType="XML"
                                from="1024" to="-320" dur="9s"
                                repeatCount="indefinite"
                                begin="walker.onload"/>
                        <animate attributeName="xlink:href"
                                attributeType="XML" fill="freeze"
                                values="#d01;#d02;#d03;#d04;#d05;#d06;#d07;#d08;
                                    #d09;#d10;#d11;#d12;#d13;#d14;#d15;#d16;
                                    #d17;#d18;#d19;#d20;#d21;#d22;#d23;#d24;
                                    #d25;#d26;#d27;#d28;#d29;#d30"
                                begin="walker.onload" dur="1.5s"
                                repeatCount="indefinite"/>
                </use>
            </svg>
```

Figure 8-20. A character swap combined with a motion animation

NOTE *Walking can prove to take a little trial and error to get right, by the way. The advantage of SVG-based animation is that the animation of a given frame is based upon a specific interval, rather than the time it takes to render a graphic. This means you can easily synchronize multiple activities simultaneously (which is where the S of SMIL really comes from). However, if the walking interval is too long, the character appears to be skating forward, and if the walking speed is too short, the character can appear to "moon-walk" backward.*

This works because the x attribute is distinct from the xlink:href. The SVG engine will automatically animate both of these quantities simultaneously because they both start at the same time—upon loading of the initial animation (which has the id of "walker"). In essence, each attribute animation works on its own thread that is independent of any other animation threads. Such threads are frequently called *timelines* or *channels* in more traditional animation terminology; *channel* will be used here.

Note one of the key points in such animations. By invoking an animation via the <use> element, you are able to abstract away the specific type of animation involved. For instance, you can use the xlink:href attribute to point to a series of text elements one at a time, such as is shown in Listing 8-20 (see Figure 8-21).

Listing 8-20. TextAnim1.svg

```
<svg xmlns="http://zzwww.w3.org/2000/svg"
     xmlns:xlink="http://www.w3.org/1999/xlink">
    <defs>
        <text id="tx01" font-size="24">
            <tspan x="0" y="0">Animation is the process</tspan>
        </text>
        <text id="tx02" font-size="24">
            <tspan x="0" y="0">of controlling time.</tspan>
        </text>
        <text id="tx03" font-size="24">
            <tspan x="0" y="0">Once you have</tspan>
        </text>
        <text id="tx04" font-size="24">
            <tspan x="0" y="0"> this understanding,</tspan>
        </text>
        <text id="tx05" font-size="24">
            <tspan x="0" y="0">creating animations in SVG</tspan>
        </text>
        <text id="tx06" font-size="24">
            <tspan x="0" y="0">becomes simple.</tspan>
        </text>
    </defs>
    <use xlink:href="#tx1" x="100" y="100" id="textBlock">
        <animate attributeName="xlink:href"
            attributeType="XML"
            values="#tx01;#tx02;#tx03;#tx04;#tx05;#tx06"
            dur="6s" begin="textBlock.load"
            repeatCount="indefinite"/>
    </use>
</svg>
```

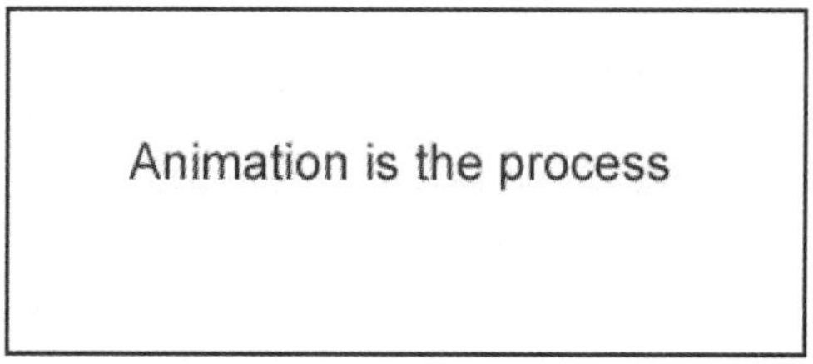

Animation is the process

Figure 8-21. Using swapping for animating text

Listing 8-20 contains a set of six text fields (#tx01 through #tx06) with the <use> element displaying them in one at a time, once per second. As with the <image> elements earlier, this approach works because the <use> element does not care about what it is referencing, only that it is in fact a valid reference.

This raises other possibilities as well. You can in fact nest animations one within another, as one example. For instance, by making a few minor modifications, you can make the same animation appear in more than one place simultaneously, as shown in Listing 8-21 (see Figure 8-22).

Listing 8-21. `TextAnim2.svg`

```
<svg xmlns="http://www.w3.org/2000/svg"
     xmlns:xlink="http://www.w3.org/1999/xlink">
    <defs>
        <text id="tx01" font-size="24">
            <tspan x="0" y="0">Animation is the process</tspan>
        </text>
        <text id="tx02" font-size="24">
            <tspan x="0" y="0">of controlling time.</tspan>
        </text>
        <text id="tx03" font-size="24">
            <tspan x="0" y="0">Once you have</tspan>
        </text>
        <text id="tx04" font-size="24">
            <tspan x="0" y="0"> this understanding,</tspan>
        </text>
        <text id="tx05" font-size="24">
            <tspan x="0" y="0">creating animations in SVG</tspan>
        </text>
        <text id="tx06" font-size="24">
            <tspan x="0" y="0">becomes simple.</tspan>
        </text>
        <rect width="300" height="48" fill="blue" stroke="black"
            stroke-width="1" id="block"/>
    </defs>
    <use xlink:href="#tx1" x="0" y="-50" id="textBlock">
        <animate attributeName="xlink:href" attributeType="XML"
            values="#tx01;#tx02;#tx03;#tx04;#tx05;#tx06" dur="6s"
             begin="textBlock.load" repeatCount="indefinite"/>
    </use>
    <svg>
        <animate attributeName="x" attributeType="XML"
            values="0;100;0" dur="5s" repeatCount="indefinite"/>
```

```
        <use xlink:href="#block" x="0" y="0"/>
        <use xlink:href="#textBlock" x="4" y="86"/>
    </svg>
    <svg>
        <animate attributeName="y" attributeType="XML"
            values="0;100;0" dur="5s"
            repeatCount="indefinite"/>
        <use xlink:href="#block" x="0" y="0"/>
        <use xlink:href="#textBlock" x="4" y="86"/>
    </svg>
</svg>
```

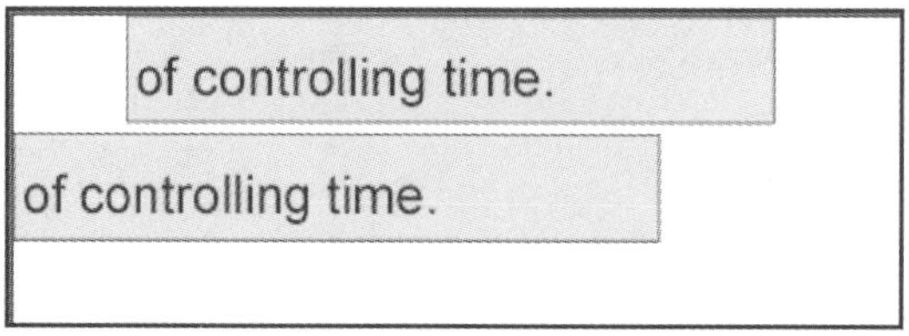

of controlling time.

of controlling time.

Figure 8-22. Referencing an animation by another animation

This animation has two blocks with the message from the previous animation: one moving up and down, the other moving left and right. In this case, the initial text animation was moved off-screen, in essence rendering outside the display area. This highlights an important point: Animations are not static entities and as such cannot be placed within <def> elements. This limitation means that in order to use an animation within another animation, it is necessary to have the initial animation run live, elsewhere within the graphics context.

CAUTION   *To reiterate, an animation can only be referenced if it is defined outside of the* <def> *element—putting an element with an animation definition in a* <def> *block will not work.*

Animating Color

Color presents a bit of a challenge to the normal animate mechanism. Setting the stroke or fill of a graphical object to a specific color (or gradient) is straightforward. In fact, it is identical to either swapping out the names of specific named colors (such as "red", "blue", "purple", and so on) with a <set> statement, or changing the url() reference of a fill or stroke object to a different object.

For instance, in the SVG graphic Listing 8-22, when the user rolls over a circle, the color of that circle will change from maroon to red (see Figure 8-23).

Listing 8-22. AnimColor1.svg

```
<svg xmlns="http://www.w3.org/2000/svg"
     xmlns:xlink="http://www.w3.org/1999/xlink">
    <g transform="translate(200,200)">
        <circle cx="0" cy="0" r="50" fill="maroon"
             stroke="black" stroke-width="4">
            <set attributeName="fill" attributeType="CSS" to="red"
                    begin="mouseover" end="mouseout"/>
        </circle>
    </g>
</svg>
```

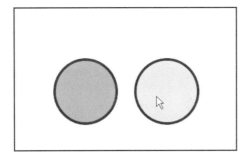

Figure 8-23. Animating color

Similarly, you can use either the hex or RGB notations when setting the colors. The same animation can be rendered as in Listing 8-23 and Figure 8-24.

Listing 8-23. AnimColor2.svg

```
<svg xmlns="http://www.w3.org/2000/svg"
     xmlns:xlink="http://www.w3.org/1999/xlink">
    <g transform="translate(200,200)">
        <circle cx="0" cy="0" r="50" fill="#800000"
             stroke="black" stroke-width="4">
```

```
                        <set attributeName="fill" attributeType="CSS"
                                to="rgb(255,0,0)"
                                begin="mouseover"  end="mouseout"/>
                </circle>
            </g>
        </svg>
```

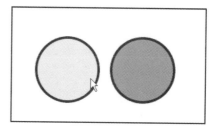

Figure 8-24. Using hex or RGB

In Listing 8-23, maroon is replaced with its hexadecimal triplet value #800000, and the color red is replaced with the RGB equivalent rgb(255,0,0).

These transitions, however, are abrupt. When the rollover is made, the fill on the circle automatically switches to red. SVG also allows for gradual transitions to be made, gradients in time, via the <animColor> element. This tag instructs the SVG render to interpolate between each of the three primary red, green, and blue portions of a color over time. For instance, Listing 8-24 will transition up from a maroon value (which is simply a dark red) to a full red over three seconds after a mouseover and then will fade back down to maroon on the mouseout (see Figure 8-25).

Listing 8-24. AnimColor3.svg

```
<svg xmlns="http://www.w3.org/2000/svg"
    xmlns:xlink="http://www.w3.org/1999/xlink">
    <g transform="translate(200,200)">
        <circle cx="0" cy="0" r="50" fill="#800000"
                stroke="black" stroke-width="4">
                <animateColor attributeName="fill"
                        attributeType="CSS" from="maroon" to="red"
                        begin="mouseover" dur="1s" fill="freeze"/>
                <animateColor attributeName="fill" attributeType="CSS"
                        from="red" to="maroon" begin="mouseout"
                        dur="1s" fill="freeze"/>
        </circle>
    </g>
</svg>
```

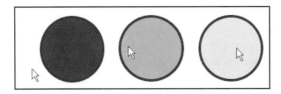

Figure 8-25. Gradual transitions in color animations

The code interpolates between each of the red, green, and blue values independently. In the previous examples (Listings 8-23 and 8-24), only the red channel changes in intensity. However, it is possible to have all three channels change at once. For instance, in Listing 8-25, the circle goes from a dark blue to yellow orange over the period of four seconds, using the RGB notations of each color to illustrate the specific numeric values (see Figure 8-26).

Listing 8-25. `AnimColor4.svg`

```
<svg xmlns="http://www.w3.org/2000/svg"
     xmlns:xlink="http://www.w3.org/1999/xlink">
    <g transform="translate(200,200)">
        <circle cx="0" cy="0" r="50" fill="rgb(0,0,128)"
                stroke="black" stroke-width="4">
            <animateColor attributeName="fill" attributeType="CSS"
                    from="rgb(0,0,128)" to="rgb(255,255,0)"
                    begin="mouseover" dur="3s"
                    fill="freeze"/>
            <animateColor attributeName="fill" attributeType="CSS"
                    from="rgb(255,255,0)" to="rgb(0,0,128)"
                    begin="mouseout" dur="3s"
                    fill="freeze"/>
        </circle>
    </g>
</svg>
```

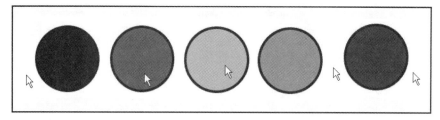

Figure 8-26. Animating each channel individually

On my system, the color transitions from navy blue to blue gray to green to yellow. This ordering may not make a lot of sense (especially the gray), but in fact the values can be seen if you manually interpolate between the colors, as shown in Table 8-1.

Table 8-1. Interpolating Colors

RED	GREEN	BLUE	FINAL COLOR
0	0	128	Navy blue
64	64	96	Dark blue gray
128	128	64	Brownish green
192	192	32	Light brown
255	255	0	Yellow

As with the other transformations, you can also employ the `values` attribute to create multiple color iterations. This can give you more control over the way that colors interpolate. For instance, in the animation Listing 8-26, the four circles each cycle through different sets of colors (see Figure 8-27).

Listing 8-26. `AnimColor5.svg`

```
<svg xmlns="http://www.w3.org/2000/svg"
     xmlns:xlink="http://www.w3.org/1999/xlink">
     <g transform="translate(100,200)">
          <circle cx="0" cy="0" r="50" fill="rgb(0,0,128)"
                      stroke="black" stroke-width="4" id="pulse">
               <animateColor attributeName="fill" attributeType="CSS"
                      values="maroon;red;maroon;maroon;maroon;maroon"
                      dur="1s" fill="freeze"
                      repeatCount="indefinite"/>
          </circle>
```

```
    <circle cx="150" cy="0" r="50" fill="rgb(0,0,128)"
            stroke="black" stroke-width="4" id="rainbow">
            <animateColor attributeName="fill" attributeType="CSS"
                    values="red;yellow;green;blue;purple;red"
                    dur="2s" fill="freeze"
                    repeatCount="indefinite"/>
    </circle>
    <circle cx="300" cy="0" r="50"
            fill="rgb(0,0,0)" stroke="black"
            stroke-width="4" id="grays">
            <animateColor attributeName="fill" attributeType="CSS"
                    values="rgb(128,128,128);rgb(64,64,64);
                            rgb(192,192,192); rgb(255,255,255);
                            rgb(128,128,128)"
                    dur="1.5s" fill="freeze"
                    repeatCount="indefinite"/>
    </circle>
    <circle cx="450" cy="0" r="50"
            fill="#0000ff" stroke="black"
            stroke-width="4" id="blueGreen">
            <animateColor attributeName="fill"
                    attributeType="CSS"
                    values="#0000ff;#00ffff;#00ff00;#0000ff"
                    dur="3s" fill="freeze"
                    repeatCount="indefinite"/>
    </circle>
  </g>
</svg>
```

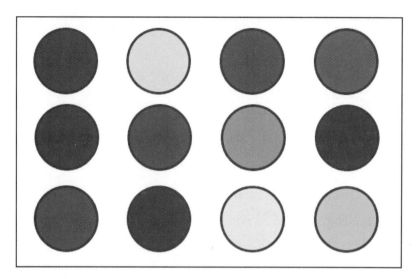

Figure 8-27. Transitioning through multiple colors

The first circle (#pulse) is usually maroon, but for about a third of a second it pulls to red before returning to its maroon state. The second circle (#rainbow) cycles through the primary colors of the rainbow, using RGB notation. The third circle (#grays) illustrates how RGB notation can also be used to work with grays in addition to colors. In the final circle (#blueGreen), the hex notation for green, cyan, and blue causes the color to flicker between blue and green.

> **TIP**   *The eye does not process all colors equally. In general, bright colors tend to dominate the eye, so they seem to last longer, and dark colors tend to recede from the eye and thus seem to last shorter, even when the actual times are the same between transitions. Additionally, some parts of the spectrum (in particular, greens) tend to remain the same over a fairly wide portion of the spectrum (probably because we usually filter the greens of forests out, so the eye is much less sensitive to variations in greens than it is variations in reds, for instance). You should thus adjust any animated chromatic spectra to take these characteristics into account if you want your spectra to appear more or less uniform.*

Animating Transformations

Movement is more than simply translation. Things spin around, grow larger and smaller, and distort. In other words, they perform a wide variety of transformations. SVG includes facilities for animating (almost) all transformations, and understanding how such animations work can significantly expand your repertoire of techniques.

The `<animateTransform>` element specifically handles changes in transformation. In form, it is almost identical to the other animate tags, providing attributes for to, from, and values elements, among others. The difference, however, is that `<animateTransform>` includes a new attribute—type—which specifies which specific transformation is being changed.

In the `<animateTransform>`, the attribute being changed (in other words, that attribute referenced by attributeName) is the transform attribute itself. However, because transform points to a number of possible transformations, each of which can have a number of possible values, the type attribute contains the specific transformation type being applied. For instance, the animation command given in Listing 8-27 will rotate a line around its origin point (see Figure 8-28).

Listing 8-27. RotateAnim1.svg

```
<svg xmlns="http://www.w3.org/2000/svg"
    xmlns:xlink="http://www.w3.org/1999/xlink">
    <g transform="translate(200,200)">
        <line x1="0" y1="0" x2="100" y2="0"
            stroke="black" stroke-width="2">
            <animateTransform attributeName="transform"
                attributeType="XML" type="rotate"
                from="0" to="360" dur="1s"
                repeatCount="indefinite"/>
        </line>
    </g>
</svg>
```

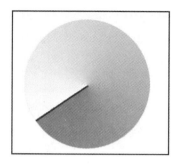

Figure 8-28. Rotation transformations around the origin

The code applies a rotation angle ranging from a value of 0° to 360°. Note that although the two values point in the same direction, they are of course different values—specifying the angle to 360 will cause the animation to increment continuously to the final value, before being restored to the initial value of 0° to do the thing all over again.

The animation occurs at the local origin point of the graphics context (0,0). If you had a graphic (such as a rectangle), for instance, then applying a rotation animation to the graphic would rotate it around the upper-left corner of the graphic—unless you changed the origin point. Listing 8-28 and Figure 8-29 show this.

Listing 8-28. AnimRotate2.svg

```
<svg xmlns="http://www.w3.org/2000/svg"
     xmlns:xlink="http://www.w3.org/1999/xlink">
    <g transform="translate(200,200)">
        <rect width="160" height="160" stroke="black" fill="red">
            <animateTransform attributeName="transform"
                    attributeType="XML" type="rotate"
                    from="0" to="360" dur="4s"
                    repeatCount="indefinite"/>
        </rect>
    </g>
    <g transform="translate(400,200)">
        <rect width="160" height="160"
            stroke="black" fill="green" x="-80"
            y="-80">
            <animateTransform attributeName="transform"
                    attributeType="XML" type="rotate"
                    from="0" to="360" dur="4s"
                    repeatCount="indefinite"/>
```

```
            </rect>
        </g>
</svg>
```

Figure 8-29. Changing the origin point

In the first instance, a red rectangle is rotating around the default origin, the upper-left corner. Note that the animation occurring here is taking place on the rectangle itself, not the graphical <g> context that contains the animation. Thus, although the graphical context of the red rectangle is displaced 200 pixels down and to the right from the origin, relative to the graphic context the origin is the upper-left corner or the rectangle.

On the other hand, in the second instance, the green rectangle is shifted 80 units to the left and up (translate(-80,-80)), but the coordinate system itself is not changed at all.

This means that the origin is now located in the exact center of the rectangle. When the same animation is applied to it, the green rectangle spins around its center, rather than along a vertex.

You can apply more complex animations using the values attribute. For instance, suppose you wanted your rectangle to spin around one complete rotation clockwise, then when it reached the end, to "unwind" back to the starting position. You can accomplish this with the values attribute, as shown in Listing 8-29 (see Figure 8-30).

Listing 8-29. `AnimRotate3.svg`

```
<svg xmlns="http://www.w3.org/2000/svg"
    xmlns:xlink="http://www.w3.org/1999/xlink">
    <g transform="translate(300,200)">
        <rect width="160" height="160"
            stroke="black" fill="green" x="-80" y="-80">
            <animateTransform attributeName="transform"
                    attributeType="XML" type="rotate"
                    values="0;360;0" dur="6s"
                    repeatCount="indefinite"/>
        </rect>
    </g>
</svg>
```

Figure 8-30. The `values` *attribute, applied to an* `<animateTransform>`

The rotation is relatively simple because it involves only one parameter: the rotation angle. Other animated transformations get to be somewhat more complex because they involve more than one parameter (all the way up to the matrix transformation, which takes six parameters). The `scale` transformation, for instance, can take a single parameter—the global scaling factor—but you can also change the x and y coordinates individually, as shown in Listing 8-30 and Figure 8-31.

Listing 8-30. `ScaleAnim1.svg`

```
<svg xmlns="http://www.w3.org/2000/svg"
    xmlns:xlink="http://www.w3.org/1999/xlink">
    <g transform="translate(100,200)" id="generalScaling">
        <circle cx="0" cy="0" r="50" fill="blue" stroke="black">
```

```
                    <animateTransform attributeName="transform"
                            attributeType="XML" type="scale"
                            from="0" to="1" dur="3s"
                            fill="freeze"/>
            </circle>
            <text x="0" y="-85" text-anchor="middle">
                    type="scale"
            </text>
            <text x="0" y="-70" text-anchor="middle">
                    from="0"
            </text>
            <text x="0" y="-55" text-anchor="middle">
                    to="1"
            </text>
    </g>
    <g transform="translate(200,200)" id="xScaling">
        <circle cx="0" cy="0" r="50"
                fill="blue" stroke="black">
            <animateTransform attributeName="transform"
                    attributeType="XML" type="scale"
                    from="0,1" to="1,1" dur="3s"
                    fill="freeze"/>
        </circle>
        <text x="0" y="-85" text-anchor="middle">
                type="scale"
        </text>
        <text x="0" y="-70" text-anchor="middle">
                from="0,1"
        </text>
        <text x="0" y="-55" text-anchor="middle">
                to="1,1"
        </text>
    </g>
    <g transform="translate(300,200)" id="yScaling">
        <circle cx="0" cy="0" r="50"
                fill="blue" stroke="black">
            <animateTransform attributeName="transform"
                    attributeType="XML" type="scale"
                    from="1,0" to="1,1" dur="3s"
                    fill="freeze"/>
        </circle>
        <text x="0" y="-85" text-anchor="middle">
                type="scale"
        </text>
```

411

```
                        <text x="0" y="-70" text-anchor="middle">
                                from="1,0"
                        </text>
                        <text x="0" y="-55" text-anchor="middle">
                                to="1,1"
                        </text>
                </g>
                <g transform="translate(400,200)" id="xAndYScaling">
                        <circle cx="0" cy="0" r="50" fill="blue" stroke="black">
                                <animateTransform attributeName="transform"
                                        attributeType="XML" type="scale"
                                        from="1,0" to="0,1" dur="3s"
                                        fill="freeze"/>
                        </circle>
                        <text x="0" y="-85" text-anchor="middle">
                                type="scale"
                        </text>
                        <text x="0" y="-70" text-anchor="middle">
                                from="1,0"
                        </text>
                        <text x="0" y="-55" text-anchor="middle">
                                to="0,1"
                        </text>
                </g>
        </svg>
```

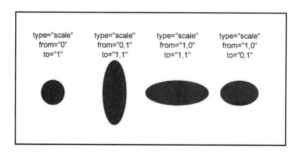

Figure 8-31. Performing a scaleX *or* scaleY

In this particular case, there are four different kinds of scaling going on. The first, a global scale from 0 to 1, causes the blue circle to expand from its center—the position (cx, cy) of (0,0) defines the origin as the center of the circle. Here, the scale factor acts as a multiplier to the dimensions of the unanimated bounding box.

When scale has a value of 0, the circle (which has a radius of 50, and hence a diameter of 100 normally) has an effective radius of 50 x 0 = 0; the circle is a single point. On the other hand, when the scale factor is 1, then the radius is 50 x 1 = 50, the unanimated value of the radius.

In the second example, however, both from and to have two values, corresponding to the x and y coordinates respectively, of the scale function. Thus, the from attribute value of "0,1" indicates that the initial horizontal radius rx should have a value of 50 x 0 = 0, having no extent. Meanwhile, the vertical radius ry has an initial value of 50 x 1 = 50, while and the final rx is 50 and ry is 50, a true circle. The animation shows an ellipse oriented along the y axis, growing outward to a full circle.

The third example does exactly the same thing, except that the animation expands along the y axis rather than the x axis, becoming taller over time before becoming a circle at the end of the animation.

The final example shows both x and y changing, with rx decreasing while ry increases: (1,0) to (0,1). Here the ellipse starts out oriented along the x axis and flattens toward the origin while the y axis expands, reaching at the end an ellipse with rx="0" and ry="1". There is no restriction on both scale parameters changing at the same time.

The values attribute, when used with a multivalue property such as scale, can also be used to change both (or all) parameters at the same time by separating each parameter in a set by a comma (,) and each set of parameters from other sets by a semicolon (;). For instance, Listing 8-31 changes both the x and y scale factors independently (see Figure 8-32).

Listing 8-31. ScaleAnim2.svg

```
<svg xmlns="http://www.w3.org/2000/svg"
     xmlns:xlink="http://www.w3.org/1999/xlink">
    <g transform="translate(300,200)">
        <circle cx="0" cy="0" r="50" fill="blue" stroke="black">
            <animateTransform attributeName="transform"
                attributeType="XML" type="scale"
                values="1,0 ; 0,1 ; 0.5,0.5 ; 2,0.5 ; 1,1"
                dur="6s" fill="freeze"/>
        </circle>
        <text x="0" y="110" text-anchor="middle">
            values="1,0 ; 0,1 ; 0.5,0.5 ; 2,0.5 ; 1,1"
        </text>
    </g>
    <text x="0" y="-55" text-anchor="middle">
        to="0,1"
    </text>
</svg>
```

413

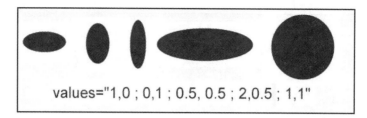

Figure 8-32. Giving values in the form sx1,sy1;sx2,sy2; ... ;sxN,syN

In this example, the first value (1,0) gives an x scale factor of 1 and a y scale factor of 2. The value (2, 0.5) gives an x scale factor of 2 and a y-scale factor of 0.5, and so forth. As with the single property values attribute, each set of values acts as a keyframe, at evenly timed intervals.

You can also animate the translate() function in this manner. Animating the translate() function is basically akin to using the <animateMotion> element, save that instead of setting the x and y values explicitly, you are changing the local coordinate system. In practice, this does not make much difference. SVG also lets you animate the skewX() and skewY() functions as well, though not the broader skew() function.

Animating Gradients

The ability to change colors obviously applies to the fill and stroke attributes of most shapes, but what is lesser known is that it also applies to the stop-color of a gradient. You can in fact set each of the colors of a gradient to change over time (or in response to a mouse event) individually, making it possible to create rolling color changes.

For instance, in Listing 8-32, the #blueGrad gradient shades from a darker to a lighter shade of blue. Each color stop in turn is set to cycle individually so that the left stop (at offset 0%) shades from navy to blue, back to navy, then to black and back again to navy. Meanwhile, the right stop (at offset 100%) cycles from blue to light blue, back to blue, navy, and returning back to blue. The combined effect is of a band of color bouncing back and forth (see Figure 8-33).

Listing 8-32. `GradientAnim1.svg`

```
<svg xmlns="http://www.w3.org/2000/svg"
     xmlns:xlink="http://www.w3.org/1999/xlink">
    <defs>
        <linearGradient id="steel"
                gradientTransform="rotate(45)">
                <stop offset="0%" stop-color="#C0C0C0"/>
                <stop offset="10%" stop-color="#808080"/>
                <stop offset="35%" stop-color="#FFFFFF"/>
                <stop offset="100%" stop-color="#808080"/>
        </linearGradient>
        <linearGradient id="blueGrad">
                <stop offset="0%" stop-color="#000080">
                        <animateColor attributeName="stop-color"
                                attributeType="CSS" dur="5s"
                                values="navy;blue;navy;black;navy"
                                repeatCount="indefinite"/>
                </stop>
                <stop offset="100%" stop-color="#8080ff">
                        <animateColor attributeName="stop-color"
                                attributeType="CSS" dur="5s"
                                values="blue;lightBlue;blue;navy;blue"
                                repeatCount="indefinite"/>
                </stop>
        </linearGradient>
    </defs>
    <g transform="translate(100,100)">
        <rect x="-30" y="-30" width="260" height="160"
                fill="url(#steel)"/>
        <rect x="0" y="0" width="200" height="100"
                fill="url(#blueGrad)"
                stroke="black" stroke-width="2"/>
        <g transform="translate(100,50)">
                <text fill="white" dominant-baseline="mathematical"
                        text-anchor="middle" font-size="20">
                        <tspan x="0" y="-15">Animated</tspan>
                        <tspan x="0" y="15">Gradients</tspan>
                </text>
        </g>
    </g>
</svg>
```

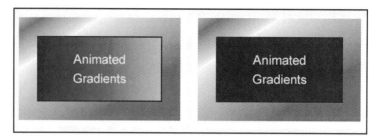

Figure 8-33. Animating the stop-color

Being able to change colors programmatically is fairly cool, admittedly, but in some cases it is not worth trying to map out complex color changes in a gradient for doing effects such as complex rolling gradients. Another solution to animating such gradients is to actually animate the transformations that can act on the gradients (those specified in the gradientTransform attribute of the <linearGradient> or <radialGradient> elements).

This is a fun example for a change. Many years ago, in the fairly forgettable TV show *Battlestar Galactica*, one of the recurrent sets of villains were the Cylons: evil, robotic creatures who had a red scanning beam instead of a set of eyes (backed with really annoying laser-sound movements . . . you would think that a technology capable of creating intelligent robots would have figured out how to put bafflers on them). The scanning eye makes for a cool graphic demo, something high tech and ominous, but something that is pretty easy to do in SVG (and it can be easily added in as eye candy to a control panel). Listing 8-33 and Figure 8-34 show the example.

Listing 8-33. CylonBeam.svg

```
<svg xmlns="http://www.w3.org/2000/svg"
     xmlns:xlink="http://www.w3.org/1999/xlink">
    <defs>
        <linearGradient id="steel"
                gradientTransform="rotate(45)">
            <stop offset="0%" stop-color="#C0C0C0"/>
            <stop offset="10%" stop-color="#808080"/>
            <stop offset="35%" stop-color="#FFFFFF"/>
            <stop offset="100%" stop-color="#808080"/>
        </linearGradient>
        <linearGradient id="cylonBand">
            <animateTransform attributeName="gradientTransform"
                    attributeType="XML" type="translate"
                    values="-0.8,0;0,0;0.8,0;0,0;-0.8,0" dur="3s"
                    repeatCount="indefinite"/>
```

```
            <stop offset="0%" stop-color="black"/>
            <stop offset="45%" stop-color="red"/>
            <stop offset="50%" stop-color="#FFD000"/>
            <stop offset="55%" stop-color="red"/>
            <stop offset="100%" stop-color="black"/>
        </linearGradient>
    </defs>
    <g transform="translate(100,100)">
        <rect x="-30" y="-30" width="260" height="80"
            fill="url(#steel)"/>
        <rect x="0" y="0" width="200" height="20"
            fill="url(#cylonBand)"
            stroke="black" stroke-width="2"/>
    </g>
</svg>
```

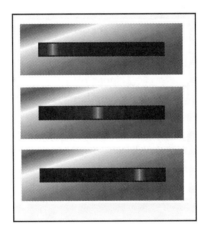

Figure 8-34. For Battlestar Galactica *fans, the infamous Cylon beam*

Pay special attention to the use of the "gradientTransform" value as the target of the attributeName property, as opposed to the "transform" value used in the previous section. You can in fact animate the transformations on gradients in much the same way.

The primary difference between the two transforms modes comes in the scale of the translations. The gradientTransform is implicitly defined on a unit square, so setting the translation value to (0.5,1) will move the gradient 50 percent to the right and 100 percent down. This is the principle used in the values attribute: The animation starts 80 percent to the left, moves to the center, then moves 80 percent to the right, moves back to the center then back to its initial position, while not moving at all along the y axis. The effect of this is to make the center of the gradient—the eye, if you will—move back and forth as well.

Gradients are treated as objects in SVG that can also be referenced via links or through the url() function. This makes it possible to swap out one gradient for another in a fill or stroke statement. For instance, in Listing 8-34, two animating gradients are defined: #blueGrad and #redGrad. When the mouse moves over the faceplate graphic, the <set> statement sets the fill attribute to "url(#redGrad)", switching from one animating gradient to the other. This is restored when the mouse moves off the graphic (see Figure 8-35).

Listing 8-34. GradientAnim2.svg

```
<svg xmlns="http://www.w3.org/2000/svg"
     xmlns:xlink="http://www.w3.org/1999/xlink">
    <defs>
        <linearGradient id="steel"
                gradientTransform="rotate(45)">
            <stop offset="0%" stop-color="#C0C0C0"/>
            <stop offset="10%" stop-color="#808080"/>
            <stop offset="35%" stop-color="#FFFFFF"/>
            <stop offset="100%" stop-color="#808080"/>
        </linearGradient>
        <linearGradient id="blueGrad">
            <stop offset="0%" stop-color="#000080">
                <animateColor attributeName="stop-color"
                        attributeType="CSS"
                        values="navy;blue;navy;black;navy"
                        dur="5s" repeatCount="indefinite"/>
            </stop>
            <stop offset="100%" stop-color="#8080ff">
                <animateColor attributeName="stop-color"
                        attributeType="CSS"
                        values="blue;lightBlue;blue;navy;blue"
                        dur="5s" repeatCount="indefinite"/>
            </stop>
        </linearGradient>
        <linearGradient id="redGrad">
            <stop offset="0%" stop-color="#000080">
                <animateColor attributeName="stop-color"
                        attributeType="CSS" dur="5s"
                        values="maroon;red;maroon;black;maroon"
                        repeatCount="indefinite"/>
            </stop>
```

```
                      <stop offset="100%" stop-color="#8080ff">
                            <animateColor attributeName="stop-color"
                                    attributeType="CSS" dur="5s"
                                    values="red;yellow;red;maroon;red"
                                    repeatCount="indefinite"/>
                      </stop>
              </linearGradient>
      </defs>
      <g transform="translate(100,100)" id="faceplate">
              <rect x="-30" y="-30" width="260" height="160"
                      fill="url(#steel)"/>
              <rect x="0" y="0" width="200" height="100"
                      fill="url(#blueGrad)"
                      stroke="black" stroke-width="2">
                      <set attributeName="fill" attributeType="CSS"
                              to="url(#redGrad)"
                              begin="faceplate.mouseover"
                              end="faceplate.mouseout"/>
              </rect>
              <g transform="translate(100,50)">
                      <text fill="white" dominant-baseline="mathematical"
                              text-anchor="middle" font-size="20">
                              <tspan x="0" y="-15">Animated</tspan>
                              <tspan x="0" y="15">Gradients</tspan>
                      </text>
              </g>
      </g>
</svg>
```

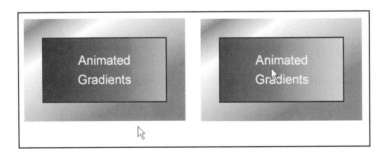

Figure 8-35. Swapping gradients by animating the xlink:href *attribute*

TIP *This technique can also come in handy when you use gradients to define custom color names. In general,* `<set ... to="url(#backgroundColor)">` *is more intuitive than* `<set ... to="rgb(12,42,214)">`, *not to mention more modular. You can change the color in the* `<defs>` *tag once and have it propagate through the rest of the document, rather than having to change each color by hand.*

Creating an Animated Stopwatch

The power of using transformative animations is particularly useful for creating cyclical events such as clocks without the use of extensive bitmap animations. You can create a surprisingly robust stopwatch (not quite a full clock, which will be demonstrated in Chapter 9, "Integrating SVG and HTML") using nothing but animation events.

The primary trick in creating a stopwatch is to recognize that there are only a few real animations involved. Creating a stopwatch in most languages can prove tricky, in part because languages such as C++ or Visual Basic do not give you the ability to cleanly work with polar (angular/radial) coordinates and in part because you need to handle multiple timing threads simultaneously. As it turns out, making a stopwatch in SVG is quite easy because the language is designed to work such that each element (such as a stopwatch hand) can maintain its own timing loop (see Figure 8-36).

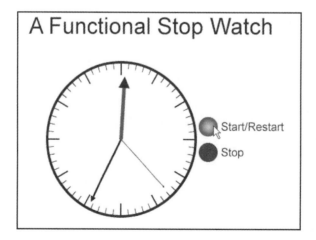

Figure 8-36. The stopwatch graphic

Listing 8-35 contains the stopwatch animation, which I will present first in its entirety and then break it down to show just how you build the watch (amateur horologists, unite!).

Listing 8-35. `StopWatch.svg`

```
<svgxmlns:xsl="http://www.w3.org/2000/svg"
        xmlns:xlink="http://www.w3.org/1999/xlink">
    <defs>
            <text id="label" font-size="36" font-family="Helvetica"
                x="0" y="36">
                A Functional Stop Watch
            </text>
            <desc>
                    These gradients indicate when a button mode
                    is currently active.
            </desc>
            <radialGradient id="startButtonOn">
                    <stop offset="0%" stop-color="lightGreen"/>
                    <stop offset="100%" stop-color="green"/>
            </radialGradient>
            <radialGradient id="stopButtonOn">
                    <stop offset="0%" stop-color="yellow"/>
                    <stop offset="100%" stop-color="red"/>
            </radialGradient>
            <desc>
                    The Triangle marker provides the pointer
                    for each hand, which in turn makes the hand
                    more like a traditional clock hand rather
                    than a simple line.
            </desc>
            <marker id="Triangle"
                    viewBox="0 0 10 10" refX="0" refY="5"
                    markerUnits="strokeWidth"
                    markerWidth="4" markerHeight="3"
                    orient="auto">
                    <path d="M 0 0 L 10 5 L 0 10 z"/>
            </marker>
            <desc>
                    This defines the clock back. Set its fill
                    to a pattern or an image to make it appear
                    more realistic.
            </desc>
```

```
<circle cx="0" cy="0" r="120"
      stroke="black" stroke-width="4" fill="white"
      id="clockBack"/>
<desc>
      This defines the three hands,
      sweep (which goes around once per second),
      secondHand (which goes around once per minute)
      and minuteHand (which goes around once an hour).
</desc>
<line x1="0" y1="0" x2="0" y2="-100"
    stroke="red" stroke-width="1"
    marker-end="url(#Triangle)"
    id="sweepHand" fill="red"/>
<line x1="0" y1="0" x2="0" y2="-100"
    stroke="black"
    stroke-width="3" marker-end="url(#Triangle)"
    id="secondHand" fill="black"/>
<line x1="0" y1="0" x2="0" y2="-80"
    stroke="green" stroke-width="6"
    marker-end="url(#Triangle)"
    id="minuteHand" fill="green"/>
<desc>
      The ticks and subticks describe the lines used
      to denote five minute and one minute intervals
      respectively.
</desc>
<line x1="0" y1="-100" x2="0" y2="-120"
    stroke="black" stroke-width="2" id="tick"/>
<line x1="0" y1="-110" x2="0" y2="-120"
    stroke="black" stroke-width="1" id="subtick"/>
<desc>
   This puts the stopWatch pieces together
</desc>
<g id="stopWatch">
      <use xlink:href="#clockBack"/>
      <desc>
             Rather than define twelve ticks and
             48 individual subticks, a group of
             one tick and five subticks are put
             together as a group called a tickSet.
             The tickSets in turn are rotated eleven
             more times to cut down on the amount of
             extraneous code.
      </desc>
```

```
<g transform="rotate(0)" id="tickSet">
    <use xlink:href="#tick"/>
    <use xlink:href="#subtick"
        transform="rotate(6)"/>
    <use xlink:href="#subtick"
        transform="rotate(12)"/>
    <use xlink:href="#subtick"
        transform="rotate(18)"/>
    <use xlink:href="#subtick"
        transform="rotate(24)"/>
</g>
<use xlink:href="#tickSet" transform="rotate(30)"/>
<use xlink:href="#tickSet" transform="rotate(60)"/>
<use xlink:href="#tickSet" transform="rotate(90)"/>
<use xlink:href="#tickSet" transform="rotate(120)"/>
<use xlink:href="#tickSet" transform="rotate(150)"/>
<use xlink:href="#tickSet" transform="rotate(180)"/>
<use xlink:href="#tickSet" transform="rotate(210)"/>
<use xlink:href="#tickSet" transform="rotate(240)"/>
<use xlink:href="#tickSet" transform="rotate(270)"/>
<use xlink:href="#tickSet" transform="rotate(300)"/>
<use xlink:href="#tickSet" transform="rotate(330)"/>
<desc>
    The minute hand applies the logic for the minute,
    second and sweep hand rotation. Note the begin and
    end attributes. The fill="freeze" is also used so
    that when the animation is stopped, it doesn't
    automatically revert back to the starting position.
</desc>
<use xlink:href="#minuteHand" x="0" y="0">
    <animateTransform attributeName="transform"
        attributeType="XML" type="rotate"
        from="0" to="360" dur="3600s"
        repeatCount="indefinite"
        begin="startButton.click"
        end="stopButton.click"
        fill="freeze"/>
</use>
<use xlink:href="#secondHand" x="0" y="0">
    <animateTransform attributeName="transform"
        attributeType="XML" type="rotate"
        from="0" to="360" dur="60s"
```

```
                                repeatCount="indefinite"
                                begin="startButton.click"
                                end="stopButton.click"
                                fill="freeze"/>
                </use>
                <use xlink:href="#sweepHand" x="0" y="0">
                        <animateTransform attributeName="transform"
                                attributeType="XML" type="rotate"
                                from="0" to="360" dur="1s"
                                repeatCount="indefinite"
                                begin="startButton.click"
                                end="stopButton.click"
                                fill="freeze"/>
                </use>
        </g>
        <desc>
                This describes a generic button, though it can
                certainly be made more complex.
        </desc>
        <circle cx="0" cy="0" r="15" id="button"/>
    </defs>
<!-- ***************** Rendering Starts Here *****************-->
    <use xlink:href="#label" x="50" y="0"/>
    <desc>
        This renders the stopwatch to the screen.
    </desc>
    <use xlink:href="#stopWatch" x="200" y="200"
        id="stopWatchInstance"/>
    <desc>
        When the start or stop buttons are pressed,
        they "light up" using the gradients defined
        at the beginning of the animation.
    </desc>
    <use xlink:href="#button" x="340" y="180"
        id="startButton" fill="green">
        <set attributeName="fill" attributeType="CSS"
            to="url(#startButtonOn)"
            begin="click" end="stopButton.click"/>
    </use>
    <use xlink:href="#button" x="340" y="220"
        id="stopButton" fill="red">
    <set attributeName="fill" attributeType="CSS"
        to="url(#stopButtonOn)"
```

```
            begin="click" end="startButton.click"/>
    </use>
    <text x="360" y="180" font-size="18"
            dominant-baseline="mathematical">
            Start/Restart
    </text>
    <text x="360" y="220" font-size="18"
            dominant-baseline="mathematical">
            Stop
    </text>
</svg>
```

The initial declaration only sets up the <defs> block and adds a headline label:

```
<svg xmlns:xsl="http://www.w3.org/2000/svg"
        xmlns:xlink="http://www.w3.org/1999/xlink">
    <defs>
            <text id="label" font-size="36" font-family="Helvetica"
                    x="0" y="36">
                    A Functional Stop Watch
            </text>
```

These gradients indicate when a button mode is currently active:

```
            <radialGradient id="startButtonOn">
                    <stop offset="0%" stop-color="lightGreen"/>
                    <stop offset="100%" stop-color="green"/>
            </radialGradient>
            <radialGradient id="stopButtonOn">
                    <stop offset="0%" stop-color="yellow"/>
                    <stop offset="100%" stop-color="red"/>
            </radialGradient>
```

The Triangle marker provides the pointer for each hand, which in turn makes the hand more like a traditional click hand rather than a simple line:

```
            <marker id="Triangle"
                    viewBox="0 0 10 10" refX="0" refY="5"
                    markerUnits="strokeWidth"
                    markerWidth="4" markerHeight="3"
                    orient="auto">
                    <path d="M 0 0 L 10 5 L 0 10 z"/>
            </marker>
```

The following code defines the clock back (set its fill to a pattern or image to make it appear more realistic):

```
<circle cx="0" cy="0" r="120" stroke="black" stroke-width="4"
fill="white" id="clockBack"/>
```

This code defines the three hands, sweepHand (which goes around once per second), secondHand (which goes around once per minute), and minuteHand (which goes around once an hour):

```
<line x1="0" y1="0" x2="0" y2="-100"
    stroke="red" stroke-width="1"
    marker-end="url(#Triangle)"
    id="sweepHand" fill="red"/>
<line x1="0" y1="0" x2="0" y2="-100"
    stroke="black"
    stroke-width="3" marker-end="url(#Triangle)"
    id="secondHand" fill="black"/>
<line x1="0" y1="0" x2="0" y2="-80"
    stroke="green" stroke-width="6"
    marker-end="url(#Triangle)"
    id="minuteHand" fill="green"/>
```

The ticks and subticks describe the lines used to denote five-minute and one-minute intervals, respectively:

```
<line x1="0" y1="-100" x2="0" y2="-120"
    stroke="black" stroke-width="2" id="tick"/>
<line x1="0" y1="-110" x2="0" y2="-120"
    stroke="black" stroke-width="1" id="subtick"/>
```

This puts the stopwatch pieces together:

```
<g id="stopWatch">
<use xlink:href="#clockBack"/>
```

Rather than define 12 ticks and 48 individual subticks, a group of one tick and five subticks are put together as a group called a tickSet. The tickSet is in turn rotated 11 more times to cut down on the amount of extraneous code:

```
<g transform="rotate(0)" id="tickSet">
                    <use xlink:href="#tick"/>
                    <use xlink:href="#subtick"
                        transform="rotate(6)"/>
```

```
            <use xlink:href="#subtick"
                    transform="rotate(12)"/>
            <use xlink:href="#subtick"
                    transform="rotate(18)"/>
            <use xlink:href="#subtick"
                    transform="rotate(24)"/>
</g>
<use xlink:href="#tickSet" transform="rotate(30)"/>
<use xlink:href="#tickSet" transform="rotate(60)"/>
<use xlink:href="#tickSet" transform="rotate(90)"/>
<use xlink:href="#tickSet" transform="rotate(120)"/>
<use xlink:href="#tickSet" transform="rotate(150)"/>
<use xlink:href="#tickSet" transform="rotate(180)"/>
<use xlink:href="#tickSet" transform="rotate(210)"/>
<use xlink:href="#tickSet" transform="rotate(240)"/>
<use xlink:href="#tickSet" transform="rotate(270)"/>
<use xlink:href="#tickSet" transform="rotate(300)"/>
<use xlink:href="#tickSet" transform="rotate(330)"/>
```

The minute hand applies the logic for the minute, second, and sweep hand rotations. Note the begin and end attributes. The fill="freeze" is also used so that when the animation is stopped, it does not automatically revert back to the starting position:

```
<use xlink:href="#minuteHand" x="0" y="0">
        <animateTransform attributeName="transform"
                attributeType="XML" type="rotate"
                from="0" to="360" dur="3600s"
                repeatCount="indefinite"
                begin="startButton.click"
                end="stopButton.click"
                fill="freeze"/>
</use>
<use xlink:href="#secondHand" x="0" y="0">
        <animateTransform attributeName="transform"
                attributeType="XML" type="rotate"
                from="0" to="360" dur="60s"
                repeatCount="indefinite"
                begin="startButton.click"
                end="stopButton.click"
                fill="freeze"/>
</use>
```

```
                                    <use xlink:href="#sweepHand" x="0" y="0">
                                        <animateTransform attributeName="transform"
                                            attributeType="XML" type="rotate"
                                            from="0" to="360" dur="1s"
                                            repeatCount="indefinite"
                                            begin="startButton.click"
                                            end="stopButton.click"
                                            fill="freeze"/>
                                    </use>
```

This describes a generic button, though you can certainly make it more complex:

```
<circle cx="0" cy="0" r="15" id="button"/>
</defs>
<!-- ***************** Rendering Starts Here *****************-->
<use xlink:href="#label" x="50" y="0"/>
```

This renders the stopwatch to the screen:

```
<use xlink:href="#stopWatch" x="200" y="200" id="stopWatchInstance"/>
```

When the start or stop buttons are pressed, they "light up" using the gradients defined at the beginning of the animation:

```
        <use xlink:href="#button" x="340" y="180"
            id="startButton" fill="green">
            <set attributeName="fill" attributeType="CSS"
                to="url(#startButtonOn)"
                begin="click" end="stopButton.click"/>
        </use>
        <use xlink:href="#button" x="340" y="220"
            id="stopButton" fill="red">
        <set attributeName="fill" attributeType="CSS"
            to="url(#stopButtonOn)"
            begin="click" end="startButton.click"/>
        </use>
        <text x="360" y="180" font-size="18"
            dominant-baseline="mathematical">
            Start/Restart
        </text>
```

```
<text x="360" y="220" font-size="18"
      dominant-baseline="mathematical">
      Stop
</text>
```

The stopwatch illustrates both the use of mouse events (clicking the start and stop buttons) and timer events (the `animateTransform` elements that control the rotations of each hand). One advantage of working with these timer events is that the SVG parser by default optimizes the rendering so that it will always start or end within the intervals specified. Thus, it will usually be accurate to within the timing error of the computer processor (typically in the neighborhood of 0.05 seconds or so with older clocks, and maybe a tenth of that for newer clocks).

Summary

There are relatively few applications that can be nicely tied up in a completely graphical language, no matter how powerful. SVG is fundamentally an interface description language, and consequently it does not by itself have the resources to create all but the simplest applications. For example, a stopwatch is possible using animations, but a clock is not unless you have some way of setting the initial time beforehand. In other words, SVG by itself lacks the ability to work with external data in any form.

However, the SVG language is more than just the XML markup tags of the language. For every element in SVG, there is a supported documented object model that lets you integrate SVG with other programming languages such as JavaScript or Java. These binding models can turn simple animations into sophisticated graphical user interfaces communicating with data from the outside: databases, XML streams, Web services . . . the list goes on and on.

Additionally, you can make even nonanimating SVG a part of a more interactive solution through the mechanism of the XML Stylesheet Language for Transformations (XSLT). An XSLT transformation can convert an XML data set (perhaps generated from a database) into just about any SVG graphic. Moreover, you can build complex applications through the use of parameterized XSLT.

Animations by themselves can still be used for a lot, everything from presentations to simple animations. You could, in fact, create fairly complex multimedia "applications" using just the material covered up to this point in the book. But to really take advantage of SVG, it is necessary to take the next step into interactivity.

CHAPTER 9

Integrating SVG and HTML

BACK IN THE EARLY **1990s,** multimedia was all the rage—it was the thing that would transform computing. It did, of course, but to such a degree that most people do not really think about it anymore. Indeed, the line between presentations, applications, and games has become exceedingly thin. You can break them down into the following (broad) categories:

- **Presentations**: A presentation may have animation and limited interactivity but is typically read-only. Thus, both PowerPoint and a DVD player are presentation applications. Presentations are typically informative or information in nature.

- **Applications**: An application is oriented around a standard graphical user interface for changing a data store. Applications are typically task oriented.

- **Games**: A game typically involves a great deal of user interaction but also involves changing the state of a data stores to some greater or lesser degree. Games are usually either educational or entertainment oriented.

Understanding both the distinctions and similarities behind these three broad categories are critical for being able to make use of SVG beyond its essential use as a graphics language. Indeed, one of the most exciting and useful aspects of SVG is that you can bind Scalable Vector Graphics (SVG) elements to specific actions using other programming languages. This in turn means you can access and modify data stores, create sophisticated applications around fairly simple interfaces, and at the same time retain the flexibility that characterizes SVG as an Extensible Markup Language (XML).

Chapters 1–7 looked at SVG from the standpoint of creating (for the most part) noninteractive graphics, and Chapter 8, "Animating SVG," began blurring the lines of animation and limited interactivity (which can be seen as animation linked to user events such as mouse clicks). However, the title of this book, SVG *Programming : The Graphical Web*, points to the use of SVG in programming environments. You have to walk before you can fly, but now you are about ready to fly.

As you have seen, SVG is powerful, but it really comes into its own when it is tied into a browser and integrated with Hypertext Markup Language (HTML) and XML content. In this chapter, I focus on how you can invoke SVG from within HTML and how SVG and HTML can interact with one another through links, JavaScript, and declarative tags.

Finally, a caveat before beginning: This is not a book on JavaScript, Java, XML Stylesheet Language (XSLT), or other programming languages. You can develop sophisticated interactivity fairly readily with SVG, but you must have a basic understanding of contemporary programming practices. Additionally, some of the code developed here is dependent to a certain extent upon the Adobe SVG Viewer rather than being a feature of SVG itself. When such extensions arise, I shall do my best to point them out.

Introducing Anchors and Links

SVG by itself was intended to be simply a language for describing graphical elements, but for a number of reasons, it has evolved instead into being a rich and robust language for describing interfaces on the Web. At its core, however, SVG shares with HTML one strong, defining characteristic: hypertext linking.

A hypertext link acts as a mechanism for relating two or more points on the Web together—it describes a relationship. HTML is built on linking—the <a> anchor tag is perhaps one of the most well known means of linking. Indeed, from a relational viewpoint, you can think of any HTML document solely as a cloud of descriptive information surrounding a set of link declarations.

Links in the XML world are currently defined using two primary standards: XLink, which describes the nature of the link and is the most important for SVG, and XPointer, which defines the syntax for links declarations themselves. XLink was first described in Chapter 2, "Getting Started: An SVG Tutorial," for referencing internally identified elements, and in Chapter 7, "Incorporating Texture," for creating links to external documents.

The <a> anchor tag serves at least one purpose in SVG that the <a> tag does in HTML—it creates a hypertext link. The syntax for <a> uses the more formal xlink syntax (and correspondingly needs to include the xlink namespace www.w3.org/1999/xlink either on the <a> tag or in the initial <svg> enclosure). Otherwise, it is functionally quite similar to the HTML tag, at least when used as a hypertext linker. This is an important distinction. The HTML <a> tag does double duty, both indicating where a link should be made and defining an explicit location in a document, given by the name attribute:

```
<a name="foobar"/>
```

In SVG this particular function is redundant—the id attribute already uniquely defines an element in an SVG document, so you cannot explicitly define a formal name attribute. Moreover, the notion of a formal location being defined (such as is performed by the scrolling of an HTML document to find a specific #name element, has no real meaning in the three-dimensional (x, y, and time) language of SVG. As such, the anchor tag actually has no real "anchor" associations; it is a link, pure and simple.

So, what does an <a> tag look like in SVG? Its form is about what you would expect for an XLink-based language:

```
<a xlink:href="url" xlink:type="simple" target="targetFrame"
    xlink:role="roleDescriptor" xlink:title="linkTitle"
    xlink:show="new|replace" xlink:actuate="onRequest"
    xlink:arcrole="arcRoleDescriptor">SVG Content</a>
```

Three lines worth of attributes to describe a link—no wonder XLink has not made huge inroads into the Web design field. Actually, however, this is pretty deceptive. Although this gives an idea of the overall structure of a link, most of these attributes have sensible defaults and consequently do not need to be specified.

For instance, the xlink:type attribute describes the type of link being discussed. The normal set of xlink:types is fairly broad, including simple, extended, locator, arc, resource, and title, but SVG only supports the simple type (in other words, the link connects to only one other link for the purpose of replacing content). Similarly, the xlink:title does not need to be supported by the browser (and consequently probably is not), and the only actuate command that xlink:actuate supports in SVG is "onRequest". The Adobe SVG Viewer, in fact, while using the XLink language, basically treats the <a> tag similarly to its HTML counterpart. Thus, in almost every case, you will use one of two forms to create a link. This format:

```
<a xlink:href="url">SVG Content</a>
```

or this one:

```
<a xlink:href="url" target="targetFrame ">SVG Content</a>
```

The first form gives (within the xlink:href attribute) the URL that will be displayed when then graphics contained within the SVG content are clicked. This will replace the whole SVG document within the browser, not just the contained graphic. You can see the first form in Listing 9-1 (see Figure 9-1).

Listing 9-1. anchorLink1.svg

```
<svg xmlns="http://www.w3.org/2000/svg"
        xmlns:xlink="http://www.w3.org/1999/xlink">
    <rect fill="black" width="100%" height="100%" x="0" y="0"/>
```

```
<svg viewBox="0 0 1000 1000" preserveAspectRatio="none">
    <g transform="translate(500,500)">
        <a xlink:href="http://www.kurtcagle.net">
            <circle cx="0" cy="0" r="75" fill="red"/>
            <text font-size="20" fill="white" text-anchor="middle"
                    dominant-baseline="mathematical">
                    <tspan x="0" y="-30">The</tspan>
                    <tspan x="0" y="0">Metaphorical</tspan>
                    <tspan x="0" y="30">Web</tspan>
            </text>
        </a>
    </g>
</svg>
</svg>
```

Figure 9-1. Using the <a> *tag to get a pointer cursor and support a link*

In this example, the <a> element points to a Web site (in this case, my own Web site) in the xlink:href attribute. Everything that is within this <a> tag, the red circle with white text, becomes an active link at that point; clicking either of these elements will cause the browser to load with the appropriate Web site. Note one interesting corollary of this: It is the boundary of the elements themselves, not the rectangle containing them, which makes up the selection area. As such, you can use paths and complex aggregates of shapes to create irregular image maps.

Whenever you set up a link, the default cursor for that link changes to a hand pointer icon. This makes it easy to both identify relevant live areas in the actual graphic and to avoid having to use the cursor element, which has only limited support in most reference implementations.

> **TIP**   *You can make the cursor appear even if you do not include the* xlink:href *attribute in the* <a> *tag. You can use this with a set of buttons that use JavaScript calls but for which you would still like to have a hand cursor.*

You can also include a target attribute to the <a> tag, which lets you use SVG graphics to either launch new windows (by setting the attribute value to "new") or by setting it to the name of a different active frame. For instance, consider an HTML frameset, as shown in Listing 9-2 and Figure 9-2.

Listing 9-2. metaphorFrame.htm

```
<html>
<head>
        <title>The Metaphorical Web</title>
</head>
<!-- frames -->
<frameset  cols="23%,*">
    <frame src="metaButtons.svg" name="toc" id="toc"
     frameborder="-1" scrolling="no" noresize marginwidth="0"
     marginheight="0">
    <frame name="display" src="splashIntro.svg" marginwidth="0"
     marginheight="0" frameborder="-1" noresize scrolling="auto">
</frameset>

</html>
```

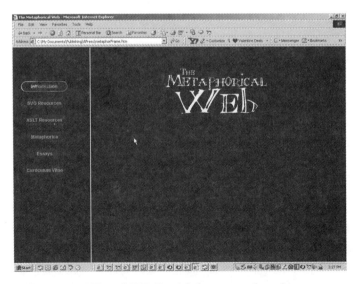

Figure 9-2. Integrating SVG and HTML with frames and anchor tags

This defines two frames, `toc` and `display`, which initially point to `metaButtons.svg` and `splashIntro.svg` (respectively). The `metaButtons.svg` file in turn contains a set of buttons, each of which is wrapped within an `<a>` tag, as shown in Listing 9-3.

Listing 9-3. `metaButtons.svg`

```
<svg xmlns="http://www.w3.org/2000/svg"
        xmlns:xlink="http://www.w3.org/1999/xlink">
    <defs>
        <radialGradient id="buttonInactiveGrad">
            <stop offset="0%" stop-color="blue"/>
            <stop offset="100%" stop-color="navy"/>
        </radialGradient>
        <radialGradient id="buttonActiveGrad">
            <stop offset="0%" stop-color="lightBlue"/>
            <stop offset="50%" stop-color="blue"/>
            <stop offset="100%" stop-color="navy"/>
        </radialGradient>
        <linearGradient id="buttonBorder" gradientTransform="rotate(15)">
            <stop offset="0%" stop-color="#808080"/>
            <stop offset="20%" stop-color="#F0F0F0"/>
            <stop offset="35%" stop-color="#606060"/>
            <stop offset="50%" stop-color="#808080"/>
            <stop offset="75%" stop-color="#505050"/>
            <stop offset="90%" stop-color="#A0A0A0"/>
            <stop offset="100%" stop-color="#808080"/>
        </linearGradient>
        <linearGradient id="textInactiveGrad">
            <stop offset="0%" stop-color="#A0A0A0"/>
            <stop offset="100%" stop-color="#A0A0A0"/>
        </linearGradient>
        <linearGradient id="textActiveGrad">
            <stop offset="0%" stop-color="#FFFFFF"/>
            <stop offset="100%" stop-color="#FFFFFF"/>
        </linearGradient>
        <rect fill="black" x="0" y="0" width="100%" height="100%"
                id="background"/>
        <rect x="0" y="0" width="140" height="30"
                fill="url(#buttonInactiveGrad)"
                rx="15" ry="15" id="buttonInactive"
                stroke-width="2"/>
        <rect x="0" y="0" width="140" height="30"
                fill="url(#buttonActiveGrad)"
```

```
                    rx="15" ry="15" id="buttonActive"
                    stroke-width="2"/>
    <text id="button0Text" x="70" y="15"
            dominant-baseline="mathematical" text-anchor="middle"
            font-size="14"  font-weight="bold" stroke-width="1">
            Introduction</text>
    <text id="button1Text" x="70" y="15"
            dominant-baseline="mathematical" text-anchor="middle"
            font-size="14"  font-weight="bold" stroke-width="1">
            SVG Resources</text>
    <text id="button2Text" x="70" y="15"
            dominant-baseline="mathematical" text-anchor="middle"
            font-size="14"  font-weight="bold" stroke-width="1">
            XSLT Resources</text>
    <!-- more button labels -->
    <g id="button0Inactive">
        <use xlink:href="#buttonInactive" x="0" y="0"/>
        <use xlink:href="#button0Text" x="0" y="0"
                fill="url(#textInactiveGrad)"/>
    </g>
    <g id="button0Active">
        <use xlink:href="#buttonActive" x="0" y="0"/>
        <use xlink:href="#button0Text" x="0" y="0"
                fill="url(#textActiveGrad)"/>
    </g>
    <g id="button1Inactive">
        <use xlink:href="#buttonInactive" x="0" y="0"/>
        <use xlink:href="#button1Text" x="0" y="0"
                fill="url(#textInactiveGrad)"/>
    </g>
    <g id="button1Active">
        <use xlink:href="#buttonActive" x="0" y="0"/>
        <use xlink:href="#button1Text" x="0" y="0"
                fill="url(#textActiveGrad)"/>
    </g>
    <g id="button2Inactive">
        <use xlink:href="#buttonInactive" x="0" y="0"/>
        <use xlink:href="#button2Text" x="0" y="0"
                fill="url(#textInactiveGrad)"/>
    </g>
    <g id="button2Active">
        <use xlink:href="#buttonActive" x="0" y="0"/>
        <use xlink:href="#button2Text" x="0" y="0"
                fill="url(#textActiveGrad)"/>
    </g>
```

437

```
                        <!-- more button definitions -->
                </defs>
                <use xlink:href="#background" x="0" y="0" width="100%" height="100%"/>
                <g id="buttons" transform="translate(25,100)">
                <a xlink:href="splashIntro.svg" target="display">
                <use x="0" y="0" xlink:href="#button0Inactive">
                    <set attributeName="xlink:href" attributeType="XML"
                                to="#button0Active"
                                begin="mouseover" end="mouseout"/>
                    <set attributeName="stroke" attributeType="CSS"
                                to="url(#buttonBorder)"
                                begin="click" end="buttons.mouseup"/>
                </use>
                </a>
                <a xlink:href="SVGResources.htm" target="display">
                <use x="0" y="50" xlink:href="#button1Inactive">
                    <set attributeName="xlink:href" attributeType="XML"
                                to="#button1Active"
                                begin="mouseover" end="mouseout"/>
                    <set attributeName="stroke" attributeType="CSS"
                                to="url(#buttonBorder)"
                                begin="click" end="buttons.mouseup"/>
                </use>
                </a>
                <a xlink:href="XSLTResources.htm" target="display">
                <use x="0" y="100" xlink:href="#button2Inactive">
                    <set attributeName="xlink:href" attributeType="XML"
                                to="#button2Active"
                                begin="mouseover" end="mouseout"/>
                    <set attributeName="stroke" attributeType="CSS"
                                to="url(#buttonBorder)"
                                begin="click" end="buttons.mouseup"/>
                </use>
                </a>
                <!-- more linked buttons -->
                </g>
        </svg>
```

In this particular case, the relevant buttons are each contained in an anchor tag of this form:

```
<a xlink:href="filename" target="display">
```

Note that such files could be HTML documents, SVG documents, or any other kind of elements. By breaking the interface into a series of targeted frames, the SVG buttons (which could additionally be generated through XSLT, as will be discussed in Chapter 10, "SVG Components"), can work independently, keeping the event management reasonable and making it possible for an SVG element to work with non-SVG elements.

NOTE   *Most Web developers have a somewhat ambivalent relationship with frames, as they tend to make both Web developing and Web indexing much more complex. It is also possible, as will be discussed in Chapter 10, "SVG Components," to embed an SVG document within HTML, though it requires a more sophisticated degree of coordination than framesets.*

Cursors, Foiled Again!

The cursor is perhaps one of the most critical pieces of feedback information you can provide to a user. That tiny graphic shows the system where the user's interest is focused and, simultaneously, provides a hint as to the current actions or states currently available to the user. An I-beam cursor, for instance, has come to universally define text entry, and the hourglass, watch, running man, or whatever happens to be the current marketing icon *du jour* has come to universally mean that your computer has frozen and you can probably go get that cup of coffee you were thinking about while it reboots (at least that is what it usually means on my system).

There are a number of different ways for setting the cursor in SVG, including the use of the `<a>` tag as shown previously. One of the simplest is to employ the `cursor` attribute. This attribute lets you set the cursor for a given element or graphical context to any of the elements in Table 9-1.

CAUTION   *The Adobe SVG Viewer 3.0 currently does not support cursor modification, so any material contained in this chapter will not work under that viewer.*

Table 9-1. The cursor *Attribute*

CURSOR NAME	USUAL CONTEXT
auto	This instructs the system to use the default cursor for the appropriate context (an I-beam over text, an arrow over neutral elements, and so on).
crosshair	This is used for precise demarcation and selection of a region, usually.
default	This gives the default cursor for the system and is almost always an arrow graphic.
pointer	This provides the "finger," which indicates that the element beneath is a link to some other resource.
move	The move cursor indicates that an element can be dragged to a different location on the screen.
(e l w l s l n l se l sw l ne l nw)-resize	This provides the direction in which dragging the appropriate element will move that element. For instance, to indicate that a graphic can be moved west only (usually toward the left of the screen) you would use the w-"resize" cursor property value.
text	This cursor indicates the location of the caret, the point of text insertion or deletion.
wait	This cursor indicates that the system is currently doing something for which you need to wait.
help	This cursor is often coupled with help systems (and is typically invoked using F1) to give an explanation of the thing being clicked.
url	SVG supports custom cursors, though these cursors must be of the appropriate graphics type for that system (unlike the <cursor> element defined later in this section).

Thus, you can theoretically use SVG to set the cursor of an element:

```
<svg xmlns="http://www.w3.org/2000/svg"
        xmlns:xlink="http://www.w3.org/1999/xlink" >
<g transform="translate(100,100)">
<rect fill="red" x="0" y="0" width="200" height="100" cursor="help"/>
</g>
</svg>
```

or, using the CSS notation:

```
<svg xmlns="http://www.w3.org/2000/svg"
        xmlns:xlink="http://www.w3.org/1999/xlink">
    <g transform="translate(100,100)">
    <rect fill="red" x="0" y="0" width="200" height="100" style="cursor:help"/>
    </g>
</svg>
```

To set the style for a specific graphical cursor for the system (such as myCursor.ico if you were in a Windows-based system), you would also use the url() notation:

```
<svg xmlns="http://www.w3.org/2000/svg"
        xmlns:xlink="http://www.w3.org/1999/xlink">
    <g transform="translate(100,100)">
    <rect fill="red" x="0" y="0" width="200" height="100"
            cursor="url(myCursor.ico)"/>
    </g>
</svg>
```

Finally, you can create a custom cursor for an element using the <cursor> tag. This tag lets you associate a transparent-backed PNG graphic with the cursor, giving you fairly dramatic control over the cursor itself:

```
<svg xmlns="http://www.w3.org/2000/svg"
        xmlns:xlink="http://www.w3.org/1999/xlink">
    <g transform="translate(100,100)">
    <rect fill="red" x="0" y="0" width="200" height="100">
        <cursor xlink:href="myCursor.png" x="0" y="0"/>
    </rect>
    </g>
</svg>
```

The cursor in this case applies to its container element. As you move the cursor into the element, the cursor changes to the specified graphic. The x and y positions contain the location of the *hotspot* on the graphic, the place that the system uses to define where the mouse is actually located. This value defaults to x="0" y="0", at the upper-left corner of the graphic. If the cursor graphic is 32-pixels wide, a value of x="16" y="16" will position the hotspot at the center of the graphic.

NOTE   *Unfortunately, all of this is basically conjecture with the Adobe SVG Viewer. Currently, the 3.0 version of this plug-in does not support cursors in any form, save for the default system behavior shown when the cursor moves over text or the pointer form of the* <a> *tag cursor.*

Using SVG and the *<embed>* Tag

You can use SVG to build both graphics and more complex multimedia presentations, but the language as it currently stands is not sufficient by itself to do many of the tasks required for a full-blown graphical user environment. Thus, at least for a while, SVG will likely end up playing something of a supporting role against other XML presentation technologies such as XHTML or XForms.

One of the tenets of this book has been to promote the idea of SVG as a way of building interface elements. In other words, beyond its ability as a convenient way of describing pictures, SVG can significantly expand the set of options that are currently in use in HTML Web pages. For instance, SVG can construct complex (potentially irregularly shaped) interactive buttons, dials, slider controls, toolbars, animations, and other components that would be difficult to do using traditional HTML means.

Moreover, and this is a point worth emphasizing, one advantage of the SVG interface is that the interfaces involved are not static, but can be generated in real time on the basis of information from the server (or the browser client). Because of this, SVG takes on much more of the characteristics of its nearest potential rival, Macromedias Flash, as a means for creating dynamic user interfaces on the fly.

Within an HTML document, the most efficient way of including SVG (as discussed in Chapter 2, "Getting Started: An SVG Tutorial") is to use the HTML <embed> tag to incorporate it into the HTML document. The <embed> tag provides a link to the relevant SVG document and can also include information for retrieving the Adobe SVG Viewer if it is not currently installed.

For instance, consider a fairly basic animation that shows a large logo element as well as additional text that appears and disappears, as shown in Listing 9-4 and Figure 9-3.

Listing 9-4. metaphoricalWebLogo.svg

```
<svg width="400" height="600" id="logo"
        xmlns="http://www.w3.org/2000/svg"
        xmlns:xlink="http://www.w3.org/1999/xlink">
    <defs>
        <text id="longLive" font-size="15" fill="yellow" text-anchor="middle">
```

```
                <tspan x="0" y="0">The Web As We Know It Is Dead!</tspan>
                <tspan x="0" y="20">Long Live the Web!</tspan>
        </text>
        <text id="decouple" font-size="15" fill="yellow" text-anchor="middle">
                <tspan x="0" y="0">The browser and HTML seems to be</tspan>
                <tspan x="0" y="20">such a simple concept -</tspan>
                <tspan x="0" y="40">Form based applications can</tspan>
                <tspan x="0" y="60">be created with little effort</tspan>
                <tspan x="0" y="80">yet can be seen universally.</tspan>
        </text>
        <text id="purists" font-size="15" fill="yellow" text-anchor="middle">
                <tspan x="0" y="0">The Web worked because it
                  made programming</tspan>
                <tspan x="0" y="20">accessible to the masses,
                  to such an extent</tspan>
                <tspan x="0" y="40">that creating a web page</tspan>
                <tspan x="0" y="60">is often not even considered
                programming . . . </tspan>
                <tspan x="0" y="90">by the purists.</tspan>
        </text>
        <text id="butItIs" font-size="24" fill="yellow" text-anchor="middle">
                <tspan x="0" y="0">But it is!</tspan>
        </text>
</defs>
<g visibility="hidden">
        <set attributeName="visibility" attributeType="CSS"
                to="visible" being="logo.load"/>
<image xlink:href="metaphoricalWeb1.png" x="0" y="0"
                width="400" height="200">
        <animate attributeName="opacity" attributeType="CSS"
                 from="0" to="1" dur="4s" begin="logo.load"
                 fill="freeze" id="logoShow"/>
</image>
</g>
<g transform="translate(200,240)">
        <use xlink:href="#longLive" x="0" y="0" opacity="0">
            <animate attributeName="opacity" from="0" to="1"
                     begin="logoShow.begin + 3s" dur="3s" fill="freeze"/>
            <animate attributeName="opacity" from="1" to="0"
                     begin="logoShow.begin + 9s" dur="3s" fill="freeze"/>
        </use>
        <use xlink:href="#decouple" x="0" y="0" opacity="0">
```

```
            <animate attributeName="opacity" from="0" to="1"
                begin="logoShow.begin + 9s" dur="3s" fill="freeze"/>
            <animate attributeName="opacity" from="1" to="0"
                begin="logoShow.begin + 15s" dur="3s" fill="freeze"/>
        </use>
        <use xlink:href="#purists" x="0" y="0" opacity="0">
            <animate attributeName="opacity" from="0" to="1"
                begin="logoShow.begin + 15s" dur="3s" fill="freeze"/>
            <animate attributeName="opacity" from="1" to="0"
                begin="logoShow.begin + 24s" dur="3s" fill="freeze"/>
        </use>
        <use xlink:href="#butItIs" x="0" y="0" opacity="0">
            <animate attributeName="opacity" from="0" to="1"
                begin="logoShow.begin + 24s" dur="3s" fill="freeze"/>
            <animate attributeName="opacity" from="1" to="0"
                begin="logoShow.begin + 27s" dur="3s" fill="freeze"/>
        </use>
    </g>
</svg>
```

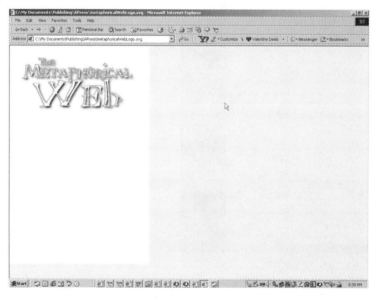

Figure 9-3. The Metaphorical Web logo

Suppose you wanted to insert this presentation into a Web page with a blue background. You could do so easily with the <embed> element, as shown in Listing 9-5 and Figure 9-4.

Listing 9-5. `simplePage1.htm`

```
<html>
<head>
    <title>A Simple Integrated SVG Page</title>
</head>

<body bgcolor="blue">

<table>
<tr>
<td>
<embed src="simpleSVGButtons1.svg" width="400" height="600"/>
</td>
<td valign="top"><h1>Here's a Simple Button Page</h1></td>
</tr>
</table>
</body>
</html>
```

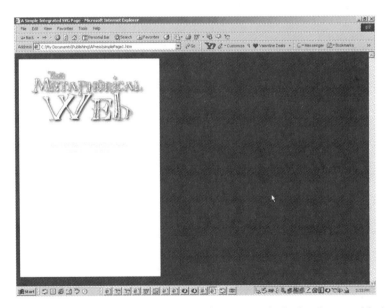

Figure 9-4. Placing an SVG graphic in a Web page, with the background being SVG

The `<embed>` element needs `width` and `height` attributes to inform the browser the dimensions of the graphic, but also to set the `width` and `height` attributes of the `<svg>` element. Note that, in general, the browser will likely not be able to ascertain the dimensions of the SVG graphic ahead of time, even if they

445

are explicitly specified within the SVG document. Thus, leaving these two attributes off in the HTML document put you at the mercy of the browser's default behavior.

Working with *wmode*

One of the first things you may notice, when looking at the output from Listing 9-5 is that the background of the SVG graphic is white against a blue background. A major selling point of SVG graphics is the creation of irregularly shaped regions, having a rectangular white background rather defeats the purpose of the whole language.

As it turns out, what you are seeing is an artifact of the windowing mode used to display the SVG. To understand windowing modes, you need a bit of background about the way in which external components are rendered in most contemporary browsers.

Typically, when HTML is drawn to a Web page, what is happening is that the browser first allocates a block of memory called a *canvas*. The HTML rendering engine then draws the HTML text, image regions, and so forth upon this particular canvas. This works fine for the basic HTML rendering, but things get more complicated when ActiveX components or Java applets get added into the mix.

Such a control creates a rectangular region within the canvas that establishes a second canvas in a separate section of memory. The browser then composites the two canvases together before sending the page to the graphics card to be displayed. The second canvas is for the most part independent of the first, with the possible exception of browser mediating script that will be discussed in Chapter 10, "SVG Components."

The most efficient operation for compositing the two canvases together is for the browser to keep track of the position and dimensions of the subordinate canvas and simply not draw anything from the first canvas into the second region. This is the default window mode and makes for the best performance by a considerable amount. You can set this value by assigning "window" to the wmode attribute in the <embed> tag.

NOTE *The* wmode *attribute is not universally supported on all browsers or SVG implementations, so before applying it make sure that you test it in your intended target browsers.*

More and more controls, however, are beginning to implement other modes of windowing, and the Adobe SVG Viewer is no exception. One problem of the default window mode comes from overlapping elements. There are times where it is handy to use an SVG document as a background—for instance, the gradient capabilities of SVG make it ideal for creating gradients for PowerPoint-like Web presentations. Yet if you used wmode="window", the windowed SVG document would simply replace anything that would normally appear in that space.

NOTE   *Windowed controls will always display above windowless controls, regardless of the value of the z-index.*

To get around this, you would use wmode="opaque". This instructs the browser to render the subordinate SVG canvas, then composite it onto the browser's canvas. Any elements that appear after the embedded SVG element would then likewise be composited on top of the top of the canvas up to that point.

For instance, suppose you had an SVG gradient that gave you a blue background fading to a dark navy:

```
<svg xmlns="http://www.w3.org/2000/svg"
        xmlns:xlink="http://www.w3.org/1999/xlink">
    <defs>
        <linearGradient gradientTransform="rotate(90)" id="bgGrad">
            <stop offset="0%" stop-color="blue"/>
            <stop offset="100%" stop-color="darkNavy"/>
        </linearGradient>
    </defs>
    <rect x="0" y="0" width="100%" height="100%" fill="url(#bgGrad)"/>
</svg>
```

This could then be composited in as a background by setting the wmode of the <embed> element to "opaque" (see Figure 9-5):

```
<html>
<head>
    <title>A Simple Integrated SVG Page</title>
</head>
<body bgcolor="blue" text="yellow" style="margin:0">
<embed src="HTMLGrad1.svg"
        width="100%" height="100%" wmode="opaque"
        style="position:absolute;top:0;left:0;z-index:-1"/>
```

```
<div style="margin:20">
<h1>The Metaphorical Web</h1>
</div>
</body>
</html>
```

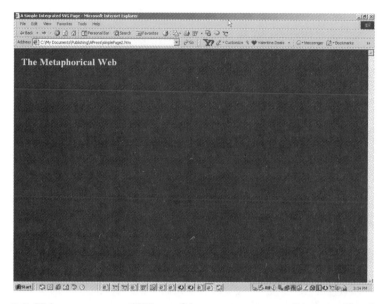

Figure 9-5. Using an opaque SVG graphic to generate a sophisticated background

You use the style attribute in the <body> element to disable the margins applied to the <body> element. This then positions the SVG element at the top-leftmost corner of the browser display window. The <embed> element itself contains a style attribute, which indicates that the graphic is positioned absolutely in the browser at (left,top) of (0,0). The z-index furthermore tells the browser that this graphic should be considered to be behind all other elements on the page (unless of course they have a z-index less than –1).

A z-index of 0 is considered to be the main display window, which would cause any additional elements to be displayed below the gradient at the bottom of the browser window (and hence the visible area of the screen). Thus, setting z-index to –1 removes the graphic from the normal element flow.

Finally, a <div> element sets the margins back to 20 so that any elements contained within the <div>will not be flush with the left of the display window.

The "opaque" windowing mode will be slower than the default "window" mode because the browser has to incorporate the graphic into the canvas before drawing any subordinate elements that may come from the HTML document if there is overlap. However, a wmode of "opaque" will still contain the bounding rectangle of the SVG container (in other words, any place in the initial graphic where the bounding rectangle is not covered with some element will appear white when wmode="opaque").

The final option, "transparent" provides the greatest degree of flexibility, but at the cost of the greatest performance loss. In the "transparent" window mode, the opacity of each pixel in the SVG graphic is calculated, then the color and alpha channel are applied to the underlying HTML canvas. Finally, other HTML (or SVG) elements can be composited on top of the graphic.

The following code demonstrates this—which is admittedly not so simple now (see Figure 9-6):

```
<html>
<head>
    <title>A Simple Integrated SVG Page</title>
</head>
<body bgcolor="blue" text="yellow" style="margin:0">
<embed src="HTMLGrad1.svg" width="100%" height="100%"
            wmode="opaque" style="position:absolute;top:0;left:0;z-index:-1"/>
<div style="margin:20">
<h1>Metaphorica</h1>
<embed src="metaphoricalWebLogo.svg" width="400" height="600"
            wmode="transparent"/>
</div>
</body>
</html>
```

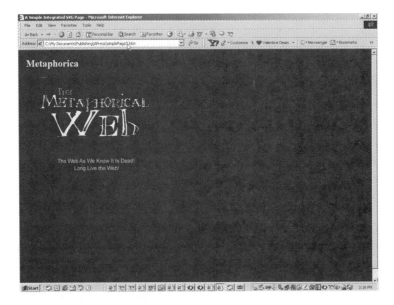

Figure 9-6. The transparent wmode

The exposed background of an SVG graphic has an implicit opacity of 0. This means that within the presentation given in Listing 9-4, which does not have any background, the only elements that are normally opaque are the opaque portions of the imported PNG graphic and the text elements. Additionally, the animations that raise the opacity to 1 and back to 0 change even these.

This example is also noteworthy because there are two distinct SVG graphics that overlap; the appearing and disappearing presentation is rendered on top of the gradient. Because the presentation itself has not had its `position` CSS property set to `absolute`, the presentation gets positioned according to the flow model of the HTML rendering . . . in this case, below the `<h1>Metaphorical</h1>` tag.

The transparent window mode opens up a number of possibilities for HTML/SVG integration. You can also do the following:

- Text title elements with drop shadows or internal gradients overlaying HTML patterned backgrounds

- Interactive arrows and other navigational controls

- Drop-down menus

- Circular or other irregularly shaped controls

- Animation sprites for help systems

- Button bars, radio buttons, and scroll bars

- Gauges, meters, and graphs

> **NOTE** *Many of these examples, such as gauges, animated sprites, and drop-down menus will be covered in more detail in Chapter 10, "SVG Components."*

Understanding SVG Events and JavaScript

SVG makes handling events relatively simple, if somewhat verbose, and the example in Listing 9-4 demonstrated how such buttons could be used to set the URL of an alternating frame through the `<a>` tag. However, to use SVG as a way of building components, the SVG has to have some way of talking to the other elements of the HTML page. This is generally handled through the SVG event mechanism and a bound language such as Java or (more typically) JavaScript.

The event mechanism that SVG uses is an interesting hybrid of HTML and SMIL. The SMIL eventing, covered extensively in Chapter 8, "Animating SVG," lets you define an animation element (such as `<animate>` or `<set>`) and within that element indicate which events (mouseup, mousedown, click, timer events, and so on) start or stop the requisite animation. However, you can also set explicit event hooks on an element in a manner similar to HTML and from there call the appropriate event handler written in a language bound to the SVG viewer.

The term *binding*, by the way, simply indicates that the language runtime library is accessible from SVG so that you can call functions or subroutines in that language. For SVG, the default binding is JavaScript, also known as *ECMAScript*. This means you can both make calls against resources available from the browser (such as a message or input window or the status message typically located at the bottom of most browsers) as well as define specific functions in that language to be called from the handlers.

CAUTION *Many of the code samples provided from here on are specific to Internet Explorer (IE) running under Windows. The Adobe SVG Viewer does not have as much functionality in Netscape or IE 5 for the Macintosh.*

For instance, you can create a simple button sequence that, when a circle is pressed, gives the color of that circle (see Figure 9-7):

```
<svg xmlns="http://www.w3.org/2000/svg"
        xmlns:xlink="http://www.w3.org/1999/xlink" >
    <defs>
        <circle cx="0" cy="0" r="20" stroke="black" stroke-width="2" id="btn"/>
    </defs>
    <use xlink:href="#btn" x="50" y="50" fill="red"
            onclick="alert('This button is red.')"/>
    <use xlink:href="#btn" x="100" y="50" fill="blue"
            onclick="alert('This button is blue.')"/>
    <use xlink:href="#btn" x="150" y="50" fill="green"
            onclick="alert('This button is green.')"/>
</svg>
```

The event handler onclick mirrors the name of the animation event tokens; thus, onclick is called whenever someone clicks on an element, onmousedown whenever someone depresses the mouse over the element, onmouseup whenever the mouse button is released over the element, and so forth. This nomenclature also mirrors the event handlers in HTML and XHTML.

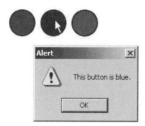

Figure 9-7. The onclick *handler*

The alert() function does not belong to SVG. Rather, these are actually methods of the window object, which is a representation of the browser window. Thus, properly the command should be this:

```
onclick="window.alert('This button is red.')"
```

which better defines the object being manipulated.

You can have more than one JavaScript statement within a given event handler. For instance, in Listing 9-6, when you click on the white button, a dialog box launches, asking you the name of a specific color. When you enter that color, the rest of the line sets the color of the circle to that color (see Figure 9-8).

Listing 9-6. boundEvents2.svg

```
<svg xmlns="http://www.w3.org/2000/svg"
        xmlns:xlink="http://www.w3.org/1999/xlink">
    <defs>
        <circle cx="0" cy="0" r="20" stroke="black"
            stroke-width="2" id="btn"/>
    </defs>
    <use xlink:href="#btn" x="50" y="50" fill="red"
            onclick="alert('This button is red.')"/>
    <use xlink:href="#btn" x="100" y="50" fill="blue"
            onclick="alert('This button is blue.')"/>
    <use xlink:href="#btn" x="150" y="50" fill="green"
            onclick="alert('This button is green.')"/>
    <use xlink:href="#btn" x="200" y="50" fill="white"
            onclick="color=prompt(
            'What color do you want to set this button?','yellow');
            evt.target.setAttribute('fill',color)"/>
</svg>
```

The following line:

```
evt.target.setAttribute('fill',color)
```

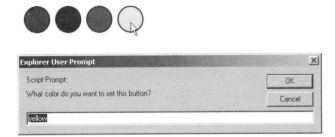

Figure 9-8. Using input prompts to change the state of your graphics

hints at a much richer structure hiding just beneath the surface of the SVG model. The keyword evt is a system-defined placeholder that always contains the event that launched the script in the first place.

If you are not familiar with event-based programming, this previous statement can seem a little counterintuitive. In essence, when an event occurs for which the appropriate handler exists, an SVGEvent object is created that contains the relevant information about that event. For instance, with the onclick event, the evt object contains the position of the event (evt.x, evt.y) and a reference to the actual SVG element that received the event (evt.target). Thus, the expression evt.target.setAttribute('fill',color) retrieves the element that was clicked (the white circle) through its event handler and sets the fill attribute to the color specified in the property() dialog box.

Note that you can use this same principle in reverse. In Listing 9-7, you can actually query an element to determine its color (see Figure 9-9).

Listing 9-7. boundEvents3.svg

```
<svg xmlns="http://www.w3.org/2000/svg"
        xmlns:xlink="http://www.w3.org/1999/xlink">
    <defs>
        <circle cx="0" cy="0" r="20" stroke="black"
            stroke-width="2" id="btn"/>
    </defs>
    <g onclick="alert('This button is ' + evt.target.getAttribute('fill'))">
    <use xlink:href="#btn" x="50" y="50" fill="red"/>
    <use xlink:href="#btn" x="100" y="50" fill="blue"/>
    <use xlink:href="#btn" x="150" y="50" fill="green"/>
    </g>
</svg>
```

This particular graphic is a little deceptive. Notice that none of the <use> elements themselves actually contain an event handler. However, if you click the blue circle, you will get the response *This button is blue.* So what gives?

Figure 9-9. The `getAttribute()` *function*

The hint to the activity comes from the event model discussed in Chapter 8, "Animating SVG." When an element is clicked (or has some other event happen to it), the SVG engine looks to see if that element has an event handler. If it does, the handler is used. If it does not, then the parent of that element is examined all the way up to the enclosing primary SVG element itself. However, although the event handler may be attached to an ancestor, the element that first receives the event is the one that populates the `evt.target` property. This can dramatically simplify the SVG scripting because you do not need to attach event handlers to every element if they perform the same activity; you can simply attach it to a graphics context `<g>` that contains the element.

Manipulating SVG can often get to be fairly cumbersome, and it is a rare application where the code can reside completely within an event handler line on an element. Perhaps more pressing, one of the principal goals of any programming effort is to consolidate code as much as possible.

SVG supports this principle with the `<script>` element. This element functions in a manner similar to that of the HTML script element, letting you define specific functions, instantiate variables, and do other related tasks. For instance, in Listing 9-8, clicking an element within the graphical context will bring up an alert box giving a summary of each the element (see Figure 9-10).

Listing 9-8. getSummary.svg

```
<svg xmlns="http://www.w3.org/2000/svg"
     xmlns:xlink="http://www.w3.org/1999/xlink">
    <script language="JavaScript">//<![CDATA[
    function getSummary(evt){
        var element=evt.target;
        buf="<"+ element.getNodeName() + " ";
        for (var i=0;i < element.attributes.length;i++){
            var attr=element.attributes.item(i);
            buf+=" "+attr.nodeName+"=\"" + attr.nodeValue+"\"";
            }
        buf +=">";
        alert(buf);
        }
//]]>    </script>
```

```
        <defs>
            <circle cx="0" cy="0" r="20" stroke="black"
                stroke-width="2" id="btn"/>
        </defs>
        <g onclick="getSummary(evt)">
        <circle cx="50" cy="50" r="40" fill="red"/>
        <rect x="150" y="50" width="30" height="30" fill="blue"/>
        <use xlink:href="#btn" x="250" y="50" fill="green"/>
        </g>
</svg>
```

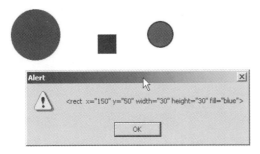

Figure 9-10. Using a standard set of functions to retrieve sophisticated information about your graphic

The <script> element requires a specific language attribute attached to it to indicate what language the scripts contained therein are using (in this case "JavaScript", which is also the default). The whole script block given in Listing 9-8 is in turn wrapped in a CDATA element:

```
<script language="JavaScript">//<![CDATA[
    function getSummary(evt){
    stuff
    }
//]]>    </script>
```

This format can seem a little confusing. The CDATA opening declaration <![CDATA[is used to "escape" the contents of the text block so that XML sensitive characters such as < or & are not interpreted as XML syntactic characters. However, the script is a JavaScript block where <![CDATA[would be considered a syntax error. Thus, to keep this expression from being interpreted as JavaScript, you need to indicate it is a comment (by using the // characters). Thus //<![CDATA[is escaped both in JavaScript and XML. Similarly, the closing expression //]]></script> means to treat everything after the // as a JavaScript comment, and]]> closes the CDATA block and </script>, now live, closes the <script> element.

TIP *The use of the* CDATA *block is not strictly required, unless your scripting code uses "dangerous" characters, most specifically the < and & characters.*

It is worth taking a closer examination of the getSummary() function because it illustrates a number of useful pieces of information about the SVG Document Object Model (DOM), which will be covered much more extensively in Chapter 10, "SVG Components":

```
function getSummary(evt){
        var element=evt.target;
        buf="<"+ element.getNodeName() + " ";
        for (var i=0;i < element.attributes.length;i++){
            var attr=element.attributes.item(i);
            buf+=" "+attr.nodeName+"=\"" + attr.nodeValue+"\"";
            }
        buf +=">";
        alert(buf);
        }
```

The event token evt is passed into the getSummary() function and from there is used to retrieve the relevant element that was clicked upon. This particular element is SVG, but it is also XML. Specifically, you can in fact manipulate the elements of SVG as W3C XML DOM-compliant XML nodes. Thus, once the element is retrieved, the name of that element can be ascertained with the .getNodeName() method, as well as the shorthand property .nodeName.

Each XML element has an associated set of attributes, the number of which can be ascertained with the length property or the .getLength() method. Each attribute can be returned through the item(n) method, which retrieves the *n*th attribute, starting from the first attribute at position 0. This attribute (as a consequence of inheriting the XMLNode interface) also has both a .nodeName and a .nodeValue property (with the appropriate getNodeName() and getNodeValue() equivalent methods) to retrieve both the name and value of the attribute.

NOTE *In Internet Explorer 5.0 and newer, the possible script languages that the Adobe SVG Viewer can run depend on the script languages installed on the client system. If you have PerlScript installed on your system, for instance, you would use this as your language attribute, and you would use an escape block looking like* #<![CDATA[*and* #]]>.

NOTE *The Adobe SVG Viewer 3.0 does include its own native JavaScript parser and will default to this if no other parser is found on the system. This makes it possible to run embedded scripts in Mozilla or Netscape 6 on Linux systems, for instance.*

Interacting with Web Pages

So far, the samples covered seem to be making fairly extensive use of the `window.alert()` method. However, real-world components typically do not communicate through such dialog boxes (though it may seem that way when you are debugging). Instead, such components need to be able to handle both talking to the HTML environment and receiving information from the same HTML environment through events and methods respectively.

Perhaps the simpler of the two operations is for SVG to raise events that can be captured by the containing Web page. To make this happen, it is worth understanding the role of the `window` object in SVG. This object is not actually a part of SVG, but rather is the container that holds SVG, the HTML page, and any other entities. It is also the container of globally defined functions.

For instance, suppose when you clicked a button, you wanted to notify the outside world that the button had been clicked and send some kind of identifier so that other applications could take action on the event. To do this properly, you need to make use of some properties of JavaScript (though, you can do this with some other languages, as well).

Specifically, a function in JavaScript is itself an object, and as such can be added to the `window` object, as shown in Listing 9-9.

Listing 9-9. `externalCalls1.svg`

```
<svg xmlns="http://www.w3.org/2000/svg"
        xmlns:xlink="http://www.w3.org/1999/xlink">
    <script language="JavaScript">//<![CDATA[
function notify_default(id){
    alert(id)
    }

if(window.notify==null){
    window.notify=notify_default;
    };

//]]>    </script>
```

```
<defs>
    <radialGradient id="greenInactive">
        <stop offset="0%" stop-color="#004000"/>
        <stop offset="100%" stop-color="#004000"/>
    </radialGradient>
    <radialGradient id="greenActive">
        <stop offset="0%" stop-color="yellow"/>
        <stop offset="50%" stop-color="green"/>
        <stop offset="100%" stop-color="#004000"/>
    </radialGradient>
    <radialGradient id="yellowInactive">
        <stop offset="0%" stop-color="brown"/>
        <stop offset="100%" stop-color="brown"/>
    </radialGradient>
    <radialGradient id="yellowActive">
        <stop offset="0%" stop-color="white"/>
        <stop offset="50%" stop-color="yellow"/>
        <stop offset="100%" stop-color="brown"/>
    </radialGradient>
    <radialGradient id="redInactive">
        <stop offset="0%" stop-color="maroon"/>
        <stop offset="100%" stop-color="maroon"/>
    </radialGradient>
    <radialGradient id="redActive">
        <stop offset="0%" stop-color="orange"/>
        <stop offset="50%" stop-color="red"/>
        <stop offset="100%" stop-color="maroon"/>
    </radialGradient>
    <circle r="20" cx="0" cy="0" stroke="black" stroke-width="2"
            id="buttonSource"/>
</defs>
<g transform="translate(50,50)"
            onmouseup="notify(evt.target.getAttribute('id'))"
                id="lights">
<use xlink:href="#buttonSource" x="0" y="0"
        fill="url(#redInactive)" id="stop">
    <set attributeName="fill" attributeType="CSS" to="url(#redActive)"
            begin="click" end="lights.click"/>
</use>
<use xlink:href="#buttonSource" x="0" y="50"
        fill="url(#yellowInactive)" id="caution">
```

```
        <set attributeName="fill" attributeType="CSS" to="url(#yellowActive)"
                begin="click" end="lights.click"/>
    </use>
    <use xlink:href="#buttonSource" x="0" y="100"
            fill="url(#greenInactive)" id="go">
        <set attributeName="fill" attributeType="CSS" to="url(#greenActive)"
                begin="click" end="lights.click"/>
    </use>
</svg>
```

In this case, when a button is clicked, the notify() function is called, with its
parameter being the id of the element being clicked. Why the id rather than the
default event object? Primarily because the likely consumer of this information is
not a function within the SVG but rather something contained in the enclosing
HTML page. In this case, you probably do not want to provide any more information about the internal state of the control than necessary; this promotes
encapsulation.

Notice in the script block that there is no explicit declaration of the notify()
function. Instead, there is a function called notify_default(), which echoes the
id in an alert box:

```
function notify_default(id){
    alert(id)
    }
```

Neither notify() nor notify_default are system functions, by the way; they
could just as easily have been called foo() and fooBar(). What is important, however, is the next block of code:

```
if(window.notify==null){
    window.notify=notify_default;
    };
```

The comparison tests to see if there is a global function declaration called
notify that has been attached to the window object. If there is not, then the
function stub for notify_default is *attached* to a new window.notify handler.
This operation is done upon initialization of the SVG document, which already
has access to the window object.

If the SVG document runs in stand-alone mode, or if a window.notify handler has not been defined already in any containing Web page, then the actions of
notify_default are used whenever the notify event is called. However, if the calling page defines a notify function handler itself, then this preempts the
notify_default function, as shown in Listing 9-10 (see Figure 9-11).

Listing 9-10. externalCalls1.htm

```
<html>
<head>
    <title>Untitled</title>
<script language="JavaScript">
    function notify(id){
        switch(id){
            case "stop":buf="You need to stop.";break;
            case "caution":buf="Proceed with caution.";break;
            case "go":buf="You may go now.";break;
            }
        display.innerHTML=buf
        }
</script>
</head>

<body background="PaperTexture.jpg">
<table border="0">
<tr>
<td>
<embed src="externalCalls1.svg" width="250" height="200"
        wmode="transparent" id="stoplight"/>
</td>
<td>
<h1 id="display"></h1>
</td>
</tr></table>

</body>
</html>
```

The HTML document defines its own notify function that supercedes the internally defined notify of the SVG component:

```
<script language="JavaScript">
    function notify(id){
        switch(id){
            case "stop":buf="You need to stop.";break;
            case "caution":buf="Proceed with caution.";break;
            case "go":buf="You may go now.";break;
            }
        display.innerHTML=buf;
        }
</script>
```

Figure 9-11. The window *object*

This function knows nothing about the internal workings of the control—
only that it should be receiving an event handler with an id value that can take
one of three possible values: "stop", "caution", and "go".

Going the other route is marginally more problematic, but not that bad. To
affect an SVG document from HTML, you need to define the methods you want
to expose, along with a method to retrieve the SVG document object. Listing 9-11
demonstrates the technique.

Listing 9-11. externalCalls2.svg

```
<svg onload="initSVG(evt)"
        xmlns="http://www.w3.org/2000/svg"
        xmlns:xlink="http://www.w3.org/1999/xlink">
    <script language="JavaScript">//<![CDATA[
var svgDoc=null;

function initSVG(evt){
    svgDoc=evt.target.parentNode;
    }

function setLight(id){
    var range=new Array("stop","caution","go");
```

```
            for (var i=0;i<range.length;i++){
                lightId=range[i];
                var activeElement=svgDoc.getElementById(lightId);
                if (lightId==id){
                    fillMode="url(#"+lightId+"Active)";
                    }
                else {
                    fillMode="url(#"+lightId+"Inactive)";
                    }
                activeElement.setAttribute("fill",fillMode);
                }
        }

//]]>    </script>
    <defs>
        <radialGradient id="goInactive">
            <stop offset="0%" stop-color="#004000"/>
            <stop offset="100%" stop-color="#004000"/>
        </radialGradient>
        <radialGradient id="goActive">
            <stop offset="0%" stop-color="yellow"/>
            <stop offset="50%" stop-color="green"/>
            <stop offset="100%" stop-color="#004000"/>
        </radialGradient>
        <radialGradient id="cautionInactive">
            <stop offset="0%" stop-color="brown"/>
            <stop offset="100%" stop-color="brown"/>
        </radialGradient>
        <radialGradient id="cautionActive">
            <stop offset="0%" stop-color="white"/>
            <stop offset="50%" stop-color="yellow"/>
            <stop offset="100%" stop-color="brown"/>
        </radialGradient>
        <radialGradient id="stopInactive">
            <stop offset="0%" stop-color="maroon"/>
            <stop offset="100%" stop-color="maroon"/>
        </radialGradient>
        <radialGradient id="stopActive">
            <stop offset="0%" stop-color="orange"/>
            <stop offset="50%" stop-color="red"/>
            <stop offset="100%" stop-color="maroon"/>
        </radialGradient>
```

```
        <circle r="20" cx="0" cy="0" stroke="black"
                    stroke-width="2" id="buttonSource"/>
    </defs>
    <g transform="translate(50,50)">
        <use xlink:href="#buttonSource" x="0" y="0"
                fill="url(#stopInactive)" id="stop"/>
        <use xlink:href="#buttonSource" x="0" y="50"
                fill="url(#cautionInactive)" id="caution"/>
        <use xlink:href="#buttonSource" x="0" y="100"
                fill="url(#goInactive)" id="go"/>
    </g>
</svg>
```

Direct your attention to the enclosing <svg> element:

```
<svg onload="initSVG(evt)"
        xmlns="http://www.w3.org/2000/svg"
        xmlns:xlink="http://www.w3.org/1999/xlink">
    <script language="JavaScript">//<![CDATA[
var svgDoc=null;

function initSVG(evt){
    svgDoc=evt.target.parentNode;
    }
```

The onload event hook is invoked when the SVG document finishes loading, but before any other handlers are called, so it is a good place to call initialization routines, in this case, the handler initSVG(). This function in turn retrieves the SVG document element through the expression evt.target.parentNode: evt.target is the root <svg> node, and the document node is that node's parent. This is assigned to a previously initialized global variable called svgDoc.

The SVG document has a number of special methods and properties, and it is to a certain extent analogous to the HTML document. For purposes of discussion, one of the most useful methods that svgDoc supports is getElementById(). With this, you can retrieve a reference to any SVG element that has an id.

The routine setLight() exploits this capability:

```
function setLight(id){
    var range=new Array("stop","caution","go");
    for (var i=0;i<range.length;i++){
        lightId=range[i];
        var activeElement=svgDoc.getElementById(lightId);
        if (lightId==id){
            fillMode="url(#"+lightId+"Active)";
```

```
                            }
                    else {
                        fillMode="url(#"+lightId+"Inactive)";
                            }
                    activeElement.setAttribute("fill",fillMode);
                        }
                }
```

In this particular case, it creates an array with the three possible states that the traffic light can be in ("stop", "caution", and "go"). It then iterates over this array and retrieves the element corresponding to each state (which not coincidentally has an id value that is the same as the state). If the state's id matches the requested id, the fill mode is set for the active state, and if it does not, the fill mode is set for the inactive state. For example, if id='go', then for the <use id="go" ..> element the variable fillMode is set to "url(#goActive)", and <use id="stop" ..> and <use id="caution" ..> are set to "url(#stopInactive)" and url(#cautionInactive), respectively. Finally, the fill attribute for each of the iterated elements is stuffed with the appropriate fillMode value (activeElement.setAttribute("fill","fillMode")).

 TIP   *This is a prime example of the value of encapsulation and abstraction. You do not need to know the colors being set, only whether you are setting the right element (#stop) to the requisite state of #stopActive or #stopInactive.*

The HTML document that invokes the appropriate methods works by retrieving the window element from the embedded control, as shown in Listing 9-12 (see Figure 9-12).

Listing 9-12. externalCalls2.htm

```
<html>
<head>
    <title>Controlling SVG From HTML</title>
</head>
<body background="PaperTexture.jpg">
<table border="0">
<tr>
<td>
<embed src="externalCalls2.svg" width="250" height="200"
 wmode="transparent" id="lights"/>
</td>
```

```
<td>
<h1>Controlling SVG From HTML</h1>
<p>Click on the appropriate word to set the right light.
<h3 onclick="lights.window.setLight('stop')">[Stop]</h3>
<h3 onclick="lights.window.setLight('caution')">[Caution]</h3>
<h3 onclick="lights.window.setLight('go')">[Go]</h3>
</td>
</tr></table>
</body>
</html>
```

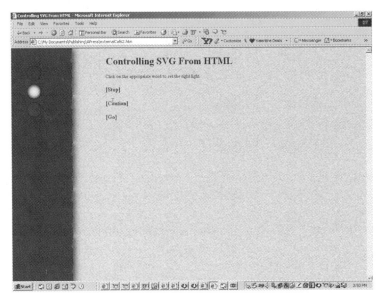

Figure 9-12. Sending information back to the SVG document

In this example, the SVG control is given the id of "lights". To get access to the methods defined within SVG script block, you need the control's window object, which is available from lights.window. Thus, lights.window.setLight() will let you call the setLights() function. Similarly, if you create a global variable in the SVG <script> element of the following form:

```
var test="This is a test."
```

then you can retrieve the value of this variable through the window handle in the HTML document. That is, the following code:

```
<h3 onclick="alert(lights.window.test)">[Test]</h3>
```

in the HTML document will cause an alert box to appear with the message *This is a test.*

One final note on this front: The window object sits at the top of the SVG DOM (as will be discussed in Chapter 10, "SVG Components") and has as one of its children, the SVG document itself. This means you can actually manipulate the document directly, rather than creating methods or properties to work with the component as an object unit. However, it should be pointed out that although this can be a temptation it is one that should generally be avoided. It is usually far better to manipulate the structure indirectly, through a well-estab- lished interface than it is to try to set each individual element's characteristics directly from a Web page.

Controlling the Title Bar

One of the advantages oft touted for XML over more traditional binary formats comes in its ability to be self-describing. A JPEG image typically does not contain any information about what the picture is about, what its purpose is, or who cre- ated it, for instance. This means that such information must be written into an external file, without necessarily a standard way of encoding this data. As distrib- uted systems become more commonplace, the inability to provide a basic level of identity to a graphic will prove more and more of a bottleneck in content man- agement systems.

This information, which essentially exists outside of the specific data neces- sary to reproduce the image, is called *meta-data.* Such meta-data exists to provide a summary of the image's subject and possible intent, authorship, or ownership, as well as current processing status (completed, under construction, a rough draft and so forth). Meta-data systems lay at the heart of most content management systems because such systems typically deal with documents and multimedia contents remotely.

SVG, being an XML language, both needs and has the capability of handling meta-data. An SVG graphic can potentially be rich in terms of its underlying structures, especially once those structures cross over from simple graphics to presentations or interfaces. Moreover, a meta-data structure can also encode code interface information, providing an indication of which methods are sup- ported and what arguments they take.

Perhaps the simplest meta-data element is the <title> element. This ele- ment, when assigned as a child of the initial <svg> container, provides a title hint for the document as a whole. Typically, this will be used to set the title bar of the browser by the SVG engine, as shown in Listing 9-13.

Listing 9-13. `metadata1.svg`

```
<svg>
    <title id="title">A Standard Green Rectangle</title>
    <rect fill="green" width="200" height="120" x="100" y="80"/>
</svg>
```

The advantage of such an element comes from the fact that if you change it, you will also change the title displayed on the title bar. Doing this is actually fairly simple, though it does require understanding a little more about the way that the XML DOM works, as illustrated in Listing 9-14 (see Figure 9-13).

Listing 9-14. `metadata2.svg`

```
<svg onload="initSVG(evt)"
        xmlns="http://www.w3.org/2000/svg"
        xmlns:xlink="http://www.w3.org/1999/xlink">
    <script language="JavaScript">//<![CDATA[
var svgDoc=null;

function initSVG(evt){
    svgDoc=evt.target.parentNode;
    }

function changeTitle(text){
    var titleElem=svgDoc.getElementById("activeTitle");
    // This sets the text.
    titleElem.childNodes.item(0).setData(text);
    }
//]]>    </script>
    <title id="activeTitle">Roll over the Green Rectangle</title>
    <rect fill="green" width="200" height="120" x="100" y="80"
        onmouseover="changeTitle('Elvis is in the building.')"
        onmouseout="changeTitle('Elvis has left the building.')"/>
</svg>
```

The initial title includes an `id` attribute identifying it as the `"activeTitle"`. When a user rolls over the green rectangle, the `changeTitle()` function is called. This retrieves the `<title>` element (through the id), then changes the text of that element with this statement:

```
titleElem.childNodes.item(0).setData(text);
```

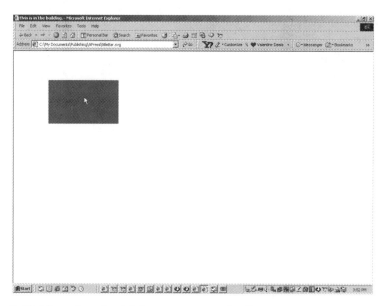

Figure 9-13. Changing the title bar content on the fly

Here, the `childNodes` collection retrieves the list of all possible XML nodes: elements, text nodes, comments . . . everything but attributes that are children of the `<title>` element. In this particular case, that happens to be just the single text node that contains the relevant text. The method `item(0)` then retrieves the first node from this collection.

NOTE *Even if* `childNodes` *contains only one item,* `childNodes` *by itself is a collection. You still have to retrieve that one item. That is why* `item(0)` *is required here. You can also use the* `firstChild` *property or* `getFirstChild()` *method to do the same thing, without the need to access the full* `childNodes` *list.*

Once you have this node, you can change the contents of that node with the `setData()` function. Thus, as you move the mouse into the rectangle, the original string *Roll over the Green Rectangle* is replaced with *Elvis is in the building.* Because the SVG engine models the current state of the browser by the state of the SVG document, this in turn causes the title bar to change to the new text.

You can also assign the <title> element to other graphic elements, such as <g> or internal <svg> tags. In this particular case, the title can act as a way for the user agent to display *tooltips*, pop-up descriptive text that appears when an element is rolled over for a certain period of time.

NOTE *The Adobe SVG 3.0 Viewer does not appear to recognize the use of* <title> *for generating tooltips.*

NOTE *Meta-data can play a major part in any SVG presentation. The subject will be revisited in Chapter 10, "SVG Components," with the* <desc> *and* <metadata> *tags.*

Passing Attributes into SVG from HTML

To build components that work effectively within HTML, in addition to making sure there is a programmatic interface, it would be nice if you could bypass this initially by placing attributes on the <embed> tag that specified the characteristics of that interface. It is "sort of" possible to do this, though certainly it is far from self-evident as to how to pass information from an HTML tag into the SVG object itself. The secret, once again, is to look at the SVG's window as, well, a window into the SVG's programmatic interface.

The trick here is to create a passback function that passes the <embed> tag back to the SVG object referenced from the tag. The tag (itself an object) can then be read for relevant information, such as attributes. For instance, consider a simple (all right, *extremely* simple) SVG component that consists of a circle and a block of text. Suppose you wanted to be able to set the position, size, and color of the circle and be able to change the text being displayed from HTML, specifically via attributes appended to the <embed> tag.

Listing 9-15 illustrates the technique of using a passback function to make this possible (see Figure 9-14).

Listing 9-15. passBackHost.htm

```
<html>
<head>
    <title>Untitled</title>
    <script language="JavaScript">//<![CDATA[
function passBackSVG(){
    var embedNodes=document.embeds;
    for (var i=0;i<embedNodes.length;i++){
        embedNode=embedNodes[i];
        if(embedNode.window.passState){
            embedNode.window.passState(embedNode);
          }
      }
    }
//]]>    </script>
</head>
<body onload="passBackSVG()">
<embed src="passBackClient.svg" width="400" height="400"
        id="bar" fill="green" cx="150" cy="100" r="30"
        text="This has been set via HTML"/>
</body>
</html>
```

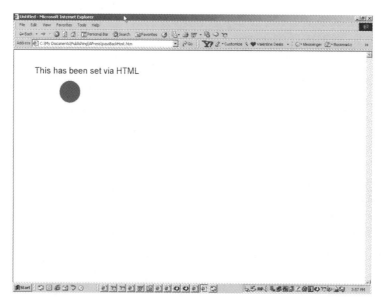

Figure 9-14. The passback *function*

First, note the <embed> element itself. I have added a number of *nonstandard* attributes to the tag, including fill, cx, cy, r, and text. If the names seem vaguely familiar, they should be—they correspond directly to SVG circle attributes (with the exception of the text). This can illustrate a couple of different techniques for using those parameters.

However, these values are *not* automatically passed to the SVG document. In general, that SVG has no idea about its container, beyond the window mode and container dimensions. Instead, you will need to pass the node with these parameters to the SVG yourself, through the passBackSVG() function. This function iterates through all the embedded elements that have been declared in the HTML document (using the JavaScript document.embeds collection, then checks to see if the embedded element supports a function called passState(). If it does, then that particular <embed> element (with its attributes intact) is passed as a parameter to the function.

The passBackSVG() function is called from the HTML <body>'s onload event handler. This event is only fired when all embedded elements have been loaded, so the SVG documents are instantiated by the time the object is received.

The SVG document itself (shown in Listing 9-16) includes a sample passState() function (see Figure 9-15).

Listing 9-16. passBackClient.svg

```
<svg onload="initSVG(evt)"
        xmlns="http://www.w3.org/2000/svg"
        xmlns:xlink="http://www.w3.org/1999/xlink">
    <script language="JavaScript">//<![CDATA[

var svg=null;
function initSVG(evt){
    svg=evt.target.parentNode;
    }


function passState(extObject){
    setText(extObject);
    setCircle(extObject);
    }


function setText(extObject){
    if(extObject.getAttribute("text")!=null){
        var textObject=svg.getElementById("titleText");
        textObject.childNodes.item(0).setData(
                extObject.getAttribute("text"));
        };
    }
```

```
function setCircle(extObject){
    var circle=svg.getElementById("circle");
    for (var i=0;i<circle.attributes.length;i++){
        var attribute=circle.attributes.item(i);
        var name=attribute.nodeName;
        if(name!="id")
            {
            circle.setAttribute(name,extObject.getAttribute(name));
            }
        }
    }

//]]>    </script>
    <g transform="translate(0,0)" id="foo">
        <circle cx="100" cy="100" r="100" fill="red" id="circle"/>
    </g>
    <g transform="translate(50,50)">
        <text font-size="24" id="titleText">Here's the default text</text>
    </g>
</svg>
```

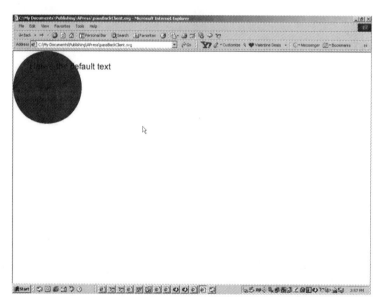

Figure 9-15. The default state of the component, as an SVG document

The function `passState()` receives the node as an argument, then illustrates two different ways of utilizing that node. The first, invoked in `setText()`, actually retrieves a specific attribute from the `<embed>` object (in this case, the `text` attribute) and then explicitly sets the text field with this value—if a text attribute is defined. If not, the default value is retained.

The second method, shown in `setCircle()`, involves iterating over the attributes in the circle element and seeing if a corresponding attribute in the `<embed>` object exists (with the single exception of `id`, which should stay unique). If one does, then the `<embed>` value takes precedence.

Note that although this example is basic, the same technique can be used to build up more complex components by passing arguments or even objects via both HTML/XML and through JavaScript. Chapter 10, "SVG Components," will explore these techniques in more depth.

Summary

The interconnection between HTML and SVG is strong and mutually beneficial. SVG by itself is a powerful language for the expression of graphics and graphical animation, but it lacks some of the aspects of form design and text flow to make it a full-fledged Web page system. HTML, on the other hand, has a rich and expressive DOM for displaying and manipulating text but is too heavily dependent upon static graphics for even the simplest nonlinear display. When you combine the two, you can get the best of both worlds.

Although you have seen some useful examples in this chapter, this chapter has been intended to lay the groundwork for the next: Chapter 10, "SVG Components." Component development, especially combining the capabilities and characteristics of both declarative languages such as XML and procedural languages such as JavaScript, brings with it both a whole new set of potential applications and potential problems. Moving on, I look a little more deeply at the way to best build not just a single component but a cohesive library that takes advantage of the unique opportunities that SVG affords.

CHAPTER 10

SVG Components

IN THE BEGINNING THERE WAS the Application Programming Interface (API) set. This set consisted of a large number of functions that, when called, did things (drew a window, saved a file, sent a byte streaming down a network connection). Such an API worked reasonably well when applications were monolithic—everything wrapped up in a nice, tight executable object. However, monolithic applications suffer from a number of limitations—they tie up a lot of memory and hard drive space in an application that may not need those specific services; updating them involves replacing conceivably large files, debugging can be ugly, and reusing just one part of an application in another application requires instantiating all of the first application.

Component-based architectures represented a first-significant step in changing all this. Instead of creating one single, large, monolithic application, a program was actually built by breaking the functionality into specific pieces and assigning to each piece its own specific functionality. Although the first such component based systems were not strictly speaking pure object-oriented entities, it did not take long before components (written primarily at the time in C) made the transition to C++ and object-oriented principles.

The concept of components thus fit hand in hand with the notion of classes, where a class could be thought of as an entity that that was either a component, a piece of that component, or a collection of components. Applications could still be monolithic, of course, by making the components encompassing enough, but the transition to seeing an application as a tree of subcomponents made the design of such applications much simpler.

Hypertext Markup Language (HTML) represented an interesting paradigm shift here. The components in HTML are conceptual, rather than code-specific—a paragraph (<p>), a bold span of text (<b>), a list (<ul>) with associated list items (<li>), and so forth. When people wrote HTML, they were not in fact consciously creating programs—they were just writing documents with specific markup indicating how such documents should be displayed.

However, perhaps because it was still so fresh in people's minds, the idea of combining an object-oriented design methodology with the ability to create container/contained relationships in HTML brought about the notion of an object model that was applied to a document—the Document Object Model (DOM). Currently, we tend to toss around the use of DOMs without really thinking about them, but at the time, the concept was actually quite radical.

Unlike most applications where the types of objects that a given parent object could host was limited and well known, DOMs worked upon the presumption that your documents could in fact be complex, if not completely open-ended. This in turn has the effect of making document object models rich in the number of objects that they support.

One other significant point about DOMs is noteworthy, especially in light of languages such as SVG. In most Extensible Markup Language (XML) object model languages—such as Scalable Vector Graphics (SVG), Extensible HTML (XHTML), Wireless Markup Language (WML), and so on—the markup language by itself should in fact carry a significant weight of the functionality of the application. In other words, you should be able to do with such languages 80 to 90 percent of all of the potential operations without ever having to resort to DOMs.

Why? DOMs (although they might be employed by the language itself through its viewer or interpreter) represent the interface between the space created by that language and some other environment. You can use DOM to create, alter, or remove pieces of the object model instance in response to some external request, but you can place too much of the responsibility for performing manipulations of the space on DOM calls and scripting code. When this happens, the markup code (SVG, HTML, whatever) becomes brittle, nonportable, and increasingly dependent upon highly specialized programming knowledge rather than markup that can be autogenerated.

Consequently, whether you are looking at SVG, HTML, or any other markup language, avoid the temptation to do too much in DOM-scripted code by seeing if there is already a way of doing it through the markup tags. SVG has a few holes, but it is in fact remarkably robust. When I started working with the language, I kept wanting to build a <script> block and resort to DOM programming because I assumed the language was just a way of drawing pretty pictures.

However, the more I wrote in SVG, the more I realized that the procedural (scripting) code that I was working with was redundant. Sure, I could change text through a DOM call, but I later found that I could create text strings, assign to them ID values, and use animation elements to switch things out in response to differing state conditions. What was even better about this approach is that it lent itself well to integration with XML Stylesheet Language for Transformations (XSLT) because I could generate the SVG markup I needed via XSLT code and then create a base XML description that could build the world exactly the way I needed it.

This book is methodological, intended to look at the best way of designing SVG for programming. The examples given in this chapter are perhaps fuller and more comprehensive (and definitely longer) than those given elsewhere in this book, but they all point to the same basic premise. If you design your SVG components so that most of the hard work is taken care of through declarative XML rather than scripting, you will have code that is portable, extensible, and much, much easier to maintain. You will need to perform some scripting, but if you use the scripting only for those parts that cannot be done easily from within SVG, you will be way ahead of the curve.

Gauging Your Progress

The digital dashboard metaphor has become something of an overused cliché in the last couple of years, but one of the best ways to understand what makes a good interface is to examine the features that seem "obvious."

In the case of the aforementioned dashboard, a little analysis reveals that you can look at a car's dashboard and, at a glance, determine whether everything is working right or if a problem is developing. For the most part you accomplish this through the use of gauges—the speedometer to indicate whether you are going too fast, the tachometer to indicate whether the engine is revving too high, a temperature gauge, fuel gauge, and battery charge indicator to show whether any of your other systems are approaching dangerous levels of performance.

Part of the reason that such gauges were created was that they were easy to build—a spring rests against a threaded spindle on which spins an arrow; as pressure is put on the spring, this pushes the arrow around. However, they are also advantageous because they are visually revealing with little examination—a crucial characteristic to driving is keeping your eyes on the road.

Such gauges can serve a similar purpose in a computer setting—indicating when disk space is getting low or when memory is being pushed to dangerous levels. Another example is banking applications that use gauges to indicate when funds are becoming perilously low.

Integrating the Gauge Control

I set out to build a gauge in SVG that I could drop into an HTML page that was able to tell me at a glance the state of pretty much any property. Moreover, I wanted a gauge that I could customize just by adding attributes to the associated <embed> tag, using the techniques discussed in Chapter 9, "Integrating SVG and HTML." Finally, as a nice touch, I wanted the background color of the gauge to change color as the needle moved from the starting position to the ending one, and I wanted to be able to set the starting and ending colors (see Figure 10-1).

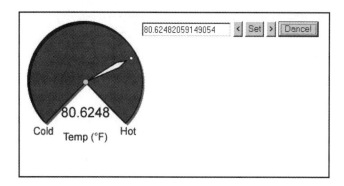

Figure 10-1. An SVG Gauge control

Complex? Not really. Listing 10-1 illustrates this principle in practice.

Listing 10-1. dialTest.htm

```
<html>
<head>
    <title>Gauge</title>
    <script language="JavaScript">
function passBackSVG(){
        if (gaugeCtl.readystate != 4)
    {
        setTimeout( passBackSVG, 50 );
        return;
    }
    gaugeCtl.window.passState(gaugeCtl);
 }


var key=0;
function dance(x){
    var minVal=parseFloat(gaugeCtl.max);
    var maxVal=parseFloat(gaugeCtl.min);
    var midVal=(maxVal-minVal)/2;
    y = minVal + midVal + midVal * Math.sin(4.4*x) *
        Math.cos(2.6 * x) * Math.cos(7.1 * x) * Math.sin(5.1*x);
    gaugeCtl.setGauge(y);
    x += 0.01;
    key = window.setTimeout("dance("+ x +")",100,"JavaScript");
    }
```

```
function updateDataWindow(){
    data.value=gaugeCtl.window.getGauge();
    }


    </script>
</head>

<body onload="passBackSVG()">
<embed name="gaugeCtl" id="gaugeCtl"
    src="Gauge.svg" width="200" height="200"
    type="image/svg+xml" style="left:10px;top:10px;position:absolute;"
    wmode="transparent"
    min="0" max="110" value="0"
    label="Temp (&#176;F)"
    minLabel="Cold" maxLabel="Hot"
    minColor="20,210,255" maxColor="255,0,0"
    onchange="updateDataWindow()"
    >
</embed>
<div style="position:absolute;left:200;">
    <input type="text" name="data" id="data" value="0"/>
    <input type="button" value="<"
            onclick="window.clearTimeout(key);
            data.value=Math.max(parseInt(data.value) - 1,gaugeCtl.min);
            gaugeCtl.setGauge(data.value);"/>
    <input type="button" value="Set"
            onclick="window.clearTimeout(key);
            data.value=Math.min(
        Math.max(parseInt(data.value),gaugeCtl.min),gaugeCtl.max);
        gaugeCtl.setGauge(data.value);"/>
    <input type="button" value=">"
                onclick="window.clearTimeout(key);data.value=
                    Math.min(parseInt(data.value) + 1, gaugeCtl.max);
                    gaugeCtl.setGauge(data.value);"/>
    <input type="button" value="Dance!" onclick="dance(0)"/>

</div>

</body>
</html>
```

The <embed> tag contains the SVG in question, and it is worth covering in its own right:

```
<embed name="gaugeCtl" id="gaugeCtl"
    src="dial1.svg" width="200" height="200"
    type="image/svg+xml" style="left:10px;top:10px;position:absolute;"
    wmode="transparent"
    min="0" max="110" value="0"
    label="Temp (&#176;F)"  minLabel="Cold" maxLabel="Hot"
    minColor="20,210,255" maxColor="255,0,0"
    onchange="updateDataWindow()"/>
```

The Gauge control includes a number of properties that are passed as parameters, with a list of the specific attributes given in Table 10-1.

Table 10-1. The Gauge Control

ATTRIBUTE NAME	DEFAULT VALUE	DESCRIPTION
value	0	The starting value of the gauge
min	0	The minimum value that the gauge can take
max	100	The maximum value that the gauge can take
label	"Percent"	The text label that appears at the bottom of the graph
minLabel	Value of min	The label for the minimum part of the gauge
maxLabel	Value of max	The label for the maximum part of the gauge
minColor	0,255,0	A decimal triplet that determines the starting color (red, green, blue) between the values of 0 and 255
maxColor	255,0,0	A decimal triplet that determines the ending color (red, green, blue) between the values of 0 and 255
onchange	No action	Thrown when the gauge's value is set

Additionally, the Gauge control also has two methods that can be called from JavaScript within HTML, as given in Table 10-2. You can add other methods, but this example is meant to be illustrative, not comprehensive.

Table 10-2. The Gauge Methods

FUNCTION	EXAMPLE	DESCRIPTION
setGauge(number)	gauge.setGauge(100)	Sets the value of the gauge, and indirectly sets the color as well
getGauge()	temperature=gauge.getGauge()	Retrieves the currently value of the gauge

It is worth noting that the embedded SVG document in this case acts much like a more traditional binary ActiveX control or Java applet—exposing methods, acting on events, and having parametric properties. You can see this in the "increaseGauge" button (marked with a > character), where the component acts in a manner indistinguishable from any other like component:

```
<input type="button" value=">" onclick="window.clearTimeout(key);
        data.value=Math.max(parseInt(data.value) + 1,
        gaugeCtl.min);gaugeCtl.setGauge(data.value);"/>
```

You can also perform fairly sophisticated actions with a component-based SVG control. For instance, the Dance! button calls the dance() procedure:

```
function dance(x){
    var minVal=parseFloat(gaugeCtl.max);
    var maxVal=parseFloat(gaugeCtl.min);
    var midVal=(maxVal-minVal)/2;
    y = minVal + midVal + midVal * Math.sin(4.4*x) *  //Continued
            Math.cos(2.6 * x) * Math.cos(7.1 * x) * Math.sin(5.1*x);
    gaugeCtl.setGauge(y);
    x += 0.01;
    key = window.setTimeout("dance("+ x +")",100,"JavaScript");
    }
```

In this case, the min and max values are read off the component to determine the possible range of values that the gauge can occupy, then the needle "dances" through a fairly complex mathematical expression, updated every one-tenth of a second (via the setTimeout property).

The passback routine here also contains code that may not be immediately intuitive:

```
    if (gaugeCtl.readystate != 4)
    {
        setTimeout( passBackSVG, 50 );
        return;
    }
    gaugeCtl.window.passState(gaugeCtl);
```

When working with the Dynamic HTML model that Microsoft exposes in the Internet Explorer interfaces, it is crucial to remember that objects such as those exposed by <embed> are loaded *asynchronously*—it may take some time for the full control to load, and there are some operations that can be performed even as the object is loading. Until the controls are loaded, you cannot perform any operations on the contents.

Consequently, the previous routine checks to see if the embed object's readyState property has cycled through from 1 (download started) through 2 (object instantiated), and then from 3 (loading) to 4 (completed). If the download is not complete (readystate!=4), then the routine will perform a callback 50 milliseconds later to check again. This lets the system perform other actions while downloading, making for a more responsive page.

Finally, when the onchange event is fired (in response to the gauge either initializing or being called through the setGauge() method), the text field automatically updates to reflect the dial's value as well:

```
function updateDataWindow(){
    data.value=gaugeCtl.window.getGauge();
    }
```

Implementing the Gauge Control

The code for the Gauge control utilizes many of the same principles that were discussed in Chapter 9, "Integrating SVG and HTML," but better illustrates how you can build such controls that are much more complete and functional (see Listing 10-2).

Listing 10-2. gauge.svg

```
<svg xmlns="http://www.w3.org/2000/svg"
     xmlns:xlink="http://www.w3.org/1999/xlink"
     version="1.0" onload="initSVG(evt)" width="220" height="220"
     viewBox="0 0 220 220"
     preserveAspectRatio="none">
    <script language="JavaScript">//<![CDATA[
var angle=0;
var curValue=0;
```

```
var minValue=0;
var maxValue=100;
var gaugeLabel="Percent"
var value=0;
var svgDoc=null;
var extGaugeEmbed=null;
var minColor="0,255,0";
var maxColor="255,0,0";

function initSVG(evt){
    svgDoc=evt.target.ownerDocument;
    }

function passState(extObject){
    extGaugeEmbed=extObject;
    extGaugeEmbed.setGauge=setGauge;
    extGaugeEmbed.getGauge=getGauge;
    minValueLocal=extObject.getAttribute("min");
    if (minValueLocal!=null) minValue=minValueLocal;
    maxValueLocal=extObject.getAttribute("max");
    if (maxValueLocal!=null) maxValue=maxValueLocal;
    gaugeLabelLocal=extObject.getAttribute("label");
    if (gaugeLabelLocal!=null) gaugeLabel=gaugeLabelLocal;
    valueLocal=extObject.getAttribute("value");
    if (valueLocal!=null) value=valueLocal;
    minLabelLocal=extObject.getAttribute("minLabel");
    if (minLabelLocal!=null) {
        minLabel=minLabelLocal;
        }
    else {
        minLabel=minValue;
        }
    maxLabelLocal=extObject.getAttribute("maxLabel");
    if (maxLabelLocal!=null) {
        maxLabel=maxLabelLocal;
        }
    else {
        maxLabel=maxValue;
        }
    var minNumberObject=svgDoc.getElementById("minValNumber");
    minNumberObject.firstChild.setData(minLabel);
```

```
        var maxNumberObject=svgDoc.getElementById("maxValNumber");
        maxNumberObject.firstChild.setData(maxLabel);
        var labelObject=svgDoc.getElementById("gaugeLabel");
        labelObject.firstChild.setData(gaugeLabel);
        minColorLocal=extObject.getAttribute("minColor");
        if (minColorLocal!=null) minColor=minColorLocal;
        maxColorLocal=extObject.getAttribute("maxColor");
        if (maxColorLocal!=null) maxColor=maxColorLocal;
        setGauge(value);
        }

function setGaugeColor(percent){
    var startArray=minColor.split(",");
    var endArray=maxColor.split(",");
    var colorArray=new Array(3);
    for (var i=0;3>i;i++){
        startColorPart=parseFloat(startArray[i]) * (1 - percent);
        endColorPart=parseFloat(endArray[i]) * (percent);
        colorArray[i]= startColorPart + endColorPart;
        }
    color="rgb("+ parseInt(colorArray[0]) +"," +  // continued
                  parseInt(colorArray[1]) + "," +    //continued
                  parseInt(colorArray[2]) + ")";
//    alert(color);
    var gaugeBackground=svgDoc.getElementById("gaugeBackground");
    gaugeBackground.setAttribute("fill",color);
    }

function setGauge(value){
    curValue=Math.min(Math.max(value,minValue),maxValue);
    angle=(value-minValue)*270/(maxValue-minValue);
    needle=svgDoc.getElementById("needle");
    var gauge=svgDoc.getElementById("gauge");
    setGaugeColor((value-minValue)/(maxValue-minValue));
    needle.setAttribute("transform","rotate("+angle+")");
    var num=svgDoc.getElementById("gaugeNumber");
    num.childNodes.item(0).setData(value);
    if (extGaugeEmbed.getAttribute("onchange")!=null){
                extGaugeEmbed.window.eval(
                        extGaugeEmbed.getAttribute("onchange"));
    }
    }
```

```
function getGauge(){
    return curValue;
    }

//    ]]></script>
    <defs>
        <path id="gaugeShape"
                d="M0,0 v-100 a100,100 0 1,1 -100,100z"
                transform="rotate(-135)"/>
        <g id="needleShape">
            <g transform="rotate(-45)">
                <path d="m0,0 L-65,5 L-80,0 L-65,-5,z"
                    stroke="black" fill="white"
                    stroke-width="2"/>
                <circle cx="-90" cy="0" r="3" stroke="black"
                    fill="white" stroke-width="1"/>
                <circle cx="0" cy="0" r="5" stroke="black" fill="lightGray"
                    stroke-width="1" id="needleCap"/>
            </g>
        </g>
        <circle cx="0" cy="0" r="5" stroke="black" fill="gray"
                stroke-width="1"/>
        <text x="0" y="60" font-size="24"
                                            id="gaugeNumber"
                                            text-anchor="middle">
                                            0
                            </text>
        <text x="-75" y="90" font-size="18"
                                            id="minValNumber"
                                            text-anchor="middle">
                                            0
                            </text>
        <text x="75" y="90" font-size="18"
                                            id="maxValNumber"
                                            text-anchor="middle">
                                            100
                            </text>
        <text x="0" y="100" font-size="18"
                                            id="gaugeLabel"
                                            text-anchor="middle">
                                            Speed
                            </text>
    </defs>
```

```
        <g transform="translate(110,110)">
            <use xlink:href="#gaugeShape" x="-3" y="-3"
                    stroke="black" stroke-width="3" fill="black"/>
            <use xlink:href="#gaugeShape" x="3" y="3" stroke="gray"
                    stroke-width="1" fill="gray"/>
            <use xlink:href="#gaugeShape" x="0" y="0"
                    fill="rgb(0,255,0)" stroke="black" stroke-width="2"
                    id="gaugeBackground"/>
            <use xlink:href="#needleShape" x="0" y="0" id="needle"/>
            <use xlink:href="#gaugeNumber" x="0" y="0"/>
            <use xlink:href="#minValNumber" x="0" y="0"/>
            <use xlink:href="#maxValNumber" x="0" y="0"/>
            <use xlink:href="#gaugeLabel" x="0" y="0"/>
        </g>
</svg>
```

Listing 10-2 defines a number of local variables that either provide defaults for specific methods or serve as holding variables for objects:

```
var angle=0;
var curValue=0;
var minValue=0;
var maxValue=100;
var gaugeLabel="Percent";
var value=0;
var minColor="0,255,0";
var maxColor="255,0,0";
var svgDoc=null;
var extGaugeEmbed=null;
```

The last two variables, svgDoc and extGaugeEmbed, hold the SVG document and the HTML <embed> tag object, the latter sent through the passState() function. The passState function performs the lion's share of the actual initialization work and also makes a little of the magic possible with this component. One of the first things that does happen within the function is the assignment of new function stubs to the embedded object itself so that when, say, the setGauge() method is called on the <embed> object, it will use the function defined within the SVG. If you did not do this, you would have to make any function calls using gaugeCtl.window.setGauge(), as shown in Chapter 9, "Integrating SVG and HTML":

```
function passState(extObject){
    extGaugeEmbed=extObject;
    extGaugeEmbed.setGauge=setGauge;
    extGaugeEmbed.getGauge=getGauge;
```

Once these functions are set, the attributes are read off of the <embed> object and assigned to internal variables. In most cases, if the attribute is not included on the <embed> object, there will be a default value that is used in its stead:

```
minValueLocal=extObject.getAttribute("min");
if (minValueLocal!=null) minValue=minValueLocal;
maxValueLocal=extObject.getAttribute("max");
if (maxValueLocal!=null) maxValue=maxValueLocal;
gaugeLabelLocal=extObject.getAttribute("label");
if (gaugeLabelLocal!=null) gaugeLabel=gaugeLabelLocal;
valueLocal=extObject.getAttribute("value");
if (valueLocal!=null) value=valueLocal;
minLabelLocal=extObject.getAttribute("minLabel");
if (minLabelLocal!=null) {
    minLabel=minLabelLocal;
    }
else {
    minLabel=minValue;
    }
maxLabelLocal=extObject.getAttribute("maxLabel");
if (maxLabelLocal!=null) {
    maxLabel=maxLabelLocal;
    }
else {
    maxLabel=maxValue;
    }
```

The next stage in the initialization involves assigning the retrieved values (or their defaulted equivalents) to the objects defined within the SVG itself. The following populate the labels and set the minimum and maximum color values:

```
var minNumberObject=svgDoc.getElementById("minValNumber");
minNumberObject.firstChild.setData(minLabel);
var maxNumberObject=svgDoc.getElementById("maxValNumber");
maxNumberObject.firstChild.setData(maxLabel);
var labelObject=svgDoc.getElementById("gaugeLabel");
labelObject.firstChild.setData(gaugeLabel);
minColorLocal=extObject.getAttribute("minColor");
if (minColorLocal!=null) minColor=minColorLocal;
maxColorLocal=extObject.getAttribute("maxColor");
if (maxColorLocal!=null) maxColor=maxColorLocal;
setGauge(value);
}
```

The setGaugeColor() function is a local function (in other words, not published to the outside world, though it is certainly accessible through the <embed> window object) that handles the assignment of color to the background. It works by splitting the minColor and maxColor strings into two arrays of three values each. The routine then iterates over each of the three values (red, green, and blue, respectively) and performs a linear interpolation between the start and end values (essentially what the SVG <animateColor> element does, though that particular tool is considerably more sophisticated). The three computed values are then combined into an "rgb(r,g,b)" string, which is passed to the gaugeBackground element's fill color:

```
function setGaugeColor(percent){
    var startArray=minColor.split(",");
    var endArray=maxColor.split(",");
    var colorArray=new Array(3);
    for (var i=0;3>i;i++){
        startColorPart=parseFloat(startArray[i]) * (1 - percent);
        endColorPart=parseFloat(endArray[i]) * (percent);
        colorArray[i]= startColorPart + endColorPart;
        }
    color="rgb("+ parseInt(colorArray[0]) +"," +
                parseInt(colorArray[1]) + "," +
                parseInt(colorArray[2]) + ")";
//    alert(color);
    var gaugeBackground=svgDoc.getElementById("gaugeBackground");
    gaugeBackground.setAttribute("fill",color);
    }
```

The setGauge() method is easily the heart of the whole component. It takes the value being passed to it and filters it to ensure that it falls within the range— truncating it if it should be too large or too small, then calculating the angle as a value between 0 and 270. The color is changed to reflect this percentage as well:

```
function setGauge(value){
    curValue=Math.min(Math.max(value,minValue),maxValue);
    angle=(value-minValue)*270/(maxValue-minValue);
setGaugeColor((value-minValue)/(maxValue-minValue));
```

The actual interaction with the SVG is pretty simple—the routine retrieves the needle (positioned so that its origin is at the needle's base), then changes the transform attribute on the needle group to reflect the rotation to the new angle. The central displayed number is likewise retrieved and set to the new value:

```
needle=svgDoc.getElementById("needle");
needle.setAttribute("transform","rotate("+angle+")");
var num=svgDoc.getElementById("gaugeNumber");
num.childNodes.item(0).setData(value);
```

The final action is fairly subtle in its implementation. If the <embed> element has an onchange attribute, this event needs to be fired when the setGauge() method is called. To do so, the <embed> object is called upon to retrieve the browser's window context. The JavaScript within the attribute is then evaluated with the window's eval() function. Calling eval() in this context is important because the JavaScript within the attribute may well include references to other objects within the HTML document or other functions defined at the HTML level:

```
if (extGaugeEmbed.getAttribute("onchange")!=null){
            extGaugeEmbed.window.eval(
                    extGaugeEmbed.getAttribute("onchange"));
    }
}
```

You can see this by reexamining the <embed> statement in the gaugetest.htm page:

```
<embed name="gaugeCtl" id="gaugeCtl"
    src="Gauge.svg" width="200" height="200"
    . . .
    onchange="updateDataWindow()">
```

which calls the updateDataWindow() function that updates the display's text box.

This is a technique, by the way, that you can use to create any event handler on an <embed> element (at least in Internet Explorer). Note that as this capability is not supported in other browsers, such code does make your SVG IE-specific.

The getGauge() function simply returns the local curValue that represents the filtered value passed into the setGauge() method:

```
function getGauge(){
    return curValue;
    }
```

In all this, it is easy to forget that this is an SVG document. Fortunately, the XMLish SVG is extremely straightforward. The Gauge shape is created with a path element, using the a arc path directive to build a 270°-filled pie. This is then rotated 135 degrees counterclockwise so that the pie slice is facing toward the bottom:

```
<defs>
    <path id="gaugeShape"
                        d="M0,0 v-100 a100,100 0 1,1 -100,100z"
                        transform="rotate(-135)"/>
```

The needle consists of a second simple path and a circle at the far end of the needle, floating a little bit for an added bit of graphical eye candy, along with a small cap over the top of the needle to make it look like it is on a spindle. This whole <g> element is similarly drawn on its side, then rotated 45 degrees counterclockwise to end up in its resting position:

```
    <g id="needleShape">
        <g transform="rotate(-45)">
        <path d="m0,0 L-65,5 L-80,0 L-65,-5,z"
                    stroke="black" fill="white"
                    stroke-width="2"/>
        <circle cx="-90" cy="0" r="3"
                    stroke="black" fill="white"
                    stroke-width="1"/>
<circle cx="0" cy="0" r="5" stroke="black"
            fill="lightGray" stroke-width="1"
            id="needleCap"/>
        </g>
    </g>
```

The labels are also declared in the <defs> arena. Because there is only one label instance per definition, you can actually change the value of the defined text labels from code while taking advantage of <use> elements in the displayed area. Note that if you use the SVG DOM, you can change the contents of text in a <text> element and have that change appear in any referenced element. In other words, you can animate a defined element through DOM:

```
<text x="0" y="60"
        font-size="24" id="gaugeNumber"
        text-anchor="middle">0</text>
        <text x="-75" y="90" font-size="18"
                id="minValNumber" text-anchor="middle">0</text>
        <text x="75" y="90" font-size="18" id="maxValNumber"
                text-anchor="middle">100</text>
        <text x="0" y="100" font-size="18" id="gaugeLabel"
                text-anchor="middle">Speed</text>
```

Once the shapes are defined, you can also start creating more abstract entities, such as the gauge shadows and the critical background:

```
<use id="gaugeShadowDark"
        xlink:href="#gaugeShape"
        x="-3" y="-3" stroke="black"
        stroke-width="3" fill="black"/>
    <use id="gaugeShadowLight"
            xlink:href="#gaugeShape"
            x="3" y="3"
            stroke="gray" stroke-width="1"
            fill="gray"/>
    <use id="gaugeBackground"
            xlink:href="#gaugeShape"
            x="0" y="0" fill="rgb(0,0,0)"
            stroke="black" stroke-width="2"/>
    </defs>
```

After all that, the final component is drawn. At this stage, any explicit
Cascading Style Sheets (CSS) characteristics are basically abstracted away so that
the actual drawing appears more like a manifest of what subordinate components are contained in the document:

```
    <g transform="translate(110,110)">
        <use xlink:href="#gaugeShadowDark"/>
        <use xlink:href="#gaugeShadowLight"/>
        <use xlink:href="#gaugeBackground"/>
        <use xlink:href="#needleShape" id="needle"/>
        <use xlink:href="#gaugeNumber"/>
        <use xlink:href="#minValNumber"/>
        <use xlink:href="#maxValNumber"/>
        <use xlink:href="#gaugeLabel"/>
    </g>
</svg>
```

There are a number of places where you can make some improvements, of
course, both from a graphical and a programmatic standpoint. Currently, you
cannot change the upper or lower values of the gauge once it is been instantiated, though that is a pretty easy fix. The gauges here have no unit tick marks
associated with them, and this could prove to be a major improvement over the
existing component. Finally, the control currently does not recognize any mouse
click events, though adding this capability is straightforward: Place an onclick

event handle on the `<svg>` element, and in the handler for that event see if an `onclick` handler attribute exists for the `<embed>` element:

```
<svg ... onclick="processClick()">
<script language="JavaScript">
function processClick(){
   if (extGaugeEmbed.getAttribute("onclick")!=null){
                   extGaugeEmbed.window.eval(
                           extGaugeEmbed.getAttribute("onclick"));
   }
     }
</script>
 ...
</svg>
```

Scrolling On Down the Boulevard

Scroll bars and sliders represent the other side to interfaces—building components that can be modified through direct actions of the users (the Gauge control was indirect—it was essentially passive). Sliders are ubiquitous in programming, but all too often they are visually pretty unexciting, consisting of a shaded *bed* and a rectangle (perhaps buttonish) that fits snuggly within that rectangle. In putting together multimedia applications, being able to easily build a custom slider that can be more visually exciting has long been something of a Holy Grail for multimedia developers.

Integrating the Scroll Bar Control

To illustrate how easy it is to create such a custom slider, I decided to create a simple application that would let me see how the images in a given folder would appear as the background of a Web page. This application is intended to run locally within the Internet Explorer browser, principally because it uses Microsoft's `File System Object` to iterate through local folders (and hence poses a massive security risk if posted on the Web).

Listing 10-3 illustrates how the scroll bar is embedded, including the use of attributes to pass parameters to the scroll bar itself (see Figure 10-2).

Listing 10-3. `scrollbar.htm`

```
<html>
    <head>
        <title>Scroll Bar</title>
        <script language="JavaScript" src="scrollBarPictures.js">
        </script>
    </head>
    <body onload="initDisplay('ApressImages/')">
    <div id="value" style="background-color:black;color:white;"></div>
    <embed src="scrollbar.svg" width="600" height="64" id="scrollbar"
        wmode="transparent" style="position:absolute;left:50;height:50;"
        value="0" minValue="0" maxValue="1"
        onbedclick="updateBackground()"
        onthumbrelease="updateBackground()"/>
    </body>
</html>
```

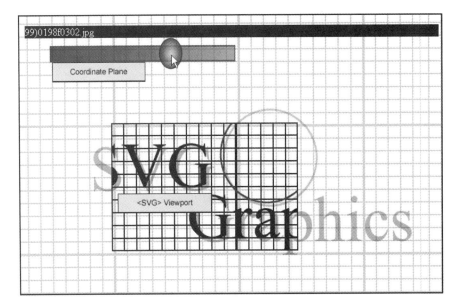

Figure 10-2. A custom scroll bar

The `scrollBar` component in Listing 10-3 is less customizable in certain respects, exposing a smaller set of properties through attributes (though more events are included), as shown in Table 10-3.

Table 10-3. Scroll Bar Attributes

ATTRIBUTE NAME	DEFAULT VALUE	DESCRIPTION
value	0	The initial value that the scroll bar will take.
minValue	0	The minimum value that the scroll bar can assume.
maxValue	100	The maximum value that the scroll bar can assume.
onbedclick	None	The event handler that is called whenever the bed (the track that the thumb rests on) is clicked.
onthumbpress	None	The event handler that is called whenever the thumb is pressed.
onthumbrelease	None	The event handler that is called whenever the thumb is released.
onthumbmove	None	The event handler that is called whenever the mouse has changed position. This may be called repeatedly during a thumb drag.

The scroll bar also supports four methods, invoked by calling the method on the object, scrollBar1.setValue(100), for instance (see Table 10-4).

Table 10-4. Scroll Bar Methods

FUNCTION	EXAMPLE	DESCRIPTION
setValue(pos)	scrollbar1.setValue(10)	Sets the value of the scroll bar and moves the thumb to the appropriate position
getValue()	var filePos=scrollbar1.getValue()	Retrieves the currently value of the scroll bar
setMinValue (minValue)	setMinValue(200);	Sets the minimum value that the scroll bar can take
setMaxValue (maxValue)	setMaxValue(300);	Sets the maximum value that the scroll bar can take

The script that translates the scroll bar movement into a background is contained in the external JavaScript file, as shown in Listing 10-4.

Listing 10-4. scrollBarPictures.js

```
var fso=null;
var Files=null;
var eFiles=null;
var scrollbar=null;

function passBackSVG(){
    var scrollbar = document.getElementById("scrollbar");

        if (scrollbar.readystate != 4)
    {
        setTimeout( passBackSVG, 50 );
        return;
    }
    scrollbar.window.passState(scrollbar);
  }
function initFSO(){
    fso=new ActiveXObject("Scripting.FileSystemObject");
    }


function updateBackground(){
    scrollbar=document.all("scrollbar");
    filePos=parseInt(scrollbar.getValue());
    eFiles.moveFirst();
    while (filePos-){
        eFiles.moveNext();

        }
    var file=eFiles.item();
    document.all("value").innerHTML=parseInt(scrollbar.getValue())+")"+file.name;
    document.body.setAttribute("background",file.path);
    }

function setFolder(folder){
    Files=fso.getFolder(folder).files;
    eFiles=new Enumerator(Files);
    scrollbar=document.all("scrollbar");
    scrollbar.setMaxValue(Files.count-1);
    }
```

```
function initDisplay(folder){
    passBackSVG();
    initFSO();
    setFolder(folder);
    updateBackground()
    }
```

To set up the system, the initDisplay function takes as an argument the folder path to the folder where the pictures reside. It then initializes the File System Object (which lets users access specific folders or files within the Windows operating system), retrieves the number of files in that folder, and passes that information to the scrollbar object through this command:

```
scrollbar.setMaxValue(Files.count-1);
```

Finally, it updates the background, based upon the position of the scroll bar, via the updateBackground() function:

```
function updateBackground(){
    scrollbar=document.all("scrollbar");
    filePos=parseInt(scrollbar.getValue());
    eFiles.moveFirst();
    while (filePos-){
        eFiles.moveNext();

        }
    var file=eFiles.item();
    document.all("value").innerHTML=parseInt(scrollbar.getValue())+")"+file.name;
    document.body.setAttribute("background",file.path);
    }
```

The scroll bar is an analog device—it returns the value between its minimum and maximum values as a floating-point number, so it is the responsibility of the application to convert it to an integer if needed:

```
scrollbar=document.all("scrollbar");
    filePos=parseInt(scrollbar.getValue());
```

The eFiles object, which contains the COM component that accesses the specific collection of files, can only be walked through via enumeration methods (moveFirst(), moveNext(), and item()). So, the updateBackground routine positions the read head at the beginning of the file list with moveFirst() and decrements a counter initially set to the slider position.

Once the appropriate file is retrieved, the name of the file is passed to a specific DIV item and displayed (along with the file position), and the background of the document is then set to the corresponding file item.

Implementing the Scroll Bar Control

The declarative portion for the scroll bar is, in some respects, even simpler than the code for the gauge. In essence, it defines two primary objects—the thumb (the item that moves) and the bed (the "track" that the thumb moves along). In the sample, both the thumb and the bed are semitransparent so that you can see underneath them, with the thumb built as a circle; however, the visual appearance of both the thumb and the bed are quite adjustable, so long as the thumb moves along the bed in a straight line (see Listing 10-5).

Listing 10-5. scrollBar.svg

```
<svg
xmlns="http://www.w3.org/2000/svg"
xmlns:xlink="http://www.w3.org/1999/xlink"
onload="initSVG(evt)" width="504" height="64" viewBox="0 0 504 64"
preserveAspectRatio="none">
    <script language="JavaScript" xlink:href="scrollbar.js"/>
    <defs>
        <linearGradient id="bedGradient">
            <stop offset="0%" stop-color="black"/>
            <stop offset="100%" stop-color="gray"/>
        </linearGradient>
        <radialGradient id="thumbGradient">
            <stop offset="0%" stop-color="yellow"/>
            <stop offset="100%" stop-color="red"/>
        </radialGradient>
        <g id="bedBase">
            <rect width="500" height="30"
                  fill="url(#bedGradient)" stroke-width="3"
                  stroke="black" x="0" y="0" opacity="0.7"
                  id="track"/>
        </g>
        <circle cx="0" cy="0" r="30" fill="url(#thumbGradient)" stroke="black"
            stroke-width="2" id="thumbBase" opacity="0.8"/>
    </defs>
    <g  onmousemove="moveThumb(evt)"
            onmousedown="beginMoveThumb(evt)"
            onmouseup="endMoveThumb(evt)"
            onmouseout="endMoveThumb(evt)">
```

```
        <g transform="translate(0,32)" id="slider">
            <use xlink:href="#bedBase" x="0" y="-15"
                    id="bed" onclick="clickBed(evt)"/>
            <use xlink:href="#thumbBase" x="0" y="0" id="thumb" width="30"/>
        </g>
    </g>
    <text x="100" y="200" id="valueText"> </text>
</svg>
```

The key to making the scroll bar work is again its external scripting calls, in this case to the file scrollBar.js (see Listing 10-6). SVG 1.0 does not include specific calls for handling drag-and-drop operations in a declarative manner, a limitation that will likely get fixed in SVG 2.0. As a consequence, you as a developer have to do a little more work in doing drag operations, including figuring out exactly where they are not in fact necessary.

Listing 10-6. scrollBar.js

```
var svgDoc=null;
var buttonPressed=false;
var bed=null;
var bedXMin=0;
var bedXMax=0;
var thumb=null;
var thumbWidth=0;
var sliderPos=null;
var value=0;
var minValue=0;
var maxValue=1;
var scaleFactor=1;
var embedId="local";
var embed;

function initSVG(evt){
    svgDoc=evt.target.ownerDocument;
    }

function passState(extEmbed){
    embed=extEmbed;
    embed.setMaxValue=setMaxValue;
    embed.setMinValue=setMinValue;
    embed.setValue=setValue;
    embed.getValue=getValue;
    sliderPos=getTranslate("slider");
```

```
      bed=svgDoc.getElementById("bed");
      track=svgDoc.getElementById("track");
      thumb=svgDoc.getElementById("thumb");
      var svgNode=svgDoc.getElementsByTagName("svg").item(0);

      embedWidth=parseFloat(embed.getAttribute("width"));
      embedHeight=parseFloat(embed.getAttribute("height"));
      bedXMin = parseFloat(bed.getAttribute("x"));
      scaleFactorX=parseFloat(track.getAttribute("width"))/embedWidth;
      scaleFactorY=parseFloat(svgNode.getAttribute("height"))/embedHeight;
      bedWidth = parseFloat(track.getAttribute("width"));
      thumbWidth=thumb.getAttribute("width");
//    alert(scaleFactorY);
      thumb.setAttribute("transform","scale("+ (scaleFactorX) + ","+(1)+")");

      if (embed.getAttribute("value")!=""){
          value=parseFloat(embed.getAttribute("value"));
          }
      if (embed.getAttribute("minValue")!=""){
          minValue=parseFloat(embed.getAttribute("minValue"));
          }
      if (embed.getAttribute("maxValue")!=""){
          maxValue=parseFloat(embed.getAttribute("maxValue"));
          }
      if (embed.id!=""){
          embedId=embed.id;
          }
      }


function beginMoveThumb(evt){
      buttonPressed=true;
      if (embed.getAttribute("onthumbpress")!=null){
          embed.window.eval(embed.getAttribute("onthumbpress"));
          }
      }


function endMoveThumb(evt){
      buttonPressed=false;
      if (embed.getAttribute("onthumbrelease")!=null){
          embed.window.eval(embed.getAttribute("onthumbrelease"));
          }

      }
```

```
function clickBed(evt){
    buttonPressed=true;
    moveThumb(evt);
    if (embed.getAttribute("onbedclick")!=null){
        embed.window.eval(embed.getAttribute("onbedclick"));
        }
    buttonPressed=false;
    }

function moveThumb(evt){
    if(buttonPressed){
        clientX=evt.clientX;
        var posX=Math.min(Math.max(clientX*scaleFactorX,
                thumbWidth),(bedWidth) - thumbWidth);
                value=minValue + (maxValue-minValue)*
                (posX-thumbWidth)/(bedWidth - 2 * thumbWidth);
    if (embed.getAttribute("onthumbmove")!=null){
        embed.window.eval(embed.getAttribute("onthumbmove"));
        }
        thumb.setAttribute("transform","translate("+posX+",0)");
        }
    }

function getTranslate(elemId){
    var elem=svgDoc.getElementById(elemId);
    var translate=elem.getAttribute('transform');
    var re=/translate\((-?[0-9]+),(-?[0-9]+)\)/;
    if(re.test(translate)){
        x=parseFloat(RegExp.$1);
        y=parseFloat(RegExp.$2);
        var obj=new Object;
        obj.x=x;
        obj.y=y;
        return obj;
        }
    else {
        return null;
        }
    }
```

```
function setValue(newValue){
    value=newValue;
    posX=thumbWidth + (bedWidth - 2* thumbWidth)*
                      ((value-minValue)/(maxValue-minValue));
    thumb.setAttribute("x",posX + sliderPos.x);
    if (embed.getAttribute("onchange")!=null){
        embed.window.eval(embed.getAttribute("onchange"));
        }
    }

function setMinValue(minVal){
    minValue=minVal;
    }

function getValue(){
    return value;
    }

function setMaxValue(maxVal){
    maxValue=maxVal;
    }
```

Surprisingly enough, that is precisely the case here, where the most obvious way to code the interface is wrong—with a scroll bar, you are not in fact dragging the thumb. Instead, the most efficiently defined scroll bar is one that retrieves the position of the mouse on the bed and then sets the position of the thumb to that position.

The passState() function in Listing 10-6 is considerably more inflated than it was in the Gauge control because it acts to initialize the various properties passed in from the HTML document. Once it retrieves the embedded node, the passState function assigns the requisite methods onto the object itself as function stubs:

```
function passState(extEmbed){
    embed=extEmbed;
    embed.setMaxValue=setMaxValue;
    embed.setMinValue=setMinValue;
    embed.setValue=setValue;
    embed.getValue=getValue;
```

With the exception of the setValue() function (called shortly), these functions simply retrieve values contained in a global variable. The next stage comes in the need to retrieve the sliderPosition offset from the <g> element called "slider". This way, you can position both the bed and the thumb anywhere

within the <svg> component using a transform on the <g> element (which consequently makes a transform on that element a necessity):

```
sliderPos=getTranslate("slider");
```

The getTranslate() function is perhaps one of the more complex functions
in the slider component—there are no clean functions that can decompose
a transformation function into the respective coordinates, so getTranslate()
takes advantage of the fact that the SVG document is also an XML document to
retrieve the transform attribute directly, then uses regular expressions to extract
the individual x and y coordinates. These are then turned into a JavaScript object
and passed pack to the client (a null is passed if no such transform exists):

```
function getTranslate(elemId){
    var elem=svgDoc.getElementById(elemId);
    var translate=elem.getAttribute('transform');
    var re=/translate\((-?[0-9]+),(-?[0-9]+)\)/;
    if(re.test(translate)){
        x=parseFloat(RegExp.$1);
        y=parseFloat(RegExp.$2);
        var obj=new Object;
        obj.x=x;
        obj.y=y;
        return obj;
        }
    else {
        return null;
        }
    }
```

Back to the passState() function—once this position object is stored, width,
height, and related attributes are also retrieved and assigned to accessible global
variables.

The movement itself is invoked by placing the appropriate event handlers on
the component's containing object (which holds both bed and thumb):

```
<g  onmousemove="moveThumb(evt)"
        onmousedown="beginMoveThumb(evt)"
        onmouseup="endMoveThumb(evt)"
        onmouseout="endMoveThumb(evt)">
```

The advantage to placing it on a super object comes when you click and drag
portions of the thumb that may be outside of the bed. Because the thumb

retrieves this value initially, it will keep from firing an onmouseout event even if the mouse strays from the bed, unless the mouse moves faster than the thumb can keep up.

NOTE *Keeping up with the mouse can prove problematic because the Adobe SVG Viewer then needs to keep track of whether the mouse was released, which puts far more burden on the speed of the event handling mechanism. This particular code consequently does not include the ability to click the thumb. If you move the mouse off the thumb, even if the mouse button is depressed, it will deactivate the current thumb's movement.*

The beginMoveThumb and endMoveThumb events perform two very simple tasks: setting a flag indicating whether the thumb has begun or finished moving and evaluating the "onthumbpress", "onthumbrelease" JavaScript contained in the <embed> element of the calling HTML document. The clickBed function performs the same purpose for the bed itself, although it also calls the moveThumb() handler (see Listing 10-7).

Listing 10-7. moveThumb *Handler*

```
function beginMoveThumb(evt){
    buttonPressed=true;
    if (embed.getAttribute("onthumbpress")!=null){
        embed.window.eval(embed.getAttribute("onthumbpress"));
        }
    }

function endMoveThumb(evt){
    buttonPressed=false;
    if (embed.getAttribute("onthumbrelease")!=null){
        embed.window.eval(embed.getAttribute("onthumbrelease"));
        }
    }

function clickBed(evt){
    buttonPressed=true;
    if (embed.getAttribute("onbedclick")!=null){
        embed.window.eval(embed.getAttribute("onbedclick"));
        }
```

```
    moveThumb(evt);
    buttonPressed=false;
    }
```

The moveThumb() function does the actual positioning, though it also calls the onthumbmove event handler. The function retrieves the x position of the mouse call and maps it to the internal coordinate system of the slider (remember that the slider can be scaled to any size). The variable scaleFactorX determines the relative distortions introduced by the differences between the internal map and the mouse position, and the position is then set using the translate function to ensure that any mouse object (including a circle) will be positioned correctly:

```
function moveThumb(evt){
    if(buttonPressed){
        clientX=evt.clientX;
        var posX=Math.min(Math.max(
                clientX*scaleFactorX,thumbWidth),
                (bedWidth) - thumbWidth);
        value=minValue + (maxValue-minValue)*
                (posX-thumbWidth)/(bedWidth - 2 * thumbWidth);
    if (embed.getAttribute("onthumbmove")!=null){
        embed.window.eval(embed.getAttribute("onthumbmove"));
        }
        thumb.setAttribute("transform","translate("+posX+",0)");
        }
```

As with the Gauge control, there is considerable room for improvement in this control. If the ratio between height and width is too far off the initial scale values, the thumb will get distorted, and the mapping between coordinate system mouse positions and the internal map are more complicated than they need to be. Finally, it should be possible to constrain the slider so it can only occupy integer positions.

Both of these sample components provide examples of visual component programming. You can also take advantage of the sophisticated power of the DOM to write extensions to SVG.

Loading External Libraries

When I first encountered SVG, one facet of the language I thought was natural for a resource such as this was the ability to create libraries of special objects in an external resource, then somehow link to that resource when you needed a specific picture, pattern, or animation definition. Unfortunately, although this is (sort of) hinted at within the specification, the Adobe SVG Viewer does not support this capability, except from the standpoint of loading complete SVG objects as static images.

However, so long as the SVG document is embedded within an HTML document viewed from Internet Explorer (which is, admittedly, an awkward restriction), you can develop an extension mechanism that will let you do a number of things within an SVG, not least of which being the loading of external libraries. The principal reason for this requirement comes in the need for an XML parser that can work with independent objects to transfer node content into the SVG.

The HTML for passing the current embedded object and window context is remarkably similar to code shown in Chapter 9, "Integrating SVG and HTML," and uses the same principle—passing the embedded object through a public method into the SVG, as shown in Listing 10-8 (see Figure 10-3).

Listing 10-8. `loadingLibrary.htm`

```html
<html>
<head>
    <title>External Libraries</title>
    <script language="JavaScript">//<![CDATA[
function passBackSVGExtended(){
        if (library.readystate != 4)
    {
        setTimeout( passBackSVGExtended, 50 );
        return;
    }
    library.window.passStateExt(library,loadObject);
    }
function loadObject(progID){
    return new ActiveXObject(progID);
    }

//]]>     </script>
</head>

<body onload="passBackSVGExtended()">

<embed src="loadingLibrary.svg" width="1024" height="768" id="library"/>

</body>
</html>
```

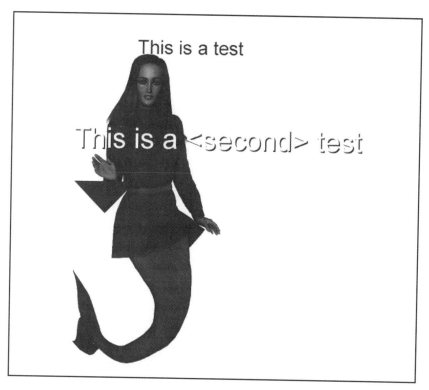

Figure 10-3. Using the DOM to import libraries of resources into your SVG documents

There are a few important distinctions, however, that dramatically increase what you can do within the SVG. One of the critical problems that the Adobe SVG Viewer 3.0 currently has lies in its inability to create COM objects. Although it is certainly possible to pass these objects in directly, from a programming standpoint it makes far more sense to pass a routine that will retrieve such COM objects (such as the MSXML object) directly from within the SVG. This also makes it possible to write routines that enable XSL Transformations directly within SVG documents, a technique used later in this chapter.

To do this, it is necessary to create a function called loadObject, which, when passed a program ID (progId) such as "MSXML2.DOMDocument", will create a new COM object of that type.

JavaScript is a useful language because you can actually pass functions themselves as parameters. This is illustrated in the function passBackSVGExtended:

```
function passBackSVGExtended(){
        if (library.readystate != 4)
    {
        setTimeout( passBackSVGExtended, 50 );
        return;
    }
    library.window.passStateExt(library,loadObject);
    }
```

As with passBackSVG from the previous chapter, passBackSVGExtended tests the <embed> object to see if the readystate is equal to 4 (loaded and ready to go). If it is ready, the function is invoked on the SVG item, passing both the current embedded object and the loadObject function in as parameters.

NOTE   *The function is passed as a stub—*loadObject*—rather than as a called function such as* loadObject(progID). *This makes the function itself an argument, which can then be invoked internally by the routines that* passStateExt *calls. It is a bit of a kludge, but it works.*

The SVG document in question, LoadingLibrary.svg, uses a little indirection of its own. The <svg:script> element has hitherto been used as a container for scripts, but you can also use it to point to an external script (in this case defsLibrary.js), as shown in Listing 10-9.

Listing 10-9. defLibrary.js

```
<svg     xmlns="http://www.w3.org/2000/svg"
         xmlns:xlink="http://www.w3.org/1999/xlink"
         xmlns:ext="http://www.kurtcagle.net/schemas/SVGextensions"
         onload="initSVG(evt)" width="100%" height="100%"
         viewBox="0 0 1024 768">
    <script language="JScript" xlink:href="defsLibrary.js"/>
    <g>
         <ext:load xlink:href="defsLibrary.xml"/>
         <use xlink:href="#mermaid" x="100" y="100"/>
         <use xlink:href="#text1" x="200" y="100"/>
         <use xlink:href="#text2" x="100" y="250"/>
         <use xlink:href="#text2" x="98" y="248" fill="white"/>
         <use xlink:href="#triangle" x="100" y="300" fill="blue"/>
    </g>
</svg>
```

Not only does this keep the scripting manageable and your SVG cleaner, but it also makes it possible to start building more extensive libraries of capabilities into your SVG (that funky modularity factor again).

The <ext:load> element in Listing 10-8 is *not* a part of SVG—it is, as the xmlns:ext namespace declaration implies, an ability to add custom tags into SVG that will be evaluated when the document is first loaded. The mechanism discussed in Listing 10-9 works reasonably well for developing any kind of extension tag, by the way, and can be freely adapted to add support for text block elements, posting instructions to the Web or related capabilities. In this case <ext:load> includes an xlink:href that points to an external XML file, defsLibrary.xml, which contains specific SVG declarations:

```
<defs xmlns="http://www.w3.org/2000/svg"
        xmlns:xlink="http://www.w3.org/1999/xlink">
        <path id="triangle" d="m0,0 l100,0 l-50,50z"/>
        <image xlink:href="SweaterMer3.png"
                width="237" height="484" id="mermaid"/>
        <text id="text1" font-size="30">This is a test</text>
        <text id="text2" font-size="45"><![CDATA[This is a <second> test]]></text>
</defs>
```

The items defined are then invoked in the calling LoadingLibrary.svg document:

```
<use xlink:href="#mermaid" x="100" y="100"/>
<use xlink:href="#text1" x="200" y="100"/>
<use xlink:href="#text2" x="100" y="250"/>
<use xlink:href="#text2" x="98" y="248" fill="white"/>
<use xlink:href="#triangle" x="100" y="300" fill="blue"/>
```

When the file LoadingLibrary.htm is then viewed in Internet Explorer, you can see that all of the elements in fact display properly, even though the declarations reside in a different document than the calling document.

So how is this done? Time to look behind the curtain at the LoadingLibrary.js script (see Listing 10-10).

Listing 10-10. LoadingLibrary.js

```
var svgDoc=null;
var embedObject=null;
var loadObject=null;
```

```
function initSVG(evt){
    svgDoc=evt.target.ownerDocument;
    }

function passStateExt(extObject,loadObject_){
    embedObject=extObject;
    loadObject=loadObject_;
    loadExternalDefs();
    }

function loadExternalDefs(){
    var nodelist=svgDoc.getElementsByTagName("ext:load");
//    alert(nodelist.length);

    for (var i=0;i<nodelist.length;i++){
        var extNode=nodelist.item(i);
        var externalURL=extNode.getAttributeNS(
                "http://www.w3.org/1999/xlink","href");
        var xmlDoc=loadObject("MSXML2.FreeThreadedDomDocument");
        xmlDoc.async=false;
        xmlDoc.load(externalURL);
        var rootNode=xmlDoc.documentElement;
//        var svgNode=parseXML(rootNode.xml);
        var svgNode=mapXMLToSVG(rootNode);
        extNode.parentNode.replaceChild(svgNode,extNode);
        }
    }

function mapXMLToSVG(xmlNode,svgParentNode){
    switch(xmlNode.nodeTypeString){
case "element":
            if (xmlNode.namespaceURI!=""){
                var svgElement=svgDoc.createElementNS(
                    xmlNode.namespaceURI,xmlNode.nodeName);
                }
            else {
                var svgElement=svgDoc.createElement(xmlNode.nodeName);
                }
            for (var i=0;i<xmlNode.attributes.length;i++){
                var attr=xmlNode.attributes.item(i);
                if(attr.namespaceURI!=""){
                    svgElement.setAttributeNS(
                            attr.namespaceURI,attr.nodeName,attr.value);
                    }
```

```
                    else {
                        svgElement.setAttribute(attr.nodeName,attr.value);
                    }
                }
            if (""+svgParentNode != "undefined"){
                svgParentNode.appendChild(svgElement);
            }
            for (var i=0;i<xmlNode.childNodes.length;i++){
                var childNode=xmlNode.childNodes.item(i);
                mapXMLToSVG(childNode,svgElement);
            }
            break;
        case "text":
            var svgText=svgDoc.createTextNode(xmlNode.text);
            svgParentNode.appendChild(svgText);
            break;
        case "comment":
            var svgComment=svgDoc.createComment(xmlNode.text);
            svgParentNode.appendChild(svgComment);
        case "cdatasection":
            var svgCDATASection=svgDoc.createCDATASection(xmlNode.nodeValue);
            svgParentNode.appendChild(svgCDATASection);
        default:break;
    }
    return svgElement;
}
```

There is a truism in magic (whether of the stage variety or the more ceremonial kind) that behind even the simplest magical acts there is usually an incredible amount of preparation and work, and this definitely holds true here. The first scripts declare three key variables: svgDoc, browserWnd, and loadObject, setting each to null:

```
var svgDoc=null;
var embedObject=null;
var loadObject=null;
```

The initSVG(evt) function, invoked from an onload(evt) handler on the containing <svg> element, simply defines the svgDoc object:

```
function initSVG(evt){
    svgDoc=evt.target.ownerDocument;
}
```

The passStateExt() function, on the other hand, should look familiar—it is the method that was invoked in the HTML call. This action first defines the embedObject variable so that it now contains a reference to the HTML <embed> element that currently hosts the SVG document. In this particular case the variable will not be needed further—the code is given to show how the same routine can in fact handle both the embed and passing of functional objects:

```
function passStateExt(extObject,loadObject_){
    browserWnd=extObject.window;
    loadObject=loadObject_;
    loadExternalDefs();
    }
```

The final function calls the loadExternalDefs() function:

```
function loadExternalDefs(){
    var nodelist=svgDoc.getElementsByTagName("ext:load");
    for (var i=0;i<nodelist.length;i++){
        var extNode=nodelist.item(i);
        var externalURL=
                extNode.getAttributeNS("http://www.w3.org/1999/xlink","href");
        var xmlDoc=loadObject("MSXML2.FreeThreadedDomDocument");
        xmlDoc.async=false;
        xmlDoc.load(externalURL);
        var rootNode=xmlDoc.documentElement;
        var svgNode=mapXMLToSVG(rootNode);
        extNode.parentNode.replaceChild(svgNode,extNode);
        }
    }
```

This function uses the getElementsByTagName function to retrieve all <ext:load> elements (a technique that can be used to retrieve any extension element from an SVG document, by the way), then iterates through this list.

NOTE *The* getElementsByTagName() *SVG method call always returns a node list so that even if there is only one node in the node list, you still have to iterate through the list to retrieve that one node.*

For each `<ext:load>` element found, it then reads the `xlink:href` attribute to obtain the location of the external library. Pay special attention to the `getAttributeNS()` function here—this retrieves the value of an attribute that has a different namespace than the current default namespace, such as the `xlink:` namespace (`http://www.w3.org.1999/xlink`). If you do not use the `getAttributeNS` function, this particular function call will generate an error and stop processing at that point. The result is then placed into the local variable `externalURL`.

The next step takes advantage of the `loadObject()` method that was passed in from the external HTML file:

```
var xmlDoc=loadObject("MSXML2.FreeThreadedDOMDocument");
xmlDoc.async=false;
xmlDoc.load(externalURL);
```

In this case, by passing `"MSXML2.FreeThreadedDOMDocument"`, you retrieve an MSXML parser object that can be used to retrieve and parse the XML of the external file. To avoid latency issues, you should set the `async` property to `false` (though this will have a slight adverse affect on your prerendering download time).

NOTE *The* `FreeThreadedDOMDocument` *object is not strictly speaking the only one you can use—the older* DOMDocument *object will work just as well here. The downside is that if you do any work with the MSXML* XSLTProcessor *object, it will only take the free-threaded version, and that version is a little more thread safe.*

In the MSXML model, the root node of a document is not the first visible load in the list, but is in fact a virtual *containing node* that holds not only this first node (called the *document element* and referred to in code as `documentElement`) but also any comments, processing instructions, or similar items that may be external to the outermost element:

```
var rootNode=xmlDoc.documentElement;
```

The `mapXMLToSVG()` function then takes this XML node and walks its tree structure, converting the XML nodes into their SVG equivalents. Once it creates the new SVG tree (as detailed next), it replaces the extension node with the corresponding SVG code, in this case the declarations in the external file:

```
var svgNode=mapXMLToSVG(rootNode);
extNode.parentNode.replaceChild(svgNode,extNode);
```

The `mapXMLToSVG()` function serves as a translator between two DOMs—the XML DOM and the SVG DOM. They are similar, in that the SVG DOM actually inherits all of the methods, properties, and events of the underlying XML DOM, but at the same time the SVG DOM includes the whole host of SVG capabilities for specialized attributes. Consequently, when you create an element in SVG (such as a `<rect>` element), that element has a number of known properties and methods (`width`, `height`, `animation`, and so on) that the corresponding XML element is not aware of—it only knows that it has attributes and child nodes.

Thus, the `mapXMLToSVG()` function is fairly complex, especially because it uses recursion to walk the XML tree. It works by taking the source `xmlNode` and the `svgParentNode` onto which to attach the new SVG node. If the `svgParentNode` argument is not given, the function returns the newly created node (with its associated tree) as a result instead:

```
function mapXMLToSVG(xmlNode,svgParentNode){
```

The action taken on the node depends upon what type of node it is, which is determined by the `nodeTypeString` of the XML source node. In the case of an element, the routine checks to see whether the node is using the default namespace or employs a different one and invokes either `createElement()` or `createElementNS` accordingly to create a new SVG element with the name of the corresponding XML element:

```
    switch(xmlNode.nodeTypeString){
case "element":
                if (xmlNode.namespaceURI!=""){
                    var svgElement=svgDoc.createElementNS(
                        xmlNode.namespaceURI,xmlNode.nodeName);
                    }
                else {
                    var svgElement=svgDoc.createElement(xmlNode.nodeName);
                    }
```

Because attributes cannot have children, it is actually easier to assign the attributes to the newly created element once it is defined. Again, it uses either a `setAttribute` or `setAttributeNS` function depending upon whether the namespace of the source attribute is the default. This is extremely important for handling linked resources, by the way, as all such linked attributes utilize the separate `xlink:` namespace:

```
for (var i=0;i<xmlNode.attributes.length;i++){
    var attr=xmlNode.attributes.item(i);
    if(attr.namespaceURI!=""){
        svgElement.setAttributeNS(attr.namespaceURI,
            attr.nodeName,attr.value);
    }
    else {
        svgElement.setAttribute(attr.nodeName,attr.value);
    }
}
```

Once the element is defined and attributes added, it is added to its parent SVG node if one exists:

```
if (""+svgParentNode != "undefined"){
    svgParentNode.appendChild(svgElement);
}
```

Then, the child nodes (elements, text nodes, CDATA sections, comments, and processing instructions) are iterated over and the same mapXMLToSVG function is applied to them, this time with the newly defined svgElement as the SVG parent element:

```
for (var i=0;i<xmlNode.childNodes.length;i++){
    var childNode=xmlNode.childNodes.item(i);
     mapXMLToSVG(childNode,svgElement);
    }
break
```

NOTE *This bit of recursion may not seem completely intuitive. Because the function adds the new element to its parent SVG node as a child, when the child element is itself passed as a parent, it already is connected to the tree. The only case where this is not true is for the first element defined because that one has no parent defined for it. This element* must *be returned to the calling routine so that it can be further processed (here, replacing the extension element).*

Elements are the most complicated nodal types, but an XML document can include a number of others. These are similarly handled, though because such nodes do not have children it is not necessary to invoke the mapXMLToSVG function again:

```
case "text":
                var svgText=svgDoc.createTextNode(xmlNode.text);
                svgParentNode.appendChild(svgText);
                break;
            case "comment":
                var svgComment=svgDoc.createComment(xmlNode.text);
                svgParentNode.appendChild(svgComment);
            case "cdatasection":
                var svgCDATASection=svgDoc.createCDATASection(xmlNode.nodeValue);
                svgParentNode.appendChild(svgCDATASection);
        default:break;
        }
```

Once all this processing is done, the final resultant SVG element with its associated tree of descendents is then passed back to replace the `<ext:load>` element:

```
return svgElement;
    }
```

Formatting Blocks of Text

One of the more tedious tasks that I have had to deal with when working with SVG is the need to position text blocks. Although SVG 1.1 will likely have some mechanism for dealing with text blocks as a native capability, this does not solve the problem of how to handle blocks of text right now. Fortunately, you can utilize the extension element mechanism to add your own text block capability (this time without needing to embed the SVG in an HTML document).

One of the tricks to effective programming in SVG is to keep as much of the functionality declarative as possible. Put another way, although it is certainly possible to write a JavaScript function that can take a block of text and insert it into SVG, it is generally preferable to create an extension element that could give you new functionality without it being obvious that this element is tied into a script. You can see an example of this in Listing 10-11 (see Figure 10-4).

Listing 10-11. `textBlockExtension.svg`

```
<svg xmlns="http://www.w3.org/2000/svg"
     xmlns:xlink="http://www.w3.org/1999/xlink"
     xmlns:ext="http://www.kurtcagle.net/schemas/extensions"
     onload="initSVG(evt);processTextBlocks()">
     <script language="JavaScript" xlink:href="textBlock.js"/>
     <defs>
     <ext:textBlock id="commentary" width="400" font-size="14"
                font-family="Verdana">
                <p>Scalable Vector Graphics (SVG) provides an
                intriguing mechanism for building not only rich
                graphics but also text content. Moreover, because
                SVG is in fact an XML language, you can, with
                some work, make the language completely extensible.</p>
            <p>These paragraphs illustrate one such example of the
                extensibility at work, through the use of JavaScript code.
                What's especially illuminating here is the fact that
                you can essentially encapsulate most of the
                functionality within an external script,
                while maintaining the source code as
                being fundamentally XML in nature.
                This has an incredible number of advantages
                over more traditional "procedural" scripting.</p>
            <p>The only real disadvantage to this method is that it
                is relatively slow, because the instantiation time of
                creating new <text> nodes is very slow
                in general. If this is a factor, you may want
                to think about generating this document ahead
                of time using XSLT instead, though you lose
                the ability to determine the runtime extents of
                text strings.</p>
     </ext:textBlock>
     <text id="title" font-size="28" font-family="Verdana">
            Text Blocks using Extensions</text>
      </defs>
        <g transform="translate(40,60)">
           <use xlink:href="#title" x="-20" y="-20"/>
           <use xlink:href="#commentary" x="0" y="0"/>
        </g>
</svg>
```

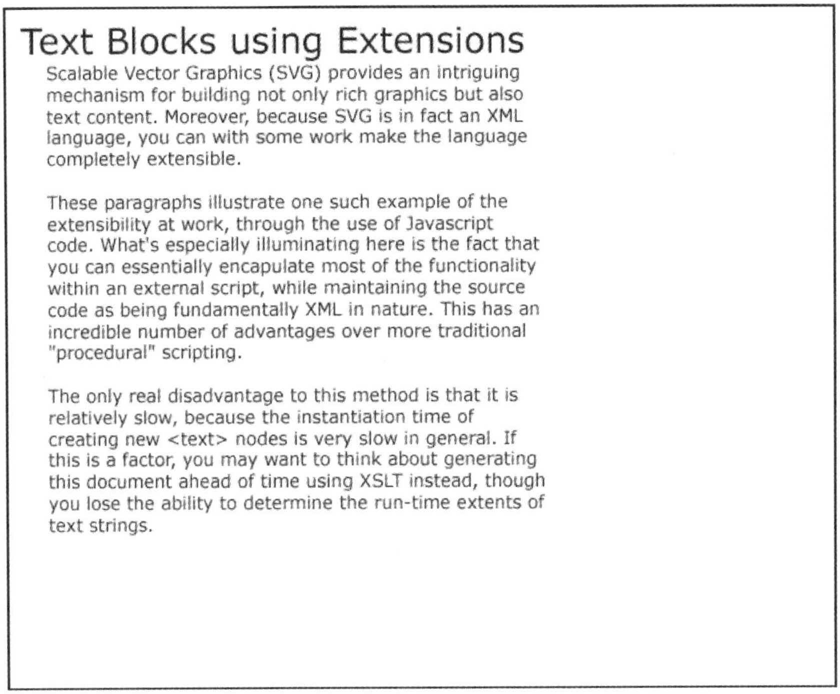

Text Blocks using Extensions

Scalable Vector Graphics (SVG) provides an intriguing mechanism for building not only rich graphics but also text content. Moreover, because SVG is in fact an XML language, you can with some work make the language completely extensible.

These paragraphs illustrate one such example of the extensibility at work, through the use of Javascript code. What's especially illuminating here is the fact that you can essentially encapsulate most of the functionality within an external script, while maintaining the source code as being fundamentally XML in nature. This has an incredible number of advantages over more traditional "procedural" scripting.

The only real disadvantage to this method is that it is relatively slow, because the instantiation time of creating new <text> nodes is very slow in general. If this is a factor, you may want to think about generating this document ahead of time using XSLT instead, though you lose the ability to determine the run-time extents of text strings.

Figure 10-4. `textBlockExtension`

In this particular case, the document defines a custom namespace (`www.kurtcagle.net/schemas/extensions`) and associates it with the `ext:` prefix. As has been repeatedly mentioned, this namespace URL does not specifically point to any given entity, it is only a unique identifier (though any of the `www.kurtcagle.net/schemas` namespaces covered in this book do point to descriptions on my Web site of the appropriate functionality).

The `<ext:textBlock>` element is a custom extension that makes it possible to create paragraphs of content. Each paragraph is in turn defined by a `<p>` child element, which can only be formatted by the `style` or other CSS attributes contained on the `<ext:textBlock>`. This element also explicitly recognizes only four attributes that must be contained on the `ext:textBlock` element: `width` (the width in current user units), `font-size` (ditto), `font-family`, and `id`. Additionally, the `ext:textBlock` can take an optional fifth attribute—`text-anchor`—which can have any of the values `start | middle | end`. For European left-to-right scripts, this corresponds to left, center, and right justification, respectively.

The paragraphs can also inherit other stylistic information such as stroke or fill colors, opacity, and related CSS properties, but if you place these attributes on the `<ext:textBlock>` they will be ignored (at least in version 1.0).

Once again, a `<script>` block is included within the document, this time pointing to the file `processTextBlocks.js` script. When the SVG document is loaded, the <svg> onload event fires, initializing a document variable (svgDoc), and calling the processTextBlocks() function defined in the JavaScript file to expand the paragraphs of text.

It is also worth noting that this element is contained within a <defs> block. This is not necessary from a functional standpoint—if you place an <ext:textBlock> element within a visible region it will display automatically— but this again illustrates the advantage of defining complex entities within the <defs> element, then invoking them with a <use> block.

Listing 10-12 shows the code that gives functionality to this element.

Listing 10-12. processTextBlocks.js

```
var svgDoc=null;

function initSVG(evt){
    svgDoc=evt.target.ownerDocument;
    }

function processTextBlocks(){
    var nodelist=svgDoc.getElementsByTagName("ext:textBlock");
    for (var i=0;i<nodelist.length;i++){
        var extNode=nodelist.item(i);
        var fontSize=extNode.getAttribute("font-size");
        var fontFamily=extNode.getAttribute("font-family");
        leading=parseFloat(fontSize) * 1.2;
        if (extNode.getAttribute("text-anchor")!=null){
            textAnchor=extNode.getAttribute("text-anchor");
            }
        else {
            textAnchor="start";
            }
        var width=extNode.getAttribute("width");
        var id=extNode.getAttribute("id");
        var gElement=svgDoc.createElement("g");
        gElement.setAttribute("font-size",fontSize);
        gElement.setAttribute("font-family",fontFamily);
        gElement.setAttribute("id",id);
        gElement.setAttribute("textAnchor",textAnchor);
        lineCount=0;
        var textElement=svgDoc.createElement("text");
        textElement.setAttribute("text-anchor",textAnchor);
        gElement.appendChild(textElement);
        lineCount=0;
        pList=extNode.getElementsByTagName("p");
```

```
for (var j=0;i<pList.length;j++){
    var pNode=pList.item(j);
    var text=pNode.firstChild.getData();
    buffer="";
    text=text+"";
    buffer="";
    while (text.length != 0){
        var tspanElement=svgDoc.createElement("tspan");
        tspanElement.appendChild(svgDoc.createTextNode("."));
        textElement.appendChild(tspanElement);
        tspanElement.setAttribute("x",0);
        tspanElement.setAttribute("y",lineCount * leading);
        while (width > tspanElement.getComputedTextLength()){
            var completedFlag=false;
            spacePos=text.indexOf(" ");
            if (spacePos != -1){
                oldBuffer=buffer;
                word = text.substring(0,spacePos);
                buffer=buffer+word+" ";
                tspanElement.firstChild.setData(buffer);
                text=text.substring(spacePos+1);
                }
            else{
                completedFlag=true;
                word=text;
                oldBuffer=buffer;
                buffer=buffer+word+" ";
                tspanElement.firstChild.setData(buffer);
                if (tspanElement.getComputedTextLength()>width){
                    tspanElement.firstChild.setData(oldBuffer);
                    lineCount++;
                    var tspanElement=svgDoc.createElement("tspan");
                  tspanElement.appendChild(svgDoc.createTextNode("."));
                    textElement.appendChild(tspanElement);
                    tspanElement.setAttribute("x",0);
                  tspanElement.setAttribute("y",(lineCount) * leading);
                    tspanElement.firstChild.setData(word);
                    lineCount=lineCount+1;
                    }
                break;
                }
            }
```

```
                        if (!completedFlag){
                            tspanElement.firstChild.setData(oldBuffer);
                            buffer=word+" ";
                            lineCount++;
                            }
                        else {
                            lineCount=lineCount+2;
                            break;
                            }

                        }
                    if (j==pList.length-1){
                        var parentNode=extNode.parentNode;
                        parentNode.replaceChild(gElement,extNode);
                        }
                    }
                }
            }
```

The processTextBlocks function is fairly complex, though it can in fact be broken into two fairly distinct processes—creating new elements and determining the breakpoints within the text itself. The routine starts by retrieving all <ext:textBlock> elements (you *can* have more than one in a document) and then iterating over each one. For each such element (contained within the extNode—extension node—variable), the relevant attributes are retrieved, with the leading (the space between the top of one line of text and the top of the next) defined as being 120 percent of the font-size attribute:

```
function processTextBlocks(){
    var nodelist=svgDoc.getElementsByTagName("ext:textBlock");
    for (var i=0;i<nodelist.length;i++){
        var extNode=nodelist.item(i);
        var fontSize=extNode.getAttribute("font-size");
        var fontFamily=extNode.getAttribute("font-family");
        leading=parseFloat(fontSize) * 1.2;
        if (extNode.getAttribute("text-anchor")!=null){
            textAnchor=extNode.getAttribute("text-anchor");
            }
        else {
            textAnchor="start";
            }
        var width=extNode.getAttribute("width");
        var id=extNode.getAttribute("id");
```

For each <ext:textBlock> element defined, the routine defines a <g> element that acts as a generic container for the text element—with the font-size, font-family, and id attributes assigned to this <g> element. This also makes it easier to add functionality such as transformations on the <g>container, rather than on the more picky <text> element:

```
var gElement=svgDoc.createElement("g");
gElement.setAttribute("font-size",fontSize);
gElement.setAttribute("font-family",fontFamily);
gElement.setAttribute("id",id);
var textElement=svgDoc.createElement("text");
textElement.setAttribute("text-anchor",textAnchor);
gElement.appendChild(textElement);
```

A single new <text> element is defined for each <g>. Because text-anchor is not an inheritable CSS attribute, it is necessary to assign the text-anchor directly to the <text> element. Once defined, the <text> element is then appended to the newly created <g>element (which is not yet connected to anything, by the way).

At this stage, a running counter is defined for keeping track of the current line being built. Additionally, a list of <p> elements are retrieved from the extNode element. It should be noted that the <p> elements do not actually correspond to any element containers in the final SVG document—they only determine the location of spaces between paragraphs. The routine iterates through each paragraph in turn, and retrieves its text to use in building the paragraphs. Additionally, a text buffer is initialized, to be used in maintaining a temporary store for each line:

```
lineCount=0;
pList=extNode.getElementsByTagName("p");
for (var j=0;i<pList.length;j++){
    var pNode=pList.item(j);
    var text=pNode.firstChild.getData();
    buffer="";
```

The text is consumed in the next routine, one that defines a new <tspan> element—with one <tspan>element corresponding to one line in the paragraph. The routine appends this <tspan>to the <text>element and then starts to set the properties on the element—initializing the x location to 0 and setting the y location to be lineCount * leading so that each line is always one leading height from the previous one. Note additionally that the <tspan> element also adds a text node with a single placeholder character in it—this character will be replaced with the content of the line, but passing empty strings to the createTextNode() function has occasionally given me odd memory problems:

```
while (text.length != 0){
                var tspanElement=svgDoc.createElement("tspan");
                tspanElement.appendChild(svgDoc.createTextNode("."));
                textElement.appendChild(tspanElement);
                tspanElement.setAttribute("x",0);
                tspanElement.setAttribute("y",lineCount * leading);
```

When text is added to the <tspan>element, this actually forces that text to render internally. This is necessary for the next function, the SVG DOM call getComputedTextLength(). This determines the actual width of the block of text within the <tspan>element (even if it is rendered in a <defs> element) in user units. So long as this length is less than the assigned width from the <ext:textBlock> width attribute, then another "word" of text can be added, where a word is any selection of characters up to the next space character:

```
while (width > tspanElement.getComputedTextLength()){
                var completedFlag=false;
                spacePos=text.indexOf(" ");
                if (spacePos != -1){
                    oldBuffer=buffer;
                    word = text.substring(0,spacePos);
                    buffer=buffer+word+" ";
                    tspanElement.firstChild.setData(buffer);
                    text=text.substring(spacePos+1);
                }
                . . .
        }
```

This routine uses a double-buffered system—the current buffer is assigned to the variable oldBuffer, then the next word is extracted from the text and appended to the new buffer (along with the delimiting space). The new buffer is then added to the <tspan> element to determine if it has exceeded the requisite width. So long as the source text does not run out, this process repeats until the width has been exceeded, with the old buffer reflecting the new buffer before each new word is added.

However, if the width is exceeded (a buffer overflow occurs), then the offending word has to be removed—which is done by swapping out the new buffer for the old. The word is then used as the initial value of a new buffer and the line count is correspondingly incremented:

```
if (!completedFlag){
        tspanElement.firstChild.setData(oldBuffer);
        buffer=word+" ";
        lineCount++;
        }
```

By the way, if the end of the text is reached, then some extra processing needs to be done. In that case, the line count is incremented by 2 to force a paragraph break, and the loop handling the display for that paragraph gets terminated with a JavaScript break keyword:

```
else {
        lineCount=lineCount+2;
        break;
        }
```

I deliberately skipped the case where the text runs out because this case is a little more complex than the normal processing loop:

```
else{
                        completedFlag=true;
                        word=text;
                        oldBuffer=buffer;
                        buffer=buffer+word+" ";
                        tspanElement.firstChild.setData(buffer);
                        if (tspanElement.getComputedTextLength()>width){
                            tspanElement.firstChild.setData(oldBuffer);
                            lineCount++;
                            var tspanElement=svgDoc.createElement("tspan");
                          tspanElement.appendChild(svgDoc.createTextNode("."));
                            textElement.appendChild(tspanElement);
                            tspanElement.setAttribute("x",0);
                          tspanElement.setAttribute("y",(lineCount) * leading);
                            tspanElement.firstChild.setData(word);
                            lineCount=lineCount+1;
                            }
                        break;
                        }
```

This routine sets the completedFlag to true, indicating that the text for that paragraph has reached its end (remember that the text is consumed by the routine). The last word is added to the buffer and the buffer is then assigned to the <tspan> element to see if it overflows. If it does not, then the routine can exit to go on to the next paragraph. If it did, however, the ‹tspan› element is refreshed with the old buffer value and a new ‹tspan› line is created. The final word, in turn is then added to this line.

One way to understand this a little better is to see that I have now covered both the normal flow and the case where a single word orphan occurs. This orphan will always by definition overflow the width of the line because trailing spaces are not counted in the ‹tspan› text's width, so it will always be on a line by itself.

This repeats for succeeding paragraphs, then for succeeding ‹ext:textBlock› elements. The final step in this routine is to replace each ‹ext:textBlock› element in the SVG source with the ‹g› container element that corresponds to it. Such a feat is accomplished with the replaceChild function, in a manner similar to that of the treewalker function—the parent node of each ‹ext:textBlock› is retrieved, then that node uses replaceChild to swap the extension node with the ‹g› element:

```
if (j==pList.length-1){
                var parentNode=extNode.parentNode;
                parentNode.replaceChild(gElement,extNode);
                }
```

The one caveat about this routine is that it is slow—normally it takes a second or more for the text to properly render on a mid-level machine (in this particular case an 800MHz laptop computer with about 200MB of free memory). There are several reasons for this—text in general renders fairly slowly in the Adobe SVG Viewer, creating text elements in particular is expensive, and each line essentially refreshes the text element between three and eight times while attempting to determine if the length has been exceeded.

There are a number of optimizations that can be done—using the number of characters in a string compared to the width and font size of the characters to make approximate where line breaks will occur before performing the test, cloning ‹tspan› elements (cloning is typically faster than full instantiation), and setting text-render and image-render attributes of the containing ‹svg› node to "optimizedSpeed" prior to rendering the text:

```
svgDoc.documentElement.setAttribute("image-rendering","optimizedSpeed");
svgDoc.documentElement.setAttribute("text-rendering","optimizedSpeed");
```

 TIP   *Note that the system usually balances speed, quality, and geometric integrity, so the hints provided here may not necessarily give you a huge boost in performance.*

Building a Slide Show Application

A book is often much like goulash: As an author you tend to throw whatever looks most interesting from your collection of goodies into it. The slide show application in this section certainly comes from that. I give a lot of presentations and talks, and one of my most pressing needs is usually a good slide presentation application. Although I have a number of commercial ones readily available, none of them readily support an XML input file, which is how I typically organize most of my materials. Ideally I would like to be able to post the same application to the Web. Given this, writing my own seemed a good idea (a slide from which is shown in Figure 10-5).

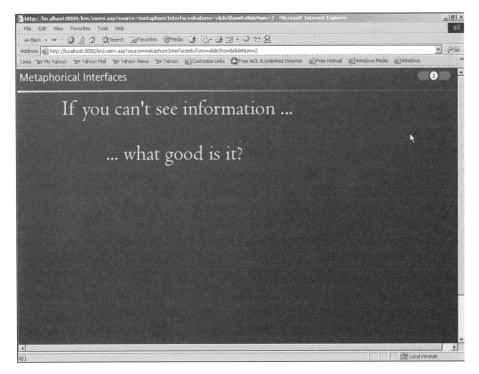

Figure 10-5. My slide show application

The requirements I faced in setting such a slide show up provided the following constraints in development:

- The application should be able to display both HTML and SVG, and the SVG should be able to access to an external environment.

- The slide show should run off of a primary XML file that could contain both raw HTML and SVG and specialized elements such as `<point>` (a bullet point).

- I would want to be able to apply customizable animation effects—fades in and out, moving from the side of the screen, and so on.

- I wanted to be able to specify multiple background templates within the presentation document.

- I would be delivering this from a server, so I would be using server-side XSLT transforms to convert the presentation document into the final output.

I also explicitly chose the following configuration because it was what I had code already written for:

- Internet Explorer 5.0+

- Microsoft IIS Server (I would eventually do an Apache version as well)

- Adobe SVG 3.0 Viewer

The architecture that I would ultimately end up using was a little indirect, but it illustrates the idea of pipelining and aggregating that I have been pushing in a lot of my talks. The idea was that the slide show was an HTML page that contained an embedded SVG document (in other words, one referenced via an `<embed>` tag). The HTML page may also contain additional HTML, possibly including other embedded SVG.

The primary SVG document, in turn would be accessed via a Web call to the server. If a template (an XSLT document) was specified, then the server (through the agency of the `xserv.asp` server script) would process the individual slide through the stylesheet. This ended up being a two-part process, first processing the background of the slide then rendering the foreground. Even if no template was specified, the slide show engine would always render the background, but by rendering the SVG of the foreground in the same document, performance would be improved dramatically in comparison to creating multiple overlays on the HTML page.

The key to making the whole process work was a script that would let me evaluate the presentation document against a stylesheet parametrically through a query string URL. This particular application, `xserv.asp`, lies at the heart of almost every piece of Web code that I write, and it (or a Java or Perl variant of it) forms the foundation of my Web site at `www.kurtcagle.net`, given in Listing 10-13.

Listing 10-13. `xserv.asp`

```
<%@language="JavaScript"%>
<%
// XServ is a JavaScript class. Everything down to
// start main() provides implementation for that class.

// This defines frequently used regular expression filters.
var squoteTrap = new RegExp("'","gi");
var ampTrap = new RegExp("&","gi");
var ltTrap = new RegExp("<","gi");
var gtTrap = new RegExp(">","gi");

function XServ(){
    this.request=requestFn;
    this.loadSource=loadSource;
    this.loadFile=loadFile;
    this.loadStylesheet=loadStylesheet;
    this.loadRequestParameters=loadRequestParameters;
    this.transform=transform;
    this.source=null;
    this.stylesheet=null;
    this.output=new ActiveXObject("MSXML2.FreeThreadedDOMDocument");
    this.getContentType=getContentType;
    this.setParameter=setParameter;
    this.setTransform=setTransform;
    this.error=null;
    }

    // This is a generalized routine for loading an XML file.
function loadFile(requestName,filePath,extension){
    var xmlDoc=new ActiveXObject("MSXML2.FreeThreadedDOMDocument");
    if (requestName==null){requestName="";}
    var requestPath=requestFn(requestName);
    if (""+requestPath != "undefined"){
        try{
            if (requestPath.indexOf(".")== requestPath.length - 4){}
            }
        catch(e){
            requestPath=requestPath + extension;
            }
        }
    else {
        requestPath=filePath;
        }
```

```
    xmlDoc.async=true;
    xmlDoc.load(Server.mapPath(requestPath))
    return xmlDoc;
    }


// This loads the XML source document

function loadSource(requestName,sourcePath){
    this.source=loadFile(requestName,sourcePath,".xml");
    }


// This creates a generalized wrapper to the current request object
// and can be overriden as appropriate.

function requestFn(requestName){
    // This should be overridden for custom request objects
    requestValue=Request(requestName);
    return requestValue;
    }


// This loads in the transform file
function loadStylesheet(requestName,xformPath){
    this.stylesheet=loadFile(requestName,xformPath,".xsl");
    }
// This retrieves the parameter names from the stylesheet and queries the
// Request object to see if any of these names are found.
// Thus, only the parameters that are relevant to the stylesheet
// are retrieved. Since the Request object also provides
// a hook into server variables and cookies, this mechanism
// can also be used by the stylesheet
// to retrieve these quantities.

function loadRequestParameters(){
    var params=this.stylesheet.selectNodes("xsl:stylesheet/xsl:param");
    for (var i=0;i<params.length;i++){
        param=params[i];
        paramName=param.getAttribute("name");
        paramValue="" + this.request(paramName);
        if (!(""+paramValue == "undefined")){
            if (paramValue.substr(1,1)=="@"){
                param.setAttribute("select",paramValue.substr(2));
                }
```

```
            else {
 paramValue=paramValue.replace(squoteTrap,"&#39;")
                param.setAttribute("select","'" + paramValue + "'");
                }
            }
        }
    }

// Set parameter makes it possible to set a given parameter with a value
// before it is processed.

function setParameter(paramName,paramValue){
    var param=this.stylesheet.selectSingleNode(
            "xsl:stylesheet/xsl:param[@name='" + paramName + "']");
    if (param){
        if (!(""+paramValue == "undefined")){
            if (paramValue.substr(1,1)=="@"){
                param.setAttribute("select",paramValue.substr(2));
                }
            else {
                param.setAttribute("select","'" + paramValue +"'")
                }
            }
        }
    }

// This retrieves the content type, either from the query string (first),
// or the @contentType attribute of the stylesheet's
//     <xsl:output> element (second).
// If neither of these are found, then the type is assumed to be "text/html".
function getContentType(defaultContentType){
    if (defaultContentType==null){defaultContentType="text/html";}
    var outputNode=this.stylesheet.selectSingleNode("xsl:stylesheet/xsl:output");
    if (""+this.request("contentType")!="undefined"){
        defaultContentType=this.request("contentType");
        outputNode=false;
        };
    if (outputNode){
        contentType=outputNode.getAttribute("media-type");
        if (contentType==""){
            contentType=defaultContentType;
            }
        }
```

```
        else {
            contentType=defaultContentType;
            }
        return contentType;
        }
// set Transform is used internally to associate
// the stylesheet with the xserv object's
// stylesheet property.
function setTransform(stylesheet){
        this.stylesheet=stylesheet;
        }


// The transform() function performs the actual transformation,
// or returns an error to
// the browser if one occurs.
function transform(){
        //this.source.transformNodeToObject(this.stylesheet,this.output);
        //return this.output;
        try {
        Response.write(this.source.transformNode(this.stylesheet));
        return "";
        }
        catch(e){
        Response.write(e.message);
        return e.message;
        }
        }


// The main() function starts the ball rolling.

// ***************** Start main()
function main(){
        Response.expires=-1;
        var xserv=new XServ();
        xserv.loadSource("source","presentation.xml");
        xserv.loadStylesheet("xform","slideShow.xsl");
        Response.ContentType=xserv.getContentType("text/html");
        xserv.loadRequestParameters();

        xserv.transform();
        }

main();

%>
```

NOTE *I do not claim that this is the most efficient such application. I present it here more in the spirit of a pedagogical exercise than as any paradigm of programming.*

The `xserv.asp` routine requires two explicit properties and one optional one to be passed via either POST (forms) or GET (query string). The primary `slideShow.xsl` file requires one other. Table 10-5 lists these files.

Table 10-5. Query String Parameters for `XServ.asp`

PROPERTY NAME	USED BY	DESCRIPTION
source	xserv.asp	This is the name of the source file to be transformed, with the .xml extension removed. If the file is XML-based but has a different extension, the extension should be left on.
xform	xserv.asp	This is the name of the transformation file, without the .xsl extension. If a different extension is used, then it should be included.
contentType	xserv.asp	This is the MIME type of the output. For XML, the output is "text/xml"; for SVG, it is "image/svg+xml"; and for HTML it is "text/html". (See also the "Hating Mimes" sidebar.)
slideNum	slideShow.xsl	This is the position of the slide in the deck.

Hating Mimes

It has become something of a cliché that, of all entertainers, pantomime artists (mimes) are perhaps the most hated (combining the worst aspects of clowns and annoying kid brothers). Mimes—specifically MIME-types—have also proved to be something of a headache to SVG developers.

Multipurpose Internet Mail Extensions (MIME) type was originally developed as a way of identifying and transporting the nontext contents of e-mail. But because of the ubiquity of e-mail, MIME has become the de-facto standard for identifying almost all forms of content on the Web. The problem with MIME is that it is something of an ad-hoc standard, and frequently the specific naming conventions for certain protocols fall through the grates. Unfortunately, SVG was one of those protocols.

Early on, the MIME protocol for specifying SVG was x-image/svg (a typical designation for an "experimental" MIME type) and then it shifted to image/svg-xml as the working draft became more solid. A number of SVG tools (including the Adobe SVG Viewer) standardized on this "image/svg-xml" designation. However, in the summer of 2001, the SVG committee, working with the IETF (the keepers of MIME) established that SVG should be given as "image/svg+xml" instead. Unfortunately, this has not completely propagated to all SVG tools yet, and there is likely to be some confusion for a while as people make the transition.

Thus, to be perfectly correct, use image/svg+xml when specifying the MIME type of an SVG document. However, if that does not work, try image/svg-xml and see if that makes the difference.

Essentially, the xserv.asp page makes it possible to transform an XML document with an XSLT stylesheet remotely, passing parameters that in turn set each named <xsl:param> in the receiving stylesheets. This provides a fairly simply RPC mechanism for manipulating the slide show from a remote server.

The source file for this transformation is a presentation as expressed in XML. The underlying design or the presentation is extremely simple—at the beginning of the document one of more master slides are defined, which set the characteristics of the background, font colors, and styles. Additionally, each master slide provides a link to a resource file consisting of SVG <defs> definitions for basic resources—bullet elements, for instance. Finally, the slide provides a reference to a CSS document that HTML markup that uses the master slide can apply. This is demonstrated in the sample presentation by two master slides (see Listing 10-14).

Listing 10-14. Two Master Slides

```
<presentation>

    <masterSlide id="metaphoricInterfaces1"
            stylesheet="metaphoricInterfaces.css">
        <masterTitle fill="yellow" font-size="24"
            font-family="Andale Sans">
                Metaphorical Interfaces
        </masterTitle>
            <masterStyle font-family="Centaur" fill="yellow"
                text-anchor="left"/>
            <background type="gradient" mode="linear"
                    foreColor="blue" backColor="black"/>
```

```
        <divider foreColor="yellow" backColor="blue"
                    stroke-width="4"/>
        <library href="metaphoricBullets.xml"/>
    </masterSlide>

    <masterSlide id="XML" stylesheet="metaphoricInterfaces.css">
        <masterTitle fill="white" font-size="24"
                font-family="Centaur">
                XML Display Languages
            </masterTitle>
            <masterStyle font-family="Centaur"
                    fill="yellow" text-anchor="left"/>
            <background type="gradient" mode="radial"
                    foreColor="green" backColor="black"/>
        <divider foreColor="yellow" backColor="maroon" stroke-width="4"/>
        <library href="metaphoricBullets2.xml"/>
    </masterSlide>
```

After the master slides are established, the actual slides of the presentation are given. The first slide in the presentation is actually pretty typical of a slide call:

```
<slide masterSlide="metaphoricInterfaces1" template="showStSlide"
        contentType=" image/svg+xml " effect="fadeIn">
    <prTitle>Metaphoric Interfaces</prTitle>
    <prSubtitle>XML Objects, Architectures and Graphical Interfaces</prSubtitle>
    <prAuthor>Kurt Cagle</prAuthor>
    <prCompany>Cagle Communications</prCompany>
    <prDatePublished>2002-03-10</prDatePublished>
</slide>
```

The `masterSlide` attribute is a reference to the appropriate master slide that the current slide uses (all slides, even ones that have no other content, must have a master slide reference in order to display). The `template` attribute, in turn, is a pointer to an XSL document (the `.xsl` extension is not included in this to emphasize the action of the transformation). Thus, `template="showStSlide"` indicates that the slide uses the XSL file `showStSlide.xsl` to transform the contents into something meaningful.

The `contentType` attribute provides the expected MIME type of the slide's content. This reflects the fact that in some cases the body of the slide will use SVG to display a slide, and in other cases HTML will be used. Thus, by setting `contentType` to `image/svg+xml`, the HTML container document will know to instantiate an SVG object from the XML being produced (this will become clearer when I focus on the actual transformation, by the way).

The final attribute in the slide is optional—an *effect*. Applications such as PowerPoint include all kinds of specialized effects—text flying in or flying out, one action starting another action on a slide, and so forth. Although not trivial to implement, SVG can similarly handle these kinds of effects. A slide by itself can implement a given effect (such as content fading in) and each subelement within the slide can additionally have its own specialized effects. The specific code that handles these effects are contained in the file effects.xsl and will be examined in more detail later in this chapter.

This slide show application is remarkably simple—there are only a few elements explicitly defined, and most of them have fairly obvious meaning: prTitle, prSubtitle, prAuthor, prDatePublished, and so on. Each specific element's implementation and action is defined in the showStSlide.xsl transformation file, which is also used by point-oriented slides (these include the additional elements point, subpoint, and para) as well as image-oriented slides through the <image> element (see Listing 10-15).

Listing 10-15. showStSlide.xsl

```
<slide masterSlide="metaphoricInterfaces1" id="metaphor4"
        template="pointsSlide" contentType=" image/svg+xml ">
    <title>Metaphor and Static User Interface</title>
    <para>The Graphical User Interface is the metaphor that is
            used to provide access to</para>
    <para>system resources. Such interfaces can be classified
            as follows:</para>
    <point>Static Ad-hoc.</point>
    <subpoint>Uses custom, low-level graphics libraries
            to build static GUI. Becoming rare.</subpoint>
    <point>Static Shared Libraries.</point>
    <subpoint>Uses system graphics library primitives to create
            fixed interfaces.</subpoint>
    <subpoint>Windows, KDE, Gnome, Mac OSX.</subpoint>
<!--        <point>Static Declarative Sources.</point>
    <subpoint>Uses unaugmented, statically
            defined HTML for rendering web pages.</subpoint>
    <subpoint>Almost All of the Web</subpoint> -->
    <image href="http://localhost/km/StaticInterfaces.png"
            width="237" height="484" x="700" y="0"/>
</slide>
```

The showStSlide.xsl file is as fairly straightforward as XSLT goes. It imports three external stylesheets—date.xsl, masterSlide.xsl, and effects.xsl—to handle date formatting, background generation, and effects implementation, respectively:

```
<xsl:stylesheet
         xmlns:xsl="http://www.w3.org/1999/XSL/Transform"
         xmlns:xlink=http://www.w3.org/1999/xlink
         version="1.0">
    <xsl:import href="date.xsl"/>
    <xsl:import href="masterSlide.xsl"/>
    <xsl:import href="effects.xsl"/>
    <xsl:output method="xml" media-type=" image/svg+xml "
            omit-xml-declaration="yes" indent="yes"/>
```

At this point, the source and xform parameters are declared, along with the slideNum parameter—these global parameters are used by xserv.asp to parameterize the stylesheet as a whole. Additionally, two global variables are defined: $slide, which retrieves the specific slide entry from the slide number (the position in the slide deck passed by $slideNum), and $masterSlide, which is retrieved from the masterSlide attribute of that same slide:

```
<xsl:param name="source" select="'metaphoricInterfaces'"/>
<xsl:param name="xform" select="showStSlide'"/>
<xsl:param name="slideNum" select="1"/>
<xsl:variable name="slide" select="//slide[position()=$slideNum]"/>
<xsl:variable name="masterSlide"
        select="//masterSlide[@id=$slide/@masterSlide]"/>
```

After these pieces are defined, the stylesheet defines a number of template matches for the primary elements in any given slide and uses that information to generate the appropriate SVG. More specifically, the showStSlide.xsl file starts by creating the background (by matching on the appropriate <masterSlide> element in the presentation) before drawing the more dynamic parts of the slide:

```
<xsl:template match="/">
    <xsl:apply-templates select="presentation"/>
</xsl:template>

<xsl:template match="presentation">
    <svg width="1024" height="720" viewBox="0 0 1024 720"
            preserveAspectRatio="none">
        <xsl:apply-templates select="//masterSlide[@id=$slide/@masterSlide]"/>
        <xsl:apply-templates select="$slide"/>
    </svg>
</xsl:template>
```

The identity template is extremely useful—it basically copies an element to the output stream of the transformation, then reapplies the same transformation to any children that it finds—unless it is overridden by some other, more clearly defined template:

```
<xsl:template match="*|@*|text()">
    <xsl:copy><xsl:apply-templates select="*|@*|text()"/></xsl:copy>
</xsl:template>
```

The rest of the templates catch specific element instances and process them accordingly. For instance, the slide template (xsl:template match="slide") catches the <slide> element, invokes the masterSlide template for the masterSlide that has an id corresponding to the slide's @masterSlide attribute, and then draws the following code:

```
<xsl:template match="slide">
        <xsl:apply-templates select="$masterSlide"/>
        <g><xsl:for-each select="$masterSlide/masterStyle/@*">
                  <xsl:attribute name="{name(.)}">
                          <xsl:value-of select="."/>
                  </xsl:attribute></xsl:for-each>
        <xsl:apply-templates select="@effect"/>
        <xsl:apply-templates select="*"/>
        </g>
</xsl:template>
```

The presentation element handlers are otherwise straightforward, with the possible exception of effects (see Listing 10-16).

Listing 10-16. Presentation Element Handlers

```
<xsl:template match="title">
    <xsl:variable name="x" select="0"/>
    <xsl:variable name="y" select="(count(preceding-sibling::*))* 50"/>
    <a href="">
    <g transform="translate({$x},{$y})" font-size="48">
            <xsl:if test="@id">
                    <xsl:attribute name="id">
                              <xsl:value-of select="@id"/>
                    </xsl:attribute>
            </xsl:if>
            <xsl:apply-templates select="@effect">
                <xsl:with-param name="x" select="$x"/>
                <xsl:with-param name="y" select="$y"/>
```

```
            </xsl:apply-templates>
            <text class="{name(.)}"><xsl:value-of select="."/></text>
    </g>
    </a>
</xsl:template>


<xsl:template match="point">
    <xsl:variable name="x" select="50"/>
    <xsl:variable name="y" select="(count(preceding-sibling::*))* 50"/>
    <a href="">
    <g transform="translate({$x},{$y})"
            font-size="36">
            <xsl:if test="@id">
                    <xsl:attribute name="id">
                            <xsl:value-of select="@id"/>
                    </xsl:attribute>
        </xsl:if>
        <xsl:apply-templates select="@effect">
            <xsl:with-param name="x" select="$x"/>
            <xsl:with-param name="y" select="$y"/>
        </xsl:apply-templates>
        <use xlink:href="#bullet1" x="0" y="0"/>
        <text class="{name(.)}"><xsl:value-of select="."/></text>
    </g>
    </a>
</xsl:template>


<xsl:template match="subpoint">
    <xsl:variable name="x" select="100"/>
    <xsl:variable name="y" select="(count(preceding-sibling::*))* 50"/>
    <a href="">
    <g transform="translate({$x},{$y})" font-size="28">
            <xsl:if test="@id">
                    <xsl:attribute name="id">
                            <xsl:value-of select="@id"/>
                    </xsl:attribute>
        </xsl:if>
        <xsl:apply-templates select="@effect">
            <xsl:with-param name="x" select="$x"/>
            <xsl:with-param name="y" select="$y"/>
        </xsl:apply-templates>
        <use xlink:href="#bullet2" x="0" y="0"/>
        <text class="{name(.)}"><xsl:value-of select="."/></text>
```

```
            </g>
          </a>
    </xsl:template>


<xsl:template match="para">
    <xsl:variable name="x" select="0"/>
    <xsl:variable name="y" select="(count(preceding-sibling::*))* 50"/>
    <a href="">
    <g transform="translate({$x},{$y})" font-size="28">
            <xsl:if test="@id">
                    <xsl:attribute name="id">
                            <xsl:value-of select="@id"/>
                    </xsl:attribute>
                </xsl:if>
        <xsl:apply-templates select="@effect">
            <xsl:with-param name="x" select="$x"/>
            <xsl:with-param name="y" select="$y"/>
        </xsl:apply-templates>
        <text class="{name(.)}"><xsl:value-of select="."/></text>
    </g>
    </a>
</xsl:template>


<xsl:template match="image">
    <xsl:variable name="x">
        <xsl:choose>
            <xsl:when test="@x"><xsl:value-of select="@x"/></xsl:when>
            <xsl:otherwise>0</xsl:otherwise>
        </xsl:choose>
    </xsl:variable>
    <xsl:variable name="y">
        <xsl:choose>
            <xsl:when test="@y"><xsl:value-of select="@y"/></xsl:when>
            <xsl:otherwise>
                    <xsl:value-of select="(count(
                            preceding-sibling::*))* 50"/>
            </xsl:otherwise>
        </xsl:choose>
    </xsl:variable>
    <g transform="translate({$x},{$y})">
            <xsl:if test="@id">
```

```
                    <xsl:attribute name="id">
                           <xsl:value-of select="@id"/>
                    </xsl:attribute>
          </xsl:if>
        <xsl:apply-templates select="@effect">
            <xsl:with-param name="x" select="$x"/>
            <xsl:with-param name="y" select="$y"/>
        </xsl:apply-templates>
        <image xlink:href="{@href}"
                width="{@width}" height="{@height}"
                x="0" y="0"/>
    </g>
</xsl:template>
<xsl:template match="prTitle">
    <g transform="translate(500,100)"
          font-family="Centaur" font-size="64"
          text-anchor="middle"
          dominant-baseline="mathematical">
        <xsl:apply-templates select="@effect"/>
        <text class="{name(.)}"><xsl:value-of select="."/></text>
    </g>
</xsl:template>

<xsl:template match="prSubtitle">
    <g transform="translate(500,300)"
             font-family="Centaur"
             font-size="36" text-anchor="middle"
           dominant-baseline="mathematical">
        <xsl:apply-templates select="@effect"/>
        <text class="{name(.)}"><xsl:value-of select="."/></text>
    </g>
</xsl:template>

<xsl:template match="prAuthor">
    <g transform="translate(500,350)"
             font-family="Centaur"
             font-size="40" text-anchor="middle"
             dominant-baseline="mathematical">
        <xsl:apply-templates select="@effect"/>
        <text class="{name(.)}"><xsl:value-of select="."/></text>
    </g>
</xsl:template>
```

```
<xsl:template match="prCompany">
    <g transform="translate(500,400)"
            font-size="40" font-family="Centaur"
            text-anchor="middle"
            dominant-baseline="mathematical">
        <xsl:apply-templates select="@effect"/>
        <text class="{name(.)}"><xsl:value-of select="."/></text>
    </g>
</xsl:template>

<xsl:template match="prDatePublished">
    <g transform="translate(500,450)"
            font-size="32" font-family="Centaur"
            text-anchor="middle"
            dominant-baseline="mathematical">
        <xsl:apply-templates select="@effect"/>
        <text class="{name(.)}">
            <xsl:call-template name="date.display">
                <xsl:with-param name="date" select="string(.)"/>
                <xsl:with-param name="showTime" select="'no'"/>
            </xsl:call-template>
        </text>
    </g>
</xsl:template>

</xsl:stylesheet>
```

If you do not include a specific template, then the passThrough.xsl transformation is implicitly invoked. This particular stylesheet copies the content of the slide to the resulting output of the transformations directly, making it possible to pass raw SVG directly to the slide show application. Note that the passThrough application creates the background elements, then overlays the foreground elements (in essence everything else) directly into the same SVG. Although it is possible to overlay one SVG document over another in the containing HTML, by incorporating the raw code directly into the background document you can get considerable improvement in efficiency and hence speed.

If the contentType of the slide is image/svg+xml, then the SVG is rendered directly.

```
<slide masterSlide="metaphoricInterfaces1"
        id="whatGood" contentType=" image/svg+xml ">
    <g font-size="48" fill="yellow">
        <g transform="translate(0,100)">
```

```
            <text>
                If you can't see information ...
            </text>
        </g>
        <g transform="translate(100,200)" opacity="0">
            <animate attributeName="opacity"
                    attributeType="CSS" to="1"
                    begin="load + 1s" fill="freeze" dur="3s"/>
            <text>
                ... what good is it?
            </text>
        </g>
    </g>
</slide>
```

In most cases, however, the slides make use of a custom-defined XML language for displaying specific elements such as bullet points, headline titles, paragraphs, and so forth (see Listing 10-17).

Listing 10-17. Custom-Defined XML

```
<slide masterSlide="metaphoricInterfaces1"
        id="metaphor2" template="pointsSlide"
        contentType=" image/svg+xml ">
    <title id="metaphor2_title">Knowledge is More
                    than Words</title>
    <point effect="slideFromRight" id="metaphor2_pt1"
        begin="metaphor2_title.click">
        The Visual Lexicon Is as Rich as the Linguistic</point>
    <point effect="slideFromRight" id="metaphor2_pt2"
        begin="metaphor2_pt1.click">
        Most Applications Provide Visual Interpretations
        of Data</point>
    <point effect="slideFromRight" id="metaphor2_pt3"
        begin="metaphor2_pt2.click">
        XML Vocabularies Can Work Across
        Sensory Modalities</point>
    <point effect="slideFromRight" id="metaphor2_pt4"
        begin="metaphor2_pt3.click">
        We are Entering the Age of
        the New Multimedia</point>
</slide>
<slide masterSlide="metaphoricInterfaces1" id="roleMetaphor"
        template="pointsSlide" contentType=" image/svg+xml ">
```

```
<title id="roleMetaphor_title" dur="2s" effect="fadeIn">
        The Role of Metaphors</title>
<para id="roleMetaphor_para1" dur="4s"
        effect="fadeIn">Semantics deals with "Meaning".</para>
<para/>
<para id="roleMetaphor_para2" dur="3s"
begin="roleMetaphor_para1.click" effect="fadeIn">
Metaphor, on the other hand, deals with the evocation
of meaning.</para>
<para id="roleMetaphor_para3" dur="3s"
        begin="roleMetaphor_para1.click" effect="fadeIn">
        We speak of desktops, files, folders, and
        even trashcans,</para>
<para id="roleMetaphor_para4" dur="3s"
        begin="roleMetaphor_para1.click" effect="fadeIn">
        yet these are metaphors that provide a context for the</para>
<para id="roleMetaphor_para5" dur="3s"
        begin="roleMetaphor_para1.click" effect="fadeIn">
        manipulation of streams of data,
        which are in turn metaphors</para>
<para id="roleMetaphor_para6" dur="3s"
        begin="roleMetaphor_para1.click" effect="fadeIn">
        for positioned fields of magnetic resonance.</para>
<para/>
<para id="roleMetaphor_para7" dur="3s"
        begin="roleMetaphor_para1.click+10s"
        effect="fadeIn">
        Any attempt at creating a semantic web,
        or even a knowledge</para>
<para id="roleMetaphor_para8" dur="3s"
        begin="roleMetaphor_para1.click+10s" effect="fadeIn">
        base, ultimately must reply on metaphor to place ontologies
        in context.</para>
</slide>
```

You can also use HTML within a slide as a whole. In this case, the HTML is rendered over the top of the SVG background elements and should not include <body>, <html>, or <head> elements (as this can create multiple instances of an HTML document at once).

```
<slide masterSlide="XML" id="svgclock" contentType="text/html">
        <h1>Time for SVG</h1>
        <h2>By building components around SVG,
                  you can both get out of the "bounding box"
                   and you can generate elements in real time.</h2>
        <embed src="cclock.svg" width="1000" height="700"
                  style="position:absolute;left:0;top:0;"
                  wmode="transparent" x="200" y="400"/>
    </slide>
</presentation>
```

It is also worth noting the use of the <embed> tag here, placing another SVG document above the first. This may prove problematic in low memory situations, so you should use it sparingly.

Summary

As my development editor can attest, the difficulty in writing this chapter was as much a question of what to leave out as it was what to put in. SVG has a fairly broad domain of usage, and each component I worked on spawned ideas for two to three more. As I continue in my own SVG exploration, I will be placing them up on the Apress site at (www.apress.com) as well as on my own Web site, The Metaphorical Web, at www.kurtcagle.net. These will not include more complete examples of the code contained herein but additional widgets, extensions, and applications built around SVG itself.

SVG is an evolving language, and like any 1.0 technology you can point to other features in the language that could definitely use some work. In the next chapter, I would like to give an overview of both the near-term prospects for the language itself and the prospects for the language in the more distant future as it becomes an integral part of the XML technologies library.

CHAPTER 11

The Future of SVG

As I write this, Scalable Vector Graphics (SVG) is at the *pre-buzz* stage, though not by much. A lot of companies are playing with SVG along the periphery, not as something central to their core products yet, but adding it in as an easy-to-create format for reading or writing graphics.

Books such as this one are being written about it. As a writer who has authored or coauthored more than a dozen books, this is significant not so much because of the capabilities of the books but because SVG is not some company's software release.

Here is a little secret about professional computer book writing: When you are developing a book, you look at the market and see what products are currently in alpha production (that is, they are not even widely available to testers). Microsoft tools and products in general are safe bets; database upgrades are usually pretty good as well. Web CGI books (Perl, ASP, and so on) used to be pretty good prospects, and at the moment there is something of a glut of Web services and security books, the one because of the current battle between Microsoft and the Java camp as to whether .NET or Java 2 Enterprise Edition (J2EE) will survive, the other because of the sorrowful events of Sept. 11, 2001, among other things.

However, there is also the gamble book. Back in 1997, Extensible Markup Language (XML) was a gamble bet, an obscure technology that had no real support to it yet, required the adoption of technology that did not really exist yet, and seemed to be something similar to what already existed. Moreover, it was only an open standard: No one was going to get rich off of XML because it was not somebody's shrink-wrapped product or hot dot-com service, right?

XML had the same kind of pre-buzz, though, that I hear about SVG now, a pre-buzz that was authentic because somebody's marketing division was not pushing it. Instead, it was coming out of the comments of programmers who were beginning to see it for what it was—a powerful new way to represent structured and semistructured data. The gurus who emerged were not from a single company but seemed to be across the board—individual developers, content managers, people with cool ideas and smart startups. The message was pretty universal: "Look at the cool stuff that you can do with this!"

Fast-forward half a decade to 2002. SVG has been a sleeper technology—an interesting idea that has largely gotten lost in the soup of World Wide Web Consortium (W3C) standards. Technologies such as Flash and PostScript completely overshadow it. Although a few companies such as Adobe have been developing a potent SVG processor, the majority of companies working with SVG are either small startups that see a niche in an admittedly full graphical market or they are companies adding SVG support into their existing graphical or presentation products.

Given that, SVG might not seem to have that much of a future, except perhaps peripherally. However, this view can be a little deceiving. The behavior of SVG is a lot like the behavior of XML before it in that it is being used in any number of different programs for any number of different applications. Need a portable way of passing vector graphics on the Web? There are SVG viewers (mainly static right now, but that is changing) for nearly every computer and operating system. Want to do a slider bar that can scale easily? You have your choice of a specialized COM component or a bit of SVG code. Want to make a more dynamic Web page . . . hmm . . . there is Flash or SVG. How about a system for creating dynamic charts and graphs? Well, you can write a complicated application that forces you into working with a distinct format, or you can go wild with an XML stylesheet transform to produce an SVG document (and even make that document linkable).

This versatility is a hallmark of XML in general, but simply because a language is built using SVG does not guarantee that it will explode into popularity (though it is a pretty good predictor). The Wireless Markup Language (WML) is based in XML, but it has gained only moderate and diminishing mind share for a number of reasons:

- Too few vendors adopted WML into their products according to the specification (making for incompatibility early on between different WML consumers).

- WML offered relatively limited functionality.

- WML's reason for existence—to provide Hypertext Markup Language (HTML)–like functionality on low bandwidth and memory devices—has been rendered obsolete as more horsepower in phones and other devices made it easier to just put an HTML renderer on the system.

SVG, on the other hand, has only one of these three limitations, in a controlled sense. SVG 1.1 (to be discussed next) recognizes that different devices may only be able to support certain types of operation. Consequently, when working with SVG 1.1, there may be specific parts that will or will not work; however, by being cognizant of which namespace is being used, any applications that work with such SVG should be aware of those limitations ahead of time.

SVG on the Road: SVG 1.0 Tiny, Basic, and Full

There is a tendency, from people who first encounter SVG, to see it as strictly a fat technology that is useful for some kinds of graphics and maybe Flash-like multimedia, and nothing else. However, there is another arena where SVG may well be instrumental in leading a revolution in the way that applications are made. If you take a look at the mobile market—Personal Digital Assistants (PDAs), handhelds, digital cell phones, and embedded system viewers within automobiles or other similar venues—you are seeing the place where, in all likelihood, SVG will become the dominant means of display within the next decade.

Currently, most mobile devices use many of the same principles that desktop systems have in terms of interface design—a framework of widgets (buttons, list controls, text areas, and so forth) provides the interfaces that all applications on these devices utilize. One limitation that such applications face, however, is that in a resource-tight arena, the storage of bitmap graphics is limited.

On the other hand, if such a device included both an SVG rendering engine and a wireless connection, then it would be capable of creating considerably more sophisticated interfaces that could be loaded off the air, changed at a moment's notice, and occupy no more space than the SVG component and a few text files.

Indeed, it is easy to identify a number of mobile applications where SVG would be an ideal fit:

- Generation of maps at arbitrary scales and levels of detail, possibly coupled with geo-positioning systems

- Creation of button bars, sliders, buttons, icons, and other standard interface graphics

- Games (of course, if you are the parent of a nine year old, this means you will lose your cell phone, PDA, and so on shortly thereafter)

- Alternative desktop interfaces

- Charts, gauges, diagnostic diagrams, and system monitoring applications

Think, for instance, of a wireless tablet for use in a refinery that would show the current state of various chemical operations or the dashboard of a car that could show speedometer/tachometer information but could be switched over to a map view, diagnostic schematic, or traffic flow view.

Although processing power continues to improve in such embedded devices, these devices will almost certainly be underpowered compared to even today's desktop for some time to come. To make SVG attractive to developers and mobile device vendors, the W3C has proposed a separate Mobile SVG.

Mobile SVG works upon a premise that has become increasingly common within the various W3C display standards—the idea of creating a modular version of each language that can then be mixed and matched to define specialized namespaces. Because the functionality in the each module remains well defined, you avoid at least some of the tag-adding feature creep that so much characterized HTML when it was first evolving (the XHTML specification is being similarly modularized).

The SVG Basic and SVG Tiny models target different classes of mobile devices but are both instances of the SVG 1.1 specification, currently (as of May 2002) in development as a working draft. SVG 1.1 contains a few new elements that will likely simplify development, but perhaps more significantly, SVG 1.1 also implements a modularization scheme to make it easier to create both lighter and heavier versions of XML-oriented display languages without spawning completely different languages.

The SVG 1.1 specification defines a number of difference modules, supported at varying levels with the Tiny and Basic models of SVG (see Table 11-1). In Table 11-1, check marks ($\sqrt{}$) indicate that a module definition exists for that model, an asterisk (*) indicates that the module inherits from the Full model, and a dash (–) indicates that the model does not support the module.

Table 11-1. SVG 1.1 Modules

MODULES	FULL	BASIC	TINY	DESCRIPTION
Core Attributes	√	*	*	Defines the standard attributes id, xml:base, xml:lang, xml:space.
Structure	√	*	√	Defines the ‹svg›, ‹g›, ‹defs›, ‹desc›, ‹title›, ‹metadata›, ‹symbol›, and ‹use› elements. Tiny does not define the ‹symbol› element.
Container Attributes	√	–	–	Defines the enable-background attribute.
Viewport Attributes	√	*	–	Defines the clip and overflow attributes.
Style	√	*	*	Defines CSS class and style attributes.
Paint Attributes	√	*	√	Defines the fill, fill-opacity, fill-rule, stroke, stroke-dasharray, stroke-dashoffset, stroke-linecap, stroke-linejoin, stroke-miterlimit, stroke-opacity, and stroke-width attributes. Tiny does not define fill-opacity or stroke-opacity attributes.
Opacity	√	*	–	Defines the opacity attribute.
Hyperlinking	√	*	*	Defines the hyperlinking ‹a› element.
XLink	√	*	*	Defines the xlink:type, xlink:role, xlink:arcrole, xlink:title, xlink:show, and xlink:actuate-opacity attributes.
External Resources	√	*	*	Defines the externalResourcesRequired attribute.
Conditional Processing	√	*	*	Defines the ‹switch› element.
Shape	√	*	*	Defines the ‹path›, ‹rect›, ‹circle›, ‹line›, ‹ellipse›, ‹polyline›, and ‹polygon› elements.
Image	√	*	*	Defines the ‹image› element.
Text	√	√	√	Defines the ‹text›, ‹tspan›, ‹tref›, ‹textPath›, ‹altGlyph›, ‹altGlyphDef›, ‹altGlyphItems›, and ‹glyphRef› elements. Basic does include the ‹gly› attributes, and Tiny only defines the ‹text› element.

(continued)

Table 11-1. SVG 1.1 Modules (continued)

MODULES	FULL	BASIC	TINY	DESCRIPTION
Text Wrapping (proposed)	√	*	–	Defines the `<tBlock>`, `<region>`, `<regionRef>`, `<flow>`, `<p>`, `<span>`, and ` ` elements.
Text Presentation Attributes	√	*	–	Defines the `writing-mode` attribute.
Text Content Presentation Attributes	√	*	–	Defines the `alignment-baseline`, `baseline-shift`, `direction`, `dominant-baseline`, `glyph-orientation-horizontal`, `glyph-orientation-vertical`, `kerning`, `letter-spacing`, `text-anchor`, `text-decoration`, `unicode-bidi`, and `word-spacing` attributes.
Font Presentation Attributes	√	*	√	Defines the `font-family`, `font-size`, `font-size-adjust`, `font-stretch`, `font-style`, `font-variant`, and `font-weight` attributes. Tiny only defines the `font-family`, `font-size`, `font-style`, and `font-weight` attributes.
SolidColor (proposed)	√	*	√	Defines the `<solidColor>` element.
Color Attributes	√	*	√	Defines the `color`, `color-interpolation`, and `color-rendering` attributes. Tiny only defines the `color` attribute.
Gradient	√	*	–	Defines the `<linearGradient>`, `<radialGradient>`, and `<stop>` elements.
Patterns	√	*	–	Defines the `<pattern>` element.
Fonts	√	*	√	Defines the `<font>`, `<font-face>`, `<glyph>`, `<missing-glyph>`, `<hkern>`, `<vkern>`, `<font-face-src>`, `<font-face-uri>`, `<font-face-format>`, `<font-face-name>`, and `<definition-src>` elements. Tiny does not define the `<font-face-uri>` and `<font-face-format>` elements.
Clip Path	√	√	–	Defines the `<clipPath>` element and the `clip-path` and `clip-rule` attributes. (Basic has a slightly different content model.)
Masking	√	*	–	Defines the `<mask>` element.
Marker	√	–	–	Defines the `<marker>` element.

(continued)

Table 11-1. SVG 1.1 Modules (continued)

MODULES	FULL	BASIC	TINY	DESCRIPTION
Document Events Attributes	√	*	*	Defines the onunload, onabort, onerror, onresize, onscroll, and onzoom attributes.
Graphical Element Events Attributes	√	*	*	Defines the onfocusin, onfocusout, onactivate, onclick, onmousedown, onmouseup, onmouseover, onmousemove, onmouseout, and onload attributes.
Animation Events Attributes	√	*	*	Defines the onbegin, onend, and onrepeat attributes.
Scripting	√	*	*	Defines the <script> element and scripting support.
Cursor	√	*	–	Defines the <cursor> element.
View	√	*	*	Defines the <view> element.
Filter	√	√	–	Defines the <filter>, <feBlend>, <feFlood>, <feColorMatrix>, <feComponentTransfer>, <feComposite>, <feConvolveMatrix>, <feDiffuseLighting>, <feDisplacementMap>, <feGaussianBlur>, <feImage>, <feMerge>, <feMorphology>, <feOffset>, <feSpecularLighting>, <feTile>, and <feTurbulence> elements. Basic only defines <feBlend>, <feFlood>, <feColorMatrix>, <feComponentTransfer>, <feComposite>, <feGaussianBlur>, <feImage>, <feMerge>, <feOffset>, and <feTile> elements.
Animation	√	*	*	Defines the <set>, <animate>, <animateColor>, <animateMotion> and <animateTransform> elements.
Extensibility	√	*	*	Defines the <foreignObject> element.

Table 11-1 does give a flavor of the primary differences between the three models. The Tiny model does not support opacity, patterns, gradients, clipping or masking, complex text blocks or custom fonts, or modifying the cursor and filters. None of this is all that surprising; many of these have an explicit or implicit dependency on alpha channel access, which is not typically supported on embedded system architectures. Similarly, the ability to define fonts or modify the cursor is limited in these systems, so not being able to work with complex font capabilities should be expected.

What is perhaps more intriguing is to look at what *is* supported. Even Tiny SVG assumes that animation, scripting, and extensibility is present—which means that any PDA supports the bare prerequisite to create interactive applications with SVG and work with external resources. It is worth thinking about what that implies. SVG accommodates a minimal footprint system reasonably well, and as long as you do not get too fancy—animated opaque operations, for instance—the same SVG you produce for a 2GHz desktop computer or kiosk can be ported to a PDA with relatively little effort—perhaps just running it through an XSLT script that maps certain effects such as patterns and gradients to something a little safer.

Adding Text Blocks

SVG is not perfect. There is one area that can induce hair pulling very quickly— the fact that you are required to handle the exact positioning of every element of text on the screen. Personally, this is one of the big areas that will keep people from adopting SVG in the short term, until a solution to this problem becomes widely available.

The SVG 1.1 specification recognizes this and proposes a reasonable solution—the creation of the <tBlock> element and its associated subelements. The purpose of <tBlock> is simple: to provide the same features that most other contemporary drawing programs do with text by creating a realistic flow mode solution for it. The specification itself gives one example of how such an element would look (see Listing 11-1).

Listing 11-1. How <tBlock> Would Work

```
<tBlock>
    <!-- You can specify regions inline via <region>
         or reference via <regionRef>.
         By default, display="none" on <region> and <regionRef>,
         but if you say display="inline" the contents will render. Only
         <rect> supported in 1.1. -->
    <region>
      <rect id="foo" x="100" y="100" width="200" height="150"/>
    </region>
```

```
<regionRef xlink:href="#Rect001"/>

<flow>
  <p>
    My initial paragraph has a
    <span fill="red">RED</span>
    word, and has these other words, also.
  </p>

  <!-- Note the <br/> element below -->
  <p>
    <span>Second<br/>paragraph.</span>
  </p>
</flow>
</tBlock>
```

This provides a model that is in fact similar to the XSL-Formatting Objects (XML-FO) model (not accidentally because Adobe has been the primary backer of both of those specifications). Within a `<tBlock>` element, a specific region is specified via the `<region>` or `<regionRef>` elements (or both). Presumably, if more than one region is defined, the flow model will fill up the first element and then flow into the second, though this is not clear from the specification.

The `<flow>` element actually contains the material to flow into the regions, using a paragraph and span model—the `<p>` element acting like an HTML `<div>` element as a local block container, and the `<span>` element acts as it does in HTML, wrapping inline content. It is likely that these elements would also support Cascading Style Sheets (CSS) class and style attributes.

The SVG 1.1 specification starts pretty modestly, assuming that the regions to be filled with text will be purely rectangular. It is not too much of a stretch to see in SVG 2.0, however, a move to where text can be flowed into any container.

I cannot stress the importance of such a flow model enough. SVG is a graphical language, but the number of instances where there is purely graphical content without some complex block of text being contained with it. With flowed text, SVG may even begin to displace HTML as the presentation language of choice over the Web.

NOTE   *The use and syntax of the `<tBlock>` element is still being worked out, so the final form may differ somewhat from that shown in this chapter. Additionally, the Adobe SVG Viewer does not currently support it.*

Moving Toward SVG 2.0

For the most part, with the real exception of the `<tBlock>` element and the `<solidColor>` element (which lets you define a single color by a specified name, rather than having to use the kludge of a gradient with identical start and end color stops as shown in Chapter 7, "Incorporating Texture"), the primary changes in SVG 1.1 are primarily structural—in other words, moving to a modular basis.

However, the wish list for SVG 2.0 shows that the SVG committee is thinking more long term about the language. There are a number of features that will improve the language in little ways, and a few that may even have a major impact, covered in the next sections.

Gradients

Currently, the way that gradient elements are defined lets you work with only two gradient forms: linear and radial. However, suggestions are currently on the table to work with gradients that follow more complex forms, such as a gradient that flowed along the contours of an irregular shape such as text. Gradients are powerful tools for building more realistic effects, and shaped gradients will definitely enhance the power of the language for developing 2.5-dimensional images (images that appear three dimensional because of layering).

Non-Affine Transformations

The SVG 1.0 specification only provides for working with *affine* transformations—transformations where all parts of the coordinate system transform in exactly the same way. Such transformations are relatively easy to compute because they can be done using relatively simple matrix mathematics.

Non-affine transformations cover every other kind of transformation and are considerably more difficult to implement. In general, non-affine transformations cover a number of different mappings: one-, two-, or three-point perspective mappings used to project three-dimensional images on a two-dimensional screen, displacement mappings where the degree of distortion for a shape is a function of a grayscale image, rectangular to polar mappings where the distance to a given line is collapsed to the distance to a given point (resulting in images that can only be viewed with a cylindrical mirror), and so forth.

Nonetheless, non-affine transformations are an integral part of most painting program toolkits, and some effects (such as three-dimensional text) can only really be accomplished with such transformations. Currently the SVG committee is exploring ways of making it possible to define such transformations easily, and it is likely that the ability to create both canned and custom transformations will be added to the language within the next year or so.

Form Elements

I remember what the Web looked like in 1993. It was, at the time, very much a read-only medium. It was not until the first graphical browsers came out did the need for CGI really become evident. Further, it was not until then that forms became a standard part of the HTML language. Since then, forms have been the differentiating factor that has kept the Web from devolving solely into a display medium, and instead turned it into a vehicle for communication: chatting, blogs, newsgroups, message board commentary, e-commerce, and so on.

Although it is possible to create forms in SVG, it is far from easy. Typically it entails a rather incredible amount of pain to create something as simple as a one line textbox (do not even think about a multiline textbox). There are currently some solutions to this: using an embedded transparent SVG beneath (or above, as the case may be) an HTML form or vice versa trying to put HTML within an SVG document's `<foreignObject>` tag, but these ad-hoc solutions are highly dependent upon the browser.

NOTE *The* `<foreignObject>` *element is one I have deliberately not covered in this book, principally because it is not supported by the Adobe SVG Viewer and because it has the potential to force SVG viewer developers into building entire Web browsers into their tools, a complicated process at best.*

Form elements will almost certainly be a part of SVG 2.0. Such elements will likely be form primitives: interactive text regions, for instance, that you would still need to wrap in a rectangular box or element. This would also include working with primitives such as list boxes (again, things you *can* do in SVG 1.0, but should not) as well as providing an easy mechanism to wrap a number of elements into a single form container that can, as with HTML, then send all of the identified elements as POST data. It should be noted that SVG would most likely inherit the XForm namespace in much the same way that it has inherited XLink or Synchronized Multimedia Integration Language (SMIL) rather than defining its own unique form set.

A number of interesting initiatives are currently underway that could shape the way such components are defined. The W3C is currently working on the XML Forms interface, which makes it possible to both define collections of interactive forms and specify the characteristics of input elements within that form.

Similarly, the OASIS organization, which sets XML technical standards for the business community and organizations such as the United Nations and the European Community, currently includes a working group for defining Web Services User Interfaces, including form content.

As with adequate text flowing, forms in SVG will go a long way in establishing SVG as a viable contender for Web interfaces, and the W3C SVG working group is seriously evaluating the various form and interface proposals to see which would be best to adapt.

Imagining the Future

It is 2012. The Web is 20 years old (with the broader Internet now closer to half a century old). In some respects the world does not look all that radically different than it did at the turn of the century—cars still race along highways, though about half of them employ fuel-cell electrical motors rather than gasoline engines, and perhaps 80 percent are now fully wired into the mobile grid.

Climbing into a 2012 Nissan Virtua or Saturn LSX Evader could prove to be a little disconcerting, though, for those of you without the 10 intervening years of experience. For instance, the small steering wheel seems to be float, only barely attached to the long, dark dashboard, rather than being attached to a steering column. The steering wheel is, in fact, a glorified joystick—and you can replace it with everything from a haptic glove (in other words, one that permits a sense of feel by pressure sensors) to an XBox control pad that works wirelessly (or the gyroscopic "magic wand" that your hacker daughter adapted from her game, as you discovered—nearly disastrously—the last time you rode with her). There are no stereos, no CD or cassette players—just two longish dark curved "screens" in front of both the driver and passenger seat.

The moment you sit down, a small keypad appears to the lower-right side of that screen, and you have to enter your Personal Identification Number (PIN) to actually get the car to recognize you. Your spouse has a different one, of course, and you assigned two to your older and younger daughters, with only the older one actually able to drive (at 12, the younger one insists she can, but you know better . . . you think).

As you type in the last number, the pad melts away and the rest of the dashboard comes alive. A full complement of dials and gauges show up, a view that does not seem much different from cars of a decade ago. However, when you click one of a couple of buttons that float just above these, the dials are replaced with numerical indicators instead. Click again and these are in turn replaced with pictures of a traffic cop and a mechanic, their faces and postures indicative of whether you are going to fast or pushing the car too hard. Holding the buttons down give you several dozen themes that you can choose from, most of them downloading as packages during the night to the onboard system.

You go back to the "traditional" controls, which then shrink and relocate to one side of the screen—still active, but deliberately staying muted so that you can concentrate on the task of driving. A diagnostic icon also flashes briefly. Brushing it, you see a schematic of the car's fuel cell system, with a yellow glow surrounding one cell that needs to have a new methane cartridge added to it within a few weeks. Switching to the structural diagnostics, you can see that the struts are beginning to exhibit signs of fatigue—given the state of the roads, that is unfortunately not surprising, but worrisome—you suspect it may be time to call the mechanic and have them looked at, as painful as it is going to be financially. The one saving grace is that you can be certain going in that this is the problem, not something completely unrelated for which they would no doubt charge much more.

You bring up the mechanic's public schedule and note that there is a time available a week from Thursday at 9 a.m. Not ideal, but workable, so you place a bid for that time slot. A few seconds later, the cartoon graphic of a mechanic pops up, telling you that time is available, with a preliminary quote and an additional offer that she would be willing to trade labor costs for some interface development work. You have made the trade before (indeed, probably about 70 percent of your compensation is in traded labor or services) and you know she has a high trust rating, so you agree. The cartoon agent winks at you and then fades away, leaving you back at the default screen.

You have a visit to another client; you do not do as many on-site trips as you used to a decade ago, but this is a long-time customer of yours who has done you some very good turns in the past. You say the name of the office, and immediately, a map pops up showing the possible routes. The map also provides traffic conditions along the way and notes that with projected congestion by the time you reach about halfway to the office, you may end up sitting in traffic for a while. An alternative route may prove better, and as you watch numerous agents flitting across the metropolitan grids constantly negotiate the best routes for all drivers that use the grid (about 80 percent at last count), with likely probabilities showing up as colors on the map. The system did not always work—the term *chaos jam* has been showing up more and more often as the complex grid develops emergent singularities as too much foreknowledge negatively influence the mix, but usually it is better than having no system at all.

As you engage the transmission, four video images appear: the view from in front (unimpeded by the hood), from each side, and from the rear, along with a schematic showing any obstacles. Four small radar guns located at cardinal points on the car actually create a three-dimensional rendering of the immediate world around you, combining it with cameras to give you both a real and a virtual image of any potential obstacles. The same system also controls the braking system; if you are approaching an obstacle too quickly, the brakes will automatically begin to slow the car down, then hand control back off to you. It is not true autodriving, where you can just get in the car, tell it where to go, and kick back—chaos again keeps rearing its ugly head to make that unworkable anywhere except perhaps along the larger highways. But it is enough of an improvement that the auto insurance industry basically subsidized the development of it, as it cut insurance claims by an order of magnitude.

Once you are on the road, you reach over and touch the entertainment icon, which gives you the option of listening to new (or favorite) music, the news, or your e-mail. Everyone else had a video option, but a spate of accidents in 2008 and 2009 quickly ended driver-side video, save for monitoring road conditions. If you select the music option, you can quickly choose graphically the characteristics you like in your music: genre; male, female, or group vocalists or instrumentals; preferences for different tempos and speeds; and you can even map it to your general mood.

Your car system regularly communicates with your studio, monitoring new mail as it comes in. A message from your client tells you there are a few elements that he wants you to think about if you can—the graphics are given only in the sketchiest level of detail to keep you from being too distracted while driving— and by the time you pull up to the office (a coffee shop on the west side), you have already begun planning how to incorporate the changes he requested into your presentation.

Everything that appears within the "dashboard" will likely end up being generated in real-time using a future version of SVG; indeed, most of it can be done with the existing specification. The display graphics and maps, for instance, are in fact easily modeled within SVG, and the fact that you can both pan graphics and prepare off-screen "buffers" can make such maps appear to have potentially infinite extents. Sensors currently can be written using SVG with JavaScript or by periodic updates of SVG via XSLT. The video is not a part of the existing specification, but the abstractions from video to schematic representation of that video certainly could be done using filters.

Moreover, other aspects of the dashboard, such as the connectivity to tomorrow's Web, would be accomplished through Web services that could be easily integrated into SVG documents, making for an interesting possibility. The dynamic representation of graphics combined with connectivity and intelligence make for interfaces that can change in response to completely novel conditions.

Looking under the Hood

Playing prognosticator is always fun, and most predictions should be taken for what they are—musings based upon changes in both technology and society that have not happened yet. The real purpose of the preceding exercise, however, was to look at how SVG will likely fit into the larger XML world schema that is beginning to emerge.

Organic Displays

Some of the most significant developments occurring in the technology field at the moment are not in fact in software; they are in hardware. Perhaps one of the most important is the emergence of a whole class of organic, rather than silicon-based, display systems.

The cost of producing a typical laptop screen today is fairly prohibitive, running to approximately 60 percent of the cost of the rest of the system. The primary reason for this cost is that the fabrication of liquid crystal displays that form the basis of such displays is expensive, especially for the blue end of the spectrum. Moreover, such systems draw an incredible amount of power because they need to be continuously refreshed.

However, a class of organic compounds has recently been developed (within the last two years) that can produce high-contrast displays that consume significantly less energy, retain information longer, and do not run into the same problems with regard to the blue colors. Perhaps more important, although the current costs of development are somewhat higher than for equivalent liquid crystal displays, the projected costs once these move into full production will be considerably less than they are today.

What this equates to is the increasing appearance of low-power, low-cost, and potentially shapeable displays that can be embedded into all sorts of different devices, from watches to car dashboards. However, one common denominator that all of these devices will have is that they will likely force designers to rethink the notion of what exactly a display means, and a dynamic display language such as SVG becomes increasingly viable as a way of quickly loading extremely complex graphics (and ultimately other multimedia) into such displays.

Asynchronous Message Systems

The second area where hardware is shifting the way that we work with interfaces (and with programming in general) comes in the twin concepts of wireless technology and synchronization. The grid—the perfect totally connected state where all items are perpetually in contact with the information network—will be a pipe dream for perhaps decades. In the real world, coverage is never perfect, which is one of the reasons why the notion of synchronous Web services will not work for the exploding numbers of mobile embedded systems. Instead, the dominant mode of mobile communication will be asynchronous—messaging systems—rather than synchronous for the foreseeable future.

E-mail is an asynchronous system that currently works over a number of different protocols, with the Simple Mail Transport Protocol (SMTP) being the most widely used. However, as XML-based systems become more commonly integrated, an increasingly percentage of e-mail will be handled via SOAP-based content. SOAP is a protocol system that transports XML content. Much of the current hype about SOAP actually focuses on the content itself being a mechanism for handling Remote Procedure Calls (something that especially infuses .NET), yet such RPC systems actually make up a fairly small part of the potential for SOAP-based communication. By 2006, it is likely that SOAP-based e-mail will dominate the messaging traffic, and SMTP will end up going the way of such venerable protocols as Archie and Gopher.

One of the characteristics that permeate messaging protocols is that they can be easily duplicated. If you take a look at the way that current software systems (especially the commercial ones) are oriented, they implement what I refer to as the *Library Model of Concurrency*. Collaboration is done as if a document exists in singularity, and in order to work with that document, you "check it out" from the system. Others can read it, but they cannot modify it.

However, if you take a look at real-world collaboration, documents often evolve through duplication and redundancy, with two or more collaborators creating an idea that gets spread out to multiple users, each of whom in turn make modifications (or additions). The whole then ends up being brought together by the agency of a designated editor.

The interesting implication of this has to do with the fact that most important standards emerge through just such a collaborative process. Beyond simply serving as a data transport mechanism, XML is a powerful tool for creating a formal codification of a standard into something programmable. As more and more code migrates from binary business logic to XML, this means that code development will likely shift into a more collaborative basis (which is in essence exactly what is happening with the open-source software movement).

Asynchronous messaging can work in one of two different ways. With schema-based programming, when a message comes in, the schema of that message's content along with a modality of operation (a method call, if you will), will help the system to process that message—with such processing potentially spawning additional messages that will be sent to other devices such as databases, other e-mail recipients, or other process initiators. The other way that such messaging works is through a process queue, where the modality of operation is determined by where the data is located—when you send an XML object to a given URL, that URL defines the operation to be done. Thus, in one case, the message contains its own processing instruction, and in the other, the location where the message is sent determines the operation to be done.

Back to the future: The car represents a good example of a truly mobile system. When it is parked at the house, the car's wireless Network Interface Card (NIC) was busily communicating with the house's much more powerful system, doing a number of tasks. High-level communication, the e-mails that the future you would receive along with the music and news information was being dumped into the car's memory all night. Prior to that dump, however, the car would synchronize with the house any relevant changes to profile information about the driver that was made while the car was not in direct communication.

This in turn makes it possible to filter out irrelevant news or entertainment content, probably through a stochastic process; news about a local dog show would probably not be of interest to the future you unless you own a dog (or had recently done research about dogs).

TIP *One of the principal goals of defining an interface is not to provide the user all the* relevant *information about the system, but instead to establish an effective mechanism for minimizing the* irrelevant *information in that same system.*

The information coming in will likely not be in any one standard format (save that it will almost certainly be in the 2012 version of XML). Instead, news stories will differ from editorials will differ from science fiction will differ from descriptive meta-data about video or audio streams will differ from advertisements. This is not a fault in XML, by the way; it is a fundamental characteristic of knowledge—the substrate, or language, of that knowledge changes based upon the requirements for that information. One consequence of this fact, however, is that a given system will need to have at least one, and potentially several, processors of that knowledge.

Contemporary programming works upon the principle that the type of objects within a system are known at runtime, and programming can consequently be done using an existing set of local processors. However, distributed applications (which are a natural consequence of asynchronous messaging architectures) often run afoul of this type of thinking because the number of types of objects coming in may be far larger than the available local library of processors. Essentially, programming at that point becomes combinatoric, the number of processors expanding roughly as the factorial of the number of objects (to within a few orders of magnitude).

One upshot of this is that the data moving through the system will need to identify, somewhere on the network, the information to process it, to cache it as usage dictates, and then purge less used information once system resources become too highly taxed. The processing information in turn must be lightweight and transparent to operating environment, development language, and hardware restraints, and it must be able to exist in an environment of incomplete information.

No languages today readily encompass all of these features, but the ones that come closest may not be the ones that people think of immediately—scripting languages such as JavaScript and declarative languages such as XSLT.

The Efficiency/Flexibility/Security Triad

One of the more peculiar facets of programming is the existence of *triads*, sets of three qualities of which only two can be optimized at any given time. Perhaps the most well known of these triads is the production triad—given the qualities of functionality, speed of development, and cost, it is nearly impossible to consistently optimize all three of these simultaneously.

A second triad that is perhaps less well known is nonetheless one that has driven software development for the better part of half a century—the triad of efficiency, flexibility, and security. You can increase the efficiency of a process by making it less flexible, holding security constant, or you can optimize for security and flexibility but at extreme cost to efficiency.

Until recently, efficiency ruled supreme. Parsers and compilers were optimized for producing the most efficient code possible, though even there it has only been within the last few years that a knowledgeable coder could not come in to tweak the performance to eke out that extra half of 1 percent improvement in speed. This was a necessity—the slow speed of computers and the amount of power that they have warranted it.

However, something happened just a couple of years ago that is beginning to change the balance, to a point where coding for efficiency may in fact be inefficient in the long run. The first desktop computer that I ever used had 4KB of memory, could store another 16KB (slooowwwlyy) on a cassette player tape and operated at a speed of roughly 2KHz—2000 operations a second, or thereabouts. This was back in 1975. A computer I purchased a few months ago had a 2.1GHz processor, with 3GHz of RAM and 240GB of hard drive space, for roughly the same amount of money.

In other words, my new computer system is by all metrics about a million times as powerful as my first system. It is so fast that applications have to clock back user interface interactions because they become too fast for human beings. (Think about the difficulty of selecting a large block of text in a typical word processing programming, and you get some idea about what I am talking about.) One consequence of this is that there are fewer applications that can really take advantage of that kind of processing power—3D graphics, complex sound processing, and data mining operations. Start throwing a few of these processors together (say 40 or 50), and you begin to get clustered computer systems that do little things such as create weather simulations or model nuclear explosions. It is something of a trip using something like this to balance my checkbook.

For all of that, the rush toward extreme efficiency has come at the cost of both security and flexibility. Security is partially a matter of good design, employing a model where access to data is controlled at a fine level of granularity. A secure system, however, is typically not an efficient system because at every stage in the process of setting up security (and security is a process, not simply a thing) there is some overhead that is imposed on operations. The current object-oriented model is particularly weak when it comes to issues of security because security adds complexity to every single class and component in a given appli-cation.

Flexible systems have likewise been overlooked in favor of the most efficient solutions. Statically typed systems—such as C++, Java, and C#—are more efficient in terms of their system resource use and performance than dynamically typed languages such as Perl, Python, JavaScript, or the whole rest of the class of scripting languages. Procedural languages are similarly more efficient than declarative languages such as LISP, Scheme, Haskell, and (yes) XSLT, which work in part by dealing with environments where knowledge of a system may be incomplete.

Yet as faster and more powerful computers become commonplace, it is very likely that you will begin to see both of these alternative types of languages become commonly used and ultimately dominant. Why? In general, dynamically typed languages trade efficiency for flexibility. This is not necessarily an ease of use issue, but rather the recognition that we are moving into programming models where you cannot rely on all components having the necessary foundation classes (or more accurately the necessary versions of those foundation classes). Instead, each node in an application network needs to be able to work with as little information as absolutely necessary, but with the ability to increase or decrease its ability to process that information on the fly. Such nodes contain very little *stateful* information because that information is basically carried by the messages coming to or leaving each node.

This is in fact the model that the Web itself initially employed, although a decade of vendors' attentions at making the Web more "efficient" has weakened this initial stateless characteristic considerably. It has meant that in many cases scaling has typically involved throwing more powerful processors at the problem rather than employing an architecture that more effectively distributes resource access. Systems such as Usenet are perhaps a better model of how such a system would have evolved in the absence of the intense commercial pressures and move toward "efficient" consolidation, though this is changing as well.

It is worth noting that XML is not efficient. It distributes resources across high-latency lines. The definition of an XML file requires parsing as well. Additionally, without the presence of other documents—schemas, RDF descriptions, transformations, and so on—XML has no real intrinsic meaning. It is text. Security is not built in, and it is an absolutely abysmal format for storing large amounts of data in. The language to do the transformations on XML, XSLT, is similarly interpreted on an as-needed basis.

The same, of course, can be said for SVG. An SVG-based system is, comparatively speaking, a resource hog. An environment has to be instantiated for it that supports scripting and the definitions of a large number of primitives, and the system does not know ahead of time what will be expected of it, so few optimizations can be made. Designing an interface around it would seem foolhardy because it makes a lot more sense to build a static interface and be done with it.

However, the argument about efficiency misses the whole point about XML, XSLT, and SVG, and in a way it misses the point about the evolution of programming over the next 10 years. What is inefficient for a single processor (that is effectively awash in efficiency) is not necessarily inefficient for a dynamic network. The computer that sits in the car will have one set of fairly well-defined XML structures that it will access, based upon the monitors that send information to intermediate nodes within the care itself. However we are reaching an age soon where car parts will upgrade just like computer parts do, with the parts themselves having a native intelligence that will communicate with the car's network. If you put in a new fuel cell system that more efficiently distributes power usage, you do not want to have to replace the entire computer system of the car as well, simply because the data format coming from the new cells is different from the old.

The advantage of an inexpensive digital screen in that car (or in the building monitor, or the cell phone screen, or the digital glasses that you are using to augment your own reality) is that it gives you the ability to display more on that screen than just a rendered equivalent of a speedometer and odometer. The more you distribute the intelligence to make this happen, the more you move the rules for generating the rendering out of static components and into context-sensitive, real-time transformations that can be updated transparently, the more uses you can get out of the hardware and the more you can tailor the information being displayed to your needs, rather than the needs of a software vendor.

The Magical Panopticon

When you think about it, this is already what has been happening with the browser for the last decade, even though a lot of people tend to dismiss the Web browser as being shallow and inadequate for "real applications." I have never really understood this sentiment. To be sure, for a while we were awash in applications showing "My CD collection" and "Why I think civilization is about to end" pages, but then again for a while we were also awash in overly produced Web storefronts selling dog-sitting services and giving away free versions of $1,000 software packages. The real beauty of the Web browser is that it made all of these things possible.

This occurred in part because it made it possible for nonprogrammers to create programmers. You did not need to know complex and specific Application Programming Interfaces (APIs) dealing with dozens or even hundreds of classes to get a Web page up and running; you only needed to know a few tags. This is a lesson that should not be lost on SVG developers, by the way. With SVG I have created complex presentations over the course of a couple of days that have taken weeks for me to even approximate using languages such as C++ or Visual Basic. What is more, I did it with a text editor and a free downloadable viewer, rather than spending several hundred dollars for the privilege.

However, the browser model also worked because it recognized that, if you can abstract out an interface to a declarative model and can work with media in digital form, then there is in practice no real difference between a sound file and animation, a dissertation, a digital video, or any other media format. They become collections of tags—nothing more, nothing less. Changing that information will change the interfaces dynamically, and by doing so in a relatively stateless manner you can create extremely sophisticated applications with comparatively little work.

You may notice, if you have slogged through this book, that I actually integrate SVG and HTML a great deal. The car example had a number of pieces that were obviously SVGish, but similarly included a number of pieces that potentially were not. SVG will not replace HTML, will not become a super language that subsumes all others, and the number of applications that are purely SVGish will always perforce be limited. However, SVG will find its way into the browser model as a piece to solve the problem of displaying graphics (and, to a certain extent, of text), just as other XML vocabularies will find their way into the rendering of voice content, the semantic description of content, the display of video, the creation of three-dimensional contexts.

I envision this magical Panopticon as a generalized environment (*browser* tends to be too passive a description of it) that is able to configure itself in response to the type of data that needs to be displayed. If it does not know how to display three-dimensional XML content, it can retrieve the necessary components to give it this capability, then can start interpreting part of the XML data stream through this filter. Ditto for voice rendering, interpretation, or the description of any other type of media. We are today defining the core standards for such systems, through languages such as SVG, X3D, VoiceML, and so forth. Different vendors may have different implementations for their Panopticons, but that should in fact be totally irrelevant to the data streams moving through the systems.

Thus it is worth seeing SVG not so much as the ultimate be all and end all of markup display languages, but only as one piece of this larger picture. It will make the rendering of graphical content both easier and more consistent, and it may even find a place in other areas such as the rendering of printed output, but it is just one manifestation of the way that we represent knowledge.

Summary

When I started this book, I envisioned it as a straightforward introduction to SVG, a technology that I was learning about even as I wrote it. The concept behind it was intriguing even as I penned the first words, but I discovered somewhere along the line a much deeper realization: We are changing our understanding of knowledge.

For eons, knowledge was absolute, something that was given from on high, fixed, and immutable. It was revealed through the musings of mystics and philosophers, the ruminations of priests and prophets, the diaries of rare adventurers, and the notations of historians.

The Renaissance began to chip away at that concept, a process that continued through the Enlightenment of the 18th century. Increasingly, knowledge was seen as something that could change, that knowledge in fact derived as much from the rules that we used to observe with as from the data that was observed. Mathematics is, at its heart, a language for the codification of those rules, and the stunning advances in mathematics from the 17th century onward changed the pace at which our society gathered and processed that information.

During the 19th century, the Industrial Age ushered in the need for better communication as colonization and the mercantile ethic displaced the authority of aristocracy and theocracy alike, and time entered into the equation. The printing press made it possible to present both words and pictures to the masses, and knowledge became synonymous with that which was presented via books; there is a reason that there is an *author* in *authority*. The dissemination of knowledge became institutionalized through a public education system (at least in the United States), but in general the dispensers of knowledge were the writers and artists who devised everything from textbooks to treatises to profound poetry and prose.

At the beginning of the 20th century (1910–1913 to be precise), Alfred North Whitehead and Bertrand Russell produced the *Principia Mathematica*, a book of logical predicates intended to show every possible logical permutation in existence. The book was a brilliant masterpiece, and as with developments in physics at the time, was taken as an indication that science and mathematics were both near their end, that shortly thereafter there could be nothing profoundly new. As with the true state in physics, it was also wrong at a structural level. Werner Heisenberg, Max Planck, Erwin Schroedinger, and a young patent clerk in Bern, Germany, named Albert Einstein looked at the inconsistencies that were hiding just under the surface of the "nearly complete realm" and discovered that things were that has completely retransformed our perceptions about the way that the universe worked.

Computer science has followed that same trajectory. In the 1950s and early 1960s, the Cyberians—a group that included such luminaries as Norbert Wiener, John McCarthy, Richard Feynman, and Grace Hopper—were convinced that aware, "thinking machines" would be a reality within a decade. Computers were several orders of magnitude more powerful in the 1970s by the time that Artificial Intelligence was declared dead, hopelessly naïve and unachievable. The irony, of course, is that the foundation of their work has gone on to fuel everything from the engines of games as diverse as chess, Quake, and SimCity to medical diagnostic knowledge systems, gene/protein sequencers, and weather modelers.

Innovation—new knowledge—begins along the edges, at the interstices between different domains of understanding. It is no accident that the areas of highest learning in the past were typically also the most volatile politically because it was there that different cultures met and compared concepts. The pace of innovation has exploded in recent years as the communication revolution has made it possible for people in different disciplines to compare notes and see the similarities in their work despite the differences in nomenclature and approach.

The ability to present that information in different ways is a key part of being able to see the commonalities. Chaos theory was spawned because a meteorologist was able to use a computer and recognize the butterfly lurking amidst seemingly unrelated data. The biotech revolution has occurred in part because it has become increasingly possible to visualize the molecules at work through simulations. The analysis of business trends (and their relationship to other "random-walk" phenomenon) has radically transformed the way that the stock market works (perhaps for the worse) by giving insight into the process.

The promise of SVG is that it is one piece of an overall set of technologies that will make it possible to work with different domains of information and see what happens when they collide. XML creates languages (namespaces) that can in turn be manipulated and transformed through the rules-based mechanisms of XSLT. SVG, along with X3D, XSL-FO, SMIL, XHTML, and similar "display" languages make it possible to see, hear, or potentially even smell or touch the nuggets of truth and the niggling details from which new insights are possible.

With SVG, a picture is a thousand words—but what glorious words.

Index

Apress Titles

ISBN	PRICE	AUTHOR	TITLE
1-893115-73-9	$34.95	Abbott	Voice Enabling Web Applications: VoiceXML and Beyond
1-893115-01-1	$39.95	Appleman	Dan Appleman's Win32 API Puzzle Book and Tutorial for Visual Basic Programmers
1-893115-23-2	$29.95	Appleman	How Computer Programming Works
1-893115-97-6	$39.95	Appleman	Moving to VB .NET: Strategies, Concepts, and Code
1-59059-023-6	$39.95	Baker	Adobe Acrobat 5: The Professional User's Guide
1-59059-039-2	$49.95	Barnaby	Distributed .NET Programming
1-893115-09-7	$29.95	Baum	Dave Baum's Definitive Guide to LEGO MINDSTORMS
1-893115-84-4	$29.95	Baum, Gasperi, Hempel, and Villa	Extreme MINDSTORMS: An Advanced Guide to LEGO MINDSTORMS
1-893115-82-8	$59.95	Ben-Gan/Moreau	Advanced Transact-SQL for SQL Server 2000
1-893115-91-7	$39.95	Birmingham/Perry	Software Development on a Leash
1-893115-48-8	$29.95	Bischof	The .NET Languages: A Quick Translation Guide
1-59059-053-8	$44.95	Bock/Stromquist/Fischer/Smith	.NET Security
1-893115-67-4	$49.95	Borge	Managing Enterprise Systems with the Windows Script Host
1-59059-019-8	$49.95	Cagle	SVG Programming: The Graphical Web
1-893115-28-3	$44.95	Challa/Laksberg	Essential Guide to Managed Extensions for C++
1-893115-39-9	$44.95	Chand	A Programmer's Guide to ADO.NET in C#
1-893115-44-5	$29.95	Cook	Robot Building for Beginners
1-893115-99-2	$39.95	Cornell/Morrison	Programming VB .NET: A Guide for Experienced Programmers
1-893115-72-0	$39.95	Curtin	Developing Trust: Online Privacy and Security
1-59059-014-7	$44.95	Drol	Object-Oriented Macromedia Flash MX
1-59059-008-2	$29.95	Duncan	The Career Programmer: Guerilla Tactics for an Imperfect World
1-893115-71-2	$39.95	Ferguson	Mobile .NET
1-893115-90-9	$49.95	Finsel	The Handbook for Reluctant Database Administrators
1-59059-024-4	$49.95	Fraser	Real World ASP.NET: Building a Content Management System
1-893115-42-9	$44.95	Foo/Lee	XML Programming Using the Microsoft XML Parser
1-893115-55-0	$34.95	Frenz	Visual Basic and Visual Basic .NET for Scientists and Engineers
1-893115-85-2	$34.95	Gilmore	A Programmer's Introduction to PHP 4.0
1-893115-36-4	$34.95	Goodwill	Apache Jakarta-Tomcat
1-893115-17-8	$59.95	Gross	A Programmer's Introduction to Windows DNA
1-893115-62-3	$39.95	Gunnerson	A Programmer's Introduction to C#, Second Edition
1-59059-009-0	$49.95	Harris/Macdonald	Moving to ASP.NET: Web Development with VB .NET
1-893115-30-5	$49.95	Harkins/Reid	SQL: Access to SQL Server
1-893115-10-0	$34.95	Holub	Taming Java Threads
1-893115-04-6	$34.95	Hyman/Vaddadi	Mike and Phani's Essential C++ Techniques
1-893115-96-8	$59.95	Jorelid	J2EE FrontEnd Technologies: A Programmer's Guide to Servlets, JavaServer Pages, and Enterprise JavaBeans
1-893115-49-6	$39.95	Kilburn	Palm Programming in Basic
1-893115-50-X	$34.95	Knudsen	Wireless Java: Developing with Java 2, Micro Edition
1-893115-79-8	$49.95	Kofler	Definitive Guide to Excel VBA
1-893115-57-7	$39.95	Kofler	MySQL

ISBN	PRICE	AUTHOR	TITLE
1-893115-87-9	$39.95	Kurata	Doing Web Development: Client-Side Techniques
1-893115-75-5	$44.95	Kurniawan	Internet Programming with VB
1-893115-38-0	$24.95	Lafler	Power AOL: A Survival Guide
1-893115-46-1	$36.95	Lathrop	Linux in Small Business: A Practical User's Guide
1-893115-19-4	$49.95	Macdonald	Serious ADO: Universal Data Access with Visual Basic
1-893115-06-2	$39.95	Marquis/Smith	A Visual Basic 6.0 Programmer's Toolkit
1-893115-22-4	$27.95	McCarter	David McCarter's VB Tips and Techniques
1-59059-021-X	$34.95	Moore	Karl Moore's Visual Basic .NET: The Tutorials
1-893115-76-3	$49.95	Morrison	C++ For VB Programmers
1-59059-003-1	$39.95	Nakhimovsky/Meyers	XML Programming: Web Applications and Web Services with JSP and ASP
1-893115-80-1	$39.95	Newmarch	A Programmer's Guide to Jini Technology
1-893115-58-5	$49.95	Oellermann	Architecting Web Services
1-59059-020-1	$44.95	Patzer	JSP Examples and Best Practices
1-893115-81-X	$39.95	Pike	SQL Server: Common Problems, Tested Solutions
1-59059-017-1	$34.95	Rainwater	Herding Cats: A Primer for Programmers Who Lead Programmers
1-59059-025-2	$49.95	Rammer	Advanced .NET Remoting
1-893115-20-8	$34.95	Rischpater	Wireless Web Development
1-893115-93-3	$34.95	Rischpater	Wireless Web Development with PHP and WAP
1-893115-89-5	$59.95	Shemitz	Kylix: The Professional Developer's Guide and Reference
1-893115-40-2	$39.95	Sill	The qmail Handbook
1-893115-24-0	$49.95	Sinclair	From Access to SQL Server
1-893115-94-1	$29.95	Spolsky	User Interface Design for Programmers
1-893115-53-4	$44.95	Sweeney	Visual Basic for Testers
1-59059-002-3	$44.95	Symmonds	Internationalization and Localization Using Microsoft .NET
1-59059-010-4	$54.95	Thomsen	Database Programming with C#
1-893115-29-1	$44.95	Thomsen	Database Programming with Visual Basic .NET
1-893115-65-8	$39.95	Tiffany	Pocket PC Database Development with eMbedded Visual Basic
1-893115-59-3	$59.95	Troelsen	C# and the .NET Platform
1-59059-011-2	$59.95	Troelsen	COM and .NET Interoperability
1-893115-26-7	$59.95	Troelsen	Visual Basic .NET and the .NET Platform
1-893115-54-2	$49.95	Trueblood/Lovett	Data Mining and Statistical Analysis Using SQL
1-893115-68-2	$54.95	Vaughn	ADO.NET and ADO Examples and Best Practices for VB Programmers, Second Edition
1-59059-012-0	$49.95	Vaughn/Blackburn	ADO.NET Examples and Best Practices for C# Programmers
1-893115-83-6	$44.95	Wells	Code Centric: T-SQL Programming with Stored Procedures and Triggers
1-893115-95-X	$49.95	Welschenbach	Cryptography in C and C++
1-893115-05-4	$39.95	Williamson	Writing Cross-Browser Dynamic HTML
1-893115-78-X	$49.95	Zukowski	Definitive Guide to Swing for Java 2, Second Edition
1-893115-92-5	$49.95	Zukowski	Java Collections
1-893115-98-4	$54.95	Zukowski	Learn Java with JBuilder 6

Available at bookstores nationwide or from Springer Verlag New York, Inc. at 1-800-777-4643; fax 1-212-533-3503. Contact us for more information at sales@apress.com.

Apress Titles Publishing SOON!

ISBN	AUTHOR	TITLE
1-59059-022-8	Alapati	Expert Oracle 9i Database Administration
1-59059-041-4	Bock	CIL Programming: Under the Hood of .NET
1-59059-015-5	Clark	An Introduction to Object Oriented Programming with Visual Basic .NET
1-59059-000-7	Cornell	Programming C#
1-59059-033-3	Fraser	Managed C++ and .NET Development
1-59059-038-4	Gibbons	Java Development to .NET Development
1-59059-030-9	Habibi/Camerlengo/Patterson	Java 1.4 and the Sun Certified Developer Exam
1-59059-006-6	Hetland	Instant Python with Ten Instant Projects
1-59059-044-9	MacDonald	.NET User Interfaces with VB .NET: Windows Forms and Custom Controls
1-59059-001-5	McMahon	A Programmer's Introduction to ASP.NET WebForms in Visual Basic .NET
1-893115-74-7	Millar	Enterprise Development: A Programmer's Handbook
1-893115-27-5	Morrill	Tuning and Customizing a Linux System
1-59059-028-7	Rischpater	Wireless Web Development, Second Edition
1-59059-026-0	Smith	Writing Add-Ins for .NET
1-893115-43-7	Stephenson	Standard VB: An Enterprise Developer's Reference for VB 6 and VB .NET
1-59059-035-X	Symmonds	GDI+ Programming in C# and VB .NET
1-59059-032-5	Thomsen	Database Programming with Visual Basic .NET, Second Edition
1-59059-007-4	Thomsen	Building Web Services with VB .NET
1-59059-027-9	Torkelson/Petersen/Torkelson	Programming the Web with Visual Basic .NET
1-59059-018-X	Tregar	Writing Perl Modules for CPAN
1-59059-004-X	Valiaveedu	SQL Server 2000 and Business Intelligence in an XML/.NET World

Available at bookstores nationwide or from Springer Verlag New York, Inc. at 1-800-777-4643; fax 1-212-533-3503. Contact us for more information at sales@apress.com.

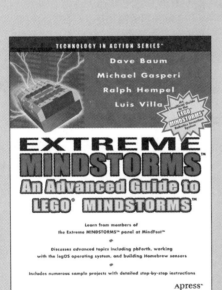

books for professionals by professionals™

About Apress

Apress, located in Berkeley, CA, is a fast-growing, innovative publishing company devoted to meeting the needs of existing and potential programming professionals. Simply put, the "A" in Apress stands for *"The Author's Press"*™ and its books have *"The Expert's Voice"*™. Apress' unique approach to publishing grew out of conversations between its founders Gary Cornell and Dan Appleman, authors of numerous best-selling, highly regarded books for programming professionals. In 1998 they set out to create a publishing company that emphasized quality above all else. Gary and Dan's vision has resulted in the publication of over 50 titles by leading software professionals, all of which have *The Expert's Voice*™.

Do You Have What It Takes to Write for Apress?

Apress is rapidly expanding its publishing program. If you can write and refuse to compromise on the quality of your work, if you believe in doing more than rehashing existing documentation, and if you're looking for opportunities and rewards that go far beyond those offered by traditional publishing houses, we want to hear from you!

Consider these innovations that we offer all of our authors:

- **Top royalties with *no* hidden switch statements**
  Authors typically only receive half of their normal royalty rate on foreign sales. In contrast, Apress' royalty rate remains the same for both foreign and domestic sales.

- **A mechanism for authors to obtain equity in Apress**
  Unlike the software industry, where stock options are essential to motivate and retain software professionals, the publishing industry has adhered to an outdated compensation model based on royalties alone. In the spirit of most software companies, Apress reserves a significant portion of its equity for authors.

- **Serious treatment of the technical review process**
  Each Apress book has a technical reviewing team whose remuneration depends in part on the success of the book since they too receive royalties.

Moreover, through a partnership with Springer-Verlag, New York, Inc., one of the world's major publishing houses, Apress has significant venture capital behind it. Thus, we have the resources to produce the highest quality books *and* market them aggressively.

If you fit the model of the Apress author who can write a book that gives the "professional what he or she needs to know"™," then please contact one of our Editorial Directors, Gary Cornell (gary_cornell@apress.com), Dan Appleman (dan_appleman@apress.com), Peter Blackburn (peter_blackburn@apress.com), Jason Gilmore (jason_gilmore@apress.com), Karen Watterson (karen_watterson@apress.com), or John Zukowski (john_zukowski@apress.com) for more information.